HAMLYN
COOKERY COURSE

HAMLYN
COOKERY COURSE

Caroline Ellwood
Rosemary Wadey

CONTENTS

USEFUL FACTS AND FIGURES

Notes on metrication

In this book quantities are given in metric and Imperial measures. Exact conversion from Imperial to metric measures does not usually give very convenient working quantities and so the metric measures have been rounded into units of 25 grams. The table shows the recommended equivalents.

Ounces	Approx g to nearest whole figure	Recommended conversion to nearest unit of 25	Ounces	Approx g to nearest whole figure	Recommended conversion to nearest unit of 25
1	28	25	11	312	300
2	57	50	12	340	350
3	85	75	13	368	375
4	113	100	14	396	400
5	142	150	15	425	425
6	170	175	16 (1 lb)	454	450
7	198	200	17	482	475
8	227	225	18	510	500
9	255	250	19	539	550
10	283	275	20 ($\frac{1}{4}$ lb)	567	575

Note: When converting quantities over 20 oz first add the appropriate figures in the centre column, then adjust to the nearest unit of 25. As a general guide, 1 kg (1000 g) equals 2.2 lb or about 2 lb 3 oz. This method of conversion gives good results in nearly all cases, although in certain pastry and cake recipes a more accurate conversion is necessary to produce a balanced recipe.

Liquid measures The millilitre has been used in this book and the following table gives a few examples.

Imperial	Approx ml to nearest whole figure	Recommended ml	Imperial	Approx ml to nearest whole figure	Recommended ml
$\frac{1}{4}$ pint	142	150 ml	1 pint	567	600 ml
$\frac{1}{2}$ pint	283	300 ml	1$\frac{1}{2}$ pints	851	900 ml
$\frac{3}{4}$ pint	425	450 ml	1$\frac{3}{4}$ pints	992	1000 ml (1 litre)

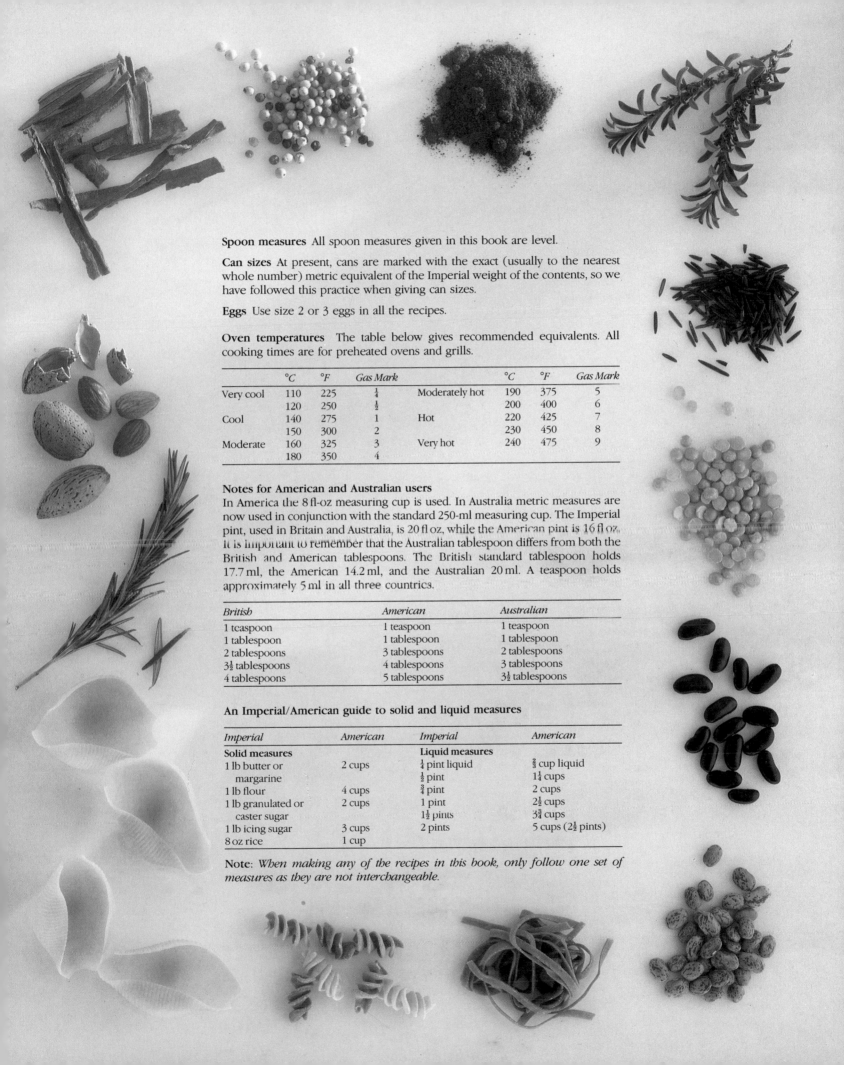

Spoon measures All spoon measures given in this book are level.

Can sizes At present, cans are marked with the exact (usually to the nearest whole number) metric equivalent of the Imperial weight of the contents, so we have followed this practice when giving can sizes.

Eggs Use size 2 or 3 eggs in all the recipes.

Oven temperatures The table below gives recommended equivalents. All cooking times are for preheated ovens and grills.

	°C	°F	Gas Mark		°C	°F	Gas Mark
Very cool	110	225	$\frac{1}{4}$	Moderately hot	190	375	5
	120	250	$\frac{1}{2}$		200	400	6
Cool	140	275	1	Hot	220	425	7
	150	300	2		230	450	8
Moderate	160	325	3	Very hot	240	475	9
	180	350	4				

Notes for American and Australian users

In America the 8 fl-oz measuring cup is used. In Australia metric measures are now used in conjunction with the standard 250-ml measuring cup. The Imperial pint, used in Britain and Australia, is 20 fl oz, while the American pint is 16 fl oz. It is important to remember that the Australian tablespoon differs from both the British and American tablespoons. The British standard tablespoon holds 17.7 ml, the American 14.2 ml, and the Australian 20 ml. A teaspoon holds approximately 5 ml in all three countries.

British	American	Australian
1 teaspoon	1 teaspoon	1 teaspoon
1 tablespoon	1 tablespoon	1 tablespoon
2 tablespoons	3 tablespoons	2 tablespoons
3$\frac{1}{2}$ tablespoons	4 tablespoons	3 tablespoons
4 tablespoons	5 tablespoons	3$\frac{1}{2}$ tablespoons

An Imperial/American guide to solid and liquid measures

Imperial	American	Imperial	American
Solid measures		**Liquid measures**	
1 lb butter or margarine	2 cups	$\frac{1}{4}$ pint liquid	$\frac{2}{3}$ cup liquid
		$\frac{1}{2}$ pint	1$\frac{1}{4}$ cups
1 lb flour	4 cups	$\frac{3}{4}$ pint	2 cups
1 lb granulated or caster sugar	2 cups	1 pint	2$\frac{1}{2}$ cups
		1$\frac{1}{2}$ pints	3$\frac{3}{4}$ cups
1 lb icing sugar	3 cups	2 pints	5 cups (2$\frac{1}{2}$ pints)
8 oz rice	1 cup		

Note: *When making any of the recipes in this book, only follow one set of measures as they are not interchangeable.*

INTRODUCTION

The Hamlyn Cookery Course aims to give a good grounding in the basics of food preparation as well as lay the foundations of the skills required for more specialised techniques.

Starting right at the beginning, choosing, buying and cooking the basic foodstuffs – meat, fish, poultry, fruit and vegetables – are covered, together with the simpler skills such as pastry-making, cakes, stocks, soups and gravies. One by one these specialised subjects are explained starting with the simple steps and moving on to tackle the recipes that many people are afraid of: soufflés, French pastries, icing and so on.

The course begins by illustrating the tools of the trade – the knives, implements, pots and pans that are available. You may not need them all but using the right tool for the

job does give a much better result. A glossary explains
culinary terms which otherwise mystify the novice. The
course then launches in to the first lesson, on stocks, the
foundation on which much good cooking is based.

Follow the detailed step-by-step instructions throughout
and success is guaranteed. Once you have mastered the
technique you will have the confidence to tackle the recipes
that are designed to build on your skills. Finally, try the
selected classic dishes that are provided in each section.

The aim throughout has been to explain basic skills
simply and easily, with illustrations to clarify difficult points.
If you have ever wished you could turn out a Victoria
Sponge, tackle marmalade or make your own bread, this is
the book for you.

EQUIPMENT

Like every profession, cookery has its own specialised tools and equipment. Always try to use the right tools for the job – and learn how to use them properly. You will find it much more efficient and the end result will be much more professional.

KNIVES & OTHER UTENSILS

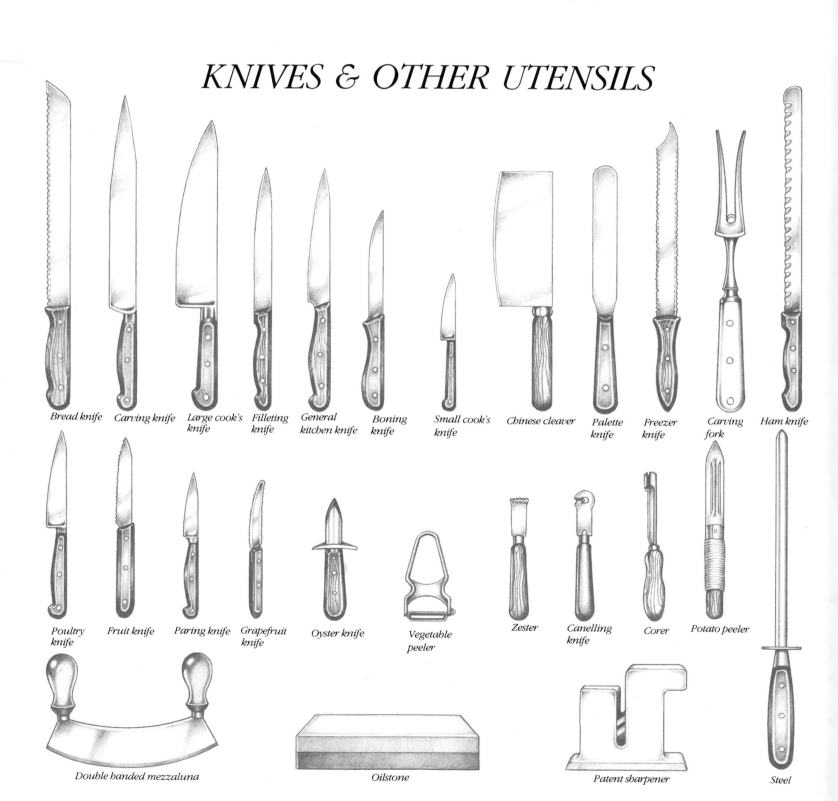

Bread knife

Carving knife

Large cook's knife

Filleting knife

General kitchen knife

Boning knife

Small cook's knife

Chinese cleaver

Palette knife

Freezer knife

Carving fork

Ham knife

Poultry knife

Fruit knife

Paring knife

Grapefruit knife

Oyster knife

Vegetable peeler

Zester

Canelling knife

Corer

Potato peeler

Double handed mezzaluna

Oilstone

Patent sharpener

Steel

Melon baller

Nutcrackers

Bean slicer

Cheese slicer

Garlic crusher

Lobster crackers

Poultry shears

Egg slicer

Butter curler

Lobster pick

Corn-on-the-cob holder

Mandoline

Tin opener

Bottle opener

Corkscrew

Bulb baster

Meat bat

Potato masher

Kebab skewer

Butcher's skewer

Larding needle

Trussing needle

Skimmer

Juicer

Wooden spoon and spatula

Wire whisk

Perforated spoon

Balloon whisk

Nutmeg grater

Box grater

Fish slice

Rubber spatula

Measuring spoons

Knives

A good set of knives is the cook's most valuable asset. It is worth investing in a well-made set, of carbon steel or stainless steel, forged in one piece, with a riveted wooden or plastic handle. Test them for good balance, a comfortable feeling in the hand and buy a steel with them to keep them at peak sharpness. Use knives only for their intended purpose and never jumble them up with other implements in a drawer – it dulls the edge. Knives should be kept separately on a wooden block or on a special magnetic rack and sharpened frequently.

Flat grater

Rotary whisk

Ice-cream scoop

Ladle

Tongs

POTS & PANS

Butter melter

Milk pan

Lipped pan

Medium copper saucepan

Pressure cooker

Chip pan with basket

Heavy duty cast iron pan

Aluminium saucepans

Frying pan

Stewing pan

Cast iron griddle

Non-stick pan

Omelette pan

Preserving pan

Paella pan

Wok

Trivet

Sauté pan

Deep fryer

Enamelled cast iron lipped frying pan

Metal heat diffuser

Anti-splash lid

Pots and pans

There is no perfect material for saucepans. Copper conducts heat well but is expensive and needs constant polishing. Cast iron gives an even heat and a good solid base but rusts easily and is heavy. Enamel is good but may crack and stain. Stainless steel won't mark but is a very poor conductor. Probably the best all-rounder is aluminium which is tough but cheap. The answer is not to buy a matching set. Instead, buy a selection of pans in various materials to suit your various needs. Whatever you choose, make sure the pans are all heavy-duty, with solid bases, insulated handles and close fitting lids.

Double boiler

Steamer

Fish kettle with steaming tray

Bamboo steamer

Couscoussière

Iron casserole

Expanding steamer

Asparagus pan

Terracotta pot

Chicken brick

Earthenware casserole

Marmite

Egg poacher

Tea kettle

Coffee pot

Tea pot

Fondue pan and fork

OVENPROOF DISHES

Terrines

Gratin dishes

Ramekin

Soufflé dish

Deep roasting pan

BAKING TINS & ACCESSORIES

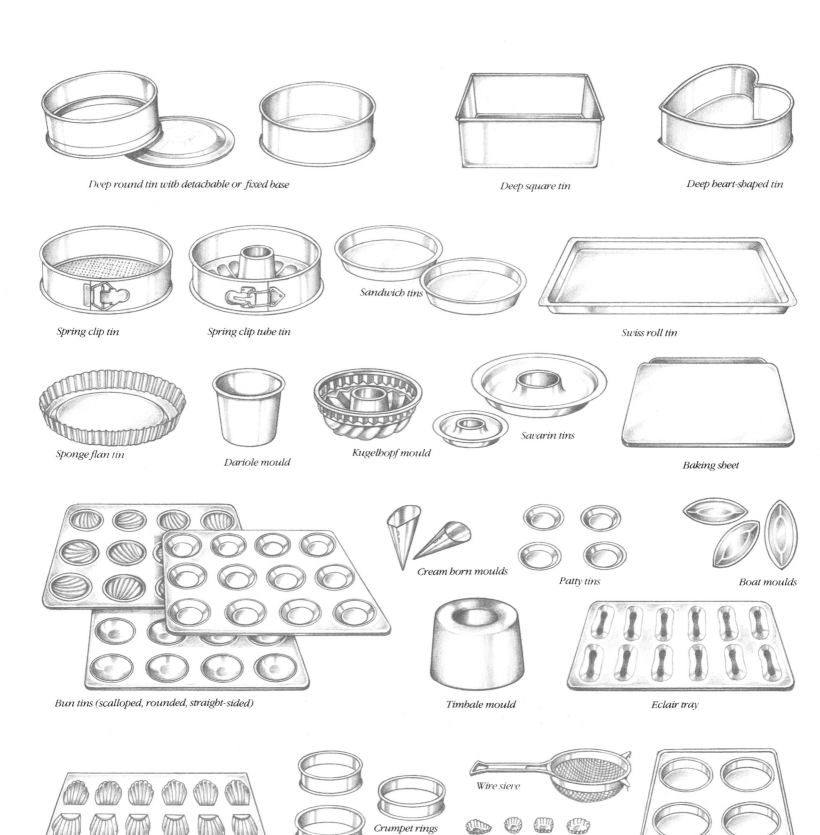

Deep round tin with detachable or fixed base

Deep square tin

Deep heart-shaped tin

Spring clip tin

Spring clip tube tin

Sandwich tins

Swiss roll tin

Sponge flan tin

Dariole mould

Kugelhopf mould

Savarin tins

Baking sheet

Bun tins (scalloped, rounded, straight-sided)

Cream horn moulds

Patty tins

Boat moulds

Timbale mould

Eclair tray

Madeleine sheet

Crumpet rings

Wire sieve

Petits-fours moulds

Yorkshire pudding tins

Baguette tin

Bread tins

Brioche tin

Flowerpot

Iron pizza tray

Fluted loose-bottomed flan tins

Flan rings

Pie dishes

Pie plate

Ceramic flan dish

Quiche tin

Raised pie mould

Copper mould

Shortbread mould

Hinged mould

Jelly mould

Fish mould

Marble pastry slab

Biscuit cutters

Pastry cutters

Gingerbread men cutters

Wire rack

Ornamental cutters

Rolling pin

Icing turntable

Icing ruler

Aspic cutters

Ravioli cutter

Pastry wheels

Pastry brush

Pastry scraper

Icing bag and nozzles

Pie funnels

Flour dredger

Baking equipment

Bright shiny tin baking equipment is cheap and effective: the shininess helps deflect the heat to get an even brownness. Buy well-made tins with few seams to harbour food scraps and wash and dry them carefully as tin is very susceptible to rust. Non-stick tins are a boon to the cook, requiring the minimum of washing and no greasing but cost substantially more. A useful starting set might be a roasting pan, two baking sheets, a flan ring, bun tin, two sandwich tins, a deep cake tin and a loaf tin. These should suit most baking needs.

ELECTRIC & OTHER MACHINES

Blender/liquidizer

Hand-held mixer with
stand and bowl

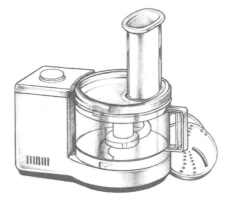

Food processor with blades

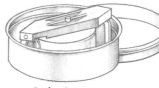

Sorbetière

Electric ice cream maker

Electric coffee grinder

Electric juicer

Hand-held beater

Electric knife sharpener

Electric coffee machine

Ice crusher

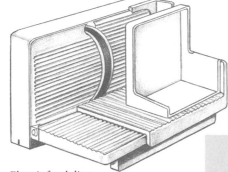

Electric food slicer

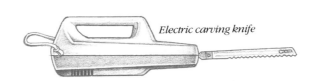

Electric carving knife

Ice cream churn

Food mill

Rotary shredder
(Mouli-légumes)

Food processors and mixers

Electrical equipment is expensive and can take up lots of space, so it is worth making quite certain its use will repay its cost before buying. Probably the most generally useful for the ordinary cook are a hand-held beater, invaluable for cake-making and beating egg whites, and a blender, which will make easy work of soups and purées. Food processors are the perfect accessory for a busy cook or someone who cooks a lot for large amounts of people. They work fast, chopping, slicing, grinding, puréeing and come with other attachments which allow more specialised work such as making juice or pasta.

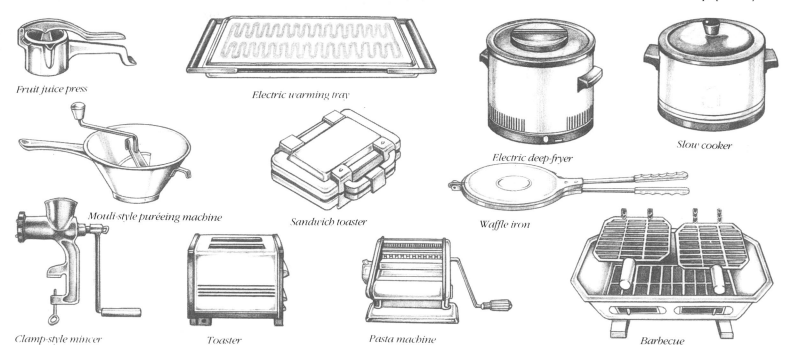

Fruit juice press

Electric warming tray

Electric deep-fryer

Slow cooker

Mouli-style puréeing machine

Sandwich toaster

Waffle iron

Clamp-style mincer

Toaster

Pasta machine

Barbecue

ACCESSORIES

Pestle and mortar

Colander

Salad spinner

Salad dryer

Chopping board

Jelly bag

Measuring jug

Egg timer

Roasting rack

Aluminium foil

Pudding basin

Meat thermometer

Kitchen scales

Sugar thermometer

Kitchen timers

Non-stick silicone paper

Greaseproof paper

Salt mill   Pepper mill

GLOSSARY

Al dente: just firm to the bite; the correct texture for pasta and many vegetables

Antipasti: Italian hors d'œuvres

Au gratin: a cheese and breadcrumb topping, browned under the grill

Bain-marie: a large, water-filled pan in which smaller dishes are set for cooking when indirect, gentle heat is required

Bake blind: to part-bake an unfilled pastry case by covering with foil or greaseproof paper and weighting down with baking beans, pulses or rice

Ballotine: boned, rolled and stuffed meat, usually poultry, served hot

Bard: to cover or wrap lean meats in a sheet of fat to prevent drying out

Baste: to spoon pan juices over meat or vegetables to moisten

Beignets: fritters

Beurre manié: flour and butter worked into a liaison to thicken soups, stew juices etc.

Beurre noir: butter heated to a light brown colour, usually served with fish

Bind: to hold dry ingredients together with egg or liquid

Bisque: smooth and thickened shellfish soup

Blanch: to immerse food briefly in boiling water to soften, remove skin, par-cook, set a colour, or remove a strong taste

Blanquette: a stew of veal, poultry or fish in a creamy white sauce

Bolognese: a rich sauce made from chicken livers and minced beef, usually served with pasta

Bouchées: small puff pastry cases, like tiny vol-au-vents

Bouillon: broth or uncleared stock

Bouquet garni: a small bunch of herbs, usually parsley, thyme and bay leaf, added to stews, soups or stocks for flavouring

Bourguignonne (à la): with mushrooms, small onions and a red wine sauce

Braise: to cook food very slowly in a little liquid in a tightly sealed pot, after initial browning

Brine: salt and water mixture for preserving

Brochette: grilled and served on a skewer

Broil: to grill (US)

Canapé: appetizer of biscuits etc. with savoury topping

Casserole: ovenproof cooking pot with lid; hence the stew cooked slowly in it

Caramelize: to cook sugar to a toffee either by boiling in a pan or melting under a hot grill

Chasseur (à la): with mushrooms, shallots and wine

Châteaubriand: roast fillet steak, for 2 persons or more

Chaudfroid: food cooked, covered in a white sauce and glazed with aspic

Chine: to loosen the backbone of a joint for easier carving

Clarify: to melt and strain butter of its milk particles and impurities; to clear stocks and jellies etc. by filtering

Cocotte: small ovenproof dish, without a lid

Compôte: fresh or dried fruit, served cold in a syrup

Consommé: concentrated clear meat or poultry stock

Court-bouillon: aromatic liquid used generally for poaching fish or shellfish

Crackling: the crisp cooked rind of a joint of pork

Cream: to beat fat and sugar together to a pale mousse-like consistency

Croustade: small cases made of bread, brushed with butter and baked or deep-fried until crisp

Croûte: a slice of fried or toasted bread on which food is served

Croûton: small dice of fried or occasionally toasted bread used as a garnish

Cut in: to distribute hard fat throughout flour in small pieces using a knife

Dariole: a small castle-shaped mould, for cakes, mousses etc

Deglaze: to free browned, solidified cooking juices and sediments from a roasting tin or dish by adding water, stock or wine and stirring over heat to make gravy

Degorge: either to sprinkle with salt or to soak, to remove indigestible or strong-tasting juices from meat, fish or vegetables

Demi-glace: basic brown sauce

Devilled: (*à la diable*) a food seasoned with a hot-tasting sauce and grilled or fried

Draw: of birds, to remove the innards

Dredge: to coat food lightly with flour, icing sugar etc.

Dress: of birds, to pluck, draw and truss; of salads, to add the dressing and toss

Dropping consistency: the stage reached when a spoonful of a mixture held upside down will drop off reluctantly

Duxelles: stuffing of finely chopped mushrooms, often with shallots or ham, used as stuffing and flavouring

Emulsion: a stable suspension of fat and other liquid – mayonnaise, for instance

En croûte: to cook food, especially meat, in a pastry case

En papillote: to cook enclosed in paper

Entrée: traditionally a dish served before the main course, now generally the main course

Entrecôte: sirloin steak

Escalope: thin slice of meat, usually veal, from fillet or leg

Espagnole: basic brown sauce

Farce: stuffing

Fines herbes: mixture of finely chopped parsley, chives, chervil and tarragon

Flake: to separate cooked meat or fish into small pieces

Flamber: to pour warmed brandy or other spirit over food and set it alight

Fleurons: small crescents of puff pastry, used as a garnish

Florentine (à la): eggs or fish served with a cheese sauce on a spinach bed

Flute: to make decorative indentations in the edges of pastry pies and flans

Fold in: to combine two mixtures gently with a metal spoon to retain their lightness

Forestière (à la): food served with mushrooms, bacon and diced potatoes fried in butter

Fricassée: a white stew, commonly of chicken or veal, fried in butter then cooked and served in a creamy white sauce

Frosting: the American term for certain types of cake icing; also egg white and sugar used to decorate glasses, flowers etc.

Fumet: a strong well reduced stock made from fish or meat

Galantine: boned, rolled and stuffed meat, usually poultry, served cold

Garnish: to decorate a savoury dish

Glace de viande: reduced strong brown stock used to add colour and flavour to sauces

Glaze: to add a shine to food with meat juices, melted jam, syrup, beaten egg or milk

Goujons: small strips of meat or fish, coated and deep fried

Grecque (à la): food, usually vegetables, cooked in stock and olive oil, often with herbs and other flavourings, then cooled

Hard ball: a stage of sugar boiling

Hollandaise: a rich emulsion sauce made with egg yolks and butter

Hongroise (à la): a cream sauce flavoured with paprika

Hors d'œuvres: the first course, or savoury morsels served with drinks

Hull: to remove the green calyx from fruit

Infuse: to extract flavour by steeping food in hot liquid

Indienne (à l'): flavoured with curry

Jardinière (à la): garnish of neatly cut, separately cooked vegetables

Julienne: matchstick strips of vegetables, citrus rind or meat, used as a garnish

Kibbled: coarsely chopped, used particularly of wheat

Knead: to work dough by stretching and folding to distribute the yeast and give springy consistency

Knock down or **knock back**: to punch or knead air from yeast dough after rising

Knock up: to separate slightly the layers of raw puff pastry with the blade of a knife, to help rising during cooking

Langues de chat: sweet long flat biscuits, served with puddings

Lard: to thread strips of fat into lean meat to moisten it

Lardons: small cooked strips or cubes of pork or bacon fat, used to flavour or garnish

Liaison: ingredients used to bind or thicken – roux, beurre manié etc.

Luting paste: a paste of flour and water used to make a good seal between dish and lid

Lyonnaise (à la): food from the Lyonnais, usually with onions

Macédoine: a mixture of diced vegetables or fruit

Macerate: to steep raw food, usually fruit, in sugar syrup or alcohol

Marinade: the liquid in which food is marinated

Marinate: to soak raw food in liquid, often wine and oil, to tenderize and give flavour

Marinière (à la): shellfish, usually mussels, cooked in white wine or, if fish, cooked with mussels and wine

Médallions: small rounds of meat, evenly cut

Ménagère (à la): applied to a dish simply made

Meunière (à la): floured food, particularly fish, cooked in butter, lemon juice and parsley

Milanaise (à la): food dipped in egg and breadcrumbs, sometimes mixed with grated Parmesan

Minute (à la): food quickly cooked, either fried or grilled

Mirepoix: a base of diced vegetables, often used in braising

Mousseline: small moulds made from poultry or fish, and served hot or cold; also a sauce lightened with cream

Niçoise (à la): food cooked or served with tomato, garlic, onions, anchovies and olives

Noisette: boneless rack of lamb, rolled and cut into rounds; nut-brown butter; or hazelnut coloured

Normande (à la): often food cooked with apples and Calvados or cider and cream; or a fish sauce with shellfish liquid and stock thickened with egg yolks and cream, often with white wine

Panada: thick white sauce used as base of soufflés etc.

Parboil: to boil for part of cooking time before finishing by another method

Pare: to peel or trim

Parisienne (à la): potato usually scooped into small balls and fried

Parmentier: containing potatoes

Pâte: French for pastry dough

Pâté: savoury paste of liver, pork, game etc.

Pâtisserie: cake shop, or sweet cakes and pastries

Paupiette: slice of meat or fish rolled around stuffing

Paysanne (à la): food with carrots and onions, or another simple combination

Poach: to cook by simmering very gently in liquid

Polonaise (à la): garnished with sieved hard-boiled egg yolk and chopped white; plus fried breadcrumbs

Praline: caramelized sugar and browned almonds ground together to a powder and used in desserts and ice cream

Prove: to put yeast dough to rise before baking

Provençale (à la): food cooked or served with garlic, tomatoes, onions, anchovies, olive oil and peppers

Pulses: the dried seeds of members of the bean and pea families, for example lentils, haricot and butter beans

Purée: cooked food, mashed or sieved to a smooth consistency

Quenelles: light fish or meat dumplings, usually poached

Ragoût: a stew

Ramekins: small individual oven dishes, usually of porcelain

Réchauffé(e): a dish of reheated leftover cooked food

Reduce: to concentrate or thicken a liquid by rapid boiling to diminish its volume

Refresh: to rinse freshly cooked food in cold water to halt the cooking process and to set colour (as with green vegetables)

Relax or **rest**: to allow pastry gluten to contract after rolling; to allow the starch cells in a batter to expand

Render: to melt and strain animal fat

Ribbon, to the: the stage reached in the beating of a mixture when a ribbon trail is left as the beaters are lifted

Roux: a basic liaison of melted butter and flour, cooked as a thickening for sauces and for soups

Rub in: to mix fat into flour, using the fingers to give a breadcrumb texture

Sabayon: a frothy, sweet sauce of whipped egg yolks, sugar, wine and liqueur

Sauter: to cook briskly in shallow fat to brown food

Scald: to heat liquid, usually milk, to just below boiling point

Scalding point: the point just before boiling, when the liquid bubbles around the edges of the pan only

Score: to make heavy cuts over the surface of meat before cooking to allow heat to penetrate and to prevent meat curling

Seal, sear or **seize**: to brown meat quickly in hot fat to seal in the juices

Seasoned flour: flour with salt and pepper added

Sieve: to pass food through a sieve

Simmer: to cook in liquid at just below boiling point, when it is just shivering

Skim: to remove scum or fat from the surface of liquid

Slake: to mix a thickening agent – arrowroot, for instance – with a small amount of cold water before adding to a hot liquid

Soft ball: a stage in sugar boiling

Soubise: onion purée, often added to a Béchamel sauce

Souse: to pickle in vinegar or brine (particularly herrings)

Spatchcock: a chicken or poussin split open and spread out flat before cooking

St Germain (à la): food with peas, or a pea soup

Steam: to cook food above boiling water, in the steam, in a perforated dish or sieve

Stew: to cook food slowly in a small quantity of liquid in a closed dish or pan in or on the stove

Stir-fry: a Chinese cooking method where food is lightly cooked in a little oil over high heat with constant stirring

Suprême: choice piece of meat, usually breast of poultry; also a rich creamy white sauce

Sweat: to soften vegetables in fat until the juices run, without browning

Terrine: a pâté or minced mixture cooked in a loaf shaped dish (a terrine)

Timbale: a dish cooked in a drum-shaped mould

Tournedos: thick steak from narrow end of fillet

Truss: to tie a joint or bird with string

Turn: to shape carrots or turnips and other root vegetables into ovals; to cut mushrooms into spiral patterns

Vanilla sugar: sugar flavoured with a vanilla pod

Vichy: mineral water or a garnish of small glazed carrots

Vinaigrette: a dressing for salad of olive oil and vinegar or lemon juice

Vol-au-vent: puff pastry case of varying size

Waffle: a crisp golden brown pancake made by baking batter in a waffle iron

Well: the hollow made in a pile or bowl of flour into which liquid, fat etc. are put prior to mixing

Zest: oily outer citrus skin

Herbs

Each herb has a particular affinity with certain foods, and it is important to be aware of these, to use herbs with complete success. Our guide shows you how to identify the different herbs, and explains their various uses in cooking.

BASIL

Basil has a unique flavour, closely related to its fragrance. It is lost on prolonged heating, so basil should be used only as a flavouring/garnish, except, paradoxically, in the case of

Basil

pesto, the Genoese sauce. Basil has a special affinity with eggs, soft cheeses, pasta, vegetable soups and creamy sauces, but its greatest partner is undoubtedly tomatoes, often served with soft cheese.

BAY

Bay leaves must be subjected to long cooking, when they release their inimitable flavour. It is strong, and often half a leaf is enough to flavour a dish. Bay leaves form part of the classic bouquet garni, and are almost always included in stocks, casseroles, pâtés and court bouillons. They make a good garnish, set in aspic on top of a pâté.

Bay

Borage

BORAGE

Borage is an annual with large hairy leaves and bright blue flowers. Nowadays it is used mainly for its decorative features. It has a refreshing cucumber flavour and is the traditional garnish for Pimms and other cups. The young leaves may also be added to salads.

CHERVIL

Chervil has a light, subtle flavour and forms part of the classic mixture called fines herbes, for use in omelettes and sauces. On its own, chervil is good in bland, creamy soups, with baked or scrambled eggs, pounded into butter for serving with grilled fish, or for flavouring a velouté sauce.

Chervil

Chives

CHIVES

Chives are the mildest of the onion family. They cannot stand heat and must be added to dishes after cooling. They make the ideal contrast to pale, creamy dishes like vichyssoise soup and scrambled eggs and are good sprinkled on salads.

Coriander

CORIANDER

Coriander looks much like flat-leaved parsley, but the leaves give off a distinctive smell when rubbed. The fresh leaves are chopped and added to curries and spiced dishes.

Garlic

Dill

DILL

Dill resembles fennel in that both have hollow stems, feathery leaves and umbels of yellow flowers. Dill leaves are best used as a flavouring/garnish, and freeze well. Dill is widely used in marinades in Scandinavia.

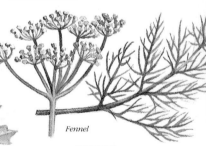

Fennel

FENNEL

Fennel leaves, with their aniseed taste are chopped and added to sauces and fish dishes. Its digestive properties have made it a traditional accompaniment to pork dishes. Fennel stalks are often laid over barbecues to flavour fish.

GARLIC

Garlic is a perennial bulb with extensive uses. It may be pounded into sauces or inserted into meat. A peeled clove will flavour a vinaigrette and it is delicious used to make garlic bread. The flavour becomes milder as it cooks.

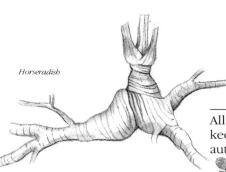

Horseradish

HORSERADISH

Horseradish has been cultivated in the UK since the sixteenth century. The root is grated and used as a condiment, like mustard, and is the traditional accompaniment to roast beef. When not available fresh, it can be bought ready grated.

Lemon Balm

LEMON BALM

Lemon balm is a perennial, with aromatic leaves which give off a strong lemon fragrance when crushed. The leaves can be chopped and added to stuffings for poultry and game, salads, desserts and fruit cups. They have a flavour somewhat like lemon rind.

Lovage

LOVAGE

Lovage is a hardy perennial growing over 120 cm (4 ft) high, with large, dark green leaves. The chopped leaves are good alone, or combined with other robust herbs, in stuffings, stews and soups, and in fresh tomato sauce for pasta. The flavour is very powerful.

MARJORAM

All marjorams dry well and keep their flavour. They give an authentic flavour to Provençal,

Marjoram

Italian and Greek dishes and go exceptionally well with tomatoes, and are the traditional flavouring for pizzas and Greek salads.

Mint

MINT

Spearmint is the mint most commonly used in the UK, for making mint sauce and jellies, and cooking with garden peas and new potatoes. Bowles' mint has a superior flavour; do not be put off by its hairy leaves.

OREGANO

Oregano is the wild marjoram, similar in taste but more powerful. It dries extremely

Oregano

well and is essential in Italian dishes especially Spaghetti Bolognese. It is also used in chilli powders.

Parsley

PARSLEY

In the UK parsley is used mainly as a garnish, but with its delicious flavour it can be used much more widely in cooking. Parsley forms part of the bouquet garni and fines herbes mixtures. Parsley sauce is the traditional accompaniment to boiled bacon and poached fish.

ROSEMARY

Rosemary is a bushy shrub with evergreen needles, dark-green

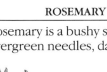

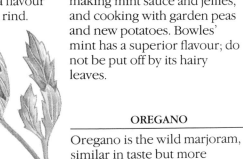

Rosemary

on top and silvery-grey underneath. Its flavour is so robust it can be overpowering. Sprigs of the herb must be removed from the dish after cooking. Rosemary is best used to flavour lamb.

SAGE

Sage has an extremely powerful flavour and can be used fresh or dried. It does not lose its taste, even after long cooking. It is used with fatty meats, such as pork and goose.

Sage

Summer savory

SUMMER SAVORY

Savory has a strong, bitter flavour and should be used in moderation. It needs long cooking to bring out and mellow its true flavour. It dries well and is said to have an affinity with bean dishes.

Tarragon

TARRAGON

French tarragon is one of the subtlest of herbs, and goes well with foods of delicate flavour, such as eggs, fish and chicken. It is part of the classic fines herbes mixture, and is good used in sauces.

THYME

Both common thyme and lemon thyme are very useful since they keep their flavour when dried or after cooking. Common thyme is good with meat and game. Lemon thyme suits chicken and fish.

Thyme

SPICES

The art of spicing food has a long and fascinating history, and is one of the most subtle techniques in cooking. Our A–Z guide shows how to use some of the lesser known as well as more familiar spices to best effect – in curry spice, pickles and marinades, as well as sweet dishes.

ALLSPICE

Allspice berries are similar to large peppercorns, with a spicy flavour mingling the tastes of cloves, cinnamon and nutmeg. It is used in smoked and

Allspice

pickled foods and traditional pork or game pies.

ASAFOETIDA

Asafoetida or 'giant fennel' is a huge odiferous member of the parsley family. When used in minute quantities it is a remarkable enhancer of other

Asafoetida

tastes and its frightful smell disappears in cooking. It is used extensively in spicy Middle Eastern dishes.

ANISEED

The small grey-green ribbed seeds of the aromatic anise annual with their spicy/sweet flavour are used in northern and eastern Europe in confectionery, desserts, biscuits, cakes and breads. Anise-flavoured alcoholic drinks are also often used in cookery. In India a small plateful of Aniseed is served with the bill to freshen the mouth and palate.

Caraway Seeds

CARAWAY SEEDS

Caraway seeds are small, oval and ribbed. Strongly aromatic, they have a warming peppery undertone and should be bought as seeds. Breads such as rye and pumpernickel frequently include caraway.

CARDAMOM

Three types of cardamom pods are available, black, green and

Cardamom

white. It is one of the essential spices of Indian cuisine, crucial in biryanis, pilaus, dals and curries. It is an ingredient of the mixture garam masala and of many Indian dishes.

Aniseed

CAYENNE

Cayenne is used as a milder alternative to chilli powder in Indian, North African and Latin American food. It has an affinity with fish and seafood and teams well with cheese and eggs.

CHILLI

Fiery chilli peppers are a very ancient spice, their cultivation stretching back 10,000 years, originating in Latin America.

Chilli

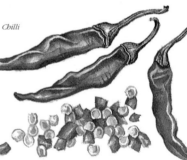

Chillis vary enormously in size, colour and strength but the ones available in this country generally come from Kenya and are very strong.

Cinnamon

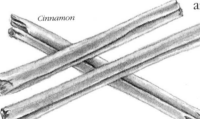

CINNAMON

Cinnamon is a universally popular spice, generally used for sweet dishes in the west and savoury ones in the East. In India it flavours curries and kormas. In Greece it is used in honeyed pastries.

Cayenne

CLOVES

Cloves are both sweet and pungent with an unmistakable aroma, but use them with restraint to avoid swamping other tastes. In British cookery a clove is used to flavour bread

Cloves

sauce and stud a ham. They blend well with apples in pies and crumbles and should be included in mulled wine mixes.

CUMIN

Cumin's spicy seeds are small, ridged and greenish-brown in colour. They have a strong unmistakable aroma, sweetish and warming. Their flavour is

Cumin

similarly pungent and penetrating and should be used in moderation, in seed or powdered form. Always buy it as whole seeds and grind only when needed.

Coriander Seeds

Ginger

CORIANDER SEEDS

Coriander seeds look like tiny ridged brown footballs. They are milder than many other spices so can be used in large quantities. The taste, fresh with a hint of bitterness, improves on keeping.

Dill Seeds

DILL SEEDS

Dill seeds have a fresh sweet aroma but a slightly bitter taste, similar to caraway seeds. They are good in pickled dishes, including the famous dill pickle, vinegars, marinades and dressing.

FENUGREEK

Roast whole fenugreek seeds lightly and grind to a golden powder. It is used most frequently in Indian food, and

Fenugreek

also in pickles and chutneys and in the Greek sweetmeat, Halva.

Fennel Seeds

FENNEL SEEDS

Fennel is best known as a vegetable but its seeds are also used in cooking, usually with fish. In the West, they are used in marinades, sauces and stuffing. In India, they are used in fish curries.

GINGER

Fresh ginger has a distinctive smell and strong taste, the fieriness of which is diminished in the powdered and crystallised form. Ground ginger is an important and traditional baking spice in the West.

Juniper Berries

JUNIPER BERRIES

Juniper berries with their spicy pine aroma and sweet resinous flavour have an affinity with robust meat dishes and are included in marinades and stuffings.

Mace

MACE

Mace is the crimson, lacy cage enclosing the shell of the nutmeg. It is available both as blades and ready ground. Because of its warm pungency it is best suited to savoury dishes.

Mustard Seeds

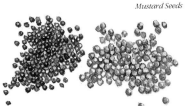

MUSTARD SEEDS

Whole mustard seeds are the basis of all prepared mustards and of the pungent mustard oil, beloved in India. They are used primarily in Indian food and to flavour pickles. Dry-fried, they lose their heat and have a warm nutty flavour.

NUTMEG

Nutmeg is milder than mace but has a similar warm sweetish taste. Grate directly

Nutmeg

over the mixing bowl or cooking pot to flavour a variety of sauces.

PAPRIKA

Paprika flavours a profusion of savoury foods – from goulashes to vegetables. The mildest kind

Paprika

is the most widely sold in Britain and imparts a wonderful reddish brown to food.

Pepper

PEPPER

Pepper is the most familiar spice of all. Black is stronger than white while green peppercorns have a mild, fresh taste. Peppercorns are added to marinades and stocks and are crushed in French recipes.

POPPY SEEDS

Poppy seeds are mild and sweetish and acquire a bitter sweet, nutty flavour when cooked. They are associated with baking and the seeds decorate many types of bread.

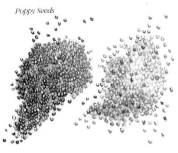
Poppy Seeds

Saffron

SAFFRON

Saffron is the world's most expensive spice. It imparts a distinctive aroma, a bitter honey-like taste and strong yellow colour to food. It is traditional in Spain's famous Paella and France's Bouillabaisse.

Sesame Seeds

SESAME SEEDS

Dried sesame seeds have a strong nutty flavour. Dry roast or fry in a little oil before use. They are popular in both Chinese and Japanese cookery and in their ground form make tahini paste.

STAR ANISE

Star anise is an attractive oriental spice especially associated with Chinese cookery. Red-cooked Chinese dishes frequently include star anise.

Star Anise

TURMERIC

Turmeric has a distinctive pungent flavour and is best known for its partnership with fish and rice: notably in traditional kedgeree, and pickles such as piccalilli.

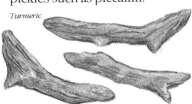
Turmeric

STOCKS & GRAVIES

The first lesson for any cook is how to make stock – a good stock is the foundation of all good soups, gravies and sauces. It is simple and easy to make, and once stored in the refrigerator, it is as handy as a stock cube only much more flavoursome.

The foundation of the best soups, sauces and gravies is a good stock. The basic ingredients are usually the raw bones of meat, fish, poultry or game, with added vegetables, herbs and seasonings and perhaps a touch of wine or sherry to give additional flavour. Stock is very simple to make, and it is as essential in the kitchen as a good knife or saucepan.

Stock cubes or powder are no substitute for a richly flavoured homemade stock. They taint the finished dish with a distinctive artificial flavour which ruins the taste and body of the recipe.

There are several basic stocks, including bone, beef, fish, chicken, veal, game and vegetable. Each one has its own particular use.

A pressure cooker is perfect for making stock, as it cuts down the cooking time considerably and saves fuel.

Basic rules

There are a few basic rules to remember when making stock. Firstly, all the ingredients should be very fresh and of good quality. The stock should be simmered for several hours to give a well flavoured, full bodied consistency.

Secondly, the finished stock should not be kept for more than 2–3 days in the refrigerator without reboiling for 15–20 minutes. Stock, in particular jellied stock, is very liable to bacterial growth which contaminates the food. The best thing to do is to make a large quantity of stock at one time and freeze it either in ice cube trays or small containers which are readily available when required. When freezing stock, it should be well reduced by boiling down, so that it is concentrated – that way it won't take up too much room in the freezer.

Never allow a stock to boil rapidly, as this will spoil the clarity of it. A long slow simmer produces a much better result. The longer the stock is cooked, the better the flavour, as the liquid reduces during cooking which concentrates the taste, and makes it more likely that the stock will gel.

Never add salt until you are actually using the stock, as cooking and reducing the stock will concentrate the flavours, and you could end up with a very salty stock.

It is important to remove any excess fat from meat and bones before cooking to prevent the stock being greasy. Once the stock is cooked, leave it to cool and then refrigerate for a couple of hours, when any fat will settle on the surface. It may then be removed by skimming a warm wet spoon, held at an angle, across the surface of the stock.

Always use a pan with a tight-fitting lid to ensure that the liquid does not evaporate too much, but allow the stock to cool with the lid half on. For further stocks see pages 26–27.

Simple Bone Stock

Makes approximately 1.5 litres (2½ pints)
450 g (1 lb) marrow bones, chopped
450 g (1 lb) shin of beef, cubed
2 onions, peeled and chopped
2–3 carrots, peeled and chopped
2 celery sticks, chopped
1 bay leaf
1 bouquet garni
4–6 black peppercorns
1.75 litres (3 pints) water
½ teaspoon salt

Preparation time: 15 minutes, plus cooling time
Cooking time: 4¼ hours

Place all the ingredients in a large pan.

Remove surface fat with paper towels.

1. Place all the ingredients in a large saucepan with a well fitting lid.

2. Slowly bring to the boil, and immediately reduce the heat to a slow simmer. Cover with a lid and simmer for 4 hours.

3. Remove from the heat, leave to cool for 30 minutes, then pour through a wire sieve set over a large bowl. Discard the solids left in the sieve.

4. Leave the stock to cool, then use a piece of paper towel to wipe over the surface of the stock to remove the excess fat.

5. Refrigerate until cold. Use a spoon to remove any of the remaining solidified fat. If not using immediately, the fat can be left to form a perfect seal and so preserve the stock until needed. Adjust the seasoning to taste.

Simple Chicken Stock

(Also for turkey or game)

**Makes approximately 1.6 litres
(2¾ pints)**
*1 large chicken carcass (or
turkey or game)*
1 onion, peeled and chopped
*1 large leek, trimmed and
sliced (optional)*
2 carrots, peeled and chopped
2 celery sticks, chopped
1 bay leaf
1 bouquet garni
4 black peppercorns
1.75 litres (3 pints) water
½ teaspoon salt

Preparation time: 15 minutes,
plus cooling time
Cooking time: 1½–2 hours

1. Place all the ingredients in a
large saucepan, breaking up
the carcass if necessary.

2. Slowly bring to the boil, and
immediately reduce the heat to
a slow simmer. Cover with a lid
and simmer for 1½–2 hours.

3. Remove from the heat, leave
to cool for 30 minutes, then
pour through a wire sieve set
over a large bowl. Discard the
solids left in the sieve.

4. Leave the stock to cool, then
use a piece of paper towel to
wipe over the surface of the
stock to remove the excess fat.

5. Refrigerate until cold, then
use a spoon, to remove any
remaining fat. Adjust the
seasoning to taste.

Meat Gravy

There is no need to use gravy
mix, gravy browning or stock
cubes, in order to make a
delicious gravy. All that is
required is the roasting tin with
its fat and juices from the meat.
The liquid used can be stock or
vegetable water, with a little
flour for thickening, if required.
It is traditional to serve a thin
gravy with beef, and a thicker
one with other roast meats. It is
important to pour the fat out of
the tin slowly, so that the rich
brown sediment remains in the
base of the pan.

Thin Meat Gravy

**Makes approximately 300 ml
(½ pint)**
salt
freshly ground black pepper
*approximately 300 ml (½ pint)
hot vegetable water or stock*

Preparation time: about 2
minutes
Cooking time: about 5 minutes

1. Ensure that all the fat is
removed from the tin, by
pouring it out slowly, leaving
the sediment and meat juices
behind.

2. Season the sediment with
salt and pepper and cook for ½
minute, stirring constantly.

3. Gradually pour in the hot
vegetable water, or stock,
stirring well.

4. Slowly bring to the boil,
scraping all the sediment from
the base of the pan. Boil rapidly
for 2 minutes, stirring
constantly. Adjust the seasoning
to taste, strain if liked, and
serve very hot.

**Makes approximately 600 ml
(1 pint)**
poultry giblets (without liver)
*about 600 ml (1 pint) cold
water*
*1 small onion, peeled and
halved*
1 carrot, peeled and halved
1 bouquet garni
2 tablespoons plain flour
salt
freshly ground black pepper
*1–2 tablespoons dry sherry
(optional)*

Preparation time: 15 minutes
Cooking time: 1¼ hours

Thick Meat Gravy

Makes 300 ml (½ pint)
*2 tablespoons fat (from
roasting the meat)*
1 tablespoon flour
*300 ml (½ pint) hot vegetable
water or stock*
salt
freshly ground pepper
*1 tablespoon sherry or wine
(optional)*

Preparation time: about 2
minutes
Cooking time: 5 minutes

1. Pour off the excess fat from
the roasting pan, leaving the
sediment and approximately 2
tablespoons of fat behind.

2. Sprinkle the flour into the
pan, and stir very well, scraping
up and mixing in all the
sediment and meat juices.
Cook for about 2 minutes,
stirring constantly, to brown
the flour, taking care not to
burn it.

3. Gradually stir the hot
vegetable water or stock into
the pan, stirring well. Bring to
the boil, stirring constantly.
Cook for 2 minutes, season

1. Put the giblets into a pan
with the water, onion, carrot
and bouquet garni. Bring to the
boil, cover and simmer for 1
hour. Strain.

2. Pour off all the fat except 1
tablespoon from the roasting
pan. Stir in the flour and cook
for 2 minutes, stirring
continually, scraping the
sediment from the base of the
pan.

3. Pour in the giblet stock, and
bring to the boil, stirring well.
Simmer for 2 minutes then
season, add the sherry if using,
and serve.

Stir in the flour, scraping
the sediment.

Gradually stir in the hot
stock and bring to the boil.

and add the sherry or wine.

4. Strain through a fine sieve
and serve very hot.

ALL-PURPOSE STOCKS

■

Stocks are the first step towards successful cooking. Used in soups, sauces, stews and many other recipes a good stock is the secret to success in producing dishes with a rich and satisfying flavour.

Stocks are made with bones, meat or fish, fresh vegetables, seasonings and flavourings, simmered slowly in water until all the goodness and flavour have been extracted. A vegetable stock can be made in a similar way with finely chopped vegetables instead of the meat, first sautéed in butter or oil and sweated over a low heat. Stock cubes may be substituted for homemade stock if you are in a hurry but you will have to accept a loss in flavour. It is far better to have a supply of the real thing on hand in the fridge or freezer.

All stocks can be reduced down for a really concentrated flavour and kept refrigerated for 3–4 days or frozen for up to 3 months. If short of time, using a pressure cooker will greatly reduce the cooking time and also save substantially on fuel bills.

Chicken or Game Stock

Use for soups, sauces and stews. This stock is suitable for game and poultry.

Makes about 900 ml (1½ pints)
1 game carcass (chicken, duck, turkey etc) broken up
giblets (minus liver), if available
50 g (2 oz) green bacon, roughly chopped
1.2 litres (2 pints) water
1 onion, peeled and quartered
2 carrots, scraped and quartered
1 leek, trimmed and roughly chopped
1 celery stick, roughly chopped
2 shallots, peeled
4 black peppercorns
1 bouquet garni
salt

Preparation time: 15 minutes, plus cooling time
Cooking time: 3½ hours

1. Place all the ingredients in a large saucepan, and bring to the boil.

2. Skim the surface of the stock with a perforated spoon to remove any scum. Cover and simmer for 3 hours, skimming occasionally.

3. Cool slightly, then strain the stock through a colander into a large bowl.

4. Rinse the pan, and return the stock to the pan. Bring to the boil and boil rapidly for 15 minutes to concentrate the flavour of the stock. Then cool slightly.

5. Pour the stock through a fine sieve. (If a very clear stock is required, the sieve may be lined with muslin.) Cool rapidly and refrigerate.

6. When completely cold, scrape off any fat which is on the surface of the stock.

Fish Stock

Beware of overcooking fish stock, as the bones can make it very bitter. For a more concentrated flavour, reduce the stock after straining.

Makes about 600 ml (1 pint)
450 g (1 lb) fish bones and trimmings (including head)
600 ml (1 pint) cold water
1 small onion, peeled and quartered
1 carrot, scraped and quartered
1 celery stick, roughly chopped
1 leek, trimmed and chopped
1 bouquet garni
salt

Preparation time: 10 minutes, plus cooling time
Cooking time: 30 minutes

1. Place the bones, trimmings and the remaining ingredients in a saucepan and slowly bring to the boil. Immediately reduce the heat, cover and simmer very gently for 30 minutes, skimming the surface of the stock occasionally to remove any scum.

2. Cool the stock slightly, then strain it through a colander into a large bowl.

3. Leave the stock to settle and then pour it through a fine sieve. (If a very clear stock is required, the sieve may be lined with muslin.) Cool rapidly and refrigerate.

Brown Stock

Use for making brown soups and sauces, beef and lamb stews, meat aspic, etc.

Makes about 2 litres (3½ pints)
1.5 kg (3 lb) beef marrow bones, sawn into pieces, fat removed
1 kg (2 lb) shin of beef, cubed, fat removed
2 large onions, skins left on
2 leeks, trimmed and roughly sliced
2 carrots, scraped and quartered
2 celery sticks, roughly chopped
1 bouquet garni
1 bay leaf
6 black peppercorns
2.25 litres (4 pints) water
salt

Preparation time: 15 minutes, plus cooling time
Cooking time: 4 hours
Oven: 220°C, 425°F, Gas Mark 7

1. Put the bones, beef and onions into a roasting pan and cook, uncovered, in a preheated oven for 30 minutes until they are well browned.

2. Place the meat, bones and onions and all the remaining ingredients in a large saucepan. Bring to the boil, cover and simmer for 3½ hours, skimming the surface occasionally to remove scum.

3. Cool slightly, then strain the stock through a colander into a large bowl.

4. Rinse the pan, and return the stock to the pan. Bring to the boil and boil rapidly for 15 minutes to concentrate the flavour of the stock. Cool slightly.

5. Pour the stock through a fine sieve. (If a very clear stock is required, the sieve may be lined with muslin.) Cool rapidly and refrigerate.

6. When completely cold, scrape off any fat which is on the surface of the stock.

For perfect Stocks

■ Raw bones should always be used as they give a better flavour. They will also help the stock to gel and will keep the stock clear in colour. Rinse the bones to remove any blood.
■ Do not use potatoes, as they tend to make the stock cloudy.
■ If a very jellied stock is required, either add a pig's trotter or a calf's foot, split.
■ Remember to skim the stock occasionally when cooking to get rid of scum.
■ Never add the liver from the giblets as it will make the stock cloudy.
■ It is important that the final cooling of the stock is done as quickly as possible. The best way to do this is to place the bowl over a roasting pan full of ice cubes.
■ Do not use oily fish such as herring and mackerel for fish stock. The best fish bones to use are plaice, sole, haddock, cod, whiting or halibut.

White Veal Stock

Makes about 2 litres (3½ pints)
1.5 kg (3 lb) veal knuckle bones, sawn into pieces
1 kg (2 lb) stewing or pie veal, cubed, fat removed
2 large onions, peeled and quartered
2 large carrots, scraped and quartered
2 celery sticks, roughly chopped
1 bouquet garni
1 bay leaf
6 black peppercorns
2.25 litres (4 pints) water
salt

Preparation time: 15 minutes, plus cooling time
Cooking time: 4 hours

1. Place the bones and veal in a large saucepan, cover with cold water, and bring to the boil.

2. Drain well and rinse the bones.

3. Rinse the pan. Return the bones and meat to the pan. Add all the remaining ingredients. Slowly bring to the boil.

4. Skim the surface to remove any scum. Cover with a tight fitting lid and simmer for 3½ hours.

5. Cool slightly, then strain the stock through a colander into a large bowl.

6. Rinse the pan, and return the stock to the pan. Bring to the boil and boil rapidly for 15 minutes to concentrate the flavour of the stock. Cool slightly.

7. Sieve the stock as above (see step 5) and remove fat from the surface when cold.

SAUCES

Sauces have an essential place in every cook's repertoire. Our complete guide to sauce-making covers all the classic sauces — Béchamel, Velouté, Demi-glace, Hollandaise, Béarnaise and Mayonnaise — together with their many variations.

A good sauce can bring life to all cooking, and is the foundation of many dishes, whether sweet or savoury. Most sauces are designed to complement a principal ingredient in a recipe, and they should never disguise or overwhelm its taste. But some sauces can be in direct contrast to the ingredients or dishes they accompany, subtly blending two flavours in one. Sauces can give endless variety to simple everyday meals as well as to special occasion dishes: a rich Béarnaise can enhance the flavour of fillet of beef or a grilled steak, but a tasty Mornay sauce can transform a selection of leftover vegetables into a delicious dish in its own right.

The white sauces tend to be used for eggs, fish and vegetables and some chicken recipes, whereas brown sauces are usually reserved for dark meats like lamb and beef, and game. However, this is not always so, as a red wine sauce may be used for poultry or for some fish, and a cream sauce may accompany pheasant.

The basic 'rule' with sauces, however, is that they should be of good flavour, good texture and made from the best ingredients. They should always be of the correct consistency for the dish, and should always add to the enjoyment of the dish. For sauces are, as Larousse said, 'liquid seasoning for food'.

For simplicity, sauces can be divided into two main categories – flour-based and butter-based.

Flour-based sauces

Most savoury sauces thickened with plain flour incorporate it into the sauce in the form of a roux. These are the white sauces such as Béchamel (made with milk), the 'blond' sauces such as Velouté (made with white stock) and the brown sauces which are made with brown stock. Sauces made by this roux method can be further enriched and thickened by adding egg yolks and/or cream or butter, usually at the end of cooking. 'Mounting' a sauce with butter just before it is served both enriches the flavour and gives the sauce a tantalizing gloss. Plain cold butter or cold savoury butter is added in small dice to the sauce and whisked through gently until it is softened and thickened.

Other thickened sauces

Sauces can also be made without the initial roux when flour, cornflour, potato flour or arrowroot are mixed with water or stock and then poured into the hot liquid to cook and thicken the liquid. Beurre manié (page 33) is another way of thickening without the initial roux.

Butter-based sauces

The butter sauces include the hot emulsified sauces such as Hollandaise, where the emulsion is of egg yolk and butter; and basic emulsified butter sauces with no egg yolks where a seasoning such as lemon juice, garlic or shallot and/or a reduction of wine, is mixed with butter.

Other sauces are the cold emulsified sauces such as Mayonnaise, where the emulsion is of egg yolk and oil, and the oil and vinegar sauces such as French dressing.

The mother sauces

Certain basic sauce techniques and recipes have become classics, and these should be mastered and learned, for they are the basis for many variations. These basic recipes are called the 'mother' sauces, and the variations the 'daughter' sauces.

The roux-based mothers are Béchamel, Velouté and Demi-glace or Fond de Veau Lié, and the emulsion mothers are Hollandaise and Mayonnaise. Many variations of these sauces can be created. Béchamel plus cheese becomes Mornay; Velouté plus cream and sometimes egg yolks, becomes Sauce Suprême; red wine and shallots plus Demi-glace makes a Bordelaise sauce; Hollandaise plus orange rind and juice becomes Maltaise; and Mayonnaise plus garlic becomes the pungent Aïoli.

Left to right: Béarnaise, Demi glace Mayonnaise, Maltaise

For perfect Sauces

■ Even the simplest sauce can transform a dish. Never wash away the juices and encrustations from a pan or roasting tin in which meat has been fried or roasted. A quick roux and some stock, some butter or simply stock alone can take advantage of this sediment to make a basic sauce which will enhance that meat.

■ Sauces like Hollandaise and the melted butter sauces are most useful when there is no sediment as above – when grilling or cooking vegetables, for instance – with which to make a sauce.

■ A bain-marie is invaluable for keeping sauces warm, especially those liable to separate if overheated.

■ Flavour is all when making sauces, so the best ingredients should always be used: butter, not margarine; a flavoured Béchamel milk rather than plain; a good strong reduced stock rather than a weak one; a good quality wine or wine vinegar; fresh herbs rather than dried.

■ If a sauce involves reduction, season towards the end rather than at the beginning, as the seasoning will concentrate as the sauce reduces.

■ In many of the 'daughter' roux-based sauces, it is not strictly a case of merely adding a flavouring to the 'mother': many ingredients like garlic or shallots, for instance, will need to be softened in the roux butter first before the flour is added. This applies to a few of the Béchamel and Velouté 'daughters' as well as to many brown and butter sauces.

Basic Sauces

∎

*Once you have mastered the basic techniques shown here,
you will feel much more confident about tackling other members
of the large sauce family.*

At this point we introduce two of the 'mother' sauces – basic sauces which can then be used as the foundation for many others. One is a classic flour-based sauce, made with a roux, and the other is an emulsified sauce.

The Roux The basic technique of making a 'roux' (liaison of flour and butter) is fundamental to many sauces, white and brown. For Béchamel the roux should never be allowed to colour. Remember always to cook a roux over gentle heat, to prevent it burning. The other main point about flour-based sauces is that they must be thoroughly cooked, after the liquid is added, to avoid a raw 'floury' taste.

Emulsified sauces are much more difficult – the basic principle being the absorption by egg yolks of oil or butter. The great secret here is patience – the instructions tell you to add the melted butter or oil drop by drop – and they mean it. Master this technique by making mayonnaise – adding the oil slowly drop by drop, and you can then go on to the more difficult sauces such as Hollandaise (see page 44).

Consistency	Uses	Quantities of Butter and Flour	Milk
Thin sauce	A basis for soups	15 g (½ oz) butter and flour	300 ml (½ pint)
Pouring sauce (medium thick)	For accompanying sauces	20 g (¾ oz) butter and flour	300 ml (½ pint)
Coating sauce (thick)	For coating foods	25 g (1 oz) butter and flour	300 ml (½ pint)
Panada (very thick)	For binding croquettes and as a basis for soufflés	50 g (2 oz) butter and flour	300 ml (½ pint)

Béchamel Sauce

Flour-based Sauces

∎ A 'roux' is a liaison of melted butter and flour. This forms a paste to which a liquid – milk, for béchamel – is added to give a sauce.
∎ A liquid that is infused with vegetables and seasonings acquires extra flavour, and adds to the final taste of the sauce and the dish.
∎ For best results, the infusion of vegetables should be left to cool in the liquid so that it has a very good flavour.
∎ For a smooth, shiny sauce, add the liquid gradually to the 'roux', beating well each time to get rid of any lumps.

Makes about 300 ml (½ pint)

300 ml (½ pint) milk
½ small onion, peeled and halved
1 small carrot, peeled and halved
½ celery stick, cut into small pieces
1 small bay leaf
1 bouquet garni
4 black peppercorns
a little grated nutmeg
⅛ teaspoon salt
25 g (1 oz) butter
25 g (1 oz) plain flour

Preparation time: 10 minutes, plus infusing and cooling time
Cooking time: 5–10 minutes

Add all the flavourings to the milk and heat

Add the flour to melted butter to make a roux

1. Put the milk, onion, carrot, celery, bay leaf, bouquet garni peppercorns, nutmeg and salt into a saucepan. Bring to the boil very slowly.

2. Remove from the heat, cover with a lid and leave until completely cold.

Mayonnaise

For perfect Mayonnaise

■ It is essential that all the ingredients are at room temperature.
■ The oil should be added to the egg yolk drop by drop. If it is added too quickly, the sauce will curdle. If this happens, place another egg yolk in a clean bowl and gradually add the curdled mixture to the yolk, whisking constantly, then add the remaining oil drop by drop.
■ The eggs should be very fresh (but not straight from the hen or the mayonnaise will not thicken).
■ The type of oil used determines the flavour of the mayonnaise. A corn or vegetable oil gives a blander flavour than a richer olive oil.
■ The type of vinegar used also varies the flavour of the mayonnaise. Choose one which complements the flavour of the food with which it is to be served.

Makes just over 150 ml (¼ pint)

1 egg yolk
¼ teaspoon salt
½ teaspoon dry mustard powder
freshly ground white pepper
150 ml (¼ pint) olive or vegetable oil
1 tablespoon white wine vinegar

Preparation time: 10 minutes

1. Place the egg yolk in a bowl, and gradually beat in the salt, mustard, and pepper, using a wire balloon whisk.

2. Add the oil, drop by drop, whisking vigorously after each addition so that it is absorbed completely before the next addition.

3. After about half the oil has been added, the mayonnaise will start to look shiny. The mixture should be thick. (If the mixture is runny after about half the oil has been added, it has curdled. See hints box for advice.) If so, the oil can now be added more rapidly, about 1 tablespoon at a time.

4. As the mixture becomes very thick, add a little of the vinegar to soften it, then add the remaining oil.

5. Blend in the rest of the vinegar. Adjust the seasoning to taste. The consistency should be as thick as lightly whipped double cream.

6. Store in the refrigerator in a covered container for up to 2 weeks. A thicker mayonnaise can be made by increasing the

First add the oil drop by drop, whisking well.

Once it has thickened, add the remaining oil

number of egg yolks used. You can also increase the amount of oil to 175 ml (6 fl oz) per egg yolk, but it is then more likely to curdle.

3. Strain the milk through a fine sieve. Discard the flavourings.

4. Melt the butter in a heavy-based saucepan over a gentle heat. Add the flour and stir well to form a 'roux' (see page 30). Do not allow the flour to colour.

5. Gradually stir in one-third of the flavoured milk, then the rest in similar quantities, blending well between each addition and stirring constantly. Bring to the boil stirring well and cook for a further 2 minutes, stirring constantly.

6. Adjust the seasoning to taste and use as required.

Blender Mayonnaise

Note that a whole egg is used for this method, sometimes with an extra egg yolk added.

Makes 450 ml (¾ pint)
1 egg
¼ teaspoon salt
½ teaspoon dry mustard
1 tablespoon wine vinegar
300 ml (½ pint) olive oil

1. Pour the egg in the goblet of the blender. Add the salt and mustard. Blend at top speed for 30 seconds, then add the wine vinegar and blend again.

2. Remove the cap of the blender and, with the blender at top speed, pour in the oil in a thin stream of drops. The sauce will begin to thicken after 150 ml (¼ pint) oil has gone in. Continue to add the oil slowly until it has all been absorbed.

3. Scrape the mayonnaise into a bowl with a rubber spatula and store, covered, in the refrigerator.

Pour in the oil through the central hole.

WHITE SAUCES Mother sauce: Béchamel or Velouté

Daughter Sauce	Ingredients		Method of Preparation	Uses
Sauce Allemande (Sauce Parisienne)	2 egg yolks 150 ml (¼ pint) white stock (either chicken or fish)	300 ml (½ pint) Velouté sauce 40 g (1½ oz) butter	Beat the egg yolks with the stock and blend into the sauce. Cook gently, without boiling, whisking all the time, until reduced and thickened. Remove from the heat and beat in the butter.	Chicken, fish, eggs, vegetables.
Sauce Aurore	300 ml (½ pint) Velouté sauce	2 tablespoons tomato purée 35 g (1¼ oz) butter	Make the basic Velouté, then whisk in the tomato purée. Season, remove from the heat, and whisk in the butter.	Eggs, chicken, pork, fish, veal, sweetbreads.
Caper Sauce	300 ml (½ pint) Velouté sauce	1 tablespoon caper or lemon juice 1 tablespoon capers	Make the basic Velouté sauce, stir in the caper juice or lemon juice, and lastly the finely chopped capers.	Fish, mutton.
Sauce Chaudfroid	300 ml (½ pint) Béchamel or Velouté sauce 150 ml (¼ pint) Aspic (see page 50)	1 teaspoon gelatine 2 tablespoons cream	Make the Béchamel or Velouté, then stir in the aspic jelly and dissolved gelatine. Remove from the heat, stir in the cream. Cool to a coating consistency, and use to coat boned, stuffed chicken etc.	Chicken, fish.
Egg Sauce	300 ml (½ pint) Béchamel sauce 1–2 hard-boiled eggs	1–2 tablespoons chopped parsley or chives	Make the basic Béchamel sauce. Stir in the finely chopped eggs and selected herb.	Fish.
Sauce à l'Estragon (Tarragon Sauce)	150 ml (¼ pint) white wine 6 tablespoons chopped tarragon 1 shallot, chopped	300 ml (½ pint) Béchamel or Velouté sauce 15 g (½ oz) butter	Place the wine, 3 tablespoons of tarragon and shallot in a pan, and heat to reduce to about 1½ tablespoons. Strain into the sauce and simmer for 2–3 minutes. Stir in the rest of the chopped tarragon and the butter off the heat.	Eggs, fish, chicken, vegetables.
Sauce Mornay	300 ml (½ pint) Béchamel sauce	50 g (2 oz) Gruyère or Parmesan cheese, grated	Make a basic Béchamel sauce. Stir in the cheese off the heat.	Chicken, veal, eggs, fish, pasta, vegetables.
Mushroom Sauce	25 g (1 oz) butter 100 g (4 oz) mushrooms, finely chopped	300 ml (½ pint) Béchamel sauce a squeeze of lemon juice	Melt the butter and fry the mushrooms gently. Drain and stir into the Béchamel sauce. Add the lemon juice.	Fish, meat, poultry.
Parsley Sauce	300 ml (½ pint) Béchamel or Velouté sauce	2 tablespoons chopped parsley	Make a basic Béchamel or Velouté sauce. Stir in the parsley and cook for 2 minutes.	Bacon, fish, eggs, vegetables.
Sauce Soubise (Onion Sauce)	40 g (1½ oz) butter 225 g (8 oz) sliced onions 25 g (1 oz) flour	175 ml (6 fl oz) white stock or milk 4 tablespoons cream salt and pepper pinch of nutmeg	Melt the butter, add the onions, and cook for 25 minutes without browning. Add flour, cook for 2 minutes. Add stock, boil. Cook for 5 minutes, stirring. Stir in cream and seasonings. Variation: add 75 g (3 oz) rice instead of flour, put in an ovenproof dish with the stock and cook covered for 45 minutes.	Poultry, vegetables, veal, lamb.
Sauce Suprême	300 ml (½ pint) Velouté sauce 2 egg yolks	2 tablespoons double cream 25 g (1 oz) butter	Make a basic Velouté sauce. Beat the egg yolks and cream together. Mix in some hot sauce, return to the pan, whisk and heat gently. Stir in the butter.	Eggs, poultry, vegetables.

ROUX-BASED SAUCES

Most thickened sauces, brown and white, are based on a butter and flour roux. The brown sauces are based on the mother Demi-glace sauce, while the white ones are based on the basic mothers Béchamel (made with milk) or Velouté (made with stock). All can be further thickened with egg, cream or butter.

General method

A roux is a liaison of butter or oil, and flour, and is the thickening agent for many sauces and soups. Firstly, the butter is melted to a foam, to which is added the flour. This is cooked slowly over a gentle heat to ensure that the flour is thoroughly cooked, thus eliminating the raw flour taste.

The roux for a Béchamel sauce is cooked without colouring, so that the basic sauce is white, or the colour of the flour. Milk is then added gradually to form the sauce.

For a Velouté, the roux is cooked a little longer until it is straw-coloured, and then the liquid – generally a white chicken, veal or fish stock – is added. The roux for a brown sauce demands longer cooking so that the butter and flour turn to a rich dark brown, giving the basic colour to the sauce. Then the liquid, a brown stock, is added.

At all times, care should be taken that the heat is fairly gentle, to prevent the roux from burning, as this would ruin the finished sauce.

Perfect roux-based sauces

■ Always use a heavy-based saucepan, as a thin pan can cause scorching. A stainless steel pan is best.
■ It is essential to cook the roux thoroughly to prevent a 'raw' flour taste in the finished sauce. This applies to both white and brown sauces. Stir well to cook evenly and prevent lumps.
■ The flavour of the finished sauce is very much dependent on the quality of the stock or infused milk used. A stock should be clear and well reduced, and the infused milk flavoured with onion, celery, carrot, bay leaf and peppercorns.
■ Whisking helps to prevent lumps and gives a shiny gloss to the sauce.
■ If the liquid is hot when added to the roux, it saves time in whisking and also helps to prevent lumps.
■ Always add seasonings (except salt) during cooking, not at the end, as they will not otherwise be absorbed into the sauce.
■ Always taste the sauce before serving.
■ If a sauce is made in advance, it may be covered with clingfilm, a butter paper or a little cold liquid (water or stock for a Velouté or brown sauce, milk for a Béchamel) to prevent a skin forming.
■ If a sauce is to be enriched by egg, cream or butter, this should be done just before serving to prevent curdling or separation.
■ If a sauce is lumpy, it can be improved by passing it through a very fine sieve.
■ If a sauce is too thick, it may be thinned down by the addition of milk, cream or stock, stirred into the sauce a tablespoon at a time.
■ Sauces can be kept covered in the refrigerator for about 3 days.

Other methods of thickening sauces

Beurre manié or kneaded butter

This is a mixture of butter and flour – slightly more butter than flour – which is added at the end of cooking rather than at the beginning. The butter is creamed with the flour to give a firm paste. This mixture is dropped, in small pieces, into the hot liquid and then whisked in vigorously. The butter melts, distributing the flour evenly throughout the liquid. By this method, the sauce can be quickly thickened to the exact consistency required, because it is added piece by piece. Simmer for at

least 5 minutes to cook the flour. Beurre manié is very useful when casseroles, soups and stews need to be thickened at the end of the cooking time, and where the exact quantity of liquid is unknown. It is seldom used for sauces on their own.

Egg yolks and cream

These are used for sauces and for soups. They enrich Velouté and Béchamel sauces, and are added at the last minute, just before serving. Great care should be taken that the sauce is not too hot otherwise it will curdle the egg. The saucepan should be removed from the heat, and a little of the hot liquid mixed with the egg/cream liaison before stirring it into the sauce. If the sauce is flour-based, the saucepan may

be returned to the heat to heat through, but do not allow the sauce to boil or it will almost certainly curdle.

Reduction

This method is used to concentrate the flavour of the sauce, at the same time producing the correct consistency. The reduction is usually carried out before the sauce is thickened, thus giving less chance of the sauce scorching or burning.

White sauces are not usually reduced in this way, but the basic brown sauces are often cooked for several hours to concentrate the flavour before they are thickened. A wide pan is always used for reduction, and the sauce is boiled hard, which also helps to give it a shine. This is the method used for Meat Glaze (see page 41).

BÉCHAMEL SAUCE

The most basic of white sauces is that made simply with a butter and flour roux and plain milk. The use of a flavoured milk, however – milk brought slowly to the boil with flavourings including onion and peppercorns – is what transforms a white sauce into a Béchamel: for a little extra trouble the ordinary becomes subtly superior.

All white sauces can be made to varying consistencies, upon which, too, will depend the success of a dish. It is the proportions of butter, flour and liquid that will make a basic sauce thick or thin – pouring consistency for an accompanying sauce, say, or very thick for a soufflé foundation (see page 30, which lists the various possible consistencies of white sauces).

The basic recipe for Béchamel sauce is also given on page 30. Here, we give a slightly different version to show how subtle changes in flavour can be achieved.

Béchamel is one of the mothers of white sauces. See the chart on page 32 for the sauces that are derived from it.

Makes 300 ml (½ pint)
300 ml (½ pint) milk
2 slices onion
1 bay leaf
2 slices carrot
½ celery stick
6 white peppercorns
1 blade mace
25 g (1 oz) butter
25 g (1 oz) plain flour
salt
a pinch of nutmeg

Preparation time: 10 minutes, plus infusing time
Cooking time: 5–7 minutes

1. Put the milk into a saucepan with the onion, bay leaf, carrot, celery, peppercorns and mace. Very slowly bring to the boil, then remove from the heat and leave to infuse for 20–30 minutes. Strain through a sieve, and discard the flavourings.

2. Melt the butter in a clean saucepan until foaming, but not coloured. Stir in the flour and cook for 2 minutes, stirring constantly, and taking care that the roux does not colour. Gradually stir in the milk, a little at a time, mixing well. Bring to the boil, stirring or whisking. Season with salt and nutmeg.

3. Simmer for 2 minutes, adjust the seasoning to taste, and use as required.

Leeks au Gratin

Make a basic Béchamel Sauce and whisk in 150 ml (¼ pint) double cream. Off the heat, stir in 25 g (1 oz) each of grated Gruyère and Parmesan cheese and stir until melted. Pour the sauce over 6–8 cooked leeks and sprinkle another 25 g (1 oz) of grated cheese on top. Place in a preheated oven (190°C, 375°F, Gas Mark 5) or under a preheated grill until golden brown.

Curried Eggs

Make the infused milk for the Béchamel Sauce (above). Melt the butter for the roux, add 1 finely chopped onion and brown for 10 minutes. Stir in 1–2 tablespoons curry powder and cook slowly for 1–2 minutes. Add the infused milk, bring to the boil and cook for 10 minutes, stirring. Stir in 2 teaspoons lemon juice and 2–3 tablespoons cream and pour over 6 hardboiled eggs.

Other methods of thickening sauces

Arrowroot or potato flour

Both arrowroot and potato flour are added, in a paste form, at the end of cooking. They are blended with cold liquid, either stock, milk, water or wine, then whisked into the hot liquid, and brought just to the boil to thicken the sauce. Both are useful for quickly thickening a roux-based sauce that is too thin, but will themselves thin if boiled for too long.

Arrowroot gives a clear sauce which is often used for glazed fruit flans.

The proportions generally used are: for 600 ml (1 pint) of liquid, 2–3 level teaspoons of arrowroot or potato flour should be blended with 2–3 tablespoons of cold liquid.

Cornflour

The same method and proportions are used as for arrowroot and potato flour. Cornflour is usually used for thickening sweet dishes.

Veal Orloff

Braised Veal with Onions and Mushrooms

This classic dish can be prepared in advance. Cook the veal the day before and carve, stuff and reshape on the day. After coating with the sauce, allow 30–40 minutes in the oven at 180°C, 350°F, Gas Mark 4 to warm through.

1.25 kg (2½ lb) fillet of veal
40 g (1½ oz) butter
1 large onion, diced
1 celery stick, diced
1 carrot, diced
150 ml (¼ pint) dry white wine
300 ml (½ pint) Veal Stock (see page 27)
salt
freshly ground black pepper
1 bouquet garni
300 ml (½ pint) Mornay Sauce (see page 32)
1 tablespoon single cream
225 g (8 oz) white button mushrooms, trimmed and washed
2 teaspoons lemon juice
1 rounded teaspoon arrowroot mixed with 1 tablespoon cold water
Sauce Soubise:
2 large onions, chopped
25 g (1 oz) butter
75 g (3 oz) long grain rice
150 ml (¼ pint) Veal Stock (see page 27)
freshly ground white pepper
1 egg yolk
1 tablespoon single cream

Preparation time: 15–20 minutes, plus assembly time
Cooking time: 3 hours
Oven: 180°C, 350°F, Gas Mark 4;
then: 160°C, 325°F, Gas Mark 3;
then: 200°C, 400°F, Gas Mark 6

1. Tie the veal up neatly with string so that it will hold its shape while being cooked. Melt 25 g (1 oz) of the butter in a casserole, add the diced vegetables and place the meat on top. Put the lid on the casserole, and cook for 30 minutes in a preheated oven.

2. Remove from the oven, pour over the white wine, and return the casserole uncovered to the oven for another 30 minutes to reduce the wine.

3. Take the casserole out of the oven again and pour the stock in so that it comes half-way up the meat. Season with salt and pepper and add the bouquet garni. Cover with greaseproof paper and the lid.

4. Lower the temperature of the oven and cook the veal for 2 hours.

5. Meanwhile, make the Sauce Soubise, Mornay Sauce and the mushroom garnish. Cook the onions for the Soubise gently in the butter in an ovenproof dish until soft but not coloured, then add the rice, stock, some salt and the white pepper. Bring to the boil, cover with a lid, and cook in the oven alongside the veal for about 30 minutes until very soft (the rice needs to be *over*cooked). Remove, cool a little, then work to a purée in a processor or blender, or push through a sieve. Stir in the egg yolk and cream.

6. Prepare the Mornay Sauce. Beat in the cream, and cover with a butter paper or greased greaseproof paper to prevent a skin forming.

7. Next prepare the mushroom garnish. Cook the mushrooms in the remaining butter with a squeeze of lemon juice for about 2–3 minutes. Add a little salt and pepper. Set aside.

8. When the veal is ready, take out of the oven and place in an ovenproof serving dish a little longer and wider than the veal, and about 4 cm (1½ inches) deep. Keep warm. Strain the stock from the casserole into a small pan and add the arrowroot and water. Set aside to make gravy.

9. Carve the meat into thin slices, keeping the order of the slices. Spread each slice with the Soubise purée and reshape the meat joint on the serving dish. Any extra filling can be spread around and over the meat.

10. Spoon the Mornay Sauce over the meat and brown in the oven at the higher final temperature for about 12–15 minutes. Heat up the mushrooms briefly, and simmer the gravy, stirring, until hot.

11. Pour a little of the gravy around the meat, and garnish with the mushrooms. Put the remaining gravy in a gravy boat and hand separately.

Fresh Vegetable Platter

450 g (1 lb) each of vegetables in season, such as carrots, French beans, courgettes, cauliflower, broccoli etc

Slice the vegetables into even-sliced pieces and steam or blanch so that they are still crisp and al dente. Arrange attractively on a serving platter and pour over 1 recipe quantity Béchamel Sauce.

This attractive vegetable platter makes a very good hors d'oeuvre, or would make an excellent accompaniment to cold sliced beef or poultry.

VELOUTÉ SAUCE

Velouté is the other mother of the roux-based white sauces (see the chart on page 32 for the variations possible on this theme). In Velouté-based sauces it is the quality of the stock used – its intensity of flavour and its clarity – that will make all the difference to the ultimate success of the finished sauce, and the dish.

This basic Velouté sauce is usually enriched with egg yolk and cream and/or butter just before serving (see page 33). For this recipe, use 1 egg yolk blended with 2–3 tablespoons of cream or 25 g (1 oz) butter.

Makes 300 ml (½ pint)
20 g (¾ oz) butter
20 g (¾ oz) flour
300 ml (½ pint) Chicken, Veal
*   or Fish Stock (pages 26–27)*
salt
freshly ground white pepper

Preparation time: 10 minutes, plus preparing the stock
Cooking time: about 25 minutes

1. Melt the butter in a saucepan until foaming. Stir in the flour and cook for 5 minutes until the roux is straw-coloured.

2. Bring the stock to the boil and gradually stir into the roux. Bring to the boil, season with salt and pepper and simmer for 15 minutes whisking, until the sauce is the correct consistency.

3. When the sauce is thick and smooth enrich with egg and cream or butter as required (see page 33).

Chicken Chaudfroid

Thin sauces

If a sauce is too thin, place it in a wide pan and boil it rapidly, stirring constantly with a wooden spoon until it has reduced down to the desired consistency. Thicken with beurre manié (see page 33) whisking the kneaded butter into the sauce.

Serves 6
6 chicken pieces
1 onion, peeled and halved
1 sprig thyme
1 sprig parsley
1 small bay leaf
1 small carrot
6 black peppercorns
1 recipe quantity Sauce
*   Chaudfroid (page 32)*
To garnish:
cucumber peel
1 large tomato
1 small green pepper
lemon peel

Preparation time: 1 hour, plus cooling overnight
Cooking time: 1½–1¾ hours

1. Wipe the chicken pieces and put in a large saucepan along with the onion, herbs, carrot and peppercorns. Cover with cold water and bring slowly to the boil. Skim to remove scum then cover with the lid. Simmer for 20–25 minutes until the chicken is tender.

2. Lift out the chicken pieces with a slotted spoon and cool, then cover with clingfilm and chill overnight. Strain the stock and cool, then chill overnight.

3. Use the chicken stock to make the Aspic (see page 50) for the Sauce Chaudfroid, allowing a little extra for the garnish. Make the sauce (see page 32) and leave until it is the consistency of thick cream, when it is ready to use for coating.

4. Remove the skin from the chicken pieces, pat them dry, and place them on a wire tray over a lipped baking sheet. Coat each piece carefully with the sauce, allowing the excess to drain off on to the sheet below. Allow about 15 minutes to set, then give the pieces a second coating if necessary, scraping up the excess sauce from the sheet, and reheating slightly to return to the correct consistency.

5. Cut the cucumber peel, tomato, pepper and lemon peel into narrow strips or shapes and dip into the remaining Aspic. Arrange them in decorative patterns on the set sauce on the chicken pieces. Allow to set in place before spooning over the remaining Aspic. Leave the chicken pieces in a cool place to set completely.

Filets de Sole Normande

**Serves 4 as a main course,
6–8 as a starter**
4 sole, about 450 g (1 lb) each
1 litre (1¾ pints) mussels
65 ml (2½ fl oz) dry cider (or
*   dry white wine)*
butter
4 shallots, finely chopped
225 g (8 oz) mushrooms, thinly
*   sliced*
salt
freshly ground white pepper
225 g (8 oz) small shrimps,
*   cooked and peeled*
Sauce:
1 recipe quantity Velouté Sauce
*   made with the stock from*
*   cooking the fish*
2 egg yolks
4 tablespoons double cream
50 g (2 oz) butter

Preparation time: at least 30
minutes
Cooking time: 20–25 minutes
Oven: 150°C, 300°F, Gas Mark 2

1. Fillet and skin the sole
(see page 96) and make a fish
stock with the heads, tails and
bones (see page 26).

2. Scrub the mussels well,
removing beards, and
discarding any that do not
close when tapped sharply
with a knife. Put them in a
large pan with the cider (or
wine) and shake over high
heat for 5–7 minutes or until
they open. Drain, reserving
the cooking liquor, then
shell the mussels.

3. Generously butter a
flameproof baking dish and
place in it the shallots and
mushrooms. Wash and dry
the sole fillets, and roll them
neatly. Place on top of the
vegetables and season with
salt and pepper.

4. Pour 600 ml (1 pint) of the
fish stock over the sole then
strain in the mussel liquid
through muslin or a very
fine sieve. Cover with
buttered greaseproof paper
or butter wrappers and
bring to the boil on top of
the stove. Cover with a lid
and poach gently for 7–8
minutes or until the fish
flakes readily.

5. Remove the fish fillets
carefully from the liquid
with a slotted spoon and
arrange in a heatproof dish.
Cover and keep warm in the
oven. If necessary, boil to
reduce the liquor in the
baking dish to 300 ml
(½ pint).

6. Make the Velouté Sauce,
using the fish liquid.
Whisk egg yolks and cream
in a bowl then stir in some
of the hot sauce. Mix, and
pour the yolk/cream liaison
into the bulk of the sauce.
Heat gently until it thickens
slightly, but do not boil.

7. Take the sauce from the
heat and add the butter, cut
into small dice. Shake the
pan until the butter has
softened into the sauce and
given it a sheen, then add
the mussels and shrimps.

8. Taste the sauce for
seasoning and pour over the
sole in the serving dish.
Glaze under a hot grill and
serve immediately.

BROWN SAUCES Mother sauce: Demi-glace or Fond de Veau Lié

Sauce	Ingredients		Method of Preparation	Uses
Sauce Espagnole	450 ml (¾ pint) Demi-glace Sauce 1½ tablespoons tomato purée 50 g (2 oz) sliced mushrooms 65 ml (2½ fl oz) jellied Brown Stock	65 ml (2½ fl oz) sherry salt freshly ground black pepper 15 g (½ oz) butter	Put the Demi-glace in a saucepan, stir in the purée and mushrooms. Simmer for 5 minutes then add the stock, bring to the boil, lower heat and simmer for 15 minutes until thickened. Stir in sherry, season. Remove from heat, beat in butter.	Red meat, poultry and game.
Sauce Madère	1½ tablespoons tomato purée 450 ml (¾ pint) Demi-glace Sauce 65 ml (2½ fl oz) Brown Stock	65 ml (2½ fl oz) Madeira 15 g (½ oz) butter salt freshly ground black pepper	Whisk purée into the Demi-glace, bring it to the boil and simmer for 7 minutes. Whisk in the stock, bring to the boil and simmer for 15 minutes until clear. Stir in Madeira, beat in butter and adjust seasoning to taste.	Grills, steaks, cutlets.
Sauce Chasseur	25 g (1 oz) butter 1 shallot, peeled and finely chopped 50 g (2 oz) button mushrooms, sliced	300 ml (½ pint) white wine 2 teaspoons tomato purée 300 ml (½ pint) Demi-glace Sauce	Melt the butter, add the shallot and cook for 2 minutes. Then add the mushrooms and cook for 5 minutes. Pour over the wine and boil rapidly for 10 minutes until reduced by ⅓. Whisk the tomato purée and Demi-glace into the sauce. Simmer for 5 minutes.	Grilled or roast chicken or meat.
Sauce Reforme	2 gherkins 15 g (½ oz) truffle 1 hardboiled egg white 25 g (1 oz) tongue 300 ml (½ pint) Sauce Espagnole	2 teaspoons redcurrant jelly 1 tablespoon port wine a pinch of cayenne	Finely chop the gherkins, truffle, egg white and tongue. Heat the sauce, then whisk in jelly, port, cayenne and other ingredients. Bring to the boil and simmer for 10 minutes.	Lamb cutlets.
Sauce Bordelaise	2 shallots, peeled and chopped 300 ml (½ pint) claret 1 bouquet garni 450 ml (¾ pint) Demi-glace Sauce	1 teaspoon arrowroot blended with 1 tablespoon water 2 marrow bones	Boil the shallots, claret and bouquet garni until reduced to ⅓. Stir in the Demi-glace, bring to the boil and simmer for 10 minutes, skimming regularly. If the sauce is too thin, add the arrowroot. Strain. Scoop out the marrow, dice and poach for 5 minutes. Drain, dry and stir into the sauce.	Roast beef or grills.
Sauce Duxelles	1 shallot, peeled and finely chopped 2 teaspoons oil 40 g (1½ oz) butter 100 g (4 oz) mushrooms, finely chopped	150 ml (¼ pint) dry white wine 450 ml (¾ pint) Demi-glace Sauce 1 tablespoon tomato purée 3 tablespoons freshly chopped parsley	Cook the shallots in the oil and 15 g (½ oz) of the butter for 2 minutes. Stir in the mushrooms and cook for a further 5 minutes. Add the wine, increase heat and boil rapidly for about 10–15 minutes, until reduced to 1 tablespoon. Stir in the Demi-glace and the purée. Bring to the boil, simmer for 5 minutes, then season and whisk in remaining butter and parsley.	Grilled chicken, veal, rabbit.
Sauce Italienne	1 small onion, finely chopped 25 g (1 oz) butter 50 g (2 oz) mushrooms, finely chopped	150 ml (¼ pint) dry white wine 300 ml (½ pint) Fond de Veau Lié 25 g (1 oz) cooked lean ham, diced	Cook the onion in the melted butter for 5 minutes, add the mushrooms and cook for a further 5 minutes, stirring occasionally. Add the wine and boil the sauce until reduced by half. Stir in the Fond de Veau Lié and bring to the boil. Stir in the ham and season.	Roast beef, steak and pasta.

BROWN SAUCES

A brown roux is generally made from either rendered fresh pork fat, oil or clarified butter (melted butter strained through muslin to remove the milky substances). If the butter is not clarified, it is likely to burn. The fat and flour roux is cooked to a deep nutty brown, which helps to impart colour and flavour to the sauce.

General method

The all-important ingredient for a brown sauce is its stock (see pages 26–27) which can be made in quantity, frozen and used as required.

Once the sauce is made, it too may be frozen, as long as frozen stock has not been used to make it.

Demi-glace is the 'mother' of many brown sauces, and is itself the basis of yet another 'mother', the classic Espagnole. It may form a simple, slightly reduced sauce – a 'half-glaze' – which can be served on its own, or it can be adapted to make its 'daughters'. This basic sauce can be reduced, either by itself, or with the addition of some more brown stock, to make a syrupy, strong tasting sauce. This is meat glaze, which sets to a solid, rubbery jelly and is used to enrich soups, sauces and stews.

Demi-Glace

Basic Brown Sauce

Always use cold stock as this helps to clear the sauce by accelerating the rising of scum. It is essential to skim the sauce frequently to produce a crystal clear result.

Makes about 450 ml (¾ pint)
3 tablespoons oil or Clarified Butter (see page 42)
1 small onion, peeled and finely diced
1 small carrot, peeled and finely diced
½ stick celery, trimmed and finely diced
15 g (½ oz) plain flour
1 teaspoon tomato purée
600 ml (1 pint) well flavoured Brown Stock (page 27)
1 bouquet garni
salt
freshly ground black pepper

Preparation time: 5 minutes
Cooking time: about 1½ hours

1. Heat the oil or clarified butter in a saucepan, add the onion, carrot and celery, and cook for 5–7 minutes, stirring constantly, until they are on the point of changing colour.

2. Stir in the flour, reduce the heat and cook for about 15 minutes until the roux is a rich nutty brown, stirring constantly.

3. Remove from the heat, cool slightly and stir in the tomato purée.

4. Return to the heat and gradually stir in two-thirds of the stock. Slowly bring to the boil, stirring or whisking constantly. Add the bouquet garni, salt and pepper, and half-cover with the lid.

5. Simmer for 35–40 minutes, skimming the surface of the sauce frequently.

6. Add half of the remaining stock, bring to the boil without stirring and skim again. Simmer for 5 minutes, half-covered with the lid.

7. Whisk in the remaining stock, bring to the boil without stirring and skim again. Strain through a chinois sieve into a clean pan, bring back to the boil and skim until clear. Season to taste and use as required.

Sauce Bigarade

Serve this sauce with roast duck, goose, pork or venison.

Makes about 450 ml (¾ pint)
15 g (½ oz) butter
1–2 shallots, peeled and finely
　chopped
200 ml (7 fl oz) red Burgundy
　wine
1 small bay leaf
1 Seville orange
450 ml (¾ pint) Demi-glace
　Sauce (see page 39)
2–3 teaspoons redcurrant jelly
a squeeze of lemon juice

Preparation time: 15 minutes
Cooking time: about 25 minutes

1. Melt the butter in a saucepan, add the finely chopped shallot and cook for 5 minutes until it is soft, but without browning, stirring occasionally.

2. Stir in the wine, add the bay leaf and the pared rind of half the orange. Bring to the boil and simmer uncovered for about 15 minutes until reduced by a quarter.

3. Strain the wine mixture through a wire sieve.

4. Put the Demi-glace and redcurrant jelly into a saucepan and dissolve over a low heat. Whisk in the strained wine.

5. Pare the remaining orange rind very thinly and cut into julienne strips. Blanch in boiling water for 5 minutes until softened, drain well and stir into the sauce.

6. Squeeze the orange juice and strain into the sauce with the lemon juice.

7. Adjust the seasoning to taste. Reheat, but do not boil, and spoon over the duck or other poultry or meat before serving.

Roast duck served with Sauce Bigarade

Fond de Veau Lié

Basic Brown Sauce

Makes 600 ml (1 pint)
15 g (½ oz) clarified butter
1 small leek, trimmed and
*   finely diced*
1 small carrot, peeled and
*   finely diced*
½ celery stick, trimmed and
*   finely diced*
1 small onion, peeled and
*   finely diced*
750 ml (1¼ pints) Veal Stock
*   (see page 27)*
2–3 tomatoes, diced
1 bouquet garni
1 tablespoon tomato purée
2 tablespoons potato flour or
*   arrowroot*
4 tablespoons Madeira or cold
*   water*
salt
freshly ground black pepper

Preparation time: 10 minutes
Cooking time: about 50
minutes

1. Heat the butter in a heavy-based saucepan, and stir in the leek, carrot, celery and onion.

2. Fry the vegetables gently for about 10 minutes until they are lightly browned.

3. Add the stock, tomatoes, bouquet garni and tomato purée, bring to the boil, and simmer for 35–40 minutes until the vegetables are very tender.

4. Strain the sauce through a fine sieve, rinse the pan, and return the sauce to the clean saucepan.

5. Blend together the potato flour or arrowroot with the Madeira or water to make a paste.

6. Gradually pour into the boiling sauce, whisking constantly and adding sufficient to give a sauce of the desired consistency. Return to the boil, whisking, and season to taste with salt and pepper. Use as required.

Veal Escalope served with Sauce Chasseur

For perfect Brown Sauces

■ If you want your sauce to be as fat-free as possible, then the stock has to be as well. After making stock, chill it thoroughly, and then remove every trace of fat that has solidified on the top.
■ The fat for brown sauces should be oil or clarified butter. If you use any old fat, it can burn during the longer cooking of the roux, and spoil the ultimate flavour. Clarified butter is best when the sauce is to accompany a food with a delicate flavour.
■ The vegetables should always be cut into very fine dice, and by frying them very

gently in the fat first before adding the flour, their flavour will be extracted gently.
■ A bouquet garni is vital for the subtle flavour of the best brown sauces. The classic bouquet garni is fresh thyme, celery, parsley and a bay leaf, tied together in a bundle; dried herbs should be used in a small muslin bag.
■ Meat glazes can be made from white stocks as well as from brown stocks. Both can be frozen in ice cube trays, and then you have your own instant 'stock cubes' to hand to enrich sauces, soups or stews.

Meat Glaze

This highly concentrated *glace de viande* or meat glaze keeps well in the fridge, and can be frozen; it can be used to glaze meats in dishes such as galantines and to flavour soups and sauces.

Large quantities of stock are needed originally because 2.75 litres (5 pints), say, will make only 300–450 ml (½–¾ pint) meat glaze. The whole process of reduction can take over 4 hours, with the pan set half off the heat.

Brown or White Veal Stock (see page 27) is boiled slowly in an uncovered pan until it has reduced through evaporation by more than half. Impurities will form a skin on the side of the pan and this should be removed. The stock is then strained into a smaller saucepan through muslin or a very fine sieve, then the slow boiling, skimming and reduction is continued until the liquid is syrupy enough to coat a spoon lightly. It will set to a solid, rubbery jelly.

HOT EMULSIFIED SAUCES

The mother sauce in this category is Hollandaise, and Béarnaise is the best known 'daughter'. Also included in this class of butter sauces is their cousin, the Sauce Beurre Blanc. Emulsified sauces, hot or cold, are considered to be the most complicated and tricky of all, due to their tendency to curdle and separate. However, one should not be deterred as they can be achieved with ease provided a few guidelines are followed. These sauces are relatively quick to make, and should be done at the last minute, although they may be kept warm in a bain-marie.

For perfect butter sauces

■ When making butter sauces, the most important thing to remember is the temperature. Too high a heat will cause the sauce to curdle or separate, or scramble the eggs, giving a grainy consistency.
■ During the cooking process, the egg yolks absorb the fat, giving a smooth cream. The safest way to achieve this is to use a double saucepan or a wire mesh pan stand over the heat source.
■ The butter should always be clarified (see right) and then cooled slightly before adding to the egg yolks as, if the butter is too hot, it will curdle the eggs.
■ A low heat should be used to cook the eggs, and the sauce should be whisked constantly to produce a light and fairly thick mousse. Once this stage has been reached, the pan should be removed from the heat, to prevent the eggs being scrambled.
■ The clarified butter should be added very slowly at first, but once the eggs have begun to absorb the fat, it may be added in a steady stream, as long as the whisking is vigorous and steady.
■ If the sauce is too thick, it may be thinned by the addition of a tablespoon of cold water. If the sauce is too thin, but not separated, it may be that the butter has been whisked in too quickly. If this

happens, it is easily remedied by placing a teaspoon of lemon juice into a clean dry bowl, and whisking in a tablespoon of the failed sauce until it is very thick. The remaining sauce may then be whisked into this in small quantities until the whole is thickened.
■ If the sauce curdles, it is almost always because it was too hot. Remove immediately from heat and whisk in an ice cube. Failing this, gradually whisk the sauce into a tablespoon of cold water in a clean pan. The sauce could be started off again with an egg yolk and a tablespoon of water over a low heat and made into a mousse; thereafter the curdled mixture can be beaten in, drop by drop. However, this does not apply to a thoroughly 'scrambled' sauce which is irretrievable and should be discarded.
■ Butter sauces which do not contain egg cannot be rescued once curdled.
■ If time is short, a Hollandaise sauce can be made in a blender. Although it lacks something in quality, it is a very acceptable equivalent. It is extremely simple to make, and is foolproof as long as the butter is added drop by drop. In this method, less butter is used as the eggs absorb less fat when they are cold.

Sauce Beurre Blanc

Makes about 300 ml (½ pint)
3 tablespoons white wine vinegar
3 tablespoons dry white wine
2 shallots, very finely chopped
225 g (8 oz) very cold, unsalted butter, diced
salt
freshly ground white pepper

Preparation time: 5 minutes
Cooking time: 5–10 minutes

1. In a small, uncovered, non-aluminium pan, boil the wine vinegar, wine and shallots until reduced to 1 tablespoon, then sieve and return to the pan.

2. Reduce the heat to very low, and start to whisk in the butter dice, a few at a time. They must soften and thicken the sauce rather than melt, so it may be necessary to remove the pan from the heat occasionally.

3. Season to taste with salt and pepper and serve immediately. If kept warm, the sauce may melt and become oily, but it can keep for a few minutes in a pan in a warm, not hot, bain-marie.

Clarified Butter

The principal reason for clarifying or ridding the butter of its impurities – salt, residues of buttermilk and sediment – is to prevent burning and sticking during cooking which butter is very prone to do.

It is an expensive cooking medium as 225 g (8 oz) of butter will produce only about 150 g (5 oz) clarified butter, but it is so pure that a little will go a long way. It keeps well in the refrigerator, so it is worthwhile making a fairly large amount.

Apart from its use in sauces and for frying, clarified butter is used to seal potted meats and fish pastes. The butter should be partly melted, then poured over the chilled paste. Leave to set then refrigerate.

1. Place the chosen amount of butter in a pan over very low heat, and let it melt gently. It must not brown, and it must not be stirred. It needs to be thoroughly heated, though, until the whole surface is bubbling, and the sediment both rises to the top in a froth and also sinks.

2. Leave it to cool for a few minutes, until the milky deposits have sunk to the bottom of the pan.

3. Line a sieve with dampened doubled muslin or cheesecloth and place the sieve over a storage jar or bowl. Pour the liquid carefully into the sieve, leaving the sediment behind. Do not force through.

4. Cover the jar or bowl and store in the refrigerator.

Sauce Blanche au Beurre

White sauce enriched with butter

It is essential that this sauce is not boiled as this would spoil the flavour. The water should be boiling and this will cook the flour. This is a simpler (and less extravagant) version of the classic Sauce Beurre Blanc (see page 42).

Makes 300 ml (½ pint)
50 g (2 oz) unsalted butter
1 tablespoon plain flour
300 ml (½ pint) boiling water
salt
freshly ground white pepper
2 teaspoons lemon juice

Preparation time: 5 minutes
Cooking time: 5 minutes

1. Melt 15 g (½ oz) of the butter in a saucepan until foaming. Stir in the flour and when smooth, remove from the heat.

2. Gradually whisk in the boiling water, whisking constantly. Do not reheat.

3. Gradually whisk in the remaining butter, stirring well.

4. Season to taste with salt and pepper, and add the lemon juice. Use immediately.

HOT EMULSIFIED SAUCES Mothers: Hollandaise and Béarnaise

Daughter Sauce	Ingredients		Method of Preparation	Uses
Sauce Choron	*300 ml (½ pint) Béarnaise Sauce*	*1½ tablespoons tomato purée*	Make the Béarnaise Sauce, then whisk in the tomato purée until well blended. Use immediately.	Steak, eggs, fish.
Sauce Foyot	*300 ml (½ pint) Béarnaise Sauce*	*1 teaspoon Meat Glaze (see page 41)*	Make the Béarnaise Sauce, then whisk in the Meat Glaze. Use immediately.	Steak.
Sauce Maltaise	*300 ml (½ pint) Hollandaise Sauce juice of ½ orange*	*rind of ½ orange, cut into julienne strips and blanched in boiling water for 5 minutes*	Make the Hollandaise Sauce, and stir in the orange juice and julienne of rind. Season to taste and serve immediately.	Asparagus and other vegetables.
Sauce Mireille	*300 ml (½ pint) Hollandaise Sauce 1½ tablespoons tomato purée*	*½ tablespoon chopped basil*	Make the Hollandaise Sauce, then whisk in the tomato purée and basil. Serve immediately.	Artichoke hearts, asparagus, eggs.
Sauce Moutarde	*300 ml (½ pint) Hollandaise Sauce*	*2 teaspoons Dijon mustard*	Make the Hollandaise Sauce, then whisk in the mustard.	Eggs, fish.
Sauce Noisette	*300 ml (½ pint) Hollandaise or Béarnaise Sauce*		After the butter has been clarified, cook it gently to a nutty brown, taking care not to burn it. Then proceed as for basic Hollandaise or Béarnaise recipe. Use immediately.	Eggs, vegetables.

HOLLANDAISE SAUCE

Of all the sauces, Hollandaise is regarded as one of the most tricky to make, due to its tendency to curdle. It is also one of the most splendid, so it is well worth mastering the art. The cardinal rule to observe is never to allow the sauce to overheat – this is why it is important to make the sauce in a bain-marie or over a very low heat. Serve with asparagus or broccoli. It is also a classic accompaniment to poached salmon, turbot or other fish.

Hot emulsified sauces such as Hollandaise are best served immediately. As soon as the sauce reaches the correct consistency, remove the pan from the bain-marie to prevent it cooking further. To keep the sauce warm for a short time, turn off the heat, till the water in the bain-marie is warm not hot, and stand the pan in the water.

Makes about 300 ml (½ pint)
175 g (6 oz) unsalted butter
2 tablespoons water
3 egg yolks
salt
a pinch of cayenne pepper
1 tablespoon lemon juice, or to taste

Preparation time: 5 minutes
Cooking time: about 5 minutes

1. Melt the unsalted butter over a low heat and clarify as explained on page 42. Strain through a fine mesh into a measuring jug and allow to cool to tepid.

2. In a small saucepan or the top of a double saucepan, whisk the water and egg yolks with a little salt and cayenne pepper for about 30 seconds until light and fluffy.

3. Set the pan over a low heat or in a bain-marie and whisk constantly until the mixture is creamy and thick enough for the whisk to leave a trail on the base of the pan. (The base of the pan should never be more than hand hot or the sauce will curdle or scramble.)

4. Turn off the heat and, very slowly, whisk the butter into the egg mixture a drop at a time. Do not add the butter too fast as this will curdle the sauce.

5. When about a third of the butter has been added, the rest may be added in a slow steady stream, but it must be whisked vigorously all the time.

6. Stir in the lemon juice to taste and serve the sauce lukewarm, never hot.

Blender Hollandaise Sauce

Makes about 300 ml (½ pint)
3 egg yolks
1 tablespoon water
1 tablespoon lemon juice
¼ teaspoon salt
a pinch of cayenne pepper
100 g (4 oz) butter, clarified, and warm, but not too hot

Preparation time: about 5 minutes

1. Place the egg yolks, water, lemon juice and seasoning into the goblet of a blender and cover with its lid. Blend at high speed for a few seconds.

2. Remove the inner part of the lid and, still blending at high, pour the melted butter in, very slowly.

3. Continue pouring and blending until all the butter has been amalgamated into the eggs, and the sauce is thick and creamy. Season to taste and serve.

Poached Turbot with Hollandaise Sauce

Serves 6–8
1.75 kg (4 lb) turbot, scaled and cleaned
2 slices lemon
600 ml (1 pint) Fish Stock (see page 26)
300 ml (½ pint) good quality dry white wine
1 bouquet garni
salt
freshly ground black pepper
double recipe quantity Hollandaise Sauce
2 tablespoons finely chopped parsley
2 tablespoons chopped chives
To garnish:
lemon slices or wedges
sprigs of parsley

Preparation time: 45 minutes, including making the Hollandaise Sauce
Cooking time: 20–25 minutes

1. Place the fish in a turbot fish kettle or large roasting pan.

2. Add the lemon, fish stock, wine, bouquet garni, salt and pepper.

3. Very slowly bring to the boil, cover with a lid or foil (for the roasting pan). Lower the heat, and simmer very gently for 20–25 minutes until the fish is just tender.

4. Meanwhile, make the Hollandaise Sauce, and stir in the chopped herbs.

5. Lift the turbot from the pan, and drain very well. Carefully remove the dark skin, peeling it away from the head to the tail.

6. Lift the fish on to a serving plate. Garnish with lemon and parsley and serve immediately with the sauce handed separately.

Mushroom Tartlets

These tartlets make delicious hot appetisers.

Makes 12 tartlets
175 g (6 oz) Rich Shortcrust Pastry (see page 261)
50 g (2 oz) butter
225 g (8 oz) mushrooms, sliced thickly
salt
freshly ground black pepper
1 recipe quantity Hollandaise Sauce

1. Roll out the pastry and use to line 12 tartlet tins. Bake blind (see page 259). Cool on a wire rack, then turn out.

2. Melt the butter and sauté the mushrooms until just tender. Season well.

3. Spoon the mushrooms into the tartlet cases and top each with 2 teaspoons of the Hollandaise Sauce.

4. Place the tartlets under a preheated very hot grill until the sauce is lightly browned. Serve immediately.

Variations

Prawn Tartlets Roughly chop 225 g (8 oz) shelled prawns, sauté in butter and top with Hollandaise Sauce as above.

Spinach Tartlets Chop 225 g (8 oz) spinach, and cook in melted butter until wilted. Chop finely, spoon into cases and top with Hollandaise.

Eggs Benedict

This makes a delicious quick snack, but served with a salad or green vegetable could make a complete meal.

Serves 6
1 recipe quantity Hollandaise Sauce
1 level teaspoon dry mustard powder
cayenne pepper
6 slices cooked ham, thinly sliced
6 muffins or 6 thick slices white bread
6 eggs
salt
50 g (2 oz) unsalted butter

Preparation time: 5 minutes, plus making sauce
Cooking time: 15–25 minutes

1. Make the Hollandaise sauce and season it with the mustard and a little cayenne. Keep warm in a bain-marie.

2. Trim the ham to fit the muffins or bread slices.

3. Toast the muffins or bread and keep warm.

4. Meanwhile, poach the eggs lightly in simmering salted water.

5. Butter the toasted muffins or bread and cover each with a slice of ham. Top with a drained poached egg and coat with the warm Hollandaise Sauce. Serve at once.

BÉARNAISE SAUCE

Béarnaise, with its distinctive tang of tarragon, wine and vinegar is one of the best-known variations of Hollandaise sauce. It can itself be used as a foundation for other sauces, such as the tomato-flavoured Choron, the orange flavoured Maltaise, or Foyot, which is further enriched by the addition of Meat Glaze (see page 41).

Makes about 300 ml (½ pint)
3 tablespoons white wine
  vinegar
3 tablespoons dry white wine
4 black peppercorns
1 small bay leaf
½ small shallot, chopped
1 blade mace
3 egg yolks
salt
freshly ground white pepper
175 g (6 oz) unsalted butter,
  clarified (page 42)
1 teaspoon finely chopped
  parsley
1 teaspoon chopped tarragon
1 teaspoon chopped chervil
½ teaspoon chopped chives

Preparation time: 15 minutes
Cooking time: 20 minutes

1. Put the wine vinegar, white wine, peppercorns, bay leaf, shallot and mace into a small saucepan. Slowly bring to the boil and then boil rapidly until the quantity is reduced to about 2 tablespoons. Remove from the heat, and set aside until cool. Then strain the liquid through a sieve.

2. Put the egg yolks into a small saucepan, stand in a bain-marie over low heat, and whisk well with a little salt and pepper. Stir in the strained vinegar.

3. Turn off the heat and whisk vigorously until the mixture begins to thicken.

4. Add the butter very gradually to the egg mixture, as with Hollandaise Sauce, whisking continuously until the sauce has thickened.

5. Stir in the chopped herbs and use as soon as possible. Béarnaise Sauce is a traditional accompaniment to chateaubriand steak, as shown.

Lamb Noisettes with Béarnaise Sauce

Serves 4
1.5 kg (3½ lb) rack of lamb
8 slices bread
100 g (4 oz) butter
4 tablespoons oil
salt
freshly ground black pepper
1½ recipe quantity Béarnaise
  Sauce
85 ml (3 fl oz) Veal Stock (see
  page 27)
85 ml (3 fl oz) dry sherry or
  Madeira
To garnish:
1 tablespoon finely chopped
  tarragon
2 teaspoons finely chopped
  parsley

Preparation time: 35 minutes
Cooking time: 15–20 minutes

1. Using a sharp boning knife make the noisettes. Carefully remove the bone by cutting away the meat, keeping the knife close to the bone, avoiding cutting into the meat. (See page 140.)

2. Roll the meat into a long cylinder, starting at the lean side. Trim the fat, if there is more than enough to wrap around once. Tie the meat with string at 2.5 cm (1 inch) intervals. Cut between each tie to make 8 noisettes.

3. Using a round pastry cutter, the same size as the noisettes, cut each slice of bread into rounds.

4. Heat half the butter and oil in a frying pan, and brown the bread croûtes quickly on each side. Drain on paper towels and keep hot.

5. Rinse the frying pan. Heat the remaining butter and oil and sauté the noisettes for 2 to 3 minutes each side. Sprinkle with salt and pepper.

6. Make the Béarnaise Sauce as described and keep warm in a bain-marie.

7. Arrange the croûtes on a serving plate, place a noisette on top of each one and keep hot.

8. Pour off the cooking fat from the pan. Deglaze the pan with the stock and sherry or madeira, adjust the seasoning to taste, and strain into a sauceboat.

9. Spoon a little Béarnaise Sauce over each noisette and serve the rest separately with the gravy.

10. Sprinkle the chopped herbs over the noisettes and serve immediately.

Monkfish with Choron Sauce

50 g (2 oz) butter
4 monkfish fillets, about 225 g
  (8 oz) each
1 tablespoon cooking oil
225 g (8 oz) tomatoes, peeled,
  seeded and finely chopped
1 recipe quantity Sauce
  Choron (see page 43)

Preparation time: 15 minutes, plus making sauce
Cooking time: about 20 minutes

1. Melt the butter in a frying pan and gently fry the monkfish fillets one at a time for about 5 minutes on each side, or until brown and tender (do not overcook). Place the fillets in a gratin dish as they cook, and keep warm.

2. Heat the oil in a small pan, add the tomatoes and cook quickly over a high heat, stirring all the time, until they have reduced to a thick purée.

3. Stir the tomato purée into the Sauce Choron and pour over the monkfish fillets. Place the dish under a preheated grill to allow the sauce to brown and glaze on top.

Vegetable Hors d'oeuvre

Serves 4
4 artichokes
  or 1 kg (2 lb) asparagus
  stems
1 recipe quantity Béarnaise
  Sauce

Preparation time: 15 minutes, plus making the sauce
Cooking time: 45–60 minutes for artichokes 15–20 minutes for asparagus

1. For artichokes, place in a large pan of boiling salted water, bring back to the boil as quickly as possible and boil, uncovered for 45–60 minutes, or until a leaf will pull out easily and the bottoms are tender when pierced with a knife.

2. Remove from the pan and drain upside down in a colander. They can be served hot or cold.

3. For asparagus, trim the stems of tough or woody parts and tie with string top and bottom in bundles about 9 cm (3½ inches) in diameter.

4. Use a pan large enough to hold the asparagus horizontally. Fill with salted water and bring to the boil. When boiling rapidly put in the asparagus bundles and bring back to the boil as quickly as possible. Reduce heat and boil, uncovered, for 12–15 minutes. The asparagus is done when a knife can pierce the ends of the stems easily.

5. Lift the asparagus out carefully, bundle by bundle, and drain. Remove the strings.

6. To serve, place each artichoke, or portion of asparagus, on individual plates and serve the sauce separately.

COLD EMULSIFIED SAUCES

Mayonnaise is one of the classic sauces. It has the reputation of being difficult, but if you follow the instructions – particularly regarding adding the oil slowly – you will achieve success. The recipe is given on page 31, one of its famous offspring, Aïoli, is given here.

Mayonnaise is the mother sauce of the egg yolk and oil emulsions, the cold emulsified sauces. Once the basic recipe is mastered, the daughters can easily be made. The best-known is perhaps Tartare, which adds chopped capers, gherkins and herbs to basic mayonnaise, and is good served with plain fried or grilled fish. Aïoli, the strong garlic mayonnaise from southern France, can be used as a dip for crudités, or can accompany hard-boiled eggs, squid or snails or a variety of vegetables.

Aïoli

Makes just over 150 ml (¼ pint)
3–4 garlic cloves
¼ teaspoon salt
½ teaspoon dry mustard
little freshly ground white pepper
150 ml (¼ pint) olive oil
2–3 tablespoons lemon juice

Preparation time: 10 minutes

1. Crush the garlic to a smooth paste.

2. Place the egg yolk in a bowl, gradually beat in the garlic, salt, mustard and pepper, using a wire balloon whisk.

3. Add the oil, drop by drop from a fork, whisking vigorously between each addition of oil so that it is absorbed completely before the next drop.

4. After about half the oil has been added, the mayonnaise will take on a shiny appearance and should look thick. If so, the oil can be added more rapidly, about 1 tablespoon at a time. If the mixture is still runny at this stage, it has curdled.

5. As the mixture becomes very thick add the lemon juice to soften it, then add the remaining oil. Adjust the seasoning to taste. The consistency should be as thick as lightly whipped double cream.

6. Store in the refrigerator in a covered container for up to 2 weeks.

COLD EMULSIFIED SAUCES Mother sauce: Mayonnaise

Sauce	Ingredients		Method of Preparation	Uses
Aïoli	150 ml (¼ pint) Mayonnaise 3–4 garlic cloves	2–3 tablespoons lemon juice	Before making the Mayonnaise crush the garlic cloves to a smooth paste and beat it into the egg yolk. Proceed as for Mayonnaise, adding the lemon juice when the sauce thickens.	With Bourride, Brandade and crudités.
Sauce Rémoulade	450 ml (¾ pint) Mayonnaise made with 1 extra tablespoon mustard 1 tablespoon each of gherkins, capers (chopped)	1 tablespoon chopped mixed parsley, chervil and tarragon 2–3 finely chopped anchovy fillets	Add the ingredients to the Mayonnaise.	Cold meats.
Sauce Tartare	150 ml (¼ pint) Mayonnaise 1 tablespoon chopped capers 1 tablespoon chopped gherkins	1 tablespoon fresh chopped mixed herbs 1 finely chopped hardboiled egg	Stir the other ingredients into the Mayonnaise.	Fried fish, deep fried mushrooms, shellfish.
Sauce Verte	450 ml (¾ pint) Mayonnaise 25 g (1 oz) mixed parsley, chervil, tarragon and chives	25 g (1 oz) watercress 50 g (2 oz) spinach	Blanch all the greenstuff for 2 minutes in boiling water, then refresh under cold water, dry, and pound or liquidize to a purée. Pass the purée through a sieve and stir into the Mayonnaise.	With salmon and other fish.

Salmon Steaks with Sauce Verte

Salmon with green Mayonnaise

Serves 6
1 large bunch watercress
3 sprigs parsley
1 bunch chives
2 sprigs tarragon
2 sprigs chervil
300 ml (½ pint) Mayonnaise
salt
freshly ground black pepper
1–2 teaspoons lemon juice
6 × 175 g (6 oz) middle cut
*   salmon steaks*
600 ml (1 pint) Fish Stock (see
*   page 26)*
150 ml (¼ pint) good quality
*   dry white wine*
1 bouquet garni
2 sprigs fennel leaves
salt
freshly ground black pepper
To garnish:
fennel leaves

Preparation time: 30 minutes
Cooking time: 2 minutes, plus
standing

1. To make the sauce put the watercress and herbs into a small saucepan of lightly salted boiling water for 2 minutes. Drain and refresh under cold water to retain their colour.

2. Drain thoroughly and pat dry in a tea-towel to remove the excess moisture.

3. Put the blanched watercress and herbs in a blender or food processor and blend to a fine purée.

4. Rub the puréed mixture through a fine sieve to get rid of any stalks and ensure that the mixture is completely smooth.

5. Beat the purée into the prepared Mayonnaise, season to taste with salt, pepper and lemon juice. Set aside.

6. Put the salmon steaks into a fish kettle or large roasting pan. Pour over the stock and wine. Add the remaining ingredients and cover.

7. Slowly bring to the boil, then immediately turn off the heat, and leave covered to cool in the cooking liquor.

8. Carefully lift the salmon from the pan, drain well and place on a serving plate.

9. Spoon a little Sauce Verte on to each salmon steak and garnish with fennel. Put the remaining sauce into a sauceboat to serve separately.

For perfect Mayonnaise

■ Ingredients must be at room temperature.
■ The oil should be added to the egg yolk drop by drop. If it is added too quickly, the sauce will curdle. If this happens, place another egg yolk in a clean bowl and gradually add the curdled mixture to the egg yolk whisking continuously, then add the remaining oil drop by drop.

■ The type of oil used determines the flavour of the mayonnaise. A corn or vegetable oil gives a blander flavour than a richer olive oil.
■ The type of vinegar used also varies the flavour of the mayonnaise. Choose one which complements the flavour of the food it is to be served with, but never use malt vinegar.

ASPIC

Clear shimmering aspic may well be the hallmark of the professional, but the technique is in fact very simple. Follow the step-by-step guide below to produce an elegant first course for a dinner party or a spectacular centre-piece for a buffet.

Aspic is used for coating meat, fish or poultry dishes, and for a garnish on top of food. It can also be used itself as a garnish, either chopped or cut into shapes using aspic cutters.

Aspic is made from a base of chicken, game, fish or meat stock. The stock itself should be well flavoured and very clear, and already set in a light jelly before using for aspic.

This is achieved by long simmering and reduction, as explained on page 33.

If necessary, gelatine is added to set the mixture so that it will coat food and set firmly

over the garnish.

Sweet jellies can also be made using the same principles as those used in making aspic (see page 55).

Basic Aspic

As a guideline 50 g (2 oz) of powdered gelatine will set 1 litre (1¾ pints) of stock. If, however, a veal stock is used as a base, which is usually set to a strong jelly, the amount of gelatine will be less. The quantity of gelatine should be reduced by 15 g (½ oz) or 25 g (1 oz) depending on what it is to be used for. If the stock is set to a firm jelly, and the food is not to be turned out, it may not be necessary to add any gelatine.

Makes about 1 litre (1¾ pints)
65 ml (2½ fl oz) dry sherry
65 ml (2½ fl oz) white wine
50 g (2 oz) powdered gelatine
1 litre (1¾ pints) well
flavoured Brown, Veal or
Fish Stock (see pages 26–27)
2 carrots, scraped and chopped
3 shallots, peeled and halved
1 teaspoon white wine vinegar,
or lemon juice
1 bay leaf
2 sprigs of parsley
2 egg whites
2 egg shells

Preparation time: 10 minutes
Cooking time: about 20–30 minutes

1. Put the sherry and wine into a small bowl, sprinkle over the gelatine, and set aside. Put the stock into a scalded saucepan, with the vegetables, vinegar and flavourings.

2. Whisk the egg whites to a froth, and stir into the pan. Place over a moderate heat and using a balloon whisk, whisk in the egg whites and shells. Continue whisking until the stock is hot.

3. Whisk in the gelatine and continue whisking until the stock reaches boiling point. Allow the liquid to rise to the top of the pan, remove from the heat, and leave to settle for 5 minutes.

4. Return to the heat, boil again and allow the foam to rise to the top of the saucepan. Remove from the heat for 5 minutes. Repeat this process once more. The liquid should now be clear.

5. Gently spoon the crust into a jelly bag or sieve lined with muslin, set over a bowl. Try to keep the crust as much in one piece as possible. Pour the stock through the crust.

6. If the aspic is not absolutely clear, strain through the filter again, then leave to cool.

Salmon Trout in Aspic

To cook the fish evenly, place the fish kettle over two hobs or burners.

Serves 8
*1 salmon trout, approx. 1.5 kg
  (3 lb), cleaned
1.75 litres (3 pints) Fish Stock
  (see page 26)
1 bouquet garni
1 carrot, scraped and sliced
1 onion, peeled and sliced
25 g (1 oz) gelatine
1 tablespoon white wine
  vinegar
2 egg whites
4 tablespoons dry white wine
  or sherry
¼ cucumber, cut with a
  canelle knife and thinly
  sliced*
To garnish:
*16 unpeeled prawns, thawed if
  frozen (optional)
1 lemon, thinly sliced
1 bunch watercress
chopped fish aspic*

Preparation time: 1 hour
Cooking time: about 1 hour
including standing and
chilling.

1. Place the salmon on the rack and lower into the kettle. Pour over the stock, add the bouquet garni, carrot and onion and cover.

2. Place the kettle over a very low heat. Slowly bring to the boil, allowing about 40 minutes. Turn off the heat and leave the salmon for 45 minutes without lifting the lid. It should then be just tender.

3. Leave to cool thoroughly in the pan.

4. Lift the fish from the stock, draining it well. Strain 1.2 litres (2 pints) of the stock into a scalded saucepan.

8. Place the fish on a tray lined with foil. Carefully cut the skin around the head without damaging the flesh. Then carefully peel the skin down towards the tail. Use the foil to flip the fish over; repeat with the other side.

9. Remove the fat gland that runs down the backbone. Place the fish on a wire rack over a tray. Check that the aspic is the correct syrupy consistency (see Basic rules, opposite), then spoon enough aspic over the fish to entirely coat it; leave to set.

10. If the remaining aspic has set, place a small amount in a bowl set over hot water until melted, then stand over ice until syrupy and ready to use. Arrange the cucumber slices over the fish, dipping each slice in aspic before putting in position. Chill.

Oeufs en Gelée

Eggs in Aspic

Serves 6
*1 × 100 g (4 oz) can liver pâté,
  chilled
6 lightly poached eggs
600 ml (1 pint) Aspic made with
  Chicken Stock (see page 50)*
To garnish:
6 sprigs fresh tarragon

Preparation time: about 40 minutes

1. Using a hot knife, slice the pâté into 6 equal slices. Place the slices of pâté in the base of 6 individual ramekin dishes. Alternatively, if using egg moulds, cut slices of pâté to fit the bases of the moulds.

2. Carefully trim the eggs and place an egg on top of each slice of pâté.

3. Melt the aspic in a bowl over hot water and cool until it is just on the point of setting. Pour the cooled aspic jelly over the eggs, leaving about 6 tablespoons in the bowl. Refrigerate the ramekins until set.

4. When the eggs are set, warm the remaining aspic jelly if it has set. Dip the tarragon into the melted aspic and place a sprig on top of each egg. Leave to set, then pour over the remaining aspic jelly. Refrigerate until set, and serve chilled.

5. Add the gelatine, vinegar and egg whites. Bring slowly to the boil, whisking constantly until a thick froth forms. Draw off the heat, and allow to settle for 5 minutes. Bring back to the boil without whisking, then again take off the heat and allow to settle. Repeat this process once or twice until the stock is very clear. Add the wine or sherry and adjust seasoning.

6. Pour the stock into a bowl through a scalded muslin cloth (see Basic Aspic, page 50). If necessary, strain again until the stock is absolutely clear.

7. Leave the stock until it is cool and the consistency of unbeaten egg white.

11. Spoon a little more aspic over the whole fish and chill until set. Set the remaining aspic on a shallow tray as described below. Then chop into large dice.

12. Carefully lift the fish, using two fish slices, on to a serving plate. Garnish with prawns, lemon twists, watercress and chopped aspic. Serve lightly chilled with Mayonnaise or Sauce Verte (page 48) and a green salad. This dish makes an ideal centrepiece for a formal buffet.

To make chopped jelly

Chopped jelly is a traditional accompaniment to galantines, aspic and jelly recipes. Pour syrupy aspic into a shallow baking tray to a depth of about 5 mm (¼ inch) thick. Allow to set until it is very firm.

Dip the tray quickly into hot water, and turn the jelly out on to a piece of wet greaseproof paper. Chop it coarsely but evenly, using a sharp, wet knife. First cut into long strips, then cut across into large dice. If it is unevenly chopped, it will lose its brilliance. To add extra sparkle, sprinkle with cold water. Do not touch with your fingers.

Basic rules

■ The saucepan should be scalded and free from grease.

■ All utensils should be scrupulously clean and the jelly bag or muslin should be scalded before use.

■ The egg whites should be free from any yolk.

■ The egg whites and shells (egg shells are not always used) are whisked through the stock to incorporate air. When the stock is heated, the egg white coagulates on top of the stock, forming a crust which traps the impurities on the surface. The egg whites, broken egg shells and scalded jelly cloth (or muslin) act as a filter, keeping back the impurities from the stock, thus producing a crystal-clear aspic jelly.

■ Ideally keep a separate jelly cloth or muslin for use with fish stock.

■ For best results, the liquid should be brought to the boil 3 times, so that the impurities are forced up into the coagulated egg white. The egg white filter must not be whisked after the initial boiling, as it will break up.

■ Avoid breaking the crust when straining the stock – spoon gently into the sieve or jelly bag.

■ The jelly should be left to settle before straining. Preferably, the jelly should be strained twice.

■ Nothing should be added after straining. Add wine, sherry or seasoning before straining.

■ Ensure that all the jelly comes through the cloth.

■ Keep the jelly in a warm place, out of draughts, while it is being strained. If the jelly does set while dripping through the cloth, place a jar of boiling water (with a lid) gently on top of the cloth.

■ When layering with aspic always make sure the first layer is thoroughly set before applying another layer.

■ Never pour hot aspic on to set aspic, as it will melt the first layer.

■ It is wise to test your aspic before using it, especially when putting it into a mould. Pour 1 cm (½ inch) layer of aspic into a chilled cup or small bowl and place in the refrigerator for 10–15 minutes until set. Cut into pieces and leave at room temperature for 10 minutes. It should remain set. If the aspic is too soft, add more gelatine and try again. If the jelly is hard and rubbery, add a little more stock, though this will affect the clarity of the aspic.

■ Aspic should be used when it is syrupy and on the point of setting. If it has begun to set, or if you are making a layered dish, place the amount you need in a bowl and stand over hot water until melted, then stand on ice until the right syrupy consistency.

■ Do not repeatedly heat and chill all the aspic, or it will go cloudy.

■ It is most important that the stock is absolutely free from fat and grease before it is used for aspic. It should be chilled, so that the fat rises to the surface, and may be easily removed with a metal spoon. To ensure that the stock is totally grease-free, a wad of paper towels may be drawn across the top surface of the set stock.

■ Try to avoid using complicated moulds as they are more likely to stick.

■ To turn out a mould, dip the bottom in warm water for 2–3 seconds. If it still sticks, lay a hot wet cloth on top of the mould for about 20 seconds – this works best with metal moulds.

Boeuf à la mode en gelée

In this classic French recipe, the beef is marinated in red wine and then cooked slowly for a long time so that it is very tender. Most recipes call for fillet of beef, but a piece of topside or top rump is equally good, and not so expensive. The dish should be prepared the day before so that the jelly sets around the sliced meat.

Serves 6–8
1.5 kg (3 lb) topside or top
   rump beef
2 garlic cloves, peeled and
   sliced
salt
freshly ground black pepper
300 ml (½ pint) dry red wine
1 pig's trotter, split
2 tablespoons vegetable oil or
   beef dripping
3 tablespoons brandy
3 shallots, peeled and chopped
2 bay leaves
300 ml (½ pint) Brown Stock
   (see page 27)
12 button onions, peeled
12 baby carrots, scraped and
   trimmed
1 tablespoon wine vinegar
2 egg whites, beaten
2 egg shells
To garnish:
parsley (optional)

Preparation time: 40 minutes, plus marinating overnight, chilling and setting of jelly overnight
Cooking time: 4½ hours
Oven: 150°C, 300°F, Gas Mark 2

1. Make small incisions in the meat and push the garlic slices into the meat. Season well. Place the meat in a large glass bowl, pour on the wine and marinate overnight, turning the meat occasionally.

2. Lift the meat from the marinade and drain well, then dry on paper towels.

3. Wash the pig's trotter and cook in boiling salted water for 10 minutes to remove any impurities. Drain well.

4. Heat half the oil or dripping in a large flameproof casserole and quickly brown the meat on all sides. Remove from the heat, pour over the brandy and set light to it. When the flames have died down, add the pig's trotter. Add the shallots and bay leaves.

5. Bring the stock and wine marinade to the boil, then pour over the meat. Cover tightly. Bring back to the boil, then cook in a preheated oven for 3 hours.

6. Turn the meat, cover and return to the oven for a further 1–1½ hours.

7. Boil the carrots and onions in salted water for 10 minutes, until just tender. Drain, refresh in cold water and drain again.

8. Lift the meat from the casserole, draining it well. Allow to cool, then wrap in foil and refrigerate. Strain the stock into a bowl and leave until completely cold.

11. Test the aspic for setting (see Basic rules, page 53) Melt a little until it is syrupy and pour a layer into a glass bowl or mould (see below). Chill until set.

12. Arrange some of the vegetables in the bottom of the dish and again spoon some aspic on top and allow to set.

13. Cut the meat into thin slices. Layer the meat slices and vegetables in the dish, covering with aspic each time.

15. When ready to serve, turn out on to a serving dish (see Prawn and Tomato Ring, step 10) and garnish with parsley, if liked, and with a selection of salads.

Prawn and Tomato Ring

9. Scrape any fat off the surface, then slowly heat through and adjust the seasoning. Add the vinegar, egg whites and shells. Bring slowly to the boil, whisking constantly, until a thick froth forms. Take off the heat to settle, then bring back to the boil without whisking.

10. Bring back to the boil twice more, without whisking, then strain the stock into a bowl through a scalded jelly bag or muslin cloth. Allow to cool and refrigerate overnight.

14. Finish with a layer of meat and pour over enough aspic to cover. Chill in the refrigerator until set.

Lining a mould

Stand the mould in a bowl of ice and add the aspic, 1 tablespoon at a time. Tilt the mould to coat the base evenly. To coat the sides, lay the mould on its side over the ice and spoon on aspic section by section, gradually turning the mould until the sides are covered.

Serves 6
1.2 litres (2 pints) melted Aspic, made with Fish Stock (see pages 50 and 26)
12 small sprigs fresh tarragon or chervil
3 small tomatoes, skinned, quartered and seeds removed
450 g (1 lb) frozen prawns, thawed and drained on paper towels
To garnish:
cress
12 unpeeled prawns

Preparation time: 15 minutes, plus making aspic
Cooking time: 1 hour

1. Set a 1.5 litre (3 pint) ring mould on a bowl of iced water and leave for a few minutes to chill and for condensation to build up in the mould.

2. Pour 150 ml (¼ pint) of the cooled aspic carefully into the mould, ensuring that bubbles do not form. Leave until set.

3. Dip the sprigs of tarragon or chervil into the remaining liquid aspic and arrange evenly on the set aspic in the mould.

4. Gently spoon 2–3 tablespoons of cold liquid aspic into the mould, being careful not to disturb the herbs. Leave to set.

5. Arrange the tomatoes in the mould, making sure that they are not too close to the edge.

6. Pour a further 150 ml (¼ pint) cooled liquid aspic carefully into the mould without moving the tomatoes. This layer of aspic should come halfway up the tomatoes – add more aspic if necessary. Leave to set.

7. Top up the mould with another 150 ml (¼ pint) cooled aspic which should cover the tomatoes. Leave to set.

8. Arrange 100 g (4 oz) of the prawns round the mould on

the layer of set jelly. Pour in enough aspic to just cover the prawns. Leave to set.

9. Continue to layer up in this way using up the remaining prawns and aspic. Leave in the refrigerator and allow to set for 2–3 hours.

10. To unmould the jelly, dip the mould into hand-hot water for a few seconds until the jelly moves when the mould is twisted. Lift out quickly, place a serving dish on the mould and invert. Shake the mould and then carefully lift it off.

11. Fill the centre of the ring mould with cress and arrange the peeled prawns round the edge.

12. Serve on its own or with a lemon mayonnaise.

Lemon and Raspberry Jelly

The principles and rules for making lemon and wine jellies are the same as for making aspic.

1.2 litres (2 pints) water
50 g (2 oz) gelatine
225 g (8 oz) lump sugar
thinly pared rind and juice of 4 lemons
1 clove
egg shells from 2 eggs
2 egg whites, lightly whipped
225 g (8 oz) large raspberries

Preparation time: 15 minutes, not including setting
Cooking time: about 2 hours

1. Measure 300 ml (½ pint) water, add the gelatine and stir to mix evenly.

2. Put the remaining water, sugar, lemon rind and clove into a very clean pan and dissolve the sugar over a very gentle heat. Leave to cool.

3. Add the gelatine, lemon juice, crushed egg shells and whipped egg whites to the pan.

4. Continue to clarify as for Aspic (steps 4–6) on page 50. Strain and cool.

5. Set a 1.5 litre (3 pint) ring mould in an ice bath and leave until condensation forms on the inside. Pour 150 ml (¼

pint) of cold lemon jelly into the mould and leave to set.

6. Arrange 8 raspberries on the set jelly. Very slowly pour in enough cool jelly to come a quarter of the way up the raspberries. Leave to set.

7. Pour in enough jelly to cover the raspberries and leave to set.

8. Arrange more raspberries on the set jelly and continue to layer up as steps 7 and 8 until the mould is full. Leave to set in the refrigerator for 2–3 hours.

9. Turn out as for Prawn and Tomato Ring. Fill the centre with any remaining raspberries.

SOUPS

Chunky or smooth, hot or chilled, there is nothing so satisfying as a well-made soup. Main-meal soups, creamed vegetable soups, hearty chowders, clear consommés, iced summer soups, even fruit soups – each type has its own technique, described in detail here.

Soup is a versatile food, and it may be served either as an appetiser or as a main course, depending on its content. It should be served either piping hot or chilled, never lukewarm.

Soup aids digestion by encouraging the flow of gastric juices, thereby stimulating the appetite. Thus it is a good food for those recovering from illness, and will make an ideal beginning for any meal. The choice of soup to serve should be governed by the main course. If a substantial main course is chosen, a light soup, such as a consommé, would be the best starter. A thicker first-course soup should be followed by a lighter main course – a salad perhaps. And if the *main* part of the meal is to be soup, it will be more satisfying and filling, thus a selection of cheeses and fruit should be adequate to follow. A first-course soup should always stimulate the appetite, but not satisfy it.

Stocks

Soup can be most nutritious. This of course depends on the ingredients which are added. A tasty soup may be made from most vegetables and pulses without even following a recipe. Many ingredients in the store cupboard or refrigerator can be used. So long as the basic stock is rich and full of flavour, a delicious soup will result.

The basis of most soups is the stock. This should be fat-free, full bodied and rich in flavour, for the stock used will contribute greatly to the end flavour of the soup. (See pages 26–27). This is why stock cubes and powders are not recommended: they have a distinctive flavour which is also rather salty. It is best to make stock in large quantities which may then be reduced, frozen and used as required. (However, it is not recommended that a soup using frozen stock should be frozen, as it may not be safe.)

Many soups, however, can be made with milk, half milk, half water, or with water alone (if the vegetables and meat, say, are fresh and good and will give their flavour to the water).

Types of soup

A soup is classified by its principal ingredients – whether they are meat, fish, vegetable, pulse or fruit – and by its thickness and texture.

Clear soups are basically well-flavoured stocks, which are clarified by egg whites (see Consommé, page 65), with a garnish which generally gives the soup its name. They are served either hot or cold.

Thick soups are generally purées of vegetables and/or pulses, or thickened soups (see right). These include both sweet (fruit) and savoury soups which may be served hot or cold.

Cream soups are made with milk and/or stock. Generally cream or egg yolk and cream is added at the end of cooking to bind the soup as well as to enrich it.

Fruit soups are light in consistency and are made from fruit purée with stock or wine. They are generally served chilled or iced.

Main-course soups are more substantial, containing pieces of meat, fish or vegetables, and may be served with savoury dumplings or scones or bread floating in the liquid.

Thickening and flavouring

Soup may be thickened by its basic ingredients – potato and other root vegetables, puréed, perhaps – or by the addition of flour, cornflour, arrowroot or in many cases egg yolks.

Many soups in the following recipes have a butter and flour roux as their basis, which does away with the need to thicken at the last minute. This can be done, though, by adding little balls of 'beurre manié' (flour and butter mixed together), and stirring well to dissolve and cook. If thickening and enriching with egg yolk, great care should be taken: if the liquid is too hot, the yolk will curdle.

The flavour of a soup may be enriched by the addition of many ingredients: wine, sherry, vermouth or lemon juice all add piquancy, and cream, single or double, gives a velvety smoothness to many soups. The *garnish* used can also add flavour (see page 67).

Puréeing soup

Food processors, liquidisers and hand-held blenders are perfect for puréeing soup. However, if these are unavailable, the soup may be passed through a mouli or sieve, which works as well, but is harder work and is a longer process. It must be remembered though that an electric blender or food processor purées *everything*, whereas a sieve or mouli retains the unwanted skin, stalk and pips. If a finer consistency is required after puréeing, the soup may need to be sieved.

Storing and freezing

Soup, once made, must be stored in the refrigerator as it deteriorates quickly. Store it for up to 2 days. If soup is made in bulk, it may be frozen in containers and stored for future use. Do not freeze for more than 3 months, and always remember to allow a good head-space (about 5 cm/ 2 inches) between the level of the soup and the lid, as the liquid swells during freezing.

Frozen soup may be thawed in the refrigerator overnight, or in a microwave oven, following the manufacturer's instructions. The frozen block can also be placed in a heavy-based saucepan placed over a wire mesh stove mat: this slows down the heating of the soup (it is very easy to burn or scorch the soup with this method, which would ruin its flavour). A large double saucepan is probably the safest way of reheating soup.

Top row: Mussel and Clam Chowder, French Onion Soup.
Bottom row: Potage Vert, Chilled Tomato and Basil Soup

PURÉES

Most soups – apart from clear and 'chunky' soups, of course – consist of a purée. The texture of puréed soups can vary, and this depends on the amount of stock used, the extent of the basic reducing to a purée (brief or lengthy blending, say), whether it is sieved after blending, and whether a final thickener is added, such as eggs or cream.

Chestnut Soup

If time is short canned whole chestnuts may be used and the cooking time reduced to 15 minutes after the chestnuts are added. It is essential, though, that the vegetables are very tender.

Serves 6–8
450 g (1 lb) whole fresh
chestnuts
25 g (1 oz) butter
100 g (4 oz) very lean bacon,
chopped
4 shallots, peeled and finely
chopped
2 celery sticks, finely chopped
3 carrots, finely chopped
1.2 litres (2 pints) Chicken or
Game Stock (see page 26)
1 bouquet garni
salt
freshly ground black pepper
To garnish:
garlic flavoured croûtons (see
page 67)

Preparation time: 25 minutes
Cooking time: 1¼ hours

1. Put the fresh chestnuts into a saucepan of cold water. Slowly bring to the boil and cook for 1 minute. Using a slotted spoon, remove from the pan.

2. Remove the outer and inner skins of the nuts by holding each one in a cloth and peeling away the skins with a knife. If the skin does not come away easily, heat the chestnuts in the pan for a further minute. Discard the skins.

3. Heat the butter in a large saucepan, add the bacon and shallots and cook for 2 minutes without browning. Add the celery, carrot and chestnuts.

4. Pour the stock into the pan, and add the bouquet garni, salt and pepper. Bring to the boil, cover and simmer for 1 hour until the chestnuts are very tender. Cool slightly, and remove the bouquet garni.

5. Purée the soup in a blender or food processor. Rinse the saucepan, return the soup to the pan and heat through. Taste the soup for seasoning.

6. Serve at once, garnished with garlic croûtons.

Broad Bean Soup

Either fresh or frozen broad beans may be used in this recipe. However, fresh ones are preferable, especially if they are young and tender. If fresh ones are used, allow about 1.5 kg (3½ lb) with their pods. Some of the pods can be added to the soup for extra flavour.

Serves 6
50 g (2 oz) butter
1 onion, peeled and finely
chopped
2 leeks, trimmed and finely
chopped
25 g (1 oz) plain flour
900 ml (1½ pints) Chicken
Stock (see page 26)
450 g (1 lb) shelled broad
beans
1 bouquet garni
salt
freshly ground black pepper
2 egg yolks
To garnish:
6 tablespoons soured cream
2 tablespoons chopped chives

Preparation time: 15 minutes
Cooking time: 50 minutes

1. Melt the butter in a large saucepan. Add the onion and leek and cook for 10 minutes without browning, stirring occasionally.

2. Stir in the flour and cook for a further 2 minutes, stirring constantly.

3. Gradually stir in the stock and bring to the boil. Add the broad beans, bouquet garni, salt and pepper then cover and simmer for 35 minutes, stirring occasionally, until the beans are very tender. Cool slightly, remove and discard the bouquet garni. Purée in a blender or food processor until very smooth, then strain to remove the bean skins.

4. Rinse the saucepan. Return the soup to the pan and heat gently.

5. Mix the egg yolks together in a bowl. Using a ladle, spoon some of the soup on to the egg yolks and blend thoroughly. Add to the soup and heat gently, without boiling, as this would curdle the soup.

6. Pour the soup into a tureen or serving bowls, swirl in the soured cream and sprinkle with chives. Serve at once.

For a perfect purée

■ Always cut the vegetables to the same size so that they cook evenly.
■ To ensure the best flavour, sweat the vegetables very gently in butter first without browning. This draws out the natural juices.
■ If using a liquidiser, remember that it quickly reduces everything to a velvet-smooth consistency. If a less uniform texture is required, a food mill gives varying textures.
■ To thicken a soup that is too thin, add one of the thickeners (see page 33), or reduce it gently by simmering with the lid off.
■ To thin down a thick soup, simply add some more well flavoured stock.
■ Beware of over-seasoning a puréed soup; if it is over salty, simmer 2 peeled, halved potatoes in the soup. These will absorb the saltiness.

Potage Vert

This soup is a beautiful colour, a rich deep green. It is essential to purée it well, and it should, preferably, be sieved afterwards to ensure that it is creamy smooth. If sorrel is unavailable, increase the quantities of spinach and watercress.

Serves 4
225 g (8 oz) fresh sorrel
225 g (8 oz) fresh spinach leaves
2 bunches watercress
1 bouquet garni
1 bunch spring onions, trimmed and chopped
3 tablespoons chopped parsley
600 ml (1 pint) Chicken Stock (see page 26)
150 ml (¼ pint) dry white wine
salt
freshly ground black pepper
40 g (1½ oz) Beurre Manié (see page 33)
150 ml (¼ pint) double cream
1 teaspoon lemon juice
To garnish:
25 g (1 oz) toasted flaked almonds

Preparation time: 15 minutes
Cooking time: 25–30 minutes

1. Place the sorrel, spinach, watercress, bouquet garni, spring onions and parsley into a large saucepan.

2. Pour over the stock and wine. Season with a little salt and pepper. Slowly bring to the boil, and simmer for 20 minutes, stirring occasionally. Cool slightly, and remove the bouquet garni.

3. Blend to a purée in a blender or food processor, then pass through a sieve. Rinse the saucepan and return the soup to the pan.

4. Bring to the boil, reduce the heat and add the beurre manié in small pieces, stirring continually until the soup has thickened. Cook for 5 minutes, stirring.

5. Remove from the heat and adjust the seasoning to taste. Stir in the cream and lemon juice and serve, sprinkled with toasted almonds.

Fennel Soup

Fennel soup has a delicate flavour and is very dependent on its stock, which should be full-bodied. A little wine or dry sherry may be added, if liked.

Serves 6
25 g (1 oz) butter
3 shallots, peeled and finely chopped
2 large bulbs fennel, trimmed and finely chopped
1 bouquet garni
900 ml (1½ pints) Chicken Stock (see page 26)
salt
3 egg yolks
150 ml (¼ pint) double cream
To garnish:
fennel fronds
puff pastry Fleurons (see page 339)

Preparation time: 10 minutes
Cooking time: about 50 minutes

1. Melt the butter in a large saucepan, add the shallots and cook for 5 minutes without browning. Stir in the chopped fennel (reserving the green fronds for a garnish).

2. Add the bouquet garni and stock. Bring to the boil, season with a little salt, cover and simmer for 30–40 minutes, until the fennel is very tender.

3. Remove the bouquet garni and cool slightly. Purée the soup in a blender or food processor, or pass through a sieve.

4. Rinse the saucepan and return the soup to the pan. Reheat slowly.

5. Blend the egg yolks and cream together in a bowl. Using a ladle, spoon some of the hot soup on to the egg mixture and stir well.

6. Pour the egg and soup mixture into the saucepan and heat very gently, stirring constantly. Make sure that the soup does not boil, as this would curdle it. Adjust the seasoning to taste.

7. Serve immediately, garnished with fennel fronds and puff pastry fleurons.

CREAM SOUPS

Cream of vegetable soups are sophisticated versions of puréed soups, in which the flavour can be enhanced and enriched by a flavoured milk – such as that used for a Béchamel sauce – and by a final addition of double cream, making them smooth, rich and delicious. Cream soups can also be made from fish and poultry purées.

Cream of Mushroom Soup

Serves 4
75 g (3 oz) butter
3 shallots, peeled and finely
*   chopped*
450 g (1 lb) mushrooms (flat
*   field if available) trimmed*
*   and chopped*
25 g (1 oz) plain flour
600 ml (1 pint) Chicken Stock
*   (see page 26)*
2 teaspoons French mustard
3 tablespoons dry sherry
salt
freshly ground black pepper
150 ml (¼ pint) double cream
To garnish:
25 g (1 oz) butter
50 g (2 oz) button mushrooms,
*   trimmed and sliced*

Preparation time: 15 minutes
Cooking time: about 20–25 minutes

1. Melt the butter in a large pan, add the shallots and cook for 5 minutes without browning. Add the mushrooms and cook for a further 10 minutes.

2. Stir in the flour and cook for 1 minute, stirring constantly.

3. Gradually add the stock, stirring well between each addition. Bring to the boil and cook for 3 minutes. Stir in the mustard and sherry.

4. Season to taste, cover and simmer for 10 minutes, stirring occasionally. Cool slightly, then blend in a blender or food processor.

5. Rinse the saucepan. Return the soup to the pan. Stir in the cream, and heat gently, without boiling. Adjust the seasoning to taste.

6. For the garnish, melt the butter in a small pan, add the button mushrooms and cook for 1 minute. Stir the mushrooms into the soup and serve immediately.

Cream of Asparagus Soup

Serves 6
600 ml (1 pint) milk
1 medium onion, peeled
1 bay leaf
3 black peppercorns
1 bouquet garni
450 g (1 lb) fresh green
*   asparagus*
450 ml (¾ pint) water
salt
40 g (1½ oz) butter
40 g (1½ oz) flour
150 ml (¼ pint) double cream

Preparation time: 15 minutes
Cooking time: about 20–25 minutes

1. Put the milk, onion, bay leaf, peppercorns and bouquet garni into a saucepan. Slowly bring to the boil, then simmer for 5 minutes. Remove from the heat and leave to cool, then strain. Discard the onion and seasonings.

2. Scrape and trim the asparagus, and remove the woody ends. Wash thoroughly and cut into 2.5 cm (1 inch) lengths.

3. Bring the water to the boil, add some salt and the asparagus stems. Cook for 5 minutes, then add the tips and cook for a further 2–3 minutes until the asparagus is tender. Drain the asparagus, reserving the tips for garnish.

4. Melt the butter in a large saucepan, stir in the flour, and cook for 2 minutes without browning, stirring constantly. Gradually add the milk, stirring well. Bring to the boil, reduce the heat and cook for 2 minutes, stirring.

5. Gradually whisk in half the asparagus liquor, then add enough of the remainder until the required thickish consistency is reached.

6. Add the asparagus and simmer very gently for 10 minutes, stirring occasionally.

7. Purée the soup in a blender or food processor, or pass through a sieve. Rinse the saucepan and return the soup to the pan.

8. Stir the cream into the soup and adjust the seasoning. Heat very gently, but do not boil. Serve immediately, with the asparagus tips on top.

MAIN-MEAL SOUPS

Some soups are substantial enough to make a meal in themselves, such as Scotch broth or the chunky Lentil and Ham Soup below. Others even provide two courses from the same pot, cooking whole stuffed chickens or joints of meat in a vegetable broth. These hearty soups originated as thrifty peasant dishes, but many are now classics.

Pot-au-Feu

Pot-au-feu provides two dishes in one. Firstly, the tender meat can be served with the vegetables, and for the next meal, the rich flavoured bouillon (soup) can have either rice or pasta or the remaining meat and vegetables stirred into it. The secret of success lies in the long and slow cooking, which makes for a strong bouillon which is clear and fat-free, and succulent non-stringy meat.

Serves 8
1.25 kg (2½ lb) shin of beef,
  boned and rolled
1 kg (2 lb) knuckle of veal
1 kg (2 lb) topside of beef
1 small beef marrow bone,
  halved
salt
12 peppercorns
450 g (1 lb) carrots, peeled
1 head celery, trimmed and
  halved
4 medium onions, peeled and
  halved
450 g (1 lb) leeks, trimmed
1 bouquet garni
150 ml (¼ pint) dry white wine
2 garlic cloves, peeled and
  sliced or crushed
a small piece of root ginger,
  peeled and finely chopped
  (optional)

Preparation time: 30 minutes
Cooking time: about 5 hours

1. Tie the meat into neat parcels with string and put into a very large saucepan with the halved marrow bone. Cover with water and season with salt.

2. Slowly bring to the boil. As the scum rises to the surface, remove it with a slotted spoon, making sure that the liquid at all times covers the meat. Continue skimming the surface until the liquid is quite clear: any scum or froth left in the stock will make it murky.

3. Add the peppercorns, all the vegetables, bouquet garni, wine, garlic and ginger (if used).

4. Slowly return to the boil, cover with a tight fitting lid, and simmer very gently for 2 hours. Check that the meat is still covered by the liquid, topping it up if necessary, then cover and continue cooking for a further 2–2½ hours until the meat is tender.

5. Lift the meat from the pan and drain well. Remove the vegetables and discard the bouquet garni. Slice the meat thickly and serve with the vegetables, accompanied by French mustard and coarse sea salt. A little of the bouillon could be used to moisten the meat.

6. Leave the bouillon to cool, then refrigerate for at least 1 hour. Carefully remove the fat from the surface, using a metal spoon, then strain.

7. To serve the soup, add pasta, meat or vegetables if liked, and heat gently to boiling point or until the added ingredients are cooked. Adjust the seasoning to taste and serve with French bread.

Lentil and Ham Soup

Serves 6
100 g (4 oz) yellow lentils
25 g (1 oz) butter
2 shallots, peeled and finely
  chopped
1 large onion, peeled and
  finely chopped
2 leeks, trimmed and chopped
4 carrots, peeled and chopped
2 celery sticks, trimmed and
  chopped
1.2 litres (2 pints) Brown or
  Chicken Stock (see pages
  26– 27)
1 bouquet garni
100 g (4 oz) cooked ham, sliced
salt
freshly ground black pepper
2 tablespoons chopped parsley

Preparation time: 20 minutes
Cooking time: 1¼ hours

1. Soak the lentils in cold water for 6–8 hours, or overnight. Rinse well and drain.

2. Melt the butter in a large saucepan, add the shallots and onion, and cook for 10 minutes until lightly browned.

3. Stir in the leeks, carrots and celery, and cook for 2 minutes, stirring occasionally.

4. Stir in the lentils, stock and bouquet garni.

5. Slowly bring to the boil, cover and simmer for 1 hour until the vegetables and lentils are soft.

6. Remove the bouquet garni and cool the soup slightly.

7. Push through a sieve or purée in an electric blender or food processor until smooth.

8. Rinse the pan and return the soup to it. Stir in the ham, add salt if necessary and season with pepper.

9. Slowly bring to the boil then cook for 5 minutes. Stir in the parsley and serve hot with crusty bread.

FISH SOUPS

Fish soups are, in general, filling, rich and nutritious, as well as delicious. Bisques are the most sophisticated, but chowders – the name is a corruption of *chaudière*, a large heavy pot used by French fishermen for soups and stews – come a close second. Bouillabaisse, perhaps the most famous fish soup of all, is rich in the flavours of Provence.

Mussel and Clam Chowder

See pages 100–102 for detailed information on preparing shellfish.

Serves 6
1 kg (2 lb) mussels in their shells
12 small clams in their shells
225 g (8 oz) plaice fillets, skinned
40 g (1½ oz) butter
4 shallots, peeled and finely chopped
2 celery sticks, chopped
1 garlic clove, crushed
25 g (1 oz) plain flour
900 ml (1½ pints) Fish Stock (see page 26)
150 ml (¼ pint) dry white wine
salt
freshly ground black pepper
1 bouquet garni
50 g (2 oz) long-grain rice, cooked
6 strands saffron, soaked in 1 tablespoon boiling water
2 egg yolks
4 tablespoons double cream
2 tablespoons finely chopped parsley

Preparation time: 20 minutes
Cooking time: 30 minutes

1. Scrub the mussel and clam shells very thoroughly to remove beards, barnacles and sand, and dry well.

2. Cut the plaice into 2.5 cm (1 inch) pieces.

3. Melt the butter in a large saucepan, add the shallots and celery, and cook for 10 minutes, without browning, stirring occasionally.

4. Add the garlic and flour, and cook for 2 minutes, stirring constantly.

5. Gradually add the stock and wine, stirring well between each addition. Bring to the boil and cook for 2 minutes. Season with salt and pepper.

6. Add the mussels, clams, plaice and bouquet garni, and simmer for 10 minutes until all the shells have opened.

If any are still closed, discard them.

7. Stir in the rice, saffron and its water. Heat through. Discard the bouquet garni.

8. Adjust the seasoning to taste. Blend together the egg yolks and cream. Using a ladle, spoon a little soup on to the eggs, remove the pan from the heat, then pour the egg mixture into the soup and stir until well incorporated. Do not reheat.

9. Stir in the parsley and serve immediately.

Lobster Bisque

A bisque is a purée of shellfish – generally lobster, crab or crayfish – served as a soup. It is creamy, spicy and full of flavour. For a good fresh taste use live shellfish (see page 102 for detailed instructions on dealing with a live lobster).

Serves 6
1 medium hen lobster (live if possible)
900 ml (1½ pints) Fish Stock (see page 26)
300 ml (½ pint) good quality dry white wine
1 bouquet garni
3 shallots, peeled
1 carrot, peeled and roughly chopped
2 celery sticks
40 g (1½ oz) butter
3 tablespoons plain flour
a squeeze of lemon juice
3 tablespoons cream
salt
freshly ground white pepper
For the lobster butter:
coral from the lobster butter (see method)
To garnish:
1 tablespoon chopped chives

Preparation time: 40 minutes
Cooking time: 1¼ hours
Oven: 150°C, 300°F, Gas Mark 2

1. Cook the lobster, if bought live.

2. Cut the lobster in half lengthways, crack the claws, remove the meat (see page 102), and cut the tail flesh into small pieces.
Carefully remove the coral and set aside.

3. Break up the shell and put it into a large saucepan with the fish stock, half the wine, bouquet garni, shallots, carrot and celery. Bring to the boil, cover and simmer for 30 minutes. Remove the lid and continue cooking for a further 30 minutes. Cool slightly, strain and reserve the liquid. Discard the vegetables, bouquet garni and shells.

4. Meanwhile, to make the lobster butter, weigh the coral and put it into a sieve and wash well. Dry on paper towels. Spread the coral on a baking sheet and place in a preheated oven for about 10 minutes to dry it, taking great care that it does not change colour (if overdried, it will spoil). Leave to cool, then pound the coral with double its weight of butter, and season to taste. Rub the mixture through a fine sieve and reserve.

5. Melt the 40 g (1½ oz) butter in a saucepan, stir in the flour and cook for 1 minute, stirring. Gradually add the strained lobster liquor. Bring to the boil and cook for 5 minutes, stirring constantly.

6. Remove from the heat, add the lemon juice, cream and remaining wine and season with salt and pepper.

7. Stir in the lobster flesh and heat gently, taking care not to boil the soup.

8. Whisk in the lobster butter without boiling, adjust the seasoning to taste and serve immediately, garnished with chopped chives.

Bouillabaisse

This recipe from Marseilles should ideally be made with fish from the Mediterranean. But any fish may be used, so long as the textures and flavours are different. The secret of making Bouillabaisse is to boil the liquid very rapidly so that the oil amalgamates with the stock. Take care not to overcook the fish, it needs very little cooking. Use a very large saucepan – a preserving pan is ideal.

Serves 8

2–3 shallots, roughly chopped
4 tomatoes, roughly chopped
4 large garlic cloves, chopped
2 large leeks, roughly sliced
2 sticks celery, roughly chopped
1/4 fennel, roughly chopped
85 ml (3 fl oz) good quality
    olive oil
2.25 litres (4 pints) Fish Stock
    (see page 26)
150 ml (1/4 pint) good quality
    dry white wine
1 bay leaf
pinch saffron strands
coarse salt
freshly ground black pepper
1 lobster, cooked and halved
1 medium-sized crab, boiled
8 large prawns
4 whole fillets plaice, skinned,
    and cut into small pieces
4 red mullet, scaled, cleaned,
    and cut into pieces
1 John Dory (optional),
    cleaned and cut into small
    pieces
16 scallops, cleaned, shells
    removed, and sliced
1 loaf French bread, sliced
Rouille:
50 g (2 oz) white breadcrumbs
4 tablespoons milk
2 garlic cloves, peeled and
    chopped
1–2 fresh red chillies, roughly
    chopped
2 tablespoons olive oil
3–4 tablespoons cooking
    liquid (bouillon)

Preparation time: 45 minutes
Cooking time: 25 minutes
Oven: 150°C, 300°F, Gas Mark 2

1. Assemble the ingredients and make sure that all advance preparations to the fish have been done. Put the shallots, tomatoes, garlic, leeks, celery, fennel and olive oil into a large pan.

2. Cook over a high heat for 2 minutes, add the stock, wine, bay leaf, saffron, salt and pepper. Bring to the boil and cook very rapidly for 15 minutes.

3. If the bouillon has been prepared in advance, bring to the boil again. Add the halved lobster, and the claws broken into pieces, the crab claws, the crab meat, and the prawns. Cook for 1 minute.

4. Add the plaice, mullet and John Dory, if using. Cook for 4 minutes then add the scallops and cook for a further 1 minute, adding some boiling water if necessary, to cover the fish.

5. Meanwhile, put the bread slices on to a baking sheet and dry in a preheated oven for 5 minutes without colouring.

6. To make the Rouille, soak the breadcrumbs in the milk for 10 minutes, put into a sieve and squeeze to remove the milk. Discard the milk.

7. Purée the bread with the garlic and chillies. Add the olive oil and blend until very smooth, adding sufficient bouillon to give a fairly thick paste. Spoon into a bowl.

8. Arrange the dried bread on a plate, or in a basket.

9. Using a perforated spoon, lift the fish from the saucepan and arrange in a heated serving dish. Strain the bouillon into a tureen and serve at once.

10. Rouille is spread on the bread, put in the soup plate, and fish and bouillon added.

BREAD SOUPS

Bread is the natural accompaniment to most soups, but sometimes it becomes a major ingredient, thickening and flavouring. Bread soups tend to be robust and hearty, usually flavoured with cheese, onion or garlic, and almost make a meal in themselves. The most famous bread soup of all is of course French Onion Soup.

French Onion Soup

Serves 6
50 g (2 oz) butter
1 kg (2 lb) onions, peeled and
  thinly sliced
1.2 litres (2 pints) Brown Stock
  (see page 27)
1 bouquet garni
salt
freshly ground black pepper
6 slices French bread, toasted
  on both sides
100 g (4 oz) Gruyère cheese,
  grated

Preparation time: 10 minutes
Cooking time: about 1 hour

1. Melt the butter in a large saucepan. Add the onions and fry very gently until golden, taking care not to burn them.

2. It will take about 30–40 minutes for the onions to reach the required stage of soft tenderness.

3. Pour the stock into the pan and add the bouquet garni, salt and pepper. Slowly bring to the boil, cover and simmer for 20 minutes. Discard the bouquet garni.

4. Adjust the seasoning to taste then ladle the soup into 6 individual, heatproof serving bowls.

5. Float a slice of toasted bread on top of each bowl of soup. Sprinkle bread slices with cheese and place under a preheated hot grill for 1 minute or until the cheese has melted. Serve immediately.

Variation

Cheese and Bread Soup Make French Onion Soup up to the end of step 3. Arrange a layer of toasted French bread in the bottom of a casserole. Cover with slices of Gruyère cheese and sprinkle with grated Parmesan and Cheddar. Top with two more layers of bread and cheese. Pour the French Onion Soup over the bread and cheese. Place the casserole in a preheated oven for 20 minutes until the cheese has melted. Serve immediately, sprinkled with chives.

CONSOMMÉ

Consommé is the French name for meat stock which has been enriched, concentrated and clarified. A large number of consommés can be made from this basic recipe, but the stock must have a good flavour and be well jellied. Chicken consommé, for instance, can be made in the same way. Consommé may be served hot, or chilled and lightly jellied.

Beef Consommé

450 g (1 lb) very lean beef,
  finely shredded
2.25 litres (4 pints) Brown
  Stock, any fat skimmed off
  (see page 27)
½ teaspoon salt
1 carrot, sliced
3 shallots
1 bouquet garni
4 egg whites
2 tablespoons dry sherry
To garnish:
*julienne strips of carrot and
  leek, blanched*

Preparation time: 30 minutes
Cooking time: 1½ hours
excluding making the stock.

For perfect Consommé

■ For best results, a jelly cloth should be used for straining the stock. However, if this is unavailable, a double piece of muslin will suffice.
■ It is essential to scald the jelly cloth or muslin thoroughly before and after use, to ensure that it is completely clean. To do this, pour boiling water over and through it, ensuring that all parts of it are scalded.
■ The bowl and colander or sieve used for straining should also be scalded.
■ It is essential to whisk continuously until a thick froth forms on the surface. If you hold the whisk in the normal fashion it can be very tiring. However, if you grip the whisk with your whole hand (see step 3) you will find it easier.

1. Place the beef, stock, salt, carrot, shallots and bouquet garni into a large saucepan. Taste the stock and season very well – remember the egg whites will absorb seasoning.

2. Lightly whisk the egg whites and add to the saucepan. Heat gently, whisking vigorously in reverse motion (see step 3).

3. Whisk continuously until a thick froth forms on top of the surface and the liquid is nearly boiling. Stop whisking when the liquid comes to the boil. Turn down the heat, add the sherry and simmer very gently for 1½ hours. Do not allow the liquid to boil during this time.

4. Remove from the heat and leave to stand for 20 minutes. A thick brown scummy crust will have formed on the surface.

5. Wet a scalded jelly cloth or double piece of muslin and drape over a colander. Fix the colander over a large bowl. Gently spoon the crust into the colander, trying not to break it, then slowly pour the consommé through the crust. Leave to stand, then strain again if necessary.

8. Chill until it has formed a jelly, or reheat and serve hot, garnished with the julienne of vegetables.

CHILLED SOUPS

Nothing could be nicer than a chilled soup on a warm summer day. It could be a lightly jellied consommé with an interesting garnish, or it could be one of the chilled soups below. And why not serve a chilled fruit soup for dessert instead of the traditional first-course soup – the idea can be adapted to many fruits such as cherries, plums or melons.

Vichyssoise

Vichyssoise is traditionally served chilled. It looks very attractive if the individual bowls are surrounded by cracked or crushed ice, with clusters of fresh herbs scattered around the edge of each bowl.

Serves 6
50 g (2 oz) butter
3 shallots, peeled and finely chopped
6 large leeks, white part only, finely chopped (use the green tops for stock or other soups)
4 large potatoes, peeled and diced
1 litre (1¾ pints) Chicken Stock (see page 26)
1 bouquet garni
salt
150 ml (¼ pint) double cream
To garnish:
1 tablespoon each chopped chives, parsley and thyme
crushed or cracked ice
bunches of fresh herbs

Preparation time: 15 minutes, plus chilling time
Cooking time: about 1 hour

1. Melt the butter in a large saucepan. Add the shallots and cook for 5 minutes without browning, stirring occasionally.

2. Stir in the leeks and potatoes and cook for a further 10 minutes without browning.

3. Stir in the stock, bouquet garni and a little salt. Bring to the boil, cover and simmer for 30–40 minutes, stirring occasionally.

4. Remove the bouquet garni and cool the soup slightly.

5. Blend to a purée in a blender or food processor, and pass through a sieve to ensure it is very smooth.

6. Pour the soup into a large bowl and chill for 4 hours. Stir in the cream, and adjust the seasoning to taste.

7. Using a ladle, pour the soup into 6 individual bowls, standing on plates. Surround the bowls with crushed or cracked ice.

8. Sprinkle the soup with the chopped herbs and decorate the ice with clusters of fresh herbs. Serve immediately.

Chilled Tomato and Basil Soup

This is a good soup to make in the summer when there is a glut of tomatoes and plenty of fresh basil available. Ensure that the flavour is very strong to begin with, as it diminishes when chilled.

Serves 6
40 g (1½ oz) butter
4 shallots, peeled and finely chopped
25 g (1 oz) plain flour
1 garlic clove, crushed
1 kg (2 lb) ripe tomatoes, or canned tomatoes, roughly chopped
300 ml (½ pint) dry white wine
150 ml (¼ pint) Chicken Stock (see page 26)
1 bouquet garni
a dash of Tabasco
a dash of Worcestershire sauce
3 tablespoons freshly chopped basil
salt
freshly ground black pepper
To garnish:
6 tablespoons double cream, lightly whipped
fresh basil, chopped

Preparation time: 20 minutes, plus chilling overnight
Cooking time: about 1 hour

1. Melt the butter in a saucepan, add the shallots and cook for 5 minutes without browning, stirring occasionally.

2. Add the flour and cook for 1 minute, stirring constantly. Add the garlic and tomatoes. Cook for a further 5 minutes, stirring occasionally.

3. Pour the wine and stock into the pan and add the bouquet garni. Bring to the boil, cover and simmer for 30 minutes, stirring occasionally.

4. Add the Tabasco, Worcestershire sauce, chopped basil, salt and pepper, and cook for a further 20 minutes, uncovered, stirring occasionally. Cool, and remove the bouquet garni.

5. Blend to a purée in a blender or food processor, then pass through a nylon sieve into a bowl to remove the skin and pips. Chill overnight, if possible.

6. Pour into 6 individual chilled bowls, and top each with a swirl of cream and a sprinkling of chopped basil.

Black Cherry Soup

This soup should be served very cold, and looks attractive if the bowls are surrounded by crushed ice.

Serves 6

750 g (1¹/₂ lb) juicy black
   cherries
1 litre (1³/₄ pints) water
150 ml (¹/₄ pint) medium red
   wine
1 tablespoon arrowroot
25 g (1 oz) icing sugar (or
   more to taste)
a squeeze of lemon juice
To garnish:
crushed ice
a few whole cherries with their
   leaves
150 ml (¹/₄ pint) soured cream
mint leaves (optional)

Preparation time: 10 minutes, plus chilling
Cooking time: 35 minutes

1. Put the cherries into a saucepan, and add the water and wine. Slowly bring to the boil, reduce the heat then simmer for 20–25 minutes until very soft. Cool.

2. Rub the soup through a nylon sieve, set over a bowl.

3. Blend together the arrowroot and icing sugar. Stir in 3 tablespoons of the soup to give a smooth paste.

4. Rinse the saucepan, return the soup to the pan and heat gently. Stir in the blended arrowroot. Slowly bring to the boil, stirring constantly. Reduce the heat and simmer, stirring, for 5 minutes.

5. Taste the soup, add more sugar if liked, then stir in the lemon juice. Chill. Leave to cool, stirring occasionally to prevent a skin forming, then refrigerate for 4 hours.

6. To serve, pour the soup into 6 individual bowls standing on plates. Surround each bowl with crushed ice. Garnish with whole cherries, and swirl a little soured cream into each bowl. Garnish with mint leaves, if liked.

For perfect Chilled Soups

■ Chilled soups rely greatly on the stock. It must be well flavoured as chilling always diminishes flavour.
■ Seasoning, too, is vital for cold soups, as this too reduces in effect with the chilling.
■ Colour is important and garnishes must contrast, eg chopped green chives on the white vichyssoise.
■ Always serve these soups thoroughly chilled, removing them from the refrigerator at the *last* moment.

Garnishes for soup

Soup can be transformed by the addition of a garnish. This can be simple or elaborate, depending on the soup's content and the occasion.

A garnish of *freshly chopped herbs* looks attractive and also adds flavour to the soup. *Fresh cream*, soured cream or yoghurt may be swirled into the soup to give a marbling effect.

Small juliennes of blanched vegetables are often added, particularly to consommés: these can include carrot, celery and leek. Use a small raw, blanched or cooked piece of the same vegetable to garnish a vegetable purée soup: an asparagus tip for asparagus, say.

Grated cheese is often added for extra flavour and to give extra protein, or sieved hard-boiled egg yolk may be sprinkled on the surface of the soup.

Toasted flaked almonds or other nuts, and sesame seeds make an unusual garnish and add a crunchy texture.

Croûtons also give a contrasting texture. These may be either small pieces of toasted bread simply cut into dice or, more usually, they are pieces of bread fried in butter until golden brown and crisp.

To make garlic croûtons, fry a few crushed cloves of peeled garlic along with the pieces of bread.

Croûtons may be made in a variety of sizes and shapes. They can be dice or larger squares, or small cutters can transform them into hearts, stars, crescents or leaf shapes.

The same cutters may be used to make *puff pastry garnishes*. The pastry is cut into attractive shapes and then baked in a preheated hot oven (230°C, 450°F, Gas Mark 8) for about 5 minutes until well risen and golden brown. They may be glazed first with beaten egg or milk, and if liked,

sprinkled with grated cheese, sesame or poppy seeds.

Crisply fried or grilled bacon is delicious in soup. To make *miniature bacon rolls*, halve lean bacon rashers lengthwise, then cut in half. Roll each piece of bacon up and secure with a cocktail stick. Grill until crisp, remove the cocktail stick and add to the soup at the last moment.

BONING

Boning is an art which should not just be the province of the professional chef or butcher. Although fairly complicated, once the basic principles are learned for all cuts of meat, poultry and fish, your repertoire will be greatly increased.

Boning meat and poultry makes it easier to carve; and boning fish makes it easier to eat. However, learning the art of boning is much more basically useful. By boning meat and fish at home, you can be assured that nothing is wasted as you will have the bones and trimmings for stocks and sauces; and you will have a boned product that will cook more evenly and often more quickly than when unboned.

Meat with its bone can be cooked in a variety of ways; but without its bone, it can be trimmed of all fat, chopped for kebabs or stews, minced for meatballs and sauces, or left

To bone a shoulder of lamb

1. Starting at the side where the hard white edge of the blade bone can be seen, cut into the flesh and gradually free it from the blade bone, keeping the knife close to the bone all the time. Cut the flesh away right up to the ball and socket joint.

2. Stand the joint on its side, with the edge of the blade bone to the work surface. Then, holding the knuckle joint firmly, press down hard on the shoulder, slightly twisting the knuckle joint at the same time. This will crack the ball and socket joint to free the blade bone.

3. Once the ball and socket joint are cracked apart, simply pull the blade bone out of the shoulder.

4. Make a long cut along the first bone of the knuckle joint, up to the ball and socket joint. Cut the flesh free from around the bone to expose it completely.

How to bone successfully

■ Firstly, examine the shape of the meat, feeling for the line of the bone, so that this can be followed throughout the boning process.
■ Use a very sharp boning knife with a flexible, thin and long blade: sharpness and flexibility both help to avoid waste when the blade is following the bone of the meat, poultry or game.

■ The choice of knife is important. Apart from the blade, it should have a handle which is comfortable to hold, and it should all be well balanced. It is worth spending time and money in the choice of any knife, as it is a good investment. Bear in mind that the price generally indicates the quality.
■ A good thick chopping

board is a great help. Keep this for meat preparation only, for hygiene purposes.
■ Always keep your fingers away from the bone, and cut away from your body.
■ Take your time. Speed will come with practice.

6. Tunnel into the meat to free the last part of the bone. Keep the knife close to the bone.

whole or stuffed before rolling for an impressive roast or braise. Fish on the bone can be simply fried or grilled; but once boned it can be stuffed in a variety of ways, or the boneless fillets can be used in many classic dishes.

Boning poultry is perhaps the most complicated technique of all, but the end result is undeniably impressive. Boned duck en croûte, chicken galantines or ballotines are all within your range once you have mastered the art of boning.

5. Using the top of the knife, work around the ball and socket joint to free the flesh.

7. Remove the last bone from the flesh by twisting and pulling it free.

Shoulder of Lamb with Rice and Kidney Stuffing

Serves 4–6
*1.5–1.75 kg (3½–4 lb)
    shoulder of lamb*
*15–25 g (½–1 oz) softened
    butter*
Stuffing:
50 g (2 oz) butter
1 onion, finely chopped
1 garlic clove, crushed
50 g (2 oz) long-grain rice
½ teaspoon dried thyme
*150 ml (¼ pint) Chicken Stock
    (see page 25)*
*4 lambs' kidneys, cored and
    sliced*
salt
freshly ground black pepper

Preparation time: about 25 minutes, plus boning time
Cooking time: 2½–2¾ hours
Oven: 190°C, 375°F, Gas Mark 5

1. Bone the shoulder as described opposite, and lay it on a board, skin side down, ready for the stuffing.

2. To prepare the stuffing, heat 25 g (1 oz) of the butter in a saucepan and fry the onion gently until softened.

3. Stir in the garlic, rice and thyme and cook for 2 minutes.

4. Pour in the stock, bring to the boil, then cover and simmer gently for about 15–20 minutes until the rice has absorbed all the liquid.

5. Meanwhile, heat the remaining 25 g (1 oz) of the butter in another pan. Toss the sliced kidneys in this for a minute over a fairly high heat.

6. Stir the kidneys into the cooked rice and season well.

7. Pack the stuffing on to and into the lamb and then roll up and tie with string as described below.

8. Place the meat in a roasting tin and smear it with the 15–25 g (½–1 oz) softened butter. Season with salt and pepper then bake in a preheated oven for 1½–2 hours.

9. Make a thick gravy from the juices left in the pan after the fat has been tipped away, to accompany the meat (see page 25).

Variations

Spinach Stuffing Mix 225 g (8 oz) cooked spinach (drained very well), chopped, with 25 g (1 oz) finely chopped fresh mint, 4 peeled and crushed garlic cloves, 1 teaspoon vinegar, salt and pepper.
Moroccan Stuffing Mix 175 g (6 oz) cous-cous grains with 25 g (1 oz) sugar, 50 g (2 oz) raisins, 50 g (2 oz) butter, melted, 2 teaspoons ground cinnamon and 50 g (2 oz) toasted almonds, ground.
Chestnut Stuffing Soften a small finely chopped onion in 25 g (1 oz) butter then mix with 225 g (8 oz) sausage meat, 75 g (3 oz) unsweetened chestnut purée, 1 tablespoon chopped mixed fresh herbs, 1 beaten egg, salt and pepper.
Apricot Stuffing Soak 100 g (4 oz) dried apricots until soft then drain and chop. Cook 225 g (8 oz) long-grain rice until tender then mix with the apricots, 2 tablespoons each of raisins and split almonds, and ½ teaspoon each of ground cinnamon, coriander and ginger.

Tying a boned shoulder

The meat can be simply rolled up lengthwise and tied as below, or it can be stuffed first.

1. Spread the chosen stuffing, if used, over the surface of the meat, pushing some into the part where the blade bone was removed.

2. Fold the shoulder into a neat shape, placing the shank meat in the centre.

3. Run a length of string under the length of the meat, bring the two ends together at the centre of the meat, twist the ends to secure and pass each end of string down the sides. Turn the meat over and secure, as for a parcel.

4. Pass the string around the meat in a spiral, turning the joint over and over and regulating the tension with your thumb, to form a neat roll.

The meat can also be formed into a ball shape – 'en ballon' – after stuffing.

1. Stuff as above, and then fold all the edges of the meat in towards the middle. Secure with skewers or sew together.

2. With the lamb skin side up, take a long piece of string – at least 3 m (9 feet) – and tie firmly around the meat, knotting at the top.

3. Tie the string again, at right angles to the first line, again tying at the first knot.

4. Continue until the ball is firmly trussed in neat segments – about 8 – all round.

To bone a chicken

This method of boning can also be used for duck, turkey and game birds.

Before starting to bone the chicken, trim off the wing tips at the second joint, remove the parson's nose, and cut off the scaly part of the legs at the first drumstick joint.

1. Place the chicken, breast side down, on a flat surface, then using a very sharp, small knife, make a deep cut right down the centre of the backbone, cutting down to the bone.

2. Cut the flesh away from one side of the chicken by carefully cutting it away from the bones, working down over the rib cage to the tip of the breast bone. Keep the knife very close to the bones all the time. As you work down the rib cage you will come to the ball and socket joint, where the leg is attached to the body, simply work the knife under the joint to free it.

3. Continue working down the rib cage until you come to the joint that connects the wing. Once again, slip the knife under the joint to cut it free. As you work down the rib cage, the joints will become exposed automatically.

4. Having removed the flesh from one side of the rib cage, repeat with the other side, then cut along the top edge of the breast bone to free the entire rib cage completely.

5. To remove the bones from the legs and wings, simply scrape the flesh away from the bones, holding the bones firmly as you do so. Once again, keep the knife close to the bones as you work.

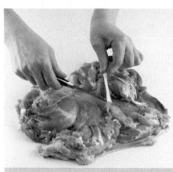

6. When all of the bones are removed, remove as many of the white sinews from the breast and legs as is possible, simply by scraping the flesh away from each one.

To bone poultry

■ Take great care not to cut or pierce the skin of the bird, otherwise the appearance of the finished dish will be spoiled.

■ Use a cloth or a paper towel to hold the bone for a firmer grip whilst breaking the joint.

■ Always keep the bones to make stocks and soups (see page 25).

■ Cut off the parson's nose, as this can impart a bitter flavour to the bird.

■ Scrape rather than cut the flesh away from the bones, using the point of the knife.

Skinning a fillet of fish

1. Place the fillet, skin side down, on a board.

2. Hold the tail of the fish in one hand – use some salt to help you get a good grip – and make a little cut close to the tail to separate flesh from skin. Do not cut *through* the skin.

3. Insert the blade of the knife gently between skin and flesh to loosen the flesh initially.

4. With the blade of the knife almost flat against the skin, use a rocking motion to cut the flesh away from the skin, ensuring that the tail is firmly held throughout the process.

5. Keep the skin for fish stock.

To fillet a Dover sole

1. Before filleting the sole the skin must be removed from each side of the fish. Starting with one side of the sole, make a small cut across the tail, then gently ease a thumb under the skin. Run your thumb along the fin edges to free the skin. Holding the tail end of the sole down firmly on the work top, pull the skin from the tail to the head end to remove it completely. Repeat with the other side.

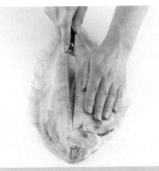

2. For 4 fillets, use a very sharp flexible filleting knife to make a long cut right down the centre of the sole, ensuring the cut goes down to the bones.

3. Remove the first fillet by cutting the flesh away from the bones, with long clean strokes of the knife, and keeping the knife very close to the bones. Work from the centre to the outside edge.

4. For 2 whole fillets, slide the knife into the stomach cavity and work down towards the fins and tail. Cut carefully along and over the ridge of the spine and work across to the other side.

To bone a trout

1. Slit the trout along the belly, then remove the entrails. Wash the fish well, and pat dry. Using a very small sharp knife, free the fine bones that lie at each side of the backbone, by gently slipping the tip of the knife under each bone to free it from the flesh.

2. Once the fine bones are free, continue to cut the flesh away from the backbone on both sides until it is free, taking care not to cut through the skin. Cut the backbone free at the head end of the fish with a pair of kitchen scissors.

3. Remove the bones completely by snipping them free at the tail end.

Boning and filleting fish

■ The first essential when skinning, filleting or boning fish is a sharp and flexible, but not too large, knife.

■ If the whole fish has not been scaled by the fishmonger, hold the fish up by the tail over the sink and scrape towards its head with a heavy non-flexible knife (or a scallop shell), to scrape the scales off. Wash off any loose scales under running cold water.

■ A separate board on which to work is particularly useful for fish preparation, but you could cover a board with greaseproof paper – this keeps the board free of fishy smells.

■ Tweezers or a small pair of pliers are a useful accessory: they can be used to pick out any small bones.

■ A clean cloth can help you get a firm grip on a slippery fish when skinning or filleting or dip your fingers in salt before starting.

Chicken Galantine

This is a most impressive looking dish which is suitable for buffet and dinner parties, al fresco eating and special occasions. It is easy to carve as it is completely boned, and the garnishing can be as simple or elaborate as you like. It should be prepared to the cooked stage the day before.

Serves 6–8
*1 oven-ready chicken, about
    1.75 kg (4 lb), boned (page
    70)*
chicken carcass and bones
1 bouquet garni
salt
175 g (6 oz) lean pork, minced
175 g (6 oz) pork sausage meat
*2 shallots, peeled and finely
    chopped*
1/2 teaspoon dried mixed herbs
*100 g (4 oz) unsweetened
    chestnut purée*
freshly ground black pepper
4 tablespoons dry sherry
*50 g (2 oz) bacon rashers, cut
    into strips*
*100 g (4 oz) cooked ham, sliced
    and cut into strips*
*100 g (4 oz) cooked tongue,
    sliced and cut into strips*
*25 g (1 oz) pistachio nuts,
    blanched*
300 ml (1/2 pint) dry white wine
1 teaspoon powdered gelatine
*600 ml (1 pint) Aspic jelly (page
    50)*
*450 ml (3/4 pint) Béchamel
    Sauce (page 34)*
3 tablespoons double cream
To garnish:
1/2 cucumber
1/2 red canned pimiento
*1 carrot, peeled and sliced
    thinly*
*a few stoned black olives, each
    cut into 8 pieces (optional)*

Preparation time: 1½ hours, excluding boning the chicken and making the aspic, plus overnight cooling
Cooking time: about 2½ hours

1. Place the chicken on a wooden board, skin side down. Carefully flatten the meat to distribute it evenly.

2. Break the carcass into small pieces, put into a very large saucepan with the bones, and cover with water. Add the bouquet garni and salt. Bring to the boil, cover and simmer while making the galantine.

10. Remove the muslin and all the string. Place the chicken on a wire rack over a tray.

11. Dissolve the gelatine in about 150 ml (¼ pint) of melted Aspic. Stir this into the cold Béchamel Sauce with the cream. Strain if necessary.

15. Using tweezers, or a wooden skewer, dip the cucumber stems into the remaining Aspic, which should be syrupy (see page 50 for hints on using Aspic). Arrange the cucumber stems up the centre of the galantine, bending them to make soft lines.

3. Mix together the minced pork and sausage meat, stir in the shallots, herbs and chestnut purée and season with salt and pepper.

4. Sprinkle the sherry over the surface of the chicken.

12. When beginning to thicken, coat the chicken with the cream sauce, ensuring that it covers all the bird. Leave to set.

16. Repeat the same process with the cucumber leaves, and the pimiento and carrot petals or flowers, and olives, if used. Leave to set (see Aspic, page 50)

5. Spread half the pork mixture over the chicken to within 5 cm (2 inches) of the edge. Arrange the strips of bacon, ham, tongue and the pistachios lengthways from head to tail. Carefully spread over the remaining pork mixture.

13. Meanwhile, slice half the cucumber skin into long thin strips, to represent flower stems.

14. Cut the remaining cucumber skin into leaves, using aspic cutters. Cut the pimiento and carrot slices into flower petals and other pretty shapes.

17. Carefully spoon syrupy Aspic over the entire galantine and leave to set. Spoon the remaining Aspic on a flat, lightly wetted tray and refrigerate until set.

18. Turn the set Aspic on to a piece of wet greaseproof paper and, using a wet knife, chop it into small pieces (see Aspic, page 53). Carefully lift the chicken on to a serving plate, surround with the chopped Aspic, and serve.

6. Fold the sides of the chicken over the stuffing and draw them together, using a trussing needle and string, ensuring that the stuffing is totally enclosed.

7. Wrap the chicken very tightly in a muslin cloth, securing the ends with string. (The chicken will shrink when cooked.)

8. Strain the stock, and discard the bones. Stand the chicken on a rack in a large pan. Add the strained stock and the wine. Cover and simmer for 2–2½ hours, turning the chicken over occasionally, until it is very tender.

9. Put the chicken on to a large plate, cover with a wooden board and put a heavy weight on top so that the weight is evenly distributed. Leave until cool, then refrigerate overnight.

BAIN-MARIE

A bain-marie is essential for foods that require gentle cooking, when ingredients might burn or curdle over direct heat. It is also useful when dishes such as sauces need to be kept warm without spoiling or further cooking.

The origins of the curious name, bain-marie, are confused. The most likely, however, is that 'marie' is a corruption of the French word for sea – '*mer*'. For using a bain-marie involves food surrounded by a 'sea' of water, a 'sea-bath', and this is a means of cooking, and keeping food hot, without spoiling or cooking further. The actual bain-marie itself is a large flat and deep vessel, in which water is kept at a controlled temperature, either on top of the stove or in the oven; into this small containers of food are placed.

A bain-marie is essential for foods that require the gentlest of cooking, when ingredients might burn or curdle if brought into direct contact with heat. It is also extremely useful when foods need to be kept warm; as the water produces steam, foods will dry out far less easily than they would in the oven, say.

General method

The temperature of the water in the bain-marie can vary according to the type of food to be cooked, both in the oven and on top of the stove. For instance, for small custards – which curdle easily – the water should barely bubble; mousselines and quenelles – both light mixtures which can include and are 'set' by eggs – require a medium heat; whereas pâtés and terrines, which are sturdier and denser, will stand a fiercer heat, with the surrounding water bubbling fairly rapidly. Where

foods are to be cooked in the oven, the water in the bain-marie is usually brought to the correct temperature on top of the stove first before placing in the oven to continue cooking. But sometimes hot water is used at the beginning of the cooking time, sometimes tepid or cold; it all depends on the recipe and to what particular use the bain-marie is to be put.

Most restaurants have commercial bain-maries which are large metal containers with the water at a controlled temperature, with metal grids at the bottom to hold the inner saucepan off the direct heat on

Crème Caramel

Serves 4–6
600 ml (1 pint) milk
1 vanilla pod, split lengthways
65 g (2½ oz) caster sugar
2 eggs
2 egg yolks
Caramel topping:
85 ml (3 fl oz) water
100 g (4 oz) caster sugar

Preparation time: about 25 minutes
Cooking time: 40–50 minutes
Oven: 180°C, 350°F, Gas Mark 4

1. First make the caramel topping. Heat the water and sugar together, without stirring, until dissolved. Boil steadily until a golden brown, again without stirring. Immediately pour into a heated ovenproof dish, 1.25 litres (2 pints) in size, or 6 individual dishes, and turn rapidly to coat the base and sides. Set aside.

2. Put the milk and vanilla pod into a saucepan, slowly bring to the boil, then remove from the heat. Cover and leave to infuse for 10–15 minutes. Remove the vanilla pod.

3. Stir the sugar into the milk until it has dissolved.

4. Lightly beat the eggs and egg yolks together, then stir into the milk. Cool the mixture slightly then strain into the prepared dish.

the base of the container.

At home, however, all that is needed for a basic bain-marie is a large roasting pan with deep sides. This can be used both on top of a stove or in the oven, and will be able to hold several small pans or containers such as ramekins comfortably. A similar principle is employed by the double saucepan in which an inner pan sits above hot water, separated from direct heat: this is particularly useful for safely making sauces, melting chocolate or for dissolving gelatine, all of which can suffer if subjected to too high a heat. Using a bain-marie, however, means that more than one process, if necessary, can be carried out simultaneously.

The bain-marie is also useful when making the bases of Genoese and other sponges, mousses and cold soufflés, and for meringue cuite. But it comes most particularly into its own for keeping delicate

sauces warm. For this the temperature of the water should be warm, not hot as the sauce can spoil.

Béarnaise Sauce will keep warm for about 40 minutes; butter sauces will only last about 5 minutes, however, before separating.

In some cases the food to be cooked in a bain-marie should be covered, so always follow the recipe.

Perfect bain-marie cooking

■ At all times, food to be baked in the oven should be surrounded generously by water, otherwise it will cook at the *oven* temperature, rather than at the temperature of the *water*.

■ Always keep an eye on the water level. If it is too low, or it evaporates, top up with *hot* water (cold will alter the cooking time). However, if the water level is too high, it could bubble over into the food containers.

■ Always keep the water at the recommended temperature: if too low for pâtés and terrines, for instance, they will take very much longer to cook.

■ For food that is cooked in a bain-marie, the cooking time starts when the surrounding water first comes to simmering on top of the stove. It will then be put in the oven at the appropriate temperature or it will

continue on top of the stove.

■ A piece of brown paper, kitchen paper, a tea-towel or thick piece of greaseproof paper placed under the food containers will further insulate the base of the containers, and protect from direct heat.

■ Do not keep food hot for too long in a bain-marie as it can eventually spoil the food.

■ Small pans are best for bain-marie cooking, not only because there's room for more of them, but because the foods will be deeper with less surface upon which a skin can form.

■ A bain-marie may be vital for many classic and complicated dishes, but it's also very useful when a large household or a large quantity of food strains the resources of one cooker; more than one pan of food can be kept over just one burner.

5. Place the dish in a bain-marie and bring to the boil on the stove.

6. Cover the dish with foil and cook in a preheated oven for 40–50 minutes, until the custard is set, and a sharp knife inserted in the middle comes out clean.

7. Remove from the bain-marie and leave to cool. Refrigerate for 1 hour or preferably overnight, before serving.

8. To serve, carefully run a knife around the edge of the dish, and turn it out on to a serving dish, allowing the caramel to run down the sides of the pudding.

Fish Mould with Butter Sauce

Serves 6
*450 g (1 lb) haddock fillets, skin
and bones removed
90 g (3½ oz) butter, softened
2 eggs, separated
salt
freshly ground white pepper
a pinch of grated nutmeg
150 ml (¼ pint) double cream
8 lemon sole fillets, skinned,
weighing about 750 g
(1½ lb)*
Sauce:
*2 tablespoons white wine
vinegar
4 tablespoons dry white wine
2 small shallots, peeled and
finely chopped
225 g (8 oz) very cold butter,
diced
a squeeze of lemon juice*
To garnish:
*12 unshelled whole prawns
1–2 lemons or limes, sliced
a few sprigs of parsley*

Preparation time: about 40
minutes
Cooking time: 35–45 minutes
Oven: 180°C, 350°F, Gas Mark 4

1. Check that the haddock does
not have any bones. Chop the
flesh very finely then purée in a
blender or food processor.

2. Add the butter, the egg yolks,
salt, pepper and nutmeg and
blend until smooth.

3. Using a wooden spoon, beat
in one egg white (the other will
not be used), then fold in the
cream and adjust the
seasoning.

4. Butter the inside of a 900 ml
(1½ pint) ring mould.

5. Place the sole fillets between
greaseproof paper and pound
with the flat side of a large
knife or the bottom of a heavy
pan.

6. Halve each fillet crosswise,
cutting diagonally. Line the
mould with the fillets broad
end to the outside of the mould
and the tail in the centre (there
will obviously be gaps between
the fillets).

7. Spoon the puréed fish
mixture into the mould, and
fold in the fillets over the top.

8. Cover the mould with
buttered foil, and place it in a
bain-marie. Bring the water to
the boil on top of the stove.

9. Transfer the bain-marie to a
preheated oven and cook for
35–45 minutes or until the
mixture is firm to the touch.
Drain off any excess liquid
from the mould if necessary,
and keep warm in the bain-
marie.

10. Make the sauce. In a small
saucepan (not aluminium) boil
the vinegar, wine and shallots
until reduced to 1 tablespoon.

11. Set the pan over a low heat,
and gradually whisk in the
diced butter. Remove from the
heat occasionally so that the
butter does not entirely melt,
but merely softens to give a
creamy smooth sauce. Stir in
the lemon juice.

12. Season to taste, and set
aside, off the heat, for as short a
time as possible.

13. To turn out, place a warm
plate on top of the mould, turn
the plate over and remove the
mould.

14. Quickly spoon the sauce
over the fish mould and serve
immediately, garnished with
prawns, lemon or lime slices
and parsley.

Petits Pots de Crème

Serves 6
*175 g (6 oz) good quality plain
chocolate
450 ml (¾ pint) milk
25 g (1 oz) caster sugar
1 tablespoon dark rum or
brandy
4 egg yolks*
To decorate:
*150 ml (¼ pint) double cream,
lightly whipped
grated chocolate*

Preparation time: 30 minutes,
plus standing and chilling
Cooking time: 35–40 minutes
Oven: 160°C, 325°F, Gas Mark 3

1. Break the chocolate into
small pieces, and place in a
small bowl over a pan of hot
water until melted. Remove
from the heat.

2. Put the milk into a saucepan,
slowly bring to the boil, then
remove from the heat
immediately. Set aside.

3. Stir the sugar and rum or
brandy into the chocolate, then
beat in the egg yolks, one at a
time.

4. Gradually stir in the warm
milk, until thoroughly blended.

5. Strain into 6 individual
ramekin dishes and cover the
tops with foil.

6. Place the dishes in a bain-
marie filled with 2.5 cm (1
inch) warm water.

7. Place in the centre of a
preheated oven and cook for
30–35 minutes until firm.

8. Remove from the bain-marie
and leave until cool.
Refrigerate for 1 hour or
overnight.

9. Decorate with swirls of
whipped cream and sprinkle
with grated chocolate. Serve
chilled.

Chicken Liver Moulds with Tomato Sauce

Serves 6
300 ml (½ pint) double cream
275 g (10 oz) chicken livers,
*   trimmed and dried*
3 eggs
2 egg yolks
1 small garlic clove, crushed
2 teaspoons fresh mixed herbs
salt
freshly ground black pepper
a little grated nutmeg
Tomato sauce:
15 g (½ oz) butter
2 shallots, peeled and finely
*   chopped*
1 garlic clove, crushed
1 kg (2 lb) ripe tomatoes,
*   roughly chopped*
150 ml (¼ pint) dry white wine

Preparation time: 30 minutes
Cooking time: about 50
minutes in total
Oven: 180°C, 350°F, Gas Mark 4

1. Lightly butter 6 × 150 ml (¼ pint) ramekins.

2. Pour about 4 cm (1½ inches) water into a bain-marie, slowly bring to the boil, then turn off the heat.

3. Put the cream into a saucepan, slowly bring to the boil, remove from the heat and set aside.

4. Put the chicken livers, eggs and yolks into a food processor or blender, and blend until the mixture is very smooth.

5. Transfer the mixture to a bowl, then gradually add the cream, whisking all the time. Stir in the garlic, herbs, salt, pepper and nutmeg.

6. Carefully spoon into the prepared ramekin dishes to about three-quarters full and place the dishes in the bain-marie. Cover the dishes with foil and fill the bain-marie with 2·5 cm (1 inch) warm water.

7. Bring to almost simmering point on top of the stove, then transfer to a preheated oven, and cook for 30–40 minutes or until a skewer inserted into the centre comes out clean.

8. Remove from the oven, keeping the ramekins in the bain-marie.

9. Meanwhile, make the tomato sauce. Melt the butter in a saucepan, add the shallots and garlic and cook for 2 minutes, stirring without browning.

10. Add the tomatoes and wine, bring to the boil, and simmer for 25 minutes, until the tomatoes are soft and the liquid reduced.

11. Adjust the seasoning to taste, blend the sauce to a purée, then pass through a nylon sieve to remove the skins and pips. Return the sauce to the cleaned pan to heat through.

12. Turn out each mould on to a serving plate and pour a little sauce over each. Alternatively, spoon a little sauce on to a plate and place the mould on top of the sauce. Hand the remaining sauce separately.

Bread and Butter Pudding

Serves 4
150 ml (¼ pint) milk
150 ml (¼ pint) single cream
1 vanilla pod
40 g (1½ oz) butter
3 large slices plain bread,
*   crusts removed*
3 tablespoons raisins or
*   chopped dried apricots*
1 tablespoon sugar
2 eggs plus 1 egg yolk
ground cinnamon

Preparation time: 45 minutes
Cooking time: 1 hour
Oven: 180°C, 350°F, Gas Mark 4

1. Bring the milk, cream and vanilla pod to a simmer over low heat. Leave to cool, then remove the vanilla pod.

2. Butter the bread, cut into fingers and layer in a shallow ovenproof dish, butter side up.

Sprinkle dried fruit between the layers of bread.

3. Pour the cooled milk on to the sugar, eggs and egg yolk and strain over the bread.

4. Leave to soak for 30 minutes. Sprinkle with cinnamon.

5. Place the dish in a bain-marie of hot water and bake in

a preheated oven for about 45 minutes or until the custard is set and the top is golden and crusty.

PÂTÉS & TERRINES

Pâtés and terrines can be made with a wide variety of ingredients. They can also range in sophistication from the homely Terrine de campagne to elaborately layered dishes such as Vegetable terrine, fit to grace the most sumptuous buffet.

Pâtés and terrines are both mixtures of chopped, minced or sieved meats, game or fish. Traditionally, pâtés were moulded by hand and baked in pastry, and terrines were moulded and cooked in a terrine dish, but the differences have eroded over the years.

Originally, pâtés and terrines were ways of preserving parts of the pig, and pork meat is still a favourite ingredient of the most basic pâtés: pork fat too is a major constituent. But nowadays pâtés and terrines are made from many other meats as well – liver, chicken, duck, venison, pheasant, rabbit – and from fish and vegetables. They can be coarse or smooth in texture, can be layered with chunks, slices or strips of meat, or dotted with nuts or vegetables. They are baked in the oven – terrines normally in a bain-marie – and meats are pressed before being served cold (although pâté en croûte can be served hot, as can some fish terrines).

Basic rules

Meat pâtés and terrines are simple to make, but they require very fresh ingredients, careful preparation – many meats require lengthy marination – and very careful seasoning. Cooking too needs meticulous attention, for meat pâtés and terrines can become very dry. For this reason, the mixture or forcemeat is wrapped either in pastry (a pâté) or in strips of barding pork fat or bacon (a terrine). This ensures that the mixture remains moist. Baking in the bain-marie also helps retain the moisture of a terrine.
Fish pâtés and terrines are generally lighter mixtures, sometimes based on a mousseline of minced raw fish, cream and whisked egg whites. They can be served hot or cold.
Vegetable terrines are characteristic of nouvelle cuisine and are very much more tricky to make successfully than traditional forcemeat terrines. Precisely cut vegetables are lightly cooked and layered with a more delicate forcemeat – of veal, say – into a terrine which will cut into attractive and variegated slices. Sometimes they can have a 'forcemeat' of a vegetable purée, or be wrapped in leaves such as vine or spinach.
Rillettes are part of the same family as pâtés and terrines and could be described as a kind of potted meat or fish. A fat meat is cooked for at least 4 hours in a cool oven until it is very tender and the fat has completely rendered down. The characteristic texture is brought about by pulling the meat into fine shreds with two forks. Never try to save time by putting the meat into a blender, or it will simply go mushy. For fish rillettes, a fairly recent innovation, the fish is flaked finely and mixed with butter.

Rillettes are generally served as a starter, but pâtés and terrines are more versatile, in that they can be served as a snack, starter, lunch or supper dish, or as part of a buffet meal.

For perfect Terrines

■ When layering a terrine mixture, place meat, fish or vegetable strips lengthwise, so that they are cut through when sliced.
■ The lid of a terrine can be sealed with a luting paste, a flour and water paste. Put 200 g (7 oz) plain flour into a bowl and gradually add 150 ml (¼ pint) cold water to make a paste. Turn on to a floured board and roll into a rope the length of the perimeter of the mould. Put this rope around the mould and press on the lid. This hardens in the heat of the oven and prevents steam escaping and seals in all the flavour and juices. To remove the lid, carefully run the point of a sharp knife around under the rim.
■ If the terrine has no lid, use foil, folded down securely round the edges.
■ Cook a terrine in a water bath (bain-marie). First boil the surrounding water and then place the bain-marie and terrine in a moderate oven to cook. Always ensure that the water level is kept topped up with boiling water.
■ Thorough cooking is essential, and care must be taken not to undercook or overcook. If the terrine is firm to the touch and the liquid (fat) surrounding the forcemeat is bubbling and clear (not pink), the terrine is cooked. Another way to test is to insert a thin skewer into the centre of the pâté or terrine and leave for half a minute; if the skewer is hot when removed, rather than cold or burning, and the juices are clear, not pink, the mixture is cooked.
■ Once cooked, allow meat terrines to cool, and then place a weight on top to flatten them evenly, and leave overnight. This ensures that there are no air spaces in the meat, and that the shapes will be easier to slice and serve.
■ Do not cut a terrine until it is thoroughly cold, or it will crumble.

Terrine de Campagne

Serves 8
225 g (8 oz) streaky bacon
   rashers
15 g (½ oz) butter
2 shallots, peeled and finely
   chopped
225 g (8 oz) lean pork, freshly
   minced
225 g (8 oz) pork fat, minced
225 g (8 oz) chicken livers,
   cleaned and finely chopped
2 garlic cloves, peeled and
   crushed
a pinch of ground cloves
a pinch of ground nutmeg
¼ teaspoon ground allspice
2 small eggs, lightly beaten
150 ml (¼ pint) double cream
1 tablespoon freshly chopped
   thyme
2–3 tablespoons brandy
salt
freshly ground black pepper
1 thick slice cooked ham, about
   225 g (8 oz) cut lengthways
   into thin strips
1 bay leaf

Preparation time: 35 minutes,
plus refrigeration
Cooking time: 1¼ hours
Oven: 180°C, 350°F, Gas Mark 4

1. Line a 2 litre (3½ pint) terrine or casserole dish (one with a tight fitting lid) with the bacon rashers, reserving enough for the top.

2. Melt the butter in a small saucepan, add the shallots and cook for 5 minutes, without browning, stirring occasionally. Leave to cool completely. Turn into a large bowl.

3. Add the pork, pork fat, chicken liver, garlic and spices and mix well.

4. Stir in the eggs, cream, thyme and brandy and season well with salt and pepper. Beat until the mixture is evenly blended.

5. To test the flavour, sauté a small amount of the mixture in a frying pan, and allow it to cool. Taste when it is cold and then adjust the seasoning if necessary.

6. Spoon a third of the meat mixture into the terrine. Place half the strips of ham lengthwise on top and cover with a further third of the meat. Place the remaining strips of ham on top and cover with the remaining minced meat. Flatten each layer as you progress.

7. Cover with the reserved bacon strips. Put the bay leaf on top of the bacon.

8. Make a luting paste (see hints, page 78) and put this around the rim of the terrine. Place the lid on top to seal.

9. Put the terrine in a bain-marie on top of the stove, and slowly bring to the boil. Transfer to a preheated oven and cook for 1¼–1½ hours or until a skewer inserted in the centre comes out hot (see hints, page 78). Run a sharp knife round the edge to unseal the lid.

10. Leave to cool, then remove the lid.

11. Place a board or plate on top of the terrine and place a heavy weight on top. Refrigerate until cold.

12. For best results make 2–3 days before it is required, to develop the flavour. Store in the refrigerator.

13. Unmould the terrine on to a serving plate and cut into thick slices. Serve with French bread and a green salad.

VEGETABLE TERRINES

Terrines based on vegetables are fresh, light and colourful, offering many opportunities for imaginative combinations, flavours, textures, shapes and colours. You can make a terrine from only two or three vegetables, while a mixture of six or seven vegetables, prepared in several different ways, will produce an attractive complexity of tastes and textures, each slice of the terrine revealing a mosaic of shapes and colours. Vegetables of varying colours can also be interleaved with a fish or chicken mousseline, or with slices of gently poached fish. (See Mousselines, page 88, for the general method, together with a recipe for a Vegetable Terrine with Veal Mousseline.)

Vegetable Terrine

Lay the vegetable strips lengthways in the terrine dish for the most attractive effect when the terrine is sliced. See the section on Aspic (see page 50) for hints on how to keep the aspic at the correct syrupy consistency while layering the terrine.

16 small broccoli florets
225 g (8 oz) carrots, scraped and sliced lengthways
225 g (8 oz) courgettes, sliced lengthways
100 g (4 oz) French beans, trimmed
1/2 cucumber, thinly sliced
600 ml (1 pint) Aspic (see page 50), made with Veal Stock (see page 27)
50 g (2 oz) radishes, thinly sliced
225 g (8 oz) sliced ham

Preparation time: 30 minutes, excluding making aspic and chilling times

1. Blanch the broccoli, carrots, courgettes and French beans in boiling, salted water until just tender. Drain and refresh in iced water. Drain again.

2. Cut the cucumber slices into fans.

3. Pour a thin layer of Aspic into the bottom of the terrine and chill until set.

4. Using tweezers, dip the radish slices and cucumber fans one by one into the remaining Aspic and use to make a decorative pattern in the bottom of the terrine. Chill until set.

5. Pour a thin layer of Aspic over the set decoration in the bottom of the terrine and chill again until set.

6. Place a layer of carrot slices in the terrine, laid lengthways, and follow with a layer of green beans, laid lengthways, a layer of ham and a layer of courgettes, also laid lengthways. Pour over a little Aspic and chill until set.

7. Continue to layer the courgettes, carrots, beans and ham in the terrine, finishing with a layer of ham. Pour a layer of Aspic over each layer and chill until set.

8. Arrange the broccoli florets on top, then slowly pour over the remaining Aspic, trying to avoid making bubbles. Place the terrine in the refrigerator and chill until set.

9. To unmould, dip the bottom of the terrine in hot water for about 30 seconds, lay a serving dish on top and quickly reverse the dishes. Give the terrine a quick shake and unmould.

Top: Vegetable terrine
Bottom: Terrine de campagne

PÂTÉS

Pâtés are savoury mixtures of pork, liver, chicken and fish. The best known, and richest in flavour of all, is pâté de foie gras, made with the liver of a specially fattened duck or goose. Cooked pâtés are generally baked in a bain-marie, or enclosed in a pastry case and baked. Uncooked pâtés – such as the Fish Pâté below – are quick and easy to make.

Fish Pâté

Serves 6
350 g (12 oz) smoked haddock
  fillet
600 ml (1 pint) Fish Stock (see
  page 26)
50 g (2 oz) butter, melted
150 ml (¼ pint) double cream
1 teaspoon finely grated lemon
  rind
2 teaspoons lemon juice
a dash of Worcestershire sauce
a pinch of cayenne pepper
freshly ground black pepper
4 tablespoons Clarified Butter
  (page 42)
To garnish:
1 thinly sliced lemon
sprigs of parsley

Preparation time: 30 minutes
Cooking time: 10–12 minutes

Fresh salmon or kippers may be used instead of smoked haddock.

1. Place the smoked haddock in a frying pan, pour over the prepared fish stock, and very slowly bring to the boil. Reduce the heat and simmer for 10–12 minutes, turning the fish over once with a fish slice.

2. Remove the fish from the cooking liquid. Remove the skin and all the bones, and flake the fish in a bowl.

3. Pour over the melted butter and mix well. Put the mixture into a blender or food processor and blend until very smooth. Allow to cool.

4. Lightly whip the cream, and fold into the fish purée with the lemon rind, lemon juice, Worcestershire sauce, cayenne and black pepper. Adjust the seasoning to taste.

5. Spoon the pâté into a serving dish, and smooth the top. Chill for 1 hour.

6. Pour over the clarified butter and refrigerate for 30 minutes or until required.

Variation

Smoked Mackerel Pâté Use the same quantity of smoked mackerel fillets and liquidise with 85 ml (3 fl oz) double cream. Soften 2 chopped shallots in 25 g (1 oz) clarified butter, then add 75 g (3 oz) tomato purée, 1 teaspoon brown sugar, 1 tablespoon fresh chopped basil, and cook gently for 4–5 minutes. Add a few drops of Tabasco, remove from the heat and allow to cool.

Add to the liquidised mixture and blend until smooth. Turn into a serving dish and leave to cool. Cover with 25 g (1 oz) clarified butter and chill until ready to serve.

Spinach and Basil Pâté

Serves 8
350 g (12 oz) fresh spinach, washed
225 g (8 oz) parsnips or turnips, peeled and blanched for 5 minutes
275 g (10 oz) carrots, scraped and blanched for 5 minutes
100 g (4 oz) curd or full fat soft cheese
3 eggs, lightly beaten
25 g (1 oz) wholemeal breadcrumbs
2 teaspoons green peppercorns, crushed
1 tablespoon freshly chopped basil
salt
freshly ground white pepper
1/2 red pepper, cored, seeded, cut into long thin strips and blanched for 2 minutes
1 teaspoon curry powder
1 large courgette, sliced lengthways and blanched for 2 minutes
sprigs of fresh basil, to garnish

Preparation time: 1 hour
Cooking time: 1¼ hours
Oven: 180°C, 350°F, Gas Mark 4

1. Select the largest leaves of the spinach, to about 100 g (4 oz) in total. Bring a saucepan of water to the boil. Dip the large leaves in this just to soften, quickly remove and dry well on paper towels.

2. Chop the remaining spinach and cook until wilted in a covered saucepan, using only the water clinging to the leaves after washing. Shake the pan occasionally.

3. Grate the parsnips or turnips coarsely into a bowl.

4. Grate the carrots coarsely into another bowl.

5. Lightly beat the curd or full fat cheese to soften it. Gradually beat in the eggs, and then stir in the breadcrumbs and peppercorns.

6. Stir in the chopped basil and season well with salt and pepper.

7. Arrange the whole spinach leaves over the base and sides of a 1 kg (2 lb) loaf tin or terrine mould, reserving some for the top.

8. Pour a third of the cheese/egg mixture over the chopped spinach; a third over the grated parsnip or turnip; and a third over the grated carrot. Mix each well.

9. Spoon the spinach mixture into the base of the spinach-lined mould. Arrange the blanched red pepper strips lengthways over the top.

10. Mix the curry powder into the parsnip or turnip mixture, then carefully spoon on top of the red peppers.

11. Spoon all the carrot mixture on top of the parsnip layer. Top with the blanched courgettes, arranged lengthways.

12. Place the reserved spinach leaves over the mixture. Cover the mould with buttered greaseproof paper and seal with foil.

13. Put the mould into a bain-marie. Heat the water to boiling on top of the stove, then place the mould in a preheated oven. Cook for 1¼ hours or until the pâté is firm.

14. Cool then chill overnight. Turn out on to a serving plate and slice thickly.

15. Serve garnished with basil sprigs.

Chicken Liver Pâté

Serves 6
50 g (2 oz) butter
100 g (4 oz) back bacon, rind removed, chopped
1–2 garlic cloves, peeled and crushed
1 shallot, peeled and finely chopped
450 g (1 lb) chicken livers
salt
freshly ground black pepper
1 teaspoon finely chopped thyme
50 g (2 oz) button mushrooms, chopped
4 tablespoons dry sherry or Madeira
3–4 tablespoons double cream
1 teaspoon lemon juice
watercress sprigs, to garnish

Preparation time: 20 minutes
Cooking time: 2 hours
Oven: 150°C, 300°F, Gas Mark 2

1. Melt the butter in a saucepan, add the bacon, garlic and shallot and cook for 5 minutes without browning, stirring occasionally.

2. Stir in the chicken livers and cook for a further 5–7 minutes, stirring. Season to taste.

3. Stir in the thyme, mushrooms and sherry or Madeira, increase the heat and boil for 2–3 minutes until the liquid has completely reduced.

4. Leave to cool, half covered with a lid.

5. Work to a purée in a blender or food processor, then stir in the cream and lemon juice.

6. Spoon into an ovenproof dish, with a tight fitting lid, and place the dish in a bain-marie containing tepid water to a depth of 2.5 cm (1 inch). Keep this level topped up as necessary.

7. Place in a preheated oven and bake for 2 hours until thoroughly cooked.

8. Leave to cool and then refrigerate. Garnish with watercress before serving.

Duck Pâté en Croûte

*1 × 1.75 kg (4 lb) duck,
  skinned and boned (see page
  70)*
225 g (8 oz) pork fillet
*225 g (8 oz) belly of pork, rind
  and bones removed*
*225 g (8 oz) chicken livers,
  cleaned and chopped*
1 garlic clove, crushed
2 eggs, beaten
2 tablespoons brandy
1 teaspoon dried mixed herbs
finely grated rind of ½ orange
*2 tablespoons green
  peppercorns*
salt
freshly ground black pepper
*225 g (8 oz) lean streaky
  bacon, rinds removed*
*450 g (1 lb) Puff Pastry (see
  page 272)*

Preparation time: 1 hour, plus
boning the duck and chilling
Cooking time: 2 hours
Oven: 200°C, 400°F, Gas Mark
6, then 180°C, 350°F, Gas
Mark 4

1. Cut the duck flesh into
small pieces and put into a
large bowl.

2. Mince together the pork
fillet and belly of pork, add
to the duck and mix well.

3. Stir in the chicken livers,
garlic, half the beaten egg
and brandy.

4. Stir in the mixed herbs,
orange rind and
peppercorns. Season
liberally with salt and
pepper.

5. Sauté a small amount of
the mixture in a frying pan
and allow to cool. Taste
when it is cold and adjust
the seasoning if necessary.

6. Using the back of a knife,
stretch the bacon rashers.

7. Roll out the pastry into a
large rectangle. Spoon the
meat into the centre of the
pastry and shape it into a
loaf.

8. Arrange the bacon over
the meat.

9. Brush the edges of the
pastry with beaten egg and
wrap around the filling, trim
the pastry if necessary.
Reserve the trimmings.

10. Place the parcel on a
dampened baking sheet,
seam side downwards.
Ensure that the pastry is well
sealed.

11. Decorate the top of the
pastry with pastry leaves or
other shapes, make a hole in
the centre for the steam.

12. Glaze the pastry with
beaten egg and place in a
preheated oven for 15
minutes until it is just
golden.

13. Reduce the oven
temperature and cook for a
further 1¾ hours.

14. Cover the pastry lightly
with foil after the first 15
minutes, after reducing the
temperature.

15. Cool on the baking sheet
and then slice thickly to
serve.

Hare Terrine

As the hare needs to marinate for 12 hours (in the refrigerator), begin the preparation 2 days before the terrine is required. The flavour mellows with keeping. The terrine will keep for up to 5 days in the refrigerator.

Serves 6–8
150 ml (¼ pint) brandy
8 juniper berries, crushed
4 small bay leaves
1 teaspoon salt
6 black peppercorns
1 hare, skinned and cleaned, with heart, liver and kidney
450 g (1 lb) lean veal
450 g (1 lb) belly of pork
350 g (12 oz) green streaky bacon, sliced and rinds removed
2 teaspoons dried mixed herbs
salt
freshly ground black pepper

Preparation time: 45 minutes, plus marinating and chilling
Cooking time: 1½ hours
Oven: 190°C, 375°F, Gas Mark 5

1. In a large bowl, mix together the brandy, crushed juniper berries, bay leaves, salt and peppercorns to make a marinade.

2. Using a sharp knife, carefully remove the meat from the saddle and legs of the hare. Cut the meat into thin slices, and put into the marinade. Stir well to coat, cover, and refrigerate for about 12 hours, turning the meat several times in the marinade to ensure that it is well impregnated.

3. Mince the veal with the hare liver, heart and kidneys. Remove the rind, bones and gristle from the belly of pork, and mince the pork meat.

4. Line a 1.2 litre (2 pint) terrine or casserole dish with a tight fitting lid with the slices of bacon, leaving 4 slices aside for the top.

5. Strain the marinade from the hare.

6. Spread half the minced veal mixture in the dish on top of the bacon, pressing it down. Sprinkle with half the herbs and season well.

7. Top with half the pork mixture and then the hare slices, arranging them lengthways. Spoon over the strained marinade.

8. Pack the remaining pork on top, followed by the veal mixture. Sprinkle with the remaining herbs and season again with salt and pepper.

9. Cover the meat in the terrine with the remaining bacon. Seal the rim with a luting paste (see hints page 78) and put on the lid.

10. Put the terrine into a bain-marie on top of the stove, bring to the boil and immediately transfer to a preheated oven. Cook for 1½ hours until a skewer inserted into the centre is hot and the juices are clear.

11. Remove the lid and paste, and return the dish to the oven for 15 minutes until the top is golden brown. Cool slightly then place a board or plate and weights on top to press the terrine.

12. Refrigerate when cool, and leave for 24 hours before turning out and serving, chilled.

Pork Rillettes

Serves 8
1 kg (2 lb) belly of pork in one piece, rind and bones removed
coarse salt
175 g (6 oz) pork fat
2 garlic cloves, peeled and crushed
1 bouquet garni
2 tablespoons dry white wine

Preparation time: 30 minutes, plus standing and chilling
Cooking time: 4 hours
Oven: 140°C, 275°F, Gas Mark 1

1. Rub the pork on both sides with salt and refrigerate for 6 hours or overnight.

2. Drain the pork, and cut it into small cubes. Cut the pork fat into small cubes and mix with the pork. Stir in the garlic and whole bouquet garni. Spoon over the wine and mix well.

3. Pile the mixture into an ovenproof dish, cover with a tight fitting lid and place in a preheated oven for 4 hours. Do not open the oven or lift the lid during this time.

4. Remove from the oven, and turn the mixture and liquid fat into a sieve set over a bowl. Drain all the fat from the meat and reserve both. Discard the bouquet garni.

5. Shred the meat, using 2 forks, until the meat becomes a coarse paste.

6. Pack the shredded meat into a large dish, and smooth the top.

7. Spoon the reserved fat over the surface of the meat to a thickness of about 1 cm (½ inch).

8. Cover with a lid and refrigerate until required.

9. Remove from the refrigerator 1 hour before serving.

For perfect Pâtés and Rillettes

■ The correct seasoning is most important for pâtés, especially those made with meat and which are to be served cold. If in doubt, after the forcemeat has been mixed, fry a little in a pan until thoroughly cooked. Cool it, taste, and adjust the seasoning.
■ Pack the mixture well into the dish, filling it completely for pâtés and terrines shrink as they cook.
■ To keep a pâté moist during cooking, wrap the forcemeat in pastry, or in barding or caul fat for terrines. Bacon can be used, but it should not be too salty or smoked, which would spoil the flavour. Poultry skin can be used for poultry pâtés or terrines.
■ Do not keep pâtés and terrines more than week after making (unless freezing) and they should be stored in the refrigetator.
■ Pâtés and rillettes can be stored in a freezer for up to 3 months. Wrap well in cling film or foil, and then in a freezer bag.

SAVOURY MOUSSES

Mousses, Mousselines and Quenelles are delicate mixtures of finely minced fish, meat, poultry or game, usually enriched with cream and lightened with egg white.

A mousse is a very light sweet or savoury cold dish, made with cream. Mousses can be made from almost anything – fish, poultry, meat, vegetables or fruit – which can be cooked or raw. The basic ingredient, as with mousselines, and quenelles, is puréed as finely as possible. Before the days of blenders and food processors the mixture was always finely minced and then pushed through a fine sieve with a scraper – a lengthy and exhausting process. Most recipes still give this method as an option, but blending finely in a blender or food processor will give a perfectly acceptable result. Egg yolk is sometimes used to enrich the mixture; whisked egg whites can be added to lighten it; and gelatine is often used to set it.

Unlike soufflés, a mousse does not sit above the rim of the dish, therefore a paper

Ham Mousse

Serves 6–8
1 litre (1³⁄₄ pints) jellied Chicken Stock or Aspic (see pages 26 and 50)
15 g (¹⁄₂ oz) gelatine (optional)
100 ml (3¹⁄₂ fl oz) dry sherry or Madeira
400 g (14 oz) lean, home-cooked ham (cold)
450 ml (³⁄₄ pint) Velouté Sauce (see page 36) made with Chicken or Veal Stock (see pages 26–27)
1 teaspoon lemon juice
freshly milled white pepper
350 ml (12 fl oz) double cream, lightly whipped
To garnish:
stuffed olives, sliced
¹⁄₂ cucumber, the skin cut into strips with a canelle knife

Preparation time: 1 hour, plus chilling time

1. Lightly oil a 1.75 litre (3 pint) dish or bowl.

2. If the stock or Aspic is not firmly jellied, soften the gelatine in 100 ml (3¹⁄₂ fl oz) of the stock in a bain-marie.

3. Warm the stock and stir in the dissolved gelatine (if using) and sherry or Madeira. Leave to cool.

4. Put the ham into a blender or food processor and work until very fine; or mince finely and push through a fine sieve into a bowl set over crushed ice.

5. Put the ham paste in a bowl. Gradually blend in the Velouté Sauce until smooth, beating with a wooden spoon, then add the lemon juice and pepper to taste.

7. Fold in the whipped cream, and turn the mixture into the prepared dish or mould. Refrigerate for 2 hours until set.

8. Spoon over a thin layer of jellied stock or aspic. Return to the refrigerator for a further 30 minutes until the top layer has set.

9. Dip the garnish into a little of the stock or aspic and arrange attractively on top of the mousse. Chill for 10 minutes, then spoon over the remaining stock or aspic.

collar is not required. Mousses can be set in moulds and turned out, or served in one large or several individual dishes.

Gelatine

Care should be taken when using gelatine, because if it is overheated it will form sticky 'ropes', which make it unusable, and will spoil the mixture into which it is to be incorporated. Always dissolve gelatine in a double saucepan or bain-marie (see page 74). As soon as the granules have dissolved, remove the bowl from the hot water and use the gelatine at once. Gelatine can also be successfully dissolved in a microwave oven.

Use a metal spoon to stir the dissolving gelatine, rather than a wooden one, as it is easier to see that it has completely dissolved.

In hot weather it may be necessary to increase the amount of gelatine to set the mixture.

For perfect Mousses

■ Ensure that the gelatine is properly dissolved before stirring into the mixture.
■ Always fold the cream thoroughly throughout the mixture, before folding in the egg whites.
■ If the mousse is to be turned out, the mould should be either wetted with cold water or lightly oiled.
■ When unmoulding a mousse, do not stand the mould in boiling water, as this will melt the mousse and spoil the shape. Quickly dip into hot water before inverting on to a serving plate – metal moulds conduct the heat quicker than china ones.
■ If the mousse is to be served in the dish it is made in, the top should be covered with aspic or jelly, to prevent it drying out.
■ Remember when using aspic that it should be melted to the consistency of unbeaten egg white (see pages 50–53).

Avocado Mousse with Prawns

6. Stir in half the melted stock or aspic, then place the bowl over iced water. Stir occasionally until the mixture starts to thicken.

10. Refrigerate for a further 1–2 hours until the mousse is completely set, and serve accompanied by toast or bread and a salad.

This should be made on the day it is to be served, as avocados discolour very quickly.

Serves 6
300 ml (¹/₂ pint) Chicken Stock (see page 26)
15 g (¹/₂ oz) powdered gelatine
2 large ripe avocado pears (or 3 small ones)
¹/₂ large onion, peeled
1 tablespoon freshly chopped thyme
1–2 teaspoons Worcestershire sauce
a dash of Tabasco
150 ml (¹/₄ pint) Mayonnaise (see page 48)
150 ml (¹/₄ pint) double cream, lightly whipped
salt
freshly ground black pepper
To garnish:
4 tablespoons olive oil
2 tablespoons lemon or lime juice
¹/₂ teaspoon French mustard
¹/₂ teaspoon clear honey
¹/₂–1 garlic clove, crushed
225 g (8 oz) peeled prawns
lemon or lime slices
a few sprigs of fresh thyme

Preparation time: about 35 minutes, plus chilling time

1. Put half the chicken stock into a bowl, over a pan of slowly simmering water. Sprinkle the gelatine over the stock, and stir until dissolved. Remove from the heat, stir in the remaining stock and set aside.

2. Halve the avocado pears, remove the stones, and scoop the flesh out into a bowl. Mash the flesh until smooth and creamy. Try to work quickly so that the avocado does not discolour.

3. Grate the onion finely on to a plate, and measure out 1 teaspoon of the juice. Stir this into the avocado with the thyme, Worcestershire sauce and Tabasco.

4. Slowly stir the gelatine and stock mixture into the avocado, stirring all the time.

5. Fold in the mayonnaise and lightly whipped cream, and season to taste with salt and pepper.

6. Spoon the mixture into a well oiled 900 ml (1½ pint) mould, or ring mould and chill until firm.

7. Make a dressing for the prawn garnish by mixing together the oil and lemon juice. Stir in the mustard, honey and garlic, and season to taste with salt and pepper.

8. Toss the prawns in the dressing and refrigerate until required.

9. Just before serving quickly dip the mould into boiling water, and unmould on to a serving plate (do not do this in advance as the avocado will discolour).

10. Spoon the prawns around the mousse, and garnish with lemon or lime slices and sprigs of fresh thyme.

MOUSSELINES

Mousseline is generally used to describe a mixture which has whipped cream added to enrich it: a Hollandaise sauce with added whipped cream is a Hollandaise Mousseline sauce, for instance. It also refers to the delicate light paste or purée of fish, poultry, veal, game or vegetables which forms the basis of a mousse, as well as the paste which is enriched with cream and lightened with egg whites, then cooked gently, as below.

The cooking of mousselines must be very gentle because of the delicacy of the mixture: it is either poached or steamed or it may also be cooked in a bain-marie.

Mousselines can be shaped and cooked in a large mould, in several smaller moulds, or can be shaped in a large spoon in the same way as quenelles (see page 91) before poaching.

A mousseline mixture may also be used in terrines or to stuff a whole fish or fillet of fish, and some vegetables.

In most cases the shaped mousseline is masked with sauce before serving. A Velouté Sauce (see page 36) is often used as the basis, with mushrooms or herbs, or a Hollandaise Sauce enriched with cream (see page 90).

Vegetable Terrine with Veal Mousseline

Serves 6
450 g (1 lb) fresh spinach,
40 g (1½ oz) butter
salt
freshly milled white pepper
grated nutmeg
350 g (12 oz) young carrots,
*   peeled*
350 g (12 oz) green beans,
*   trimmed and chopped*
225 g (8 oz) turnips, peeled
*   and chopped*
Mousseline:
450 g (1 lb) lean veal, chopped
1 egg, separated
20 g (¾ oz) butter, softened
150 ml (¼ pint) double cream

Preparation time: 1¼ hours
Cooking time: 35–40 minutes
Oven: 180°C, 350°F, Gas Mark 4

1. Wash the spinach thoroughly and remove thick stems. Blanch the spinach in boiling salted water for 1 minute, then drain, refresh under cold water and drain again thoroughly.

2. Pat the leaves dry on paper towels. Select the largest ones, and use to line a lightly buttered 1.5 litre (2½ pint) ovenproof terrine dish, overlapping the leaves slightly. Finely chop the remaining leaves.

3. Melt 15 g (½ oz) of the butter in a pan, add the chopped spinach and cook for 2 minutes, stirring constantly. Season well with salt, pepper and nutmeg.

4. Shape each carrot into a rectangle, and slice very thinly, lengthways. Cook the strips in boiling salted water for 10 minutes. Drain thoroughly.

5. Cook the beans in a pan of boiling salted water for 10 minutes. Drain thoroughly then purée in a blender or food processor. Melt 15 g (½ oz) butter and stir the bean purée into this. Season well with salt, pepper and nutmeg, and cook for 2 minutes, stirring, until the mixture is dry.

6. Cook the turnips in boiling salted water for 10 minutes, then purée as for the beans. Melt the remaining butter and cook the purée until dry.

7. Put the veal into a blender or food processor and blend until smooth.

8. Place the mixture in a bowl set over crushed ice and beat in the egg yolk and softened butter. Beat in the egg white and beat until the mixture is really cold.

9. Gradually beat in the cream, whisking well until the cream is incorporated.

10. Season well with salt, pepper and nutmeg, then spread a layer of veal mousseline over the spinach leaves.

For perfect Mousselines

■ Well butter the mould before use.

■ Always season the mixture after the egg whites and cream have been folded into the mixture.

■ The consistency should be that of whipped cream.

■ The water in the bain-marie (see page 74) should be a slow simmer.

■ Allow the mousseline to stand for 5 minutes before turning out on to a plate.

■ Do not overcook a mousseline as this will spoil its texture.

■ Always mince or blend the main ingredient – the fish, veal, poultry or game – twice, so that the mixture is fine.

■ If the mixture is not fine enough, force it through a sieve, into a bowl.

■ Mix the ingredients for a mousseline in a bowl set over ice or iced water as the cold helps the mixture to thicken.

■ To test if the mousseline is cooked, insert a skewer into the centre. If it comes out clean, the mousseline is cooked.

11. Spoon a layer of green bean purée over this. Arrange half the carrots lengthways on top, followed by half the turnip purée and lastly half the spinach purée.

12. Repeat these layers until all the mixtures are used.

13. Cover with buttered foil, place the terrine in a bain-marie on top of the stove, and bring to the boil. Place the terrine, in its bain-marie, in a preheated oven for 30–35 minutes, until the mousseline is set.

14. Drain off any excess fat from the terrine dish and turn the terrine out on to a warmed serving plate. Put the plate on top of the terrine and invert plate and dish. Leave to stand for 5 minutes before slicing.

Mousseline of Rabbit with a Julienne of Vegetables

Serves 4
2 carrots, peeled
4 celery sticks
1 leek
2 courgettes
750 g (1½ lb) boned rabbit
3 egg whites, lightly beaten
300 ml (½ pint) double cream
salt
freshly ground white pepper
*1 recipe quantity Velouté Sauce
    (see page 36), made with
    Veal or Chicken Stock (see
    pages 26–27)*
*50 g (2 oz) white button
    mushrooms finely chopped*

Preparation time: 45 minutes
Cooking time: 40 minutes

1. First prepare the vegetable julienne. Cut the carrots, celery, leek and courgettes into fine julienne strips (see page 171). Cover with a damp tea-towel.

2. Put the rabbit into a blender or food processor and blend until smooth, or pass through a mincer twice. Add the egg whites and blend again. If necessary, rub the mixture through a fine sieve.

3. Place the mixture in a bowl over crushed ice. Gradually beat in the cream, and season to taste.

4. Turn the mixture into a well buttered 900 ml (1½ pint) ring mould. Using a palette knife, smooth over the surface, then cover with buttered foil.

5. Put into a bain-marie (see page 74) and cook on top of the stove at a slow simmer for 40 minutes, until a skewer inserted into the mixture comes out clean. Leave for 5 minutes.

6. Meanwhile blanch the julienne of vegetables in boiling salted water for 3 minutes. Drain well and keep warm.

7. Make the Velouté Sauce as described on page 36. Stir in the chopped mushrooms and cook for 2 minutes.

8. Turn the mousseline out on to a heated serving plate and spoon the vegetables into the centre.

9. Spoon the sauce over the mousseline, taking care not to coat the vegetables, and serve immediately.

Mousselines of Chicken with Roquefort Cheese

These mousselines can also be cooked in small ramekins. Place them in a roasting tin of simmering water on top of the stove, cover with foil and leave for 15 minutes.

Serves 4
25 g (1 oz) shelled walnuts
2 tablespoons milk
*20 g (¾ oz) ripe Roquefort
    cheese, crumbled*
1½ teaspoons brandy
*100 g (4 oz) chicken breasts
    boned and skinned*
300 ml (½ pint) double cream
3 egg whites, lightly beaten
salt
freshly ground white pepper
1 dessert apple
25 g (1 oz) butter
*1 litre (1¾ pints) Chicken Stock
    (see page 26)*
Mousseline sauce:
*1 quantity Hollandaise Sauce
    (see page 44)*
*5 tablespoons double cream,
    whipped*
To garnish:
sprigs of fresh chervil

Preparation time: 50 minutes
Cooking time: 15 minutes
Oven: 160°C, 325°F, Gas Mark 3

1. Put the walnuts into boiling water for 5 minutes, then drain thoroughly and remove their skins.

2. Soak 4 walnut halves in the milk and finely chop the rest. Mix the chopped nuts into the cheese and stir in the brandy.

3. Form the cheese mixture into 4 small egg shapes, put on to a saucer and refrigerate until required.

4. Put the chicken flesh into a blender or food processor and blend until very smooth. Alternatively rub the purée through a fine sieve, set over a bowl surrounded by crushed ice. Place the mixture in a bowl set over crushed ice. Gradually work in the cream, fold in the egg whites and season with salt and pepper.

5. Peel and core the apple, and cut the flesh into matchsticks, cutting them as evenly as possible. Melt the butter in a small saucepan, and sweat the apple for 2 minutes, without colouring.

6. Using a large tablespoon and a palette knife, shape the chicken mousse into 6 even sized mousselines, the size of a very large egg. Make a small cavity in the base of each one and place a cheese and walnut shape in each cavity. Carefully smooth the chicken mixture over to completely enclose the cheese.

7. Bring the stock to the boil, then lower the heat to a slow simmer. Poach the mousselines for 5 minutes on each side, taking great care when turning them over, as they are very fragile. Drain on paper towels.

8. Make the Hollandaise Sauce. Whisk in the whipped cream very gradually, and keep warm in a bain-marie.

9. Spoon the cooked apple matchsticks into the base of a shallow ovenproof dish. Carefully arrange the mousselines on top, and cover the dish with buttered paper. Place in a preheated oven for 2 minutes.

10. Carefully lift the mousselines and apple from the cooking dish.

11. Arrange the apple on individual plates, and place a chicken mousseline on top. Spoon over the sauce, and serve immediately, garnished with sprigs of fresh chervil and the drained walnut halves.

QUENELLES

Quenelles are a particular speciality of Nantua, on the French-Swiss border, where they are made with pike and served with a local crayfish sauce. Quenelles are light dumplings made of finely minced and pounded fish, meat, poultry or game and they are cooked by poaching in simmering salted water. The mixture is very similar to that of a mousseline, and in fact a basic mousseline recipe may be adapted to make quenelles.

Traditionally, quenelles are oval in shape, and they may be cooked in special quenelle moulds, or shaped into ovals using two dessertspoons.

The ingredients for quenelles should be mixed over ice or iced water. The cold makes the mixture thicken slightly, as for mousselines.

Great care should be taken in cooking, as they break up very easily if the water boils. The liquid should barely simmer.

When the quenelles are cooked they rise to the surface of the water, detaching themselves from the moulds if these are used.

Fish Quenelles with Prawn Sauce

Serves 4–6
750 g (1½ lb) fresh haddock fillets
3 egg whites, lightly beaten
300 ml (½ pint) double cream
salt
freshly ground white pepper
1 recipe quantity Velouté Sauce (see page 36), made with Fish Stock (see page 27)
50 g (2 oz) peeled prawns, finely chopped
To garnish:
6 whole prawns, unpeeled
a few sprigs of chervil

Preparation time: 45 minutes
Cooking time: 7 minutes, or 14 minutes if cooked in batches

For perfect Quenelles

■ Butter the moulds very thoroughly if using.
■ Do not overfill moulds.
■ Use a large shallow pan to cook the quenelles. The water should be at least 6–7.5 cm (2½–3 inches) deep.
■ Do not put in too many at a time. Cook in batches.
■ Cook for about 7 minutes with the water barely simmering, shaking the pan from time to time.
■ Lift them out of the water carefully in a slotted spoon and drain thoroughly on paper towels or dry muslin.

1. Remove the skin and bones from the fish.

2. Mince the fish finely, or work in a blender or food processor until very fine. Mix in the egg whites.

3. Rub the purée through a fine sieve set over a bowl of crushed ice, then gradually work in the cream. Season with salt and pepper. The consistency should be similar to whipped cream.

4. Turn the mixture into well buttered quenelle moulds, or shape into ovals using 2 dessertspoons.

5. Slip the bowl of one spoon under each quenelle to loosen it, then place carefully on a dampened tray. Heat a large shallow pan of water to a simmer.

6. Carefully drop the filled moulds, or shapes, into the water, and cook for 7 minutes or until the quenelles rise to the surface, shaking the pan gently.

7. Using a perforated spoon, lift the cooked quenelles out of the water and drain on paper towels or muslin.

8. Make the Velouté sauce as described on page 36, adjust the seasoning to taste, and stir in the chopped prawns.

9. Arrange the quenelles on a serving plate, coat each one with a little sauce, and serve immediately, garnished with whole prawns and sprigs of chervil.

Bass

Bream

Carp

Cod

John Dory

Dover Sole

Flounder

Haddock

Halibut

Herring

Mackerel

Plaice

Red Mullet

Salmon

Skate

Sprat

Squid

Trout

Turbot

Whiting

FISH

Versatile and healthy, fish is in many ways the ideal food. Use the fisherman's guide to help you identify all the different types, from everyday whiting and cod to luxurious halibut and turbot, and try out our suggestions for cooking methods and serving ideas.

There are so many different sizes and shapes of fish available at the fishmonger, that it is difficult to choose which one to buy. Fish are generally categorised as white or oily, but they may also be divided into freshwater, salt-water (or sea), flat or round.

White fish – a category which includes fish such as cod, plaice, haddock and halibut – have firm white flesh, and a low fat content. Oily fish have a much richer flesh which is darker in colour and has a slightly coarser texture. Fish in this category include herring, mackerel, salmon and trout.

The main difference between white and oily fish is that in the latter the oil is distributed throughout the flesh; they are thus more nutritious, but not always so easily digestible. In white fish, the oil is found largely in the liver; this is usually discarded – and explains why we have cod liver oil, not herring liver oil.

See the charts on pages 94–95 for general listings of some of the more common white and oily fish, and smoked or pickled fish.

Fish is a valuable source of first class protein, although not as high as meat. Fish is also a useful source of calcium, phosphorus (in the edible bones of whitebait, sardines etc), and many of the B vitamins. Cod liver oil, for instance, is the major source of Vitamins A and D; and D, which occurs in very few foods, is contained in most oily fish. Many fish supply iodine and fluorine.

Nutritionally fish are also important because they contain little fat. Even oily fish seldom have more than a 20 per cent fat content (much less than an equivalent weight of meat). This means that it is more easily digestible and contains few calories. White fish, especially, is valuable for slimmers, and when cooked simply, is an ideal food for the very young, the old, and the convalescent.

The structure of fish flesh is composed of muscle fibres which vary in length and thickness depending on the fish. These fibres are shorter and finer than those of meat, and moreover, are packed together in flakes, with a small amount of connective tissue. This means that fish must never be overcooked or cooked too vigorously, as it will become dry and disintegrate. It also means that fish cooks very quickly – a bonus for the busy cook.

METHODS OF COOKING FISH

As fish has such a small amount of connective tissue, it requires very little cooking. If it is overcooked, the flakes fall apart and the fibres become tough, dry and tasteless.

There are several ways of cooking fish, but the cooking process should, in general, be short and gentle. Although fillets are more popular, most cooks agree that fish on the bone – as with meat – has more flavour.

Frying This is a popular method, and fish can be both shallow- or deep-fried. For both processes the flesh of the fish must be coated with egg and breadcrumbs, batter, flour or oatmeal – to protect the delicate flesh. Usually fillets of fish are cooked in this way. A vegetable oil should be used (if deep-frying, the oil should only be used for fish), but a combination of butter and oil is best and tastiest for shallow-frying. It is a quick method of cooking fish – fillets, for example, will only take 5–8 minutes to deep fry; whitebait takes only 2–3 minutes.

Grilling This method is used for whole fish, steaks, fillets and cutlets, particularly of oily fish. The flesh is usually scored with a knife (if the fish is on the bone) to ensure even and thorough cooking. The fish should be dotted with butter to prevent it drying out. The grill should be set at a moderate heat, rather than high, so that the fish does not dry. The smaller the fish, the higher the grill. Line the grill with foil so that the pan and the rack don't have lingering fish flavours.

Baking Fish can be baked whole, brushed with butter or oil, and stuffed; they may be open or lightly covered with buttered foil for protection. They can also be cooked in a liquid (milk, sauce, wine, stock).

Poaching This method ensures that the fish remains moist throughout the cooking time. The fish is cooked in a liquid, such as fish stock, wine, water or milk, which can be flavoured with herbs, a little onion or lemon juice. The fish may be cooked on top of the stove in a covered or uncovered pan (or fish kettle) or in the oven. If the pan is not covered the fish should be basted frequently. The cooking liquor is usually used as a basis for the accompanying sauce.

Steaming The fish should be placed between 2 buttered plates, or on a heatproof plate and covered in foil. This prevents the natural juices escaping into the boiling water.

En papillote Fish, whole or in fillets or steaks, can be wrapped up in foil, greaseproof paper or cellophane with various flavourings (butter, lemon juice, wine, onion, garlic, herbs) and poached, steamed, baked or deep-fried. All the essential flavours and juices are retained making it one of the best ways to cook fish.

WHITE FISH

Bass: Best in mid-June to mid-March. A round fish, silver in colour. The flesh is white and delicate in flavour and texture. Sold whole. To cook: bake, steam, poach or grill. Serve with butter sauces.

Bream, Sea: Best mid-June to mid-March. A round fish with very coarse big scales, it is identifiable by a black spot behind the eyes. The flesh is pink and delicate. Sold whole or in fillets. To cook: steam, bake or fry. Particularly good steamed with herbs.

Brill: A salt-water flat fish, similar to turbot in appearance but smaller, with a brownish yellow skin with small scales. The flesh is a creamy white, and delicate, breaking up easily. Sold whole or filleted. To cook: bake, steam, poach, fry or grill. Good with Mornay Sauce (see page 32).

Cod: Available all year round. A very large round salt-water fish with a silver-grey skin with small yellow and brown spots. The flesh should be pure white and firm with a coarse texture. Available fresh, as steaks or fillets, and salted, smoked and dried. To cook: use in pies, grill, fry, poach or steam. Good with parsley, egg or Mornay Sauce (see page 32).

Coley (Saithe): Available all year round. A round salt-water fish with a very dark charcoal-grey skin and a greyish-pink flesh, which turns white when cooked. Always sold in fillets. To cook: fry, bake, use in soups and pies.

Dab: Best April to November. A flat salt-water fish, smaller than a plaice, and similar in shape and colouring, but with rough scales, and a white flesh. Sold whole. To cook: best grilled or fried.

Dogfish (Huss, Rock Salmon, Rock Eel): Available all year round. Always sold skinned and split through. This salt-water fish is related to the shark family. It has a white flesh which is soft and a little oily in texture. To cook: use for soups and pies and for deep-frying.

Flounder: Available all year round. Related to the plaice and brill. A flat salt-water fish with a rounded body. The underside is cream coloured, the top pale brown. Sold whole. To cook: best grilled or fried.

Haddock: Available all year round. A round salt-water fish, related to the cod family. It has a greyish-silver skin with a dark line which runs along both flanks. A white flesh, which is firm and tasty but coarse in texture. Available whole, in fillets and cutlets. To cook: grill, fry, poach or bake.

Hake: Available all year round. A round salt-water fish with a thin, sleek body and pointed nose, and large fins. The skin is a silver grey and the flesh is firm, white, flaky and easy to digest. Sold as fillets, steaks and cutlets. To cook: bake, poach, stew or casserole.

Halibut: Available all year round, it is the largest flat salt-water fish. The flesh is firm, coarse and white; that of smaller fish – known as chicken halibut – is finer. Available in steaks, fillets and whole for small ones. To cook: grill, poach, fry, bake or steam.

Monkfish (Angler Fish): Available all year round. A deep-sea fish with such an ugly head, usually only the tail is sold. The skin is blackish; the flesh is white, firm and succulent. To cook: poach, steam, fry, grill, stew or bake.

Plaice: Best from June to January. A flat salt water fish with a brownish-grey upperside with bright orange spots; the underside is a creamy colour. The flesh is white and easily digested. Sold whole or in fillets. To cook: fry, poach, steam, bake or grill.

Skate: Available from October to April. A flat salt-water fish, it is ray shaped. Only the wings are sold. Flesh is pinkish cream. To cook: fry, poach or grill.

Sole, Dover: Available all year round. A flat salt-water fish with an oval body and fairly small fins. The skin on one side is brownish-grey, the underside is creamy white. The flesh is fine textured with a delicate flavour: it is considered the finest of the flat fish. Sold whole or in fillets. To cook: poach, fry, steam or grill.

Sole, Lemon: Best from December to March. Considered inferior in flavour and texture to Dover Sole. It is wider and with a more pointed nose than Dover Sole. Sold whole or in fillets. To cook: poach, fry, steam or grill.

Turbot: Available all year round, best July to March. A large flat salt-water fish, with a dark brown/black skin; the underside is white. The flesh is firm and white with a delicate flavour. Sold whole (chicken turbot) or in cutlets, steaks or fillets. To cook: bake, steam, poach, fry or grill.

Whiting: Available all year round. A member of the cod family. This round salt-water fish has a greyish-green upper skin, which is silvery cream underneath. Rather bland flavour with a flaky texture. To cook: steam, poach, bake or fry. Good served with sauces.

SMOKED FISH

Arbroath Smokies: Small whole haddock which are smoked to a rich brown. To cook: poach in milk or steam.

Bloater: Whole herring, salted, dried and lightly cold-smoked. To cook: grill or fry.

Buckling: Brined, hot-smoked herring. Moist flesh under a tough skin. No need to cook.

Kipper: The best known smoked herring. Before cold-smoking the fish is split, gutted, then soaked in brine. To cook: grill, fry or poach.

Mackerel, Smoked: Hot-smoked whole or in fillets. Ready to eat. Can also be bought cold-smoked, when it needs to be grilled.

Smoked Eel: Sold whole or in fillets. Dutch is best. Serve with brown bread and butter and lemon.

Smoked Haddock: Haddock fillet, or on the bone (Finnan haddock) is smoked until pale yellow. If the colour is deeper yellow it has probably been dyed, giving a poor flavour. To cook: poach or steam.

Salmon, Smoked: filleted salmon, cold- or hot-smoked and sold in the piece or very thinly sliced. Should be soft and moist, with a delicate pink colour. Serve with brown bread and butter.

Smoked Trout: Rainbow trout, hot-smoked. Does not freeze well. Serve whole or in fillets.

OILY FISH

Carp: Best mid-June to mid-March. A freshwater fish whose habitat is generally muddy ponds, lakes and rivers, it is a round fish with coarse scales, a small mouth and no teeth. Available whole, or in steaks and fillets. To cook: soak in salt water for 4–6 hours before cooking to remove the muddy flavour and aroma. Best stuffed and baked whole.

Eel, Common: Available all year round, best in autumn. Freshwater fish with a long thin body. The skin is a shiny grey-black colour, and the flesh white, firm and rich. Also available jellied from stalls and specialist shops, and smoked. Sold whole or in fillets. To cook: steam, deep-fry or braise.

Eel, Conger: The most common salt-water eel. Best March to October. The flesh is very firm and white, stronger in flavour than the freshwater eel and the skin is pale silvery grey to black. Can be smoked. Sold whole or in chunks. To cook: steam or boil; use for soups and stews.

Herring: Best in the summer. A smallish silvery-blue skinned salt-water fish, with a brownish white flesh. The skin should be shiny. Very bony, but delicately flavoured. Sold whole or filleted. To cook: grill, fry or bake. Rollmops are salted herring fillets, rolled up with onion and pickled in jars of vinegar and spices. Serve with rye bread and butter.

Mackerel: Available all year round. A silver-skinned salt-water fish with blue and black stripes from the head to the tail along its back. The flesh is pinkish brown and firm, the flavour is fairly rich. Sold whole. To cook: grill, fry, barbecue or bake. Best served with a sour or mustard sauce.

Mullet, Grey: Available all year round. A salt-water fish with large scales, and a grey skin. The flesh is greyish white, firm and rather fatty. Sold whole. To cook: steam, bake, poach or grill.

Mullet, Red: Best in the summer. A small salt-water fish with pinky-red skin and large scales. The flesh is white and firm. Difficult to buy fresh – usually frozen. Sold whole. To cook: grill, or fry, with the liver left inside for flavour.

Pike: Best mid-June to March. Freshwater fish, with a long lean body, a large pointed mouth and numerous teeth. The flesh is white, coarse, and may require soaking in water before cooking if from muddy waters. Sold whole or in fillets. Boil, bake, poach, fry or grill. Often used to make quenelles.

Pilchard: An adult sardine, this salt-water fish is similar to a herring in shape and colouring, but much smaller. Seldom sold fresh, usually canned in oil or tomatoes.

Buying fish

■ Always buy on the day it is to be cooked.
■ Choose fish that has bright shiny eyes and a plump, firm body.
■ The scales and skin should be shiny and moist.
■ The flesh should be firm.
■ The smell of the fish is an excellent guide to the freshness. It should smell slightly sweet, certainly not unpleasant, nor too fishy.
■ Choose a fishmonger who has a good turnover, and take his advice on the freshest fish to choose. The shop itself should not have an unpleasant stale fish smell.

Serve on toast or in salads if canned; fry or grill if fresh.

Salmon: Best February to November. A fish which matures in the sea, but which spawns in fresh water. The skin is silvery with small scales, the flesh pink to dark red and close textured, with a delicate flavour. Scotch salmon is the best. Sold whole or in steaks or cutlets. Also frozen and smoked. To cook: poach, steam or grill.

Sardine: Available all year round. A silver-skinned small salt-water fish, which is a young and immature pilchard. Sardines are sold fresh or canned. To cook: when fresh they are best grilled. Canned, whether in oil or tomato sauce, they can be served on toast or in salad.

Smelt (Sparling): Available in winter. Small, silver-skinned salt-water fish, a member of the salmon family, which spawns in rivers. The flesh is white and sweet-smelling, and less oily than salmon. It is eaten whole. To cook: deep- or shallow-fry.

Sprat: Best November to March. A member of the herring family. A small silvery skinned salt-water fish. Young sprats (brisling) are salted, canned or smoked. To cook: deep- or shallow-fry or grill.

Trout, Rainbow: In season March to November, farm-reared available all year round. A silver-skinned freshwater fish with rainbow colours flecked over the body. The skin should be slimy, the flesh is firm and either pink or creamy white. Sold whole. To cook: grill, fry, poach or bake.

Trout, River or Brown: Available March to November. A brown-skinned freshwater fish with dark brown spots. The flesh is finer than that of the rainbow trout. To cook: grill, fry, poach or bake.

Trout, Sea or Salmon: In season March to August. Freshwater river trout which has spent a season or more at sea, it has a silver skin with silvery scales and a pale pink flesh - because of diet of crustaceans – with a flavour similar to salmon. To cook: steam, poach or bake. Fry or grill fillets.

Tuna (Tunny): Best in early summer. A large fish, found only in warm seas, it is occasionally sold frozen as steaks with firm, 'un-fishy', pink flesh. More usually it is canned in oil. To cook: grill, bake or braise fresh; use canned tuna in salads etc. principally Salade Niçoise.

Whitebait: Best in spring and summer they are the fry of young sprats or herring. These tiny seawater fish are silver in colour with a fine white flesh. Eaten whole. Available fresh and frozen. To cook: deep-fry whole, ungutted, in batter.

CEPHALOPODS

Squid Available frozen all year round. 7.5–15 cm (3–6 inches) in length. Covered with a fine purplish membrane which must be removed to reveal the white flesh. The tentacles are edible. The ink sac can be used to colour the cooking liquid. Fry in oil or stew. Large ones can be stuffed.

Octopus Available all year round. Bluish-grey, with 8 tentacles covered with knobs. Needs preliminary cooking to remove the skin and the knobs from the tentacles. Flesh is pinkish white and very tender. Boil, stew or fry.

How to skin a sole

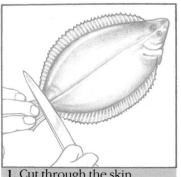

1. Cut through the skin above the tail

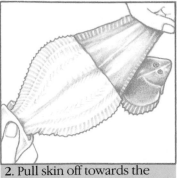

2. Pull skin off towards the head

1. Put the sole on a board, dark side up, head away from you, and wipe the skin dry.

2. Using a sharp knife, cut through the skin at the tail. With the point of the knife, loosen and ease up the skin around the cut edge of the tail.

3. Sprinkle the loosened skin with salt, and hold the tail firmly with one hand.

4. With the other hand, very gently lift the skin and pull it upwards towards the head. (The skin may be held with a cloth, to give a firmer grip.)

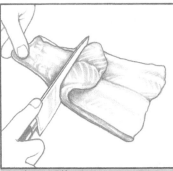

3. Skin a fillet by easing flesh away with a knife

5. Turn the fish over, and repeat on the other side.

How to fillet a flat fish

To cut 4 fillets from a plaice or sole, lay on a board and cut off the head and fins. Cut along the backbone from the head to the tail. Keeping the knife close to the bone work out from the backbone with long firm strokes. Remove the other fillet in the same way. Turn the fish over and remove the other 2 fillets in the same way.

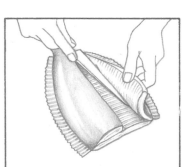

1. Cut along the backbone with a sharp knife.

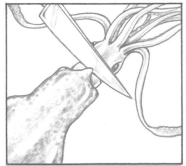

2. Work outwards from the backbone.

How to bone a herring or mackerel

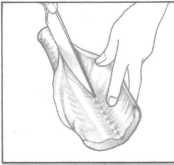

1. Open up the fish

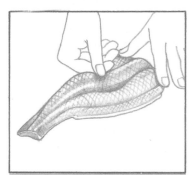

2. Press down with thumb along its backbone

1. To bone a round fish like a herring or mackerel, first cut off the head and tail and cut down the belly to open it completely. Remove gut.

2. Lay it down flat, skin side up, and press firmly with your thumb along the backbone, to loosen it.

3. Turn the fish over and use a sharp knife to lift out the backbone.

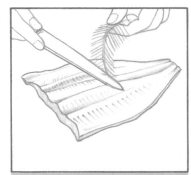

3. Ease out backbone with a knife

How to prepare squid for cooking

The edible parts of a squid are the tentacles and body. The head and inner part of the body must be removed and discarded. The body is usually cut into rings for cooking, or it can be stuffed whole.

1. Hold the squid in one hand and pull the head and tentacles away sharply from the body with the other. This will bring most of the innards with it.

2. Peel the thin skin off the body part, and discard. This is easily done by scraping gently with a sharp knife.

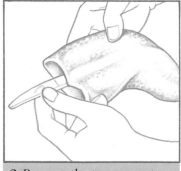

1. Remove the head and tentacles

2. Remove the transparent backbone and the innards

Special Fish Pie

Serves 6–8
750 g (1½ lb) potatoes, peeled
salt
100 g (4 oz) butter
about 100 ml (3½ fl oz) milk
  or single cream
freshly ground white pepper
450 g (1 lb) fresh haddock fillet
350 g (12 oz) smoked haddock
  fillet
300 ml (½ pint) dry white wine
1 bouquet garni
2 shallots, peeled and halved
2 small leeks, cleaned, trimmed
  and thinly sliced
25 g (1 oz) plain flour
4 tablespoons double cream
½ teaspoon made English
  mustard
100 g (4 oz) mature Cheddar
  cheese, finely grated
100 g (4 oz) peeled prawns
2 tablespoons chopped parsley

Preparation time: 30 minutes
Cooking time: 45 minutes
Oven: 200°C, 400°F, Gas
Mark 6

1. Cut the potatoes into small pieces, put into a saucepan with sufficient cold water to cover, add some salt, and bring to the boil. Reduce the heat and simmer for 12–15 minutes until tender. Drain.

2. Melt half the butter in the potato pan, add the drained potatoes, and mash until very smooth. Beat in the milk or single cream, and season to taste with salt and pepper. Cover and set aside until required.

3. Cut the fish fillets into halves, if large, and place in a buttered ovenproof dish. Pour over the wine, and add the bouquet garni and shallots. Cover with a lid, or foil, and bake in a preheated oven for 12 minutes until the fish is tender. Remove from the oven, and leave to cool.

4. Lift the fish from the cooking liquor, remove and discard the skin and bone, and flake the flesh. Strain the cooking liquor and reserve.

5. Heat the remaining butter in a saucepan, add the leeks and sauté for 5 minutes without browning. Add the flour and cook for 2 minutes, stirring.

6. Gradually stir in the reserved fish liquor, stirring well between additions. Bring to the boil and simmer for 5 minutes, stirring constantly. Season to taste with salt and pepper.

7. Remove from the heat, and stir in the cream, mustard and finely grated cheese. Stir in the flaked fish, peeled prawns and parsley.

8. Spoon into a lightly greased ovenproof dish, and smooth the top. Spoon the mashed potato over the fish, and fork to make a pattern.

9. Bake in the oven for 30 minutes until golden brown and bubbling. Serve immediately.

Squid with Tomato Sauce

It is important not to overcook squid, as this will toughen the flesh and spoil the texture.

Serves 6
750 g (1½ lb) prepared squid
Sauce:
25 g (1 oz) butter
2 shallots, peeled and finely
  chopped
450 g (1 lb) tomatoes, peeled,
  seeded and chopped
1–2 garlic cloves, peeled and
  crushed
150 ml (¼ pint) dry white wine
1 bouquet garni
salt
freshly ground black pepper
To garnish:
2 tablespoons chopped parsley

Preparation time: 10 minutes, excluding preparing the squid
Cooking time: about 1½ hours

1. Cut the prepared squid into 5 mm (¼ inch) slices; halve or quarter the tentacles.

2. To make the sauce, melt the butter in a saucepan, add the shallots and cook for 5 minutes, without browning, stirring occasionally.

3. Stir in the tomatoes, garlic, and wine, and slowly bring to the boil. Add the bouquet garni, salt and pepper.

4. Lower the heat and cook, uncovered, for 35–40 minutes until the sauce has reduced and thickened. Adjust the seasoning to taste.

5. Stir the prepared squid into the sauce, increase the heat to just below boiling, and cook for 30 minutes.

6. Spoon the squid and sauce into a heated serving dish, sprinkle with parsley and serve immediately.

3. Pull out the thin transparent backbone from the body, and scoop out any remaining innards.

4. Rinse the body cavity well, to ensure that all the matter inside has been rinsed away. Drain and pat dry.

5. Cut the tentacles off the head. Discard the head. Scrape the tentacles free of skin if they are large. Wash well and dry.

6. The squid is now prepared and ready to cook.

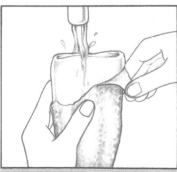

3. Peel off the skin and rinse well

4. Cut the body into rings or chunks

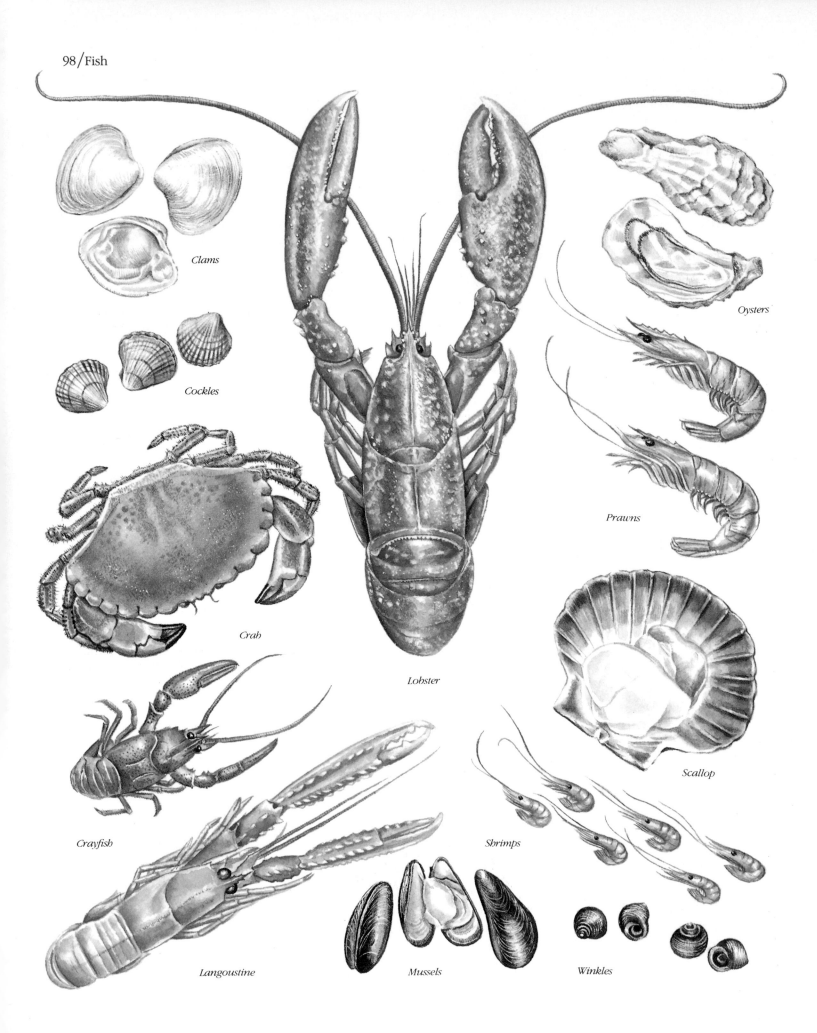

Clams

Cockles

Crab

Crayfish

Langoustine

Lobster

Mussels

Shrimps

Winkles

Scallop

Prawns

Oysters

SHELLFISH

There's nothing quite like the sea taste of fresh shellfish but it's vital to make sure it's absolutely fresh. This section tells you what to look for when buying, and preparation techniques, cooking methods and serving suggestions are given for every type of seafood.

SHELLFISH

Shellfish are divided into two main groups: crustaceans and molluscs. Crustaceans are animals like crabs and lobsters which have a protective external skeleton and legs: many have jointed shells. Molluscs have shells, mostly hinged, and no legs, and they include mussels, oysters, cockles and clams.

To ensure freshness and flavour, it is best to choose live shellfish and kill and cook them yourself. Lobsters, crabs, crayfish, oysters, cockles, clams and mussels can all generally be bought alive. Lobsters and crabs should be lively, and the tail of the lobster should curl under the body. Live mussel, clam and oyster shells should close tightly when tapped; any which do not are dead and should be discarded.

Crustaceans, however, are often sold cooked, a relief to the cook too squeamish to kill a crab or lobster. They should have dry bright shells, and should feel heavy for their size. Cooked shrimps and prawns should be bright pink, and smell fresh and pleasant.

As with all seafood, it is essential to buy shellfish and cook or use it on the day it is to be eaten. It deteriorates quickly, and if not absolutely fresh can be toxic.

Careful cooking is important too as, if overcooked, the flesh of shellfish becomes tough. It cooks surprisingly quickly. It is easier to tell when mussels and clams are cooked as they open up in the liquor; if any do not open, they should be discarded.

Crawfish (Spiny/Rock Lobster): Similar to a lobster but without the large claws, and it has a very rough spiny back. It is known in France as *langouste*. All the edible meat is on the tail. The flesh is cream-coloured and fairly coarse, but of good flavour. It is prepared in the same way as lobster (see page 102). Usually sold frozen and available April to September.

Grill topped with butter and breadcrumbs. Steam or boil. Use in starters, soups, hors d'oeuvres, and main course salads.

Crayfish: A freshwater animal, known as *écrevisse* in France. Rarely available fresh, but the raw tails are available frozen.

The main ingredient of the classic Nantua sauce, but can be used in starters, sea-food salads, etc. Can be poached or fried.

Clam: Large and small available, and soft or hard shelled, usually the latter. They have a greyish thick, very tightly fitting shell, and are usually sold live. In some parts of the country they are available throughout the year, but best in autumn.

As they are sandy, they must be washed several times in cold water, then soaked in cold water with a little oatmeal. Scrub before cooking.

To open a raw clam: work over a basin to catch the juices, prise the shell open with a sharp knife to sever the hinge. Carefully run the point of the knife between the clam and the shell to remove it. Also available canned and smoked.

To cook whole, simmer in lightly salted water or wine for 5–10 minutes until the shells open (depending on size).

Use in soups, such as chowders, fish stews, or as a starter. Also eaten raw, as oysters, with lemon juice.

Cockle: Tiny shellfish enclosed in a whitish fluted shell.

Available throughout the year, but best from September to April.

Usually sold cooked. If fresh, soak in a bucket of salt water for at least 1 hour before cooking to remove the sand. Scrub the shells before cooking.

If cooked, they are usually served with vinegar, or on their own. To cook, simmer in lightly salted water for 4–5 minutes until the shells open. Use in fish soups, pies or as a starter. Can be eaten raw.

Crab: A raw crab is pinkish brown when alive, the shell turning to an orange-red when cooked. Usually sold cooked, but they are available alive (see page 101 for how to cook and prepare). The body contains soft brown meat; and the white meat comes from the legs and claws. The male crab has larger claws than the female, but the female or 'hen' crab is generally considered superior.

Always shake a crab lightly when buying; it should feel heavy for its weight with no water inside.

Allow 1 large crab for 2 people or 1 small to medium crab per person for a main course dish. Best served freshly cooked, and dressed, or cold with Mayonnaise (see page 31). Also may be grilled with butter and breadcrumbs on top.

It is used in soups, pâté, mousse, fish dishes, or in sandwiches or salads.

Lobster: Dark blue-black when live, which cooks to a bright red. The male, although smaller than the female, has larger claws. The flesh of the female is finer than that of the male, and the body contains the coral (bright orange when cooked) which is highly prized. It is used to make sauces with a lovely pink colour, or for garnish.

Sold both live and cooked. Available all the year frozen, which spoils the texture of the flesh, but best fresh from April to August. Avoid lobster with white blemishes on the shell, which is a sign of age.

See page 102 for how to prepare and cook a lobster. Use in salads, soups or starters. It can be grilled. It is especially good cold, served with Mayonnaise (see page 31)

SHELLFISH

Mussels: Deep blue-purple to black shells. Usually sold live in the shell by the litre (pint or quart). 2.25 litres (2 quarts) is usually sufficient for 4 people. They should be put into a bucket of cold water, with a sprinkling of flour or oatmeal to plump them, and left for a few hours to remove any sand or grit. Wash well, scrub the shells, and pull off the beards. Discard any shells that are broken, or do not close swiftly when tapped. Available usually from September to March. Simmer in boiling water or wine for 5 minutes until the shells open. Discard any that have not opened.

Oysters: The most prized of molluscs. There are many varieties, and the English and French are often claimed to be the best. The shells should be tightly closed when bought. Available September to April. Usually served raw, although sometimes cooked, very lightly. The shell should be opened just before the oyster is eaten.

Serve raw in half shell on a bed of crushed ice with pepper, lemon or Tabasco sauce. Allow 6 per person as a starter. Add to steak pies, or serve in creamy sauces.

Prawns: Grey hinged shell which turns pink when cooked. Only the body and tail are edible. To prepare, pull off the head and legs, and carefully peel away the shell on the body and tail. Usually sold cooked or frozen. Available throughout the year.

If uncooked, simmer in water for about 5 minutes, until pink. Use in salads, prawn cocktails, or sauces

Prawns, Dublin Bay (scampi; langoustine): The best come from the North Atlantic. About 10 cm (4 inches) in length, often with claws (like a mini

1. Insert an oyster knife into the hinge and twist

2. Loosen the oyster from its shell

lobster). The prawn shell is pale pink when live, turning to a deeper pink when cooked. Prepare in the same way as prawns (below), with only the tail section being eaten. Sold fresh or frozen. Available throughout the year. If cooking

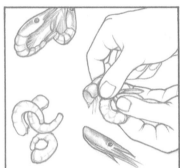

Pull off head and legs from prawns and remove shell

from raw, boil for 10–12 minutes.

Prawns, Pacific: The largest of the prawn family, measuring up to 15 cm (6 inches) long. The pinkish orange shell encloses the fine pink flesh. Imported frozen, available throughout the year either cooked or uncooked. Prepare as prawns.

Delicious served with Hollandaise Sauce (see page 44), or cooked in garlic butter.

If bought uncooked, cook in boiling water for 15 minutes and peel as other prawns.

Scallop: A large flat fan-shaped shell – on which the fish sits – is topped by a rounded shell – in which the fish is usually served. The scallop is a creamish white nugget of firm flesh with a bright orange coral (roe). Choose large scallops as the smaller ones are under-developed. They should look plump and firm too. Also available in closed shells and frozen off the shell. Remove from shells as for oysters.

Available throughout the year if frozen, but the fresh ones are best from September to March.

Scallops require very little cooking, as the flesh becomes tough if it is overcooked. Suitable for poaching, baking and grilling, as well as for use in soups and stews. Often served in the round shell in a creamy sauce with a piped border of creamed potatoes browned under the grill.

Shrimps, Brown Common: Tiny transparent crustaceans, much smaller than prawns. The shell turns brown when cooked, either fresh or frozen. Available throughout the year.

Usually served with brown bread and butter, in salads, or potted with butter and mace.

Shrimps, Pink: Usually sold cooked, these grey-shelled shrimps are slightly larger than the brown or common variety. The flesh turns bright pink when cooked. Serve as above.

Whelks: Snail-shaped brown or grey shells which are quite large. The flesh is brownish in colour. Usually sold cooked but they can be found uncooked. Available throughout the year, but best from September to February. To cook, boil in salted water for 5–7 minutes, and remove from the shell before serving. Usually served with vinegar and brown bread and butter.

Winkles: Similar to whelks, but much smaller. The shell is greyish brown. Usually sold cooked, but can also be found uncooked. Available throughout the year, but best from October to May.

Cook in boiling salted water for about 4 minutes. A pin is required to remove the flesh from the shell. Serve with vinegar and brown bread and butter.

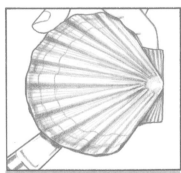

1. Insert knife into scallop shell and twist

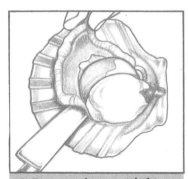

2. Remove the greyish fringe

How to prepare a crab

1. Choose a live crab that is fairly active, has a clean shell and is heavy for its size. (To pick up a live crab, grip it at the tail end.)

2. Put the crab into a large saucepan with a few flavouring vegetables, if liked, cover with cold water, and add a little salt.

3. Cover with a lid, slowly bring to the boil and simmer gently for 10–12 minutes per 450 g (1 lb).

4. Leave to cool in the cooking liquor, which may be used as a base for fish stock (see page 26) or a sauce.

5. When cold, rinse the crab shell under cold water. Place it shell down on a large board, with the legs uppermost.

6. Twist off the legs and claws at the joint with the body.

7. With the tail flap facing you, hold the crab firmly with both hands, and using the thumbs push and prise the body section or 'apron' upwards so that the whole body section is released from the hard back shell.

8. Pull away and discard the greyish-white stomach sac (just behind the mouth) and the long white pointed 'dead men's fingers'. These are very obvious and should be removed.

9. Using a small spoon, scoop out all the meat from both shells, keeping white and brown meats separate, in bowls. Reach in carefully to all the crevices with a lobster pick or metal skewer. Be careful to remove all pieces of shell.

10. Place the empty hard shell on the board, and using the thumbs, or a small hammer, push or tap the shell to remove the thin undershell. This should come away easily, following a visible line on both sides.

11. Crack the claws, using a hammer or shellfish crackers, and remove the white meat. Break the legs at the joints, and extract the meat.

12. For dressed crab, wash and dry the hard shell. Mix the brown meat with a little mayonnaise and seasoning, and spoon it down the centre of the shell. Season the white meat and arrange on either side of the brown meat. Garnish with finely chopped parsley and hard-boiled egg.

1. Twist off the legs

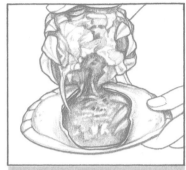

2. Pull the body away from the shell

3. Remove the 'dead men's fingers' and intestines

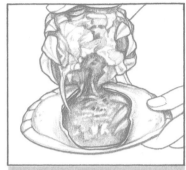

4. Scrape out brown meat from the body shell

Stuffed Crab

Serves 4
*2 large cooked crabs each
　about 1 kg (2 lb)*
75 g (3 oz) unsalted butter
*6 shallots, peeled and finely
　chopped*
*3 large garlic cloves, peeled
　and crushed*
2 tablespoons chopped parsley
1 tablespoon chopped chives
150 ml (¼ pint) dry white wine
*4 tablespoons Calvados or
　brandy*
salt
freshly ground black pepper
*4 tablespoons fresh
　breadcrumbs (white or
　brown)*
To garnish:
1 lemon, cut into slices
sprigs of fresh parsley

Preparation time: 15 minutes, excluding cooking and preparing the crabs
Cooking time: 8–10 minutes
Oven: 220°C, 425°F, Gas Mark 7

1. Prepare the crabs (see above) and wash and dry the shells.

2. Mix together the white and brown meat from the crab.

3. Melt 25 g (1 oz) of the butter in a saucepan, add the shallots and garlic, and fry gently for 5 minutes until softened.

4. Stir in the crab meat, parsley and chives, then pour in the wine. Cook gently for 5 minutes, stirring occasionally.

5. Pour in the Calvados or brandy and set light to it.

6. Spoon the mixture into the two crab shells, and place them on a baking sheet.

7. Mix together the seasoning, breadcrumbs and the remaining butter, melted, and sprinkle over the crabs to cover the top of the filling.

8. Bake in a preheated oven for 8–10 minutes.

9. Place the shells on to a serving plate, garnish with lemon slices and parsley, and serve immediately, from the shells.

How to prepare a lobster

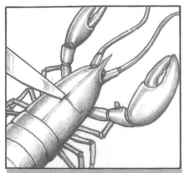

1. To kill the lobster, pierce its head with a sharp knife

2. Cut the boiled lobster in two down its length

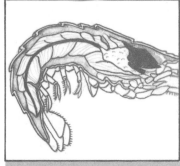

3. Remove the intestinal vein, gills and stomach sac

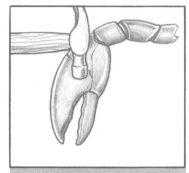

4. Crack the claws to extract meat

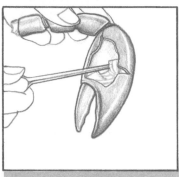

5. Remove meat from claws with a lobster pick

There are two ways of killing a lobster. One is to pierce its head, at the well defined cross mark, with a sharp strong knife. This goes straight into the brain, and kills it instantly. The other method is given below.

1. Tie the claws together with string or with a rubber band.

2. Place the lobster, dead or alive, in a large pan of lightly salted water with flavouring vegetables, if liked, and slowly bring to the boil. Cover with a lid and simmer for 15–20 minutes until the dark shell turns bright red.

3. Leave the lobster to cool in the cooking liquor.

4. Twist off the claws, and remove the legs. Using shellfish crackers, or a hammer, crack the claws, and pull out the meat.

5. Cut away the thin undershell of the tail section, using sharp scissors, and carefully pull out the flesh.

6. Place the lobster on a board and cut in half along its length with a sharp knife. Remove the thin grey vein of intestine running along its length.

7. Scrape out the red coral (if present) and reserve.

8. If liked, add the liver to the flesh. This is the grey-green flesh near the head, which is delicious.

9. Carefully lift out the bony part of the head and break it into pieces. Using a lobster pick or skewer pick out the flesh and any remaining liver and roe.

10. Pull away the grey spongy gills and stomach sac from the top of the head and discard.

11. Wash the shell and dry well. This method of preparation means that both the head and tail sections of the lobster may be used to hold and serve the meat.

Lobster Newburg

Serves 6
2 large cooked lobsters each about 1.5 kg (3 lb) in weight
150 g (5 oz) butter
6 large slices white bread, cut into large rounds
150 ml (¼ pint) dry sherry or Madeira
1 tablespoon brandy
salt
freshly ground black pepper
3 egg yolks
300 ml (½ pint) double cream
To garnish:
flat leaf parsley

Preparation time: 10 minutes, excluding cooking and preparing the lobsters
Cooking time: about 6 minutes.

1. Cook and prepare the lobsters, as described left.

2. Cut the flesh into 4 cm (1½ inch) pieces. Save the coral for garnish.

3. Melt half the butter in a large frying pan. When it is bubbling, add the bread and fry on both sides until golden brown. Drain on kitchen paper and keep hot.

4. Melt the remaining butter in a saucepan, stir in the lobster pieces and pour over the sherry or Madeira and brandy,

and season with a little salt and pepper.

5. Bring to the boil and boil rapidly for 3 minutes to reduce the liquor.

6. Whisk together the egg yolks and cream.

7. Remove the saucepan from the heat, cool slightly, then stir in the egg and cream mixture.

8. Place over a very gentle heat for 1 minute, to thicken the sauce. Do not allow the sauce to boil as this will ruin it. Adjust the seasoning to taste.

9. Arrange the fried croûtes of bread on a serving plate, spoon over the lobster and sauce, and serve immediately, garnished with parsley.

Avocado with Curried Prawns

Serves 4
225 g (8 oz) peeled prawns,
    thawed if frozen
a squeeze of lemon juice
2 avocados
Sauce:
1 teaspoon Madras curry
    powder
1 garlic clove, peeled and
    crushed
150 ml (¼ pint) Mayonnaise
    (see page 31)
4 tablespoons plain
    unsweetened yogurt
1–2 drops Tabasco sauce
1 tablespoon chopped parsley
salt
freshly ground black pepper
½ teaspoon thin honey
To garnish:
lime slices or wedges
sprigs of fresh thyme

Preparation time: 15 minutes,
plus standing

1. Make the sauce first. Put the curry powder into a bowl, add the garlic, and stir in the Mayonnaise and yogurt.

2. Add the Tabasco, parsley, salt, pepper and honey. Mix and cover, then refrigerate for 4 hours to allow the flavours to blend and mature.

3. Stir in the prawns and lemon juice.

4. Cut the avocados in half, remove the stones and skin, and cut the flesh into slices lengthwise.

5. Arrange the avocado slices in flower shapes on 4 individual plates. Spoon the prawn mixture into the centre of the flower.

6. Serve immediately, garnished with lime slices and sprigs of thyme.

Scallops with Leeks

Serves 4
12 scallops, removed from their
    shells
6 thin leeks, white part only
50 g (2 oz) butter
1 shallot, peeled and finely
    chopped
4 tablespoons dry white
    vermouth
6 tablespoons good quality dry
    white wine
6 tablespoons double cream
1 bunch chervil, chopped
salt
freshly ground black pepper
To garnish:
sprigs of chervil

Preparation time: 10 minutes
Cooking time: 8 minutes

1. Wash the scallops well and pat dry. Remove the coral and set aside. Slice each scallop in half horizontally.

2. Cut the leeks into julienne strips (see page 171).

3. Melt the butter in a saucepan and fry the shallot and leeks gently for 5 minutes, stirring constantly, taking care not to brown them.

4. Pour the vermouth and wine over them, and slowly bring to the boil. Simmer for 5 minutes.

5. Stir the scallops into the pan and cook for 1 minute.

6. Pour over the cream, and stir in the chopped chervil, and slowly bring to the boil. Boil for 1 minute, adding the coral half-way through. Season with salt and pepper to taste.

7. Spoon the scallops, coral, leeks and sauce into a heated serving dish and serve immediately garnished with chervil sprigs.

Mouclade

Mussels with White Wine and Cream Sauce

Serves 4
2.75 litres (5 pints) fresh
    mussels
400 ml (14 fl oz) good quality
    dry white wine
1 bouquet garni
25 g (1 oz) butter
2 large shallots, peeled and
    finely chopped
1 garlic clove, peeled and
    crushed
1 teaspoon curry powder
a pinch of cayenne pepper
150 ml (¼ pint) double cream
3 egg yolks
salt
freshly ground black pepper
To garnish:
chopped parsley

Preparation time: 15 minutes,
plus cleaning mussels
Cooking time: about 15
minutes

1. Scrub the mussels, remove the beards and discard any that are broken, or do not close when tapped. Wash several times to remove sand or grit.

2. Put the wine into a large saucepan, add the bouquet garni and bring slowly to the boil.

3. Add the mussels, and shake them over a high heat until they open, about 2–3 minutes. Discard any which have not opened.

4. Using a perforated spoon, remove the cooked mussels from the saucepan. Remove the top half of each shell and set aside the bottom halves with their mussels still attached.

5. Boil the cooking liquor rapidly until it has reduced by about a third. Discard the bouquet garni.

6. Melt the butter in a saucepan, add the shallots and cook slowly for 10 minutes, stirring, without browning. Stir in the garlic and curry powder and cook for a further 2 minutes, then add the cayenne pepper. Cook for a further minute, taking care not to burn the shallots or spices.

7. Strain the cooking liquor through a fine sieve lined with muslin, and stir into the pan with the shallots.

8. Lightly whisk the cream into the egg yolks, and season to taste. Gradually whisk in 4 tablespoons of the hot liquor from the saucepan.

9. Place the saucepan of cooking liquor over a very gentle heat, whisk in the egg mixture and heat gently, stirring constantly. Do not allow the sauce to boil as this will scramble the eggs.

10. Adjust the seasoning to taste, stir in the mussels, and shake the pan constantly to coat the mussels. Continue cooking over a very gentle heat without boiling, until the mussels are hot.

11. Spoon the mussels and their sauce into a heated serving dish and serve immediately, sprinkled with chopped parsley.

SEAFOOD RECIPES

The joy of fish is that it's right for every occasion – as starter or main course, for family meals or the most extravagant entertaining. For a special occasion try Coquilles St Jacques, a French classic with scallops, or be extravagant with Lobster Thermidor, in a cream sauce.

Coquilles St Jacques à la Provençale

Scallops Gratinéed with Wine, Garlic and Herbs

This scallop dish can be prepared in advance and gratinéed just before serving. The following proportions are sufficient for a first course. Double them for a main course. Serve with a chilled rosé, or a dry white wine such as Côtes de Provence.

Serves 6
75 g (3 oz) butter
1 medium onion, chopped
1½ tablespoons chopped shallots or spring onions
1 garlic clove, chopped
24–30 medium scallops, washed, or 450 g (1 lb) frozen scallops
salt
freshly ground black pepper
50 g (2 oz) flour
1 tablespoon olive oil
150 ml (¼ pint) dry white wine or 65 ml (2½ fl oz) dry white vermouth and 4 tablespoons water
½ bay leaf
generous pinch of thyme
25 g (1 oz) Parmesan cheese, grated

Preparation time: 15 minutes
Cooking time: 20 minutes

1. Melt 25 g (1 oz) of the butter in a small saucepan and cook the onion slowly for 5 minutes or so, until tender and translucent but not browned. Stir in the shallots or spring onions, and garlic, and cook slowly for 1 minute more. Take the pan off the heat and reserve.

2. Dry the scallops and cut into slices 5 mm (¼ inch) thick. Just before cooking, sprinkle with salt and pepper, roll in flour, and shake off the excess.

3. Melt 25 g (1 oz) of the remaining butter with the olive oil in a frying pan and fry the scallops quickly for 2 minutes to brown them lightly.

4. Pour the wine, or the vermouth and water, into the frying pan with the scallops. Add the bay leaf and thyme and the cooked onion mixture. Cover the frying pan and simmer for 5 minutes. Uncover and remove the scallops with a slotted spoon. If necessary, boil down the sauce rapidly for a minute until it is slightly thickened. Correct the seasoning, and discard the bay leaf.

5. Divide the scallops between 6 buttered scallop shells or porcelain shells and spoon the sauce over. Sprinkle with cheese and dot with the remaining butter.

6. Just before serving, place under a moderately hot grill for 3 to 4 minutes to heat through, and to brown the cheese lightly.

Moules Marinières

Mussels are best eaten the day they are bought, but if it is necessary to keep them overnight, wash and scrub them well, then put in a bucket full of sea or salted water. Sprinkle with fine oatmeal, cover the bucket with a teatowel and leave in a cool place.

Serves 6
3.5 litres (6 pints) mussels
40 g (1½ oz) butter
3 shallots or 1 small onion, peeled and finely chopped
1 garlic clove, peeled and crushed
1 sprig parsley
1 sprig thyme
300 ml (½ pint) dry white wine
freshly ground black pepper
1 tablespoon finely chopped fresh parsley, to garnish

Preparation time: 30 minutes
Cooking time: about 10 minutes

1. Wash and scrub the mussels well, discarding any open or cracked ones. With a small, sharp, strong knife, scrape away the beard and anything else attached to the shell. Wash them again in several changes of water until there is no sand at the bottom of the bowl. Drain them well.

2. Melt half the butter in a large saucepan and soften the shallot or onion and the garlic over a low heat. Add the herbs, wine and pepper and bring to the boil.

3. Tip in the mussels, cover the pan, and shake over a brisk heat for about 5 minutes until all the shells have opened.

4. Take the mussels out with a slotted spoon and divide between 4 hot soup plates or bowls and keep hot while you reduce the liquor by boiling for 3 minutes. Adjust the seasoning, and whisk in the remaining butter.

5. Strain over the mussels through a muslin-lined sieve, and sprinkle with parsley. Serve with plenty of crusty French bread.

Variation

For a thicker sauce, stir in 3 tablespoons double cream or 25 g (1 oz) Beurre Manié (see page 33) after reducing the liquor, then reheat until thickened.

From the top: Moules marinières, Coquilles St Jacques à la provençale

Bourride Provençale

Fish Soup with Aïoli

This robust Provençal soup with its golden garlic sauce has been known for over 200 years. The soup is so substantial it can be served as a main dish, and like most peasant dishes is very versatile, suiting any fairly firm-fleshed fish. Brill, turbot, mullet, John Dory, rock salmon, bream, even scallops or sardines can all be used, and although Bourride can be made with just one type of fish it is best with at least two or three varieties. Despite being inexpensive and quite simple to prepare, it makes an extra special dish for a dinner party.

Serves 6
2 kg (4 lb) fish (e.g. whiting, bass, monkfish, etc.), cleaned and cut into large pieces
450 g (1 lb) potatoes, peeled and cut in chunks
6 slices hot toast, to serve
Court bouillon:
2 tablespoons olive oil
2 leeks (white part only), thinly sliced
2 medium onions, peeled and thinly sliced
1 carrot, scraped and thinly sliced
1 celery stick, thinly sliced
fish heads and trimmings
1 litre (1¾ pints) water
750 ml (1¼ pints) dry white wine
1 bay leaf
1 fennel sprig
1 sliver fresh or dried orange peel
salt
Aïoli:
10 garlic cloves, peeled
6 egg yolks
400 ml (14 fl oz) olive oil

Preparation time: 30 minutes
Cooking time: 50 minutes

1. Make the Court bouillon: heat the oil in a large pan, add the leeks, onions, carrot, celery stick and fish trimmings and heads and cook gently for 5 minutes. Add the water, wine, bay leaf, fennel and orange peel, and salt to taste. Bring to the boil, then lower the heat and simmer uncovered for 20 minutes.

2. Meanwhile, make the Aïoli: crush the garlic and 4 pinches of salt to a paste using a mortar and pestle. Add 2 egg yolks and mix well.

3. Beat in the oil a little at a time, with a wire whisk, as when making Mayonnaise (see page 31), then pour it in a thin stream as the Aïoli becomes thick. Divide the Aïoli in half and whisk the remaining egg yolks into one half.

4. Strain the Court bouillon through a fine sieve, pressing firmly to extract as much of the juice as possible. Discard the fish trimmings and vegetables. Return the stock to the rinsed-out pan and reheat gently.

5. Add the fish to the stock, putting in those that take longest to cook first (e.g. monkfish, turbot, eel), and those with shorter cooking times (e.g. whiting, John Dory) after about 5 minutes. Add the potatoes at the beginning. Simmer for 15–20 minutes until the fish and potatoes are tender.

6. Remove the fish and potatoes from the stock with a slotted spoon and place in a deep soup tureen. Keep hot. Strain the stock again through a fine sieve and return to the rinsed-out pan. Reheat gently, then stir 1 tablespoon into the Aïoli and egg yolk mixture. Whisk this mixture back into the stock and reheat gently, whisking vigorously all the time. Do not allow the stock to boil or it will separate. Taste and adjust seasoning, then pour into the tureen over the fish and potatoes.

7. To serve, place a slice of toast in the bottom of a hot soup plate. Place a portion of fish and potatoes on the toast. Pour some of the soup over each plate. Serve the remaining Aïoli separately.

Truites aux Amandes

Trout with Almonds

Serves 4
4 trout, about 225 g (8 oz) each, cleaned, with heads and tails left on but fins removed
1 tablespoon seasoned flour
1 tablespoon oil
150 g (5 oz) butter
salt
freshly ground black pepper
100 g (4 oz) blanched almonds
lemon slices, to garnish (optional)

Preparation time: 2 minutes
Cooking time: 14 minutes

1. Coat the trout with the flour. Shake to remove excess flour.

2. Heat the oil and 100 g (4 oz) of the butter in a heavy frying pan. Add the trout and cook gently for 5 minutes on each side, taking care that the butter does not burn.

3. Remove the trout from the pan and place on a warmed serving platter. Sprinkle with salt and pepper to taste. Keep hot.

4. Melt the remaining butter in the rinsed-out pan. Add the almonds and cook over moderate heat for about 2 minutes, stirring constantly, until golden on all sides. Sprinkle the almonds and butter over the trout and garnish with lemon slices, if liked. Serve immediately.

From the top: Truites aux amandes, Bourride Provençale

Lobster Thermidor

The ultimate in luxurious richness, Lobster Thermidor was created in France during the Third Republic. See page 102 for instructions on how to cook and prepare lobster.

Serves 4
one cooked lobster about 1 kg (2 lb) or two 450 g (1 lb) lobsters, halved and cleaned
50 g (2 oz) butter
1 small onion, peeled and finely chopped
pinch of cayenne pepper
1 tablespoon dry white wine
1 teaspoon tomato purée
2 tablespoons double cream
150 ml (¼ pint) Béchamel Sauce (see page 34), warmed
salt
freshly ground black pepper
2 tablespoons grated Parmesan cheese

Preparation time: 45 minutes
Cooking time: 20 minutes

1. Pick all the meat out of the shells and crack the claws of the lobster to remove the meat. Cut into 1 cm (½ inch) pieces.

2. Melt the butter in a frying pan and add the onion. Soften the onion in the butter for 5 minutes, then add the lobster, cayenne and wine. Simmer gently for 5 minutes, stirring constantly.

3. Stir the tomato purée and cream into the Béchamel sauce and add salt and pepper to taste.

4. Pour the sauce over the lobster in the frying pan and mix well. Spoon this mixture evenly into the lobster shells and sprinkle the tops with Parmesan cheese.

5. Place the shells under a preheated grill and cook until bubbling and golden.

Raie au Beurre Noir

Poached Skate with Black Butter

Skate wings have a delicate flavour and soft, easily managed bones. Black butter is the traditional accompaniment.

In spite of its name, black butter should be a dark nutty brown, not black. It is best made with clarified butter (see page 42) which will ensure that there are no dark, gritty specks in the sauce from the milk solids in the butter.

Serves 4
4 small wings of skate, about 225 g (8 oz) each
1 small onion, peeled and sliced
1 bay leaf
1 sprig thyme
1 sprig parsley
3 tablespoons white wine vinegar
salt
freshly ground black pepper
50 g (2 oz) butter
2 tablespoons capers
1 tablespoon finely chopped fresh parsley

Preparation time: 5 minutes
Cooking time: 25 minutes

1. Place the fish in a large pan. Add the onion, bay leaf, thyme, parsley and 1 tablespoon of the wine vinegar. Cover with water and add salt and pepper. Cover and poach over low heat for about 20 minutes until the fish is tender.

2. Remove carefully from the pan and drain well. Take off the skin and, if possible, the large bones at the top of each piece of skate. Keep hot.

3. Slowly melt the butter in a pan and cook until dark golden brown. Pour on the remaining wine vinegar.

4. Sprinkle the capers and chopped parsley over the fish. Strain the sauce over the fish and serve immediately with plain boiled potatoes.

From the top: Raie au beurre noir, Lobster thermidor

POULTRY & GAME

Poultry and game were once strictly seasonal but, with the advent of freezers, they are now available throughout the year. However, fresh poultry has a superior flavour to frozen and game is best in season. These recipes with their rich sauces give superb results.

Basic rules

For the best flavour, all poultry should be hung for 2–3 days after killing before it is drawn and put on sale. It is usually hung, ready plucked, and this helps develop the flavour and tenderise the flesh of the bird. This is one reason why fresh birds are generally considered superior to frozen where the speed of the killing, chilling and freezing processes allows no time for hanging.

When buying poultry, the larger the bird, the better the value as the proportion of meat to bone is higher. And always make sure you are given the giblets. These include the heart, liver, neck and gizzard, and are used to make an excellent stock for the gravy, or are chopped and added to the gravy, to stuffings and soups etc. Wash them carefully before use and cut off any fat and the yellow bits on the liver or gizzard which contain bile.

This is very bitter and will spoil the flavour of the stock.

Frozen poultry When cooking poultry that has been frozen it is absolutely essential to make sure it is fully thawed first. You can be sure that it is completely thawed when all the limbs are flexible and there are no ice crystals left in the body cavity. If poultry is cooked whilst still partly frozen, it slows down the cooking and the deepest parts of the body do not get cooked through.

Salmonella, a common cause of food poisoning, can lurk in the intestines of all birds, and is normally quickly destroyed by heat. The body cavity, however, is more insulated by the surrounding flesh, and if this is still frozen, the heat may not penetrate enough to destroy the bacteria. It is very important to cool down a cooked bird as quickly as possible and then chill it until needed. It is also possible to cook poultry a second time as a

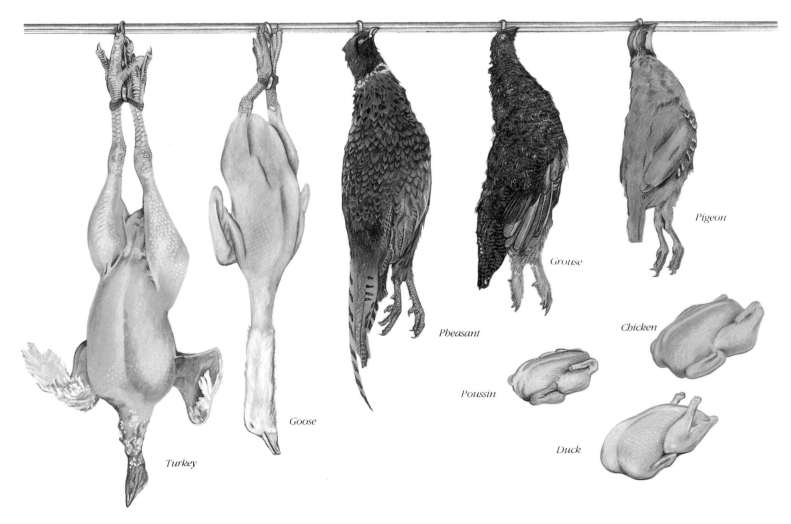

Turkey

Goose

Pheasant

Grouse

Pigeon

Poussin

Chicken

Duck

CHICKEN

Chickens are sold under different names according to their age, ranging from the poussin of a few weeks old to the boiling fowl, which is usually at least a year and a half old. In between are spring chickens, and roasters and broilers. Any chicken younger than 6 months is best grilled, sautéed or roasted, to develop the best flavour.

reheated dish, but the important point to remember is that it must be recooked and not just reheated. Put it into a sauce and boil for at least 5 minutes, or put it into the oven in a sauce and make sure it bubbles for at least 5 minutes. Cooked poultry meat can be refrozen even if it was a frozen bird to start with, but again do thaw properly and then recook it before serving.

Thaw a frozen bird completely, still in its wrappings either at room temperature or in a cool place, allowing about 12 hours for a 900 g (2 lb) bird and longer according to size.

To thaw in the refrigerator, the time allowed must be at least doubled and even then you may still find ice crystals present. Chicken portions take about 6–9 hours to thaw depending on size and longer in the refrigerator.

Fresh poultry is always more expensive but is thought to have a better flavour. A fresh bird will keep for up to 2 days in the refrigerator before cooking, but remove any tight wrappings, and cover loosely to allow air to circulate. Remove the giblets too, and store separately.

If buying a fresh chicken – one that has not been frozen in any way – the way to tell its age is to feel the breast bone with your thumb and finger: a young bird's should feel soft and flexible. The feet should be small with smooth small scales.

There are several types of chickens and these are given different names mainly to describe the size and age of the bird.

Poussins These are very small chickens weighing from 350–900 g (¾–2 lb) each and are usually only 4–8 weeks old. The larger ones (sometimes called double poussins) are served one per portion, but the really tiny ones may need to be served in pairs. They are very tender and have a delicate flavour so do not cook with overpowering ingredients. Best to roast, pot roast, casserole, or grill.

Broilers. These are smallish birds, too, usually about 12 weeks old, and are most often sold ready frozen. They weigh from 1.25–1.5 kg (2½–3½ lb), are extremely versatile, and can be cooked by any method. One bird should serve 3–4 portions. The flavour is not so good as a chicken which has been properly hung, but they are very cheap and always tender.

Spring chickens. These are small broilers, from 6–8 weeks old, and weighing about 900 g (2 lb). They can be cooked in a variety of ways, and will serve 2–3 people.

TYPES OF CHICKEN

Large roasters. These are usually hens or young cockerels which have been specially fed so they grow large quickly. They are aged about 10–15 weeks, and vary in size from 1.75–2.25 kg. (4–5 lb) and should feed 5–6 portions quite easily. They are also available cut into portions. They have a good flavour and are usually tender. They can be roasted, pot roasted and casseroled.

Capons. True capons are no longer produced. Capons were roaster cockerels of about 7–10 months old, which were neutered and then specially fattened so they grew much larger than normal chickens. Available now are specially fattened birds, usually called 'capon-style' chickens, and their flavour is always good and the flesh tender. They tend to

weigh 3.5–4.5 kg (8–10 lb) and should be sufficient to feed up to 10 portions.

Boiling fowl. These are older birds which are much tougher than the others as they are often over 18 months old and may have been former egg-layers. However they have an excellent flavour and, if cooked properly, will be tender. It is essential to remove any fat from inside the cavity before cooking. They usually weigh from 1.75–3 kg (4–7 lb) and should be cooked by boiling (in reality a gentle simmering) or stewing for about 3 hours or until tender. Add vegetables towards the end of the cooking time.

POULTRY ROASTING CHART

Type of Bird	Oven Temperature	Cooking Time
Chicken	200°C, 400°F, Gas Mark 6	20 minutes per 450 g (1 lb), plus 20 minutes over
Guinea Fowl	200°C, 400°F, Gas Mark 6	20 minutes per 450 g (1 lb), plus 20 minutes over
Duck	190–200°C, 375–400°F, Gas Mark 5–6	25–30 minutes per 450 g (1 lb)
Goose	Either 200°C, 400°F, Gas Mark 6 Or 180°C, 350°F, Gas Mark 4	15 minutes per 450 g (1 lb), plus 15 minutes over 25–30 minutes per 450 g (1 lb)

How to truss a chicken

Trussing keeps the bird in a good shape for roasting.

1. Insert a skewer widthwise right through the body of the bird just below the thigh bone so that the ends stick out at either side. Turn the bird over on to its breast.

2. Take a piece of string and first catch in the wing tips, then pass it under the ends of the skewer and cross it over the back.

3. Turn the bird over and tie the ends of the string together round the tail, at the same time securing the legs.

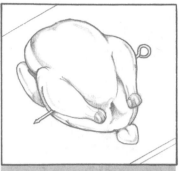

Insert skewer just below the thighs.

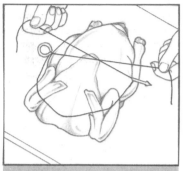

Turn chicken over and loop string round skewers.

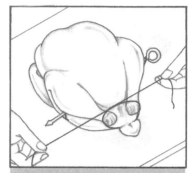

Turn over again and tie in legs and parson's nose.

Cooking chicken

■ When calculating the cooking time (see chart, page 111), always allow at least 15 minutes for possible extra cooking. Sometimes if the legs are trussed very tightly against the body, this will increase the cooking time. Some birds are much 'thicker' whilst others are more slimline, and the cooking times will vary slightly with these different shapes.
■ If taking the bird straight from the refrigerator to the oven, increase the cooking time by 10–15 minutes to allow the bird to warm up before it starts to cook.
■ To test if the chicken is cooked, take a fine skewer and pierce the thickest part of the thigh. If the juices run clear the bird is cooked; but if they are tinged pink, however slightly, return to the oven for a further 10 minutes and test again.
■ Like meat, poultry should be allowed to stand and set for about 10 minutes before carving.

Cutting up Chicken or Duck

If you want to cook poultry in portions it is much more economical to cut it up yourself. Individual portions bought in a butcher or even supermarket are always more expensive, weight for weight, than buying a whole bird. Learn how to do this at home and save money.

All you need is a chopping board and a heavy knife. Poultry shears are also useful. The secret is to first find the joints and so cut through the tendons and cartilage, rather than hacking through bones.

1. Place the bird with the legs facing you and pull one leg away from the body. Cut through the skin down to where the thigh joins the body. Bend the leg outwards to expose the ball and socket joint and cut down between the ball and socket to free the whole leg. Repeat with the other leg. A large leg can then be cut into drumstick and thigh.

2. Press down through the shoulder joint attaching the wing to the body, then cut down through the skin at the base of the wing. Repeat with the other wing.

Cutting off the leg joint

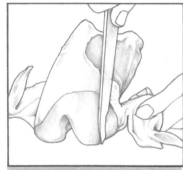

Cutting through the wing joint

Detaching breast from the rest of the carcass

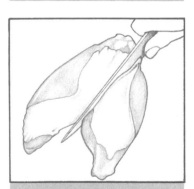

Cutting down along the breastbone

3. Place the knife inside the carcass and carefully slit along the ribs on both sides to separate the breast from the lower carcass. Pull the breast away from the back to expose the shoulder bones and cut down to detach the breast.

4. Place the breast skin side up on the board and cut down on one side or other of the breastbone to give two breasts. With larger birds the breast portions can then be cut widthways to give 4 or 6 portions.

Roast Chicken

Serves 4
1 oven-ready chicken
1 slice raw onion or ½ lemon
(optional)
softened butter or oil
salt
freshly ground black pepper
streaky bacon rashers
(optional)
dripping

Preparation time: about 10 minutes
Cooking time: see chart (page 111)
Oven: see chart (page 111)

1. If the bird was frozen make sure that it is completely thawed and that no ice crystals remain inside the cavity. Remove the giblets and any loose fat from inside the cavity.

2. If using stuffing (see page 114), it is better to only stuff the neck end of the bird, making any excess stuffing into balls to cook around the bird or press into an ovenproof dish and cook below the bird for about 30 minutes. Fold the neck skin over the stuffing to enclose it, then truss the bird as usual. A piece of onion or lemon can be put inside the cavity for extra flavour and to help keep it moist.

3. Weigh the bird and calculate the cooking time from the chart, allowing time to 'set' before carving etc. Put the bird into a roasting tin with the breast upwards. Rub or brush all over with softened butter or oil. Season lightly with salt and pepper, and lay a few rashers of streaky bacon over the breast to help keep it moist during cooking, if liked. Add a little dripping to the roasting pan and add peeled parboiled potatoes to roast if wished.

4. Roast in a preheated oven for the recommended time, basting occasionally with the fat in the tin. If stuffing balls are to be cooked, place on a baking sheet or around the bird for the last 20–30 minutes of cooking. Remove the bacon, if used, about 15 minutes before the end of cooking time, to allow the breast to brown.

5. When ready, remove the chicken and the potatoes to a serving dish. Spoon off the fat from the pan and use the juices for the base of a gravy.

6. If you prefer to roast a chicken in foil, wrap the weighed bird loosely in buttered foil and stand in a roasting tin. Increase the cooking time by about 5 minutes per 450 g (1 lb) and fold back the foil for the last 15–20 minutes of cooking time to brown up the bird.

Accompaniments to roast chicken

Bacon rolls; stuffing balls or stuffing in the neck end of the bird; bread sauce; thin gravy.

Bread Sauce

1 medium onion, peeled
5–6 whole cloves
450 ml (¾ pint) milk
1 bay leaf
6 black peppercorns
25 g (1 oz) butter
75 g (3 oz) fresh white
breadcrumbs
salt
freshly ground black pepper

Preparation time: about 15 minutes, plus infusing
Cooking time: about 15 minutes

1. Stud the onion evenly with the cloves. Put into a saucepan with the milk, bay leaf and peppercorns and bring up to the boil.

2. Remove from the heat and leave in a cool place to infuse for about 20 minutes or longer, if time allows.

3. Remove the peppercorns and bay leaf, and add the butter and breadcrumbs.

4. Bring slowly back to the boil, stirring continuously, and cook very gently for about 10 minutes until thick and creamy, stirring from time to time.

5. Discard the onion and season to taste. Serve hot with roast chicken, turkey or game birds.

How much to allow

For raw oven-ready chicken, allow at least 225 g (8 oz) per portion plus some extra to serve cold. A 1.25–1.5 kg (2½–3 lb) oven-ready chicken should therefore serve 3–4 portions.
For portions, allow 1 quarter, a wing or leg per portion, or one breast portion, whether boned or partly boned.
For drumsticks, allow 2–3 per portion, depending on size.
For wings, allow 2–3 per portion, again depending on size.
For thighs, allow 2 per portion.

Carving chicken

Follow the general rules for carving meat on page 128, and stand firmly on a board or large plate. Allow to rest and 'set' for about 5–10 minutes. Special poultry carvers are available and poultry shears are also good if you want to cut a chicken into quarters once it is cooked.

1. Stand the bird with the breast diagonally towards you.

2. Keeping the bird steady with the flat of the knife, prise the leg outwards with the fork to expose the thigh joint. Cut through this cleanly to remove the leg. The leg is then usually cut in half.

3. Hold the wing with the fork and cut through the outer layer of the breast, trying to judge where the wing joint comes, so that the wing is cut through cleanly in one go.

4. Slice the breast thinly parallel to the breast bone. When stuffing has been cooked in the neck of the bird it should be sliced from the front of the breast and the remainder removed with a spoon.

5. Turn the bird around and carve the other side in the same way.

TURKEY

This is probably the most versatile and economical of all the various kinds of poultry. Although large, it can be cooked in many different ways apart from the traditional roast. It is now also available cut into pieces of all shapes and sizes to suit all occasions – wings, thighs, drumsticks, escalopes, fillets, steaks etc, as well as rolled, boned 'roasts'.

Turkey is now available all year round, although the larger fresh birds are more readily available at Christmas, Easter and around bank holidays. The size of whole turkeys varies enormously from the mini birds of around 2.25 kg (5 lb) up to the very large ones of 13.5 kg (30 lb). An average domestic cooker can handle a turkey of about 10.5 kg (23 lb), but not much more. Always buy the giblets with a whole bird.

Portions available include wings, thighs (boned and with bone), drumsticks, escalopes, fillets, steaks, etc as well as the many types of rolled roasts.

Turkeys are available fresh, frozen and chilled as with most other poultry; but they do vary a little. Basically a fresh turkey is the one seen hanging up ready plucked but with the head still on. When it is bought it is then drawn and dressed, ready to cook. Fresh turkeys are always hung before preparation. Frozen turkeys, like frozen chickens, are killed, plucked, drawn and prepared all in one process which ends up with them being sealed into polythene bags and blast frozen. A chilled turkey goes through a similar process but is packed into a different sort of bag and then chilled and despatched to the stores immediately, for its shelf life is very limited.

Both fresh and chilled birds will keep in the refrigerator (out of any wrappings) for about 2 days before cooking. A frozen turkey, however, must be thawed out completely and preferably at room temperature or in a cool place. This should *not* be done in the refrigerator for, because of the size of the bird, the extra cold will lengthen the thawing process quite dramatically. Follow the chart for the recommended thawing times.

When stuffing a turkey, it is imperative that you only stuff the neck of the bird and not the body cavity. If the cavity is stuffed, it may mean that the turkey has to be really overcooked to ensure that the stuffing itself is cooked, and this ruins the texture of the flesh.

TURKEY THAWING TIMES AND SERVINGS

Oven-Ready Weight	Thawing Time at Room Temperature	Approx. Number of Servings
2.25–3.5 kg (5–8 lb)	15–18 hours	6–10
3.5–5 kg (8–11 lb)	18–20 hours	10–15
5–6.75 kg (11–15 lb)	20–24 hours	15–20
6.75–9 kg (15–20 lb)	24–30 hours	20–28
9–11.25 kg (20–25 lb)	30–36 hours	28–36

How to stuff and truss a turkey

1. Put the stuffing in the neck end only and fold the neck flap over so it completely encloses the stuffing. It can be secured with a small skewer or wooden cocktail sticks.

2. The bird can be trussed in a similar way to a chicken with the wings folded under the body, but do not tie the legs too tightly to the body or the heat of the oven will find it hard to penetrate the deepest part of the body and will increase the cooking time.

3. Put a quartered onion or lemon in the body cavity for flavour and to help keep it moist.

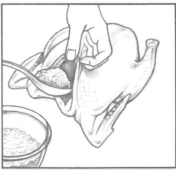

Stuff the neck end of the turkey

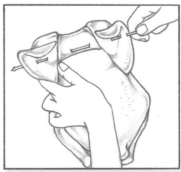

Fold over the neck flap and secure with a skewer.

Apricot Stuffing

Combine 100 g (4 oz) dried apricots, soaked, cooked and chopped with 1 onion, finely chopped and sautéed in butter. Add grated rind of ½ lemon, 2 tablespoons parsley, salt, pepper and pinch of mixed spice. Stir in 75 g (3 oz) fresh breadcrumbs and bind with beaten egg.

Pecan Stuffing

Mix together 40 g (1½ oz) boiled rice, 1 onion, chopped and sautéed in butter, 1 tablespoon chopped parsley, ½ teaspoon dried thyme, 40 g (1½ oz) chopped pecan nuts, ¼ teaspoon ground coriander and bind with beaten egg.

Roast Turkey

It is recommended that all sizes of turkey should be cooked at 180°C, 350°F, Gas Mark 4.

1 oven-ready turkey
softened butter
salt
freshly ground black pepper

Preparation time: about 10 minutes
Cooking time: see chart
Oven: 180°C, 350°F, Gas Mark 4

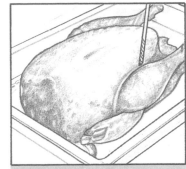
Use a skewer to test if the turkey is cooked

1. Once completely thawed (if frozen, and at room temperature), wipe out the inside of the bird with a clean cloth. Remove the giblets and use to make stock for the gravy.

2. Stuff the neck end of the bird only and truss; then weigh and stand in a greased roasting tin. Rub the bird all over with softened butter and season lightly.

3. Cook in a preheated moderate oven following the chart timings, either as it is or wrapped in foil, if preferred. Baste several times during cooking and, when sufficiently browned (if not cooked in foil), lay a sheet of foil or wet greaseproof paper over the breast. If cooking in foil, fold back the foil for the last 15–20 minutes of cooking to brown.

4. Check the bird is cooked by inserting a skewer in the deepest part of the thigh and then remove to a serving dish and allow to 'set' for about 10 minutes. If the bird was taken straight from the refrigerator allow an extra 15 minutes cooking time. Pour off the fat from the pan juices and use the juices with the giblet stock to make gravy.

6. Serve with bacon rolls, chipolata sausages, roast potatoes, Brussels sprouts, and cranberry sauce.

RECOMMENDED COOKING TIMES FOR TURKEY

Weight	Without foil	Wrapped in foil
2.25–3.5 kg (5–8 lb)	2–2½ hours	2½–3½ hours
3.5–5 kg (8–11 lb)	2½–3¼ hours	3½–4 hours
5–6.75 kg (11–15 lb)	3¼–3¾ hours	4–5 hours
6.75–9 kg (15–20 lb)	3¾–4¼ hours	5–5½ hours
9–11.25 kg (20–25 lb)	4¼–4¾ hours	Not recommended

How to carve a turkey

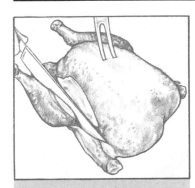
First remove the drumstick, leaving the thigh

Remove the wings and cut off the meat

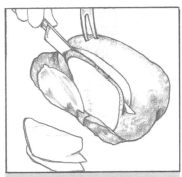
Carve slices from the breast lengthways

Stand on a board or a large plate with the breast facing upwards. Allow to 'set' for about 10 minutes.

1. Remove a drumstick, leaving the thigh on the bird and slice the meat from the drumstick.

2. Carve slices from the thigh and then remove the wings and strip the meat off neatly.

3. Carve thin slices from the breast, taking in slices from the stuffing as it is reached.

4. Serve a mixture of dark and white meat for each portion plus some stuffing. Finish carving one side before turning the bird round to do the other.

Cranberry Sauce

For an orange cranberry sauce, use orange juice in place of all or part of the water and add the grated rind of ½ orange.

175 g (6 oz) sugar
150 ml (¼ pint) water
225 g (8 oz) cranberries, fresh or frozen
1–2 tablespoons port (optional)

Preparation time: about 5 minutes
Cooking time: about 15 minutes

1. Dissolve the sugar in the water in a saucepan, and bring up to the boil. Stir occasionally and boil for about 5 minutes.

2. Add the cranberries, cover the pan and simmer gently until they have all popped. Remove the lid from the pan and continue simmering for about 5 minutes, until they are quite tender.

3. If liked add 1–2 tablespoons port, and leave to cool. Serve with roast turkey, lamb, game.

DUCK

The domestic duck or duckling is available all year round, both fresh and frozen as a whole bird and as portions. Duck has dark meat with a good rich flavour, a thick skin and plenty of fat. There is always very much less flesh on a duck than it might appear, thus anything that is less than 1.5 kg (3 lb) in weight is not a good buy for it is likely to be all bone with very little flesh. An average duck will weigh from 1.75–2.25 kg (4–5 lb) and, in general, one duck will not feed more than 4 people, if that. Larger birds are now being bred which will make duck even more popular.

When selecting a duck, it should be young with soft pliable feet, not rough or tough, and the feet and the bill should be yellow; a dark orange indicates age. A duckling is a bird between 6 weeks and 3 months old and the majority of ducks sold are, in fact, duckling. They tend to toughen as they age. Always try to get the giblets, as they can add flavour to the gravy.

Fresh ducks, like chickens, are always better than frozen. As there is so much fat on ducks, this can turn rancid if the bird is frozen for longer than 3 months. This fat content worries many when cooking duck, but if prepared and roasted carefully, the fat will flow out – and indeed has a wonderful flavour and should be kept to use for shallow-frying and roasting.

It is not traditional to stuff duck for roasting, although some cooks like to add a sage and onion stuffing to the duck rather than cook it separately. A stuffing will absorb a lot of fat. It is quite usual, though, to put a quartered onion inside the cavity of the duck before roasting.

Duck with Black Cherries

Serves 4
4 breast portions of duck or 4 halves of duck, if small
salt
freshly ground black pepper
1 × 425 g (15 oz) can black cherries, pitted
duck or chicken stock (optional) or water
grated rind of 1 orange
juice of 2 oranges
1 tablespoon lemon juice
1½ tablespoons cornflour
2–3 tablespoons port
To garnish:
orange wedges
watercress

Preparation time: about 30 minutes
Cooking time: about 50 minutes
Oven: 200°C, 400°F, Gas Mark 6

1. Season the duck with salt and pepper and prick the skin lightly with a fork. Put into a lightly greased roasting tin, and cook in a preheated oven for 10 minutes.

2. Meanwhile, drain the cherries, and make up the juice to 200 ml (7 fl oz) with water or stock. Add the orange rind and orange and lemon juices and pour over the duck. Return to the oven for 20 minutes, basting once.

3. Add the cherries to the roasting tin, baste the duck again, and continue to cook for 10–20 minutes or until the duck is tender.

4. Transfer the duck and cherries to a serving dish and keep warm. Spoon off any fat from the cooking juices and heat in a saucepan.

5. Blend the cornflour with the port and add to the juices. Boil for a minute or so then season to taste.

6. Spoon some of the sauce over the duck and serve the remainder separately. Garnish with orange wedges and watercress.

Roast Duck

First of all, if the duck was frozen, make absolutely sure that it is completely thawed.

Serves 4
1 oven-ready duck
salt
freshly ground black pepper

Preparation time: about 5 minutes
Cooking time: 25–30 minutes per 450 g (1 lb)
Oven: see chart (page 111)

1. Truss the duck if not already done, after removing the giblets and any extra fat from the cavity. Dry the skin thoroughly with paper towels: this allows it to crisp up during cooking.

2. Pierce deeply all over the skin of the duck with a fine skewer, and season with salt and pepper.

3. Stand the bird on a rack in a roasting tin. It is not necessary to add any fat to the pan, for as the duck begins to cook the fat will run copiously from the skin.

4. Roast in a preheated oven for the time recommended in the chart. Baste once, after about 45 minutes of the cooking time.

5. When ready, remove the duck to a serving dish and leave to 'set' for a few minutes. Spoon off all the fat from the tin before making gravy, otherwise it is likely to taste very fatty.

Carving duck

1. The easiest way to carve a duck is to cut it into quarters, once it has been cooked, using a pair of poultry shears. A sharp kitchen knife can also be used.

2. Begin at the neck and cut along the length of the breast bone. Split it in half completely by cutting through the backbone and then make a diagonal cut through the wings and legs to give the four portions.

3. Another way is to remove the legs and wings in a similar way to a chicken, and then carve the breast meat in long slices the whole length of the body, keeping parallel with the breast bone.

GOOSE

This is a rather expensive bird which was once rather difficult to obtain. However, it is becoming much more readily available now, both fresh and frozen. It is a large bony bird with a very poor flesh to body size ratio. The flesh, though, has a very fine flavour and texture. It is usually very tender, although it can be a little greasy if insufficient care is taken before and during cooking. Like duck, goose is very fatty and should always be pricked all over with a skewer and then stood on a rack to cook so that it doesn't stew in its own fat.

An oven-ready goose should weigh about 4.5 kg (10 lb) and will feed 6–8 people only, so it is an extravagant bird to serve. The bird must be young, preferably under 6 months old, with soft yellow feet, a yellow bill and yellowish fat.

Truss it with skewers and string after cutting off the feet and wings at the first joint. Put a skewer through the wing then through the body and out again through the opposite wing. Put a second skewer through the end of the wing joint on one side, through the thick part of the leg, through the body and out the other side in the same way. Put a third skewer through the loose skin near the end of the leg, through the body and out the same way. Wind string around the skewers to keep the body in shape, but do not take the string over the breast. Tuck the neck skin under the string.

A goose for roasting – the best way of cooking them – can be stuffed with a sage and onion stuffing, but the stuffing is more often cooked and served separately. A prune or apple stuffing tastes good, as does a stuffing containing the liver of the bird. A quick and simple way of cutting down on richness and adding flavour is to put some peeled and cored sour apples in the cavity.

Roast Goose

Serves 6–8
1 oven ready goose
salt

Preparation time: about 5 minutes
Cooking time: see chart (page 111)
Oven: see chart (page 111)

1. Dry the skin very well with paper towels. Sprinkle the bird all over with salt and stand on a rack in a roasting tin. Prick the skin lightly with a skewer – not as much as for a duck – to help the fat run out and then cover with a sheet of lightly greased greaseproof paper.

2. Add about 4 tablespoons water to the roasting tin and then cook by either of the methods on the chart. The goose may be basted once or twice if liked (you'll probably have to remove some fat from the tin anyway), and the paper should be removed for the last 20 minutes or so of cooking to crisp up the skin.

3. Pour off virtually all the fat from the tin and retain. (It's a delicacy, wonderful for roasting or sautéing potatoes.) Use the juices to make a thin gravy, preferably with stock from the giblets.

4. Serve with a thin gravy, apple or gooseberry sauce, fried apple rings and sage and onion stuffing.

How to carve a goose

Follow the general principles for carving meat on page 128, and stand the bird on a board with the breast upwards. Allow to 'rest' and 'set' for about 15 minutes.

1. Take off the trussing string and remove the skewers and then remove the legs and wings.

2. Carve thickish slices from either side of the breast bone taking the slices the whole length of the body. Carve the meat off the legs and wings and serve with the breast meat.

3. If the bird is stuffed, carve off the slices with the breast meat and remove the rest with a spoon.

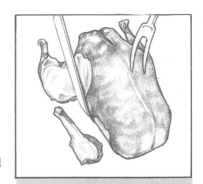
Remove the legs and wings before carving

Place the goose on a rack before roasting

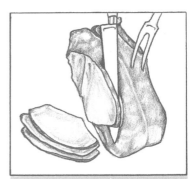
Carve long slices along the whole length of the body

GAME

The term 'game' is generally applied to animals and birds that live in the wild, and that are hunted and killed for food or sport. They are protected by rigorous game laws which allow them to be shot only at certain times of the year – not during the breeding season, or when they are rearing their young. The wide variety of feathered game includes all the game birds and water fowl, and furred game includes venison and hare.

Preparation and selection of game

Game is mainly available fresh, and is displayed by butchers and game dealers as well as some fishmongers whilst it is in season. It is always hung in feather or fur (apart from venison), and undrawn for birds and hares. Birds are hung by their neck and hares and rabbits by their feet. Hanging is essential to help to tenderize the meat and to improve the characteristic flavour associated with game. The length of time required for the hanging varies greatly, depending on a number of factors: the type of game; whether it was well or badly shot (badly torn flesh will not last as long); the weather conditions – (cold weather slows down the ripening process whilst warm muggy weather hastens it – sometimes quite dramatically); and on the degree of ripeness preferred. For birds, they are usually ready when one of the tail feathers can be plucked out quite easily.

Some Game Seasons

Pheasant: October 1–February 1
Partridge: September 1–February 1
Red Grouse: Ptarmigan: August 12–December 10
Black Grouse (Blackcock): August 20–December 10
Wild Duck: mainly September 1–January 31
Pigeon: No close season
Quail: No close season
Hare: No close season
Rabbit: No close season
Venison: some type of venison is available all year.

Partridge These are small game birds which will serve only 1 portion. The flavour of partridge is delicate and natural, and the birds are thought to be at their best in October. They are available fresh and frozen.

Young plucked birds weigh up to 400 g (14 oz). They are best roasted, but are also good when spatchcocked (see page 119) to cook under the grill or on a barbecue. Older birds will weigh up to 450 g (1 lb) or more.

Wild Duck Wild ducks are frequently not hung at all, but may be hung for about 24 hours. Because of their diet, it is unwise to keep them hanging for longer; the flesh deteriorates very quickly, and the flavour can become rancid.

All wild duck have very dry flesh because they are virtually fat-free. For this reason, when they are roasted, the skins should not be pricked like domestic duck; instead cover liberally with fat to prevent them drying out.

Roast wild duck should be served only just barely done, sometimes slightly underdone (fine unless you've acquired a tough old bird which would have been better braised). Timing is important, for if they are too underdone they will be inedible; and if overcooked they will be dry, tasteless and a complete waste of time.

A mallard or large wild duck should serve 2 people whilst the smaller birds will serve only 1 portion.

Serve roast wild duck (of all

TYPES OF GAME

varieties) with a thin gravy made using the giblets and pan juices and often flavoured with orange and port; or a Bigarade or orange-flavoured brown sauce; game chips or creamed potatoes; orange wedges or an orange salad.

Grouse There are several species of grouse in Britain, the best known being the red grouse – to many, the finest of all game birds. Other varieties of grouse are the black grouse – known also as the blackcock (male) and greyhen (female) – the ptarmigan and capercaillie.

As with most other game, it is much better if well hung, for about 4–5 days on average, sometimes even as long as 2 weeks for those who prefer a really gamey flavour.

They are usually only available fresh. Young birds should have bright eyes, soft pliable feet and smooth legs, and the breast bone should feel soft and pliable too. They are best roasted. As the birds age the breast bone hardens and the feet and legs become hard and scaly. Older birds can be marinated and casseroled, made into pâtés or pies, or potted. One grouse will usually serve only 1, although sometimes the really large ones will serve 2.

Grouse to be roasted should be well barded (see page 128) and should be cooked until only just done, but if it was hung until 'high' it should be cooked really well. The liver is considered such a delicacy, that it is generally fried lightly, mashed and spread on an oval

slice of bread. This is slipped under the bird towards the end of cooking time and it absorbs many of the delicious juices. Serve roast grouse with a thin gravy made from the giblets.

Quail These are the smallest European game birds (like tiny partridges). In the wild they are migratory, so only available in Europe during the summer, but they are now bred for the table at rearing farms. As they are so small, 2 can be served for a good portion, but 1 is usually enough, and eating them in the fingers is almost obligatory.

Quails must be eaten really fresh – within 24 hours of being killed – and they are most usually roasted, well barded (see page 128). Their meat is soft and tender, with more flavour than chicken.

Pigeon Wood pigeon are in season all year, but are considered best from March to September when birds are young. A young bird is recognizable by its small pink legs, fat breast and flexible beak. Pigeons do not need to be hung but, if freshly killed, hanging head downwards for an hour or so will lighten the flesh. They should be plucked and drawn immediately.

If plump and young, 1 bird will serve a portion; 2 squabs (fledglings) are needed per portion, and an older larger bird will serve 2 portions if casseroled with other ingredients. A roast bird will need to be barded well with streaky bacon.

Roast Pheasant

This is probably the best known and most popular of all the game birds. It is available fresh and frozen and now can often be found in larger supermarkets. Birds are often available – and cheaper – by the brace, meaning a cock and a hen. The cock is larger, with brightly coloured plumage, while the dull brown hen is plumper and more succulent, and generally considered the better for eating. Pheasant should be hung for at least 3 days for a good flavour to develop, but it can be as long as 3 weeks if the weather is exceptionally cold.

Young birds are best roasted but more mature birds – which have a better flavour – will be tougher, so need the longer cooking of casseroling, braising or pot-roasting to ensure they are tender. One pheasant will serve 2–3 people when roasted, and larger mature birds may serve up to 4 when casseroled with other ingredients.

1 oven-ready young pheasant
butter
a wedge of lemon or onion
salt
freshly ground black pepper
3–4 rashers streaky bacon or a
  piece of pork fat, beaten
  thinly
plain flour (optional)
watercress, to garnish

1. Wipe the pheasant inside and out and place a knob of butter and the lemon or onion in the cavity.

2. Tie the legs together with string and stand the bird in a roasting tin. Pour or spoon some melted butter (or dripping) over the bird and season lightly if liked. Lay the bacon rashers or pork fat over the breast.

3. Cook in a hot oven for the time recommended on the chart, basting every 15 minutes. Test the deepest part of the thigh with a fine skewer to check it is cooked through. The bacon rashers or fat can be removed 15 minutes before the end of cooking, and the breast lightly dredged with flour and left to brown up before serving. Pheasant should be completely cooked, not underdone as with some game.

4. Remove the string from the bird and serve garnished with watercress.
Accompaniments should be game chips, fried breadcrumbs, bread sauce and a thin gravy made using the pan juices and giblets.

GAME BIRD ROASTING CHART

Type of Game	Oven Temperature	Cooking Time
Pheasant	220°C, 425°F, Gas Mark 7	45–60 mins, depending on size
Partridge	220°C, 425°F, Gas Mark 7	30–45 mins, depending on size
Grouse	220°C, 425°F, Gas Mark 7	30–45 mins, depending on size
Wild Duck	220°C, 425°F, Gas Mark 7	30–50 mins for mallard 30–40 mins for widgeon 20–30 mins for teal and other small birds
Pigeon	200°C, 400°F, Gas Mark 6	about 30 mins, depending on size
Quail	180°C, 350°F, Gas Mark 4	20 mins

How to spatchcock

1. Cut along one side of the backbone

2. Cut along other side to remove backbone

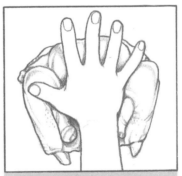

3. Lay the bird breast up and flatten with your hand

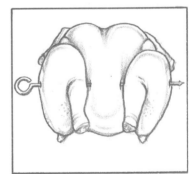

4. Skewer through beneath thighs to anchor wings

Most poultry and game are suitable for spatchcocking and it is a particularly good way of serving poussins or small game birds which are then served as a whole portion.

Spatchcocked birds, marinaded in oil, spices and herbs, can be cooked under a conventional grill or cooked over a barbecue. To prevent the birds drying out, baste frequently with oil or with the marinade.

POULTRY & GAME RECIPES

*Ring the changes with two unusual casseroles –
Pheasant with Chestnuts, and Pigeon with Juniper and
Raisins – and perfect your technique with two great
classics – Coq au Vin, chicken and mushrooms
in red wine, and tangy Duck à l'Orange.*

Pigeon with Juniper and Raisin Sauce

Juniper berries are a traditional accompaniment to game and are worth adding to marinades and beefy pies, to give extra flavour. Pigeons are now widely available, and can often be found in supermarkets.

Serves 4
50 g (2 oz) butter
4 plump pigeons, plucked, drawn and trussed
4 rashers streaky bacon, rinded and diced
1 small onion, peeled and finely chopped
1 celery stick, trimmed and chopped
1 tablespoon plain flour
150 ml (¼ pint) red wine
150 ml (¼ pint) Chicken Stock (see page 25)
8 juniper berries, crushed
8 coriander seeds, crushed
salt
freshly ground black pepper
50 g (2 oz) seedless raisins, soaked in 4 tablespoons port for 3–4 hours
1 tablespoon redcurrant jelly
To garnish:
4 slices fried bread, cut into triangles
4 bay leaves
whole juniper berries

Preparation time: 15 minutes, plus soaking
Cooking time: about 1¾–2 hours
Oven: 150°C, 300°F, Gas Mark 2

1. Melt the butter in a flameproof casserole and fry the pigeons gently until lightly browned on all sides. Remove from the pan and reserve.

2. Add the bacon to the casserole and cook until the fat begins to flow, then add the onion and celery and cook for 4–5 minutes until soft and lightly browned. Sprinkle in the flour and stir over a moderate heat for 1 minute.

3. Remove the casserole from the heat and gradually blend in the red wine and stock. Return to the heat, bring to the boil and simmer for 1 minute, stirring. Add the juniper berries and coriander seeds, stir together well and season with salt and pepper. Return the pigeons to the pan and coat with the sauce. Bring back to the boil.

4. Cover closely with a lid or foil and cook in the oven for 1 hour. Stir in the raisins and port. Cover again and return to the oven for a further 30 minutes or until very tender.

5. Transfer the pigeons to a heated serving dish. Skim any fat from the sauce, stir in the redcurrant jelly and reheat if necessary. Pour a little sauce over the pigeons and garnish with a border of fried bread, bay leaves and juniper berries. Serve the remaining sauce separately in a heated sauce-boat.

Duck à l'Orange

One of the best known duck recipes is this roast duck decorated with fresh orange and accompanied by a rich, orange-flavoured brown sauce. Remember duck serves less meat for its weight than chicken.

Serves 4
1 duck, about 2.5 kg (5½ lb)
salt
freshly ground black pepper
1 orange
½ onion, peeled and sliced
1 tablespoon plain flour
150 ml (¼ pint) giblet stock (see Poultry Gravy, page 25)
juice of 2 oranges
juice of 1 lemon
2 tablespoons cognac or curaçao
2 tablespoons sugar
2 tablespoons water
To garnish:
fresh orange segments
watercress sprigs

Preparation time: 20 minutes
Cooking time: about 2½ hours
Oven: 180°C, 350°F, Gas Mark 4

1. Prick the duck all over with a fork and season inside and out with salt and pepper. Thinly pare the orange rind and reserve. Remove all the pith and cut the orange into slices. Add the orange slices to the duck cavity along with the onion.

2. Place the duck on a rack in a roasting tin and roast until tender, allowing 20 minutes per 450 g (1 lb) plus 30 minutes. Drain off the fat that drips into the tin from time to time.

3. When the duck is cooked, remove to a heated dish and keep warm. Drain off all but 2 tablespoons of the fat from the tin and over gentle heat stir in the flour, scraping all the sediment from the base and sides of the tin with a wooden spoon. Gradually stir in the stock, then the orange and lemon juice and cognac. Cook gently, stirring, until thickened.

4. Meanwhile, blend the sugar and water in a small saucepan and stir until dissolved over gentle heat. Raise the heat and boil without stirring until the sugar caramelizes and becomes a dark brown. Add this to the sauce and stir in well.

5. Blanch the reserved orange rind in boiling water for 2 minutes, then cut into fine shreds.

6. Place the duck on a heated serving dish. Strain over the sauce and sprinkle with the orange rind. Garnish with orange segments and watercress sprigs and serve immediately.

From the top: Duck à l'orange, Pigeon with juniper and raisin sauce

Pheasant in Red Wine with Chestnuts

The season for pheasant is from the 1st October to 1st February though it can be bought frozen outside these times. It should have been hung for 5–7 days after being shot.

Serves 5–6

2 oven-ready pheasants
salt
freshly ground black pepper
3 tablespoons oil or dripping
2 large onions, peeled and
*   sliced*
2 tablespoons plain flour
450 ml (³/4 pint) red wine
450 ml (³/4 pint) Brown Stock
*   (see page 27)*
1 tablespoon redcurrant jelly
3–4 tablespoons brandy
*   (optional)*
1 bay leaf
1 × 440 g (15¹/2 oz) can whole
*   peeled chestnuts, drained*
Stuffing balls:
50 g (2 oz) butter or margarine
2 onions, peeled and very
*   finely chopped*
175 g (6 oz) celery, very finely
*   chopped*
2 tablespoons chopped fresh
*   parsley*
2 teaspoons dried thyme
350 g (12 oz) fresh white
*   breadcrumbs*
2 eggs, beaten
a little lemon juice (optional)
parsley sprigs, to garnish

Preparation time: about 40 minutes
Cooking time: about 1³/4 hours
Oven: 180°C, 350°F, Gas Mark 4

1. Wipe the pheasants inside and out and season well with salt and pepper. Heat the oil in a large frying pan, add the pheasants one at a time and fry, turning, to brown all over. Transfer to a large casserole dish.

2. Add the onions to the pan and fry over a gentle heat for about 7 minutes until lightly browned. Sprinkle in the flour and cook for 1–2 minutes. Gradually stir in the wine and stock and bring to the boil. Stir in the redcurrant jelly and brandy, if using, season well with salt and pepper and add the bay leaf. Simmer for 2 minutes.

3. Add the chestnuts and pour the contents of the pan over the

pheasants. Bring back to the boil. Cover and cook in a preheated oven for about 1¹/4 hours or until tender and cooked through.

4. Meanwhile make the stuffing balls: melt the butter in a frying pan, add the onion and celery and fry over a gentle heat until soft. Turn into a bowl, season well with salt and pepper and add the herbs. Add the breadcrumbs and stir in the eggs to bind, with a little lemon

juice if using. Form the mixture into 20 balls.

5. Arrange the stuffing balls in a greased tin and cook above the pheasants for the last 30 minutes of cooking time.

6. Transfer the pheasants to a large warmed serving dish. Garnish with the stuffing balls and parsley sprigs. Pour the juices from the roasting tin with the onions and chestnuts into a heated sauce boat.

Coq au Vin

A variety of wines will suit this recipe – even a white will do if red is unavailable. Use a fresh chicken for best results and serve with boiled potatoes.

Serves 6–8

2 tablespoons oil
50 g (2 oz) butter
1 chicken, about 1.75 kg (4 lb),
*   cut into serving pieces (see*
*   page 112 for how to cut up*
*   chicken)*
24 small pickling onions,
*   peeled*
100 g (4 oz) smoked bacon,
*   rind removed and cubed*
1 tablespoon brandy
1 bottle good red wine
300 ml (¹/2 pint) Brown Stock
*   (see page 27)*
1 bouquet garni
2 garlic cloves, peeled and
*   crushed*
1 tablespoon tomato purée
pinch of freshly grated nutmeg
salt
freshly ground black pepper
24 button mushrooms
25 g (1 oz) butter and 25 g
*   (1 oz) flour, blended to form*
*   Beurre Manié (see page 33)*
2 tablespoons finely chopped
*   parsley, to garnish*
triangles of fried bread, to serve

Preparation time: 20 minutes
Cooking time: 1¹/2 hours

1. Heat the oil and butter in a large flameproof casserole, add the chicken pieces and fry gently until golden on all sides. Remove from the casserole with a slotted spoon and reserve.

2. Pour off half the fat from the casserole, then add the onions and bacon. Fry over moderate heat until lightly coloured. Return the chicken pieces to the casserole and season. Cover and cook gently on top of the stove for 10 minutes.

3. Uncover the pan and pour in the brandy. Averting your face, ignite with a lighted match. Shake the casserole until the flames subside.

4. Pour in the wine and add enough stock to cover the chicken. Add the bouquet garni, garlic, tomato purée and nutmeg, salt and pepper to taste. Lower the heat, cover and simmer for 15 minutes.

5. Add the mushrooms, then continue cooking gently for a further 30 minutes or until the chicken is tender. Remove the chicken, onions and mushrooms with a slotted spoon and keep warm.

6. Skim the fat off the surface of the sauce, then raise the heat and boil rapidly for about 5 minutes, until the liquid has been reduced to about 600 ml (1 pint).

7. Beat the beurre manié piece by piece into the sauce with a wire whisk, whisking well between each addition. Bring the sauce to simmering point – it should be thick enough to coat the back of a spoon.

8. Return the chicken pieces to the casserole, place the onions and mushrooms around and baste with the sauce. Sprinkle with the parsley and serve hot, with triangles of fried bread.

From the top: Pheasant in red wine with chestnuts, Coq au vin

Roast Turkey with Chestnut Stuffing

Chestnuts, with their distinctive, slightly sweet flavour, are often used in stuffings for poultry. Fresh chestnuts should be peeled and simmered in stock for about an hour, until tender.

Serves 8
1 turkey, about 5.5–6.5 kg (12–14 lb), defrosted if frozen
50 g (2 oz) butter, softened
175 g (6 oz) fat bacon rashers
Chestnut stuffing:
50 g (2 oz) streaky bacon, rinded and finely chopped
25 g (1 oz) butter or margarine
1 turkey liver, finely chopped
1 tablespoon chopped onion
1 tablespoon chopped celery
450 g (1 lb) cooked fresh or canned chestnuts, chopped
1 tablespoon chopped parsley
100 g (4 oz) fresh white breadcrumbs
4 teaspoons grated lemon rind
salt
freshly ground black pepper
lemon juice, to taste
2 eggs, beaten
Gravy:
giblets, from the turkey
1 bay leaf
sprig of parsley
1 small onion or shallot, peeled
8 black peppercorns
salt
freshly ground black pepper
1 teaspoon cornflour (optional)

Preparation time: 45 minutes
Cooking times: Stuffing: 7 minutes
Turkey: 3¾–4¼ hours if frozen
2¾–3¼ hours if fresh
Oven temperatures: 160°C, 325°F, Gas Mark 3, if frozen; 220°C, 425°F, Gas Mark 7, if fresh

1. Make the stuffing: cook the bacon gently until the fat runs. Add the butter or margarine and fry the chopped turkey liver, onion and celery until slightly coloured.

2. Stir in the chopped chestnuts. Add the chopped parsley, breadcrumbs and lemon rind and mix well. Season to taste with salt and pepper and sharpen with lemon juice. Bind with the beaten eggs.

3. Stuff the neck of the turkey and secure with skewers, following the instructions on page 114. Place the turkey in a greased roasting pan. Spread softened butter all over the bird and cover the whole of the breast and the top of the legs, with the bacon rashers.

4. Cover the bird with oiled foil, place in the preheated oven and cook for the given time. About 30 minutes before the end of the cooking time remove the foil and bacon and allow the bird to brown. Test for doneness by inserting a skewer into the thickest part of the thigh. When the juices run clear, the bird is cooked.

5. Make the gravy: while the bird is cooking put all the gravy ingredients in a small pan with enough water to cover. Simmer for 20 minutes, strain and reserve.

6. Place the turkey on a warmed serving platter and spoon off the fat from the pan, leaving the juices at the bottom. Add the giblet stock, scrape up the juices from the pan and boil briskly until the liquid is reduced and the gravy is a good colour. Thicken with cornflour, if liked.

7. Serve the turkey with the bacon, stuffing and gravy.

Jugged Hare

Boiled or mashed potatoes or forcemeat balls are the classic accompaniment to jugged hare. It is such a rich dish that it is best served with only the plainest of vegetables. Ask the butcher for the hare's blood, if using. The blood must not be allowed to boil, or it will curdle.

Serves 6
2 tablespoons red wine vinegar
2.5 kg (5 lb) hare, jointed and blood reserved (optional)
65 g (2½ oz) butter
2 tablespoons vegetable oil
100 g (4 oz) smoked bacon, rind removed and diced
18 small pickling onions, peeled
225 g (8 oz) button mushrooms, thinly sliced
2 tablespoons brandy
2 tablespoons plain flour
salt
freshly ground black pepper
ground mixed spice
Marinade:
4 carrots, scraped and roughly chopped
2 onions, peeled and roughly chopped
1 garlic clove, peeled and crushed
1 bay leaf
2 parsley sprigs
1 thyme sprig
1 rosemary sprig
1 litre (1¾ pints) full-bodied red wine

Preparation time: 40 minutes, plus marinating
Cooking time: 1½ hours

1. Add the vinegar to the blood, if using, to prevent it coagulating.

2. Put all the ingredients for the marinade in a large bowl with pepper to taste and stir well. Add the pieces of hare and mix well. Leave in a cool place (not in the refrigerator) for 24 hours, turning the hare over from time to time.

3. Remove the pieces of hare from the marinade and dry thoroughly on paper towels. Reserve the marinade.

4. Melt the butter in a large flameproof casserole, add the oil, then the bacon and whole onions. Fry gently until the onions are lightly coloured on all sides, then remove with a slotted spoon and drain on paper towels. Add the mushrooms to the casserole, fry gently for 1–2 minutes, then remove and drain with the bacon and onions.

5. Pour off half the fat from the casserole, then add the pieces of hare and fry briskly until lightly coloured on all sides. Sprinkle in the brandy, then the flour, and stir until the fat is absorbed.

6. Strain the reserved marinade over the hare, pouring in just enough to cover. Add salt, pepper and spice to taste, then the drained onions, bacon and mushrooms. Bring to the boil, then lower the heat, cover and simmer gently for 1 hour or until the hare is tender. Stir occasionally during cooking.

7. Stir about 4 tablespoons of the cooking liquid from the hare into the blood, if using, adding only a little at a time to prevent it curdling. Pour this mixture slowly back into the casserole, stirring constantly. Reheat carefully without boiling for 2 minutes.

8. Taste and adjust the seasoning of the sauce, then transfer to a warmed deep serving dish. Serve immediately, with redcurrant jelly and mashed potatoes.

From the top: Roast turkey with chestnut stuffing, Jugged hare

BEEF

Roast beef with Yorkshire pudding is undoubtedly everyone's favourite. But there are so many other ways of cooking beef, with an abundance of different cuts to choose from. This section includes carving details, roasting times and classic recipes.

When you buy beef, the lean of the meat should be bright to dark red with the fat a creamy white. Small flecks of fat should be visible throughout the lean. Flesh that has a dark red colour indicates that the carcass has been well hung, essential if the meat is to have a good flavour and be very tender. Bright red meat often indicates that it is very fresh and unhung or not hung long enough for the flavour to develop properly.

Freezing meat

Joints and cuts of meat can be bought ready frozen from a butcher or supermarket to simply transfer to your own freezer. However, if you want to freeze the meat you have just bought, do check with your butcher that it hasn't already been frozen. If so, it would be very unwise to refreeze it. Before freezing meat at home, it is important to wrap it very securely with polythene or foil, making sure there are no tears in the wrapping (if there are sharp bones, pad these first with foil before wrapping). Make sure too that all air has been excluded from the pack, then label clearly giving the cut, amount and date of freezing.

Meat keeps well in the freezer, but it must be of top quality and very fresh if pork or veal; lamb or beef should have been hung for the requisite time. The fat on the meat will turn rancid after a time, so it is wise to remove any excess visible fat before freezing. Joints of lamb, beef and veal will freeze well for up to 1 year; steaks and chops are best used within 6–8 months. Boneless braising or stewing meat can be stored in the freezer for about 6 months. Pork does keep well but the flavour can deteriorate quickly.

Guide to the cuts of beef

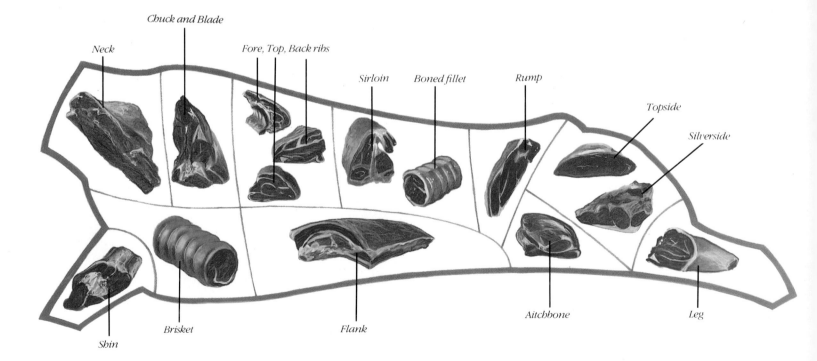

Neck · Chuck and Blade · Fore, Top, Back ribs · Sirloin · Boned fillet · Rump · Topside · Silverside · Shin · Brisket · Flank · Aitchbone · Leg

CUTS OF BEEF

In different parts of the country and in other countries such as France the same cuts of beef and other meats are often given a different name. Those used here are generally the most commonly known in Britain.

Sirloin A boned and rolled joint with a good layer of fat to protect it, coming from the back of the animal. It is very suitable for roasting. It is also sold on the bone and can be bought with the 'undercut' on it (fillet). The joints can be cut to any size required. Usually it makes a round of about 18 cm (7 inches) across, but this can be larger or smaller depending on the size of the animal it is taken from. Steaks can also be cut from the sirloin.

Ribs come as wing rib, top rib, back rib and fore rib joints and they too can be bought on the bone or as boned and rolled joints. The flavour is particularly good when cooked on the bone and this joint makes a most impressive centrepiece. Roast for preference, but these joints can also be pot-roasted or braised.

Topside or top round This joint is usually boned and rolled. As it is a very lean cut with little or no fat of its own, a strip of extra fat (barding fat) is often tied on by the butcher to prevent it from becoming over-dry when cooked. It can be roasted, although pot-roasting or braising often gives a better result, for the liquid involved keeps it more moist.

Silverside or round This is a popular joint, always boneless, which can also be bought salted to serve for the traditional boiled beef and carrots. It needs the long slow cooking achieved by boiling or braising, or if preferred, pot-roasting.

Aitchbone or top rump This is also known as thick flank. These are usually boned and rolled joints, but they can be bought on the bone if you ask your butcher. It is a little fatty on the top, but has a good flavour and also can be salted. Best to pot-roast, braise or grill joints, but slices can be fried or grilled.

Brisket has an excellent flavour, but tends to be fatty so always look for a lean piece. It is best boned and rolled when some of the excess fat can be discarded, but it can also be cooked on the bone. It is best cooked by a long slow method such as braising or pot-roasting. It is also available salted or pickled. It is good served hot and cold.

Rump This is the joint next to the sirloin and one of the most usual cuts made into steaks and used for grilling and frying. The 'point' is considered the best part for flavour and tenderness – the flavour of rump is always good, but it may not always be as tender as it should. There is a layer of fat all along the top edge of this steak and it is usually cut from 2–3 cm (¾–1¼ inches) thick.

Fillet This is cut from the centre of the sirloin. It is probably one of the best known and most expensive cuts of beef, and steaks cut from it have no fat at all. It is very tender, but the flavour is probably not as good as that of rump.
Different parts of the fillet are called by different names, according to what end of the fillet they are cut from; sometimes the name depends on the thickness of the steak (as

Stewing meats These include leg and shin which are the cheapest cuts and need the longest and slowest of cooking to really tenderize them, though the flavour is excellent. Neck and clod are also good for stews, but have less flavour and are less gelatinous than shin. Skirt and flank are boneless cuts which can be stewed but are normally made into mince. Chuck and blade steak are the best cuts of stewing steak and they require less cooking. These cuts should not have too much thick fat on the outside, but the flesh of the meat should be well 'marbled' or streaked with flecks of fat. For all stewing steak, either stew, braise or casserole. It can also be used in meat pies, and boiled for stock.

TYPES OF STEAKS

with Chateaubriand, see below). What we call, in general, fillet steaks are cut from the tail end of the fillet, and are known by the French as filets, tournedos and filets mignons.
Fillet steaks are generally slices of 2.5–5 cm (1–2 inches) thick and they are often shaped into rounds known as tournedos. These weigh from 150–225 g (5–8 oz).

Sirloin This is cut into two parts to give the porterhouse steak and the T-bone steak. The upper part of the sirloin is cut into thin steaks which are called 'minute' steaks. Thicker slices cut from the sirloin joint about 2.5 cm (1 inch) thick resemble the shape of a large boneless lamb chop. All these steaks have a layer of fat along the top edge.

Entrecôte This is really the part of the meat between the ribs of

Minced or ground beef Various qualities of mince are available, some of which, at the top end of the price market, are almost fat free. At the other end of the market is the cheapest quality which does contain a lot of fat. It is also sold finely minced, medium minced and coarsely minced; each to be used for different purposes. The best way to remove any excess fat from mince is to begin the cooking in a pan without any extra fat. As it heats gently the fat flows out and can then be spooned off.

Steaks come in several different cuts, and are all suitable to grill or fry. Only fillet steaks are completely fat free.

beef, but a slice from the sirloin or rump, which is thin rather than thick, can also be termed an entrecôte steak. The flavour is good and the steak is very versatile, often used with a variety of sauces.

Chateaubriand This is a thick slice taken from the end of the fillet, weighing from 350 g (12 oz) upwards, which can be grilled or roasted. It is an excellent cut and well worth trying for a special occasion. It is often offered in restaurants as a 2-portion serving, so that it can be cooked in the piece to keep it succulent.

CARVING

This is a little appreciated culinary art but it is one that may easily be mastered with a little practice.

Good carving should never be underestimated, as without it meat can lack flavour and can be wasted. The first essential is a very good sharp knife with a slightly flexible blade, which is made of best stainless or carbon steel. It should be well balanced and feel 'comfortable' in the hand. It is just as important to have a good carving fork – with a guard for protection in case the knife slips – and a steel for sharpening the knife.

The next essential is some knowledge of the anatomy of the cut that you are to carve. As a general principle, most meat is carved across the grain because this shortens the meat fibres, making each slice more tender. Leg of lamb is an exception as this can be carved either parallel to or at right angles to the bone. In general, butchers prepare joints in the easiest way for them to be carved, and they will often give hints on carving if asked.

Barding

To prevent a joint drying out tie pieces of pork fat, or fatty bacon rashers, round it. This technique can also be used on game birds.

Barding a lean joint with pork fat

For wing rib

1. Remove the chine bone at the thickest end of the joint.

2. Lay the meat fat uppermost and carve in narrow slices, loosening it from the rib bones as you go.

For boned and rolled joints

1. Remove any skewers and any string which runs along the length of the joint as opposed to around it, and take off the first string that will come in the way.

2. Carve downwards in neat, and fairly thin slices, removing more string as it becomes necessary. If carving a cold joint, all the string may be removed before you begin. An electric carving knife is ideal to use with a boned, rolled joint.

Larding

A lean piece of meat such as fillet should be larded with fat to prevent it drying out during roasting. Cut pork fat into short narrow strips which are then threaded one by one into a larding needle. Thread the pieces of fat into the meat, taking 'stitches' about 1 cm (½ inch) deep.

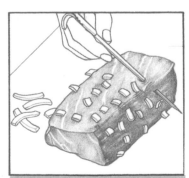

Lard beef by threading in short pieces of fat

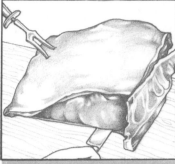

1. Cut the chine bone off the wing rib.

2. Lay flat and carve in narrow slices.

For rib roasts

1. Remove any string, and stand the joint on its wide end, holding it securely with a carving fork. If necessary, remove the chine bone with a sharp knife.

2. Cut across the joint in even, fairly thick slices until the blade of the knife reaches the rib bone. Cut down close to the bone to loosen each slice.

How much to allow

For beef on the bone allow 225–350 g (8–12 oz) raw per person, plus a little extra for some to serve cold.

Stand the rib roast on its wide end to carve.

For boned and rolled beef allow about 175 g (6 oz) raw per person, plus a little extra for some to serve cold.
For steaks allow 150–175 g (5–6 oz) raw per portion.

For perfect carving

■ Always stand up to carve a joint – it is so much easier than sitting down.
■ Let the joint rest for at least 5 minutes and up to 15 minutes before carving, to allow the juices to settle, and make carving very much easier.
■ Make sure your knife is really well sharpened before carving: the blade will slide through the meat instead of sawing and tearing at the fibres.
■ Remove any string and/or skewers which will be in the way as you start to carve.
■ Stand the joint on a flat non-slip surface, such as a wooden board, or on a plate with spikes to hold it in position. A carving fork will help to hold it steady.
■ Remove any outer bones, which will be in the way of carving, but not the main bone to which the flesh is attached.
■ Don't lose heart if you don't make a wonderful job the first time you try to carve. With a little practice, it will soon become much easier.

Roast Beef

Serves 6–10
about 1.25–2.75 kg (2½–5 lb)
prime joint of beef on the
bone, e.g., sirloin, ribs or
aitchbone or 1.25–2.25 kg
(2½–4½ lb) prime joint of
beef, boned and rolled, e.g.,
sirloin, ribs, topside or top
round
50 g (2 oz) dripping
freshly ground black pepper

Preparation time: about 10
minutes
Cooking time: see chart
Oven: 190°C, 375°F, Gas Mark
5; or 220°C, 425°F, Gas Mark 7

1. Wipe the meat all over and
trim if necessary. Calculate the
cooking time from the chart
after deciding whether to use
the fast or slower method of
roasting.

2. Stand the joint in a roasting
tin and spread all over with the
dripping. Sprinkle lightly with
pepper, to taste.

3. Cook the joint in a hot or
moderately hot preheated oven
for the times suggested in the
chart. The joint should be
basted with the fat in the tin
several times during cooking.
Peeled parboiled potatoes, or
parsnips can be placed around
the joint for the last hour of
cooking – they should be
basted at the same time as the
meat.

4. When the beef is ready,
remove to a serving dish and
keep warm. Allow to stand for
at least 5 minutes and up to 15
minutes before carving. Serve
with a selection of
accompaniments.

Accompaniments to roast beef

Horseradish sauce or cream, or
one of the horseradish
mustards; Yorkshire puddings,
either individual ones or a
large one; a good thin gravy
made from the meat juices,

ROASTING TIMES FOR BEEF (slow and fast methods)

Meat on the bone	Moderately hot 190°C, 375°F, Gas Mark 5	Hot 220°C, 425°F, Gas Mark 7
Rare	20 minutes per 450 g (1 lb) plus 20 minutes	15 minutes per 450 g (1 lb) plus 15 minutes
Medium	25 minutes per 450 g (1 lb) plus 25 minutes	20 minutes per 450 g (1 lb) plus 20 minutes
Well done	30–35 minutes per 450 g (1 lb) plus 30 minutes	25–30 minutes per 450 g (1 lb) plus 25 minutes
Meat boned and rolled		
Rare	25 minutes per 450 g (1 lb) plus 25 minutes	20 minutes per 450 g (1 lb) plus 20 minutes
Medium	30 minutes per 450 g (1 lb) plus 30 minutes	25 minutes per 450 g (1 lb) plus 25 minutes
Well done	35–40 minutes per 450 g (1 lb) plus 35 minutes	30–35 minutes per 450 g (1 lb) plus 30 minutes

Yorkshire Puddings

Makes 4 large or 12 small
puddings
50 g (2 oz) plain flour
a pinch of salt
1 egg
150 ml (¼ pint) milk
a little dripping or vegetable oil

Preparation time: 5 minutes
Cooking time: about 25
minutes
Oven: 220°C, 425°F, Gas Mark 7

1. Sift the flour and salt into a
bowl and make a well in the
centre.

2. Add the egg and a little milk
to the well and gradually work
in the flour to give a smooth
thick batter, beating hard to
remove any lumps that may
appear. Add the rest of the milk

and beat until smooth.

3. Put some dripping from the
joint or a little oil into 4
Yorkshire pudding tins or 12
patty or muffin tins and put into
the oven until the fat is really
hot. Pour the batter into the

tins so they are not more than
two-thirds full and bake in the
oven (above the joint) for
about 25 minutes or until well
puffed up, and golden brown.

4. Remove to a warm plate
and serve with the beef.

Spoon a little oil or dripping
into the tins

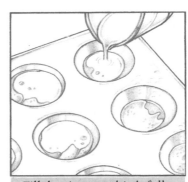
Fill the tins two-thirds full
with batter

Pour on the marinade and leave for up to 24 hours.

Brown the meat on all sides to seal.

Pot Roast of Brisket

Serves 4–6
1.5 kg (3 lb) lean joint of
  brisket of beef, boned and
  rolled
150 ml (1/4 pint) red wine or
  cider, or half red wine
  vinegar and half stock
2 tablespoons vegetable oil or
  dripping
10 whole cloves
2 bay leaves
2 garlic cloves, crushed
salt
freshly ground black pepper
150 ml (1/4 pint) Bone Stock
  (see page 24)
8–12 small onions, peeled and
  thickly sliced or 2–3 large
  onions, peeled and thickly
  sliced
4 carrots, peeled and cut into
  thick sticks
4 celery sticks, thickly sliced
2 turnips, peeled and
  quartered (optional)
1 tablespoon cornflour

Preparation time: about 20
minutes, plus marinating
Cooking time: 3–3½ hours
Oven: 160°C, 325°F, Gas Mark 3

1. Put the joint into a deep dish
and pour the wine, cider or
vinegar and stock over it. Leave
to marinate for at least 6 hours
and preferably up to 24 hours
in a cool place, turning the
joint once or twice.

2. Remove the meat from the
marinade and dry it well. Heat
the oil or dripping in a frying
pan and fry the joint all over
until it is well sealed and a
good golden brown.

3. Put the joint into a large
casserole with sufficient room
to add the vegetables. Add the
cloves, bay leaves, garlic and
seasonings and then pour over
the marinade and the stock.

4. Cover the casserole tightly
and cook in a moderate oven
for 2 hours.

5. Arrange the prepared
vegetables around the joint.
Cover again, and continue
cooking for 1–1½ hours or
until the meat is very tender.

6. Remove the meat and the
vegetables to separate serving
dishes, and keep warm. Strain
the cooking liquor into a small
pan and skim off any fat from
the surface. Blend the
cornflour with 2 tablespoons
cold water, add to the sauce
and bring to the boil. If too
thick, add extra stock or water
to achieve the correct
consistency and bring back to
the boil. Adjust the seasoning
and serve with the joint. Boiled,
mashed or jacket potatoes
make a good accompaniment
along with a green vegetable.

Meat Sauce for Pasta

Serves 4
450 g (1 lb) lean minced beef
1 large onion, peeled and
  finely chopped
1–2 carrots, peeled and
  chopped
1–2 garlic cloves, crushed
2 tablespoons tomato purée
1 tablespoon flour (optional)
1 × 425 g (15 oz) can peeled
  tomatoes or 450 g (1 lb) fresh
  tomatoes, peeled and sliced
1 teaspoon Worcestershire
  sauce
1 bay leaf
salt
freshly ground black pepper
4–5 tablespoons red wine,
  cider or stock
100 g (4 oz) mushrooms,
  chopped or sliced
mixed herbs (optional)
grated Parmesan cheese, to
  garnish

Preparation time: about 20
minutes
Cooking time: about 1 hour

1. Put the minced beef into a
heavy-based saucepan without
any extra fat and heat gently
until the fat begins to run. Stir
frequently, and continue
cooking until the mince loses
its red colour – about 4
minutes.

2. Add the onion, carrots and
garlic and continue to cook for
about 5 minutes, stirring
occasionally.

3. Stir in the tomato purée and
flour (if used) and cook for
about a minute, stirring
constantly; then add the
tomatoes and their liquid, the
Worcestershire sauce, bay leaf,
seasonings and 4 tablespoons
wine and bring to the boil.

4. Cover the pan and simmer
gently for about 20 minutes,
giving an occasional stir.

5. Add the mushrooms, a little
more stock or wine if
necessary, and a sprinkling of
herbs if used, and continue to

Boiled Salt Beef and Carrots

Serves 6–8
1.75 kg (4 lb) joint of salted
  silverside of beef
4–6 small onions, peeled
6–8 medium carrots, peeled
1 leek, trimmed and cut into
  5 cm (2 inch) lengths or 3
  celery sticks, cut into thick
  slices
1–2 turnips, peeled and
  quartered
Herb dumplings:
100 g (4 oz) self-raising flour
a good pinch of salt
1 tablespoon mixed herbs or 1
  teaspoon dried mixed herbs
50 g (2 oz) shredded suet
about 4 tablespoons cold water

Preparation time: about 20
minutes
Cooking time: about 3 hours

1. Wash the beef and place in a
large saucepan with sufficient
room around the joint for the
vegetables, and cover with cold
water. Bring to the boil,
remove any scum from the
surface with a spoon, then
cover the pan and simmer,
allowing 45 minutes per 450 g
(1 lb).

2. About 30 minutes before the
end of cooking time add the
prepared vegetables to the
saucepan, distributing them
evenly around the joint.
Continue to simmer.

Steak and Kidney Pie

cook for another 30 minutes, stirring occasionally.

6. Taste, and adjust the seasoning if necessary. The sauce is now ready to serve with spaghetti, noodles or other pasta, garnished with Parmesan cheese, or to use for lasagne in conjunction with a cheese sauce.

Serves 4–6
675 g (1½ lb) stewing or braising steak, cut into 2 cm (¾ inch) cubes
100–175 g (4–6 oz) ox kidney, chopped
1 tablespoon flour
1 large onion, peeled and thinly sliced
1 meat extract cube or stock cube
1–2 tablespoons tomato purée
600 ml (1 pint) water
1 teaspoon Worcestershire sauce
salt
freshly ground black pepper
100 g (4 oz) mushrooms, sliced (optional)
1 recipe quantity Puff, Flaky or Shortcrust Pastry (see pages 261–265)
beaten egg, to glaze

Preparation time: about 30 minutes
Cooking time: about 2¼ hours, plus cooling of the meat
Oven: 220°C, 425°F, Gas Mark 7
then: 190°C, 375°F, Gas Mark 5

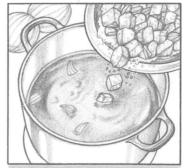

Place the floured steak and kidney in a large casserole.

Spooning the cooked meat into the pie dish.

1. Place the steak and kidney in a bowl with the flour and toss until well coated.

2. Place the meat in a large pan or ovenproof casserole and add the onion, crumbled stock cube, tomato purée and water and bring to the boil. Add the Worcestershire sauce and seasoning and cover the pan. Simmer gently for about 1½ hours or until tender. Alternatively cook in a moderate oven (180°C, 350°F, Gas Mark 4) for 2 hours.

Crimping the edges of the pastry lid.

3. If using shortcrust pastry, put a pie funnel into the centre of the chosen pie dish. If using the mushrooms, stir through the beef and then spoon the meat around the funnel, adding as much of the liquid as possible. Leave to cool.

4. Roll out the pastry and use to cover the pie. Decorate with pastry trimmings, flake and crimp the edges, and brush with beaten egg. Chill for 15–20 minutes. (See page 260 for how to decorate a pie.)

5. Cook in a preheated hot oven for 25 minutes (15 minutes for shortcrust pastry) or until beginning to brown, then reduce the temperature and continue cooking until the crust is a good golden brown and well risen. If the pastry seems to be over-browning, lay a sheet of wet greaseproof paper over the top.

---

3. For the dumplings, sift the flour and salt into a bowl and mix in the herbs and suet. Add enough of the cold water to mix to an elastic dough. Divide into 10–12 pieces and form into balls.

Remove the scum from the surface of the boiling meat.

4. About 15 minutes before the end of the cooking time, add the dumplings to the saucepan, placing them around the meat. If the pan is too full to hold them, bring another saucepan of water to the boil and add the

Place the dumplings on top around the meat.

dumplings to this. Cover the pan and simmer for 15–20 minutes or until they swell and rise to the surface of the pan; they should look very fluffy.

5. Remove the dumplings carefully to a serving dish. Take out the meat and put on a serving plate. Strain the vegetables and either arrange around the meat or put into another serving dish. Strain the cooking juices and serve as they are; or use them to make a mustard or parsley sauce, using half cooking liquor and half milk. Serve with boiled or mashed potatoes and English mustard.

PORK & HAM

Rich, succulent pork is one of Britain's most popular meats. The distinction between pork, gammon, ham and bacon can be confusing: this section makes the differences clear and gives a useful round-up of all the various cuts, with instructions on carving the different types of joint.

When selecting a joint or piece of pork, it should have a good layer of firm white fat with a thinnish elastic skin around the pale pink, smooth and fine-grained lean. A roasting joint should have a good rind that can be scored (cut into narrow parallel lines with a very sharp knife) to give a good crackling when cooked – the butcher should do this.

Bacon and ham is the flesh of the pig which has been salted or cured in brine and then smoked. Green or unsmoked bacon is cured, but not smoked and is consequently less strong in flavour and will not keep for the same length of time as its smoked counterpart.

Gammon is the hind leg of the pig which is cured on the side of bacon; if the leg is then cut off and cooked and served cold, it is known as ham. A true ham, however, is the hind leg of the pig, detached before curing, and which is then cured, salted, matured, hung or smoked, depending on the manufacturer's process. Many countries produce different types of ham, each with its own properties and flavour. Shoulder and collar joints are far less expensive than gammon and they can be served in a similar way and are again called ham. Special pigs are bred as bacon pigs and they have small bones, a long back, small shoulders and large plump gammons or hams. Good fresh bacon should have a pleasant aroma with firm, white fat and pink coloured lean, that is firm with a good bloom. The rind should be a good pale cream colour if unsmoked or green; or light to dark golden brown for smoked bacon.

Methods of cooking

Remember that pork must always be thoroughly cooked – on no account should it be underdone. All pork joints are suitable for roasting – the leg and loin are often boned and stuffed first – while gammon and ham joints can be boiled or baked. Steaks and chops are usually grilled or braised.

Guide to the cuts of pork and ham

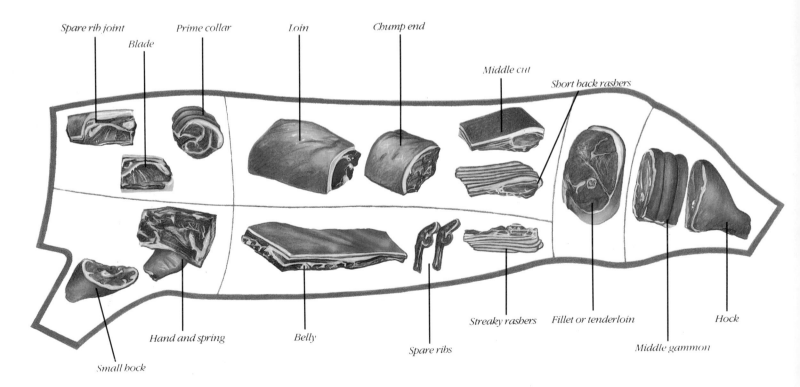

Spare rib joint · Blade · Prime collar · Loin · Chump end · Middle cut · Short back rashers · Streaky rashers · Fillet or tenderloin · Hock · Middle gammon · Spare ribs · Belly · Hand and spring · Small hock

CUTS OF PORK

Leg A large lean joint often boned and rolled, although excellent when cooked on the bone. It can be cut into various sizes of joints which are usually roasted.

Loin This is a prime roasting joint which can be bought on

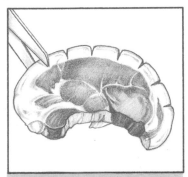

Snip the fat on chops to prevent it curling.

or off the bone. It sometimes includes the kidney and can be excellent if stuffed and rolled. The loin is also cut into chops and also boneless chops (or steaks as they are often called) which can be grilled or fried.

Spare rib Not to be confused with spare ribs, this joint comes from the shoulder. A fairly lean joint, but sometimes with more fat than other joints, should be moderately priced, and has an excellent flavour. Good to roast; and it can be cut up to braise, casserole or stew.

Blade Shoulder of pork is often sub-divided into spare rib and blade. This is a tender cut, available on the bone or boneless. It can be roasted, stuffed, grilled or casseroled.

Fillet or tenderloin A prime piece of meat with very little fat. Very versatile, and excellent for kebabs, escalopes, pan-frying and for grilling or frying. It can also be sliced lengthways and stuffed. Quite expensive but it goes a long way.

Hand and spring This is the foreleg of the pig and is suitable for roasting, boiling, stewing and casseroling. It is relatively inexpensive and is the cut to buy if you want to mince pork to use for meatballs or pâtés.

Belly Cheap and fatty but full of flavour. It can be used on and off the bone, either as a joint or cut into slices. Bone and roll it with a stuffing to roast or pot-roast; or use the slices to grill

or fry or casserole or cook on a barbecue. For some recipes it can be salted. The butcher will do this if 3–4 days notice is given.

Spare ribs Taken from the belly, they are removed in one piece and then cut up into ribs with the meat left all around the bones. These are very popular and are usually barbecued, grilled, or casseroled.

CUTS OF BACON AND HAM

Back bacon can be sub-divided into short back, top back and long back. It is taken from the back of the pig, and boned out ready to slice into rashers, to grill or fry. Short back rashers are the prime cut and are the most expensive. They can also be cut up to 2.5 cm (1 inch) thick when they are known as bacon chops. It should have a good eye of meat and a distinct layer of fat. Back bacon can also be used rolled into a joint, with or without a stuffing, to boil or bake.

Middle or throughcut These are long rashers that combine the back and the streaky. The amount of fat varies for it can be cut from the leaner prime streaky from the front, or the fatter hind or thin streaky. It gives a true 'throughcut' of the whole, or in fact half, side of the pig. This is also good to use as a joint, for it is long and will easily wrap around a stuffing to bake, roast or boil.

Streaky bacon These are narrow rashers which have lean and fat streaked together. They are taken from the belly part of the pig. The amount of fat to lean differs widely, and they vary from long to short. They have good flavour, smoked or unsmoked, and can be fried, grilled, added in cubes to casseroles or minced for pâtés etc.

Collar Prime collar from the shoulder, when boned and

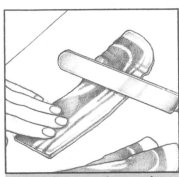

Stretch bacon rashers with the back of a knife.

rolled, makes one of the best boiling joints, for it is full of flavour and not too fatty. Joints vary in size from small at 450 g (1 lb) upwards to very large at 3.5 kg (8 lb) or more, and they can be boiled, baked, braised or pot-roasted. Collar rashers are fairly substantial – round or square in shape – and basically lean with just fat around the side.

Forehock Whole hocks – the front legs – can be bought very cheaply with the bone still in, ready to cook; including the knuckle, they weigh about 3–3.5 kg (7–8 lb). They are more often sold boned and rolled, when they can be cut into any size of joint. The flavour is good and it is fairly lean. Boil, braise, bake or pot-roast.

Gammon or ham The most prized part of the side of bacon both for its leanness and for its fine texture, with very little fat. It is often sold ready cooked,

either boned or on the bone, but can be bought raw as a whole or half gammon, or as smaller cuts which are known as the slipper, middle, corner and gammon knuckle. Most of these joints are ready boned. Boil, bake or braise. Gammon steaks and rashers are cut off this joint after it has been boned and rolled and are suitable for grilling and frying.

Boiling bacon can be bought in large or small joints, the large ones usually being sold on the bone, the smaller ones boned and rolled. Large joints should be soaked in cold water for 12–18 hours. Boil-in-the-bag bacon is also available, its advantage being that the shape of the joint is retained during cooking, and juices and flavours do not get lost in the cooking water.

CARVING PORK

Follow the basic rules on page 128 and allow the meat to stand and 'set' for 5–10 minutes before carving. Stand it squarely on a board or large plate.

Loin

1. Sever the chined bone from the chop bones and put aside.

2. Divide into chops cutting between the rib bones and the scored crackling and serve as chops.

3. Alternatively, loosen the meat from the bones (after cutting off the chined backbone) and then cut off in slices without dividing into chops. It is easier to cut the crackling off first and cut into portions before slicing the meat, if you use this method.

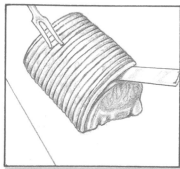

1. Remove the crackling first to make carving easier.

2. Without the crackling, cut in thin slices.

Leg

1. Use the knife to cut through the crackling and remove it before actually carving the meat; this makes it much easier. Do not take off more crackling than meat to be carved.

2. Carve in a similar way as for leg of lamb (see page 141), keeping the slices fairly thin. For half legs it is probably easier to start at one end of the joint and work to the other end, then turn over and carve the under side of the joint.

Spare rib

1. Cut between the score marks into fairly thick slices.

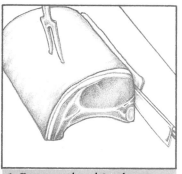

1. Remove the chine bone first.

2. Carve the loin into chops.

CARVING HAM AND BACON

All cooked ham and bacon should be carved thinly; thick slices and chunks do not look appetising and do not do justice to the texture and flavour of the meat. The knife must be very sharp and the experts will use a special ham carving knife which is fairly long and thin (see page 10) but a good large cook's knife will do just as well.

Whole gammon

There are several methods of carving a whole gammon or ham. The simplest is probably to remove a small slice from the knuckle end of the bone and then carve in long oblique slices to the bone on either side. An alternative method is to carve slices at an angle from either side of the bone. Hold the knife at an oblique angle and cut long thin slices from each side.

Prime forehock

1. This is best carved keeping the fat side underneath. Hold the protruding bone firmly with the fork or a cloth and carve in vertical slices up to the bone, then repeat from the other end.

2. When the bone is reached carve long, downward slanting slices at an angle to the bone. Turn over and carve the remaining slices down to the bone.

Gammon hock

1. Hold the shank end (or bone) firmly with the fork or a clean cloth and carve in wedge-shaped slices from one side of the bone.

2. Turn the joint over and repeat, again holding the shank end firmly.

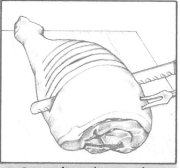

1. Cut in slices down to the bone.

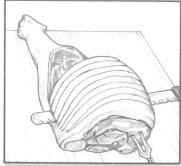

2. Release the slices by cutting flat along the leg bone.

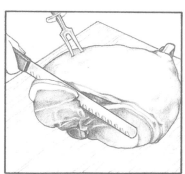

1. Cut a slice from one side of the bone.

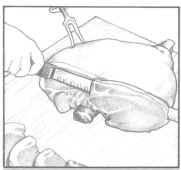

2. Carve slices alternately from each side of the bone.

Roast Pork

Serves 6
*a prime joint of pork (leg, loin
or spare rib), on the bone or
boned and rolled, weighing
about 1.75–2.25 kg (4–5 lb)*
oil
salt

Preparation time: about 5
minutes
Cooking time: see chart
Oven: see chart

1. Trim the pork of any excess
fat, then weigh and calculate
the cooking time from the
chart.

2. Rub the well scored rind of
the joint with oil and then rub
in a good layer of salt to ensure
crackling. (Make sure the
butcher has scored the rind
properly when you buy the
joint: this is easier than
attempting to do it yourself.)

3. Stand the joint in a roasting
tin and cook for the time
suggested in the chart, either in
a preheated moderate or hot
oven. Thin joints which are
boned and rolled can also be
cooked in the hot oven but for
any 'wide' boned and rolled
joint, or one that is stuffed, it is
essential to cook it at the lower
temperature.

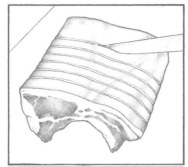

Score the skin of the joint
with a sharp knife.

4. Baste the joint several times
during cooking and roast
potatoes around it for the last
hour of cooking, if liked.

5. When ready, transfer to a
serving dish and keep warm.
Leave to stand and 'set' for at
least 5 minutes before carving.
Serve with apple sauce and
sage and onion stuffing, and a
gravy using the pan juices after
spooning off the excess fat.

Accompaniments to roast pork

These are traditionally apple
sauce and sage and onion
stuffing, together with a gravy.

ROASTING TIMES FOR PORK

Pork on the bone	Hot 220°C, 425°F, Gas Mark 7	25–30 minutes per 450 g (1 lb) plus 25 minutes, depending on the thickness of the joint.
Pork boned and rolled	Moderately hot 190°C, 375°F, Gas Mark 5	30–35 minutes per 450 g (1 lb) plus 30 minutes depending on the thickness of the joint.

Roasting temperature

Pork cooked on the bone is
best cooked in a hot oven,
whilst boned and rolled joints
are better cooked at a lower
temperature as they take
longer to cook through. It is
essential that all pork is really
well cooked – never serve
underdone.

How much to allow

For joints on the bone allow
225–350 g (8–12 oz) raw pork
per portion.
For joints boned and rolled
allow about 175 g (6 oz) raw
pork per portion plus some
extra to serve cold.
For chops allow 1 per portion
For cutlets or boneless pork

slices allow 1–2 or about 100–
175 g (4–6 oz) raw pork per
portion.
For hand and spring allow
350 g (12 oz) raw pork per
portion.
For tenderloin allow 100–175 g
(4–6 oz) per portion.
For belly allow 100–225 g (4–
8 oz) raw pork per portion.
For rashers of bacon, allow 2–4
per portion, depending on size
and what else is to be served
with them.
For bacon chops, allow 1–2
depending on size.
For gammon steaks, allow 1
per portion; for gammon
rashers 1–2 depending on size.

Apple Sauce

*450 g (1 lb) cooking apples,
peeled and cored*
2–3 tablespoons water
25 g (1 oz) butter or margarine
a little sugar (optional)

Preparation time: about 5
minutes
Cooking time: about 10
minutes

1. Slice the apples into a small
saucepan, and add the water.
Cover the pan and cook gently
until very soft and pulpy –
about 7–10 minutes – stirring
occasionally.

2. Beat the apple with a
wooden spoon until quite
smooth, or rub through a sieve,
or purée in a blender.

3. Return to a clean pan and
beat in the butter or margarine
and a little sugar, to taste.

Sage and Onion Stuffing

*2 large onions, peeled and
chopped*
25 g (1 oz) butter
100 g (4 oz) fresh breadcrumbs
2 teaspoons dried sage
salt
freshly ground black pepper

Preparation time: about 15
minutes
Cooking time: about 50
minutes
Oven: as the pork

1. Put the onions into a pan of
water, bring to the boil and
simmer for 5 minutes; drain
well.

2. Melt the butter in a pan, add
the onions and fry for a minute
or so.

3. Put the breadcrumbs into a
bowl and mix in the sage and
seasonings. Add the onions and
the butter and mix well
together.

4. Press lightly into a greased
ovenproof shallow dish and
cook in the oven below the
pork for 30–40 minutes or
until lightly browned on top
and crisp. Cut into wedges to
serve.

Spiced Spare Ribs

American or Chinese spare ribs are cut from the belly, and are the actual ribs of the animal. The rind and excess fat are removed, and the ribs are sold either in sheets or as separate bone strips, with a varying amount of meat adhering. Chinese cooks chop them up individually into shorter lengths.

Serves 4
2 tablespoons oil
900 g (2 lb) pork spare ribs (American-style)
2 large onions, peeled and thinly sliced
4 tablespoons soft brown or demerara sugar
1½ teaspoons salt
1 teaspoon paprika
1 tablespoon tomato purée
1 tablespoon Worcestershire sauce
2 tablespoons vinegar
4 tablespoons lemon juice
200 ml (7 fl oz) water or stock
175 g (6 oz) no-need-to-soak stoned prunes
12–16 green olives, plain or stuffed
25 g (1 oz) blanched almonds, cut into strips and toasted

Preparation time: about 25 minutes
Cooking time: about 1½ hours
Oven: 200°C, 400°F, Gas Mark 6

1. Heat the oil in a pan and fry the ribs quickly all over to brown. Transfer to a fairly shallow ovenproof casserole or large roasting tin.

2. Fry the onions in the same fat until lightly browned, then drain off the excess fat.

3. Add all the other ingredients except the prunes, olives and almonds and bring up to the boil. Simmer for 3–4 minutes and then pour over the ribs.

4. Cover the casserole with a lid or foil and cook in the oven for 45 minutes.

5. Remove the foil, stir in the prunes and olives, and baste the chops well with the juices. Return to the oven, uncovered for 20–30 minutes, until the ribs are well browned and really tender.

6. Remove the casserole from the oven. Sprinkle with the toasted almonds just before serving. Spoon off any fat from the surface and blot with kitchen paper to remove the last traces of fat or grease.

Roast Stuffed Loin of Pork

Serves 5–6
1.5 kg (3 lb) loin of pork joint, with belly flap still attached, boned and rolled, with the skin well scored
salt
freshly ground black pepper
parsley or celery leaves, to garnish
Stuffing:
25 g (1 oz) butter or margarine
1 onion, peeled and chopped
1–2 celery sticks, chopped
75 g (3 oz) breadcrumbs, brown or white
25 g (1 oz) walnut halves, chopped
40 g (1½ oz) raisins
½ teaspoon curry powder or ground coriander
1 egg, beaten
oil or dripping, for roasting

Preparation time: about 20 minutes
Cooking time: see chart
Oven: see chart

Trim off excess fat on meat side

Bring up belly flap to enclose stuffing

Re-roll the joint and sew up with string

1. Unroll the pork and cut the flesh a little if necessary to provide a pocket for the stuffing. Season the inside of the meat lightly.

2. For the stuffing, melt the fat and fry the onion and celery gently until soft – about 5 minutes. Turn into a bowl and mix in the breadcrumbs, some salt and pepper, the walnuts, raisins, curry or coriander and mix until evenly distributed. Add the egg to bind the mixture together.

3. Spread the stuffing over the inside of the pork and then re-roll the joint to enclose the stuffing. Secure with skewers and string, and then remove skewers unless absolutely necessary to hold it together.

4. Weigh the joint and calculate the cooking time. Stand the joint in a roasting tin, rub with oil or dripping and then rub liberally with salt.

5. Cook as for roast pork following the chart on page 135. Cook parboiled potatoes around it for the last hour and baste from time to time.

6. Serve the joint surrounded with potatoes and garnish with parsley or celery leaves. Make a gravy from the pan juices and serve apple sauce (page 135) as an accompaniment.

Boiling Bacon

Large smoked joints should be soaked in cold water for 12–18 hours. Smaller joints can be soaked if you prefer a less salty taste. With the milder cures or green or unsmoked joints there should be no need to soak at all – or do so for about 4–6 hours if you are worried. After soaking always discard the soaking water and cook in clean water.

Instead of soaking, the joint may be placed in a large saucepan of cold water, brought to the boil, and then the water (including some of the salt from the joint) thrown away, and the joint started off again in clean cold water.

The joint should always be weighed for the length of cooking time depends entirely on the weight. For joints up to 4.5 kg (10 lb), allow 20–25 minutes per 450 g (1 lb), plus 20 minutes over – giving the longer time for really thick joints. For larger joints still, allow 15–20 minutes per 450 g (1 lb), plus 15 minutes over.

1. Place the joint of bacon in a large saucepan, skin side down, cover with cold water and bring to the boil.

2. Remove any scum from the surface with a slotted spoon and add 1 bouquet garni and, if liked, 1–2 chopped onions, 1–2 chopped carrots and 6 black peppercorns. Start timing from the minute the water comes to the boil. Cover and simmer gently until cooked, adding extra water if necessary. Do not fast boil.

3. To serve cold, leave in the water (off the heat) for an hour or so, then remove and leave to cool completely. When cold, strip off the skin. To serve hot, drain well and carefully ease away the skin (if an unsmoked joint it can be left on). Serve with a parsley or mustard sauce.

Remove the scum from the surface.

Add herbs, spices and vegetables.

Baked Gammon

Whole joints of bacon or gammon should be soaked for 2–3 hours before being cooked. To bake, joints are first parboiled for half the cooking time. Calculate the total cooking time as for boiling bacon.

Serves 8
1.75 kg (4 lb) gammon joint or prime collar joint
6 black peppercorns
1–2 bay leaves
2 tablespoons white wine vinegar or cider vinegar
1 tablespoon clear honey
100 g (4 oz) demerara sugar
whole cloves
watercress or parsley, to garnish

Preparation time: 15 minutes, plus soaking
Cooking time: about 1¾ hours
Oven: 180°C, 350°F, Gas Mark 4; then 220°C, 425°F, Gas Mark 7

1. Boil the joint as above with the black peppercorns and bay leaves for half the cooking time, then drain the joint, wrap loosely in foil and stand in a roasting tin or shallow casserole dish.

2. Cook in a preheated oven until 30 minutes before the end of cooking time. Then increase the oven temperature.

3. Unwrap the foil and strip the skin off the joint. Score the fat into diamonds and stick a clove into the point of each diamond. Heat the vinegar and honey together and use to brush liberally over the fat. Then sprinkle generously with the sugar, pressing it well in all over the fat.

4. Return to the oven, uncovered, for the remainder of the cooking time. Serve hot or cold garnished with watercress or parsley.

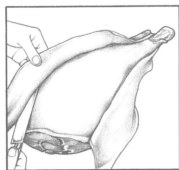
Peel the skin off the gammon when cooked

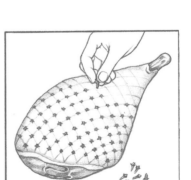
Score a diamond pattern and stud with cloves

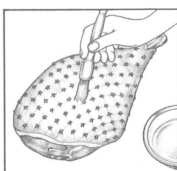
Baste the joint with the honey to glaze

LAMB

Lamb is one of the most versatile of meats, and this is reflected in our recipe selection. All the lamb cuts, ranging from the more expensive leg to economical scrag end of neck, are described in full, with exciting cooking ideas for each.

When you buy lamb, the age of the animal is indicated both by its weight (obviously the heavier a joint, the larger and older the animal), and by the colour of the lean meat. Pale pink flesh denotes young lamb, and this turns to light red as the age of the animal increases. Mutton, once so popular in Britain and one of our traditional dishes, is now hard to obtain; the demand for it has decreased so lambs are killed very much younger. Lamb is

generally from an animal under a year, mutton from an animal under 2 years, but more often mutton is defined as coming from an animal weighing over 36 kg (79 lb). However, if you can find it, the flavour of mutton is distinctive and extremely good.

The best of the home-produced lamb is obviously the new season or spring lambs which are generally under 6 months old. Welsh lamb, for instance, is renowned for its

flavour and tenderness. As the year progresses the price drops and for those interested in buying a whole carcass to freeze, it is worth asking the butcher the best time to buy when it is both good in quality and low in price.

Legs and shoulders of lamb should be plump with a thin layer of fat covering the flesh; this fat should be white to pale cream, not a dark yellow. If you buy New Zealand lamb that is still frozen, do take time to

thaw it out very slowly so that the meat is in prime condition when you cook it. If it is thawed fast, the flavour will deteriorate and more often than not it will be tough when cooked.

Sometimes roast or grilled lamb is served in the French style, with the flesh still pink inside. The cooking times given allow for a completely cooked piece of meat, but cut the cooking time by about 20 minutes on a joint if you want to serve it pink.

Guide to the cuts of lamb

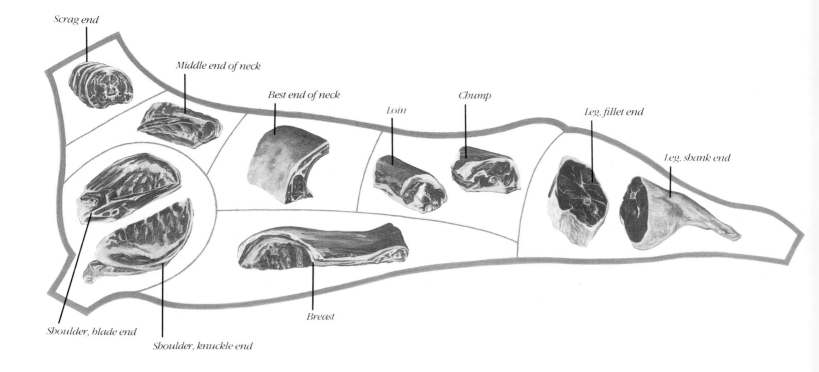

Scrag end

Middle end of neck

Best end of neck

Loin

Chump

Leg, fillet end

Leg, shank end

Shoulder, blade end

Shoulder, knuckle end

Breast

CUTS OF LAMB

With lamb the cuts and joints are more universally named than with some of the other meats, apart from the chops which can vary in name from butcher to butcher. There are also some very new and inventive cuts of lamb which are sometimes on display in butchers and supermarkets – if you see something you don't recognize, simply ask the butcher what it is.

Because lamb is young, almost all the cuts are prime, thus suitable for frying and grilling.

Leg This is a prime joint which is quite large and always rather expensive. It is often cut in half and sold as half legs, as the fillet end (or top half) and the shank end (or lower half). The fillet half is sometimes boned out and it is good for kebabs, for casseroling, and it can be cut into leg steaks.

Leg of lamb, whether whole or in halves, is usually roasted although it can also be pot-roasted with great success.

Shoulder One of the sweetest and most tender parts of the animal but it does have a fair amount of fat on it and is one of the most difficult of all joints to carve. It is always succulent and most often roasted either on the bone, or boned and rolled when some of the fat can be discarded. It can also be pot-roasted and boiled to serve with caper sauce. It is a cheaper joint than the leg and again can be cut in half to buy as the blade end and knuckle end. Shoulder meat can also be boned to use for kebabs, casseroles and mince etc., when excess fat can be trimmed off before cooking.

Loin This is a prime cut which is usually roasted on the bone or boned and rolled with or without a stuffing. It can also be pot-roasted. This part of the animal can be cut up and made into an assortment of chops (see right).

Best end of neck This is again a prime roasting joint either on the bone or boned and rolled. It is from this joint that the spectacular crown roast of lamb and guard of honour roasts are made. It can be cut into cutlets which are left as they are or can be trimmed.

Breast of lamb This is a versatile and cheap cut of lamb which is very tasty but also very fatty. Some scorn it, but others enthuse about its flavour, provided a little trouble is taken to bone and remove all the visible fat and membrane. It is ideal for casseroling, but should be cooked the day before required, so it can be cooled and the resulting layer of fat on the surface removed before the dish is reheated. It can be boned, stuffed, rolled and slow roasted or pot-roasted with great success. It will also cut into pieces or 'riblets' still on the bone to bake in the oven or on a barbecue: the fat pours out, leaving crunchy brown morsels of lamb.

Middle and scrag end of neck These are the cheap cuts with a rather high percentage of bone and some fat, but again with a good flavour. Well worth using for casseroles. Chops can be cut from the middle neck.

CHOPS AND CUTLETS

Loin These contain part of the backbone, and are cut from the loin as single or double loin chops (also known as butterfly chops).

Chump These chops come from between the loin and the leg and are the largest and leanest.

Leg These chops are slices taken straight across the leg joint and have an 'eye' of bone in the centre.

Cutlets These are taken from the best end of neck. They have a small eye of meat and a long bone which can be left with meat on it or be trimmed both in length and free of meat.

All chops and cutlets are ideal for grilling and can also be fried. Because of the layer of fat they need very little extra fat added for cooking. They can also be pan-fried, braised and used in casseroles, as in the traditional Lancashire hot-pot of onions, potatoes and lamb.

Boneless chops These include noisettes, which are taken from a boned-out best end of neck (or sometimes a small loin): the meat is rolled up tightly and secured with cocktail sticks or string and then cut into slices which have a layer of fat all round the outside and the eye of the meat in the centre. Sometimes a kidney is rolled into the centre of the meat for extra flavour. Grill, fry or pan-fry.

Lamb steaks are slices taken from a boned leg of lamb. They can be beaten out between two layers of cling film to make them thinner, if required, prior to grilling, frying, braising or pan-frying.

To bone a breast of lamb

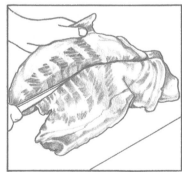

1. Lay the breast with bones uppermost and the breast bone nearest to you. First cut loose the flap of flesh at the end of the joint, opening it up to form a pocket. Insert the knife blade under the breastbone and work along the length of the bone.

2. Hold the breast at the thickest end and cut the bone and ribs away from the flesh. Scrape along the ribs to free them from the flesh and cut away the last piece attached to the meat.

NOISETTES

Noisettes are rolled boneless chops taken from a boned best end of neck. The meat is rolled up tightly, tied, and then cut into slices for frying or grilling. To prepare noisettes, first chine the best end, i.e. remove the backbone with a cleaver or heavy knife. Next, using a small sharp knife cut along both sides of each rib bone to release it. Keep the knife pressed close to the bone to avoid cutting into the meat. When the bones are out, roll the piece of meat up tightly, starting at the meaty chined end. Trim off the meatless flap at thin end and trim away any excess fat. Tie the meat securely at 2.5 cm (1 inch) intervals with fine string, knotting each loop separately. Cut midway between each loop to make the noisettes. Grill as for lamb cutlets.

1. Cut off the chine bone, using a sharp knife.

2. Remove the rib bones one by one.

3. Cut off the meatless flap and trim off excess fat.

4. Tie the joint and cut into slices.

Guard of honour

This is prepared from 2 best ends of neck. The bones are trimmed clean of meat for 6 cm (2½ inches) and the two best ends are then folded together, skin outside and sewn along the bottom. The bones are criss-crossed together on top. Tie with string to hold it in shape while cooking.

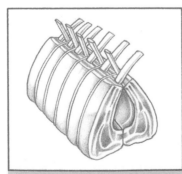

Prepared guard of honour. Cover the bones with foil.

CARVING LAMB

Follow the general rules on page 128, and stand the joint neatly and squarely on a board or large plate. Allow to 'set' before carving.

Lamb should not be carved too thinly; try to aim for about 5 mm (¼ inch) thick. With loin and best end of neck joints on the bone, ask the butcher to chine the joint first. This simply means he partly chops through the backbone lengthwise so the bone can easily be removed before carving to make it easier to carve between the rib bones. If removed before cooking the meat would shrink from the bones, and look rather unattractive. Alternatively, the joint can be chopped which means the individual or every other chop is partly chopped through so when it is cooked the cut has just to be completed: this does not give such a good looking or well cooked joint.

For loin or best end of neck

1. Stand the chined joint (see above) squarely on a plate or board and remove the back-bone with a sharp knife.

2. Carve between the ribs to divide the joint neatly into cutlets. Sometimes slices will have no bone if the joint is from a large animal.

3. You could also cut the meat really quite thick to give two bones per portion which gives a 'mini' joint for each serving.

For shoulder

The shoulder is probably the most difficult joint to carve. To simplify carving, you can loosen around the blade bone in the raw joint with a small sharp knife, but do not remove it. When cooked, this loosened bone can then be pulled out to make carving easier.

1. Lay the joint skin side uppermost and make a series of parallel cuts, starting at the elbow and ending at the shoulder blade.

2. Run the knife horizontally along the length of the bone so as to free the slices

3. Turn the joint over, remove any fat, and then carve in horizontal slices.

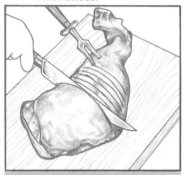

Make parallel cuts down to the bone.

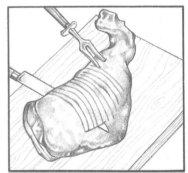

Cut along the bone to release slices.

Turn over and carve horizontal slices.

Begin carving from the narrow end of the leg.

Turn over and carve in long slices.

ROASTING TIMES FOR LAMB (slow and fast methods)

	Moderate oven 180°C, 350°F, Gas Mark 4	Hot oven 220°C, 425°F, Gas Mark 7
Meat on the bone	30–35 minutes per 450 g (1 lb), depending on the thickness of the joint	20 minutes per 450 g (1 lb), plus 20 minutes
Meat, boned and rolled	40–45 minutes per 450 g (1 lb), depending on the thickness of the joint	25 minutes per 450 g (1 lb), plus 25 minutes

For leg

1. Hold the knuckle end firmly with the carving fork.

2. Carve a wedge-shaped slice from the centre of the meatiest side. Carve slices from each side of the cut, gradually turning the knife to get larger slices and ending parallel to the bone.

3. Turn the joint over and carve in long horizontal slices.

For boned and rolled joints

Simply remove any skewers and string as you come to them and cut the meat in straight vertical slices. Keep them thickish, but not quite so thick as when carving meat on the bone.

How much to allow

For leg, loin, shoulder and best end of neck on the bone, allow 350 g (12 oz) raw per portion, with perhaps a little more for the loin and best end joints, plus extra to serve cold.
For boned leg, loin, shoulder and best end of neck, which are rolled (before adding any stuffing), allow 175–225 g (6–8 oz) raw per portion, plus extra to serve cold.

For stewing lamb and breast of lamb, allow 225–350 g (8–12 oz) raw per portion.
For chops and cutlets, allow 1–2 per portion, depending on size, but 1 double loin or chump chop should be sufficient. With noisettes, again allow 1 or 2 depending on size.

Roast Lamb

As lamb is fattier than other meats it requires no extra fat for roasting. Some seasoned flour can be sprinkled over the joint which will help absorb surplus fat.

Serves 6
about 1.75 kg (4 lb) prime joint of lamb (leg, shoulder, or loin)
salt
freshly ground black pepper
crushed or sliced garlic (optional)
fresh or dried rosemary (optional)

Preparation time: about 5–10 minutes
Cooking time: see chart
Oven: see chart

1. Trim the meat if necessary, and weigh it. If the joint is boned and rolled and is to have a stuffing added, add the stuffing before weighing the joint. Calculate the cooking time from the chart and decide whether to fast or slow roast.

2. Stand the joint in a roasting tin with the thickest layer of fat upwards and season with a little salt and pepper. If using garlic, rub all over the surface of the lamb with a cut or crushed garlic clove; and if using rosemary either make tiny slits and insert small sprigs of fresh rosemary (you could do this with slivers of garlic too), or simply sprinkle dried or fresh rosemary over the surface.

3. Roast the lamb either in a hot or moderate oven, following the times on the chart, and baste the joint several times during cooking. Parboiled potatoes may be roasted around the joint for the last hour or so of the cooking time; turn them over once when basting the meat.

4. When cooked, remove the meat to a serving dish, keep warm and allow to stand and 'set' for at least 5 minutes and preferably longer, before carving.

5. Serve with mint sauce or jelly, or redcurrant jelly and a slightly thickened gravy. Peas are a traditional vegetable to serve with lamb, but any green vegetable goes well.

Accompaniments to roast lamb

Traditionally mint sauce or mint jelly are served with lamb although many prefer redcurrant jelly; some will even serve both. Onion sauce is the traditional accompaniment for mutton, but it should be fairly thick, and rich in onions. Where the joint has been spiked with garlic and/or herbs the accompaniments are usually omitted and just a good gravy, made from the pan juices and slightly thickened, served with it.

Crown of Roast Lamb

The crown looks magnificent when cooked, but a surround of the chosen accompanying vegetables makes it look even better. Peas, French beans, baked whole tomatoes, braised celery, or cauliflower florets can be used, or a selection, choosing them for their colour contrast.

It is wise to order a crown of lamb from your butcher in advance although you may be lucky enough to pick one up from the larger supermarkets without ordering. To prepare it yourself, see illustrations on right. It is, in fact, two best ends of neck of lamb that are chined and turned inside out, then tied or sewn together so the bony structure is on the outside and the meaty part inside.

Serves 6
1 prepared crown of lamb
a little oil or melted dripping
accompanying vegetables, to
garnish (see below)
Stuffing:
75 g (3 oz) butter
1 onion, peeled and finely
chopped
1 large cooking apple, peeled,
cored and finely chopped
175 g (6 oz) breadcrumbs,
lightly toasted
100 g (4 oz) no-need-to-soak
stoned prunes, chopped
40 g (1½ oz) shelled walnuts,
chopped
2 tablespoons freshly chopped
parsley
½ teaspoon dried thyme
salt
freshly ground black pepper
1 egg yolk
lemon juice (optional)

Preparation time: about 30 minutes
Cooking time: about 50 minutes allowing 10 minutes per 450 g (1 lb), plus 20 minutes over
Oven: 180°C, 350°F, Gas Mark 4

1. Trim meat and fat 5 cm (2 inches) from end of bone

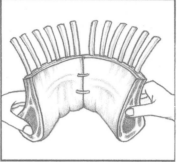

2. Place best ends back to back and sew together

3. Spoon stuffing into centre of crown

1. Brush the roast all over lightly with oil or melted dripping.

2. For the stuffing, melt the butter and fry the onion gently until soft. Add the apple and continue cooking for a few minutes. Turn into a bowl and mix in the breadcrumbs, prunes, walnuts, parsley, thyme

and seasonings and mix well. Add the egg yolk to bind and, if necessary, a few drops of lemon juice.

3. Use the stuffing to fill the centre of the crown, piling it up into a dome in the centre. Weigh the joint to calculate the cooking time and stand it in a well greased roasting tin.

4. Cover the bone tips and the stuffing with foil and cook in the oven for the calculated time. Baste the outside of the joint once or twice during cooking and roast parboiled potatoes around the joint if liked, for the last hour. Remove the foil from the stuffing for the last 20–30 minutes of cooking time.

Lamb Kebabs

Serves 4
1.25 kg (2½ lb) piece of top leg
of lamb or 2 fillets of lamb
8 thick slices from small, peeled
raw onions
8 squares green pepper
8 large mushrooms
8 bay leaves
Marinade:
4 tablespoons oil
2 tablespoons wine vinegar
2 tablespoons lemon juice
2 tablespoons red wine
1 garlic clove, crushed
salt
freshly ground pepper
1 teaspoon coarse grain
mustard
To garnish:
wedges of lemon
watercress
tomato quarters

Preparation time: about 20 minutes, plus time for marinating
Cooking time: about 20 minutes

1. Trim the lamb and cut into cubes of about 2.5 cm (1 inch), keeping as neat as possible and as close to the bone as you can if using top leg of lamb.

2. For the marinade, put all the ingredients into a bowl and whisk until thoroughly mixed. If liked, ½–1 teaspoon mixed herbs or oregano or marjoram may be added to the marinade.

3. Add the cubes of meat, mix well, cover and put into a cool place to marinate for at least 2 hours, preferably longer, giving the meat a good stir two or three times.

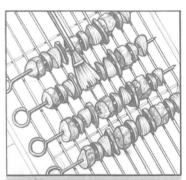

Brush kebabs at least once with marinade

4. Drain the cubes of meat. Dip the slices of onion, pepper and mushrooms in the marinade and then thread the meat onto 8 long skewers, alternating with the vegetables and bay leaves.

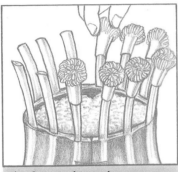

4. After cooking, decorate bones with cutlet frills

5. To serve, stand the crown on a serving dish and top each bone tip with a cutlet frill after removing the pieces of foil. Arrange hot cooked vegetables around the base of the crown and use the pan juices, after pouring off the excess fat, to make a gravy. Serve about 2 chops per person, and offer mint sauce or redcurrant jelly to accompany.

5. Cook under a moderate preheated grill for about 10 minutes each side or until well browned and cooked through. Brush with the marinade at least once during cooking. The kebabs can also be cooked on a barbecue over charcoal.

6. Serve on the skewers with boiled rice or a savoury rice, with lemon, watercress and tomato to garnish and with a variety of salads.

Moussaka

There are about as many ways of making moussaka as there are of making shepherd's pie, and moussaka has been called the Greek equivalent of the latter. Many claim that potatoes are not traditional; some say the topping should be a custard rather than a cheese sauce. It can also be made with cooked lamb – a tasty way of using up leftovers.

Serves 6–8
1.5 kg (3 lb) aubergines
salt
olive oil
3–4 medium potatoes, boiled in their skins, peeled and thinly sliced (optional)
Meat Sauce:
450–675 g (1–1½ lb) lean raw lamb, minced
225 g (8 oz) onions, peeled and chopped
1 × 400 g (14 oz) can peeled tomatoes
½ teaspoon dried oregano
2 garlic cloves, crushed
freshly ground black pepper
150 ml (¼ pint) red wine
Topping:
600 ml (1 pint) thick Béchamel Sauce (see page 30)
½ teaspoon made mustard
2 eggs
75 g (3 oz) Cheddar cheese, grated

Preparation time: about 1¼ hours
Cooking time: about 1¾–2 hours
Oven: 180°C, 350°F, Gas Mark 4

1. Cut the aubergines into 5 mm (¼ inch) slices and arrange them in a colander. Sprinkle in between the layers with salt. Put a plate on top and leave them for about an hour to degorge, or get rid of the bitter juices.

2. Rinse the aubergine slices, pat dry with kitchen paper and then fry, on one side only, in some olive oil until golden. They 'eat' oil and frying them on one side only reduces the ultimate fattiness of the dish. (Alternatively, the slices could simply be blanched in water.) Drain them well on kitchen paper.

3. Meanwhile, make the meat sauce. Heat the lamb mince in a large frying pan until the fat runs out. Fry until uniformly brown. Remove to a plate with a slotted spoon and set aside.

4. Fry the onions in the fat until soft and golden, then strain off the fat.

5. Put the meat back in the pan with the onions, and add the tomatoes and their juice, oregano, garlic, salt and pepper. Simmer, uncovered, for about 30 minutes until thick and rich. Add the wine and boil fiercely for a few moments. Taste for seasoning.

6. For the cheese sauce, warm the Béchamel sauce gently, and stir in the mustard. Beat the eggs into the sauce off the heat. Stir in the cheese.

7. To assemble the dish, line the bottom of a wide, shallow ovenproof dish with a layer of aubergine slices, cooked side down, then put in a layer of meat sauce. Put in a layer of potato, if used, and continue the layers until all the ingredients are finished. Pour the cheese sauce over the top.

8. Bake in a preheated oven for about 40–60 minutes, or until the topping is golden brown.

Lamb Hotpot

Serves 4–5
8–12 middle neck of lamb chops or best end chops
225 g (8 oz) onions, peeled and finely chopped
2–3 carrots, scraped and sliced
2 lamb's kidneys, skinned, cored and diced (optional)
salt
freshly ground black pepper
½ teaspoon dried rosemary (optional)
450–675 g (1–1½ lb) potatoes, peeled and thinly sliced
300 ml (½ pint) stock or half stock and half white wine or cider
25 g (1 oz) butter, melted
chopped parsley, to garnish

Preparation time: about 20 minutes
Cooking time: about 2½ hours
Oven: 160°C, 325°F, Gas Mark 3, then: 220°C, 425°F, Gas Mark 7

1. Trim the lamb of excess fat and layer the chops in a casserole with the onions, carrots, kidneys, seasonings and rosemary.

2. Arrange a neat layer of sliced potato over the ingredients in the casserole.

3. Bring the stock to the boil and pour over the potatoes; then brush the potatoes with melted butter.

4. Cover the casserole with a lid or foil and cook in a moderate oven for 2 hours. Remove the lid, increase the oven temperature to hot and continue cooking for about 20 minutes or until the potatoes are well browned. Finish browning under a moderate grill, if liked. Serve sprinkled with chopped parsley.

VEAL

Escalopes that melt in the mouth, creamy fricassée, classic Italian ossobuco braised in a rich tomato and wine sauce . . . these are just some of the delicious veal dishes you'll find in this section. A complete guide to the cuts will bring you up to date on this tender, lean, no-waste meat.

Veal is the meat from a very young calf and because the calf should be very young, and thus milk-fed (although this is not always so), the flesh should be a very light pink in colour, and soft and moist with only very little fat which should be firm and either white or faintly pink. Do not buy veal that is over-flabby and really wet looking. As the animal ages, the flesh becomes deeper pink, slightly mottled, often taking on a slightly bluish tinge and more mature veal does not have the melting tenderness of good young veal. If veal looks dry, brownish, or has a very mottled appearance, it is stale.

Veal has a lot of bone in proportion to flesh and these bones make an excellent pale gelatinous stock to use in all sorts of soups, sauces and gravies. Never discard any veal bones that come with the joint; they may be used for stock, either raw or cooked, and the resulting stock will form a really solid jelly. The feet of calves are particularly gelatinous, and are used to make aspic, or the calf's foot jelly that used to be served to invalids.

Because veal has very little fat, great care must be taken during cooking to prevent it drying out and roasting meat is usually barded (see page 128) with pork fat or fatty bacon. For this reason, veal is rarely grilled, unless very carefully moistened by basting. Whatever method of cooking you choose, make sure there is sufficient fat for roasting or frying, and liquid for casseroling or pot-roasting. The meat should not be cooked too fast or over a fierce heat, this would make it dry and tasteless and a waste of money, for all cuts of veal tend to be expensive.

Guide to the cuts of veal

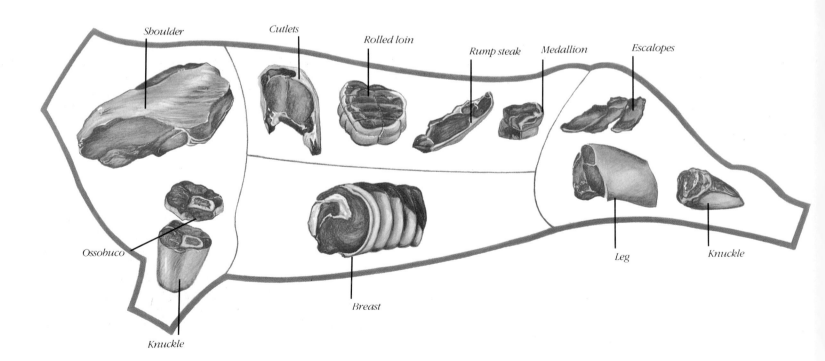

Shoulder   Cutlets   Rolled loin   Rump steak   Medallion   Escalopes

Ossobuco   Leg   Knuckle

Knuckle   Breast

CUTS OF VEAL

Leg This is a prime cut, and can be subdivided into other cuts, including the knuckle. A leg joint is often boned and rolled, sometimes with a stuffing added before rolling. It can also be cooked on the bone, although this is not usual. It is suitable for roasting, pot-roasting, or braising.

Loin Another prime cut for roasting – from the back – which again is more often boned and rolled with or without stuffing rather than cooked on the bone. It has more fat on it than most of the other joints. It is also cut into cutlets from the neck end, and chops as you move further down the joint.

Shoulder This is often boned and rolled and roasted or pot-roasted. It is also cut into pieces to use for pies, fricassées, casseroles, etc. It is a more economical joint because of its rather awkward shape.

Fillet This is the prime cut of the calf, from the hindquarters, and is usually sliced into escalopes to fry or grill. However, it can be used as a very expensive roasting joint or cut into cubes for kebabs.

Knuckle This is a cheaper cut from the end of the leg. It is bony, but is good for stewing, for pies and casseroles and to mince; it is the traditional cut used for ossobuco (see page 147) when it is sawn across into small pieces, each one a ring of bone surrounded by meat. The flavour is good, coming both from the meat and the bone with its marrow. It can also be boned and rolled to pot-roast or braise, but not roast.

Breast Another fairly cheap cut that is usually boned, stuffed and rolled and then pot-roasted or braised.

Chops These come from the loin. Those from the bottom end, with a small round bone, are known as chump chops; those from the other end are called cutlets although one cutlet is quite large. All chops are suitable for frying, grilling (if basted well) and pan-frying, but need good flavourings or a good sauce as accompaniment.

Veal escalopes These are probably the most popular cut of veal and are the most expensive. The escalopes should be cut from the best part or fillet end of the leg, and they should be cut between 5 mm (¼ inch) and 1 cm (½ inch) thick. They should always be cut across the grain of the meat, not along it. However, not all veal escalopes are cut from the correct part of the leg, mainly for cost reasons.

Once cut, escalopes are usually beaten so they are very much thinner. Usually the butcher will do this for you, but if not it is quite simple to do yourself. Put the escalopes, one at a time, between two sheets of damp greaseproof paper or cling film and, with the flat side of a meat chopper or the rolling pin, beat out the meat evenly thin. Do not continually

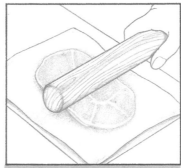

Beat escalopes thinly between sheets of paper

Dip in egg and coat with breadcrumbs

beat in one place or the fibres will break.

Each escalope is then dipped in beaten egg and coated with fresh white breadcrumbs. Sauté in butter over medium heat for about 4 minutes on each side.

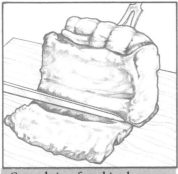

Carve loin of veal in the same way as beef

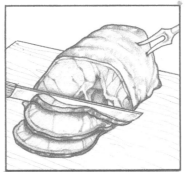

Carve a rolled and boned joint in thin slices

How much to allow

For roasting joints on the bone allow 225–350 g (8–12 oz) raw per portion.
For roasting joints, boned and rolled allow 175–225 g (6–8 oz) raw per portion, plus extra to serve cold.
For fillets or escalopes (boneless) allow 100–150 g (4–5 oz) raw per portion.
For chops allow 1 veal chop taken from the loin; or 1–2 cutlets taken from the neck end or top of loin, depending on the size of the animal.
For breast of veal on the bone, knuckle on the bone, and best end of neck on the bone allow about 450 g (1 lb) raw per portion; or, when boned, allow 100–175 g (6–8 oz) raw per portion.

Carving veal

Veal is similar in shape to beef and therefore is carved in a similar way. However, it is a lot more tender than some meats, so should carve much more easily, providing you have a sharp knife. Most roasted or pot-roasted veal joints are boned and rolled, so all that is necessary is to remove any skewers and the string as each piece is reached. The joint is carved in fairly thin vertical slices. When on the bone, carve in a similar way to beef or pork (for loin joints). Remember to leave the joint to stand and 'set' for 5–10 minutes before carving.

Accompaniments to roast veal

Forcemeat balls made with a mixture of herbs and lemon rind are the most common accompaniment; prunes are sometimes used (use the ready soaked and stoned variety, sautéed in butter); glazed onions; and sometimes a spinach or sorrel purée. Lemon is a predominant flavouring for all veal dishes.

Roast Veal with Stuffing Balls

As veal is a very dry meat with very little fat of its own to keep the flesh moist, it is a good idea to wrap it in bacon first; this has a good proportion of fat to help keep the meat moist.

Serves 6
about 1.75 kg (4 lb) prime roasting joint of veal, boned and rolled
8–10 rashers streaky bacon
salt
freshly ground black pepper
about 50 g (2 oz) dripping or other fat
stuffing balls (see below)
1 tablespoon lemon juice

Preparation time: about 20 minutes
Cooking time: about 2 hours
Oven: 220°C, 425°F, Gas Mark 7; then 180°C, 350°F, Gas Mark 4

1. Trim the joint, weigh it, then stand it in a roasting tin. Lay the rashers of bacon evenly over the joint, tying in place with string, if necessary. Season lightly, if liked, and spread the dripping liberally over the whole joint.

2. Calculate the cooking time, allowing 30 minutes per 450 g (1 lb). Place in the preheated oven for 15 minutes, then reduce the temperature and continue cooking, basting every 15 minutes. Potatoes may be roasted around the joint for the last hour of cooking. For a larger joint that will take longer than 1½ hours, lay a sheet of foil over it after 1¼–1½ hours of the cooking time, to prevent it drying out.

3. About 45 minutes before the end of the cooking time, put the stuffing balls on a greased baking sheet in the oven below the joint to cook.

4. Remove the joint to a serving dish and, if preferred, remove the bacon. Allow 5–10 minutes to 'set' before carving, and serve with the stuffing balls, a garnish of lemon wedges and parsley, and a green vegetable, perhaps spinach, or celery in a white sauce. Make a fairly thin gravy from the pan juices and flavour it lightly with lemon juice.

Stuffing Balls

1 small onion, peeled and finely chopped
25 g (1 oz) butter or margarine
25 g (1 oz) mushrooms, finely chopped
25 g (1 oz) walnut halves, finely chopped
1 tablespoon chopped parsley
1 tablespoon freshly chopped thyme or 1 teaspoon dried thyme
grated rind of ½–1 lemon
salt
freshly ground black pepper
75 g (3 oz) fresh breadcrumbs
1 egg, beaten
a little lemon juice (optional)

Preparation time: 15 minutes
Cooking time: about 45 minutes

1. Fry the onion gently in the melted fat until soft. Add the mushrooms and continue cooking for a minute or so. Turn into a bowl and leave to cool.

2. Add the walnuts, parsley, thyme, lemon rind, seasonings and the breadcrumbs and mix well.

3. Add the beaten egg to bind with a few drops of lemon juice if necessary to moisten. Shape into balls about the size of a large walnut.

4. Place the stuffing balls on a greased baking sheet and cook below the joint in a hot oven for about 45 minutes or until lightly browned and firm.

Fried Veal Escalopes

Veal escalopes are delicious by themselves with only a wedge of lemon – as with the classic Wiener Schnitzel – but other garnishes or toppings may be added to transform the simple escalope into Veal Viennoise or Veal Holstein.

Serves 4
4 veal escalopes, beaten
salt
freshly ground black pepper
1–2 eggs, beaten
about 100 g (4 oz) fresh white breadcrumbs
100 g (4 oz) butter
4–6 tablespoons oil
Wiener Schnitzel:
lemon wedges
watercress
Viennoise:
1 hard-boiled egg
1–2 tablespoons capers
a few anchovy fillets
Holstein:
4 eggs
oil, for frying
a few anchovy fillets
parsley, to garnish

Preparation time: about 20 minutes, plus chilling time
Cooking time: about 15 minutes, or a little longer for Veal Holstein

1. Make sure the escalopes have been beaten until evenly thin all over, either by the butcher or by yourself (see page 145).

2. Season the beaten egg, if preferred, and then dip the escalopes into it, one at a time. Immediately coat each one in fresh breadcrumbs, pressing them in firmly. Any places that have been missed should be dabbed with beaten egg and extra crumbs pressed in. At this stage the escalopes may be chilled for several hours before cooking.

3. Melt the butter and about half the oil in a frying pan and fry the veal escalopes gently two at a time only, until golden brown on one side – about 5 minutes. Turn over carefully and fry the second side until golden brown and cooked through – again about 5 minutes. Drain on absorbent kitchen paper and keep warm whilst frying the remainder. It may be necessary to add more oil to the pan.

4. To serve the escalopes as Wiener Schnitzel, garnish the escalopes simply with wedges of lemon and watercress.
  To serve the escalopes as Veal Viennoise, garnish each with a small pile of sieved egg yolk surrounded by finely chopped egg white and capers with 2 fillets of anchovy laid over the garnish or rolled up and placed on top.
  To serve the escalopes as Veal Holstein, fry 4 eggs, preferably without basting them so they are yellow-faced, and put one on top of each escalope. Add a criss-cross of anchovy fillets and sprig of parsley.

Ossobuco

Braised Knuckle of Veal

Ossobuco comes from Milan, and should traditionally be accompanied by a Risotto (see page 190). Don't forget to eat the marrow from the centre of the bones – it's delicious!

Serves 4
4 large meaty pieces knuckle of veal, about 5 cm (2 inches) thick
25 g (1 oz) plain flour
3 tablespoons olive oil
1 large onion, finely chopped
1 large carrot, finely chopped
1 celery stick, finely chopped
150 ml (¼ pint) dry white wine
300 ml (½ pint) Veal Stock (see page 27)
2 garlic cloves, crushed
a strip of lemon peel
2 teaspoons tomato purée
salt
freshly ground black pepper
350 g (12 oz) ripe tomatoes, peeled and chopped
1 bouquet garni
To garnish:
1 tablespoon finely chopped parsley
½ small garlic clove, peeled and very finely chopped (optional)
1 teaspoon finely grated lemon peel (optional)

Preparation time: about 15 minutes
Cooking time: about 2 hours

1. Coat the pieces of veal with flour and then brown on all sides in 1 tablespoon of the oil in a flameproof casserole large enough to hold the pieces in one layer. Remove to a plate as they are browned.

2. Gently cook the chopped onion, carrot and celery in the casserole in the remaining oil until just soft then remove with a slotted spoon and reserve.

3. Sprinkle any remaining flour into the casserole and stir well.

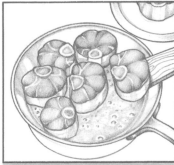
Flour the veal and brown on all sides.

Add the veal to the stock and vegetables.

Sprinkle the finished dish with the garnish.

Pour in the wine and stock and boil briskly for about 3 minutes, stirring, then add the garlic, lemon peel, tomato purée, seasoning, chopped tomatoes and vegetables.

4. Bring back to the boil and place the veal pieces in the liquid. Tuck the bouquet garni in as well and cover.

5. Simmer gently on top of the stove for 1½ hours or until the meat is very tender.

6. Remove the veal and keep warm in a shallow serving platter, covered with foil. Boil the sauce rapidly, after removing the bouquet garni, to reduce and thicken it, and then push through a sieve if liked. Pour over the meat and serve piping hot, sprinkled with a mixture of parsley, garlic and lemon rind.

Veal Fricassée

Serves 6
1 tablespoon oil
50 g (2 oz) butter
900 g (2 lb) stewing or pie veal, cut into 2.5 cm (1 inch) cubes
225 g (8 oz) back bacon, rinded and cut into small dice
1 onion, peeled and finely chopped
300 ml (½ pint) Veal Stock (see page 27)
salt
freshly ground black pepper
2 tablespoons flour
2 tablespoons lemon juice
6 tablespoons double cream
To garnish:
turned mushrooms, fried (see right)
watercress or chopped parsley
fried bread triangles (optional)

Preparation time: about 20 minutes
Cooking time: about 2 hours
Oven: 180°C, 350°F, Gas Mark 4

1. Melt the oil and half the butter in a pan and fry the veal until well sealed but not at all coloured. Remove from the pan to a casserole. Fry the bacon in the same fat until sealed but not browned and add to the casserole.

2. Add the onion to the fat left in the pan and fry very gently until soft, but not coloured. Transfer to the casserole.

3. Bring the stock to the boil, and pour over the contents of the casserole. Season, cover tightly and cook for 1½ hours.

4. Strain off the liquor and keep the ingredients in the casserole warm.

5. Melt the remaining butter in a small pan and stir in the flour. Cook for a minute or so stirring constantly. Gradually add the cooking liquor and bring back to the boil for a minute or so. Add the lemon juice and mix well then stir in the cream and reheat gently without boiling. Adjust the seasonings.

6. Turn the meat and onion into a shallow serving dish and pour the sauce over. Garnish with fried turned mushrooms and watercress or chopped parsley. Triangles of fried bread may also be used as a garnish.

To turn mushrooms

Take a medium sized button mushroom and, beginning in the centre of the mushroom, carefully pare off a thin strip of the skin taking it at an angle to the outer edge. Do this evenly around the cap, using a small sharp knife, until there is a stripy pattern. Simply toss in melted butter for a minute or so and use as a garnish.

OFFAL

Liver and kidney, brains and tripe, sweetbreads, oxtail and tongue: make the most of nutritious, value-for-money offal by following our detailed instructions on what to look for, how to prepare it and how best to cook it.

The word offal – which means, literally, the 'off-fall' or off-cuts from a carcass – puts many people off trying any of these delicious cuts.

It is usually taken to mean liver and kidneys, and people don't realize how wide a selection of other parts of the animal it includes: brains, sweetbreads, glands, tails, tongues etc. Although they do not sound appetizing, they are very rich in nutrients which are vital for everybody from the smallest child upwards. The most important is iron, found in abundance in liver particularly.

Offal is relatively inexpensive (apart from calf's liver). However, it is extremely perishable and should be bought and consumed on the day of purchase, or at the very latest within 24 hours, provided it is kept in the refrigerator. Offal can be bought and frozen provided it is fresh and has not already been frozen; and it will keep for up to 2 months in the freezer. As with all meats it is best thawed out slowly and then cooked as soon as possible.

There is very little waste on offal and most of it is quick to cook and easy to prepare. There are one or two forms which need a little more preparation before the actual cooking.

Most offal is easily digestible and is, therefore, a valuable food to serve to invalids, children and to the elderly. It is also useful during pregnancy, but it should feature in a good sensible diet at least once a week, as it is extremely versatile as well as nutritious.

TYPES OF OFFAL

Liver

There are several types of liver available and all are good value. They vary in flavour and texture, however, and therefore require different types of cooking to serve at their best. Whatever type, liver should be smooth and glossy, and it should not have a strong smell if it is fresh. Always wash it to rinse away any excess blood and cut out any tubes, or membranes. Take care not to overcook liver or it can become hard and dry.

Ox liver. This is the cheapest of the livers, has a strong flavour, and can be tough because the texture is rather coarse. It needs to be soaked or blanched before cooking to

Cut away any tubes or membrane from the liver

help remove some of the strong flavour. It is best used for slow braising or casseroling, rather than for frying or grilling.

Calf's liver. The finest and most expensive of all the livers, it is not always easy to obtain. It is very tender with a delicate flavour and is best simply and lightly fried in butter, grilled, or pan-fried with various flavourings.

Pig's liver. This is fairly cheap, and has a very distinct and rather strong flavour with a much softer texture than some of the other livers, which not everyone likes. It can be fried or grilled, but is better braised or casseroled; it is the most popular liver (along with chicken livers) for making pâtés and terrines. It is possible to remove some of the strong flavour prior to cooking by soaking in milk for about 30 minutes.

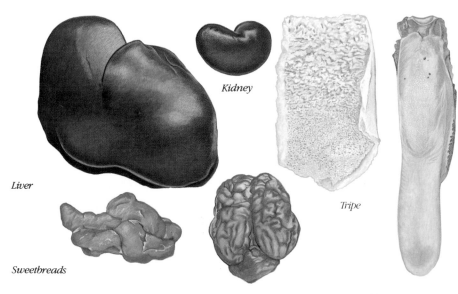

Liver

Kidney

Sweetbreads

Brains

Tripe

Tongue

Lamb's liver. This is probably the most popular of the livers, with a good flavour which is not as strong or pronounced as pig's or ox liver. Although not as tender as calf's liver, it is much cheaper.

Chicken or turkey livers are very tender and easily obtained. They make excellent pâté and are good fried. Remove any greenish patches (from the gall bladder) or the liver will taste bitter.

These livers are very rich in flavour and are therefore often used in very small quantities. They can be bought either loose or frozen in cartons. After freezing the texture is very soft, and they are then best used in pâtés or sauces.

Kidneys

Kidneys are sometimes sold still in their casing of suet which must be removed. They should smell mild, be smooth and shiny with no discoloured patches, and be soft to the touch.

All kidneys are covered in a thin transparent skin which must be removed before cooking, as must the fatty core. It is best to snip out the core with a pair of scissors.

Kidneys can be grilled or fried, pan-fried and sautéed as well as being added to casseroles along with other meats, added to stuffings, risottos and many other foods. They should not be

overcooked, though, as they are virtually fatless and therefore shrivel and dry out easily.

Ox kidney. This is the largest and cheapest. It has a fairly strong flavour and needs a little more cooking than the smaller kidneys. It looks different, too, for it is made up of many joined lobes and a whole kidney weighs about 675 g (1½ lb). However, ox kidney is sold cut up in pieces by butchers to suit your needs. It is also available mixed with braising steak ready to make into steak and kidney pudding or pie.

Calf's kidney. Similar in multi-lobed shape to ox kidney, but much smaller and paler in colour. It is more tender and more delicate in flavour, but can be cooked in the same ways. It is in very short supply.

Lamb's kidney. Usually the best and most popular of all the kidneys. They are small and well flavoured but do not have a harsh or overpowering taste. The flavour blends well with many other foods and is enhanced by the addition of wine, herbs, and citrus fruits amongst others. They can be cooked whole or halved or cut into pieces, simply by frying in butter or grilling, but do not overcook or they will become tough and dry. They are available both fresh and frozen.

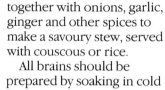
1. Soak brains in cold water for 15 minutes

2. Remove the membrane after blanching

Pig's kidney. This is larger than lamb's kidney, more elongated in shape and slightly lighter and more orangey in colour. They are also stronger in flavour, but can still be fried or grilled, as well as being diced to add to casseroles for flavour. They make a good soup.

Suet is the hard fat from around the kidneys of beef or mutton. Beef suet is better flavoured and more often used in cooking. Fresh suet used to be an important ingredient in dishes such as suet pudding, roly poly pudding or dumplings etc. Nowadays suet is usually bought ready-shredded in packets, but fresh suet still has the best flavour. See page 264 for how to make Suet Crust.

Brains

It is essential to buy these really fresh and to use them at once. Some butchers will only sell them to order, for they cannot be kept or sold unless they are very fresh. Calf's are the best and most expensive, followed by lamb's. Calf's can be crumbed and fried or poached and served with a delicately flavoured sauce; lamb's are best if braised or casseroled, pig's brains are not so good nor so popular.

Two French methods of cooking brains are either tried in brown butter (à la meunière) or poached in red wine and served sliced with a

rich wine sauce. In Algeria, brains and tongues are chopped up and cooked together with onions, garlic, ginger and other spices to make a savoury stew, served with couscous or rice.

All brains should be prepared by soaking in cold water for 15 minutes. They should then be put into clean water and brought to the boil. This will enable the membrane to be removed before cooking further.

Blanch sweetbreads then press until compact

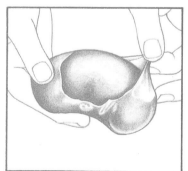
1. Peel off the fine membrane

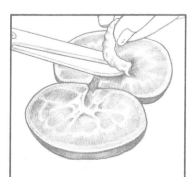
2. Cut in half and snip out the core

Tripe

This comes from the stomach lining of a cow or ox. There are two types – ordinary or blanket and honeycomb – and they come from the first and second stomachs respectively. Tripe is a light and easily digested meat but it must be prepared carefully. It is usually bought ready 'dressed' which means it has been cleaned and parboiled, but it still requires further slow, gentle cooking. It should be thick, firm and very white. Grey, slimy or strong-smelling tripe should be avoided.

It is traditionally served in a white onion sauce as tripe and onions; but it is equally good served shallow fried after dipping in egg and breadcrumbs. It can also be casseroled, and a tomato and herb sauce with a hint of garlic is a good accompaniment.

Hearts

These make an excellent casserole or pot-roast, being a very economical meat with no fat, but as the heart itself is a strong muscle, it requires very long slow cooking to serve it at its tender best. Hearts must be very thoroughly washed and soaked in cold water to remove the blood, and all the tubes and veins should be trimmed off. Once cooked the gravy or sauce has a marvellous flavour.

Ox heart. This is the largest and consequently the toughest of the hearts. It is best to cut it into strips or dice rather than to cook it whole. If to be pot-roasted, it is best halved and parboiled before a stuffing is added; cook thereafter on a bed of flavoursome vegetables with a good stock. A whole heart will weigh about 1.5–2 kg (3–4½ lb), and be bluish-red in colour.

Calf's heart. Smaller and therefore more tender than ox

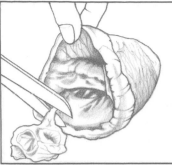

1. Snip out any tendons or tubes from the heart

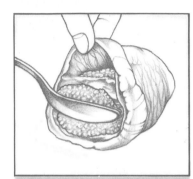

2. Spoon in a stuffing and sew up before cooking

heart, but it still needs slow cooking for preference. It can be stuffed and braised or pot-roasted whole, or even roasted if it has a lid of foil.

Lamb's heart. The smallest and most tender of all the hearts, with a very good flavour. They are usually stuffed and then braised, pot-roasted or casseroled; they can also be roasted with care.

Tongue

Always look for a tongue that has as smooth a skin as possible, for as the animal ages, so its tongue roughens and will consequently be tough. Tongues are available fresh, salted or pickled and sometimes smoked. They should be soaked in cold water overnight before cooking, and a fresh tongue will need to cook twice as long as a salted or smoked one.

The best flavoured tongue is an ox tongue, and the texture is

good too. It can be boiled or braised to serve hot or cold. Traditionally, when served cold, an ox tongue is skinned, then curled and pressed into a tin and covered with an aspic made from its own liquor; when set, it looks good and will carve easily into thin slices.

Calves' and lambs' tongues are smaller, are sold fresh, and can be boiled or braised to serve hot or cold. The small tongues, once cooked, can be skinned before returning to a sauce to serve.

Sweetbreads

Sweetbreads are the thymus glands (in the throat) and the pancreas glands (near the stomach) of young animals. The latter are considered to be the finer. Again these must be bought really fresh and should be used at once. Lamb's sweetbreads are thought to be best followed by calf's (probably because the latter are rarer and thus more expensive). Ox sweetbreads, available cheaply, are less tender than calf's or lamb's, and are very much stronger in flavour.

All sweetbreads need to be as white and blood-free as possible and thus require a good soaking of up to 4 hours, with the water changed frequently to remove all the blood from between the lobes. This soaking also softens the membrane or skin, making it easier to remove. Drain and put into a pan of cold salted water and bring it slowly to the boil. Remove the sweetbreads and carefully pick out all the veins and peel off the membrane or skin. Put the blanched sweetbreads between two plates to flatten them as they cool. They are best cooked by lightly frying in butter to serve with a delicately flavoured sauce, or dipped in egg and breadcrumbs and shallow fried, to serve garnished with lemon.

Oxtail

This part of the animal speaks for itself but it has an excellent flavour and makes a wonderful casserole as well as a traditional soup. It has a high proportion of bone and is usually rather fatty, but some of this can be trimmed off before starting to cook. It should look fresh and bright when bought, with good red flesh and creamy white fat. If he has not already done so, the butcher will cut it up for you into slices which are usually about 4–5 cm (1½–2 inches) thick. The dish should have a long slow cooking to bring out the flavour and to really tenderize the meat; for preference, it should be cooked the day before required, so that the layer of fat can form on the surface and then be removed before reheating to serve.

How much to allow

For liver, allow 100–150 g (4–5 oz) raw per portion.
For kidneys, allow 100–150 g (4–5 oz) raw per portion for ox kidney; 1 calves' kidney will serve 1–2 portions; 2 lamb's will serve 1 portion; allow 1–2 pig's kidneys per portion, depending on size.
For hearts, a whole ox heart will serve 4–6 portions; 1 calf's heart will serve 2 portions; allow 1 lamb's heart per portion.
For sweetbreads, allow about 100 g (4 oz), or a pair per portion.
For brains, allow 1–2 sets per portion.
For tripe, allow 100–175 g (4–6 oz) raw per portion.
For tongue, an ox tongue weighs about 1.8 kg (4 lb) so will serve up to 8 portions if served hot, more if served cold; calves' tongues weigh from 450–900 g (1–2 lb) so each will serve 3–4 portions; allow one lamb's tongue per portion.
For oxtail, 1 oxtail will serve 4 portions.

Pressed Tongue

Serves 8–10
1 salted or pickled ox tongue,
weighing about 1.5 kg
(3–3½ lb)
2 medium onions, peeled and
each studded with 2 cloves
2 bay leaves
2 carrots, peeled and sliced
8 black peppercorns
2 tablespoons vinegar
1 tablespoon brown sugar

Preparation time: about 20
minutes, plus soaking and
chilling
Cooking time: about 3½ hours

Soaking the tongue in cold
water overnight

To test, plunge a skewer into
the root

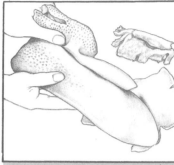
After cooking, peel off the
skin and remove bones

1. Soak the tongue in cold
water for 12–24 hours. Drain,
place in a saucepan and cover
with cold water.

2. Add the onions, bay leaves,
carrots, peppercorns, vinegar
and sugar to the pan and bring
up to the boil. Remove any
scum from the surface, then
cover the pan tightly and
simmer very gently for about

3½ hours, adding a little more
boiling water if necessary to
keep the tongue covered. The
tongue should be very tender –
check with a fine skewer
inserted into the root.

3. Drain the tongue and
immediately plunge it into cold
water. Remove the skin, and
any bones and gristle from the
thick end of the tongue.

4. Arrange the tongue in a
round 15 cm (6 inch) cake tin,
curling it round to fit neatly.
Spoon over a little of the
reduced cooking liquor.

Curl into a cake tin and add
a little stock.

5. Stand a saucer or small plate
on top of the tongue and put a
heavy weight on the saucer.
Leave until quite cold and then
chill overnight at least.

6. To serve, turn the tongue
carefully out of the tin and
place on a plate. Serve with a
selection of salads and new or
boiled potatoes. Carve the
tongue horizontally in thin
slices.

Lambs' Kidneys with Orange

Serves 4
10–12 lambs' kidneys,
skinned, halved and cored
4 rashers streaky bacon, rinded
and chopped
2 onions, peeled and thinly
sliced
40 g (1½ oz) butter or
margarine
2 tablespoons seasoned flour
½ teaspoon paprika
300 ml (½ pint) beef stock
finely grated rind and juice of
1 large orange
salt
freshly ground black pepper
2 teaspoons tomato purée
100 g (4 oz) button
mushrooms, halved or sliced
chopped parsley and slices of
orange, to garnish

Preparation time: about 20
minutes
Cooking time: about 30–40
minutes

1. Cut each kidney half in half
again and dry well.

2. Fry the bacon and onions in
the melted butter in a frying
pan, until soft.

3. Coat the kidneys in seasoned
flour, reserving the excess. Add
the kidneys to the pan and
cook gently for about 5
minutes, turning frequently,
until well sealed.

4. Stir in the remaining flour
and paprika and cook for about
a minute. Gradually add the
stock, orange rind and juice
and bring slowly to the boil.
Season well and add the
tomato purée.

5. Cover the pan and simmer
gently for 10 minutes. Stir in
the mushrooms, recover the
pan, and simmer for a further
5–10 minutes or until tender,
stirring occasionally and
adding a little extra stock if
necessary.

6. Adjust the seasonings and
garnish. Serve with boiled rice
or noodles and a green salad.

M EAT

Here we take you on an international cook's tour – to France for Blanquette de veau, to Italy for cold stuffed veal in tuna sauce and stuffed veal escalopes, to Belgium for a hearty beef casserole and to India for a mouthwatering creamy Korma.

Gigot à la Bretonne

Leg of Lamb with Haricot Beans

Haricot beans go particularly well with lamb. As an alternative, braise the lamb in wine and stock, parcook the beans and then add to the casserole and let them finish cooking with the lamb.

Serves 6
1 leg of lamb, about 2 kg (4 lb)
2 garlic cloves, peeled and sliced
rosemary sprigs
4 tablespoons olive oil
salt
freshly ground black pepper
450 g (1 lb) dried white haricot beans, soaked overnight in cold water
3 onions, peeled
1 whole clove
1 bouquet garni
750 g (1½ lb) tomatoes, skinned and roughly chopped
85 ml (3 fl oz) white wine
25 g (1 oz) butter, softened

Preparation time: 15 minutes plus soaking beans overnight
Cooking time: 1¼ hours
Oven: 230°C, 450°F, Gas Mark 8, then 200°C, 400°F, Gas Mark 6

1. Using a small sharp knife, make several incisions over the surface of the lamb and press a garlic sliver and rosemary sprig into each.

2. Place the lamb in a roasting pan, then sprinkle with half the oil and salt and pepper to taste. Roast in the hot oven for 10 minutes, to sear the meat, then turn the heat down and roast for a further 45–60 minutes, basting from time to time, until the lamb is done to your liking (allow 15 minutes per 450 g (1 lb) for rare meat, 20 minutes per 450 g (1 lb) for medium-done).

3. Meanwhile, drain the beans, rinse under cold running water and drain again, then place in a large pan and cover with fresh water. Add 1 onion stuck with the clove and the bouquet garni. Bring to the boil, then lower the heat, cover and simmer for 45 minutes to 1 hour until tender. Add salt to taste halfway through the cooking time (the skins will be tough if the salt is added too early).

4. Chop the remaining onions. Heat the remaining oil in a heavy pan, add the onions and fry gently for 10 minutes until soft and lightly coloured. Add the tomatoes and wine, with salt and pepper to taste, then cook gently for 10–15 minutes until thick.

5. When the beans are tender, drain and discard the onion, clove and bouquet garni. Add the beans to the tomato mixture with the butter and stir well to mix. Heat through gently, then taste and adjust seasoning.

6. Place the lamb on a warmed serving platter and surround with the beans and tomatoes. Skim the fat from the juices in the roasting pan, then deglaze with a little boiling water or stock, and pour into a warmed sauceboat. Serve hot.

Saltimbocca alla Romana

Saltimbocca means 'jump in the mouth' – a reference to the delicious tenderness of this dish. Although it originated in Lombardy it has long been known as a Roman speciality.

Serves 6
12 thin escalopes of veal
juice of 1 large lemon
freshly ground black pepper
12 fresh sage or basil leaves or 2 teaspoons dried marjoram
12 thin slices of prosciutto (or other ham if not available)
75 g (3 oz) butter
3 tablespoons Marsala
fried croûtons, to garnish

Preparation time: 20 minutes
Cooking time: about 30 minutes

1. Ask the butcher to bat out the veal escalopes to about 10 × 13 cm (4 × 5 inches). Season with lemon juice and pepper. Place a sage or basil leaf or a little marjoram in the centre of each slice of veal and cover with a slice of ham. Roll up and secure firmly with a wooden cocktail stick.

2. Melt the butter in a frying pan just large enough to take the rolls in a single layer, packed fairly tightly to keep the rolls in good shape. Gently fry the veal rolls, turning once or twice, until golden brown on all sides. Do not overheat the butter. Add the Marsala. Bring to simmering point, cover the pan and simmer gently for 25–30 minutes, or until the veal rolls are tender. Serve hot, garnished with fried croûtons.

From the top: Gigot à la Bretonne, Saltimbocca alla Romana

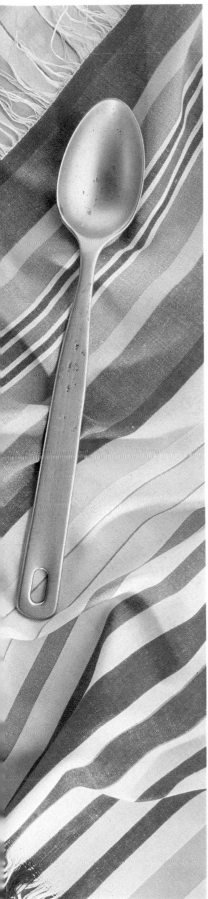

Shahi Korma

Royal Lamb Curry

This rich, creamy korma is called 'Royal' because of the luxuriousness of its ingredients. It incorporates costly spices like cardamom and saffron with cream, almonds and tender lamb to make a dish fit for a king.

Serves 6
750 g (1½ lb) boneless lamb,
trimmed and cubed
juice of 1 lemon
1 teaspoon saffron strands
120 ml (4 fl oz) boiling water
50 g (2 oz) fresh ginger,
scrubbed and chopped but
not peeled
100 g (4 oz) cashew nuts
4 green chillies, stalks removed
1 teaspoon cardamom seeds
10 cloves
2 teaspoons ground coriander
2 teaspoons coriander seeds
1 teaspoon cumin seeds
1 teaspoon ground cinnamon
300 ml (½ pint) plain yogurt
50 g (2 oz) clarified butter (see
page 42)
2 medium onions, peeled and
thinly sliced
4 cloves garlic, peeled and
thinly sliced
2 teaspoons salt
1½ teaspoons freshly ground
black pepper
300 ml (½ pint) double cream
50 g (2 oz) blanched almonds
sprig of fresh coriander, to
garnish

Preparation time: 20 minutes, plus standing
Cooking time: 1¼ hours

1. Sprinkle the cubes of lamb with the lemon juice and set aside.

2. Immerse the saffron in the boiling water and allow to stand for 10 minutes to release the flavour and colour.

3. Put the ginger, cashew nuts, chillies, cardamom seeds, cloves, ground coriander and seeds, cumin seeds, cinnamon and yogurt into a liquidizer and blend to a smooth paste. Add any excess lemon juice from the lamb.

4. Heat the clarified butter in a heavy-based saucepan and fry the lamb gently, until browned and well sealed on all sides. Remove the lamb with a slotted spoon and reserve.

5. Fry the onions and garlic in the butter until soft, then add the spiced yogurt mixture and bring to the boil. Add the saffron and its water. Stir in well and add the lamb.

6. Sprinkle in the salt and pepper, bring to the boil, cover and simmer for 45 minutes, or until the lamb is tender.

7. Reduce the heat and stir in the cream and almonds. Cook gently for a further 2–3 minutes, but do not allow to boil. Turn into a heated serving dish and garnish with fresh coriander. Serve with Basmati rice (see page 188).

Fegato alla Veneziana

Calves' Liver with Onions

Tender calves' liver, cut into the thinnest possible slices, makes for a dish of melting delicacy. Beware of over-cooking the liver, or it will become tough.

Serves 4
450 g (1 lb) calves' liver, thinly
sliced
salt
freshly ground black pepper
2 tablespoons lemon juice
450 g (1 lb) onions, peeled and
sliced
3 tablespoons olive oil
1 tablespoon seasoned flour
120 ml (4 fl oz) red wine
1 tablespoon chopped fresh
parsley

Preparation time: 10 minutes
Cooking time: 20 minutes

1. Sprinkle the liver with salt, pepper and lemon juice and leave to marinate while cooking the onions.

2. Heat the oil in a large frying pan. Add the onions and fry gently for 10 minutes, until softened and lightly coloured.

3. Dust the liver lightly with the seasoned flour and add to the pan. Fry for about 5 minutes, until lightly browned, turning the liver once.

4. Sprinkle over the red wine, parsley, salt and pepper. Simmer gently for 5 minutes, stirring the onions and turning the liver. Serve piping hot.

From the left: Fegato alla Veneziana.
Shahi korma

Navarin d'Agneau

Lamb Stew

This wonderful lamb stew was traditionally made in the spring when vegetables were young and tender. Nowadays of course, it can be made all year round, thanks to the deep-freeze, but it still tastes best with fresh young vegetables.

Serves 6
1½ kg (3 lb) middle neck of lamb, trimmed and cut into neat pieces
25 g (1 oz) plain flour
salt
freshly ground black pepper
50 g (2 oz) dripping or vegetable fat
1 onion, peeled and thinly sliced
6 carrots, scraped and sliced
1 small piece of turnip, peeled and sliced
2 garlic cloves, peeled and crushed
a pinch of sugar
bouquet garni
750–900 ml (1¼–1½ pints) Brown Stock (see page 27)
3 tablespoons tomato purée
18 button onions, peeled
100 g (4 oz) green peas
100 g (4 oz) French beans, cut into 1 cm (½ inch) pieces
350–450 g (¾–1 lb) small new potatoes, scraped, or old potatoes, peeled and cut into large dice

Preparation time: 30 minutes
Cooking time: about 2–2½ hours
Oven: 160°C, 325°F, Gas Mark 3

1. Coat the meat pieces with seasoned flour, then melt the dripping in a heavy frying pan. Add the meat in batches and brown briskly on all sides. Remove from the pan, and put into a large casserole.

2. Add the onion, carrot, turnip and garlic to the fat in the frying pan along with the sugar. Fry gently until coloured. Remove with a slotted spoon and place in the casserole along with the meat. Add the bouquet garni.

3. Pour off all but 1 tablespoon of the fat from the frying pan, and stir in any remaining seasoned flour. Cook for a few moments, then gradually stir in the hot stock. Add the tomato purée and bring to the boil.

4. Pour the sauce from the pan over the meat and vegetables, and season with salt and pepper. Cover with a lid and place in a preheated oven. Cook for 1¼–1½ hours.

5. Meanwhile, blanch the button onions, peas and beans, separately, in salted boiling water. Drain well.

6. Remove the stew from the oven, and skim off fat. Add the blanched onions and the potatoes, stirring them in, and cook for a further 30 minutes or until the vegetables are tender.

7. About 10 minutes before the stew is ready, add the blanched peas and beans to the casserole. Stir them in a little so they cook in the sauce. Let the stew continue to cook its allotted time, then serve immediately from the casserole.

8. The stew can be cooked in advance and refrigerated overnight, then reheated for 30 minutes at 200°C, 400°F, Gas Mark 6.

9. This dish will freeze better without the potatoes. Thaw in a refrigerator or cool room overnight and continue with step 5 as above.

Boeuf Stroganoff

This is one of the few dishes of international repute that Russia has given the world. it is the ideal dish if you have to entertain important guests in a hurry.

Serves 4–6
1 kg (2 lb) fillet or rump steak
freshly ground black pepper
2 tablespoons finely chopped onion
50 g (2 oz) butter
225 g (8 oz) button mushrooms, sliced
salt
good pinch of freshly grated nutmeg
300 ml (½ pint) soured cream
3 tablespoons finely chopped parsley

Preparation time: 15 minutes
Cooking time: about 20 minutes

1. Cut the beef across the grain into 5 × 1 cm (2 × ½ inch) strips about 1 cm (½ inch) thick. Season to taste with salt and pepper.

2. In a large heavy frying pan melt 40 g (1½ oz) of the butter and fry the onion for a few minutes until softened, then add the mushrooms and cook for a few minutes until softened. Using a slotted spoon, transfer the vegetables to a heated plate and keep hot.

3. Melt the remaining butter in the pan, add the beef, and sauté over a brisk heat for a few minutes until well browned but still pink inside. Do this in batches unless the pan is very large. The beef must not be overcooked or it will toughen and the texture and flavour of the dish will be impaired.

4. Return the vegetables to the pan and season with salt, pepper and nutmeg. Stir in the soured cream, heat through without boiling and transfer to a heated serving dish. Sprinkle with the parsley and serve with plain boiled rice.

From the top: Navarin d'agneau, Boeuf Stroganoff

Boeuf en Daube Provençal

Provençal Beef Stew

Although daube is simply a method of cooking meat very slowly in wine, it has become almost synonymous with beef as this is the meat that suits this method best. Serve this dish with a rich full-bodied wine.

1 kg (2 lb) lean chuck or blade-bone steak, trimmed and cut into 4 cm (1½ inch) cubes
2–3 onions, peeled and sliced
3 carrots, scraped and sliced
1 strip orange rind, without pith
1 bay leaf
4–5 black peppercorns
300 ml (½ pint) red wine
4 tablespoons cognac
4 tablespoons olive oil
2–3 garlic cloves, peeled and crushed with a little salt
300 ml (½ pint) Bone Stock (see page 24)
100 g (4 oz) black olives, pitted
freshly ground black pepper
2 tablespoons finely chopped fresh parsley, to garnish

Preparation time: 20 minutes, plus marinating overnight
Cooking time: 2–2½ hours
Oven: 160°C, 325°F, Gas Mark 3

1. Place the beef in a deep dish with 1 sliced onion, the carrots, orange rind, bay leaf and peppercorns. Pour on the red wine and cognac, cover and leave to marinate in the refrigerator overnight.

2. Remove the meat and vegetables from the wine and drain well, reserving the marinade.

3. Heat the oil in a flameproof casserole, add the beef in batches and brown on all sides. Remove from the casserole with a slotted spoon and set aside.

4. Add the remaining onions and the crushed garlic to the casserole and cook gently until golden brown.

5. Return the beef to the casserole together with the wine, vegetables, orange rind and bay leaf used in the marinade. Discard the peppercorns. Add the stock, salt and pepper. Bring to the boil.

6. Cover tightly, bring to the boil and place in the preheated oven. Cook for 2–2½ hours until tender.

7. Discard the bay leaf and orange rind. Skim any fat from the surface of the sauce. Remove the beef from the pan and boil the sauce until reduced by half.

8. Return the meat to the casserole with the olives and pour the sauce over. Taste and adjust the seasoning and sprinkle with the chopped parsley.

9. Serve with noodles, macaroni or creamed potatoes.

Porc Normande

Cows fed on Normandy's rich pasture produce superlative milk and cream, while the region's apples produce the famous cider and Calvados. This recipe combines Normandy's finest ingredients with rich pork.

Serves 4–6
1.5 kg (3 lb) boned and rolled loin of pork
salt
freshly ground black pepper
2 tablespoons water
4 tablespoons dry cider
1 kg (2 lb) cooking apples, peeled, cored and cut into quarters
25 g (1 oz) butter
2 tablespoons double cream

Preparation time: 20 minutes
Cooking time: 2¼ hours
Oven: 190°C, 375°F, Gas Mark 5

1. Place the pork in a greased roasting pan and sprinkle with salt and pepper. Add the water, then roast in the preheated oven for 1¾ hours, basting frequently.

2. Remove the pork from the pan and drain off the cooking juices. Pour the cider into the pan, add the pork, then surround with the apples. Sprinkle with salt and pepper, then dot with the butter. Return to the moderately hot oven and roast for a further 20 minutes or until the pork is tender.

3. Transfer the pork to a warmed serving platter and surround with the apples. Stir the cream into the juices in the pan, then cook on top of the stove for 2 minutes, stirring constantly. Taste and adjust seasoning, then pour over the apples. Serve immediately.

From the top: Boeuf en daube Provençal, Porc Normande

Blanquette de Veau

This lovely, delicately-flavoured dish is usually made from a mixture of breast and shoulder meat. Only best quality veal should be used, of the palest pink colour.

Serves 6
1.5 kg (3 lb) boneless veal
    (breast or shoulder),
    trimmed and cut into 3.5 cm
    (1½ inch) cubes
1.2–1.5 litres (2–2½ pints)
    Veal Stock (see page 27)
juice of 1 lemon
1 onion, peeled and quartered,
    stuck with 1 clove
1 carrot, scraped and
    quartered
1 garlic clove
1 bouquet garni
salt
freshly ground black pepper
24 pickling onions, peeled
225 g (8 oz) button
    mushrooms, wiped
40 g (1½ oz) butter
25 g (1 oz) plain flour
2 egg yolks
150 ml (¼ pint) double cream

Preparation time: 30 minutes
Cooking time: 2 hours

1. Put the veal in a large saucepan, pour in enough cold water to cover and bring slowly to the boil, skimming off the scum as it rises to the surface. Simmer for 2 minutes. Drain the veal and rinse quickly with cold water to remove all scum. Place the veal in a heavy flameproof casserole and add enough stock to cover. Add the lemon juice, onion, carrot, garlic and bouquet garni, season to taste and simmer, skimming if necessary from time to time, for 1–1¼ hours or until the veal is nearly tender.

2. Using a slotted spoon, remove and discard the vegetables and bouquet garni. Add the pickling onions and mushrooms to the pan and

cook for a further 15 minutes until they are tender.

3. Strain the cooking liquid and measure out 600 ml (1 pint). Keep the veal and vegetables warm in a deep serving dish.

4. Melt the butter in a saucepan, add the flour and cook over gentle heat, stirring, for 1–2 minutes. Allow to cool until the bubbles subside. Whisk in the reserved cooking liquid and bring to the boil, stirring constantly. Simmer gently until thickened and smooth.

5. Beat the egg yolks with the cream and whisk in a little of the hot sauce. Whisk the mixture back into the sauce and cook very gently, stirring constantly, until the mixture thickens, but on no account allow to boil or it will curdle.

6. Taste and adjust the seasoning and pour the sauce over the veal and vegetables turning the meat to coat in the sauce. Keep warm, making sure that the sauce does not boil or become too hot. Serve with noodles or plain boiled rice.

Tournedos Rossini

Legend has it that this superlative, extravagant dish was invented by the composer Rossini, a renowned gourmet who loved to create new dishes. If truffles are beyond your means, use thinly sliced sautéed mushrooms instead, for the topping.

4 slices pâté de foie gras, 1 cm
    (½ inch) thick and 4 cm
    (1½ inches) in diameter
1 × 15 g (½ oz) can truffles,
    sliced (optional)
175 ml (6 fl oz) Brown Stock
    (see page 27)
100 g (4 oz) butter
4 small slices white bread,
    crusts removed
1 tablespoon olive oil
4 tournedos or medallions of
    fillet steak, 2.5 cm (1 inch)
    thick and 6 cm (2½ inches)
    in diameter
1 teaspoon arrowroot
3 tablespoons Madeira
salt
freshly ground black pepper
watercress sprigs, to garnish

Preparation time: 30 minutes
Cooking time: about 20 minutes
Oven: 120°C, 250°F, Gas Mark ½

1. Place the foie gras slices and the sliced truffles in a small heatproof dish, baste with 25 ml (1 fl oz) stock and cover. Place the dish over a pan of barely simmering water to heat through gently.

2. Melt 50 g (2 oz) butter in a small frying pan and sauté the bread slices over medium heat until lightly browned. Remove the slices from the pan and keep warm in a low oven.

3. Heat 1 tablespoon oil in a large heavy-based frying pan over moderately high heat and add 25 g (1 oz) of the remaining butter. Dry the steaks on paper towels. When the oil and butter are sizzling, add the steaks and sauté quickly for about 3–4 minutes on each side, depending on taste (they will be medium rare if they have a suggestion of resistance and spring back when pressed with the finger).

4. Arrange the bread croûtes on a warm serving dish and place a steak on each. Over each steak lay a warm slice of foie gras and top with slices of truffle, if using. Keep warm in a low oven while the sauce is made.

5. Pour the fat from the frying pan and add the remaining stock and the juices from the foie gras and the truffles. Boil down rapidly, scraping up all the coagulated juices, until reduced by half. Blend the arrowroot with the Madeira, stir into the sauce and simmer for 1 minute. Correct the seasoning. Away from the heat, swirl in the remaining 25 g (1 oz) butter. Pour over the steaks and serve, garnished with watercress.

From the top: Blanquette de veau, Tournedos Rossini

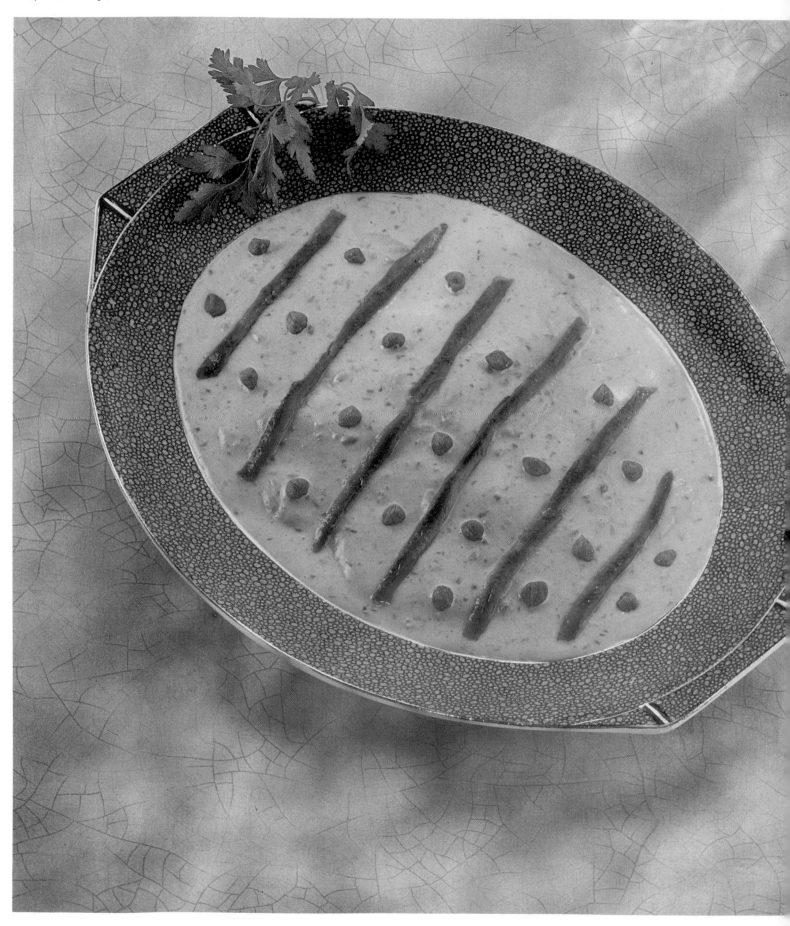

Vitello Tonnato

In Italy, this striking dish of cold sliced veal dressed with a tuna mayonnaise is often served in mid-summer.

Serves 6–8
1.5 kg (3–3½ lb) boned leg of veal, rolled and tied
3 anchovy fillets, cut into 2.5 cm (1 inch) lengths
1–2 garlic cloves, peeled and cut into thin slivers
900 ml (1½ pints) Chicken Stock (see page 25)
450 ml (¾ pint) dry white wine
450 ml (¾ pint) water
2 onions, peeled and quartered
2 carrots, scraped and chopped
3 celery stalks, chopped
2 bay leaves
6 parsley sprigs
10 whole peppercorns
Tuna mayonnaise:
150 ml (¼ pint) olive oil
1 egg yolk
75 g (3 oz) canned tuna fish in oil
4 anchovy fillets, drained, soaked in milk for 10 minutes, then finely chopped
1–2 tablespoons lemon juice
3 tablespoons double cream, whipped
3–6 tablespoons veal cooking liquid
1½ tablespoons capers, rinsed, drained and lightly chopped
salt
freshly ground white pepper
To garnish:
anchovy fillets
capers

Preparation time: 15 minutes, plus cooling and chilling time
Cooking time: about 2 hours

1. Using a small, sharp knife, make deep slits along the length of the veal and insert a piece of anchovy and a garlic sliver into each one.

2. Put the veal into a large saucepan, cover with cold water and bring to the boil. Drain, then return to the rinsed-out pan, add the chicken stock, wine, water, vegetables, herbs and peppercorns and bring to the boil. Reduce the heat and simmer, partially covered, for about 1¾ hours, until the veal is tender and cooked through. Remove the pan from the heat and leave the veal to cool in the cooking liquid.

3. To make the tuna mayonnaise, place the oil, egg yolk, tuna fish, anchovies and lemon juice in a blender and process at high speed for about 10 seconds until puréed.

4. Transfer the mixture to a bowl and gradually stir in the cream and enough of the veal cooking liquid to give the consistency of thick cream. Stir in the capers and taste and adjust the seasoning.

5. Remove the cooled veal from the cooking liquid, drain well and carve into neat, thin slices.

6. Spoon some of the tuna mayonnaise over a serving platter, arrange the veal slices on top and spoon over the remaining mayonnaise, making sure each slice is evenly coated. Cover with clingfilm and chill in the refrigerator for 2–3 hours or overnight before serving.

7. Garnish the dish with anchovy fillets and capers.

Flemish Carbonnade of Beef

To the Belgians must go the credit of having discovered the marvellous affinity beef has with beer, producing a rich, dark stew. Carbonnade literally means 'glowing coals' from the days when the dish would be cooked buried in the hot coals of the range.

Serves 4

50 g (2 oz) dripping
750 g (1½ lb) top rump or
*   chuck steak, cut into 2.5 cm*
*   (1 inch) cubes*
225 g (8 oz) onions, peeled
*   and sliced*
100 g (4 oz) mushrooms,
*   washed and sliced*
2–3 tablespoons flour
2 teaspoons brown sugar
300 ml (½ pint) brown ale
about 300 ml (½ pint) Brown
*   Stock (see page 27)*
salt
freshly ground black pepper
bouquet garni
6 thick slices French bread
40–50 g (1½–2 oz) butter
French mustard
parsley sprigs, to garnish

Preparation time: 15 minutes
Cooking time: 2 hours, 20 minutes
Oven temperature: 160°C, 325°F, Gas Mark 3; then 190°C, 375°F, Gas Mark 5

1. Heat the dripping in a flameproof casserole and quickly fry the cubes of beef in batches until brown on both sides, then remove and set aside. Add the onions and mushrooms to the casserole and fry until the onions are lightly browned. Remove the casserole from the heat and stir in sufficient flour to absorb the fat. Add the sugar.

2. Return the casserole to the heat and cook, stirring, until the roux is caramel coloured. Reduce the heat and pour in the ale. Bring to the boil, add the beef and sufficient stock to cover. Season to taste with salt and pepper and add the bouquet garni. Cover and cook in the centre of a preheated oven for 1½ hours. Remove the bouquet garni.

3. Spread one side of the bread slices with the butter and the other with mustard. Arrange the slices, butter side uppermost, on top of the meat. Increase the oven temperature. Continue cooking, uncovered, for 20–30 minutes on the top shelf of the oven until the beef is tender and the bread is crusty on top.

5. Garnish with parsley. Serve hot.

Steak au Poivre

To intensify the peppery flavour, cover the peppered steaks with greaseproof paper and let them stand for 2–3 hours, so that the flavour penetrates the meat.

Serves 4

25 g (1 oz) black peppercorns,
*   coarsely crushed*
4 rump or entrecôte (sirloin)
*   steaks, 175–225 g (6–8 oz)*
*   each*
50 g (2 oz) butter
1–2 tablespoons brandy
150 ml (¼ pint) dry white wine
4 tablespoons double or
*   whipping cream*
salt
chopped fresh parsley, for
*   sprinkling*

Preparation time: 5 minutes
Cooking time: 10–15 minutes

1. Press the crushed peppercorns well into each side of the steaks. A potato masher is ideal for this.

2. Melt the butter in a frying pan, add the steaks and cook for 1–2 minutes on each side or according to preference.

3. Pour off any surplus butter, retaining all the peppercorns in the pan. Warm the brandy by pouring it into a jug and placing this in hot water for 1 minute. Pour over the steaks and carefully ignite.

4. When the flames subside, remove the steaks from the pan and place on a hot serving dish. Keep hot.

5. Add the wine to the pan, bring to the boil and cook until it has reduced by half. Pour in the cream, mix well and reheat without boiling. Add salt to taste.

6. Pour the sauce over the steaks, sprinkle with parsley, if using, and serve at once with sauté potatoes.

From the top: Flemish carbonnade of beef, Steak au poivre

VEGETABLES

Fresh vegetables, cooked or raw, are the healthiest addition to the daily diet. From the humble potato to exotic okra and mangetout, this section lists each vegetable alphabetically, giving details on nutritional value, preparation techniques, cooking methods and availability.

ARTICHOKES (GLOBE)

Available in summer. The base of this thistle-like plant is edible, as is the heart, which is highly prized. Cook in boiling salted water for 45 minutes, or until a leaf pulls away easily.

ARTICHOKES (JERUSALEM)

Available between October and March. A tuber, whose flesh is creamy-white and similar to a turnip in texture. The flavour is sweet. Scrub under cold water and put immediately into acidulated water as the cut surfaces discolour quickly.

ASPARAGUS

This is an expensive vegetable and considered a luxury. The tips are the most tender part and should be tightly closed and well formed. English asparagus has the best flavour, but limited availability. Imported asparagus is available most of the year.

AUBERGINES

The deep purple skin of this vegetable should have a slight bloom on it. Prior to cooking, the cut flesh of the aubergine should be rubbed in salt and left for 30 minutes, then rinsed, to extract the bitter juices.

AVOCADOS

This is, in fact, a fruit, but it is often used as a vegetable. Avocados are available throughout the year, but are generally at their cheapest in midsummer. The flesh is high in protein, vitamins and minerals. Once cut, always brush the flesh with lemon juice to prevent discoloration.

BEANS (RUNNER)

The pod of the runner bean should be young and tender enough to snap in half. They should be topped and tailed before cutting diagonally into thin pieces and either steamed or boiled until just tender. They freeze well for up to 9 months.

BEANS (FRENCH)

These beans should be bright to darkish green in colour, and no more than 10 cm (4 inches) in length. Treat and cook as for runner beans. They may be served as an accompaniment or in salads – the best known is Salade Niçoise – or added to soups and casseroles.

BEAN SPROUTS

These are the sprouts of green mung beans, and are widely available. They are white, thin and very crunchy, and should be cooked or used on the day of purchase. They are used for salads and stir-fry dishes.

BEETROOT

Beetroot has a high sugar content which gives the vegetable its distinctive flavour. It is usually sold cooked, but some greengrocers do sell it raw. It is often steeped in spiced vinegar to serve with salads.

BROAD BEANS

Fresh broad beans are available from June to September. The pods should be free from any blemishes and plump. The beans should be steamed or cooked in boiling salted water for about 15 minutes. Broad beans freeze very well.

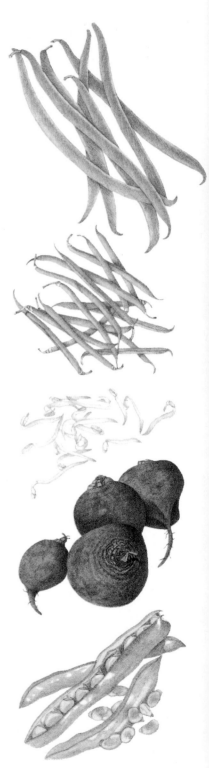

BROCCOLI

Trim broccoli stems, and cut each floret into even sized pieces. Cook by steaming or boiling in salted water for 6–7 minutes until just tender – overcooking will spoil the flavour. The stems should be slightly crisp. Drain well.

BRUSSELS SPROUTS

Brussels sprouts are an autumn and winter vegetable. To prepare, remove the outer leaves (if necessary) and cut a cross in the base of each sprout. Steam, or cook in boiling salted water for 8–15 minutes. They should be still crunchy.

CABBAGE

This is the best known of the brassica family. There are many varieties ranging from spring cabbage, spring greens, winter, red, white and savoy. The best way to cook cabbage is to shred it and stir-fry it for a couple of minutes in butter.

CHINESE CABBAGE

This vegetable has become increasingly popular over the past few years. Often called Chinese leaves, it is used extensively in Chinese recipes and for steaming, stir-fries and salad and for stuffings.

CARROTS

Carrots are inexpensive and high in nutrients, which include Vitamins A and C, carotene, minerals and fibre. All the vitamins are just below the skin so it is best just to scrub them. At their best in spring and summer.

CAULIFLOWER

The cauliflower is much prized for its delicate flavour, which, if properly cooked, is delicious. It is an all-year vegetable, which is equally good eaten raw or cooked. When cooked, the florets should be just soft and the stem fairly crunchy.

CELERIAC

This has a similar flavour to celery and is grown for the swollen base of the stem. It is equally good served raw or cooked. It may be puréed and creamed and used in soups, stews and casseroles. Steam or boil for about 20 minutes.

CELERY

Celery is at its best during the winter months. It may be braised, added to stews and casseroles and made into soups. It is also a useful addition to salads and is traditionally served with cheese at the end of a meal.

CHICORY

This is a conical shaped vegetable with white fleshy leaves packed closely together. The flavour is quite bitter although when cooked it is more bland. Used mostly in salads.

COURGETTES

Courgettes are a versatile vegetable which can be steamed, baked, deep fried or boiled, either cooked whole, stuffed or sliced. Due to their high water content, cooking should be kept to a minimum.

CUCUMBERS

Choose cucumbers that are straight and fairly light green in colour. They should be very firm and have a slight bloom on the skin. They are available throughout the year, but are at their best in late summer.

ENDIVE

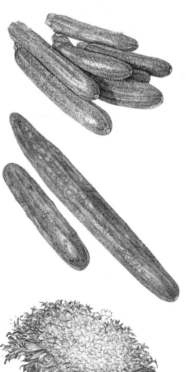

There are two varieties available, the curled-leaved (Staghorns) or plain-leaved (Batavia). The former is the most popular, although the Winter Batavia is more mild. Endive is nicest served on its own, tossed in a French dressing well flavoured with grain mustard and garlic just before serving.

FENNEL (FLORENCE)

Florence fennel has a mild rather sweet flavour, similar to aniseed. Use raw in salads, toss in lemon juice, or steam, poach or boil. Best in mid-summer.

KOHLRABI

A root vegetable with a fine delicate turnip-like flavour. Do not peel but carefully scrape away any blemishes and put into acidulated water, then steam or boil in salted water. When young, kohlrabi may be coarsely grated, tossed in lemon juice and eaten raw. Available July to April.

LEEKS

Members of the onion family – young leeks are delicious served thinly sliced in a salad; usually they are steamed or boiled – beware of over-cooking.

LETTUCE

Several varieties are available – cos, Webb, iceberg and soft-leaved. The cos is crisp and oblong with long pointed leaves; the Webb has crinkled outer leaves with a firm heart. The iceberg lettuce resembles a white cabbage, while the soft leaf lettuce has floppy leaves and a crisp yellow heart.

MANGETOUT

Sometimes called sugar peas. A member of the pea family cultivated for their pods, rather than for the peas. They should be no more than 9 cm (3½ inches) long, and if young may be eaten raw. To prepare, top and tail. Steam or boil in salted water or stir-fry.

MARROWS

There are two types, trailing and bush. Young small marrows may be cooked with the skin, otherwise they should be peeled. Halve lengthways and, if large, remove the seeds and the pithy flesh from the centre. Steam, sauté or boil.

MUSHROOMS

The button mushroom and flat field mushroom are the best known. To prepare, simply wipe the stalk and cap. Always eat mushrooms on the day of purchase. Use raw in salads, cook in melted butter or add to casseroles, stews and soups. Available throughout the year.

OKRA (LADIES' FINGERS)

These are small green seed pods. Avoid cutting, or they will have a slimy texture. Usually used in curries, soups or sautéed in butter. Available December to June.

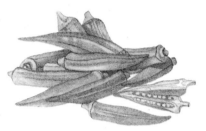

ONIONS

There are several varieties, ranging from the strong-flavoured English onion, the large bulbous Spanish onion, the red Italian onion to the small pickling onion and the spring onion. Onions have firm but juicy flesh and many uses. Available throughout the year.

PARSNIPS

Root vegetables with fibrous cream flesh, parsnips are sweet-flavoured, high in sugar and carbohydrate. Choose small parsnips which will be more tender. Thinly peel away the skin, and steam, bake or boil in salted water. They are excellent roasted. Available September to April.

PEAS

Peas are available fresh or dried, frozen or canned. The best tasting are petits pois. When young, peas may be eaten raw in salads, steamed or boiled. Available May to October.

PEPPERS (CAPSICUMS)

This brightly coloured vegetable (red, green, white, black or yellow) should be firm and unblemished. To prepare, remove the core and seeds. Use either raw in salads, stuffed and baked, or stewed.

POTATOES

Potatoes are available all the year – home-grown new potatoes from May throughout the summer and the larger maincrop from August to May. Always cook potatoes in their skin, as the nutrients are contained just underneath and steam rather than boil them.

PUMPKINS

These large gourds have dark yellow fibrous flesh. To prepare, remove the seeds and fibrous matter, then cut away the skin, and chop the flesh. Steam or boil for about 20 minutes until soft, drain and purée. Used for sweet and savoury dishes.

RADICCIO

A member of the chicory family with a slightly bitter flavour, this purple and white leaf vegetable looks like a small lettuce. The stems are fairly thick and should be removed before eating in salads. Available from autumn to spring.

RADISHES

The small red and white ones are the most common, others may have white, black or violet skins but the flesh is white and the flavour strong and pungent. Used mostly for salads, dips and snacks and available throughout the year.

SALSIFY

A white skinned vegetable with soft white flesh. The Scorzonera variety has a black skin and white flesh. Both have a turnip-like flavour. Best peeled after steaming. May be grated to add to a salad.

SHALLOTS

A member of the onion family. The bulbs have a pungent flavour with a hint of garlic. The flesh is firm and deep purple or whitish green. Available September to March.

SORREL

Sorrel has small fleshy light green rounded leaves. It looks similar to spinach and is prepared in the same way. Serve raw in salads, steamed or cooked in the water remaining on the leaves after it has been washed. Available mid-summer.

SPINACH

Wash the dark green fleshy leaves very thoroughly to get rid of all the soil, drain and cook in the water left on the leaves or steam. Available all the year, but best in March and April.

SWEDES

A winter vegetable with purple and orange skin and yellow flesh. Peel before cooking and dice or cube then steam or boil until tender. Usually served mashed with butter. Available September to May.

SWEETCORN (CORN ON THE COB)

Sweetcorn should be yellow and firm, encased in white silky threads and light green leaves. Remove the leaves and silk, and cook in unsalted boiling water for about 5 minutes until the kernels are soft. Drain and serve hot with melted butter or in salads, casseroles and soups. Available July to November.

TOMATOES

Scientifically classed as a fruit, but used as a vegetable. Varieties range from the tiny 'cherry' tomatoes to the large continental beef tomatoes. Available all the year but best midsummer to early autumn.

TURNIPS

A root vegetable with a tough skin. The flesh is white and delicately flavoured. Early turnips have a mustardy flavour and may be eaten raw or cooked. Maincrop turnips available August to March, are best in soups and stews.

PREPARING AND COOKING VEGETABLES

Vegetables should really be 'prepared' as little as possible. Vegetables are good sources of vitamins and other nutrients, but these tend to concentrate in the outer darker leaves and just under the skin. Trim as little as possible, and scrub rather than peel.

Many of the nutrients of vegetables, especially Vitamin C, are water soluble, and can be lost in soaking as well as cooking water. Always wash vegetables – if you must – as briefly and speedily as possible, before cooking in a minimum of water (steaming is a better and healthier method and any cooking water can be used in stocks, gravies or sauces). To boil vegetables perfectly, the rule is to cook root vegetables in cold water to start, with a lid; green vegetables in hot water to start, no lid, and refresh in cold water when just tender. Another 'rule' to retain the nutrients is to prepare a vegetable as soon before cooking or eating as possible: once cut or peeled, and exposed to the air, the vegetable rapidly loses much of its goodness. (Indeed, once plucked from ground or parent plant, the vegetable starts to lose its nutrients – the best reason of all for growing your own vegetables.)

Degorging aubergines

1. Trim both ends and slice or dice.

2. Sprinkle with salt, leave for 30 minutes, then rinse.

To prepare Brussels sprouts

1. Trim off bruised or damaged leaves.

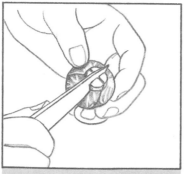

2. Make a cross-cut in base of stems.

How to chop onions

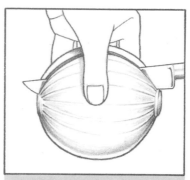

Cut the onion in half through the root.

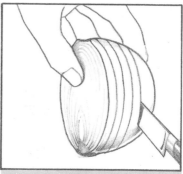

Slice downwards, leaving the root intact.

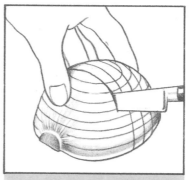

Place cut side of onion on board and cut across slices.

Turn round and slice across again.

1. Peel away the brown skin, leaving the root end on, to hold the leaves together.

2. Cut the onion in half lengthways from the top.

3. Place the cut side of the onion down on to a board.

4. Hold it firmly and cut it into narrow strips from near the root to the stalk end, leaving the root uncut.

5. Still holding the onion firmly, cut slices across the strips, so that they cut into tiny squares. Discard the root end.

How to crush garlic with salt

Crush garlic and salt with the flat of the knife.

1. Peel off the skin of the garlic and discard.

2. Place the garlic clove on a chopping board, sprinkle with fine salt.

3. Lay the flat of a knife on top of the garlic, press down heavily with the flat of the hand on to the flat of the knife blade, which will totally crush the garlic.

How to skin green peppers

1. Hold the pepper over a flame on a fork (or place under the grill) until lightly charred.

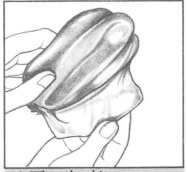

2. When the skin starts to blister, remove the pepper from the heat. Peel off the skin when it is cool enough to handle.

How to prepare artichokes

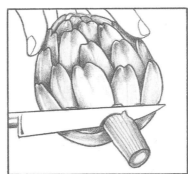

1. Cut off the stalk at the base of the artichoke.

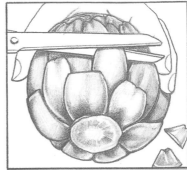

2. Trim the points off the lower leaves with scissors. If you are preparing the artichoke in advance, rub the cut surfaces with a half lemon to prevent discoloration.

How to cut julienne strips

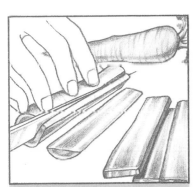

Cut the vegetables into lengths.

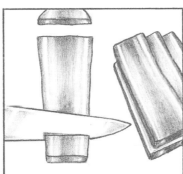

Trim off the ends to make even-size lengths.

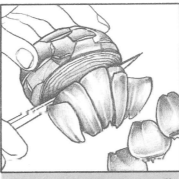

3. Using a sharp knife, cut off the top leaves about one-third from the top.

4. For stuffed artichokes, open out the leaves after cooking and scoop out the hairy 'choke' and the fibres, using a teaspoon.

1. Peel and trim the vegetable. If using a carrot or similar rounded shaped vegetable, cut the rounded edges off to square up the vegetable.

2. Cut the vegetable into 4 cm (1½ inch) to 5 cm (2 inch) lengths and stack together.

3. Cut the block into 3 mm (⅛ inch) lengths holding the block firmly in one piece.

Line up lengths to cut lengthways into strips.

4. Turn the block a quarter turn, ensuring that all the slices are evenly together. Slice 3 mm (⅛ inch) lengthways to give 'Julienne strips'.

5. If slicing leek, it is not necessary to make the vegetable into a block first.

How to skin tomatoes

1. Immerse in boiling water for 8–10 seconds.

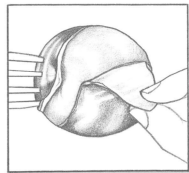

2. Remove from hot water and peel off the skin.

VEGETABLE & SALAD RECIPES

Starters, vegetable accompaniments and main course hot dishes and salads are featured here, from Greek-style spiced mushrooms marinated in wine, and all-American Caesar Salad to peas braised the French way with lettuce and onions; and two classic potato dishes.

Braised Peas with Lettuce and Onions

This is the king of pea dishes with a delicious flavour and creamy consistency. To taste this dish at its best, use only fresh young garden peas.

Serves 6
75 g (3 oz) butter
1 kg (2 lb) shelled peas
12 small pickling onions, peeled
finely chopped parsley, savory and thyme, to taste
1 firm lettuce heart
2 pinches of sugar
salt
freshly ground black pepper

Preparation time: 10 minutes
Cooking time: about 30 minutes

1. Melt the butter in a pan and add the peas, onions and herbs. Cook gently for 10 minutes, shaking the pan.

2. Tie the lettuce with fine string, to hold the leaves in shape, then add to the pan. Add the sugar and salt and pepper to taste. Pour in enough boiling water just to cover the peas and simmer gently, covered, until the peas are tender.

3. Untie the lettuce heart and stir the leaves into the peas and onions. Serve immediately.

Salade Niçoise

Serves 4
1 firm round lettuce
3 firm tomatoes (skinned if preferred), quartered
3 hard-boiled eggs, quartered
6 anchovy fillets, halved lengthways
12 black olives
2 teaspoons capers
1 × 200 g (7 oz) can tuna fish in oil, drained
1 medium red pepper, cored, seeded and cut into strips
6 tablespoons good quality green olive oil
1 tablespoon wine vinegar
1 large garlic clove, peeled and crushed
salt
freshly ground black pepper
1 tablespoon chopped fresh tarragon

Preparation time: 15–20 minutes

1. Keeping the lettuce whole, wash it well and shake dry. Remove the outer leaves and arrange them around the edge of a salad bowl; cut the remaining lettuce heart into quarters and place in the middle of the bowl.

2. Add the tomatoes, hard-boiled eggs, anchovy fillets, black olives, capers, tuna fish in chunks, and the strips of pepper.

3. Mix the oil with the vinegar, garlic, salt and pepper to taste, and the chopped tarragon. Spoon the dressing evenly over the salad, and toss lightly before serving.

Mushrooms à la Grecque

Serves 4
4 tablespoons lemon juice
4 tablespoons olive oil
300 ml (½ pint) dry white wine
2 teaspoons coriander seeds
2 sprigs parsley
2 sprigs thyme
1 small celery stick with leaves
2 bay leaves
12 black peppercorns
450 g (1 lb) button mushrooms
finely chopped parsley

Preparation time: 2–3 minutes, plus cooling
Cooking time: 10 minutes

1. Combine all the ingredients except the mushrooms and parsley in a small saucepan and bring to the boil.

2. Add the mushrooms to the pan and simmer for 5 minutes over a gentle heat.

3. Remove the mushrooms from the pan with a slotted spoon and arrange in a serving dish. Boil the liquid rapidly until reduced to 150 ml (¼ pint) and strain over the mushrooms.

4. Cover and leave to cool completely in the liquid – at least 2–3 hours – and chill overnight. Sprinkle with parsley before serving.

From the top: Salade Niçoise, Braised peas with lettuce and onions, Mushrooms à la grecque

Mushrooms with Tomatoes

Serves 4
6 tablespoons olive oil
6 tablespoons water
4 tomatoes, skinned, seeded
  and chopped
6 black peppercorns, coarsely
  crushed
8–12 coriander seeds, crushed
1 bay leaf
2 sprigs fresh thyme
a pinch salt
450 g (1 lb) very small button
  mushrooms
To garnish:
chopped parsley

Preparation time: 10 minutes
Cooking time: 20 minutes

1. Put the oil, water, tomatoes, peppercorns, coriander seeds, bay leaf, thyme and salt into a large saucepan.

2. Bring slowly to the boil and simmer for 5 minutes.

3. Stir in the mushrooms, and simmer for a further 5 minutes. Using a perforated spoon, lift the mushrooms out of the pan, letting the juices return into the saucepan. Place the drained mushrooms into a serving dish.

4. Increase the heat, and boil the sauce rapidly for about 10 minutes until it has reduced and thickened.

5. Spoon the sauce over the mushrooms.

6. Cover and leave until cold. Refrigerate until required.

7. Remove from the refrigerator at least 30 minutes before it is required. Sprinkle with parsley and serve.

Ratatouille Niçoise

French vegetable stew

Serves 6
2 large aubergines, trimmed
  and cubed
4 courgettes, trimmed and
  cubed
salt
150 ml (¼ pint) olive oil
2 large onions, peeled and
  sliced
2 large red peppers, cored,
  seeded and sliced
2 garlic cloves, peeled and
  crushed
4 large tomatoes, skinned and
  chopped
4–6 coriander seeds, crushed
2 tablespoons freshly chopped
  basil
To garnish:
chopped parsley

Preparation time: 1½ hours
Cooking time: 1 hour 5
minutes

1. Put the aubergine and courgette cubes into a colander and sprinkle liberally with salt, to extract the excess moisture. Leave for 1 hour, rinse thoroughly under cold water and pat dry.

2. Heat the oil in a large, heavy-based shallow pan, add the onions and cook for 3 minutes without browning, stirring occasionally.

3. Add the aubergines, courgettes, peppers and garlic, cover the pan, and simmer for 40 minutes, stirring occasionally.

4. Stir in the tomatoes, coriander seeds and basil, adjust the seasoning to taste. Simmer for a further 20 minutes, until the vegetables are soft, but not mushy.

5. Spoon into a serving dish, serve hot or cold, sprinkled with chopped parsley.

Leek and Cream Flan

Serves 6
175 g (6 oz) plain flour
a pinch of salt
75 g (3 oz) butter
2–4 tablespoons iced water
1 kg (2 lb) leeks, trimmed
50 g (2 oz) butter
50 g (2 oz) cooked ham, diced
3 egg yolks
300 ml (½ pint) double cream

freshly ground black pepper
a knob of butter

Preparation time: 30 minutes
Cooking time: 1 hour 10
minutes

1. Sift the flour and salt into a bowl. Rub in the butter until it resembles fine breadcrumbs.

2. Add the water, a little at a time, to bind the dough together. Form into a ball. Do not knead the pastry, but spread it directly into a 20 cm (8 inch) flan tin, with a loose bottom.

3. Spread the pastry over the base and up the sides of the tin using the knuckles, until it is evenly distributed.

4. Prick the base with a fork, bake 'blind' in a preheated oven for 20 minutes (see page 259).

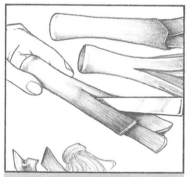

To clean leeks, cut down lengthways.

Dunk upside down in cold water to remove dirt.

5. Meanwhile, prepare the leeks. Remove the green leaves and use for soup.

6. Cut the white part into thin slices.

7. Melt the butter in a saucepan, and sauté the leeks for 1 minute, stirring constantly, without browning.

8. Remove the baking beans

Parsnip Croquettes

Serves 6
450 g (1 lb) parsnips, topped,
tailed and peeled
75 g (3 oz) butter
2 eggs
seasoned flour
100 g (4 oz) wholemeal
breadcrumbs
salt
freshly ground black pepper
2 tablespoons vegetable oil

Preparation time: 20 minutes,
plus chilling
Cooking time: 25–30 minutes

1. Cut the peeled parsnips into
even pieces, and simmer in
salted water until tender, about
15 minutes.

2. Drain and return to the pan
to dry out over a low heat.

3. Mash the parsnips with 25 g
(1 oz) of the butter and 1 egg
yolk.

4. Form the mixture into 6
sausage shapes, about 5 cm (2
inches) long and 2.5 cm (1
inch) in diameter.

5. Roll the croquettes in the
seasoned flour and then in the
remaining egg and egg white,
beaten together.

6. Season the breadcrumbs
with a little salt and pepper and
roll the croquettes in these.
Leave to chill for at least 3
hours.

7. Heat the oil and the
remaining butter in a frying
pan and fry the croquettes on
all sides for about 10 minutes.
Drain on paper towels before
serving hot.

from the pastry. Spread the
leeks evenly over the base,
sprinkle with the ham.

9. Beat together the egg yolks,
cream, salt and pepper, and
carefully pour over the leeks;
dot with butter.

10. Return to the oven and
cook for a further 30–40
minutes until set and lightly
golden brown.

11. Serve hot or cold.

Baked Garlic Mushrooms

Serves 4
450 g (1 lb) flat mushrooms
175 g (6 oz) butter, softened
2 large garlic cloves, crushed
1 tablespoon lemon juice
2 tablespoons finely chopped
fresh parsley
salt
freshly ground black pepper

Preparation time: 10–15
minutes
Cooking time: 10–15 minutes
Oven: 220°C, 425°F, Gas Mark 7

1. Wipe the mushroom caps
briefly and remove the stalks.

2. Arrange the caps in a
buttered ovenproof dish, and
scatter the stalks around them.

3. Mash the butter to soften it
further, and mix in the crushed
garlic.

4. Add the lemon juice, parsley
and salt and pepper to taste.
Mix together well.

5. Place a little of the garlic
butter mixture in each
mushroom cap, spreading it to
cover. Dot the stalks with a
little of the butter as well.

6. Place the dish in a preheated
oven and cook for 10–15
minutes until the butter is
melted and sizzling. Serve
immediately.

Celeriac Purée

Parsnips, carrots, potatoes,
swede, turnip, Brussels sprouts
and cauliflower can all be
made into a purée in the same
way. Vary the final sprinkled
topping: try tiny dice of red or
green peppers, chopped nuts,
grated cheese or ground
nutmeg or coriander.

Serves 4
450 g (1 lb) celeriac
salt
25 g (1 oz) butter
150 ml (¼ pint) single cream
25 g (1 oz) pine kernels, toasted

Preparation time: about 20
minutes
Cooking time: 10 minutes, plus
reheating

1. Top and tail the celeriac, and
then peel. Chop into even
small dice of about 6 mm (¼
inch).

2. Add the dice to simmering
salted water and bring back to
the boil. Cover and boil for 6–8
minutes.

3. Drain the celeriac, and put
back in the pan with the butter

to dry out over a low heat.

4. Reduce to a purée with the
cream in a liquidizer or
blender. To ensure that it is
really smooth, push the purée
through a fine, non-metal,
sieve.

5. Reheat gently in the top of a
double saucepan or in a pot or
pots in a bain-marie (see
page 74).

6. Serve each portion sprinkled
with a few toasted pine kernels
to add crunch and flavour.

Glazed Onions

Serves 4
450 g (1 lb) button onions
50 g (2 oz) unsalted butter
40 g (1½ oz) caster sugar
chopped parsley

Preparation time: 10–15
minutes
Cooking time: about 5 minutes

1. Wash the onions well, and
place in a saucepan, pour over
sufficient boiling water to
cover them.

2. Bring to the boil and simmer
for 8 minutes, drain and peel
away the skin.

3. Melt the butter in a
saucepan, stir in the onions and
toss well to coat them. Cook
over a gentle heat for 2
minutes, shaking the pan.

4. Sprinkle over the sugar,
increase the heat a little and
toss the onions for 5 minutes
until golden brown.

Stuffed Cabbage Leaves

Savoy cabbage with its strong colour and attractive crinkled leaves is probably the best choice for this dish and blanching will help retain its bright green colour and also soften the leaves for easier rolling. Vegetarians can substitute dried chestnuts, soaked, boiled and chopped, for the meat and replace the beef stock with a vegetable bouillon cube.

Serves 4
1 large, firm green cabbage
salt
450 g (1 lb) minced lamb or beef
100 g (4 oz) long-grain rice, cooked
1/2 onion, peeled and grated
2 tomatoes, skinned and chopped
4 tablespoons finely chopped parsley
1/2 teaspoon ground mixed spice
freshly ground black pepper
1 × 400 g (14 oz) can tomatoes, chopped
150 ml (1/4 pint) Bone Stock (see page 24)
1 tablespoon red wine vinegar
1 tablespoon soft light brown sugar

Preparation time: 30 minutes
Cooking time: 1 hour
Oven: 180°C, 350°F, Gas Mark 4

1. Separate the cabbage into leaves, discarding the outer ones and choosing suitable-sized leaves. Blanch the leaves for 2 minutes in boiling salted water, then drain, refresh under cold running water and drain again.

2. In a bowl mix together the meat, rice, onion, fresh chopped tomatoes, parsley and spice. Season well with salt and pepper.

3. Lay the cabbage leaves vein side up on a board or work surface and trim away the stalk end.

4. Put a tablespoon of filling towards the end of each leaf and roll up, tucking the outer edges of the leaf over the filling as you do so, to make neat parcels.

5. Arrange the cabbage rolls seam side down in an ovenproof dish, packing them closely together.

6. Combine the canned tomatoes with their juice, stock, vinegar, sugar and salt and pepper to taste. Pour over the cabbage rolls.

7. Cover and cook in the preheated oven for about 1 hour, or until the rolls are tender, topping up with a little extra hot stock if necessary. Serve hot.

Glazed Carrots

Carrots have often been used as a sweetening agent, notably in plum pudding and carrot cake. Here, their sweetness is accentuated by cooking in a light sugar syrup.

Serves 6
750 g (1 1/2 lb) carrots, scraped and cut into 5 cm (2 inch) lengths
300 ml (1/2 pint) Brown Stock (see page 27)
salt
freshly ground black pepper
25 g (1 oz) butter
1 teaspoon soft light brown sugar
2 tablespoons finely chopped parsley

Preparation time: 15 minutes
Cooking time: 15 minutes

1. Place the carrots in a heavy-bottomed saucepan with the stock, salt and pepper to taste, and the butter and sugar.

2. Cover and bring to the boil. Remove the lid and boil rapidly until the carrots are tender and the liquid has reduced to a syrupy glaze (about 10 minutes). Correct the seasoning.

3. Just before serving, roll the carrots gently in the pan until well coated with the glaze. Serve sprinkled with parsley.

From the top: Gratin Dauphinois, Glazed carrots, Stuffed cabbage leaves

Gratin Dauphinois

Layered Potatoes with Cream and Garlic

Serves 4–6
1 garlic clove, peeled and halved
40 g (1 1/2 oz) butter
1 kg (2 lb) waxy potatoes, peeled and sliced into very thin rounds
freshly grated nutmeg
salt
freshly ground black pepper
1 egg
250 ml (8 fl oz) hot milk
250 ml (8 fl oz) double cream
50 g (2 oz) Gruyère cheese, grated

Preparation time: 30 minutes
Cooking time: 1–1 1/4 hours
Oven: 180°C, 350°F, Gas Mark 4; then 200°C, 400°F, Gas Mark 6

1. Rub the inside of an earthenware baking dish with the cut surface of the garlic, then grease with the butter.

2. Place the potato slices in layers, sprinkling each layer with nutmeg, salt and pepper to taste.

3. Whisk the egg with the milk and cream, then pour over the potatoes, making sure they are completely covered with the liquid. Cover the top with the cheese.

4. Place on a baking sheet and bake uncovered for 1–1 1/4 hours, until the potatoes are tender when pierced with a skewer. Increase the heat for the last 10 minutes' cooking time to brown the top layer of potatoes. Serve hot, straight from the baking dish.

Tian de Légumes

Spinach au Gratin

The tian is a shallow earthenware dish from the Provence region of France. It has given its name to gratin dishes such as this spinach one.

Serves 6
4 tablespoons olive oil
1.5 kg (3–3½ lb) fresh spinach
2 garlic cloves, peeled and
*   bruised*
salt
freshly ground black pepper
1 egg, beaten
50 g (2 oz) fresh breadcrumbs
50 g (2 oz) Gruyère cheese,
*   grated*

Preparation time: 10 minutes
Cooking time: 15 minutes

1. Heat half the oil in a large heavy pan. Add the spinach with just the water clinging to the leaves after washing, the garlic and a little salt and pepper. Cook, uncovered, over brisk heat for 10 minutes until all the water from the spinach has evaporated.

2. Discard the garlic, then leave the spinach to cool slightly. Stir in the beaten egg, reheat gently, then taste and adjust seasoning.

3. Transfer the spinach to an oiled gratin dish and level the surface. Mix together the breadcrumbs and cheese, sprinkle over the top, then sprinkle with the remaining oil.

4. Put under a preheated hot grill for 5 minutes or until the topping is golden brown. Serve hot.

Caesar Salad

The classic American salad, said to have come originally from Mexico.

Serves 4
4 tablespoons vegetable oil
6 slices white bread, crusts
*   removed, cubed*
1 cos lettuce
salt
freshly ground black pepper
50 g (2 oz) Roquefort or blue
*   cheese, crumbled*
3 tablespoons lemon juice
6–8 tablespoons olive oil
1 garlic clove, peeled and
*   crushed*
1 egg, well beaten

Preparation time: 15 minutes
Cooking time: 5 minutes

1. Heat half the vegetable oil in a frying pan and fry the bread cubes in 2 batches until golden, adding the remaining oil for the second batch. Drain on paper towels.

2. Separate the lettuce leaves and tear very large ones in half. Put the lettuce leaves into a serving bowl. Add salt and pepper, the cheese, lemon juice and half the olive oil. Toss the leaves gently so that they do not break.

3. Pour the remaining oil with the garlic over the croûtons.

4. Pour the egg over the salad and toss gently. Add the croûtons and toss again. Taste and adjust seasoning and serve at once.

Stuffed Aubergines

Serves 4
4 aubergines, weighing about
*   1 kg (2 lb)*
225 g (8 oz) lean lamb or
*   beef, minced*
75 g (3 oz) long-grain rice,
*   cooked*
2 large tomatoes, skinned and
*   chopped*
1 medium onion, peeled and
*   finely chopped*
2 tablespoons finely chopped
*   parsley*
½ teaspoon ground
*   cinnamon*
pinch of grated nutmeg
salt
freshly ground black pepper
3 tablespoons tomato purée
4 tablespoons olive oil
2 tablespoons lemon juice

Preparation time: 30 minutes, plus draining
Cooking time: 1 hour

1. Cut the aubergines in half lengthways and scoop out the centres, being careful not to pierce the skin. Sprinkle the cut surfaces with salt and leave to drain for at least 30 minutes.

2. Rinse the aubergine halves and pat dry with paper towels.

3. Mix together the meat, rice, tomatoes, onion, parsley, cinnamon and nutmeg in a bowl, and season to taste. Stuff the aubergines with the filling and level the tops. Arrange the aubergine halves in an ovenproof dish or roasting tin.

4. Mix the tomato purée, oil and lemon juice with a little water. Pour this mixture into the dish around the aubergines, adding more water if necessary – the liquid should come half-way up the aubergines. Place in the preheated oven and bake for 15 minutes, then reduce the heat and bake until the aubergine flesh is quite tender, about 45 minutes. Top up the liquid if necessary halfway through the cooking time.

From the top: Tian de légumes, Stuffed aubergines, Caesar salad

Braised Celery

Serves 4
4 celery hearts
25 g (1 oz) butter
1 tablespoon olive oil
*100 g (4 oz) carrots, scraped
    and sliced*
*100 g (4 oz) onions, peeled
    and sliced*
*300 ml (1/2 pint) Chicken Stock
    (see page 25)*
bouquet garni
sea salt
freshly ground black pepper

Preparation time: 10 minutes
Cooking time: 1¼–1½ hours
Oven: 180°C, 350°F, Gas Mark 4

1. Trim the celery hearts and blanch by plunging them into a bowl of boiling water for 2–3 minutes. Drain.

2. Melt the butter and oil in a flameproof dish. Add the carrots and onions and fry gently for 10 minutes until tender. Arrange the celery hearts on top, and spoon some of the carrots and onions over the celery.

3. Pour in the stock. Add the bouquet garni and season with salt and pepper. Cover the dish closely and bake in the preheated oven for 1–1¼ hours until the vegetables are tender.

4. Remove the bouquet garni and serve with roast or grilled meat, fish or chicken.

Red Cabbage with Apple

Serves 5–6
*1 medium red cabbage, cored
    and finely shredded*
25 g (1 oz) butter
*1 large onion, peeled and
    chopped*
*2 medium cooking apples,
    peeled, cored and sliced*
*1 tablespoon soft light brown
    sugar*
1 teaspoon vinegar
150 ml (1/4 pint) cider
salt
freshly ground black pepper

Preparation time: 30 minutes
Cooking time: 1¼–1½ hours
Oven: 180°C, 350°F, Gas Mark 4

1. Blanch the red cabbage in boiling water for 1 minute, then drain.

2. Melt the butter in a flameproof casserole, add the onion and fry gently until transparent. Add the apple and shredded cabbage, cover tightly and cook gently for 5 minutes.

3. Remove the casserole from the heat and stir in the sugar, vinegar, cider and salt and pepper to taste. Cover tightly and cook in the oven for about 1¼ hours, or until the cabbage is very tender. Taste and adjust the seasoning before serving.

Duchesse Potatoes

Serves 6
These potatoes are often piped as a decorative border round meat or fish dishes.

*1 kg (2 lb) potatoes, peeled and
    cut into chunks*
salt
100 g (4 oz) butter
2 eggs, beaten
freshly ground black pepper
pinch of grated nutmeg
a little milk, if necessary

Preparation time: 15 minutes
Cooking time: 45 minutes
Oven: 200°C, 400°F, Gas Mark 6

1. Cook the potatoes in boiling salted water for 15–20 minutes. Drain them well.

2. Sieve or mash them and beat to a smooth, lump-free purée. Beat in the butter, eggs, seasoning and nutmeg. Add a few teaspoons of milk to soften the purée, if necessary.

3. Cool the mixture, then spoon it into a piping bag fitted with a large rosette nozzle. Pipe tall rosettes on to a greased baking sheet. Cook in a preheated oven for about 25 minutes, until set and golden brown.

From the left, clockwise: Duchesse potatoes, Red cabbage with apple, Braised celery

PASTA

Quick-cooking and very versatile, pasta is ideal for all kinds of meals. Choose from an amazing variety of dried pasta shapes or make your own fresh pasta as described here – it's much easier than you might think! Just follow our simple cooking and serving instructions.

The word 'pasta' means 'dough' in Italian, and is the generic name for all forms of spaghetti, macaroni, ravioli etc. Although many other national cuisines feature forms of pasta, Italy is indisputably the world's major producer and consumer.

Pasta falls mainly into two main types: the factory-produced dried pasta (*pasta secca*) made from hard-wheat flour; and the homemade pasta of flour and eggs (*pasta all'uovo*), which is also now available dried in packets. Although pasta is generally a natural pale yellow in colour, it can be green (with added spinach) or red (with added tomato purée); it can also be made with buckwheat or wholewheat flour.

Dried pasta

Dried pasta is made from strong (usually durum) wheat flour and water. Although it comes in what appears to be a bewildering assortment of shapes and sizes, all these may be classified as long and narrow, short and broad, flat or tubular, solid or hollow, smooth or ridged. These various shapes are not merely decorative, they are specifically designed to affect the body, character and taste of the pasta, and determine how it will be served, as each pasta shape has a certain form of sauce it will particularly suit, or a filling that has been specifically designed for it.

Cooking pasta

Pasta should always be cooked in plenty of boiling salted water. Allow at least 4 litres (7 pints) of water for 450 g (1 lb) of pasta. This may seem a lot of water, but the pasta must cook evenly and be able to move in the boiling water without sticking.

The water should be boiling rapidly when the pasta is added, and returned to the boil as quickly as possible.

Add the pasta as quickly as possible, but not all at once, as this will cool the water. When adding long pasta, hold it in a bunch at one end and coil the strands around the sides of the saucepan as they soften until all the pasta is in the pan.

Do not cover the pan, as there is more chance of the water boiling over.

Always test the pasta throughout cooking and as soon as it is 'al dente', drain it immediately into a large colander. The pasta will continue cooking after draining, so always allow for this. There should be no need

Hold long pasta in a bunch and lower into boiling water

To cook perfect Pasta

■ The addition of 1–2 tablespoons of olive oil in the cooking water helps prevent the pasta sticking.
■ Never overcook pasta. Freshly made pasta cooks in seconds, while dried pasta takes up to 12 minutes, depending on its type. It

should always be cooked *al dente*, just tender, but firm. Filled pasta such as ravioli takes a little longer.
■ Toss in butter before coating in the chosen sauce. This gives the pasta a delicious flavour and texture.

to wash it in either boiling or cold water, which will spoil it, just toss the cooked pasta in butter or oil.

Do not cook pasta that is to be coated in a sauce – Spaghetti Bolognese, for instance – in advance. It should be prepared and cooked only when it is required.

Suggested cooking times for dried pasta

These times are a rough guide. As stated before, it is necessary to use your own judgement.
Spaghetti: 9 minutes
Long macaroni: 10 minutes
Lasagne: 10 minutes (add a

sheet at a time)
Cannelloni: 10–12 minutes
Ravioli: 15 minutes
Tagliatelle: 10 minutes
Vermicelli: 5 minutes

Homemade pasta needs much less time – from seconds, to 7 minutes for dumpling or stuffed ravioli types.

Some manufacturers produce a dried lasagne which requires no pre-cooking like fresh lasagne (the dried needs to be boiled before baking). Always allow a little extra sauce to moisten, and help it to cook.

Pasta should never be reheated, as this will make it overcooked and soggy.

Storing pasta

Freshly made pasta should be eaten preferably on the day it is made or purchased, but it can be stored in the refrigerator for up to 24 hours. The dough, or shaped dough, stores well in the freezer for up to 3 months.

Dried pasta keeps well in sealed jars or containers for up to 9 months. Ensure that the storage container is dry and airtight. It is best to store pasta in a dark cupboard.

When cooked, toss the hot pasta in butter

Wholewheat Rigatoni

Ziti

Ravioli

Conchiglie

Spaghetti

Wholewheat Spaghetti

Farfalle

Macaroni

Capelli d'angeli

Penne

Gnocchi

Bozzoli

Ditali

Bucatini

Elbow macaroni

Rigatoni

Cannelloni

Ruoti

Ruotini

Spirale

Semini

Cannelloni

Lasagne

Tomato Tortellini

Pastina

Wholewheat Tagliatelle

Tagliatelle Verde

HOMEMADE PASTA

Homemade pasta is very simple to make and has a completely different texture and taste to dried pasta. Ready-made 'homemade' pastas are now available in some supermarkets: Tagliatelle, Lasagne and many of the stuffed pastas are often on offer, sometimes accompanied by the appropriate sauces.

Homemade pasta is often made from a softer flour than dried, although a strong bread flour will give the best results. The recipe varies from region to region in Italy: in some places it is made with flour and eggs; in the Italian Riviera it is made with fewer eggs and with the addition of water; in some other regions it is made without any eggs at all.

Homemade pasta can be made with or without a machine. A machine will roll and cut the dough into flat sheets or strips of varying thicknesses, or form it into a number of shapes. By hand, the shapes possible to make are limited, and it is quite hard work to roll the dough evenly and thinly. However, the sense of achievement – as well as the superior taste – will make it very worthwhile.

Basic Egg Pasta Dough

Makes 450 g (1 lb)
450 g (1 lb) plain flour
a large pinch of fine salt
2 large or 3 medium eggs
1 teaspoon olive oil
3–4 tablespoons water

Preparation time: about 25 minutes

1. Sift the flour and salt into a large bowl (using one attached to a large electric mixer will save you kneading).

2. Make a hollow in the centre and drop in the eggs. Add the oil, and draw the flour into the centre using your hand. Gradually add the water, a tablespoon at a time. It may not be necessary to add all the water, as this depends on how absorbent the flour is. Knead to a firm smooth dough (firmer than a pastry or bread dough).

3. Continue kneading until the dough is very elastic, smooth and shiny – about 15–20 minutes. (A dough hook is ideal for this.) It is essential to knead the dough very thoroughly so that it rolls out evenly without breaking.

4. Wrap the dough in cling film and leave to rest for a minimum of 15 minutes and a maximum of 2 hours, before using (see below).

Wholemeal pasta dough

Follow the directions for the basic egg pasta dough above, but use 450 g (1 lb) wholemeal flour, a large pinch of salt, 3 large eggs, and about 4–5 tablespoons of water. A little oil may be added, if liked.

Colouring

Spinach and tomato purée colour and flavour pasta. For spinach pasta, beat puréed spinach into the dough (see recipe, right). For tomato pasta replace 1 egg with 3 tablespoons tomato purée. Herbs could be added for herb pasta. Cooked, puréed beetroot can also add a rich colour and flavour. For beetroot, boil 2 small beetroot for 50 minutes or until tender. Peel, chop and purée and stir into the dough.

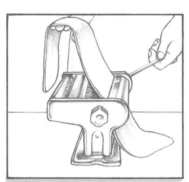

Rolling pasta using a machine.

SOME COMMON HOMEMADE PASTA TYPES

Cannelloni. Rectangles of dough rolled into a tube which is stuffed with meat, fish or vegetables in a Béchamel Sauce (see page 34).

Cappelletti. Pasta dough made into little peaked hat shapes, and usually stuffed with a variety of the following: chicken, pork, Mortadella or Bologna sausage, cheeses and nutmeg. Similar to Tortellini.

Fettucine. The Roman version of egg noodles, a little narrower than Tagliatelli.

Lasagne. The broadest strips of pasta dough. It can be bought fresh, dried, green or wholewheat, smooth, ridged or ruffled. It is cooked in layers with a filling of meat, fish or vegetables and a Béchamel Sauce.

Quadrucci. Egg pasta rolled thinly and cut into 5 mm (¼ inch) squares, and used in soups and broths.

Ravioli. Little squares of pasta encasing a filling, which can be fish, meat or vegetables.

Tagliatelli. The classic ribbon egg noodle, a specialty of Bologna.

Tortellini. Small crescents of stuffed pasta, formed into 'navel'-shaped rings, which look rather like Cappelletti. They can be made larger (Tortelli and Tortelloni). They are usually stuffed with green vegetables such as spinach and Ricotta cheese or with finely minced chicken or pork.

Egg and Spinach Pasta Dough

Makes 450 g (1 lb)
350 g (12 oz) plain flour
a large pinch of salt
100 g (4 oz) leaf spinach, cooked, drained and finely chopped or puréed
2 large, or 3 medium, eggs
1 teaspoon oil

Preparation time: about 25 minutes

Follow the directions for the Basic Egg Pasta Dough, adding the spinach with the eggs.

This recipe may be the best one to try if you have not made pasta before, as it is easier to make, and does not dry out so quickly.

Rolling out the dough

Either roll out the dough on a lightly floured board or marble slab, or with a pasta machine. If using a machine, follow the manufacturer's instructions. The more the pasta is rolled, the better the end result. It is worth taking time with this process, as the rolling not only ensures that the dough is even in thickness but also helps to make it more elastic, essential when making pasta. It is often easier to do this in 2 batches.

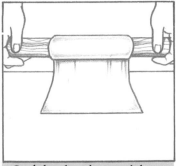

Curl the dough round the rolling pin and stretch.

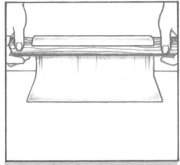

Turn dough sideways and roll and stretch again.

4. Continue rolling up until all the dough has been wrapped around the pin. Give the pin a quarter turn, so that it points towards you, and unfurl the sheet of dough, to open it out flat.

5. Repeat the rolling and stretching until the dough is again wrapped around the rolling pin. Give the dough a quarter turn and unwrap as before.

1. Place the kneaded dough on a floured board and flatten it with a long floured rolling pin. Roll out, giving the dough a quarter turn between each rolling, always rolling away from yourself, until the dough measures 20–23 cm (8–9 inches) in diameter. It should be about 3 mm (⅛ inch) thick.

2. This next stage takes a little practice. The objective is to stretch the pasta with a sideways pressure of the hands as you wrap it around the rolling pin. Curl the far end of the sheet of pasta around the centre of the rolling pin, and roll it towards you, with both of the palms of the hands cupped over the centre of the rolling pin. When about a quarter of

the dough has been rolled on to the pin, do not roll any more.

3. Quickly roll the pin backwards and forwards and at the same time slide the palms of your hands away from each other, towards the end of the rolling pin. Do not roll the dough but stretch it all the time.

6. Continue the process until the sheet of dough measures 40–45 cm (16–18 inches) square.

7. This process must be done with great speed to prevent the dough drying out as it will be ruined. Roll out the dough paper-thin and use as required.

SOME COMMON DRIED PASTA TYPES

Most of the shapes and types of pasta mentioned below are available at specialist Italian shops and supermarkets.

Bucatini (also known as Perciatelli). Thick hollow spaghetti.

Capelli d'angeli Angels' hair is the literal translation, and these are very fine noodles, usually served in a meat broth.

Conchiglie The literal translation is 'seashells', and this is exactly what they look like. Available large or small, smooth or ridged, they have a cavity which is ideal for sauces or stuffings.

Farfalle Butterfly or bow-tie shaped pasta. The small version, Farfallini, are used to thicken soups.

Fusilli (also known as Tortiglioni or Rotelle). Corkscrew-shaped spaghetti, ideal for thick creamy sauces which cling to it (rather than tomato or oil-based sauces).

Linguine Similar to a noodle, it is flat and long.

Lumache Snail shapes which are similar to Conchiglie (seashells).

Macaroni The name in English for 'maccheroni', the general term for tubular hollow pasta, available large, small, long, short, smooth or ridged.

Pastina This is the general term for tiny pasta used in soups (*in brodo*), and it comes in many miniature shapes – stars, circles, butterflies, letters of the alphabet, etc.

Penne Means quills, and the pasta comes in hollow quill-shaped lengths, cut diagonally at both ends (usually smooth but sometimes ridged).

Rigatoni Hollow macaroni which is stubby and slightly curved and ridged. It is generally served with a meat sauce.

Ruoti Pasta shaped into wheels, large or small.

Spaghetti The word means 'little strings', and it is a long pasta with no hole in the middle. It can vary in length and in thickness: Spaghettini is much thinner than spaghetti.

Ziti A short tubular shape, similar to Rigatoni, but narrower and unridged. It is usually used in baked dishes.

Perfect Homemade Pasta

■ Always wrap homemade pasta dough in cling film or polythene to prevent it drying out. Leave it for a while to rest and relax the gluten.
■ A long rolling pin is vital for successful pasta rolling.
■ If rolling the pasta dough in one piece is daunting, divide the dough into smaller pieces which will be easier to work with.
■ An easy way of cutting noodles is to roll the dough up, well floured, and then cut through as for a jam roll.
■ Allow all shaped and cut homemade pasta to dry for a while before cooking. Hang long ribbon noodles over the back of a chair.
■ Allow 100 g (4 oz) fresh pasta per person, 50 g (2 oz) for a starter.

Chicken and Ham Ravioli

Special ravioli trays are available, but it is just as easy to make ravioli without.

Serves 4 for a main course, 6 for a starter
100 g (4 oz) butter
2 shallots, peeled and finely chopped
1 garlic clove, peeled and crushed
50 g (2 oz) button mushrooms, finely chopped
500 g (1¼ lb) cooked chicken, minced
150 g (5 oz) cooked ham, minced
150 ml (¼ pint) dry white wine
120 ml (4 fl oz) double cream
1 tablespoon chopped thyme
3 tablespoons chopped parsley
salt
freshly ground black pepper
1 recipe quantity Basic Egg Pasta Dough (see page 184)
1 egg, beaten
4–6 tablespoons freshly grated Parmesan cheese

Preparation time: 30 minutes, excluding making the pasta
Cooking time: 5–7 minutes

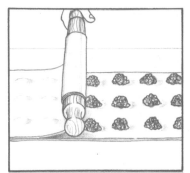
Unfold the second layer of pasta over the filled sheet

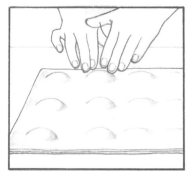
Press down edges and between fillings to seal

Cut out the pasta squares with a pastry wheel.

1. Melt 25 g (1 oz) of the butter in a large saucepan, and add the shallots and garlic. Cook for 5–7 minutes without browning, stirring occasionally.

2. Stir in the mushrooms, and cook for a further 2 minutes. Remove from the heat and cool.

3. Add the chicken, ham, wine, cream, thyme and 1 tablespoon of the parsley. Season to taste with salt and pepper.

4. Divide the pasta dough in half. Wrap one piece in cling film and set aside.

5. Roll out the pasta thinly on a floured board.

6. Place teaspoons of the chicken mixture about 5 cm (2 inches) apart in lines down the length of the pasta. Brush with beaten egg between the filling.

7. Roll out the second piece of pasta, slightly larger than the first, and carefully lay it on top, pressing down between the filling to seal.

8. Using a pastry wheel or knife, cut around the little filling piles to give ravioli squares.

9. Check that each ravioli is thoroughly sealed, and place on a floured board to dry for 15 minutes.

10. Cook in boiling salted water, with the addition of a little oil or butter for 5–7 minutes until *al dente*.

11. Carefully drain into a colander. Add the remaining butter and half the Parmesan cheese to the pan. Toss in the ravioli, sprinkle with the remaining parsley, and serve immediately, accompanied by the remaining Parmesan cheese.

Spinach and Ricotta Ravioli

Serves 4 for a main course, 6 for a starter
450 g (1 lb) spinach, washed, stalks removed
salt
175 g (6 oz) fresh Ricotta cheese
25 g (1 oz) fresh Parmesan cheese, finely grated, plus 1 tablespoon
2 eggs, lightly beaten
freshly ground black pepper
1 recipe quantity Basic Egg Pasta Dough (see page 184)
50 g (2 oz) melted butter

Preparation time: 20 minutes, excluding making the pasta
Cooking time: 5–7 minutes

1. Put the spinach in a large pan with only the water adhering to the leaves. Add the salt and cook, shaking the pan occasionally, for 5–7 minutes until the spinach is well reduced in volume. Drain thoroughly and squeeze it between 2 plates to remove as much moisture as possible.

2. Chop the spinach very finely and mix with the Ricotta cheese and 25 g (1 oz) Parmesan cheese, and eggs. Season to taste with salt and pepper.

3. Fill and cook the ravioli as described above in Chicken

and Ham Ravioli. Serve immediately, tossed in melted butter and the remaining Parmesan cheese, as above.

Ravioli variations

The fillings for ravioli – and indeed many of the other (more complicated) stuffed pasta types – can be varied, but those made from Ricotta cheese will not keep, and should be eaten on the same day as they are made. Another filling possibility is a bolognese *ragù* or sauce, carefully reduced.

Sauces for stuffed pasta can be varied as well. The simplest is butter and Parmesan cheese as above. Cream and butter with Parmesan is smooth and rich, and some onion could have been fried gently in the butter first. A fresh tomato sauce would be good, too.

Tagliatelle with Pesto

Tagliatelle strips are easily cut from pasta dough. Roll up and slice as shown, then allow the strips to dry for 30 minutes by draping them over the back of a chair.

Whenever fresh basil is in season – very briefly – pesto sauce should be made in quantity as it keeps very well in the freezer.

The best pestos are made from a combination of Parmesan cheese and the slightly saltier, less readily available Pecorino cheese; if the latter is included, be very careful about adding salt.

Serves 4 for a main course, 6 for a starter
1 recipe quantity Basic Egg
Pasta Dough (see page 184),
rolled and cut into
tagliatelle (see illustrations)
salt
3 tablespoons oil
For the pesto sauce:
75 g (3 oz) fresh basil leaves
25 g (1 oz) pine kernels
2 garlic cloves, peeled
coarse salt (optional)
8 tablespoons olive oil
50 g (2 oz) fresh Parmesan
cheese, finely grated
2 tablespoons Pecorino cheese,
finely grated (optional)
40 g (1½ oz) softened butter

Preparation time: about 10–20 minutes, plus making and cutting the tagliatelle
Cooking time: about 5 minutes

1. Prepare the pesto sauce first.

2. If you have a blender or liquidizer, put the basil, pine kernels, garlic, a little salt (if using) and the oil into the goblet and mix at high speed. You may have to stop it from time to time to scrape the mixture down to the bottom of the bowl. When evenly blended, scrape into a bowl, and beat in the cheeses by hand, followed by the butter.

Flour the pasta and roll up loosely

Cut across the roll in slices, open out each strip

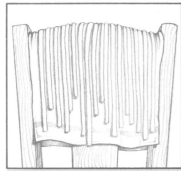
Hang the strips over a chair back to dry

3. If making the sauce in a mortar – as is traditional – put the basil, pine kernels, garlic and salt (if using) in the mortar and pound them to a paste with a pestle. Add the grated cheese and continue pounding until evenly blended. Then beat in the oil a few drops at a time at first, using a wooden spoon. When all the oil has been added, beat in the butter.

4. Cook the tagliatelle in plenty of boiling salted water with the oil added. Drain well when just tender – if very fresh, within about 10 seconds of the water returning to the boil.

5. If the sauce looks a little thick, add a tablespoon or so of the hot pasta water before pouring over the pasta and tossing together.

6. Serve immediately.

Spaghetti Bolognese

For a true bolognese *ragù* or meat sauce, a long slow cooking is vital so that the grains of meat literally melt in the mouth. The sauce can be made well in advance and will keep in the refrigerator for up to 4 days; it also freezes very well.

Serves 4 for a main course, 6 for a starter
450 g (1 lb) spaghetti
salt
3 tablespoons oil
15 g (½ oz) butter
50 g (2 oz) fresh Parmesan
cheese, finely grated
For the bolognese sauce:
2 medium onions, finely
chopped
3 tablespoons olive oil
40 g (1½ oz) butter
1 celery stick, finely chopped
1 carrot, finely chopped
450 g (1 lb) lean chuck steak,
finely minced
salt
300 ml (½ pint) dry white wine
8 tablespoons milk
freshly grated nutmeg
1 × 400 g (14 oz) can Italian
plum tomatoes

Preparation time: about 15 minutes
Cooking time: just over 4 hours

1. Make the bolognese sauce first. In a heavy-based deep saucepan, fry the onion gently in the oil and butter until translucent. Add the celery and carrot and cook gently for 2 minutes.

2. Add the minced steak and a little salt, and cook and stir only until the meat has lost its red colour.

3. Add the wine and turn the heat up to medium to high. Stir occasionally and cook until the wine has evaporated.

4. Turn the heat down again to medium, and add the milk and a little freshly grated nutmeg. Cook until the milk too has evaporated, stirring more frequently.

5. Chop the canned tomatoes and add them and their juice to the pan. Stir thoroughly and when the sauce begins to bubble turn the heat down as far as it will go.

6. Cook at the gentlest simmer, uncovered, for about 4 hours, stirring occasionally. Check for seasoning.

7. Cook the spaghetti in plenty of boiling salted water with the oil, until just tender. Drain well and toss immediately with butter.

8. Turn into a warm serving dish, add the bolognese sauce and the cheese, and toss.

9. Serve immediately with extra grated Parmesan cheese to sprinkle over each serving.

RICE

Cooking rice just right is an easily acquired skill – four foolproof methods are given in this section. There is also information on the different types of rice and rice products available, and the dishes for which they are suitable.

The world total of rice varieties is said to be over seven thousand – in India alone there are up to a thousand varieties in cultivation – but the basic choice in Britain is between brown and white, and a selection of grain sizes. Rice is an important staple food for over half the world's population and grows well in wet soil with warm conditions. It is most commonly grown on submerged land, in paddy fields, and the leading rice-growing countries are China, India, Indonesia, Bangladesh, Japan and Thailand. It is also grown in America, and in parts of Europe, particularly the Po Valley in Northern Italy. It cannot, as yet, be grown successfully very much farther north.

Rice is generally rather bland in flavour, so it combines well with many other types of sweet and savoury foods, and may be used as an accompaniment to replace vegetables. It may also be used in soups, main courses, salads and puddings. The type of rice chosen for a dish should be matched carefully to the result desired: pudding rice will not produce the separate grains vital for a *pilau*; and a long-grain Basmati will not produce the moist clinging texture characteristic of the best risottos, which need Italian Arborio rice.

Brown rice is the grain with nothing but the outer inedible husk removed. Because it retains the bran, brown rice is greatly superior in food value, and has a nutty texture and flavour when cooked. White, polished or pearled rice is produced when the bran is removed by milling. Both white and brown rice come generally in three grain sizes: long, medium and short.

Long-grain The varieties most commonly available include Carolina, Patna, and Basmati. The grains are up to five times as long as they are wide, and are fluffy and separate when cooked. They are ideal, therefore, for use in salads, and with curries, stews, chicken and meat dishes. Basmati has a delicate flavour and is traditional in Indian cooking.

Medium and short-grain Although some rices are occasionally defined as medium-grain, short-grain can more easily be used to define the shorter, fatter and stubbier varieties such as the Italian rices, white or brown, the glutinous rices widely used in Chinese cookery, and pudding rice. Because they are stickier, medium-grain rices are generally used for savoury dishes where the rice needs to cling or to be moulded or bound together – such as risottos, stuffings, rice rings and croquettes – whereas the short-grain pudding rice is best for sweet dishes.

TYPES OF RICE

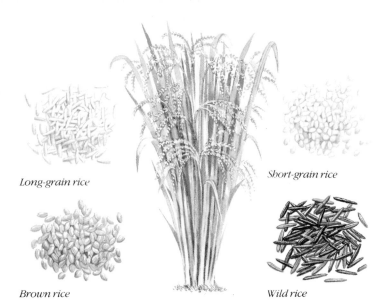

Long-grain rice

Short-grain rice

Brown rice

Wild rice

Glutinous or sticky rice Widely used in Chinese cookery, these grains stick together and thus are easy to pick up with the fingers or chopsticks. It is also used, because of its sweetness, in baking and confectionery.

Par-boiled or converted rice was introduced to counteract the nutritional deficiencies that arose when peoples reliant on unprocessed rice changed to polished rice.

The brown grain is cooked before milling by a special steam pressure process, which impregnates the inner grain with some of the nutrients of the bran and thus helps it to retain its food value.

This type of rice takes longer to cook than white rice, but the benefit is that it produces plump, fluffy and separate grains.

Instant rice or pre-cooked rice only needs soaking in boiling water for 5 minutes, following the manufacturers' instructions. It is useful for quick snacks and salads.

Rice flakes are produced by steaming and rolling, and can be made from whole or white rice. They are used for cereals, for baking and for muesli.

Ground rice or rice flour The rice is ground to a fine powder, and is used for thickening and in cakes, puddings and biscuits.

Wild rice is not actually rice, but the seeds of a grass grown in the United States and the Far East. It is used for savoury dishes, particularly poultry and game stuffings, and is a blackish-brown in colour. Not widely sold, it is expensive.

PREPARING AND COOKING RICE

Most varieties of white rice should be washed before cooking. This ensures that the loose starch, which is a white powder, is removed. If the rice is not washed it is more likely that the grains will stick together. Put the rice in a large sieve and rinse under cold running water, until the water running through the sieve is clear.

Some brown rices contain bits of husk etc, so the rice should be put into a bowl of water. Any foreign bodies will float to the top and can easily be skimmed off.

There are several methods of cooking rice. It is a matter of choice which one you use, and will depend also on the type of rice used. If possible, follow the manufacturers' instructions or a good recipe for the specific rice. Allow approximately 50 g (2 oz) of raw rice per person.

Absorption method

This is an easy way of cooking rice, and it ensures that the grains stay separate and fluffy. Both white and brown rices can be cooked in this way, but brown rice will take longer.

Measure the amount of rice required in a cup, and for each cup of rice use 2 cups of water or stock plus ½ teaspoon salt.

Bring the water to the boil in a large saucepan, add the salt and then the rice which has

been washed under cold running water and stir well to separate the grains. As soon as the water boils, reduce the heat, cover with a very tight-fitting lid, and cook for 15 minutes (45 for brown). Do not be tempted to lift the lid at all during this time, or the steam will escape, and alter the cooking time.

When the 15 or 45 minutes have elapsed the rice will be perfectly cooked, the liquid completely absorbed and the rice tender and fluffy. Stir in a small knob of butter and use immediately.

Oven method

Brown and white rices may also be cooked by the absorption method in the oven, and once again brown rice takes longer to cook than white.

Use the same proportions – 1 of rice to 2 of water – as the first method, but put the rice into an ovenproof dish with a tight-fitting lid. Cover with the required amount of boiling water or stock and salt. Stir well. Cover the dish with foil and a lid.

Cook the rice in a preheated oven (180°C, 350°F, Gas Mark 4) for 30–40 minutes (1 hour for brown) until all the liquid has been absorbed and the rice is tender, then stir in some butter to taste and serve immediately.

Add the rice to boiling water in a saucepan

When it returns to the boil, cover and turn heat down

Steaming

Steaming is a popular Chinese method of cooking rice so that the grains stay separate and fluffy. First soak the rice in cold

Line the steamer basket with muslin

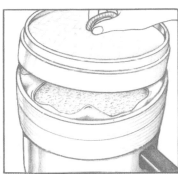

Fold over the muslin and cover with the lid

water for at least 1 hour, then drain. Fill the bottom half of a steamer, or a large pan, with water. Line the steamer, or a Chinese steamer basket, with muslin. Spoon in the rice and fold the muslin ends over the rice. Cover and steam for 25–30 minutes, or until the rice is tender.

Cooking wild rice

Wild rice takes about twice as long to cook as ordinary white rice. Use the same proportion of grains, water and salt as suggested for boiled rice, but boil for 25 minutes. Check it is cooked, then drain in a sieve, return to the pan and stir in a knob of butter, if liked.

Boiling rice

Per 50 g (2 oz) rice, use 600 ml (1 pint) of water and ½ teaspoon salt.

Bring the water to the boil, add the salt, sprinkle in the rice, return to the boil and simmer for 12–13 minutes (25 for brown) until 'al dente' (see page 18). A tablespoon of oil in the water helps prevent it boiling over and the rice grains from sticking together. Drain the rice in a sieve, return to the saucepan, stir in a knob of butter and serve immediately.

Open the hinged boiler and fill one half with rice.

Close the boiler and lower into boiling water.

To simplify draining, the rice can also be cooked in a rice boiler which is suspended by a chain which hooks over the side of the pan. Cook as for boiling rice, above. When the rice is cooked simply lift the boiler out of the pan and drain.

Rissotto

The method of making Italian risotto goes against all the rules set down on page 191. It is essential that the rice is stirred for the entire cooking time and that the liquid is added in small quantities, so that it is absorbed slowly by the rice. The rice is cooked when it is 'al dente'. It should be creamily bound together but not swamped in liquid – practice and experience of making this dish will enable you to judge when it is perfectly cooked.

Extra ingredients can be added to risotto – diced chicken, mushrooms, etc, as liked.

Serves 6
1 litre (1³/4 pints) Chicken Stock (see page 25)
75 g (3 oz) butter
2 tablespoons oil
2–3 shallots, peeled and finely chopped
50 g (2 oz) Prosciutto (Parma) ham, diced (if available)
400 g (14 oz) Arborio rice, washed and drained
¹/2 teaspoon saffron strands soaked in 1 tablespoon hot stock
salt
freshly ground black pepper
75 g (3 oz) freshly grated Parmesan cheese
2 tablespoons finely chopped parsley

Preparation time: 10 minutes
Cooking time: 30 minutes

1. Bring the stock slowly to the boil, reduce the heat, and simmer for 5 minutes, skimming if necessary. Turn off the heat.

2. In a large heavy-based saucepan, melt 40 g (1½ oz) of the butter, add the oil, and heat gently. Fry the shallots gently for 5 minutes without browning, stirring occasionally.

3. Add the Prosciutto, and cook for a further 5 minutes, stirring occasionally.

4. Stir in the rice, and cook over a medium heat for 3 minutes until the rice is well coated in the butter and oil.

5. Pour over 150 ml (¼ pint) of the hot stock, and cook over a high to medium heat, stirring constantly, until the liquid is absorbed. Stir in a further 150 ml (¼ pint) of stock and continue stirring until the liquid is absorbed, ensuring that the rice does not stick to the base of the pan.

6. Continue adding stock as before, and stirring constantly, for 30 minutes until the rice is dry and tender and most of the stock has been used.

7. About 10 minutes before the end of the cooking time, stir in the soaked saffron, and season with salt and pepper.

8. Taste and adjust the seasoning, then stir in the remaining butter and 25 g (1 oz) of the Parmesan cheese. Sprinkle with chopped parsley and serve immediately. Serve the remaining grated Parmesan cheese in a separate bowl, to be sprinkled over the top of the risotto.

Kedgeree

Serves 6–8
750 g (1¹/2 lb) smoked haddock
1 bay leaf
a few parsley sprigs
1 lemon, sliced
4 black peppercorns
100 g (4 oz) butter
1 onion, peeled and finely chopped
2 teaspoons curry powder
450 g (1 lb) long-grain rice
1.2 litres (2 pints) fish liquor (from cooking the haddock)
2 hard-boiled eggs, chopped
4 tablespoons single cream
3 tablespoons chopped parsley
To garnish:
lemon slices or wedges
a few whole unshelled prawns

Preparation time: 15 minutes
Cooking time: about 45 minutes

1. Put the haddock, cut up into pieces if necessary, into a large saucepan, with the bay leaf, parsley, lemon slices and peppercorns. Cover with just over 1.2 litres (2 pints) of boiling water. Bring to the boil, turn the heat down immediately and simmer for 10 minutes until the fish is just tender.

2. Using a slotted spoon or fish slice, remove the fish from the pan and cool. Carefully remove the skin and bones and roughly flake the flesh.

3. Strain the fish liquor and reserve for cooking the rice. Taste to check the seasoning, and adjust accordingly.

4. Melt 75 g (3 oz) of the butter in a large saucepan, add the onion, and cook for 10–15 minutes until lightly browned. Stir in the curry powder and cook for a further 2 minutes, stirring constantly.

5. Add the rice and cook quickly for 1 minute, stirring all the time, then pour in the fish liquor. Slowly bring to the boil, then reduce the heat, cover, and simmer for 10 minutes. Test that the rice is nearly cooked, increase the heat and cook for a further 2 minutes until the liquid is absorbed.

6. Fold in the flaked fish, chopped hard-boiled eggs, single cream and parsley and adjust the seasoning to taste. Serve immediately, garnished with lemon slices or wedges, and prawns.

Traditional Rice Pudding

Serves 4–6
50 g (2 oz) pudding rice, washed and drained
25 g (1 oz) demerara sugar
a pinch of salt
1 large can evaporated milk, made up to 900 ml (1¹/2 pints) with water
grated nutmeg
15 g (¹/2 oz) butter

Preparation time: 10 minutes
Cooking time: 3½–4 hours
Oven: 150°C, 300°F, Gas Mark 2

1. Put the rice into a 900 ml (1½ pint) lightly greased pie dish or ovenproof dish.

2. Sprinkle over the sugar and salt, then slowly pour in the diluted evaporated milk. Mix well and sprinkle with grated nutmeg.

3. Dot with the butter and bake in a preheated oven for 3½–4 hours until golden brown.

4. Serve hot or cold.

Fried Rice

Serves 4
3 tablespoons vegetable oil
*175 g (6 oz) long-grain rice,
  cooked*
50 g (2 oz) lean bacon, diced
*50 g (2 oz) peas, blanched for 2
  minutes and drained*
*50 g (2 oz) button mushrooms,
  sliced*
2 eggs, beaten
100 g (4 oz) fresh beansprouts
50 g (4 oz) peeled prawns
To garnish:
*2 tablespoons chopped spring
  onions*

Preparation time: 5 minutes,
excluding cooking the rice
Cooking time: 8 minutes

1. Heat the oil in a wok or large
frying pan until smoking.

2. Quickly stir in the cooked
rice and stir-fry for 1 minute,
then add the bacon, peas and
mushrooms. Stir-fry for 5
minutes, stirring.

3. Pour over the beaten eggs,
and add the beansprouts and
prawns. Stir-fry for 1–2
minutes until the eggs have set.

Stir the cooked rice into the
hot oil in the wok.

Add bacon, peas and
mushrooms and stir-fry.

4. Serve immediately,
sprinkled with spring onions.

To cook rice perfectly

■ When using the absorption
methods, do not increase the
amount of water or stock, or
the rice will be soggy.
■ Don't be tempted to open
the lid of the saucepan or
casserole when using the
absorption method, as vital
steam will escape and this will
increase the cooking time.
■ Don't stir the rice whilst it
is cooking, as this tends to
break the grains.
■ To test if rice is cooked,
remove a grain from the pan,
and squeeze it between the
fingers. It should be soft on
the outside but still retain its
shape and a certain amount of

firmness in the centre.
■ Always serve freshly
cooked rice within 10
minutes of cooking, to
prevent it from sticking. If the
rice is to be served cold, put
into a sieve and run warm
water over it until the grains
are quite separate. Leave to
drain and cool.
■ Rice may be cooked in
water, chicken, fish or beef
stock, or in tomato juice.
There are numerous
flavourings which can be
added to rice, including fruit
juices, meats and fish, herbs,
spices, vegetables, dried fruit
like raisins and nuts.

Almond Cake

This cake is very moist and
improves with keeping. As
soon as it is out of the oven,
turn it out on to a wire tray, and
then turn it over so that the top
is not marked.

Makes 1 × 20 cm (8 inch) cake
*100 g (4 oz) soft margarine or
  softened butter*
100 g (4 oz) caster sugar
2 large eggs, beaten
50 g (2 oz) self-raising flour
1 teaspoon baking powder
50 g (2 oz) ground rice
50 g (2 oz) ground almonds
a few drops of almond essence

Preparation time: 15 minutes
Cooking time: 35–40 minutes
Oven: 180°C, 350°F, Gas Mark 4

1. Lightly grease and line a
20 cm (8 inch) shallow cake tin,
about 5 cm (2 inches) deep
(see page 311).

2. Cream the margarine or
butter, then beat in the sugar.
Continue beating until the
mixture is light and fluffy.

3. Gradually beat in the eggs, a
little at a time, until the mixture
is light.

4. Sift together the flour and
baking powder. Fold into the
mixture with the ground rice
and ground almonds. Stir in
the almond essence.

5. Spoon the mixture into the
prepared tin and bake in the
centre of the oven for 35–40
minutes, until well risen and
golden brown.

6. Turn out on to a wire tray,
and immediately invert so that
the top is not marked. Cool,
and store in an airtight tin.

To make a rice ring

Cold cooked rice can be used
to make a ring of rice which
may be served hot or cold. Toss
the rice in sufficient French
dressing to moisten it, add a
few cooked peas, or blanched
red and green peppers, and
lightly press into a metal ring
mould. Smooth the top, cover
and chill in the refrigerator for
1 hour.
  If the rice is to be served hot,
it may be warmed in the mould

in a bain-marie (see page 74)
for 10–15 minutes.
  To turn out, place a serving
plate on top of the mould, and
turn it upside down. Carefully
remove the metal ring and use
as required. The inside may be
filled with a salad of vegetables,
cold curried chicken, flaked
fish or prawns or shellfish.

Press the rice mixture into
the mould with a spoon.

To turn out, place a plate on
top and turn it upside down.

PULSES

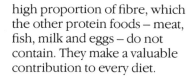

Dried beans, peas and lentils are exciting to cook in different ways – in soups and stews, salads, burgers and dips. Follow the handy hints to help you cook pulses correctly. The alphabetical guide provides information on identification and nutritional value.

Pulses – the general term for all ripe, dried and edible seeds of légumes (peas, beans and lentils) – are becoming more popular, principally because of their high nutritive value. They are cheap to buy and are a major source of vegetable protein; they are also a good source of iron, phosphorus and a selection of the B vitamins. The fat content of pulses is lower than any other protein food, and they provide a very high proportion of fibre, which the other protein foods – meat, fish, milk and eggs – do not contain. They make a valuable contribution to every diet.

Buying and storing

It is a myth that pulses have a long shelf life: long storage causes them to harden to such an extent that they will not soften during cooking. For this reason, it is best to buy small quantities at a time, and use them as soon as possible. Buy from a shop that has a quick turnover, which will ensure freshness.

Kidney beans, chick peas, flageolets, butter beans, cannellini beans and borlotti beans can be found in cans, already cooked and ready to use. Although fairly expensive, they are a good standby to keep in the store cupboard. You can then use them in a salad or add them to a casserole.

Store dried pulses in airtight containers in a dark cupboard or larder. Do not push them to the back of the cupboard to be forgotten.

Freshly cooked pulses will store for a couple of days in a covered container in the refrigerator. They also freeze well in their cooked form. Rissoles and croquettes are best cooked from frozen, rather than thawing them first.

Adzuki beans

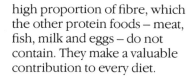

Broad beans

Flageolet beans

Dried peas

Black beans

Butter beans

Haricot beans

Pinto beans

Black-eyed beans

Cannellini beans

Continental lentils

Red kidney beans

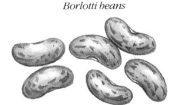

Borlotti beans

Chick peas

Red lentils

Mung beans

Split peas

Soya beans

Soaking pulses

Most pulses benefit from an initial soaking prior to cooking. This not only speeds up the

Soak pulses overnight in cold water

cooking time, but also makes them more digestible. It also enables 'foreign bodies' to be seen and removed.

There are two methods of soaking pulses. The first, the long soak, means covering the pulses completely with cold water and leaving them to soak

Always rinse pulses well after soaking

for between 6–8 hours or overnight. With the short soak method, the pulses are put into a saucepan, covered with plenty of water and slowly brought to the boil. They are boiled vigorously for 3 minutes, then removed from the heat, covered with a lid, and left to soak in the water for 1 hour. After soaking, the pulses should be drained thoroughly, and then rinsed in a sieve under cold running water until the water runs clear. This gets rid of residual starch.

Cooking pulses

Put the soaked and rinsed pulses into a large saucepan or casserole and cover generously with stock or water. If using stock, ensure that it does not contain any salt, as this toughens the outer skin of the pulse and prevents it cooking properly. Salt should be added at the end of cooking when the pulses are soft. Lemon juice, vinegar and other acids, including tomatoes, have a similar effect and should be added at the end of cooking time.

Pulses may be cooked on top of the stove or in the oven. A pressure cooker is ideal for speeding up the cooking time, in most cases reducing it by two-thirds.

TYPES OF PULSES COMMONLY AVAILABLE

Pulse	Description	Cooking Time
Adzuki Beans	Small reddish-brown beans, which are rounded with a slightly squared edge. The flavour is sweet and nutty. They are used a lot in oriental dishes: a Japanese rice has a mixture of beans and rice, the rice a delicate pink from the bean-cooking water. Also used in some cakes and sweetmeats.	30 minutes after soaking
Black Beans	A member of the kidney bean family. These shiny black beans may be substituted for red kidney beans in any recipe. They have a strong and meaty taste, and are particularly effective when cooked with rice. They may be mixed into salads, casseroles, soups and main dishes.	1 hour after soaking
Black-eyed Beans	These beans are smaller than kidney beans, but similar in shape. They are known in the States as black-eyed peas, where they are a major savoury ingredient in Creole cooking. They are cream coloured with a black spot, which gives the bean its name. Use in salads, stews, and soups.	35 minutes after soaking
Borlotti Beans	A member of the kidney bean family. Very popular in Italy, they have pinkish-orange flecks on a cream-pink skin, and a fairly sweet flavour. Very good in salads and stews.	1 hour after soaking
Broad Beans	Large flat kidney-shaped beans, sold in their brownish-tan skin (which should be removed after cooking, as it is very tough) or, better, skinned. Use in soups and casseroles.	1½ hours after soaking
Butter Beans	Also known as Lima beans. Very large, flat, oval beans with slightly pointed ends. They are off-white in colour and have a meaty texture and good flavour. Best used in casseroles, soups and stews. They tend to go mushy if overcooked.	1¼ hours after soaking
Cannellini Beans	A member of the kidney bean family. These beans are small and creamy white. They are very similar to haricots and are interchangeable with them. They may be used in soups, stews and casseroles. They are particularly good in salads.	1 hour after soaking

Pulse	Description	Cooking Time	Pulse	Description	Cooking Time
Chick Peas	Similar in size and shape to a small hazelnut. They are yellowish-brown in colour, and are very nutritious. Use as a vegetable accompaniment or in salads and stews. Common in Indian curries, North African stews, and Mediterranean dishes – the Middle Eastern hummus, for example.	1¼–1½ hours after soaking	Peas	Dried whole peas look like pale green fresh peas with wrinkled skins. They have a sweet flavour. The peas break down to a purée during cooking, which is why they are used to make 'mushy peas' and soups.	45 minutes after soaking
Flageolet Beans	A member of the kidney bean family. They are young haricot beans, a pale greenish-yellow in colour, and very tender. They are probably the most expensive pulse. Mixed with other beans in a salad, they add colour, and are good as a delicate vegetable accompaniment.	1¼ hours after soaking	Pinto Beans	A member of the kidney bean family. These oval beans are slightly rounded and pinkish peach in colour with darker speckles. They are related to Borlotti beans, are pink when cooked, and have a distinctive flavour. Use for salads, stews and casseroles.	1–1¼ hours after soaking
Haricot Beans	A member of the kidney bean family. Creamy-white, oval-shaped small beans, which are used in 'baked' beans. They have many other uses – in casseroles, classic cassoulets, stews and soups.	1¼–1½ hours after soaking	Red Kidney Beans	A member of the kidney bean family. Deep maroon in colour, these beans have a meaty texture and delicious flavour. They hold their shape well during cooking, but must be well cooked (boiled for at least 15 minutes of their cooking time). Use for salads, soups, casseroles and stews. Best known for their use in Chilli con Carne.	1 hour after soaking
Lentils, Continental	Often referred to as whole green or brown lentils, although they can be other colours. Flat and round, they retain their shape well during cooking. They have a good flavour which is useful in soups, salads, rissoles, stews and casseroles. Lentils are second only to soya beans in food value, and are a staple in India where they are made into dhal.	30–45 minutes after soaking 1½ hours if unsoaked	Soya Beans	These beans are the hardest of all the pulses. They require 3–4 hours' cooking after a long soaking. The richest natural vegetable food, very high in protein, they are small, round, and yellowish-cream in colour. They are used to make bean curd or *tofu*, much used in oriental cooking, soy oil (the basis of margarine), soy milk and soy sauce. They are also ground down to a high protein flour, and are used in TVP foods (textured vegetable protein). To save time in soaking and cooking, 'soya splits' are available which only require 30 minutes' cooking. Use whole for soups and casseroles which require long cooking.	3–4 hours after 3–6 hours' soaking
Lentils, Split Red	Split lentils do not need to be soaked before cooking, but this can speed up the cooking time. Known also as Egyptian lentils, they are orangey-red in colour, cook to a yellowish-brown and break down to a rough purée. Excellent for soups, croquettes and rissoles.	15–20 minutes if soaked 25–30 minutes if unsoaked			
Mung Beans	Small, olive green, oval-shaped beans, which are sweet tasting and have a soft texture. They may be cooked without soaking. Best known in their sprouted form as beansprouts, which are used in salads and stir-fry dishes.	20–30 minutes if soaked 30–40 minutes if unsoaked	Split Peas	Green and yellow are available. These peas have been split in half, and the skin removed. During cooking the pea breaks down into a coarse purée. Yellow are more often seen than green. Use for soups, dhals, rissoles, croquettes. They do not need soaking before cooking.	30 minutes if soaked 40–45 minutes if unsoaked

Three Bean Salad

Serves 6
*1 × 425 g (15 oz) can
cannellini beans*
*1 × 425 g (15 oz) can red
kidney beans*
*1 × 425 g (15 oz) can flageolet
beans*
*3 spring onions, trimmed and
chopped*
*3 celery sticks, trimmed and
chopped*
*1 small green pepper, seeded
and chopped*
*1 small red pepper, seeded and
chopped*
*50 g (2 oz) button mushrooms,
thinly sliced*
For the dressing:
*150 ml (¼ pint) Mayonnaise
(see page 31)*
*1 teaspoon finely grated lemon
peel*
2 teaspoons lemon juice
*1–2 garlic cloves, peeled and
crushed*
*1 tablespoon chopped fresh
thyme*
*1 tablespoon chopped fresh
parsley*
*2 tablespoons chopped fresh
basil*
salt
freshly ground black pepper
To garnish:
*50 g (2 oz) black olives, stoned
fresh basil*

Preparation time: 20–30
minutes

1. Place the contents of the cans
of beans in a colander and
rinse under running cold
water to remove the starch.
Drain thoroughly and put into
a large salad bowl.

2. Add the spring onions,
celery, red and green peppers,
and the mushrooms.

3. Put the mayonnaise into a
basin, and stir in the lemon
peel, lemon juice, garlic, herbs
and salt and pepper to taste.

4. Spoon the dressing over the
beans and other ingredients,
and toss well.

5. Arrange the black olives over
the surface and garnish with
the fresh basil. Serve
immediately.

Chilli con Carne

Serves 6
*350 g (12 oz) red kidney beans,
soaked*
4 tablespoons oil
*1 kg (2 lb) lean stewing beef,
trimmed and cubed*
*2 onions, peeled and thinly
sliced*
*1–2 garlic cloves, peeled and
crushed*
1 tablespoon chilli powder
*1 dried red chilli, crushed
(optional)*
2 tablespoons plain flour
*300 ml (½ pint) well flavoured
Bone Stock (see page 24)*
*1 × 400 g (14 oz) can
tomatoes*
salt
freshly ground black pepper

Preparation time: 1 hour
(including cooking the beans)
Cooking time: 3¼ hours
Oven: 160°C, 325°F, Gas Mark 3

1. Rinse the soaked beans and
drain well. Cook them in
boiling water for 50 minutes
until nearly tender, then drain
thoroughly.

2. Heat the oil in a flameproof
casserole, and fry the meat in 2
batches until browned on all
sides. Drain on paper towels
and set aside.

3. Fry the onion in the oil in the
casserole for 5 minutes until
translucent, stirring
occasionally. Stir in the garlic.

4. Sprinkle over the chilli
powder and cook for a further
2 minutes, stirring constantly.

5. Stir in the crushed chilli if
using, along with the flour, and
cook for 2 minutes, stirring
constantly.

6. Heat the stock and gradually
pour into the casserole, stirring
constantly.

7. Return the meat to the
casserole, stir in the tomatoes
and their juice, and slowly
bring to the boil.

8. Season with a little salt and
plenty of pepper, cover with a
lid, and place in a preheated
oven for 2¾ hours until the
meat is tender.

9. Stir the kidney beans into the
casserole, and return to the
oven for a further 30 minutes.

10. Adjust the seasoning to
taste, and serve with boiled
rice.

Cooking Pulses

■ Dry pulses may be used to
line a pastry case when
baking 'blind'. Once used for
this purpose, they should be
cooled and stored in an
airtight tin or jar and kept for
that specific purpose.
■ Vegetable stock cubes are a
good medium in which to
soak pulses. The salt content
is very low, and they add
flavour.
■ Always use a large heavy-
based saucepan, casserole or
ovenproof dish, which will
hold sufficient liquid to cover
the pulses completely during
soaking and cooking.
■ Soaking pulses not only
speeds up the cooking
process, it also makes them
more digestible. If you still
find pulses indigestible,
change the water several times.
■ The addition of a bouquet
garni to the cooking water
adds real flavour to the
cooked pulse.
■ When sprouting pulses,
only do so a few at a time, as
they increase by up to six
times in volume.
■ Although most pulses cook
down to a purée, most pulse
soups have a better texture if
they are puréed after cooking,
either in a blender or food
processor, then pushed
through a sieve.
■ When cooking pulses for
rissoles and croquettes, it is
important not to make the
mixture too wet. Steaming
rather than boiling is better
therefore: put the pulses into
a bowl, just cover with water,
and place over a saucepan of
boiling water. Give them an
occasional stir.
■ When making salads, toss
the cooked pulses in French
dressing while still warm.

PASTA RICE & PULSE RECIPES

Five exciting rice dishes illustrate just some of the ways it can be cooked, from fried Chinese style to simmered Italian-style to make creamy risotto. Two Middle Eastern dishes, together with a great Italian pasta dish, Spaghetti alla carbonara – complete this section.

Jambalaya

This is one of the glories of Creole cooking – from Louisiana and New Orleans – which combines French, African and Spanish influences to produce spicy, highly seasoned dishes.

Serves 4
2 tablespoons olive oil
4 chicken quarters
2 large onions, peeled and chopped
1 green pepper, cored, seeded and chopped
2 garlic cloves, peeled and finely chopped
100 g (4 oz) cooked ham, diced
350 g (12 oz) smoked sausage, sliced
2 bay leaves
2 tablespoons finely chopped parsley
¼ teaspoon dried thyme
½ teaspoon cayenne pepper
pinch of ground cloves
salt
freshly ground black pepper
275 g (10 oz) long-grain rice
900 ml (1½ pints) hot Chicken Stock (see page 25)
225 g (8 oz) peeled prawns
To garnish:
parsley sprigs
bay leaves

Preparation time: 30 minutes
Cooking time: 1¼ hours

1. Heat the oil in a very large, heavy-based saucepan, add the chicken pieces and brown on all sides. Remove and drain.

2. Add the onions, green pepper and garlic to the pan and fry gently for about 10 minutes, stirring from time to time, until the onions are soft and browned. Add the ham, sausage, herbs, spices and seasoning and cook for a further 5 minutes, stirring.

3. Add the reserved chicken pieces, rice and stock to the pan. Stir well to mix, then bring to the boil. Lower the heat, cover the pan and cook gently for 45 minutes, stirring from time to time.

4. Raise the heat to moderate, uncover the pan and cook for a further 10 minutes, stirring frequently, until most of the liquid is absorbed. Add the prawns and heat through gently for a few minutes. Adjust the seasoning.

5. Pile the jambalaya on to a heated serving dish, garnish with parsley and bay leaves and serve immediately.

Felafel

These little spiced fritters are a Middle Eastern speciality. During Lent the Christian Copts of Egypt consume them in large quantities. They can be served at any meal – breakfast, lunch or supper. Felafel are also delicious as an informal snack tucked inside pitta bread with salad or served with a tahini dip.

Makes about 20
1 kg (2 lb) cooked chick peas
1 medium onion, peeled and grated
1 garlic clove, peeled and crushed
1 teaspoon ground cumin
1 teaspoon ground coriander
¼ teaspoon chilli powder
½ teaspoon caraway seeds
salt
freshly ground black pepper
3 tablespoons chopped fresh parsley
1 egg, beaten

75 g (3 oz) wholemeal flour
vegetable oil, for shallow frying

Preparation time: 20 minutes
Cooking time: 20 minutes
Oven: 110°C, 225°F, Gas Mark ¼

1. Blend the chick peas in a food processor to a smooth paste.

2. Put into a bowl with the onion, garlic, cumin, coriander, chilli, caraway seeds, salt and pepper. Mix to a firm paste then stir in the chopped parsley.

3. Form the mixture into small balls then pat them into small flat cakes about 4 cm (1½ inches) across. The uncooked felafel can be prepared up to 8 hours in advance and kept in the refrigerator, lightly covered with clingfilm. Dip in beaten egg and then into flour.

4. Shallow fry in oil in batches for about 5 minutes, turning once, until crisp and brown. Drain on paper towels and keep hot in the oven while frying the rest.

Left to right: Felafel, Jambalaya

Risotto alla Milanese

The bone marrow is not an essential ingredient, but it does add a rich quality to the risotto – ask your butcher to give you a good beef or veal bone, sawed through. Roast the bones in a hot oven for 30 minutes to allow the marrow to soften – it will then be easy to scoop it out.

Serves 4–6
½ teaspoon saffron strands
3 tablespoons hot water
2 tablespoons olive oil
100 g (4 oz) butter
1 small onion, peeled and
    finely chopped
1 tablespoon bone marrow
    (optional)
450 g (1 lb) round-grain
    Italian rice (Arborio for
    preference)
150 ml (¼ pint) dry white wine
1.5 litres (2½ pints) hot
    Chicken Stock (see page 25)
salt
freshly ground black pepper
50 g (2 oz) Parmesan cheese,
    grated

Preparation time: 3 minutes, plus soaking the saffron and roasting the marrow bone
Cooking time: 35 minutes

1. Soak the saffron in the water for 15–20 minutes.

2. Heat the oil and half the butter in a large saucepan and gently fry the onion for 3 minutes. Add the bone marrow if using and rice and stir over a gentle heat for 5 minutes, making sure that the rice does not colour.

3. Add the wine and cook over a brisk heat until the wine has almost evaporated.

4. Add 250 ml (8 fl oz) of the stock to the rice and cook steadily until absorbed. Continue adding the stock in this way for about 20 minutes, or until all the stock has been used up and the rice is tender – it should be 'creamy' and not dry. Add salt and pepper to taste and strain the saffron water into the rice. Stir in the remaining butter and the Parmesan cheese. Serve immediately.

Moors and Christians

Black Beans and Rice

This dish comes from the Caribbean where it is usually served with fried plantains (green bananas).

Serves 4
2 tablespoons olive oil
1 medium onion, peeled and
    finely chopped
1 garlic clove, peeled and
    crushed
1 green pepper, cored, seeded
    and chopped
2 tomatoes, peeled, seeded and
    chopped
salt
freshly ground black pepper
225 g (8 oz) black beans,
    cooked
225 g (8 oz) long-grain rice
450 ml (¾ pint) water

Preparation time: 10 minutes
Cooking time: about 30 minutes

1. Heat the oil in a heavy pan, add the onion, garlic and pepper and cook gently until the onion has softened. Add the tomatoes and cook, stirring, until the mixture is quite thick. Season to taste with salt and pepper.

2. Stir in the beans, mixing well. Add the rice and water and mix in lightly. Bring to the boil, then cover and cook over a very low heat until the rice is tender and all the water has been absorbed.

3. To serve, fluff up the rice with a fork and pile on to a serving dish.

Tabbouleh

Cracked Wheat and Mint Salad

A highly popular Lebanese party dish, often served piled high on a large platter. It can be decorated with tomatoes, olives, cucumber slices, parsley sprigs or strips of green peppers.

Serves 4–6
225 g (8 oz) burghul (cracked
    wheat)
4 large spring onions, finely
    chopped
1 large garlic clove, peeled and
    crushed
4 tablespoons chopped fresh
    parsley
4 tablespoons finely chopped
    fresh mint
6 tablespoons olive oil
4 tablespoons lemon juice
salt
freshly ground black pepper
coriander or mint sprig, to
    garnish

Preparation time: 15 minutes, plus soaking and draining

1. Put the burghul into a bowl and add sufficient cold water to cover. Leave to stand for 45 minutes–1 hour. The burghul will swell up considerably.

2. Drain the burghul and squeeze out as much moisture as possible, then drain more thoroughly by spreading it out on a clean tea towel.

3. Mix the drained burghul with the spring onions, garlic, parsley and mint.

4. Mix the olive oil with the lemon juice and salt and pepper to taste. Stir this dressing into the burghul mixture.

5. Taste and adjust the seasoning – tabbouleh should be lemony and well-seasoned. Garnish with a sprig of fresh coriander or mint and serve with a selection of salads.

From the top: Tabbouleh, Moors and Christians, Risotto alla Milanese

Yangchow Fried Rice

Chinese mushrooms have a taste and aroma quite distinct from ordinary English field mushrooms. These dried mushrooms are available in Chinese stores and supermarkets and will give this dish the authentic flavour.

Serves 4
5 tablespoons vegetable oil
2 medium onions, peeled and finely sliced
2 slices root ginger, peeled and diced
100 g (4 oz) minced pork
salt
1 tablespoon light soy sauce
1 teaspoon sugar
450 g (1 lb) cooked rice
2 eggs, lightly beaten
2 tablespoons cooked green peas
2 tomatoes, chopped
3 dried Chinese mushrooms, soaked for 20 minutes, drained, stemmed and chopped (optional)
freshly ground black pepper

Preparation time: 20 minutes, plus soaking
Cooking time: about 10 minutes

1. Heat the oil in a large wok or frying pan. Add the onions and ginger, and stir-fry for 1 minute. Add the minced pork and stir-fry for 3 minutes. Add ½ teaspoon salt, soy sauce and sugar and stir-fry for 1 minute.

2. Add the rice to the wok to heat through, turning and stirring well.

3. Heat the remaining oil in a frying pan. Season the beaten eggs with salt and pepper and add to the pan. Stir and turn the eggs gently. As soon as they have set, add the peas, tomatoes and mushrooms.

4. Stir for about 1 minute, then turn the egg mixture into the wok containing the rice. Mix lightly together, then serve in a heated bowl.

Risi e Bisi

Risi e Bisi is rather more liquid than an ordinary risotto. It should not be stirred too much or the peas will break up. It is a Venetian dish served to the Doges on the feast of St Mark. Bisi is a local dialect word for peas, and traditionally the dish should be made only with Venetian peas. While this is a counsel of perfection, fresh peas will give the best results.

Serves 4–6
75 g (3 oz) butter
1 onion, peeled and finely chopped
350 g (12 oz) shelled fresh or frozen peas
350 g (12 oz) short-grain Italian rice (preferably Arborio)
100 g (4 oz) cooked smoked ham, diced
1.5–1.75 litres (2½–3 pints) hot Chicken Stock (see page 25)
salt
freshly ground black pepper
50 g (2 oz) Parmesan cheese, finely grated

Preparation time: 15 minutes
Cooking time: 35–40 minutes

1. Melt 50 g (2 oz) of the butter in a heavy-based saucepan. Add the onion and cook, stirring frequently, until transparent but not browned.

2. Add the fresh peas, rice and ham. Cook, stirring, for 1–2 minutes.

3. Add 600 ml (1 pint) of the stock and cook, stirring gently, until absorbed. Add a further 600 ml (1 pint) and again cook, stirring, until the stock is absorbed. Add a little more stock and continue until the rice is cooked. If using frozen peas, add 5 minutes before the end of the cooking time. Season with a little salt and plenty of pepper.

4. Stir in the remaining butter and Parmesan cheese and serve immediately.

Spaghetti alla Carbonara

A classic Roman dish which can be made with any shaped pasta, spaghetti or noodles. The sauce, a creamy amalgam of egg, cream and cheese, should never contain flour.

Serves 4
350 g (12 oz) spaghetti
salt
freshly ground black pepper
175 g (6 oz) streaky bacon rashers, cut into 1 cm (½ inch) strips
4 tablespoons double cream
3 eggs
50 g (2 oz) Parmesan cheese, finely grated
40 g (1½ oz) butter, softened

Preparation time: 10 minutes
Cooking time: 15–20 minutes

1. Lower the spaghetti into a large saucepan of briskly boiling salted water and cook for about 10 minutes until *al dente*. Drain thoroughly and rinse with hot water.

2. Meanwhile fry the bacon gently in a frying pan without added fat until crisp and golden. Drain on paper towels. Bring the cream to simmering point and keep hot.

3. Beat the eggs with the cheese and season with a little salt and plenty of pepper.

4. When the spaghetti is ready, transfer to a heated serving bowl and stir in the butter, tossing and turning the spaghetti to coat all the strands evenly.

5. Mix the bacon with the hot cream and quickly stir into the spaghetti, immediately followed by the egg and cheese mixture. Toss thoroughly (the egg will set as it comes into contact with the hot ingredients) and serve immediately.

From the left, clockwise: Risi e bisi, Yangchow fried rice, Spaghetti alla carbonara

EGGS

Still relatively cheap, eggs are probably the most indispensable ingredient in all kinds of cooking, and egg cookery is an art of its own. This section shows how to boil, coddle, poach, scramble, fry and bake the perfect egg, as well as make omelettes and pancakes.

How to test for freshness

The fresher the egg, the higher the food value. It is best to buy from a reliable source where there is a quick turnover, and for preference choose free-range eggs where the birds have been fed high-quality food.

Each egg has an air space at the 'blunt' end which increases as the egg ages, therefore the fresher the egg, the smaller the air space. If an egg is placed in a tumbler (or similar container) of water, it should lie completely flat in the base. If it tilts slightly, it is slightly stale. If the egg floats to the top of the water, it is not suitable to use for boiling and should be cracked before use. If a pungent smell comes from the egg, it should be discarded.

When an egg is broken, the white should be translucent and thickly clinging to the yolk. If the white runs away from the yolk, it is not as fresh as it should be.

Storing eggs

Always store eggs in a cool place, preferably not the refrigerator, with the blunt end up, pointed end down. Store away from strong smelling and flavoured foods, as the porous shell absorbs these. Try not to keep them for more than two weeks. Buy eggs frequently, in small quantities.

Left-over whites and yolks may be stored in small covered containers in the refrigerator. The yolks, if whole, should be covered in a little cold water;

they will store in the refrigerator for up to 1 day. Whole eggs in their shells cannot be frozen but, as they are so plentiful, there is no need for this anyway. However, whole eggs, beaten together, freeze well. To 6 beaten eggs, add either ½ teaspoon of salt or sugar, depending on their ultimate use. Egg whites may be frozen as they are in covered containers, but egg yolks will coagulate during freezing.

Grading of eggs

Eggs are now graded by weight throughout the EEC. Most of the recipes in this book use either size 1 or 2.

Uses of eggs

Eggs have many culinary uses. An egg yolk acts as a *binding agent* for stuffings, fish cakes, rissoles, etc. They also *aerate*, the white having the ability to hold air and to increase its volume by many times (as in meringue). Eggs act as a *thickening agent*, for soups, sauces and stews as well as for custards, where the yolk coagulates as it is heated to hold the liquid in suspension. The yolk *emulsifies* and is capable of holding oil or butter in suspension (the beaten yolk will hold tiny globules of fat, such as in mayonnaise). A whole egg or yolk is also used for *coating* foods or *glazing* them.

How to whisk egg whites

The more egg white is whisked, the more air is incorporated. However, care must be taken that the egg is not over-beaten as this can cause the mixture to collapse during cooking. The amount of whisking should be gauged according to the recipe for which it is required. The general rule is that the texture of the egg white should be similar to the consistency of the mixture it is being added to.

It is essential that all the utensils used – the bowl, whisk and spoon – are completely free of grease and very clean, as the smallest amount of grease, and that includes egg yolk, can spoil the end result.

Egg whites should ideally be beaten by hand in a copper bowl with a balloon whisk, though an electric hand-held beater can also be used.

The copper gives the egg white a strong texture, enabling it to hold up longer. Aluminium or stainless steel is the best alternative.

A metal spoon or spatula should be used to fold in the whisked egg, as it has a sharp thin edge which cuts through into the mixture. A wooden spoon tends to break down the air in the mixture.

Always have the eggs at room temperature before whisking.

Make sure when following a recipe whether the whites should be whisked to soft or firm peaks.

Generally, soft peaks are required for soufflés, where the egg white is whisked until it is slightly translucent and holds soft peaks. For meringue, however, the whites are whisked until the mixture is opaque and holds very firm peaks.

Use whisked egg white immediately, as it can collapse if left for a short time. If the cook is interrupted, the bowl should be turned upside down on to the work surface to exclude the air. This method is only suitable for whites whisked to firm or stiff peaks.

Whisking by hand with a balloon whisk

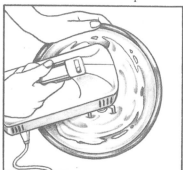
Whisking with a hand-held electric beater

How to separate an egg

Always break an egg into a cup or basin before adding to a mixture, rather than breaking it directly into the food, in case it is bad.

To separate an egg, give the egg a firm sharp knock against the side of a basin or cup, to break the shell cleanly in half. Carefully pass the yolk from one half of the shell to the other, so that the white of the egg drops into the basin. Then place the yolk into a cup or basin.

If the yolk of the egg breaks, use a very clean teaspoon (or the shell half) to remove all

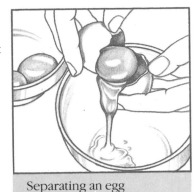

Separating an egg

specks of yellow from the white, as this can spoil the whisking ability of the white.

Folding in egg whites

1. First stir in a big spoonful of whites into the mixture to lighten it. Then scoop the rest of the egg whites on top.

2. Using a metal spoon or spatula, cut down into the centre of the bowl.

3. With a scooping action, bring the spoon up towards you, turning the mixture bottom to top. Continue, turning the bowl and working clockwise, until completely folded in.

Folding in egg whites with a spatula

BASIC COOKING TECHNIQUES FOR EGGS

Boiled eggs Eggs may be soft, medium or hard-boiled. Soft-boiled eggs have a softly set white and runny yolk. Medium-boiled have a set firm white with just soft yolk, and hard-boiled eggs are firm throughout, the white being dry and the yolk solid.

It is essential that the eggs are not cold as the shell will crack in the hot water. If the eggs are to be peeled, they should be a couple of days old. Otherwise, they are very difficult to peel, with the white adhering to the shell during peeling.

The fresher the eggs, the longer they should be cooked.

Lower eggs at room temperature into boiling water, and reduce the heat to a simmer. Cook the eggs for 3 minutes for a light set, and 4½ minutes for a firmer set.

Eggs that are to be hard-boiled should be lowered into cold water, and slowly brought to the boil. Simmer and time from this point for 10–12 minutes. As soon as the eggs are cooked, place them in a bowl under cold running water. As soon as they are cool,

peel and use at once. This method helps to prevent the egg becoming tough and also reduces the chance of a dark black line forming around the yolk.

Coddled eggs With this method, the eggs are cooked in a china 'egg coddler' which is similar in shape to a large egg cup with a lid. Place a knob of butter in the base of the coddler and drop in the whole egg. Sprinkle a little salt and pepper on top, and screw the lid on. Place the coddler in simmering water which comes about three-quarters up the sides of the coddler. Turn off the heat and leave in a covered pan for 8–9 minutes for size 1–3 eggs, 6–7 minutes for size 4–7 eggs. Remove the coddler from the pan. Unscrew the lid and serve the egg in the coddler.

Poached eggs There are two methods of poaching eggs: in a deep frying pan filled with simmering water, or in a 'poacher', where the eggs are placed in individual cups and steamed over water, with a lid.

Frying pan method Pour water into the pan to a depth of approximately 4 cm (1½ inch) and bring to simmering point. Break each egg on to a saucer, and carefully lower into the water. Cook for about 3 minutes until cooked to your liking. A lid may be used to cover the eggs, or they can be basted with the hot water during cooking. Using a fish slice or perforated spoon, carefully lift the egg from the pan, draining it well, and serve immediately.

Poacher method Place a knob of butter in each cup, half fill the lower part of the pan with water, and place the cups in position. Bring to the boil, lower the heat, break the eggs into the cups and simmer, covered, for about 4–5 minutes. Loosen each egg with a blunt-ended knife and tip the eggs out of the cups.

Scrambled eggs The art of scrambling eggs is not to overcook or over stir the mixture. The eggs should be large creamy flakes.

For 2 people, break 3 or 4

eggs into a bowl, and whisk lightly with a fork. Season with salt and pepper and stir in 2 tablespoons of milk or single cream. Melt about 25 g (1 oz) of butter in a pan over a low heat. Pour in the eggs and leave for about ½ minute before gently stirring with a wooden spoon. Cook for a further ½–1 minute, stirring, until the eggs are just set. Serve immediately.

Baked eggs Eggs cooked in this way are cooked in individual cocotte or ramekin dishes. Lightly grease the dishes with a little butter. Place the dishes into a roasting pan with 2.5 cm (1 inch) of warm water in it. Break an egg into each dish and season well. Dot the surface with a little butter or a tablespoon or two of cream and cook in a preheated oven – 180°C, 350°F, Gas Mark 4 – for 8–10 minutes until just set. Remove from the water at once (they will go on cooking) and serve immediately.

These eggs are even nicer if a small amount of flaked fish, fried onion, chopped bacon, etc are placed in the bottom of each ramekin.

French Omelette

A French omelette is a plain, lightly cooked omelette with a golden brown outside and a creamy soft inside. For best results, an omelette pan, or round-sided frying pan, should be used for this purpose only. The pan should not be washed after use, just wiped clean with paper towels.

For best results, the butter should be foaming when the egg is added so that it cooks the egg as soon as it goes into the pan. However, it is essential that the heat is not too high as this will toughen the egg and ruin the omelette.

Serves 1
2 eggs
1 tablespoon cold water
salt
freshly ground black pepper
about 15 g (½ oz) butter

Preparation time: 2 minutes
Cooking time: about 2 minutes

Whisk the eggs and water lightly with a balloon whisk

Add butter and tilt pan to coat the surface

Use a palette knife to draw mixture into the centre

Cook until underside is golden brown

1. Break the eggs into a basin and whisk lightly with a balloon whisk.

2. Whisk in the water and season well. Do not over-beat as this will spoil the texture of the finished omelette.

3. Place the pan over a gentle heat and when it is hot, add the butter. Tip the pan so that the entire inner surface is coated with the butter. When the butter is foaming, but not coloured, tip in the eggs.

4. Leave for about 2 seconds, then using a palette knife, draw the setting mixture away from the edge of the pan into the centre, allowing the egg to run into the sides.

5. Repeat the process twice more, by which time the egg should have set. Cook for a further ½ minute until the underside of the egg is golden brown, and the top of the omelette is still slightly runny and creamy.

6. Tilt the pan, and with the help of a palette knife, carefully turn the omelette on to a plate, folding it in half in the process.

Spanish Tortilla

This Spanish version of omelette can be eaten warm or cold.

Serves 4
450 g (1 lb) potatoes, peeled and cut into 1 cm (½ inch) dice
225 g (8 oz) onion, peeled and finely chopped
olive oil
1 medium green pepper, seeded and finely chopped
100 g (4 oz) Chorizo (or similar) sausage, diced
6 eggs
salt
freshly ground black pepper

Preparation time: about 10 minutes
Cooking time: 25–30 minutes

1. Mix the potato and onion dice together and then heat enough olive oil to cover the bottom of a 20 cm (8 inch) frying pan.

2. Fry the potato and onion gently in the oil for about 10 minutes, turning them over occasionally.

3. Add the green pepper and sausage dice, and fry gently for another 10 minutes. They should all be evenly – but lightly – browned.

4. Beat the eggs in a large bowl, adding seasoning to taste, then mix in the fried vegetables and sausage, draining from the oil in the pan with a perforated spoon.

5. If the oil in the pan is clean, pour the egg mixture in and leave to cook. If not, discard the oil, clean the pan and heat up more fresh oil. Pour in the eggs.

6. After 2–3 minutes, lift up the sides of the omelette to see if they and the undersides are browned. If so, slide the pan under a preheated grill to set and brown – but do not overcook.

7. Serve from the pan, or slide out on to a plate to serve or cool.

BATTERS

The literal translation of batter is to beat. This name is given to mixtures of flour with sufficient liquid to give a cream-like consistency, and which generally contain ingredients such as eggs and milk, sometimes fat and sugar. Batters are used to make Yorkshire pudding, pancakes, fritters, dropped scones and sometimes creamed cakes.

Basic Batter

This is the batter to use for Yorkshire puddings; the same recipe can be used for toad-in-the-hole.

Makes 1 large or 12 individual puddings
100 g (4 oz) plain flour
a pinch of salt
1 egg
just under 300 ml (¹/₂ pint) milk
2 tablespoons water
a little oil or dripping

Preparation time: 10 minutes plus standing
Cooking time: 15 minutes
Oven: 220°C, 425°F, Gas Mark 7

1. Sift the flour and salt into a mixing bowl, make a hollow in the centre and break the egg into it.

2. Mix the milk and water together, add a quarter of the milk to the hollow, and, using a wooden spoon, draw the flour into the centre, beating well to incorporate the flour completely into the egg and liquid.

3. Gradually beat in the remaining milk, beating well between additions, to form a smooth batter. Leave to stand for 15 minutes.

4. For Yorkshire Pudding, pour a little oil into an 18 cm (7 inch) roasting tin. Place in a preheated oven for 5–7 minutes until the oil is smoking.

5. Pour the batter into the tin, and cook for about 25 minutes until well risen and golden brown.

Basic Pancake Recipe

The quantities for the Basic Batter recipe are identical for pancakes, so follow the recipe to the end of stage 3. This amount of batter will make 12 pancakes, using an 18 cm (7 inch) pancake or crêpe pan.

Makes 12 pancakes
Preparation time: 10 minutes, plus standing
Cooking time: about 25 minutes

1. Make up the batter as described opposite.

2. Heat a little oil or lard in a frying pan until really hot, running it around to coat the pan. Pour off any excess.

3. Pour or spoon just enough batter into the pan to cover the base, to give a thin even layer.

3. Cook quickly until tiny bubbles form on the upper surface of the pancakes, and the underside is golden brown.

4. Toss or turn the pancake over and cook the other side for about 1 minute until golden brown.

5. Slip the pancake out of the pan, and keep warm inside a teatowel on a plate. Use as required. Repeat the process with the remaining batter.

6. If the pancakes are to be used at a later date, they may be stacked on top of each other, interleaved with greaseproof paper or foil, and frozen.

Crêpes

The batter for crêpes is richer than a normal pancake mixture. It is enriched with butter and is lighter in texture. This recipe is particularly light, making crêpes that are so thin they are transparent. They are very similar to the delicious crêpes sold on the streets of Normandy and Brittany.

Makes 12–14 crêpes, depending on thickness
3 eggs
100 g (4 oz) plain flour
300 ml (¹/₂ pint) milk
2 tablespoons melted butter
a pinch of salt
oil or lard for frying

Preparation time: 5 minutes plus standing
Cooking time: about 20 minutes

1. Place the eggs in the goblet of an electric blender.

2. Sprinkle the flour over the eggs, then add the milk, melted butter and salt.

3. Blend for 2 minutes on high. Leave to stand for 30 minutes.

4. To cook, follow the instructions for pancakes (above).

Pour in just enough batter to give a thin layer

Cook until bubbles form on surface, then turn over

SOUFFLÉ BASICS

A soufflé is a popular and spectacular show-stopper for any occasion. Pay no attention to the idea that they are for the experts only – if you follow the basic principles set out here, you will have no cause for anxiety. Instead you will have added to your repertoire an extremely attractive and versatile dish. You can choose the traditional cheese flavour shown here or follow your personal preferences and experiment freely.

Although thought to be a difficult and unmanageable dish to serve to more than two people, chefs everywhere can whip up a soufflé without panic for any number, or as any course of a menu. And so can you, but there are a few basic rules to follow to ensure complete success. The first is to try out your soufflé on the family before making it for an important dinner party – just in case you have not got it quite right!

There are two types of soufflé. The best known is the hot soufflé, savoury or sweet, which comes to the table steaming and well risen, ready to eat immediately. The point most commonly made concerning hot soufflés is that they will not wait for the guests, that the guests should be seated ready and waiting to greet the soufflé. In reality, however, once the soufflé is cooked, it will not come to too much harm if left in the turned-off closed oven to wait for about 5 minutes. But, once *out* of the oven, it must be served at once, for otherwise it will simply collapse before your very eyes.

The second type of soufflé is a cold one, set with gelatine, which is explained on pages 211–213.

Hot savoury soufflés

A hot soufflé consists of a thick sauce made of butter, flour and milk (known as a panada) which then has egg yolks beaten into it and stiffly whisked egg whites folded through it immediately before baking. It is important, firstly, to cook the fat and flour together before adding the milk, and then to boil the resulting sauce, beating constantly, in order to cook the flour properly, thus avoiding an uncooked flour taste in the finished dish.

The eggs used should be at room temperature to encourage more volume in the beaten whites. The whites should be separated very carefully from the yolks: the tiniest speck of yolk can prevent the whites whisking properly. And the bowl used should be immaculately clean. Beat the whites so that they fluff up to about 7 times their original volume. It is the air incorporated *now* into the egg whites that will make the soufflé rise. Fold the beaten whites with a metal tablespoon evenly and lightly through the mixture to retain as much volume as possible. Pour the mixture immediately into a greased dish and bake at once.

Cheese Soufflé

Serves 4
2 tablespoons grated Parmesan
 cheese
25 g (1 oz) butter
3 tablespoons plain flour
300 ml (½ pint) milk
75 g (3 oz) mature Cheddar
 cheese, finely grated
4 eggs, separated
salt
freshly ground black pepper
½ teaspoon dry mustard
 powder

Preparation time: about 20 minutes
Cooking time: 35–40 minutes
Oven: 200°C, 400°F, Gas Mark 6

1. Grease a 1.2 litre (2 pint) soufflé dish and sprinkle the inside with 1 tablespoon grated Parmesan.

2. Melt the butter in a saucepan (which should be large enough to hold the whisked egg whites). Add the flour and cook for 2–3 minutes, stirring continuously.

1. Make a roux and gradually stir in the milk.

2. Remove from the heat and stir in the cheese.

4. Whisk the egg whites until stiff.

5. Fold the egg whites into the mixture.

3. Gradually stir in the milk and bring slowly to the boil, stirring all the time. The sauce will be very thick. Cook gently for 1 minute, still stirring.

4. Remove from the heat and stir in the cheeses until just melted; if overheated, cheese tends to become stringy. Then beat in the egg yolks, one at a time, beating until evenly

Flavouring

Flavourings can be added in different ways. Grated, finely chopped or puréed ingredients can be added to the basic sauce before folding in the egg whites. Use cooked meats, fish, seafood, cheese, vegetables, herbs etc (or, for sweet soufflés, chopped, grated or puréed fruits, nuts, liqueurs, essences etc). Flavouring ingredients – a cooked vegetable, say, or a mixture of vegetables – can be put into the base of the soufflé dish, and then a basic or minimally flavoured soufflé mixture is baked on top. (Remember,

when doing this, to use a larger dish to allow for the space taken up by the extra ingredients.)

To test

Do not open the oven door before the cooking time stated in the recipe. Test for doneness by giving the dish a shake. If the soufflé wobbles, it is still runny inside. If it only shakes slightly, the centre is creamy and almost set. You can also test by inserting a trussing needle into the side of the puff. If the needle comes out clean it is ready. When closing the oven door do so gently or the cold

3. Beat in the egg yolks one by one.

6. Make a groove for a 'top-hat' effect.

mixed. Add salt and pepper to taste, and the mustard.

5. In a large, clean, grease-free bowl whisk the egg whites until very stiff. Stir a spoonful of the

egg whites into the sauce to lighten it, then scoop the remainder into the pan and fold through quickly and evenly using a metal spoon.

6. Pour into the prepared dish and cook in the centre of the preheated oven for 35–40 minutes. Serve at once.

Variations

Herb Add 3 tablespoons freshly chopped mixed herbs to the sauce with the egg yolks.
Cheese and Bacon Grill or fry 100–175 g (4–6 oz) streaky bacon rashers until crisp, then crumble or chop finely. Fold in with the egg whites.
Ham and Horseradish. Finely chop or mince 75–100 g (3–4 oz) cooked ham, and beat into the sauce in place of the cheese with 1–2 teaspoons horseradish sauce.
Chicken. Finely chop or mince 100 g (4 oz) cooked chicken meat, and beat into the sauce in place of the cheese.

blast of air will either make the soufflé sink or cease rising.

To serve

Once baked, a soufflé *has* to be eaten quickly. All that air, beaten into the egg white before baking, has expanded to make the soufflé puff up in the traditional way; but once the soufflé is out of the oven, and the heat is removed, that trapped air will slowly be released. As a result the soufflé will sink and become tough and rubbery.

Soufflé dishes

Traditionally they are round with straight sides, and they are often decorated with a fluted design. Usually made of porcelain, glass or earthenware, they come in a wide variety of sizes ranging from individual ramekins upwards. The depth varies, but those of about 6–9 cm/2½–3½ inches are better than very deep ones.

Always grease the inside of the soufflé dish well with butter, margarine or oil before filling and to make a most impressive soufflé, only fill the dish to about three-quarters up the sides. This way it will puff up well above the rim. Don't be tempted to overfill the dish for the soufflé will rise too much and collapse over the edges of the dish, leaving the best part on the oven shelves.

It is important that the soufflé starts to rise straight away. The best way to ensure this is to have a preheated baking sheet in the oven at the correct height. When the soufflé is placed on the hot surface it will have the requisite 'kick' of bottom heat.

A soufflé made with 5–6 eggs requires a dish of about 1.75–2 litre (3–3½ pint) capacity. One made with 3–4 eggs needs a dish of about 1.2–1.5 litre (2–2½ pint) capacity.

For perfect soufflés

■ Have everything prepared before you start. Heat the oven in advance and put the shelf at the right height, allowing plenty of room for the soufflé to rise.
■ Don't cook anything else in the oven at the same time.
■ Butter the dish well so that the mixture will slip up the sides easily.
■ Fill the dish to three-quarters up the side only, so that the soufflé will rise well above the dish. Level the surface with a metal spatula.
■ For a 'top hat' effect, run a round-bladed knife round the edge to make a groove.
■ Serve a soufflé immediately. It will collapse less readily if you cook it until a thin skewer plunged into the centre comes out clean.
■ To test if the soufflé is ready, shake it gently. If it quakes all over it is not done.
■ Have the egg whites at room temperature – they will mount more rapidly. Ideally beat them in a copper bowl. Failing that, add a small pinch of cream of tartar to the whites halfway through the beating.
■ Handbeating with a wire balloon whisk achieves the greatest volume of egg whites. The whites will not rise stiffly if they contain any particle of yolk, or if the bowl or whisk have any trace of grease.
■ Correctly beaten egg whites mount to 7–8 times their original volume and are firm enough to stand in peaks when lifted on the wires of the beater.
■ Don't be too thorough when folding in the egg whites. The whole process should not take more than a minute.

HOT & COLD SOUFFLÉS

■

The basic techniques of soufflés mastered, it is an easy step to trying something spectacular which, since the soufflé is an infinitely variable dish, may be sweet or savoury, hot or cold. A hot soufflé should be served immediately, but a cold soufflé, set with gelatine, may be made well in advance.

Basic information about soufflés – beating, flavouring, dishes to choose, testing etc – is given on pages 206–207. In this section we continue with more elaborate soufflés, hot and cold. Hot sweet soufflés look spectacular, and are often considered to be one of the triumphs of classic cooking. They are usually lighter and airier than hot savoury soufflés, but the general idea is the same: a flavoured sauce into which you fold stiffly beaten egg whites. All the basic hints regarding savoury soufflés given previously also apply to sweet soufflés.

Chocolate Orange Soufflé

Serves 4–6
100 g (4 oz) chocolate dots, or plain chocolate, broken up
2 tablespoons rum or orange juice
450 ml (¾ pint) milk
50 g (2 oz) caster sugar
4 tablespoons flour
15 g (½ oz) butter
grated rind of 1 orange
4 eggs, separated
icing sugar, to dredge

Preparation time: about 25 minutes
Cooking time: about 45 minutes
Oven: 180°C, 350°F, Gas Mark 4

1. Grease a soufflé dish of about 1.75 litre (3 pint) capacity or 18 cm (7 inches) in diameter.

2. Put the chocolate and rum or orange juice into a small heatproof bowl and stand over a pan of gently simmering water until melted. Stir until smooth.

3. Heat most of the milk to just below boiling point. Stir in the caster sugar until dissolved then pour in the chocolate mixture and stir until well blended.

4. Blend the flour with the remaining milk until smooth and gradually add to the chocolate mixture. Return to the saucepan and bring to the boil, stirring frequently. Simmer for 2 minutes.

5. Add the butter and orange rind, stir until the butter is melted, then leave until lukewarm, covered with cling film or foil. Beat the egg yolks into the sauce until evenly mixed.

6. Whisk the egg whites until very stiff and fold quickly and evenly through the chocolate sauce, using a metal spoon.

7. Pour into the dish and cook in a preheated oven for about 45 minutes or until well risen and just firm to the touch. Dredge the top with sifted icing sugar and serve immediately.

Hot Fruit Soufflé

Serves 4–6
225 g (8 oz) raspberries, or strawberries, sliced
1–2 peaches or nectarines, sliced or chopped
2 tablespoons brandy or liqueur
50 g (2 oz) caster sugar
4 eggs
4 tablespoons flour
300 ml (½ pint) milk
½ teaspoon vanilla essence
icing sugar, to dredge

Preparation time: 20–25 minutes
Cooking time: about 45 minutes
Oven: 180°C, 350°F, Gas Mark 4

1. Grease a 19–20 cm (7½–8 inch) soufflé dish. Put the raspberries or sliced strawberries and the sliced or chopped peaches or nectarines into the dish and pour the brandy or liqueur over.

2. Cream the sugar with 1 whole egg and 1 egg yolk until pale in colour, stir in the flour, then gradually add the milk and mix until completely smooth.

3. Transfer to a saucepan and bring very slowly to the boil, stirring constantly. Simmer for 2 minutes then remove from the heat and cool a little.

4. Separate the 2 remaining eggs and beat the yolks into the sauce followed by the vanilla essence.

5. Put the 3 egg whites into a clean grease-free bowl and whisk until very stiff. Fold the egg white quickly and evenly through the sauce using a metal spoon, and pour over the fruit in the dish.

6. Cook in a preheated oven for about 45 minutes until well risen and browned. Do not open the oven for the first 35 minutes. Remove from the oven, dredge with icing sugar and serve immediately.

■ Have the dish ready and oven on at the correct temperature before you start.
■ It is a good idea to heat a baking sheet in the oven to stand the dish on to help the soufflé to cook evenly.
■ Make sure the sauce is thick and smooth and has boiled to cook the flour, before beating in the eggs.
■ If adding cheese, this should be done off the heat to prevent it becoming at all stringy whilst melting. Beat until melted.
■ Whisk the egg whites until stiff and dry and standing in peaks.
■ To help when folding the whites into the mixture, and to keep the maximum bulk, beat in 2 tablespoons of whites first until well incorporated. You will then find the mixture accepts the rest much more easily.
■ Turn quickly into the dish and cook at once. Do not open the oven door at all if you can help it, but at least not until about 5–10 minutes before the end of the cooking time.
■ Make sure there is no draught around the oven door before opening it and close it very carefully. A bang or draught will certainly cause a sudden collapse!
■ Always work quickly when making hot soufflés. Have your guests waiting for the soufflé, rather than vice versa, for it must be served immediately with no 'waiting time' at all if it is to be served at its best.

Asparagus and Prawn Soufflés

Serves 6
350 g (12 oz) fresh asparagus, trimmed, or 225 g (8 oz) frozen asparagus
salt
50 g (2 oz) butter
4 tablespoons plain flour
350 ml (12 fl oz) milk
freshly ground black pepper
1 teaspoon dry mustard powder
6 eggs, separated
2–3 tablespoons grated Parmesan cheese
100 g (4 oz) peeled prawns
To garnish:
12 whole prawns

Preparation time: about 30 minutes, including cooking the asparagus
Cooking time: about 25–30 minutes
Oven: 180°C, 350°F, Gas Mark 4

1. Cook fresh asparagus in boiling salted water for 10–15 minutes until just tender; or frozen asparagus following the directions on the packet. Drain well and cut into small pieces, discarding the tough part of the fresh asparagus stalk.

2. Melt the butter, stir in the flour and cook for 1–2 minutes. Gradually add the milk and bring up to the boil, stirring constantly. Cook for 1 minute.

3. Stir the asparagus into the sauce, season well with salt and pepper, and add the mustard. Remove from the heat.

4. Cool the sauce a little, then beat in the egg yolks, one by one, followed by the cheese.

5. Grease 6 individual ramekin or soufflé dishes of about 150 ml (¼ pint) capacity, and divide the prawns between them. Stand on a baking sheet.

6. Whisk the egg whites until very stiff and fold carefully through the soufflé mixture. Spoon over the prawns.

7. Cook in the preheated oven for 25–30 minutes or until well risen and golden brown. Serve immediately on saucers with 2 prawns at the side of each dish.

COLD SOUFFLÉS

Cold soufflés are made in much the same way as hot soufflés but they are not baked. They are set with gelatine, and the base is usually egg yolks and sugar.

Like hot soufflés, these cold ones usually rise about 7.5 cm (3 inches) above the rim of the dish. To achieve this effect the soufflé is set with a high paper collar round the outside.

Flavourings in the form of grated fruit rind or fruit purée, melted chocolate, liqueurs etc are added, followed by lightly whipped cream and, finally, stiffly whisked egg whites. The latter should, as always, be at room temperature to achieve the maximum volume, and must be whisked in a scrupulously clean bowl, absolutely free of any grease.

Cold soufflés are usually sweet, but cold savoury soufflés can also be made. These are usually based on a well-flavoured white sauce with puréed or minced flavourings added, along with whipped double or soured cream and, of course, the whisked egg whites.

Decorating cold soufflés

The mixture for a cold soufflé usually stands about 7.5 cm (3 inches) above the rim of the dish, and this is achieved by adding a collar to the dish before filling (see right). This helps give a spectacular appearance to the finished dish. You can grease this collar for a smooth-sided soufflé, or leave it ungreased for a soft matt surface to the soufflé sides. When the soufflé is set and ready to serve, the collar is gently peeled off and the sides, although they can be left plain, are often decorated with chopped nuts, grated chocolate, toasted coconut etc. The tops of cold sweet soufflés can be dredged with icing sugar or decorated with whirls of cream and small pieces of fruit, grated peel, angelica or sugar shapes etc.

Using gelatine

It is essential to dissolve the gelatine completely. Do this, with the stated liquid, either in a small bowl over a pan of gently simmering water, or in a microwave oven set on Cool. Cool the gelatine to lukewarm before adding to the soufflé base: this should be at room temperature – not chilled or hot – otherwise the gelatine can form into strands in the setting mixture and completely spoil the texture. Stir the gelatine briskly into the base to avoid this.

Do not use raw pineapple in gelatine mixtures as they will not set. Canned or precooked pineapple, however, will set perfectly.

Cold soufflé dishes

The size of the soufflé dish determines the height of the finished soufflé and often with a new recipe, if you are experimenting, it may be necessary to move the mixture to a smaller dish if it doesn't stand up above the rim sufficiently; next time you make the recipe you will know which dish to use. As a rough guide a 3-egg soufflé will fit a 13–15 cm (5–6 inch) soufflé dish (unless it is particularly deep), and a 6-egg mixture can be put into an 18 cm (7 inch) or slightly larger dish. Small individual dishes can also be used.

To make a collar for a soufflé dish

1. Cut a strip of foil, greaseproof paper or non-stick silicone paper which is wide enough to fold in half lengthwise and still stand 7.5 cm (3 inches) above the rim of the dish, and long enough to fit around the dish with an overlap of at least 5 cm (2 inches). If a smooth edge is required on the sides of the soufflé, brush the inside of the collar with oil (not necessary if non-stick).

2. Put the strip, folded edge at the foot, around the outside of the dish and hold in place with string or sticky tape. It must fit tightly to the sides of the dish to prevent the mixture from running down between the paper strip and dish.

3. To remove the collar, first cut string or sticky tape then ease the collar away from the side of the soufflé (see Lemon Soufflé, Step 8).

Folding in egg whites

1. Using a metal spoon or spatula, cut down into the centre of the bowl.

2. Using a scooping action, bring the spoon up towards you, turning the mixture bottom to top. Continue, turning the bowl and working clockwise, until folded in.

Lemon Soufflé

Note that with acid-based soufflés it is advisable to fold in the cream first before adding the lemon and gelatine mixture, to ensure a light result.

Serves 4–6
3 eggs, separated (size 1 or 2)
225 g (8 oz) caster sugar
2 large firm juicy lemons
1 tablespoon powdered
*   gelatine*
1 tablespoon water
150 ml (¼ pint) double or
*   whipping cream*
To decorate:
50 g (2 oz) shelled walnuts,
*   finely chopped (optional)*
4–8 tablespoons double or
*   whipping cream*
angelica
mimosa balls or julienne strips
*   of lemon peel*

Preparation time: about 30 minutes plus time for setting

Variations

Lime Replace the lemons with 3–4 limes or 2 limes and 1 lemon, and continue as above.
St Clements Use the rind of 1 lemon and 1 orange with the juice of the lemon in the initial whisking and orange juice in place of lemon juice and water with the gelatine.

1. Prepare a 13 cm (5 inch) soufflé dish with a collar. Put the egg yolks and sugar into a large heatproof bowl standing over a saucepan of gently simmering water.

2. Grate the rind from both lemons and add to the bowl with the squeezed and strained juice of 1 lemon.

3. Whisk the mixture over the heat using a hand-held electric mixer or rotary whisk until very thick and pale in colour and the whisk leaves a heavy trail when lifted. Remove the bowl from the heat and continue to whisk until cool. (If the mixture is put originally into a large free-standing electric mixer, no heat is required.)

4. Put the gelatine into a small bowl with the water and juice of the remaining lemon, and place over a pan of simmering water until dissolved. Alternatively, put into a microwave oven set on Cool for ½–1 minute until dissolved. Leave to cool a little, but it must not begin to set.

5. Whip the cream until floppy, but not too stiff, and fold through the mixture.

6. Stir the gelatine quickly and evenly into the lemon mixture – which should be neither too hot nor too cold – and leave until beginning to thicken.

7. Whisk the egg whites until standing in peaks and then fold evenly through the lemon mixture. Pour quickly into the prepared dish and chill until set.

8. To serve, carefully peel off the collar from around the soufflé. Press the nuts (if used) around the side of the soufflé. Whip the cream until stiff and pipe alternate large and small whirls around the top edge of the soufflé, using a large star nozzle.

9. Complete the decoration with diamond shapes of angelica and clusters of mimosa balls stuck into the larger cream whirls, or scatter lemon peel over the centre of the soufflé. This soufflé freezes very successfully and makes a good party dish that can be prepared in advance. To freeze, prepare up to step 7 but do not remove collar or decorate. Open-freeze, then wrap in cling film and freeze for up to 2 months. Thaw overnight in the refrigerator, remove collar, decorate and serve.

Cranberry Soufflé

Fresh cranberries, imported from the United States, are available October to February. Choose deeply coloured bright red berries that are firm and smooth – avoid any that look at all mushy. In the States, cranberry sauce is the traditional accompaniment to the roast turkey at Thanksgiving. Their tart flavour also goes well with cheese, and cranberries make a very successful tart or teabread.

Serves 6–8
175 g (6 oz) cranberries, fresh or frozen
150 ml (¼ pint) water
175 g (6 oz) caster sugar
4 eggs, separated
2 tablespoons orange juice
4 teaspoons powdered gelatine
5 tablespoons water
150 ml (¼ pint) double or whipping cream
To decorate:
a little whipped cream
whole fresh cranberries

Preparation time: about 30 minutes plus time for cooling and setting

1. Cook the cranberries with 150 ml (¼ pint) water in a covered pan until very tender, about 10–15 minutes. Stir in 50 g (2 oz) sugar until dissolved, then allow to cool. Either rub through a sieve or purée in a blender or food processor.

2. Prepare a 14–15 cm (5½–6 inch) soufflé dish with a collar. Put the egg yolks, remaining sugar and orange juice into a heatproof bowl standing over a pan of gently simmering water (or into the bowl of a large electric mixer, when no heat is required). Whisk until very thick and creamy and the whisk leaves a heavy trail when lifted. Remove from the heat and whisk until cool.

3. Dissolve the gelatine in the 3 tablespoons water over a pan of simmering water, or in a microwave oven set on Cool. Allow to cool a little then stir into the cranberry purée.

4. Stir the cranberry mixture into the egg yolk mixture and leave until very thick but not setting.

5. Whip the cream until thick but not stiff and fold through the mixture.

6. Whisk the egg whites until standing in peaks, and fold quickly and evenly through the soufflé. Pour into the dish and chill until set.

7. Before serving remove the paper from around the soufflé and decorate the top with whirls of cream (using a large star nozzle) and whole fresh cranberries.

Coffee Walnut Soufflé

Serves 6
3 eggs, separated
75 g (3 oz) caster sugar
3 tablespoons coffee essence
1 tablespoon powdered gelatine
2 tablespoons Tia Maria or Kahlua
150 ml (¼ pint) single cream
300 ml (½ pint) whipping cream
75 g (3 oz) shelled walnuts, finely chopped
To decorate:
a little whipped cream
6 walnut halves

Preparation time: about 25 minutes plus time for setting

1. Prepare 6 individual soufflé or ramekin dishes – 100 ml (4 fl oz) in capacity – with collars to stand 5 cm (2 inches) above the rim of the dishes.

2. Put the egg yolks, sugar and 2 tablespoons of the coffee essence into a heatproof bowl. Stand over a pan of gently simmering water and whisk until very thick and creamy, and the whisk leaves a heavy trail when lifted. (If using a large electric mixer, no heat is required.)

3. Dissolve the gelatine in the remaining coffee essence with the liqueur over a pan of simmering water or in a microwave oven set on Cool. Allow to cool a little, then stir into the single cream.

4. Stir the cream mixture evenly into the egg yolk mixture and leave until beginning to set.

5. Whip the whipping cream until very thick, but not too stiff, and fold through the mixture followed by 25 g (1 oz) of the chopped walnuts.

6. Whisk the egg whites until very stiff and dry, and fold quickly and evenly through the mixture. Pour into the prepared dishes and chill until set.

7. Before serving remove the collars and decorate the sides with the remaining chopped walnuts. Complete the decoration with a whirl of cream topped with a walnut half in the centre of each soufflé.

MERINGUES

■

Meringue-making is where the cook becomes artist, creating delightfully frivolous, light and airy confections out of egg white and sugar. Despite what you might think, it is child's play to make.

Meringue is a light sugary confection which forms the basis of many desserts. It can also be made as individual cakes to serve plain or sandwiched together with cream or other fillings.

There are basically three types of meringue. Meringue Suisse, the most commonly used, is made by whisking egg whites until very stiff then whisking in part of the sugar

and folding in the remainder (usually allowing 50 g (2 oz) sugar to each egg white). It can be piped or spread as required for all shapes and sizes of meringue, from large discs to mini meringues.

Meringue Cuite, the professional's meringue, is rather more complicated and, as the name implies, is 'cooked'. It is made by whisking the egg whites and

sugar (usually icing sugar rather than caster) in a bowl over gently simmering water until thick and stiff. It is then removed from the heat and whisked until cold. As it is very stable – the heat partly coagulates the egg whites – it is most often used for meringue baskets and nests. It can also have 'extras' such as chopped nuts added to it before baking, which other types of meringue

will not accept so easily. With a few adaptations, Meringue Cuite forms the basis of Pavlova, a meringue with a soft marshmallowy centre.

Meringue Italienne is a very light soft meringue which can be piped, but is usually used in pâtisserie or ice cream making. It is made by pouring a boiling sugar syrup on to lightly whipped egg whites and beating until cold.

Meringue Suisse

4 egg whites (size 1 or 2)
225 g (8 oz) caster sugar

Preparation time: about 15 minutes, plus piping or shaping
Cooking time: about 2 hours
Oven: 110°C, 225°F, Gas Mark ¼

1. Put the egg whites into a clean grease-free bowl and whisk until the mixture is thick, white, dry and stands in stiff peaks.

2. Gradually whisk in a quarter of the sugar, a tablespoon at a time, until completely incorporated. Whisk until the meringue is stiff again each time, before adding further sugar.

3. Fold in the rest of the sugar all at once, using a large metal spoon. The meringue is now ready for use.

4. Put the meringue into a piping bag fitted with a large star vegetable nozzle or a 1–2 cm (½–¾ inch) plain nozzle. Line at least 2 baking sheets with non-stick silicone paper.

5. Pipe the shapes required on to the lined baking sheets (see opposite). Bake the stars, whirls, shells and bars in a cool preheated oven for about 2 hours, reversing the trays in the oven after an hour.

6. They are ready when the meringues will lift easily off the paper. Makes 18–30 depending on size. Bake the larger discs at the same temperature, but for about 2½–3 hours, again reversing the sheets in the oven after an hour.

Meringue Shapes

For stars and whirls. Use the star nozzle. Pipe a small star straight on to the paper, or for a larger whirl twist the nozzle round as you pipe to give a larger and more elaborate shape. Always slightly dip the nozzle and pull off quickly as you finish to leave a neat top.

For shells. Put the nozzle on to the paper, pipe out a little at the same time moving the

nozzle along a little then touch the paper again and quickly lift off to leave a shell shape.

For bars. Use a star or plain nozzle and pipe out straight lines of mixture about 10–13 cm (4–5 inches) long. Alternatively squiggle the piping bag to give zig-zag bars, or pipe in a continuous twisted line to give an elegant shape. These can be made to the size you prefer.

Variations

Brown sugar meringues. Use a proportion of soft light brown sugar, not more than half. Beat in the caster sugar then fold in the sieved brown sugar. This will give a delicate coffee coloured result with a delicious nutty taste. Use in various shapes as above.

Coffee meringues. This again gives a pale brown meringue but with the flavour of coffee. At the last minute fold in ½–1 teaspoon instant coffee powder (not granules), per egg white

For meringue discs. Cover 2 baking sheets with non-stick silicone paper and draw circles on each of 20–23 cm (8–9 inches). Turn the paper over so that the pen or pencil marks do not come off on the meringue. Other sizes can be made if preferred. Fill the piping bag, fitted either with the star or plain nozzle with meringue and, beginning in the centre of the circle, pipe a continuous line round and round to fill the drawn circle keeping the outside edge very neat and even. Alternatively pipe a series of circles of rosettes, each touching the next to cover the circles. Repeat with the second circle. A two egg mixture is sufficient for one circle and more can be made depending on the number of discs required.

just before piping or spreading, then continue as above.

Chocolate meringues. A pale brown meringue with a light chocolate flavour. Add ½–1 teaspoon of sifted cocoa powder per egg white to the meringue just before piping or spreading. Continue as above.

Coloured meringues. Just before piping or spreading and baking, mix a few drops of any liquid food colouring into the meringue.

For perfect Meringues

■ Always use a clean, grease-free bowl and grease-free utensils – any traces of fat or oil will prevent egg whites whisking properly. It helps to rub a little lemon juice or a lemon skin round the bowl, then rinse with cold water.

■ Make sure there is no trace of yolk in the whites when separating the eggs, for again the yolks contain fat and will inhibit the bulk.

■ Use eggs at room temperature, not straight from the fridge – cold inhibits the whisking and bulk.

■ The stiffer and drier the egg white the better. The less moisture in the whipped whites the less chance there is of the sugar 'weeping' from the meringues as they bake.

■ For best results with Meringue Suisse use a copper bowl and large balloon whisk, although a glass bowl and rotary whisk still give good results. Hand-held electric mixers make the job easier but do not incorporate as much air and consequently give less rise. Large electric mixers give even less bulk, and the bowl must have no trace of grease. If used for cake making etc, the fat is often almost impregnated into the side of the bowl unless it is glass or metal.

■ Once prepared, Meringue Suisse should be used as soon as possible or it will separate, weep and be difficult to handle. Meringue Cuite will hold up for a short while as it is already part cooked.

■ Do not overfold when adding the sugar or it will become runny when piped. For ease of removal, pipe or

spread all types of meringue on to baking sheets lined with non-stick silicone paper. Newish baking sheets with a special non-stick surface are also good. Alternatively use greased greaseproof paper or foil dusted with flour.

■ Cook meringues at the lowest possible setting, even on a pilot light (apart from Pavlovas) for they should in fact dry out rather than cook. Meringue Cuite bakes at a higher temperature than Meringue Suisse and should not be baked too slowly. Reverse the trays in the oven after an hour of cooking to give even cooking all round and keep the colouring even. The oven may be shut off when they are ready and the meringues left to dry out further as the oven cools.

■ If the day is damp or very rainy, the atmosphere in the kitchen could become muggy or damp, and this will affect the finished meringues, making them go soggy. Excess steam in the kitchen will have the same result.

■ Meringues are ready when they will peel easily off the paper or tray on which they were baked. Leave until they are cold before removing. Store in an airtight container between layers of greaseproof paper. They will store quite satisfactorily for 2–3 weeks before use.

■ Egg whites freeze very well and usually make better meringues. They also keep well in the refrigerator for 3–4 weeks, and the older the egg white the better the meringues (some of the moisture will evaporate).

Meringue Cuite

250 g (9 oz) icing sugar
4 egg whites
a few drops of vanilla essence
(optional)

Preparation time: about 20
minutes
Cooking time: see individual
recipe
Oven: 130°C, 275°F, Gas Mark 1

1. Sift the icing sugar once
or twice. Put the egg whites
into a fairly large, clean and
grease-free heat-proof bowl,
and whisk until just frothy.

2. Add the icing sugar
gradually and whisk until
blended.

3. Stand the bowl over a
saucepan of very gently
simmering water and whisk
the mixture until it is very
thick and white and stands
in peaks. Remove from the
heat and whisk until cold.
Whisk in the vanilla essence,
if using it.

Meringue Nests

Serves 8
1 recipe quantity Meringue
Cuite
Filling:
475 ml (16 fl oz) double or
whipping cream
16 marrons glacés
about 75 g (3 oz) plain
chocolate made into mini
curls with a potato peeler

Preparation time: about 20
minutes
Cooking time: about 1–1½
hours
Oven: 150°C, 300°F, Gas Mark 2

1. Make up the Meringue Cuite.
Cover a baking sheet or sheets
with non-stick silicone paper
and draw 8 circles of about 10–
13 cm (4–5 inches). The nests
can be made in two ways. The
first is to put an eighth of the
meringue on each circle and
spread into a nest shape with
raised sides. The second is to
put the meringue into a piping
bag fitted with a plain or star
vegetable nozzle and pipe a
circle to cover the base; then a
simple ring or a circle of piped
stars can be piped on top

around the edge to make the
nest.

2. Bake in a preheated oven for
1–1½ hours or until they are
crisp and dry and will easily
peel off the paper. Leave until
cold.

3. To assemble, remove the
nests from the paper and stand
on a serving dish or on
individual plates. Whip the
cream until stiff. Cut 4 marrons
glacés in half for decoration
and chop the rest. Fold the
chopped marrons through the
cream and spoon into the
nests. Sprinkle the mini
chocolate curls over the cream
and place half a marron glacé
in the centre of each. Serve
within 2 hours of assembling.

Hazelnut Meringues

Serves 12 or makes 20–24
meringues for teatime
1 recipe quantity Meringue
Cuite
100 g (4 oz) hazelnuts, toasted
and finely chopped
Topping:
300 ml (½ pint) double or
whipping cream
12 large or 350 g (12 oz) small
strawberries

Preparation time: about 20
minutes
Cooking time: about 40
minutes
Oven: 150°C, 300°F, Gas Mark 2

1. Make up the Meringue Cuite.
Line a baking sheet or sheets
with non-stick silicone paper.

2. Fold the chopped nuts into
the meringue mixture. Spoon
the mixture into 12 even
rounds on the paper. (For
teatime meringues simply
spoon into 20–24 even-shaped
rounds.)

3. Cook in a preheated oven for
about 40 minutes (the smaller
ones should only need about
30 minutes) until a pale cream
colour and they can be easily
removed from the paper. Leave
until cold.

4. To serve, peel the meringues
off the paper and stand on a
serving dish. Whip the cream
until stiff and spread or pipe
over the top of each meringue.
Top each with a whole large
strawberry or sliced or halved
smaller ones. The smaller
meringues should be topped
with half a strawberry or a few
slices of strawberry. Other
fruits or nuts may be used for
the decoration.

Pavlova

Pavlova is an Australian confection named after the ballerina Anna Pavlova, and the way in which the meringue is spread out and pulled up at the sides is said to represent a ballerina's tutu. It is usually filled with fresh (or canned) fruit and cream. The traditional fruits are strawberries and passion fruit, but nowadays any colourful fruits can be used.

Pavlovas are made from Meringue Cuite but with caster rather than icing sugar, and cornflour and vinegar are added: the cornflour to help keep the centre soft and light, and the vinegar to encourage the volume. It is also baked at a higher temperature than traditional Meringue Cuite.

Serves 6
3 egg whites
175 g (6 oz) caster sugar
1/2 teaspoon vanilla essence
1/2 teaspoon vinegar
1 teaspoon cornflour
Filling:
250 ml (8 fl oz) double or
*   whipping cream*
175 g (6 oz) strawberries
2 kiwi fruit
a few mint leaves (optional)

Preparation time: about 20 minutes
Cooking time: about 1 hour
Oven: 150°C, 300°F, Gas Mark 2

1. Put the egg whites and sugar into a large ovenproof bowl and whisk until well mixed.

2. Stand the bowl over a large saucepan of gently simmering water and whisk until the mixture becomes thick and white and stands in peaks.

3. Remove the bowl from the heat and beat in the vanilla essence, vinegar and cornflour.

4. Line a baking sheet with non-stick silicone paper and draw an 18 cm (7 inch) circle on it. Spread the meringue over this circle, pushing it up at the sides and leaving a dip in the middle.

5. Bake in a preheated oven for about an hour or until firm. Leave until cold and then carefully peel off the paper if to be used at once, otherwise store as it is in an airtight container for a few days.

6. To serve, peel the meringue carefully off the paper and stand on a serving dish. Whip the cream until stiff and use to spread or pipe over the meringue especially in the dip. Slice the strawberries if large, and peel and slice the kiwi fruit. Use these fruits to decorate the centre of the Pavlova, finishing with mint leaves, if used. Serve the dessert within an hour of assembling or it will collapse.

Filling variations

The fillings for Pavlova can vary widely. Try some of the following:

Chocolate and Chestnut. Mix a can of sweetened chestnut spread with 250 ml (8 fl oz) whipped double cream and fold in 100 g (4 oz) coarsely grated plain chocolate.

Hazelnut and Orange. Whip 300 ml (1/2 pint) double cream until stiff and then fold in 1 tablespoon caster sugar, 50–75 g (2–3 oz) toasted and chopped hazelnuts and the grated rind of 1/2 orange. Decorate the top with slices or segments of orange.

Lemon Cheese and Grape. Soften 75 g (3 oz) soft cream cheese and beat in 2 tablespoons caster sugar and the finely grated rind of 1 lemon. Halve and pip about

350 g (3/4 lb) grapes – black or green – and fold about a third into the cheese mixture together with 250 ml (8 fl oz) whipped double cream. Use the remainder of the grapes to decorate the top.

Hazelnut Pavlova

Serves 6
3 egg whites
175 g (6 oz) caster sugar
1/2 teaspoon vanilla essence
1/2 teaspoon vinegar
1 teaspoon cornflour
75 g (3 oz) finely ground
*   hazelnuts*
Filling:
300 ml (1/2 pint) double cream
2 tablespoons brandy or Kirsch
350 g (12 oz) fresh apricots,
*   halved and stoned, or a*
*   425 g (15 oz) can apricot*
*   halves, drained*
Chocolate sauce:
100 g (4 oz) plain chocolate
40 g (1 1/2 oz) butter
4–6 tablespoons top of the milk
*   or single cream*

Preparation time: about 25 minutes
Cooking time: about 1 hour
Oven: 150°C, 300°F, Gas Mark 2

1. Make up the meringue as for Pavlova, remove from the heat and fold in the finely ground hazelnuts.

2. Draw a 20 cm (8 inch) circle on a piece of non-stick silicone paper on a baking sheet and spread the meringue over it. Make a dip in the middle and push the sides up a little. Bake in a preheated oven for an hour. Leave to cool on the paper.

3. For the filling, whip the cream and brandy or Kirsch together until stiff. Prepare the apricots.

4. For the chocolate sauce, melt the chocolate either in a small basin over simmering water or in a microwave set on Cool then stir in the butter until

melted, followed by the milk or cream. Leave to cool. The sauce should be thick when cold but not set. If it appears to be too thick add a little more milk or cream.

5. To assemble, peel the Pavlova off the paper carefully. With the nuts in it, it is likely to sink a little. Stand on a serving plate and fill the centre with the whipped cream, either piped or spread. Decorate with the apricot halves and then drizzle a little of the chocolate sauce over the whole thing. Serve the rest of the sauce separately. Do not assemble more than an hour before required; it's best made just before serving.

Meringue Basket

Serves 10

*2 recipe quantities Meringue
Suisse, made up separately
(see page 214)*

Filling and topping:
300 ml (½ pint) double cream
*2 tablespoons Kirsch or other
liqueur*
*1 small Ogen or Charentais
melon, deseeded and
scooped into balls or cut into
dice*
*2 oranges, peeled and
segmented*
*100–175 g (4–6 oz)
strawberries or raspberries*

Preparation time: about 1½
hours
Cooking time: 2–3 hours
Oven: 110°C, 225°F, Gas Mark ½

1. Make up one quantity of
Meringue Suisse. Line 2 (or
4) large baking sheets with
non-stick silicone paper and
draw two 20 cm (8 inch)
circles on each sheet. Turn
the paper over so that the
pen or pencil circles do not
mark the meringue.

2. Put the meringue into a
piping bag fitted with a plain
1 cm (½ inch) nozzle and
outline 3 of the circles.
Completely cover the fourth
one beginning in the centre
and working out to the edge.

3. Bake in a preheated oven
for about an hour or until
the meringue will lift off
the paper. The disc will
probably need a little
longer.

4. Make up the second batch
of Meringue Suisse and put
into a piping bag fitted with
a large star vegetable nozzle.
Leave the meringue disc on
the non-stick paper still on
the baking sheet.

5. Peel off the other 3 rings
(handling with extreme care)
and place on top of each
other on the meringue disc,
using some of the second
batch of meringue as 'glue'
to hold them in position.

6. Using the remainder of
the Meringue Suisse in the
piping bag, carefully pipe
vertical lines all round the
outside of the basket.

7. Cook in the same oven for
about an hour until the
meringue is cooked. Leave
until cold, then peel off the
paper.

8. To assemble, stand the
basket on a serving dish.
Whip the cream with the
Kirsch or liqueur until thick
and stiff. Spread about two-
thirds of it over the base and
up the sides inside the
basket. Combine the fruits
and spoon into the basket so
it is almost overflowing.

9. Complete the decoration
by piping the remaining
cream using a star nozzle,
around the top and possibly
the base of the basket.

Variation

The first amount of meringue
can have 40 g (1½ oz) finely
ground toasted hazelnuts or
almonds beaten into it before
piping; or each amount may be
flavoured with 2 teaspoons
instant coffee powder; or the
meringue may be flavoured
with 2 level teaspoons ground
cinnamon or ginger, or mixed
spice.

Instead of the double cream
for the filling, you could use
crème fraîche. Its slightly acidic
taste contrasts well with the
sweetness of the meringue.

Heat 600 ml (1 pint) whipping
cream and 1½ tablespoons
buttermilk gently in a large pan
until it registers 24–29°C/75–
85°F. Cover and leave in a
warm place overnight. It can be
whipped, provided the cream,
the bowl and whisk are all very
cold.

Meringue basket

Lemon Meringue Pie

Serves 4

½ recipe quantity Rich
   Shortcrust Pastry (see
   page 261)
25 g (1 oz) cornflour
300 ml (½ pint) milk
caster sugar
2 egg yolks
grated rind and juice of 1
   lemon
½ recipe quantity Meringue
   Suisse (see page 214)

Preparation time: about 20
minutes
Cooking time: about 25 minutes
Oven: 190°C, 375°F, Gas Mark
5: then : 170°C, 325°F, Gas
Mark 3

1. Roll out the pastry and use to
line a 15 cm (6 inch) flan tin.
Chill for 30 minutes.

2. Bake the flan case blind (see
page 259) until about half
done, and then remove
the baking beans and

the foil. Return to the oven
briefly.

3. Meanwhile, mix the
cornflour with 1 tablespoon
milk and heat the remaining
milk. Pour this on to the
cornflour paste and return all
to the pan. Boil for 3–4
minutes, stirring continuously.

4. Add 25 g (1 oz) sugar, then
allow to cool a little, before
beating in the egg yolks, lemon
rind and juice.

5. Pour immediately into the
warm pastry case and return to
the oven to set for 2 minutes.
Reduce the oven temperature.

6. Make up the meringue and
pile it on to the pie, making
sure that it covers the filling
completely. Sprinkle with a
little extra sugar.

8. Return to the reduced oven
for 10 minutes or until the
meringue is a pale biscuit
colour.

CHEESE

The variety of cheeses is almost endless — and there are just as many ways of using cheese in cooking. Follow our handy chart to identify the different cheeses, learn about their texture and flavour, and discover new ways of cooking and serving them.

Choosing and buying cheese

There is a vast choice of cheese available throughout Britain, either home produced or imported from the continent. A few years ago, it was difficult to buy freshly cut cheeses, but with the ever growing demand for fresh cheese, rather than the prepacked type, more and more supermarkets and delicatessens are prepared to cut portions from the whole cheese.

Choose a supplier who has a quick turnover, so that the cheese is in prime condition. Avoid anything that looks dry, sweaty or has blue mould on the surface.

When choosing soft cheeses such as Brie and Camembert, press the top surface lightly with the fingertips. The cheese should yield slightly. It should be creamy in texture throughout, without any chalkiness in the centre. This chalkiness means that the cheese has not been ripened sufficiently and will remain in this condition. Goat's milk cheeses should be consumed on the day they are purchased, as the flavour soon becomes 'soapy'. Both English and French goat cheeses (the French ones called 'chèvre') have become more widely available, some of them flavoured with fresh herbs.

Storing

Ideally, cheese should be stored in a cool, draught-proof larder – the refrigerator is the next best thing. Cheese should be removed from the refrigerator and unwrapped at least 1 hour before it is required so that it has time to come to room temperature, which is best for appreciating the full flavour and the texture of the cheese.

Freezing

Most cheeses freeze well. They should be well wrapped and labelled prior to freezing. Hard cheeses tend to become more crumbly but the flavour is good. Soft and cream cheeses should not be frozen for more than 6 months. It is not recommended to freeze cottage cheese as it deteriorates. Allow plenty of time for the cheese to thaw in the refrigerator, and remove an hour before it is required. Cheese that has been frozen does not keep as well as unfrozen cheese, so it should be consumed quickly. Never re-freeze cheese.

Cooking

Although many cheeses cook well, care should be taken that the heat applied is not too fierce, as the protein breaks down, causing the cheese to become stringy and rather rubbery. It should be melted rather than cooked. Hard cheeses should be finely grated before cooking so that they melt into the sauce. It is best to have the other ingredients hot before adding the cheese.

Emmenthal

Edam

Sage Derby

Feta

Dolcelatte

Tomme au Raisin

CHARACTERISTICS	USES

BRITAIN

Blue Dorset

| A fairly strong-flavoured cheese with blue veining. Made from skimmed milk, which gives it a sharp flavour. It is a hard, white cheese, with a crumbly texture. | Use uncooked. |

Caboc

| A white full-cream soft Scottish cheese. Rolled in toasted oatmeal. It may be difficult to obtain outside Scotland. | Use uncooked. |

Caerphilly

| A semi-hard cheese which has a slightly salty mild flavour. It is crumbly and has a close texture. It is one of the fastest ripening British cheeses. | Perfect for a cheese board, but may be used for cooking. |

Cheddar

| Probably the most popular of British cheeses. Its flavour ranges from very mild to a fully matured strong nutty flavour. Canadian Cheddar has the strongest flavour. | Ideal for grating and cooking, and for eating in salads or with fruit. |

Cheshire

| A red or white hard cheese with a crumbly texture and a slightly salty taste. Sometimes Blue Cheshire is available. It is a whitish cheese with blue veining, and has a similar flavour to Stilton. | Use uncooked or in cooking. Ideal for grilling and for sauces. Blue Cheshire is best uncooked. |

Cottage cheese

| A mild-flavoured cheese, very low in calories, as it is made from skimmed milk curds and is therefore low in fat. It is pure white, very moist and lumpy and is sold in cartons. It is often flavoured with herbs or fruit. | Usually used uncooked but it may be used for flans, cheesecakes and some sweet or savoury dishes. |

Cream cheese

| Usually a full fat cheese. It has a rich creamy flavour which is rather bland. Generally sold in small foil containers or from a bulk container. | Use cooked or uncooked. Ideal for savoury and sweet dishes including cakes and icings. |

Crowdie

| A high protein cottage cheese made from skimmed milk. Made in Scotland. A finer textured cheese than ordinary cottage cheese. | Use as above for cottage cheese. |

Curd

| A soft unripened, slightly grainy cheese, with a clean acid bland taste. | Used generally for cooking, in sweet and savoury dishes. Often in cheesecakes. |

Derby

| A mild-flavoured close-textured hard cheese. The flavour becomes stronger with age. | Best used uncooked. |

Sage Derby

| This cheese has the same characteristics as Derby, but has layers of chopped fresh sage incorporated during the making. It gives the cheese a green marbled effect. | Not recommended for cooking. |

Double Gloucester

| A hard cheese with a close crumbly texture. It is pale orange and has a mild flavour similar to Cheddar. | Use uncooked or crumble for savoury flans, pies and sauces. |

Dunlop

| A moist soft-textured hard Scottish cheese, pale yellow in colour. Similar to Cheddar, but milder in flavour. | Ideal for grilling. Uses are the same as for Cheddar. |

Hramsa

| A soft Scottish cheese made from double cream flavoured with wild garlic gathered from the Highlands. | Serve as a dessert cheese, or uncooked in dips, etc. |

Islay

| A miniature Dunlop made in Scotland. Best eaten when it is well matured. | Use cooked or uncooked. It melts easily and is perfect for sauces. |

Lancashire

| A white open-textured cheese with a crumbly texture. Mild flavoured when new, but becoming fairly strong when fully matured. | Use cooked or uncooked. A good grilling cheese and for any cooked dish. |

CHARACTERISTICS	USES

Leicester

A flaky textured cheese. Bright orange in colour. The flavour is fairly strong but sweet.	Good for cooking.

Lymeswold

A creamy soft cheese similar to Brie in texture and consistency. It has a mild flavour and is one of the newer popular cheeses available.	Use uncooked.

Morven

A smooth textured mild-flavoured Scottish cheese. Similar to Dutch Gouda. Sometimes flavoured with caraway seeds.	Use uncooked.

Orkney

Made in 500 g (1 lb) whole cheeses. A mellow-flavoured close-textured firm cheese made in white or red. Also made with a smoked flavour.	Best used uncooked.

Red Windsor

A fairly rare English cheese with a mild flavour similar to Cheddar. It has red veining throughout, which is caused by the injection of red wine. It has a crumbly texture.	Not recommended for cooking.

Stilton

The Queen of English cheeses. It should be very creamy and not dry in texture. The blue veining should be evenly distributed throughout the pale cream cheese. If the cheese is white in colour, it is a sign of immaturity.	Best served uncooked, but it may be used in some flans. Serve accompanied by port.

Wensleydale

A crumbly cheese, varying in colour from white to butter colour depending on its maturity. It has a mild clean and slightly sweet flavour.	A perfect accompaniment to apple pie or rich fruit cake.

Blue Wensleydale

A rich-flavoured creamy cheese with blue veining.	Best used uncooked.

CHARACTERISTICS	USES

FRANCE

Brie

A soft whitish cheese, made from cow's milk, with a white crust. It should be soft throughout, without any 'chalky' solid centre.	Generally, Brie is eaten uncooked but it may be cooked (with the crust removed) as for Brie Tart.

Blue Brie

This is generally a thicker cheese than plain Brie, with blue veining throughout.	As above.

Boursin

A triple cream cheese which is thick and soft, flavoured with garlic, herbs or pepper.	Perfect for a cheese board, or may be used in cooking, particularly the garlic and herb ones.

Camembert

A stronger flavoured cheese than Brie. As with Brie, it should bulge but not run when the top surface is pressed. It is usually about 2.5 cm (1 inch) thicker than Brie.	Perfect with bread, biscuits or salad. It may be cooked, e.g. Fried Camembert with gooseberry or cranberry sauce.

Livarot

A soft, yellow cheese with a reddish-brown rind. Made from skimmed milk, it has a stronger flavour than Camembert.	Perfect for a cheese board – not recommended for cooking.

Munster

A strong-smelling cheese with a sharp flavour. It is semi-soft and has a reddish coloured rind. Sometimes, it is flavoured with aniseed or cumin.	Best eaten uncooked.

Petit-Suisse

Made from whole milk with added cream. It has a creamy flavour and texture and is sold in little rolls of paper.	May be used for cooking, but is perfect when served with cooked fruit or sugar. It is particularly good with figs or grapes.

Pont l'Evêque

A semi-soft pale yellow cheese with a yellow crust. It has a rich creamy flavour, stronger than Camembert.	Best used uncooked.

CHARACTERISTICS	USES

Port Salut

A cheese with an orange rind. It is semi-hard and has a creamy bland flavour which gets stronger when it is fully ripe.	Suitable for a cheese board and for cooking.

Roquefort

Made from ewe's milk curds. It has bluish green veins. A crumbly, semi-soft cheese with a strong flavour.	May be used cooked or uncooked. Perfect for dressing (e.g. blue cheese dressing) or crumbled over salads.

Saint Paulin

Similar to Port Salut, with a fairly bland flavour.	Use cooked or uncooked.

Tomme au Raisin

A semi-hard cheese, covered with grape pips and skins. The cheese has a slightly chewy texture.	Use uncooked.

ITALY

Bel Paese

One of the best-known Italian cheeses. A delicately-flavoured cheese, with a slightly salty taste. Close-textured, it is pale yellow in colour, with a dark yellow rind.	Use cooked or uncooked. It melts very easily.

Dolcelatte

A creamy white cheese with blue/green veins, a robust strong flavour and a creamy moist texture.	Usually used uncooked, but may be used for cheese sauces, especially with pasta.

Fontina

One of the few really great cheeses. A soft fat cheese, straw coloured, with a few holes. It has an orange rind. The flavour is nutty and delicate. Variations are called Fontinella and Fontal.	Use uncooked or for cooking. It melts easily and is perfect for grating and sauces.

Gorgonzola

A strongly flavoured pale yellow cheese with bluish green marbling and a coarse brown rind. Although it is a semi-soft cheese, it should be firm and fairly dry.	Best used uncooked.

CHARACTERISTICS	USES

Mozzarella

A soft compact curd cheese, moulded into a ball, egg or flask-shape and tied with raffia. It is also sold in oblong blocks, sealed with plastic. This type is not to be recommended as the texture and flavour are rubbery. It forms long strands during cooking, and becomes rather hard if overcooked.	Served in salads or as a topping for pizzas.

Parmesan

A very hard cheese, yellowish in colour and fairly grainy. It is strong-flavoured and should be grated just before it is required. When fresh, it has a fairly soft texture, similar to Cheddar.	If very fresh, it is a good dessert cheese. The mature cheese (3–4 years old) is usually used for cooking and serving with pasta and soups. It is low in fat and therefore ideal for topping dishes where other cheeses would be too heavy.

Pecorino

A whole family of ewe's milk cheeses come under this name, the best known being Pecorino Romano. They have a pronounced piquant flavour.	Pecorino goes particularly well with fresh country bread, and is used grated in many regional dishes.

Provolone

A creamy/white cheese with a brownish rind. This is a hard curd cheese made into shapes, ranging from cone, pear, round and sausage. When mildly matured, the flavour is delicate and sweet. After further maturing, the flavour becomes sharp and spicy.	Usually used for cooking.

Ricotta

Made from ewe's milk, this cheese has a soft bland flavour and texture. It has a low fat content. The rind is distinctively ridged and white.	Used a great deal in Italian cooking. It can be mixed with spinach and made into gnocchi or used as a filling for ravioli and cannelloni. It also makes a delicious base for cheesecake.

SWITZERLAND

Emmenthal

A buttery-yellow cheese with large holes. It is slightly rubbery in texture and has a mild to strong nutty flavour.	Ideal uncooked or cooked. It melts well.

CHARACTERISTICS	USES

Gruyère

A pale yellow cheese with small holes, similar in texture to Emmenthal. It has a rich, full flavour with a little sweetness.	An excellent cooking cheese as it melts well. Equally good used uncooked.

Raclette

A pale brown rind encloses a semi-soft cheese which is straw coloured with tiny holes.	Use cooked or uncooked.

Sapsago

A clover-leaf-flavoured cheese which makes the cheese green. This is a very hard cheese.	Suitable for cooking.

HOLLAND

Edam

Made from partly skimmed milk, this yellow cheese has a bright red rind and a rubbery texture. It has a mild creamy flavour. Fairly low in calories.	Suitable for cooking or for eating uncooked.

Gouda

A hard cheese with a buttery yellow colour. The rind is fairly thin and a brighter yellow than the cheese itself. It has a slightly rubbery texture, with a fairly mild flavour.	Use uncooked or cooked.

Tilsit

Originally made by the Dutch, this cheese is now made by the Germans and is also produced in Switzerland and Scandinavia. A loaf-shaped cheese, open-textured and straw coloured, it has a sharp, sour flavour.	Used mainly for slicing.

VARIOUS

Bergkäse (German)

A high-fat-content cheese with a mild nutty flavour. It is a pale yellow, with a dark brown rind.	Use uncooked.

Danbo (Danish)

A firm textured mild cheese with regular, even-sized holes. Sometimes the cheese is flavoured with caraway seeds.	Use uncooked.

CHARACTERISTICS	USES

Edelpilz (German)

A crumbly textured cheese with blue mottles at the centre and white around the edges. It has a strong flavour.	Use uncooked.

Feta (Greek)

A semi-soft curd cheese made from sheep's milk. Brilliant white in colour, with a flaky texture. It has a salty bland flavour.	Use uncooked in salads or in cooked dishes.

Gjetost (Norwegian)

A goat's milk cheese with a strong, pungent flavour, with a slight sweetness. A hard, brown cheese.	Best used uncooked.

Jarlsberg (Norwegian)

A mild flavoured cheese, slightly sweet. A semi-hard cheese with irregular holes, pale yellow in colour.	Best used uncooked.

Limburger (Belgian)

A strong-smelling cheese with a spicy flavour. Made from whole cow's milk. Semi-hard, with a smooth texture. Bright orange/brown rind.	Use uncooked.

Molbo (Danish)

A cheese with a red rind, similar to Edam. Pale yellow cheese with irregular large holes. A mild flavour with an acidic after-taste.	Use cooked or uncooked.

Quarques (Austrian)

A piquant-flavoured yellow to white cheese made in small round discs (similar to patties).	Use uncooked.

Samsoe (Danish)

A yellow cheese with a sweet, nutty flavour. It has a firm texture, with irregular holes. The rind is a deeper yellow.	Use uncooked.

Schlosskäse (Austrian)

The rind is very creased. The cheese is pale yellow and has a mild flavour.	Use uncooked.

Swiss Cheese Fondue

Ideally, cheese fondue should be cooked in an earthenware fireproof dish, specially made for the purpose, with a burner to keep it hot at the table.

Serves 4–6
1 garlic clove, peeled and halved
300 ml (½ pint) good quality dry white wine
1 tablespoon lemon juice
225 g (8 oz) Emmenthal cheese, finely grated
225 g (8 oz) Gruyère cheese, finely grated
1 tablespoon cornflour
4 tablespoons Kirsch
salt
freshly ground white pepper
freshly grated nutmeg
To serve:
French bread or crusty white bread, cut into cubes

Preparation time: 10 minutes
Cooking time: 15–20 minutes

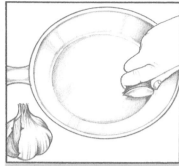
Rubbing the dish with a cut garlic clove

Adding the grated cheeses to the wine mixture

Dipping a cube of bread into the Fondue

1. Rub the cut side of the garlic around the inside of the fireproof dish. Discard the garlic.

2. Pour the wine and lemon juice into the dish and place over a gentle heat. Add the grated cheeses and stir until melted.

3. Blend the cornflour and Kirsch together to give a smooth paste. Stir into the dish. Slowly bring to the boil, stirring constantly. Cook for 2 minutes, then add the salt, pepper and nutmeg.

4. Place the dish over its burner at the table and serve immediately with cubes of bread.

5. Each person has a long handled fork to spear the bread, which is then dipped into the cheese mixture.

Quiche au Roquefort

With this recipe, the pastry is moulded into the flan tin, rather than rolled out. It gives a very light texture.

Serves 4–6
Pastry:
175 g (6 oz) plain flour
½ teaspoon salt
75 g (3 oz) butter, diced
1 egg yolk
1–2 tablespoons iced water
1 beaten egg
Filling:
25 g (1 oz) butter, softened
75 g (3 oz) Roquefort cheese
150 g (5 oz) cream cheese
75 g (3 oz) ripe Camembert cheese, crusts removed
3 tablespoons double cream
2 eggs, beaten
2 tablespoons chopped chives
salt
freshly ground black pepper

Preparation time: 20 minutes
Cooking time: 40–45 minutes
Oven: 200°C, 400°F, Gas Mark 6

1. Sift the flour and salt into a bowl. Rub in the butter until the mixture resembles fine breadcrumbs.

2. Mix in the egg yolk and 1 tablespoon of water to give a firm, soft but dry dough. If necessary, add a little more water. Form into a ball. Do not knead or chill.

3. Lightly press the pastry into the base and sides of a 20 cm (8 inch) flan tin. Prick the base with a fork. Bake 'blind' for 15 minutes (see page 259).

4. Brush the base and sides of the pastry with a little beaten egg. Return to the oven for a further 2–3 minutes.

5. Meanwhile, make the filling. Beat the butter until creamy, then beat in the crumbled cheeses until well blended.

6. Stir in the cream, eggs, chives and salt and pepper.

Pour the filling into the pastry case.

7. Return to the oven and cook for 20–25 minutes until well risen and golden brown. Serve immediately.

Potted Cheese

This is a good recipe for using up any leftover cheese.

50 g (2 oz) softened butter
100 g (4 oz) mature Cheddar cheese or Stilton, finely grated
2 tablespoons dry sherry
freshly milled black pepper
pinch of ground mace

Preparation time: 10 minutes

1. Cream the butter until very soft. Beat in the chosen cheese until well blended.

2. Stir in the sherry, pepper and mace.

3. Spoon into a small pot, cover and refrigerate until required.

4. Serve with biscuits or bread.

Three highlights of egg cookery are featured here – Pipérade, a delicious version of scrambled eggs, omelette with the classic fines herbes mixture, and delicate Oeufs en cocotte. Eggs also team with cheese to make the perfect cheese soufflé.

Crêpes aux Fruits de Mer

Seafood Pancakes

See page 205 for detailed instructions on making pancakes and how to keep them warm.

Serves 4–8
300 ml (1/2 pint) Crêpe batter (see page 205)
225 g (8 oz) haddock or cod, skinned and boned
150 ml (1/4 pint) white wine
4 scallops
50 g (2 oz) butter, plus extra for greasing
1 medium onion, peeled and finely chopped
100 g (4 oz) button mushrooms, thinly sliced
1 teaspoon lemon juice
salt
white pepper
25 g (1 oz) plain flour
about 150 ml (1/4 pint) milk
4 tablespoons double or whipping cream
100 g (4 oz) peeled prawns
4 tablespoons grated Gruyère cheese
To garnish:
8 whole prawns
finely chopped fresh parsley (optional)

Preparation time: 20 minutes
Cooking time: 40–45 minutes, including making pancakes
Oven: 200°C, 400°F, Gas Mark 6

1. Make 4 large pancakes or 8 smaller ones and keep warm.

2. Place the haddock in a pan with the white wine and poach over a gentle heat for 10–12 minutes.

3. Cut the scallops into 4 and add to the pan. Cook for a further 2–3 minutes. Drain, reserving the liquor. Flake the haddock and reserve.

4. Meanwhile, melt 25 g (1 oz) of the butter in a pan. Add the onion and cook gently until soft but not coloured.

5. Melt the remaining butter in another pan and add the mushrooms, lemon juice, salt and pepper. Cover and cook for a few minutes until soft.

6. When the onion is soft, add the flour. Cook for 1–2 minutes, stirring, then add the fish cooking liquor and milk. Bring to the boil and cook for 2–3 minutes, stirring.

7. Add the cream, haddock, scallops, mushrooms and prawns. Reheat, and thin the sauce if necessary with a little more milk. Taste and adjust the seasoning.

8. Place some of the mixture on each pancake. Roll up and place in a buttered ovenproof dish. Sprinkle the cheese over the top.

9. Place in a preheated oven and cook for 7–10 minutes or under a preheated hot grill to allow the cheese to melt.

10. Serve hot, garnished with the whole prawns and chopped parsley, if liked.

Classic Cheese Soufflé

See pages 206–213 for detailed instructions on making soufflés.

Serves 4
50 g (2 oz) butter, plus 1 tablespoon
75 g (3 oz) Parmesan or Gruyère cheese, grated, plus 1 tablespoon for sprinkling
40 g (1 1/2 oz) flour
300 ml (1/2 pint) milk
salt
pepper
pinch of cayenne pepper
pinch of grated nutmeg
4 egg yolks
5 egg whites

Preparation time: 30 minutes
Cooking time: 30–35 minutes
Oven: 190°C, 375°F, Gas Mark 5

1. Butter a 1.5 litre (2 1/2 pint) soufflé dish and sprinkle the inside with 1 tablespoon grated cheese.

2. Melt the 50 g (2 oz) butter in a pan, stir in the flour and cook over moderate heat for 2 minutes without browning.

3. Remove the roux from the heat and pour in the milk, beating vigorously with a wire whisk until well blended. Add seasoning, return to the heat and simmer for 5 minutes, stirring well until smooth.

4. Remove the pan from the heat and allow to cool slightly. Beat in the egg yolks one by one. Add the cheese and beat well. The sauce will now be very thick.

5. Put the egg whites in a large dry bowl, add a pinch of salt and whisk until stiff. Stir a large spoonful of the whites into the sauce, then fold in the remainder gently.

6. Pour the mixture into the prepared dish, and level the top with a metal spatula.

7. Place the dish in the preheated oven and bake for 25–30 minutes, or until the soufflé is well puffed up and golden brown. Serve immediately.

Top: Classic cheese soufflé
Bottom: Crêpes aux fruits de mer

Pipérade Basquaise

Fried bread croûtons are also a traditional garnish to this dish and may be used to replace the ham.

Serves 3–4
25 g (1 oz) butter
2 tablespoons olive oil
1 large Spanish onion, peeled and chopped
2 large garlic cloves, peeled and finely chopped
2 small red peppers, cored, seeded and sliced
2 small green peppers, cored, seeded and sliced
450 g (1 lb) tomatoes, skinned and chopped
good pinch of dried marjoram
salt
freshly ground black pepper
6 eggs, lightly beaten
6 wafer-thin slices raw Bayonne ham

Preparation time: 30 minutes
Cooking time: about 20 minutes

1. Heat the butter and oil in a large heavy frying pan. Add the onion and garlic and fry gently until softened but not coloured. Add the peppers, tomatoes and marjoram and salt and pepper. Cover and cook gently for 10–15 minutes, until thick and pulpy. Drain off any excess liquid.

2. Pour in the beaten eggs, return the pan to low heat and stir with a wooden spoon until the eggs are just set and creamy. Pile the mixture on to a heated serving dish, garnish with the ham and serve immediately.

Omelette aux Fines Herbes

See page 204 for detailed instructions on making omelettes.

Serves 1
2 eggs
1 tablespoon chopped fresh herbs (parsley, tarragon, chervil and chives)
1 teaspoon water
salt
freshly ground white pepper
small knob of butter

Preparation time: 5 minutes
Cooking time: 5 minutes

1. Beat the eggs with a fork. Mix in the herbs, water and salt and pepper to taste. Heat the butter in an 18 cm (7 inch) pan until it sizzles but do not allow it to brown. Pour in the beaten egg mixture.

2. Leave for 10–15 seconds until beginning to set round the edges. Then with a fork or a palette knife, draw the mixture from the sides to the middle of pan and tilt the pan so that the uncooked egg runs underneath and sets.

3. When the underneath is set but the top still slightly runny, fold the omelette in half. Slide the omelette on to a warm plate. Serve immediately.

Cheese Sablés

Sablé literally means 'sanded' and is a reference to the appearance of these crispy cheese bites. Serve them with drinks before dinner.

75 g (3 oz) plain flour
salt
freshly ground black pepper
pinch of cayenne
75 g (3 oz) butter
50 g (2 oz) mature Cheddar cheese, finely grated
25 g (1 oz) Parmesan cheese, finely grated
1 egg, lightly beaten

Preparation time: 10 minutes
Cooking time: 10–12 minutes
Oven: 190°C, 375°F, Gas Mark 5

1. Sift the flour with a pinch of salt, pepper and cayenne into a mixing bowl. Cut the butter into the flour with a palette knife, then rub in with the fingertips, until the mixture resembles fine breadcrumbs. Stir in the cheeses and press together to make a dough.

2. Shape into a 2.5 cm (1 inch) roll, wrap in clingfilm and chill for 30 minutes.

3. Cut the dough into slices 5 mm (¼ inch) thick and place on greased baking sheets. Brush with the beaten egg. Bake for 10–12 minutes, until light golden-brown. Remove from the oven and allow to cool on the sheets for a few minutes, then transfer to a wire tray to cool completely.

Oeufs en Cocotte

As a variation, add a teaspoon of chopped, fresh parsley, chives and tarragon to the cream.

Serves 4
40 g (1½ oz) butter
8 tablespoons double cream
4 eggs
salt
freshly ground black pepper

Preparation time: 5 minutes
Cooking time: 12–15 minutes
Oven: 180°C, 350°F, Gas Mark 4

1. Butter generously 4 ovenproof ramekins and add 1 tablespoon cream to each one.

2. Break 1 egg into each ramekin, season with salt and pepper and place another tablespoon of cream on top with a dot of butter.

3. Place in a shallow roasting pan and pour in hot water to come two-thirds of the way up the sides of the ramekins. Bake for 12–15 minutes, until the eggs are just set (the eggs will go on cooking when the ramekins are removed, so do not overcook). Serve immediately.

From the top: Cheese sablés, Omelette aux fines herbes, Pipérade Basquaise, Oeufs en cocotte

FRUIT

The alphabetical guide lists every kind of fresh fruit, from the most familiar orchard and soft fruits to the exotic varieties now widely stocked by greengrocers and supermarkets. Each type is described in full, with details on availability, hints on buying and testing for ripeness.

APPLES

Dessert apples are available throughout the year, cookers most of the year. The best known include Cox's Orange Pippin, Granny Smith, Worcester Pearmain, Laxton Superb and Bramley Seedling. Apples are used in pies, sauces, mousses, crumbles and jams and preserves.

APRICOTS

Small yellowish orange stoned fruits with a slightly furry skin, and a juicy flesh. Eat raw or poach for pies, crumbles, fools and jams. Available May to September or October.

BANANAS

Bananas are creamy in colour and mealy in texture. As the fruit ripens it becomes sweeter and softer. Usually eaten uncooked, but if it is to be baked or fried, it is best to choose slightly under-ripe fruit. Available all year.

BLACKBERRIES

These blackish purple soft berried fruits are usually cooked, unless they are very sweet. Cook by poaching or boiling. Used for pies, flans, tarts, ice cream, preserves, jellies and wine. Available July to October.

BLACKCURRANTS

These blackish purple berries with a slight bloom to the skin are usually sold stripped from their stems. Cooked with sugar to make pies, fools, mousse, ice cream, and jellies.

CHERRIES

The sweet dessert cherry is available from mid June to the end of July. The morello cherry, available from July to August, is slightly sour and ideal for preserves and jams. Use for flans, pies, gâteaux, ice cream, fruit salads.

CRAB APPLES

Small bright red fruits touched with yellow. They have an acid flavour and are not eaten raw. Generally used for making preserves, jellies and pickles.

COCONUTS

A large nut with a woody fibrous shell, enclosing succulent pure white flesh and coconut juice. Puncture the 3 indentations at the top of the nut to pour out the colourless juice. Crack open the nut by hitting it with a hammer one third of the way from the top. Use the flesh raw, or dried and shredded. Available all year.

DATES

Sold fresh or dried. Fresh dates, available in winter, should have a shiny brown skin and soft, sweet flesh. Dried dates have a wrinkled skin. Eat raw or use in cooked dishes and cakes.

FIGS

A Mediterranean fruit, figs are deep purple, white or red skinned, with pinkish flesh. Available from August to December and eaten raw with cheese, ham or in fruit salads. Dried figs are used in cooking.

GOOSEBERRIES

There are dessert and cooking types. The green hairy berries are generally used for pies, flans, fools, mousses, ice creams and preserves. The dessert gooseberry has a red skin with sweet juicy flesh. Available May to September.

GRAPEFRUIT

There are two types, yellow-skinned with yellow flesh, and yellow skinned with pink flesh. It is the largest of the citrus fruit family; available throughout the year.

GRAPES

There are many varieties ranging from black, red, white, amber and green. The skin should have a whitish bloom. Usually eaten uncooked. Grapes are generally peeled if used in flans and desserts. Available throughout the year.

KIWI FRUIT (CHINESE GOOSEBERRIES)

This fruit resembles a large gooseberry, but with a brown hairy skin. The flesh is green with dark seeds around a light core. Peel before use with a sharp knife. Generally used sliced for desserts and ice creams or in fruit salads. Available July to February.

LEMONS

Choose smooth skinned lemons which are likely to contain more juice than the knobbly ones. The skin is bright yellow and can be used for flavouring, grated finely. Lemons are invaluable for both sweet and savoury dishes. Available all the year.

LIMES

A citrus fruit, similar in shape to a lemon, but much smaller. The flesh is green and the skin, which is quite thin with little pith, is greenish yellow and used in the same way as a lemon. Available all year.

LOGANBERRIES

Elongated deep red berry with a white core. Very juicy and fairly tart. Usually stewed or poached with sugar and used for pies, tarts, mousses, fools and preserves. Available summer and autumn.

MANGOES

A large stoned fruit with a thick yellow-green or orange-red skin. The flesh is deep orange with a distinctive flavour. Peel the skin and slice the fruit away from the stone. Generally eaten raw; also used in preserves and pickles. Available January to September.

MELONS

Several varieties – Honeydew has thick rough skin and yellowish pink flesh. Ogen melon has thick green striped skin, and sweet juicy flesh. Charentais melon is round and small, with yellow-green skin and a dark orange fragrant flesh. Cantaloup melon is slightly flattened in shape with rough green to yellow skin. Available all year.

NECTARINES

A variety of peach, with a smooth deep red skin, tinged with yellow and juicy, fragrant flesh. Served raw. Homegrown are available from July to September.

ORANGES

Two types are available, bitter or sweet. The bitter (Seville) orange is thin-skinned, and is best used for marmalade. Available January and February. The dessert oranges are available all year.

PEACHES

Yellow peaches have a pink furry skin flecked with yellow, and a pinkish orange juicy flesh. White peaches have a pinky skin and white flesh. Homegrown are available July to September.

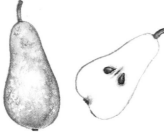

PEARS

Varieties of dessert pears are Conference, Comice and William. Both William and Conference may be cooked by poaching. Pitmaston Duchess is the main cooking pear, with a thick yellow or green skin, spotted with reddish brown, and a creamy yellow flesh. Available throughout the year.

PERSIMMONS

Similar to a tomato in shape with a large leafy stem. The skin is reddish-orange and thick. The flesh is orange to yellow and is soft and juicy, with a sharp flavour. Available October to January.

PINEAPPLES

Large oval fruit, with a yellowish orange pinc skin, with dark green prickly leaves. The flesh is yellow and juicy with a thick core running through the centre. When ripe, it is sweet and fragrant, and a leaf should come away easily. Available all year.

POMEGRANATES

The size of an apple, with a brown tough leathery skin. The flesh is bright reddish-pink, packed with seeds, very juicy. Slice in half, and spoon out the flesh. Use as a dessert or add to sauce.

QUINCES

A relative of the pear. With large pear-shaped yellow fruits. A sharp flavoured fruit only suitable for jellies and preserves, or cooked with stewed apples to give a piquant flavour. Available early autumn.

RASPBERRIES

Oval fruit with pinkish-red berries. The core (or hull) should be removed before eating. Do not wash the fruit. Best served fresh with cream or in a fruit salad, flan, ice cream, or in sauces. Available summer and autumn.

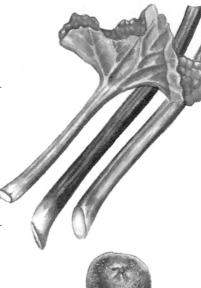

REDCURRANTS

Bright red, slightly translucent berries. Usually cooked by stewing or poaching, and sweetened to taste with sugar. Used in pies, sauces, compote, fruit salads, preserves and jellies. Available July to August.

RHUBARB

Really a vegetable. There are two types. Forced or early, is available from mid December to mid April, and has pink thin stalks with yellow leaves. Maincrop rhubarb is thicker-stemmed, reddish-green with dark green leaves, and is available from mid March to end of June. Use only the stem. Steam, poach or stew with sugar. Used for pies, tarts, crumbles, fools, wine and preserves.

SATSUMAS

Similar to a tangerine, it is a member of the citrus family. Orange green thin skin, and orange flesh. There are no pips. Use as a dessert fruit or in preserves. Available October to February.

STRAWBERRIES

This bright oval red berry is sweet and juicy, with a distinctive aroma. Usually served with cream, but also used for flans, pies, tarts, ice cream and preserves. Homegrown available from the end of May to September.

TANGERINES

A citrus fruit with bright orange to red skin and small juicy orange segments. Usually served as a dessert, but sometimes used for preserves. Available October to March.

WATERMELONS

The largest of the melon family, either round or oval, with a dark green or yellow skin. The fruit is bright pink and juicy, studded with black seeds. Available May to September.

Fruit Fools

There are two methods of making fools, either with a basis of freshly whipped cream or homemade custard and cream.

The fruit is generally sieved or made into a purée before folding in the other ingredients. Serve these light summery desserts with homemade shortbread or crisp biscuits.

Serves 4
450 g (1 lb) gooseberries, black or redcurrants, rhubarb, raspberries or strawberries
2–3 tablespoons water
75–100 g (3–4 oz) caster sugar
300 ml (½ pint) double cream
food colouring (optional)
To decorate:
whipped cream
a few ratafia biscuits or toasted chopped nuts

Preparation time: 15 minutes plus chilling
Cooking time: 5–15 minutes, depending on the fruit

1. Prepare the fruit, according to type.

2. Put the prepared fruit into a saucepan with the water, slowly bring to the boil, cover with a lid, and simmer for 5–15 minutes, depending on the fruit, until very soft.

3. Remove from the heat, stir in sufficient sugar to sweeten the fruit. Leave to cool.

4. Blend the fruit to a purée, and strain into a large bowl, through a nylon sieve to remove any pips.

5. Whip the cream until it forms soft peaks, and carefully fold into the purée. Use a little food colouring if liked.

6. Spoon the fool into a serving bowl, or divide between 4 individual dishes and chill for 1 hour.

7. Just before serving, pipe rosettes of cream on to the fool and decorate with ratafia biscuits or toasted, chopped nuts.

How to prepare pineapple

1. Using a medium-sized very sharp knife cut off the leaf end and the stem of the pineapple.

2. Thinly pare away the skin of the pineapple, cutting from top to bottom, leaving the 'eyes' exposed.

3. Cut out the eyes with a potato peeler or a sharp knife.

4. Slice into rings and stamp out the core using a 2 cm (¾ inch) diameter biscuit cutter.

5. Alternatively, slice off the leaf end, loosen and remove the flesh without slitting the skin

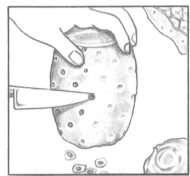

Remove the eyes with the tip of a sharp knife.

and cut into chunks. Serve the chunks in the pineapple shell.

How to segment an orange

1. Hold the orange in one hand and, using a very sharp knife, cut off one end of the orange, to the flesh. Insert the knife at a 45° angle, and carefully remove the skin and pith in a long spiral, turning the orange whilst cutting.

2. Discard the skin, unless it is to be used for julienne strips (see page 171)

3. Cut away any remaining pith from the flesh.

4. Hold the orange in one hand, with the segments vertical. Hold the orange over a bowl to catch the juice.

5. Insert the knife into the orange between the flesh and the membrane and cut through to the centre.

6. Continue this process around the orange until all the segments are removed.

7. Squeeze the juice into the bowl.

Fresh Fruit Salad

Any other fruit may be added, such as cubed melon, or watermelon, strawberries, raspberries, cherries, peaches, nectarines or plums, depending on the time of the year.

Serves 6
2 large oranges, peeled and cut into segments
2 dessert apples
2 ripe pears
100 g (4 oz) green grapes, halved, pips removed, skinned if liked
100 g (4 oz) black grapes, halved, pips removed, skinned if liked
2 kiwi fruit, skinned and sliced
2 bananas
Syrup:
50 ml (¼ pint) water
100 g (4 oz) caster sugar
juice ½ lemon
2 tablespoons Kirsch or brandy (optional)

Preparation time: 30 minutes, plus chilling
Cooking time: about 5 minutes

1. First make the syrup. Put the water into a small saucepan, sprinkle over the sugar, and add the lemon juice. Stir over a low heat, until the sugar has dissolved. Bring to the boil and simmer for 2 minutes.

2. Remove from the heat, and leave to cool. Stir in the Kirsch or brandy, if using.

3. Pour the cooled syrup into a serving bowl, stir in the orange segments and the juice.

4. Peel, core and slice the apples and pears and add to the bowl.

5. Stir in the grapes and kiwi fruit.

6. Peel the bananas and cut the flesh into slices. Add to the other fruit and stir gently. Stir in any of the other chosen fruit and refrigerate for 1–1½ hours.

7. Serve with whipped cream.

SWEET MOUSSES

Sweet mousses are among the lightest and easiest of cold puddings. Their light but creamy textures comes from the whisked egg whites or whipped cream, or a combination of both, which are blended into a smooth sauce or purée made from chocolate, fruit, or nuts.

Chocolate Mousse with Macaroons

Serves 6
175 g (6 oz) bitter chocolate, broken into small pieces
150 g (5 oz) caster sugar
4 tablespoons water
5 egg yolks
1 egg
120 ml (4 fl oz) double cream, whipped
18 ratafias
3 tablespoons rum

Preparation time: 50 minutes, plus chilling time
Cooking time: 30 minutes

1. Put the chocolate into a double saucepan or bain-marie filled with simmering water (see page 74), and stir until melted.

2. Put the sugar and water into a heavy-based saucepan and set over a low heat until dissolved. Do not stir.

3. Increase the heat and bring to the boil. Skim the surface, and continue boiling until the temperature reaches the soft crack stage (138°C/280°F) on a sugar thermometer. Remove from the heat immediately and plunge the saucepan into cold water for a few moments to prevent further cooking.

4. Put the egg yolks and egg into a bowl, and whisk until pale and frothy, using an electric hand mixer. Increase the speed and quickly whisk in the hot syrup, whisking continuously. Continue whisking at a lower speed until the mixture is lukewarm.

5. Using a wire whisk, beat in the melted chocolate until incorporated.

6. Fold the cream into the mixture.

7. Put 12 ratafias on to a plate, sprinkle with the rum and leave to soak for 5 minutes.

8. Spoon a little mousse into the base of 6 individual serving dishes or glasses, to come about half-way up.

9. Crush the remaining ratafias and spoon on top of the mousse. Pour over the remaining mousse.

10. Top each one with 2 soaked ratafias and chill for 2 hours.

11. Serve chilled.

Apricot and Orange Mousse

Serves 4–6
225 g (8 oz) dried apricots
600 ml (1 pint) boiling water
grated rind of 1 orange
juice of 2 oranges
15 g (1/2 oz) powdered gelatine
50–75 g (2–3 oz) caster sugar,
*   to taste*
150 ml (1/4 pint) double cream,
*   lightly whipped*
2 egg whites
To decorate:
150 ml (1/4 pint) double cream,
*   whipped*
rind of 1/2 orange, cut into
*   julienne strips and blanched*
*   for 5 minutes*

Preparation time: 30 minutes,
plus chilling and soaking
Cooking time: 40 minutes

1. Put the apricots into a
saucepan, pour over the
boiling water, and leave to soak
for 2 hours, covered with a lid.

2. Slowly bring the apricots and
soaking water to the boil, then
add the grated rind of 1 orange.
Cover and simmer very gently
for 40 minutes until the
apricots are very soft, stirring
occasionally to break up the
fruit. Remove from the heat.
Stir in half the orange juice.

3. Put the gelatine into a bowl,
pour over the remaining
orange juice and leave to soak
for 5 minutes. Put into a bain-
marie (see page 74), and stir
until dissolved.

4. Stir sugar to taste into the
apricots, then push the fruit
and juice through a nylon sieve
set over a bowl.

5. Stir the dissolved gelatine
into the apricot purée, then
leave until cool, and just
beginning to thicken.

6. Fold the lightly whipped
cream into the purée.

7. Whisk the egg whites until
they are holding their shape,
and fold into the mixture.

8. Spoon into a serving bowl or
dish, and refrigerate for 1½–2
hours until set.

9. Pipe swirls of whipped
cream around the edge of the
dish, and scatter the orange
julienne in the centre.

10. Serve chilled.

Blackberry Mousse

Serves 6
450 g (1 lb) fresh or frozen
*   blackberries*
100 g (4 oz) caster sugar
3 tablespoons lemon juice
5 tablespoons cold water
15 g (1/2 oz) powdered gelatine
150 ml (1/4 pint) double cream
2 egg whites
To decorate:
whipped cream
a few fresh blackberries, if
*   available*

Preparation time: 35 minutes
Cooking time: 10 minutes

1. Put the blackberries, sugar
and lemon juice into a
saucepan, and slowly bring to

the boil. Cover and simmer
gently for 10 minutes until the
fruit is soft, shaking the pan
occasionally. Remove from the
heat and leave to cool.

2. Pass the blackberries and
juices through a nylon sieve,
pressing the sieve to extract all
the purée and juices. Discard
the pips in the sieve.

3. Put the water into a bowl
over a pan of slowly simmering
water or a bain-marie (see page
74). Sprinkle on the gelatine,
and stir until dissolved.
Remove from the heat, and stir
into the blackberry purée.
Leave until cold.

4. When the purée is just
starting to thicken, lightly whip
the cream and fold into the
purée.

5. Whisk the egg whites until
they hold their shape and
carefully fold into the purée.

6. Spoon the mixture into a
large serving dish, or 6
individual ones, and chill until
set.

7. Decorate the top of the
mousse with swirls of whipped
cream and fresh blackberries.
Serve chilled.

Chocolate and Hazelnut Mousse

This is a much simpler, and
quicker, version of the classic
chocolate mousse, but it is
none the less very rich.

Serves 4–6
100 g (4 oz) plain chocolate,
*   broken into pieces*
1–2 tablespoons dark rum
3 eggs, separated
40 g (1 1/2 oz) hazelnuts,
*   toasted, skinned and ground*
To decorate:
whipped cream
a few toasted whole hazelnuts

Preparation time: 15 minutes
Cooking time: 10 minutes

1. Place the chocolate and rum
in a heatproof bowl over a pan
of hot water, and stir until
melted.

2. Stir in the egg yolks, and
continue stirring for 5 minutes
until the mixture has thickened
slightly. Remove from the heat
and leave to cool.

3. Whisk the egg whites until
fairly thick, then fold into the
chocolate mixture alternately
with the ground hazelnuts.

4. Pour into a serving dish, or 4

large or 6 small dishes.

5. Chill until set.

6. Pipe rosettes of whipped
cream around the top and
decorate with whole hazelnuts.
Serve chilled.

SORBETS

A home-made sorbet is a revelation: a delicious smooth concoction of sugar syrup and flavouring quite unlike anything made commercially. Most sorbets are flavoured by fruit juices or purées, but delicious sorbets may also be made from leaves, as here, wines and coffee.

Sorbets or water ices – or sherbets, as they are known in the USA – are water-based ices, often thought to be the best of all frozen ices. Granite or granita are similar, but use less sugar and are more granular in texture.

General method

The basis of a water ice is a syrup made from sugar and water to which some strongly flavoured fruit juice and/or fruit purée and sometimes a small quantity of whisked egg white are added. In the true sorbet, the ingredients are similar, but the proportion of egg white is greater, giving a much softer texture to the finished ice. Granita does not normally have any egg white added. All varieties can also be flavoured with wines, champagne or liqueurs, as well as tea and coffee.

Sorbets can be served in a variety of ways. The simplest is to serve a scoop or two in a dish or glass, but they look more attractive if frozen in the fruit shell corresponding to the flavour. They can be spooned or scooped into tall glasses alternating with crushed miniature meringues, macaroons or ratafias; they can also be spooned or scooped into shells of a brandy snap or tuile mixture. Make the biscuits larger than for petits fours. When baked, shape while still warm over an upturned cup until firm to get the shape.

Basic rules

Sorbets are a little complicated to make, and do take time, but they are worth it. An ice-cream maker is a great help when making sorbets. The different types of ice cream makers are described on pages 238–9 and there is no question that a machine gives better results than hand whisking. Small ice cream makers will make up to about 1 litre (1¾ pints) sorbet at a time. However, sorbets can easily, if more lengthily, be made in the freezer, taking them out every so often to beat them by hand – or, preferably, with an electric hand beater.

Lemon Water Ice

Serves 4–6
225 g (8 oz) caster sugar
600 ml (1 pint) water
3 lemons
1 egg white

Preparation time: about 30 minutes, plus freezing time

1. Put the sugar and water into a saucepan and heat gently until the sugar has completely dissolved, stirring continuously.

2. Pare the rind thinly from the lemons using a potato peeler, and add to the syrup. Simmer gently for 10 minutes. Leave until cold.

3. Squeeze the juice from the lemons and add to the syrup. Strain into a shallow freezing container and freeze until mushy.

4. Turn the mixture into a cold bowl and whisk until evenly mushy and the ice crystals are broken up. Return to the container and freeze until mushy again. Repeat the whisking.

5. Whisk the egg white until stiff and fold evenly through the mixture. Return to the freezing container and freeze until firm.

Variations

Use 300 ml (½ pint) of the syrup as above. Mix with an equal quantity of strained fruit purée (raspberry, strawberry, blackcurrant, gooseberry, apricot, etc), and add the strained juice of ½–1 lemon. Continue from Step 3.

Blackcurrant Leaf Water Ice

For a perfect Sorbet

■ Use fresh, well flavoured fruits, fruit purées and other ingredients and colourings if necessary to achieve a good colour as well as a good flavour.
■ Alcohol freezes at a lower temperature than water, so sorbets or ices containing alcohol will stay softer and melt faster.
■ Do not be tempted to make the sugar syrup sweeter or the extra sweetness will hinder the freezing process. The finished ice might be too sweet as well – they are far more refreshing when slightly tart. Sugar quantities are critical: too much produces an over-soft sorbet or ice; too little a rock-hard one.
■ The addition of whisked egg whites to sorbet and water ice mixtures helps to prevent the formation of large ice crystals, and slows up melting.
■ Do not hurry the freezing process. You must wait until sufficient ice crystals have formed before beating the sorbet mixture.
■ You must beat at least twice for a really smooth ice, and preferably more often if using the freezer and electric mixer method. Allow to freeze completely before use – it is best to make it at least 2 days before you want to serve it.
■ Chill the freezing container, the bowl and the whisk in the freezer if you can. The colder the better.
■ Ice cream and water ices often need a short time in the refrigerator to 'come to' before serving – about 30–60 minutes. You don't want them melting, but neither do you want them rock-hard!

This is an attractive water ice both in colour (pale green) and flavour, well worth making when the leaves are available.

Serves 4–6
600 ml (1 pint) water
175 g (6 oz) caster sugar
thinly pared rind of 2 lemons
3–4 handfuls blackcurrant leaves, washed and well dried
juice of 3 lemons
a few drops of green liquid food colouring
1 egg white (optional)

Preparation time: about 30 minutes, plus infusing and freezing time

1. Put the water and sugar into a saucepan with the lemon rind, and bring to the boil, stirring continuously until dissolved. Boil for 5–6 minutes then add the leaves, remove from the heat and leave until cold. Remove the leaves from the syrup, squeezing out the excess liquid.

2. Strain the lemon juice and add to the syrup together with a few drops of green food colouring to give the required colour. Turn into a shallow freezing container and freeze as for Lemon Water Ice.

3. This ice should have 3 whiskings and, if preferred, may have a stiffly beaten egg white folded through it after the final whisking. Freeze until firm.

China Tea Water Ice

Any interestingly flavoured tea can be used for water ices or sorbets. Try Earl Grey, Orange Pekoe, Oolong, Indian teas or some of the new fruit-flavoured teas. Always strain through muslin to avoid leaves.

Serves 4
750 ml (1¼ pints) water
150 g (5 oz) caster sugar
1 tablespoon China tea leaves
juice of 1 orange

Preparation time: about 20 minutes, plus infusing and freezing time

1. Put 600 ml (1 pint) water into a saucepan with the sugar and bring to the boil slowly, stirring until the sugar has dissolved. Boil for 3–4 minutes. Boil the remaining water, pour over the tea and leave to infuse for 5–10 minutes.

2. Strain the tea through a muslin lined sieve into the syrup with the orange juice and leave until quite cold.

3. Pour into a shallow container and continue as for Blackcurrant Leaf Water Ice.

Coffee Granita

Granita uses less sugar than sorbets and water ices, and is stirred – with a fork or spoon – rather than whisked, so that it retains its gritty texture of tiny ice crystals.

Serves 6
100 g (4 oz) caster sugar
1.2 litres (2 pints) water
100 g (4 oz) coarsely ground coffee
2 tablespoons Tia Maria or brandy (optional)
lightly whipped cream (optional)

Preparation time: about 30 minutes, plus infusing and freezing time

1. Put the sugar and water into a saucepan and heat gently until the sugar has dissolved. Bring to the boil and boil hard for about 3 minutes. Remove from the heat, stir in the ground coffee, stir well and leave to infuse for 15 minutes, stirring occasionally.

2. Strain the mixture through a fine sieve lined with muslin or a coffee filter paper. Cool and then chill.

3. Add the Tia Maria or brandy and pour into 1 or 2 shallow containers. Freeze until beginning to become granular. Stir the mixture until slushy and then return to the freezer for about 30 minutes until beginning to solidify again.

4. Repeat the stirring of the mixture at about 30-minute intervals until thick and slushy and finally firm but still granular. Serve spooned into tall glasses and decorate each with a spoonful of whipped cream, if liked.

ICE CREAMS & BOMBES

There's no comparison between real homemade ice cream and the commercial varieties. Once you have mastered the basic process, whether by machine or hand, you'll want to progress to making a spectacular party Bombe. Here is all you need to know about equipment, ingredients and techniques.

Ice creams aren't difficult to make at home. Once you have mastered the basics, you can extend your repertoire with any of the variations listed below – or you can make peach, pistachio, spiced banana, mango, lime, peppermint, or an infinite variety of ice creams. And they can be presented in an infinite number of ways too: as sundaes with fruit, sauces and nuts; swathed in meringue for a Baked Alaska; served in delicate biscuit, chocolate or cake bases, for a contrast in texture; and layered in a cake tin to make a rainbow ice-cream cake.

There are two main types of ice-cream mixture: an egg custard base which is usually flavoured with vanilla, chocolate, coffee, chopped nuts etc; or an egg mousse base which has a hot sugar syrup with egg yolks, cream and added flavourings, such as praline, browned breadcrumbs or a fruit purée. The custard base is the least suitable if an ice-cream churn is not available as it has a higher water content and will freeze very hard. There are also other types of mixture that can be frozen such as one containing condensed milk.

A proper ice-cream scoop makes it much easier to serve the ice cream.

Churns To obtain a very smooth light ice cream, a churn should be used as this keeps the mixture moving as it freezes, and ensures that no large crystals of ice form in the mixture. There are several varieties of churn available, from the old-fashioned bucket type to an expensive ice-cream machine. The bucket churns have to be packed with a mixture of ice and salt around the central container. The ice cream is poured into the container, a paddle fitted, and a close-fitting lid with a handle or motor on it.

Ice-cream machines By contrast, the most expensive machine requires no ice and salt: the ice-cream mixture is poured into a container in the machine, two switches are pressed, and 20–40 minutes later the ice cream is ready.

There are several other types of ice-cream machines available, one where the container is frozen for 8 hours and then fitted on to a motor for churning. However, only one batch of ice cream can be made before the container has to be frozen again. There are other machines which have an electric motor that are designed to operate inside the freezer or ice box of a refrigerator, the electric cable coming through the door. Most

Fruit Ice Cream

This ice cream can be made satisfactorily without an ice-cream machine.

Serves 6
Makes 1.2 litres (2 pints)
90 g (3½ oz) granulated sugar
120 ml (4 fl oz) water
3 egg yolks
450 ml (¾ pint) cold fruit purée (blackcurrant, raspberry, damson, apricot etc.)
450 ml (¾ pint) single cream

Preparation time: 30 minutes, excluding making of purée and freezing time
Cooking time: 10 minutes

1. Dissolve the sugar in the water and bring to the boil. Boil steadily to the thread stage (107°C, 225°F). Pour on to the egg yolks in a bowl, whisking constantly. Do not let the sugar boil past the thread or it will set.

2. Continue to whisk the yolk and sugar mixture until the bowl is cold and the mixture will leave a faint trail over itself.

3. Add the fruit purée and cream to the yolk mixture and taste for sweetness.

4. Freeze in a shallow container until slushy and beginning to freeze round the edges. Remove from the freezer and beat until even in texture.

machines cut out when the mixture has frozen to the correct consistency.

Making ice cream by hand
Ice creams can be made without the use of an ice-cream churn, but their smoothness and soft texture cannot be guaranteed. They need to be beaten several times by hand, or with an electric whisk, to prevent the mixture freezing as a solid block. The ice-cream mixture should be poured into a wide, reasonably deep container and placed in the freezer or ice-making compartment. When the mixture begins to freeze around the edge of the dish, remove from the freezer and beat the mixture until it becomes even in texture. Freeze again and repeat the beating as the mixture firms up again. A third beating may be necessary, and the freezing process will take 2–4 hours.

No ice cream should be eaten straightaway, but should be allowed to mellow in the freezer for at least an hour.

Vanilla Ice Cream

This recipe is not so good made by hand as it has a high water content and will not freeze very smoothly.

Makes 900 ml (1½ pints)
6 egg yolks
75 g (3 oz) caster sugar
600 ml (1 pint) milk
5–6 drops vanilla essence
150 ml (¼ pint) single cream

Preparation time: 5 minutes, excluding chilling and freezing
Cooking time: 15 minutes

1. Work the egg yolks and sugar together with an electric whisk until white and light.

2. Pour on the milk that has been heated to just below boiling point, and mix well. Wipe out the milk pan and pour the custard back into it.

3. Heat gently, stirring well, until the frothy surface disappears and the mixture lightly coats the back of a spoon. Do not allow the custard to boil. Pour the custard through a strainer into a bowl. Add the vanilla essence and leave until cool. Refrigerate until cold.

4. Add the cream to the cold custard, taste for flavour and freeze according to the instructions for the machine.

Rich ice cream

Make this as for the Fruit Ice Cream (see below) using the following proportions:
750 ml (1¼ pints) single cream well flavoured with vanilla essence
75 g (3 oz) sugar
120 ml (4 fl oz) water
4 egg yolks

Variations

Chocolate Melt 150 g (5 oz) chocolate in the milk or cream and proceed as recipe.
White Coffee Heat 150 g (5 oz) crushed coffee beans in the milk or cream and leave to cool for several hours. Then proceed as recipe.
Chocolate Chip Add 100 g (4 oz) grated milk or plain chocolate to the ice cream when it is frozen to a soft slush.
Browned Breadcrumb Place 75 g (3 oz) brown breadcrumbs on a baking tray with 25 g (1 oz) natural cane sugar and bake in a hot oven (190°C, 375°F, Gas Mark 5) for 10–15 minutes until toasted and caramelized. Leave to cool. Add to the semi-frozen ice cream as above.

5. Return to the freezer, removing twice more to beat when the mixture becomes slushy.

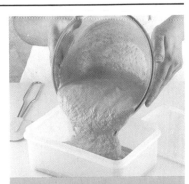

6. When frozen pour into a suitable freezer container, pack down, cover and leave in the deep freeze for at least an hour before serving.

For perfect ice cream

■ When making ice creams that contain dairy products, always ensure that all equipment used is kept scrupulously clean.
■ Single cream (18 per cent minimum butter fat) is usually the best and most economical for ice cream. Higher butter fat creams do not give such a smooth result, but obviously a richer ice cream is obtained.
■ Always taste the mixture for sweetness, particularly in the case of fruit purées. Too little sugar in the mixture will cause the mixture to be very hard and it will not have a good flavour whereas too much sugar will mean the mixture may not freeze properly and will stay soft.
■ If flavourings are added to the ice cream make sure that the mixture is well flavoured as a little of the flavour is lost in the freezing.
■ If a fruit purée is being used, check that the consistency is correct.
■ Never overfill the containers of ice-cream machines. Remember the mixture will expand on freezing. Check manufacturers' specifications for quantities.
■ If the ice cream has been stored in the freezer for any length of time, remove it at least 30 minutes before serving and keep in the refrigerator so that it softens, making it easier to scoop.
■ Do not allow ice cream to melt and then re-freeze it.
■ Ice creams should not be kept in the freezer for longer than 6 months.

BOMBES

Bombes are basically a frozen dessert. They originally always consisted of ice cream but nowadays they can be any frozen dessert. The basic idea is to use two or more ice creams of varying colours and textures, and to freeze them in layers, one inside the other, in the mould. When cut, a slice should show the number of colourful layers.

General method

Traditionally bombes were made in a bombe mould before the days of refrigeration and deep freezes. A true bombe mould is made of copper with a tin lining. It has a lid with a ring on it to cover the base, and at the other rounded end, there is a screw with a flat surface. The ice cream is packed into the mould with the screw in place, and then the lid is put on. At one time the mould would have been smeared in grease, usually lard, around the lid and screw to keep it water-tight as it would have to be buried in crushed ice for several hours to freeze it. Nowadays the mould does not need to be larded as it is frozen in the freezer. Once the bombe is frozen the lid is pulled off using the ring. The mould is then placed on the serving dish and the screw unscrewed from the top end to let in air. A warmed cloth is wrapped around the mould to help release the ice cream

which should slide out of the mould. Another way of releasing a bombe – although it doesn't sound very hygienic – is to place the lips around the screw-hole and to blow into the mould!

Bombes can be made quite satisfactorily without a bombe mould, however, as a pudding basin is a perfectly good substitute. The ice cream mixture should be well packed into the basin and it must be well covered before freezing. The quickest way to turn out the bombe is to lower the basin into a bowl of hot water for a few seconds, and then invert quickly on to a plate. If the ice cream does not drop out, repeat the process in hot water but do not allow the basin to stay in for too long as the ice cream will start to melt.

Once turned out, bombes can be decorated with whipped cream or melted cooled chocolate can be poured over them. They are cut into slices for serving.

For perfect Bombes

■ Check that the mould or pudding basin is scrupulously clean, and that there is no sign of rusting if an old copper mould is used.
■ Allow the ice creams to soften for about 30 minutes in the refrigerator before using to make up the bombe.
■ Pack the ice creams firmly and evenly into the mould. If making a layered bombe use a lightly warmed spoon to shape and smooth the first, outer layer of the ice cream

on to the sides and bottom of the mould. The outside layer of ice cream should be about 2.5 cm (1 inch) thick. Inner layers may be less thick.
■ If the ice cream softens too much when shaping, place the mould back in the freezer for a short time before filling with the next mixture.
■ Freeze for at least 3–4 hours before turning out.

Chocolate Fruit Bombe

Serves 6
85 ml (3 fl oz) brandy or rum
50 g (2 oz) raisins
50 g (2 oz) currants
25 g (1 oz) sultanas
25 g (1 oz) glacé cherries, quartered
15 g (½ oz) candied peel, chopped
15 g (½ oz) flaked almonds
15 g (½ oz) pecan, Brazil nuts or walnuts, chopped
1 recipe quantity Chocolate ice cream, made to the soft slush stage (see page 239, Vanilla Ice Cream Variations)

Preparation time: 10 minutes excluding fruit soaking time, making of ice cream, and freezing.

1. Put the brandy or rum into a bowl, add all the prepared fruit and nuts and leave to soak for several hours while preparing the ice cream.

2. When the ice cream is frozen to a slush, work all the soaked fruits into the mixture.

3. Fill a 900 ml (1½ pint) bombe mould or bowl and freeze for 3–4 hours minimum.

4. About 30 minutes before serving, take the mould from the freezer and leave in the warm kitchen for 5 minutes.

5. If using a bombe mould, pull off the lid and remove the screw. If the bombe doesn't slide out, wrap a warm cloth round it.

6. If using a bowl, dip the bowl into hot water for about 10 seconds. Place the serving plate on top, turn over and remove bowl. Repeat dipping in hot water if necessary. Put the bombe in the refrigerator until ready to serve.

Three-Layered Bombe

Choose 3 compatible flavoured and coloured ice creams such as chocolate, chocolate chip and vanilla, or raspberry, strawberry and orange water ice flavoured with Grand Marnier (see Lemon Water Ice, page 236–237)
300 ml (½ pint) double cream, whipped, for decoration

Preparation time: about 20 minutes, excluding making of ice creams, chilling and freezing

1. Chill the chosen mould and put the ice creams to be used in the refrigerator for 30 minutes.

2. Remove one ice cream from the fridge and spoon it into the mould, packing it down well against the sides. If the mould is too cold to hold comfortably wrap it in a tea towel.

3. Warm a spoon in some hot water and use to smooth out the ice cream and push it evenly round the mould. The first layer should be almost 2.5 cm (1 inch) thick. If the ice cream has become too soft, chill in the freezer for 15 minutes or so.

4. Take the second ice cream and fill the mould in the same way, leaving a hollow in the centre.

5. Fill the hollow with the third ice cream, packing it down well so that there are no gaps.

6. Cover the mould with the lid or cover tightly with foil. Freeze for 3–4 hours or as long as liked.

7. About 30 minutes before serving, take the mould from the freezer and leave in the warm kitchen for 5 minutes.

8. If using a bombe mould, pull off the lid and remove the screw. If the bombe doesn't slide out, wrap a warm cloth round it.

9. If using a bowl, dip the bowl into hot water to the level of the ice cream for about 10 seconds. Place the serving plate on top, turn over and remove bowl. Repeat dipping in hot water if mixture doesn't come out immediately.

10. Keep the turned out bombe in the refrigerator – but not for *too* long – until ready to serve, then decorate with the whipped cream.

Left: Chocolate, vanilla and coffee bombe
Right: Raspberry ice cream

SWEET SAUCES & FILLINGS

There's nothing smoother than a rich homemade custard sauce, or a custard-based filling for fruit flans and pastries. Making these successfully is a skill you'll have no difficulty in mastering with the help of our guide to ingredients, cook's tips and delicious recipes.

Sweet sauces and fillings are fundamental to many French pastries and desserts. It would be as difficult to imagine a choux pastry dessert without its pastry cream filling, say, as it would be Christmas pudding without its brandy or rum butter. Sweet egg-yolk based fillings are often used in flans, tarts and gâteaux, and sweet accompanying sauces can be pouring custards, frothy sabayons and colourful fruit sauces.

Egg-based sweet sauces and fillings

Although the simplest sweet sauce or filling is whipped cream (perhaps flavoured with vanilla to make Crème Chantilly), most sauces or fillings are egg-based. Crème Anglaise is a liquid or pouring custard sauce, the French version of the British egg custard. Crème Pâtissière is a thick custard (also known as pastry cream or confectioner's custard), which is used to fill choux pastry shapes, flans, gâteaux etc.

Both are made from egg yolks, milk and sugar. Crème Pâtissière is thickened with flour, whereas Crème Anglaise is generally made without any other thickening agent than the egg yolk (although in some cases, a small amount of arrowroot or cornflour may be added to stabilize the mixture to prevent scrambling).

Both these basic sauces may be adapted and flavoured in numerous ways. Although Crème Anglaise is usually flavoured with vanilla, it can also be made with orange or lemon rind, chocolate or liqueurs. It also forms the basis of a cream pudding, a bavarois. A Crème Pâtissière with egg whites folded into it becomes a Crème St-Honoré, and a Frangipane (almond custard) is a Crème Pâtissière with ground almonds or crushed macaroons.

An accompanying Sabayon sauce is also an egg-based sauce, made with white wine or fortified wine, the amount of sugar depending on the sweetness of the wine used.

These egg-based sauces should be cooked in a bain-marie (see page 74) or a double saucepan. Ideally a copper bowl should be used over the hot water. The

Crème Pâtissière

Unlike Crème Anglaise, this sauce may be brought to the boil, and indeed should be to cook the flour. This is a much thicker mixture, and is used as a filling for choux pastry, fruit tarts, flans, gâteaux etc.

Makes about 600 ml (1 pint)
5 egg yolks
150 g (5 oz) vanilla sugar
70 g (2¾ oz) plain flour, sifted
450 ml (¾ pint) boiling milk
15 g (½ oz) unsalted butter

Preparation time: 5 minutes
Cooking time: 15 minutes

1. Put the egg yolks into a bowl in a bain-marie (see page 74) or into the top of a double saucepan.

2. Heat the water in the bain-marie to a slow simmer.

3. Gradually whisk the sugar into the egg yolks until the mixture forms a ribbon (see hint, opposite).

4. Beat in the flour until well blended.

6. Remove from the heat, and pour the sauce into a bowl.

7. Dot the top of the sauce with butter to prevent a skin forming. Leave to cool and use as required.

temperature of the water is most important, as if it is too hot the mixture will curdle. Whisking is also important to combine the ingredients and to incorporate air to create lightness.

Vanilla sugar

Vanilla is often used as the flavouring in sweet sauces. A vanilla pod placed in sugar in a jar for a week gives a mild flavour. For a more positive taste, steep a vanilla bean in the hot milk for 20 minutes for a stronger flavour.

5. Gradually beat in the boiling milk. Pour the sauce into a heavy-based saucepan, and slowly bring to the boil, stirring constantly. Lower the heat and simmer for 3 minutes, stirring.

Variations

Similar flavourings may be used for Crème Pâtissière as the Crème Anglaise, using 5–6 teaspoons of liqueur, 75 g (3 oz) of chocolate or 3 tablespoons of coffee.

Crème Anglaise

This sauce is either served warm or chilled, depending on the dessert it is to accompany. It is used on fruit desserts, puddings, ice cream, fresh fruit and moulded creams, and is less rich than fresh cream. It can be enriched by additional egg yolks, sugar and double cream, and used as the base for ice cream. If a stronger vanilla flavour is required a few drops of vanilla essence can be used.

Makes about 450 ml (¾ pint)
4 large egg yolks
75 g (3 oz) vanilla sugar
1 teaspoon cornflour or potato flour (optional)
450 ml (¾ pint) hot milk

Preparation time: 5 minutes
Cooking time: 15 minutes

1. Put the egg yolks into a bowl in a bain-marie (see page 74) or into the top of a double saucepan.

2. Heat the water in the bain-marie to a slow simmer.

3. Gradually whisk the sugar into the egg yolks until it forms a ribbon.

4. If using the cornflour, or potato flour, beat it into the mixture until the mixture is pale and light and the sugar has dissolved.

5. Continue beating with a wooden spoon and very slowly beat in the hot milk until all the milk has been incorporated into the sauce. At this stage the custard will be very frothy. When the custard is about to thicken the froth will disappear. Use a sugar

thermometer as a guide for temperature (see page 245) and cook slowly until the sauce just coats the back of the spoon.

6. Remove from the bain-marie, and continue beating for 5 minutes until the sauce has cooled a little.

7. Strain the sauce through a fine sieve, into a cold bowl, whisk well and serve.

Variations

Crème Anglaise can also be flavoured with brandy, rum, Kirsch or orange liqueurs, adding about 4 teaspoons to the above quantity, or with chocolate or coffee. To the above quantity add 50 g (2 oz) of plain chocolate, which is melted in the hot milk, or 2 tablespoons strong black coffee, added to the boiling milk.

Crème St Honoré

This custard is used as a dessert cream filling for Gâteau St Honoré and other cakes. It may be flavoured with liqueurs, chocolate, grated orange rind or praline.

Makes about 750 ml (1¾ pints)
8 egg whites
a large pinch of salt
2 tablespoons granulated sugar
1 recipe quantity Crème Pâtissière

Whisking sauces

■ To whisk 'until the mixture forms a ribbon', in the following recipes, add the sugar slowly to the yolks whilst whisking with a metal whisk or electric hand mixer for 3 minutes. By this time the mixture will be pale in colour, and will have thickened sufficiently so that when the whisk is lifted from the mixture, the 'cream' will fall back into the bowl, forming a slow dissolving ribbon on the surface. Once this stage has been reached the liquid may be added. It is essential to add the sugar slowly to prevent the mixture becoming granular.
■ For the strongest vanilla flavour of all, grind 2 vanilla beans to a powder in a food processor with 100 g (4 oz) sugar lumps. Sieve before use.

1. Whisk 8 egg whites with a pinch of salt until they have formed soft peaks. Gradually whisk in the sugar, a little at a time, and continue whisking until stiff peaks are formed.

2. Stir about a quarter of the whisked egg whites into the Crème Pâtissière, and then fold in the rest. Use cold.

Bavarois à l'Orange

Orange Bavarian Cream

Serves 8
2 large sugar lumps
2 large oranges, well washed
*   and dried*
15 g (½ oz) powdered gelatine
5 egg whites
a pinch of salt
2 tablespoons caster sugar
150 ml (¼ pint) double cream
2 tablespoons orange liqueur
Crème Anglaise:
7 egg yolks
175 g (6 oz) sugar
2 teaspoons cornflour
450 ml (¾ pint) boiling milk
To decorate:
4 oranges, peeled, all pith
*   removed, cut into segments*
3 tablespoons orange liqueur

Preparation time: 30 minutes
Cooking time: 20 minutes

1. Rub the sugar lumps over the rind of the oranges until they are impregnated with the zest. Put the sugar into a large mixing bowl and crush until fine.

2. Squeeze the juice from the oranges and strain into a measuring jug to give 150 ml (¼ pint). (If the oranges are not very juicy, squeeze another one to make up to the specified amount.)

3. Sprinkle the gelatine over the orange juice and set aside.

4. Follow the method for Crème Anglaise, given on page 243. Put the bowl containing the orange-flavoured sugar into a bain-marie of simmering water. Add the egg yolks, and gradually whisk in the sugar. Whisk until the mixture forms a ribbon (see hint, page 243).

5. Beat in the cornflour, then gradually whisk in the hot milk and bring to just below boiling point.

8. Lightly whisk the cream until it forms soft peaks.

9. Whisk the egg whites and salt until they form soft peaks. Continue whisking and gradually add the sugar, whisking constantly, until stiff peaks are formed.

10. Add the orange liqueur to the custard then quickly and lightly mix in the egg whites and cream, taking alternate scoops from each in turn until all mixed in.

11. Turn the mixture into a wet or oiled 1.75 litre (3 pint) mould. Smooth the surface. Cover with greased greaseproof paper and chill for 4 hours.

Frangipane

Almond Custard Filling

This is a very thick type of Crème Pâtissière used for filling tarts or crêpes. Finely crushed macaroons may be used instead of the ground almonds.

Makes about 750 ml (1¼ pints)
1 egg yolk
1 egg, beaten
100 g (4 oz) sugar (not vanilla sugar)
50 g (2 oz) plain flour
300 ml (½ pint) boiling milk
40 g (1½ oz) unsalted butter
75 g (3 oz) ground almonds
¼ teaspoon almond essence (or to taste)
2 tablespoons Kirsch

Preparation time: 10 minutes
Cooking time: 20 minutes

1. Put the egg yolk and whole egg into a bain-marie (see page 74) or into the top of a double saucepan.

2. Heat the water in the bain-marie, and gradually whisk the sugar into the egg until it forms a ribbon. Beat in the flour until well blended. Gradually beat in the boiling milk.

3. Pour the sauce into a heavy-based saucepan, and slowly bring to the boil, stirring constantly, whisking out any lumps that may form. Continue whisking until it forms a thick paste. Reduce the heat and simmer, beating with a wooden spoon for 3 minutes to cook the flour. Take care that the heat is not too high.

4. Remove from the heat, beat in the butter, ground almonds, almond essence and Kirsch.

5. If the sauce is not to be used immediately, dot the top of it with butter (see page 242) to prevent a skin forming.

6. Stir until the sauce coats the back of the spoon. Remove from the heat, and stir in the softened gelatine until it has completely dissolved.

7. Pour the custard into a clean mixing bowl. Stand the bowl over a tin or bowl filled with ice, and leave to cool, stirring occasionally to prevent a skin forming.

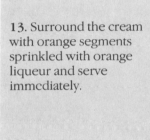

13. Surround the cream with orange segments sprinkled with orange liqueur and serve immediately.

12. Quickly dip the mould into very hot water and unmould on to a serving plate.

Sabayon Sauce

Sabayon sauce may be served warm or cold. The amount of sugar depends upon the choice of wine and upon individual taste. Serve it with pies, flans and fruit.

For Sabayon au Madère, use Madeira instead of white wine.

Makes about 300 ml (½ pint)
4 egg yolks
about 50 g (2 oz) sugar
  (depending on sweetness of wine)
150 ml (¼ pint) white wine
grated rind of 1 orange or 1 lemon

Preparation time: 5 minutes
Cooking time: about 15 minutes

1. Put the egg yolks into a bowl, and beat lightly. Put in a bain-marie (see page 74) half filled with hot, but not boiling, water.

2. Beat in the sugar and wine and whisk until the mixture is frothy and forms a ribbon.

3. Remove from the bain-marie and mix in the grated orange or lemon rind.

4. If serving the sauce warm, serve it immediately. If serving the sauce cold, whisk it until cool off the heat, then set the bowl over a pan of iced water. Continue whisking until the sauce is cold. It will hold up for about 1 hour before separating.

Perfect sauces and fillings

■ Use eggs at room temperature. If they have been stored in the refrigerator, remove them at least 3 hours before they are required.
■ When using milk to make a sauce, it should be at boiling point, and added very gradually to the eggs, whilst whisking constantly.
■ A sugar thermometer is helpful; as a guide, the maximum temperature for a Crème Anglaise without starch should be 160°C/320°F and for a crème pâtissière, 170°C/340°F.
■ Do not use too large a bowl for making a sauce. If it is too big the sauce is more likely to separate. If the pan is too small the sauce is likely to splatter.
■ Use a fairly small whisk which can reach into the edge of the bowl.

CLASSIC DESSERTS

Perfect your technique with these classic desserts. Strawberry Malakoff, a superb version of strawberries and cream, Crème brûlée, rich cream under a brittle burnt sugar crust, or a Savarin ring soaked in Kirsch syrup, filled with fresh fruit.

Strawberry Malakoff

Use only the very best quality sponge fingers for this delicious dessert. Although it looks so impressive, it is in fact quite simple to make.

Serves 10–12
225 g (8 oz) unsalted butter
175 g (6 oz) caster sugar
175 g (6 oz) ground almonds
1 teaspoon almond essence
450 ml (15 fl oz) double cream
450 g (1 lb) small strawberries, hulled
about 21 sponge fingers
100 ml (4 fl oz) orange or almond liqueur

Preparation time: 30 minutes

1. Cream the butter and sugar until light and fluffy. Beat in the ground almonds and almond essence.

2. Whip the cream until it stands in soft peaks. Fold into the almond mixture. Reserve 4–12 strawberries for decoration. Fold the rest into the mixture (cut in half if large).

3. Cut a circle of greaseproof paper to fit the base of a 1.8 litre (3 pint) charlotte tin or soufflé dish.

4. Dip the sponge fingers one at a time into the liqueur and place them sugar side out around the inside edge of the dish. Add any remaining liqueur to the strawberry and almond mixture.

5. Spoon the strawberry and almond mixture into the centre of the prepared tin or dish, pressing down lightly. Cover and chill until required.

6. Invert the dish on to a serving plate and allow to stand at room temperature for about 10 minutes before removing the mould and the paper. Decorate with strawberries.

Crème Brûlée

This delicious pudding should be served after a comparatively light main course as it is very rich. It is particularly useful for dinner parties as it must be prepared the night before, and only needs the sugar crust adding on the day. In summer, this pudding is the perfect companion for soft fruit like raspberries or strawberries.

Serves 4
300 ml (½ pint) double cream
1 vanilla pod
4 egg yolks
2 tablespoons caster sugar
Topping:
caster sugar

Preparation time: 10 minutes, plus cooling and chilling overnight
Cooking time: 30 minutes
Oven: 160°C, 325°F, Gas Mark 3

Variation

As an alternative presentation, make a cartwheel of sponge fingers to fit the base of the mould. You will need approximately 20 extra sponge fingers. Cut the biscuits slightly to form the design and arrange them on top of the greaseproof paper in the mould. Soak the remaining biscuits in liqueur

1. Put the cream with the vanilla pod into a saucepan and heat to just below boiling point. Remove from the heat, cool, and discard the vanilla pod.

2. Beat the egg yolks with the sugar until pale and creamy. Stir in the warm cream. Transfer to the top of a double boiler and cook, stirring, until the mixture is sufficiently thick to coat the back of the spoon (on no account allow it to boil).

3. Pour into a flameproof dish or individual ramekins and bake in the oven for about 12 minutes for a large dish, 5 minutes for ramekins, until a skin has formed on top. Chill overnight in the refrigerator.

4. Sprinkle the custard with sugar, to make an even 5 mm (¼ inch) layer. Heat the grill to high.

and proceed as above. The fruit and liqueur may be varied according to taste, for example fresh raspberries and Framboise, blackberries and Kirsch.

5. Set the custard under the grill, as near to the heat as possible, so that the sugar melts and caramelizes evenly, turning the dish if necessary.

6. Allow to cool completely before serving, so that the topping hardens.

From the top: Strawberry Malakoff, Crème brûlée

Pêches Cardinal

Compôte of Fresh Peaches with Raspberry Purée

This is an especially nice colourful dessert when both peaches and raspberries are in season. Though the taste is not quite as good, you can use canned peaches and frozen raspberries.

Serves 10
1.5 litres (2½ pints) water
450 g (1 lb) sugar
2 tablespoons vanilla essence or a vanilla pod
10 firm, ripe, unblemished, fresh peaches about 6 cm (2½ inches) in diameter
450 g (1 lb) fresh raspberries
225 g (8 oz) icing sugar
fresh mint leaves (optional)

Preparation time: 30 minutes, plus cooling and chilling
Cooking time: 12 minutes

1. Put the water, sugar and vanilla essence or pod in a saucepan over gentle heat and stir until the sugar has dissolved. Bring to the boil and simmer for 2–3 minutes. Remove vanilla pod and discard.

2. Add the unpeeled peaches to the simmering syrup. Bring again to simmering point, then maintain at just below the simmer for 8 minutes or until the peaches are tender.

3. Remove pan from heat and allow peaches to cool in syrup for 20 minutes. (Syrup may be used again for poaching other fruits.) Drain the peaches on a rack; peel while still warm, and arrange in a serving dish. Chill.

4. Purée the raspberries with the icing sugar in a liquidizer at top speed, then sieve. Chill.

5. When both purée and peaches are chilled, pour the purée over the peaches and return to refrigerator until serving time. Decorate with fresh mint leaves, if using.

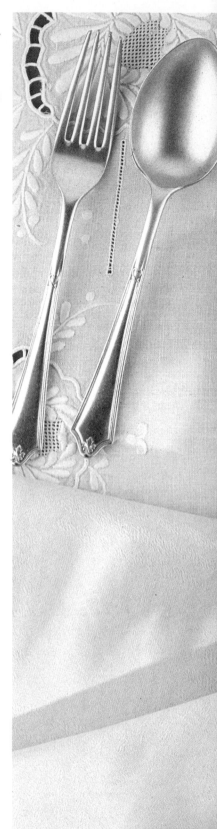

Crêpes Suzette

Legend has it that this dish was created for Edward Prince of Wales when dining with a certain lady.

The crêpes for this dish should be as thin and delicate as possible. It does look spectacular if you flambé the crêpes at the table, with a chafing dish, but it would be a good idea to practise the technique well beforehand.

Serves 4–6
12 crêpes (see page 205)
75 g (3 oz) unsalted butter
25 g (1 oz) caster sugar
finely grated rind of 1 orange
2 tablespoons orange juice
2 tablespoons Curaçao
Flambé:
caster sugar
2 tablespoons Curaçao
1 tablespoon brandy

Preparation time: 30 minutes
Cooking time: 40 minutes

1. Make the crêpes, following the instructions on page 205. Stack them on a plate and keep warm over a pan of simmering water.

2. Put the butter, sugar, orange rind and juice and Curaçao into a large frying pan and simmer gently for 2 minutes.

3. Put a crêpe into the frying pan and fold in half and in half again, to form a triangle, using a spoon and fork. Push to the side of the pan. Repeat until all the crêpes have been folded in the same way.

4. Arrange the crêpes overlapping in the pan, sprinkle with a little sugar and pour over the Curaçao and brandy. Avert your face and ignite. Shake the pan gently to and fro and when the flames have died down, serve immediately.

From the left: Crêpes Suzette, Pêches cardinal

Savarin aux Fruits en Kirsch

See page 308 for detailed information on yeast doughs and savarins.

Serves 8
225 g (8 oz) strong plain flour
pinch of salt
10 g (¼ oz) easy-blend dried
  yeast
1 teaspoon sugar
6 tablespoons milk, warmed
  slightly
4 eggs, beaten
100 g (4 oz) butter, creamed
Syrup:
175 g (6 oz) sugar
250 ml (8 fl oz) water
strip of lemon rind
6 tablespoons Kirsch
Filling:
225 g (8 oz) fresh fruit
  (pineapple, strawberries or
  cherries), marinated in
  3 tablespoons Kirsch
sugar to taste
300 ml (½ pint) double cream

Preparation time: 25 minutes, plus proving time
Cooking time: 30–40 minutes
Oven: 190°C, 375°F, Gas Mark 5

1. Sift the flour and salt into a large warmed bowl. Add the yeast and sugar.

2. Mix the milk and eggs together and add them to the flour. Using the hands, work the mixture to a smooth dough. This dough should be very soft, almost runny.

3. Beat the dough vigorously until the texture is smooth and elastic.

4. Cover the dough with oiled clingfilm and leave in a warm place for 45 minutes to rise until doubled in bulk.

5. Beat the well-creamed butter into the risen dough until it is thoroughly incorporated.

6. Turn the dough into a well buttered ring mould 20 cm (8 inches) in diameter. Cover with oiled clingfilm and leave in a warm place until the dough has risen to the top of the mould.

7. Bake in a preheated oven for 30–40 minutes until golden and firm to the touch.

8. Turn the savarin mould on to a wire tray and leave upside down until the sponge drops out.

9. To make the syrup, gently heat the sugar with the water in a small saucepan, stirring frequently until the sugar has dissolved. Add the lemon rind and boil for 5 minutes.

10. Stir in the Kirsch and remove the pan from the heat.

11. Put a plate under the savarin (still on the wire tray) and prick the savarin all over with a fork. Pour the syrup evenly over the top. Spoon it over again until the savarin has soaked up all the syrup.

12. Fill the centre of the savarin with fruit, sugar to taste and cream. If preferred, whip the cream and pipe on.

Roulade au Chocolat

The texture of this dessert is like a mousse rather than a sponge and it cracks on rolling.

Serves 6–8
175 g (6 oz) plain chocolate
3 tablespoons hot water
5 eggs, separated
175 g (6 oz) caster sugar
sifted icing sugar, for dredging
450 ml (¾ pint) double or
  whipping cream, whipped
chocolate caraque (curls), to
  decorate (optional)

Preparation time: 25 minutes, plus cooling and standing overnight
Cooking time: 20–25 minutes
Oven: 180°C, 350°F, Gas Mark 4

1. Grease and line a 38 × 23 cm (15 × 9 inch) Swiss roll tin.

2. Gently warm the chocolate and water together until melted and smooth.

3. Whisk the egg yolks and sugar together until thick and pale, about 10 minutes, then stir in the chocolate mixture until evenly blended.

4. Whisk the egg whites until stiff and fold into the chocolate mixture. Pour into the prepared tin and bake in a preheated oven for 15–20 minutes until just firm.

5. Cover with a sheet of greaseproof paper and a damp tea towel and leave until completely cold, preferably overnight.

6. Turn out on to a large piece of greaseproof paper dusted with icing sugar. Remove the lining paper, spread with half the cream and roll up like a Swiss roll.

7. Place on a serving plate and pipe with the remaining cream. Decorate with chocolate caraque, if liked.

From the top. Savarin aux fruits en Kirsch, Roulade au chocolat

DESSERT CAKES

Sophisticated Sachertorte and wickedly rich Devil's food cake are two of the all-time great chocolate cakes, while in Croquembouche a pyramid of cream-filled profiteroles is encased in a web of spun sugar.

Sachertorte

Sachertorte was the invention of Franz Sacher, who owned a hotel in Vienna in the 1880s. For a long time the cake was the exclusive speciality of the hotel, the recipe being a closely guarded secret.

Serves 6–8
150 g (5 oz) plain dessert chocolate, broken into pieces
100 g (4 oz) butter
150 g (5 oz) caster sugar
4 eggs, separated
75 g (3 oz) plain flour, sifted
1/2 teaspoon baking powder
100 g (4 oz) apricot jam, sieved
Icing:
175 g (6 oz) plain dessert chocolate, broken into pieces
175 ml (6 fl oz) water
15 g (1/2 oz) butter
100 g (4 oz) sugar
25 g (1 oz) milk chocolate, melted

Preparation time: 1 hour
Cooking time: 1 hour 20 minutes
Oven: 160°C, 325°F, Gas Mark 3

1. Melt the chocolate in a microwave oven or in a bowl set over gently simmering water, then allow to cool slightly.

2. In a mixing bowl, cream the butter with the sugar until light and fluffy, then beat in the chocolate. Gradually beat in the egg yolks one at a time.

3. Whisk the egg whites until they form stiff peaks and fold into the mixture, alternately with the flour and baking powder.

4. Pour the mixture into a greased and floured 22 cm (8½ inch) springform tin and bake in the centre of a preheated oven for 1 hour, or until risen, firm to the touch and a skewer inserted into the centre comes out clean. Turn out on to a wire rack and leave to cool completely, then spread the top and sides of the cake with the apricot jam. Stand on a thin cakeboard to ice.

5. Make the icing: melt the chocolate with 2 tablespoons water in a bowl set over gently simmering water. Stir in the butter until smooth.

6. Boil the remaining water with the sugar to a temperature of 104°C, 221°F – the thread stage. Pour the sugar syrup over the melted chocolate, stirring with a wooden spoon until the icing is of a consistency that will coat the back of the spoon. Allow to cool very slightly, then pour over the cake, to coat the top and sides evenly, and allow to cool and set at room temperature.

7. Put the melted milk chocolate into a paper icing bag; cut off the tip and use to pipe the word 'Sacher' on top of the cake.

Strawberry Shortcake

The classic American dessert. In some versions the shortcake layers are lavishly buttered, before being covered with cream and strawberries.

Serves 6–8
225 g (8 oz) plain flour
3 teaspoons baking powder
1/2 teaspoon salt
50 g (2 oz) caster sugar
50 g (2 oz) butter or margarine
150 ml (1/4 pint) milk (approximately)
350 g (12 oz) ripe strawberries, hulled
300 ml (1/2 pint) whipping cream, whipped with 1 teaspoon caster sugar (optional)

Preparation time: about 15 minutes
Cooking time: 10–12 minutes
Oven: 225°C, 425°F, Gas Mark 7

1. Sift the flour, baking powder and salt together and stir in the sugar. Cut in the fat with a pastry blender or round-bladed knife.

2. Stir in just enough milk to make a soft dough. On a lightly floured board, pat – do not roll – the dough out to a 30 cm (12 inch) wide oblong. Cut out two 15 cm (6 inch) rounds.

3. Lay the pastry rounds on a lightly greased baking sheet and bake in a preheated oven for about 10 minutes, until risen and brown.

4. Reserve 12 of the best berries for the top of the shortcake. Slice the remaining berries. Spread some of the whipped cream on one shortcake layer and cover with the sliced berries. Add a little more cream and then place on the second shortcake layer. Pipe the remaining cream on top of the shortcake and round the sides. Decorate with the reserved berries.

From the top: Strawberry shortcake, Sachertorte

Gâteau St Honoré

This gâteau is named after the patron saint of pastry cooks and bakers. The pastry base and the choux ring and buns can be made in advance (see page 278 for detailed instructions on making choux paste) but the gâteau must be eaten the same day it is filled.

Serves 8
Pastry base:
100 g (4 oz) plain flour
pinch of salt
50 g (2 oz) butter
25 g (1 oz) vanilla sugar
1 egg yolk
Choux paste:
50 g (2 oz) butter
150 ml (¼ pint) water
65 g (2½ oz) plain flour
pinch of salt
2 eggs, beaten
Filling:
450 ml (¾ pint) double or
  whipping cream, whipped
Glaze:
225 g (8 oz) sugar
150 ml (¼ pint) water
Crème St Honoré:
300 ml (½ pint) milk
1 vanilla pod
1 egg and 1 egg yolk
50 g (2 oz) caster sugar
20 g (¾ oz) plain flour
15 g (½ oz) cornflour
15 g (½ oz) butter
2 egg whites, stiffly beaten
To decorate:
glacé fruit
angelica

Preparation time: 1 hour plus chilling, cooling and infusing
Cooking time: 1½ hours
Oven: Base: 180°C, 350°F, Gas Mark 4. Choux paste: 230°C, 450°F, Gas Mark 8 then 190°C, 375°F, Gas Mark 5

1. Make the pastry base: sift the flour with the salt on to a work surface. Make a well in the centre, add the butter and sugar and work together with the fingertips of one hand.

2. Add the egg yolk and mix to a soft dough with the heel of one hand. Wrap in clingfilm and chill for 30 minutes.

3. Roll out the dough to a 21 cm (8½ inch) round. Place on a baking sheet, prick with a fork and crimp the edge with the fingers. Bake for about 20 minutes in a preheated oven, until light golden. Cool on the baking sheet until beginning to firm, then transfer carefully to a wire rack and leave to cool completely.

4. Meanwhile, place the butter and water for the choux paste in a saucepan and melt over low heat. Sift the flour with the salt on to a sheet of greaseproof paper.

5. Bring the butter and water mixture in the pan to the boil, remove from the heat and tip the flour quickly into the pan. Beat with a wooden spoon until the mixture forms a paste and leaves the sides of the pan clean. (Take care not to overbeat or the mixture will become oily.) Allow to cool until tepid.

6. Gradually add the eggs, beating hard between each addition until the paste is glossy and of a smooth piping consistency.

7. Grease and flour two baking sheets. Press the rim of a 21 cm (8½ inch) flan ring on one of the baking sheets, to make an imprint. Remove the ring.

8. Spoon the choux paste into a piping bag fitted with a large plain nozzle. Using the floured ring as a guide, pipe two-thirds of the paste in a circle on the baking sheet.

9. With the remaining choux, pipe out 12 small buns on to the second baking sheet. Bake the buns and the ring in a preheated oven for 15 minutes, then reduce the oven and bake for a further 20 minutes, or until puffed and golden.

10. Pierce the bases of the buns and the ring to release the steam and cool on a wire rack. Split the choux ring when cold and use a teaspoon to scoop out any soggy or uncooked pastry.

11. Meanwhile, place the milk and vanilla pod for the Crème St Honoré in a saucepan and bring just to the boil. Remove from heat and leave to infuse for 30 minutes, then discard the vanilla pod.

12. To make the glaze, dissolve the sugar with the water over gentle heat, then bring to the boil and boil rapidly to 127°C, 260°F or until a caramel colour. Using tongs, dip the tops and sides of the buns into the syrup and leave on a rack to harden.

13. Place the pastry base on a serving plate, position the choux ring base on top and pipe whipped cream into the base. Replace the top of the choux ring and arrange the glazed buns on top of the ring, dipping your fingers in iced water so that the syrup does not stick.

14. To make the Crème St Honoré, cream the egg and yolk, sugar, flour and cornflour together. Reheat the vanilla-flavoured milk and pour on to the mixture. Mix well, then return to the pan and bring to the boil, stirring continuously, until the mixture thickens. Boil gently for 2–3 minutes, then

stir in the butter until melted. Allow to cool, then fold in the egg whites and spoon into the centre of the pastry ring.

15. Decorate with small glacé fruits and angelica.

Croquembouche

This pyramid of choux buns is often served at an Italian wedding. The buns are filled with a delicious liqueur-flavoured cream and the whole edifice is swathed in spun sugar. See page 278 for detailed information on choux pastry.

Serves 20
Choux pastry:
100 g (4 oz) butter
300 ml (½ pint) water
150 g (5 oz) plain flour, sifted
pinch of salt
4 eggs, beaten
Filling:
450 ml (¾ pint) double cream
3 tablespoons orange liqueur
3 tablespoons icing sugar, sifted
Spun sugar:
350 g (12 oz) sugar
150 ml (¼ pint) water
5 teaspoons liquid glucose
Preparation time: about 40 minutes, plus spinning of sugar
Cooking time: about 1 hour
Oven: 220°C, 425°F, Gas Mark 7

1. For the choux paste: melt the butter in a saucepan, add the water and bring to the boil.

2. Add the flour and salt all at once and beat well until the mixture forms a smooth paste and leaves the sides of the pan clean. Remove from the heat.

3. Spread the paste out over the base of the pan and leave to cool until lukewarm.

4. Gradually beat in the eggs until the mixture is smooth and glossy and gives a piping consistency. A hand-held electric mixer is ideal for this task.

5. Spoon the choux paste into a piping bag with a plain 2 cm (¾ inch) nozzle. Pipe the mixture into small buns on greased baking sheets, keeping them well apart.

6. Place in a preheated oven and bake for about 20–25 minutes or until well-risen, golden brown and firm to the touch. Pierce each bun once to allow the steam to escape, return to the oven and bake for a further 2 minutes. Cool on a wire tray.

7. Whip the cream with the liqueur until stiff, then stir in the sugar. Use to fill the choux buns. A piping bag fitted with a 5 mm (¼ inch) plain nozzle makes filling the buns easier than splitting and filling them; you can simply insert the nozzle in the steam escape hole.

8. Put half the spun sugar ingredients into a heavy-based saucepan and heat gently until dissolved. Bring to the boil and boil rapidly until a temperature of 154°C, 312°F is reached on a sugar thermometer. Remove from the heat immediately.

9. Arrange a layer of choux buns on a silver board or dish attaching them with a little sugar syrup. Then gradually build up the pyramid by dipping the base of each choux bun into the syrup so it will stick to the previous layer of buns. Continue until all the buns are used.

10. Using the remaining spun sugar ingredients, heat as before to the same temperature. Remove the pan from the heat and dip 2 forks into the syrup. Pick up a small amount and wind it round and round the pyramid of buns so the sugar pulls into thin threads which stick to the buns. Repeat until all the syrup is used and a faint haze of spun sugar hangs all over the pyramid. If there is not enough spun sugar, then make up another half quantity and repeat the process. Serve as soon as possible.

Devil's Food Cake

This favourite American cake has a lovely rich moist texture. It is traditionally filled and covered with a soft chocolate butter icing. It is also sometimes covered with white frosting.

Serves 8
5 tablespoons cocoa powder
1 egg yolk
300 ml (½ pint) milk
100 g (4 oz) butter, softened
350 g (12 oz) caster sugar
1 teaspoon vanilla essence
2 eggs
250 g (9 oz) flour, sifted
2 teaspoons baking powder
¼ teaspoon bicarbonate of soda
½ teaspoon salt
Chocolate butter icing:
350 g (12 oz) plain dessert chocolate, broken into pieces
175 g (6 oz) unsalted butter, softened
350 g (12 oz) icing sugar, sifted
3 egg yolks

Preparation time: 40 minutes, plus cooling
Cooking time: 45 minutes
Oven: 180°C, 350°F, Gas Mark 4

1. In a double boiler mix the cocoa smoothly with the egg yolk and half the milk. Cook gently, stirring, until smooth and thickened. Allow to cool.

2. In a mixing bowl, cream the butter with the sugar until light and fluffy. Add the vanilla essence, then the eggs one at a time, beating well after each addition. Beat in the cocoa mixture.

3. Sift the flour with the baking powder, soda and salt and fold into the creamed mixture, alternately with the remaining milk.

4. Turn the cake mixture into two greased and lined 23 cm (9 inch) sandwich tins, dividing it equally between them. Smooth the tops and bake for 30 minutes, or until risen and firm to the touch.

5. Remove from the oven and cool in the tins for 5 minutes, then turn out on to a wire rack and leave to cool completely.

6. To make the icing, melt the chocolate in a bowl set over gently simmering water. In a mixing bowl, cream the butter with the icing sugar until light and fluffy. Beat in the egg yolks, then the melted chocolate. Use half the icing to sandwich the cakes together and swirl the remainder over the whole cake. Leave to set.

Variation

This cake can also be covered with a white butter cream or glacé icing, or the top can simply be dusted with icing sugar.

Left to right: Devil's food cake, Croquembouche

PASTRY

Pastry-making is one of the skills which every cook should master. To have a 'light hand with pastry' has always been considered a great accomplishment and it can be achieved, with practice, if you follow the detailed instructions.

Pastry-making is an art and to be a successful pastrycook, it is essential to learn the basic techniques. There are no secrets to guarantee instant success, but with a little care, and plenty of practice, it can be a quick and simple process.

In this section we cover the simpler pastries which everyone should be able to tackle. See pages 266–293 for Hot-Water Crust, Strudel and the more difficult French pastries

Basic rules

Plain flour is used for all pastries, except suet crust. Wholewheat flour can be used for most pastries but extra water will be needed to bind, and the pastry will be heavier.

Self-raising flour *can* be used, but the pastry will be sponge-like in texture when baked. The fats used should be butter for flavour or hard margarine. Lard can be used in some pastries to give a short, crisp texture when baked. If using lard, use a quarter or one third of the total fat content. Choose hard fats as they are easier to rub in – avoid soft spreading margarines and vegetable fats.

Keep everything cool Try to make the pastry in the morning when the kitchen is cool. It should be made as quickly as possible, handled with speed and agility. The fats should be cold when used and chilled water will help to keep the pastry cold while working with it. When rubbing the fat into the flour, always use only the

Meat Pie

Steak and Kidney Pudding

Eccles Cakes

Lattice-Topped Jam Tart

Bakewell Tart

Sausage Rolls

finger tips, as this is the coolest part of the hand. (If you have 'hot' hands, try running them under a cold tap to cool down before starting.)

Rubbing or cutting in the fat can be done with two round-bladed knives used to cut the fat into small pieces in opposite directions, shaking the bowl from time to time to bring the larger lumps to the surface. Finish the rubbing in using the fingertips. A food processor or food mixer will give the same results in seconds.

Binding The amount of water added to the pastry will vary each time as some flours will absorb more water than others. But make sure that enough water is added, as too dry a mixture will make the pastry crumbly and impossible to handle, and too wet a mixture will make a tough, hard result to eat. Add the water a little at a time, stirring it quickly into the flour with a round-bladed knife. Ensure that at least two-thirds of the given liquid is added.

The pastry is moist enough when it will gather together to form a soft ball without much kneading. If the pastry is dry and crumbly, then add a drop more water to bind it together. Turn the dough out of the bowl on to a lightly floured work surface and knead quickly until smooth, handling the pastry as little as possible. Wrap in clingfilm and chill for 10–15 minutes before using – this allows the pastry to firm up and relax before being used, and

makes rolling easier.

Rolling out

Roll out carefully using light even pressure with both hands on the rolling pin – light flowing movements are better than heavy abrupt actions. Always roll away from yourself. Keep the pastry in a round shape and lift and turn it often to make sure that it does not stick to the work surface and that it keeps its shape. Sprinkle with a little flour to prevent it sticking to the table or rolling pin, but do not turn the pastry over, as this will incorporate too much flour into the pastry. Before baking, the pastry should be lightly chilled in its finished shape to prevent excessive shrinkage.

To bake

It is essential to bake the pastry in a preheated oven at a fairly high temperature to ensure quick rising and 'set' before it has a chance to shrink and collapse.

Proportions If a recipe calls for 225 g (8 oz) pastry, this means 225 g (8 oz) flour and not all the ingredients added together. Any pastry recipe can be doubled or halved, but always keep the proportions the same in each case. Try to master shortcrust pastry before attempting any others.

Lining a flan tin

1. Choose a flan tin with a loose bottom, or a flan ring used on a baking sheet. China flan dishes do not conduct the heat quickly enough.

2. Roll the pastry out thinly, about 3 mm (⅛ inch) thick to a circle 4 cm (1½ inches) larger than the diameter of the flan tin.

3. Lift the pastry on the rolling pin and lower it into

the flan. Press it carefully into the base and sides, taking care not to stretch it at any time.

4. Trim the edges, using a rolling pin to roll the pastry level with the rim.

5. Prick the base with a fork to allow any steam to escape while cooking.

6. Chill the lined flan tin for at least 10 minutes.

Baking blind

1. The flan case is baked blind when the filling is to be cooked for only a short time or not at all.

2. Line the pastry case with greaseproof paper, foil, or a double layer of absorbent kitchen paper.

3. Weight it down with dried beans (kept specially for this purpose, they can be used indefinitely). You can also buy special ceramic or aluminium beans. Take care to put in enough beans to compensate for the filling. Push them well to the edges to support and hold up the sides.

4. Bake the pastry case in the centre of a preheated oven at 200°C, 400°F, Gas Mark 6 for about 15 minutes.

Line pastry case with paper and weigh down with beans.

5. Remove the beans and paper and bake for a further 10 minutes or until the pastry is dry and golden brown.

6. Allow to cool on a wire rack before carefully removing from the flan tin.

For perfect Pastry

■ The fats for Flaky Pastry should be at room temperature and not straight from the fridge, as this will make it easier to blend them with the flour.
■ Chill Flaky and Rough Puff Pastry between rollings, if the fats become too soft to roll.

■ Self-raising flour is used for Suet Crust to give it a light, spongy texture.
■ Do not chill Suet Crust before using, as this will make the pastry difficult to handle. It should be made quickly and rolled out and used quickly for the best results.

■ For an even lighter Suet Crust, omit 50 g (2 oz) of the measured flour and substitute the equivalent weight in fresh white breadcrumbs.
■ For Steak and Kidney Pudding make sure that you have a large enough pan to hold the basin, and allow for a

5 cm (2 inch) rising and still be able to keep the lid on tightly.
■ Make sure that the greaseproof paper on a suet crust pudding does not come in contact with the boiling water at any stage of the cooking.

Decorations for pies and flans

Knocking up pastry edges with knife blade.

Knocking up This is done to seal the edges of a pie. Hold a sharp knife blade horizontally to the cut edge and make a series of shallow cuts all the way round, while pressing down the pastry edges with the forefinger of the left hand. The finished result should look like the pages of a closed book.

This technique is also known sometimes as 'flaking' the edges.

Use back of the knife to make a scalloped pattern.

To make a scalloped pattern press a thumb or back of a decorative spoon handle around the edges at 1 cm (½ inch) intervals, drawing the back of a knife between each towards the centre of the pie. Or press the edges together with the index finger of one hand and make a pointed, crimped edge with the other thumb and index finger.

The dog-tooth edge, suitable for plate pies. Cut the edge of the pastry at 2 cm (¾ inch) intervals then fold each piece diagonally to form a triangle. Press down with the handle of a spoon, or with the tines of a fork.

The tops of pies can be decorated with any pastry trimmings. Roll out thinly and cut into small shapes with pastry cutters or try some leaf shapes or tassels.

Making pastry leaf shapes.

To make leaves cut the pastry into 2.5 cm (1 inch) strips and then diagonally across into diamond shapes. Mark with the back of a knife to indicate veins on the leaves.

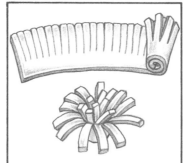

Making a pastry tassel for a pie.

To make a tassel cut a 2.5 cm (1 inch) strip, then cut three-quarters of the way through at intervals of 5 mm (¼ inch) and roll up neatly. Open out like a flower and place on the pie.

Glazing Brush the decorated pie or flan with glaze before baking, to give it a really professional look. A whole egg, beaten with a large pinch of salt, gives pastry a rich golden colour. Egg yolk, diluted with a drop of water or milk, will give a deeper glaze. For sweet pies, brush with a little milk or beaten egg white and dust with caster sugar, before baking, to give a frosted sparkly look.

Circular or leaf edging Cut a series of plain or fluted small circles of pastry, about 1–2 cm (½–¾ inch) in diameter, damp the pastry edge and lay the circles evenly all round the rim, just overlapping each other. An edging of leaves can be made in the same way. Suitable for all pastries, but flaky pastry should be cut a little larger to allow for the shrinkage which takes place during cooking.

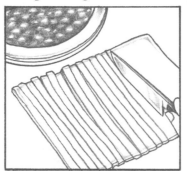

1. Cut strips long enough to cover the flan.

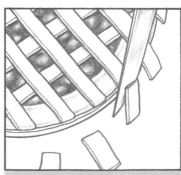

3. Trim off the edges and seal.

To make a lattice pattern for open flans cut pastry into 5–10 mm (¼–½ inch) wide strips long enough to cover the flan. Moisten the edges of the flan case with water and lay half the strips over the filling, about 2.5 cm (1 inch) apart, then lay the remaining strips diagonally across these. Trim off excess and press edges together neatly.

For a more decorative effect the strips can be twisted before being laid in position. Seal and trim as before.

The strips can also be interwoven to give a really professional effect. For this, lay the first layer of strips, then lay a strip at right angles across the centre. Lift up alternate strips of the first layer on one side and lay another strip at right angles. Replace the top strips and repeat with the other side to give the woven effect. Glaze the strips with egg white and sugar.

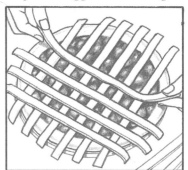

2. Place 2 layers of strips to form the lattice.

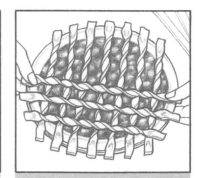

4. Twist each strip for a twisted lattice effect.

SHORTCRUST PASTRY

Shortcrust is the basic pastry used for pies, tarts and flans. It should be made with two parts flour to one part fat – the fat can be butter, lard, margarine or a combination of any two.

Ideally it should be 'short', i.e. crisp and crumbly in texture. For sweet tarts and flans use Rich Shortcrust, which has a higher proportion of fat and is enriched with egg yolk.

225 g (8 oz) plain flour
a pinch of salt
100 g (4 oz) butter
3–4 tablespoons cold water

Preparation time: 5 minutes

1. Sift the flour and salt together into a large mixing bowl.

2. Cut the butter into small cubes and mix in, then using two round-bladed knives, cut the fat into the flour in opposite directions until the pieces are very small and coated with flour.

3. Rub the butter into the flour with the fingertips until it resembles fine breadcrumbs.

4. Stir in 3 tablespoons of the water. Add the extra water if necessary, but do not allow the pastry to become too wet. Gather together into a soft pliable dough.

5. Turn out on to a lightly floured board and knead until smooth. Wrap in clingfilm and chill for 10–15 minutes before using.

Cut the butter into cubes.

Rub the butter into the flour with fingertips.

Gradually stir in the water.

Gather together to form a soft dough.

Rich Shortcrust Pastry

225 g (8 oz) plain flour
a pinch of salt
175 g (6 oz) butter, cubed
1 tablespoon caster sugar
(sweet recipes only)
1 egg yolk
1–2 tablespoons cold water

Preparation time: 5 minutes

1. Sift the flour and salt together into a large mixing bowl. Add the butter and cut into the flour with two round-bladed knives, then rub in with the fingertips until the mixture resembles fine breadcrumbs.

2. Stir in the sugar, if using. Mix the egg yolk with 1 tablespoon of the water and stir into the flour to make a soft pliable dough, adding the remaining water as needed.

3. Turn on to a floured board and knead lightly until smooth. Chill for 15 minutes before using.

Traditional Apple Pie

750 g (1½ lb) cooking apples,
peeled, cored and sliced
50 g (2 oz) caster sugar
3 tablespoons water
1 recipe quantity Shortcrust
Pastry
Glaze:
milk
caster sugar

Preparation time: 10 minutes
Cooking time: 40 minutes
Oven: 200°C, 400°F, Gas Mark 6

1. Layer the apples in a 900 ml (1½ pint) pie dish, adding the sugar halfway through. The apples should dome slightly above the dish. Add the water.

2. Roll out the pastry to 5 mm (¼ inch) thick and cut a strip long enough to lay round the edge of the pie dish. Brush the pastry with water and press the band firmly on to the edge and wet again.

3. Lift the remaining pastry on the rolling pin and lay loosely over the pie. Press on to the wet pastry band, trim off the excess with a sharp knife and decorate, if liked. Chill for 10–15 minutes.

4. Brush the top with milk and dust with caster sugar. Put the pie on a baking sheet and bake in a preheated oven for 35–40 minutes until well risen and golden brown. Serve hot or cold with whipped cream, ice cream or custard.

Variations

Add 4 or 5 whole cloves to the pie, or ¼ teaspoon ground cinnamon, or the finely grated rind of half a lemon or orange to the apple filling.

Double-Crust Meat Pie

1 recipe quantity Shortcrust
Pastry, well chilled
Filling:
2 tablespoons cooking oil
350 g (12 oz) lean minced beef
1 medium onion, peeled and
finely chopped
2 medium carrots, scraped and
coarsely grated
2 teaspoons flour
5 tablespoons water
1/2 teaspoon salt
freshly ground black pepper
a pinch of mixed herbs
beaten egg, to glaze

Preparation time: 20 minutes,
plus making pastry
Oven: 200°C, 400°F, Gas Mark 6

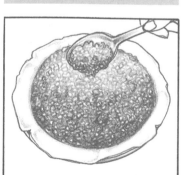

Line the pie plate without
stretching the pastry.

1. Heat the oil in a pan, add
the beef, onion and carrots
and brown gently.

2. Stir in the flour and then
the water and bring to the
boil. Season, add the herbs
and leave to cool
completely.

3. Divide the pastry in 2
portions. Roll out one piece
to about 2.5 cm (1 inch)
wider than the diameter of an
18 cm (7 inch) pie plate.

4. Line the plate, being
careful not to stretch the
pastry. Spoon on the cold
filling, doming it slightly in
the centre.

5. Roll out the remaining
pastry for the lid, allowing
about 1 cm (½ inch) beyond
the rim. Brush the edge of
the pastry base with beaten
egg, then lift the lid and lay it
carefully over the filling.
Seal the edges by pressing
together and trim off the
excess pastry with a knife.
Use the trimmings to make
leaf decorations, if liked. Cut
a slit in the centre of the lid
for the steam to escape.
Brush with beaten egg to
glaze, and chill for 10–15
minutes.

6. Bake in a preheated oven
for 30 minutes, until golden
brown. Serve hot or cold.

Spoon on the filling doming
in the middle.

Brush the edges with beaten
egg.

Bakewell Tart

1 recipe quantity Rich
Shortcrust Pastry
Filling:
40 g (1½ oz) butter
75 g (3 oz) caster sugar
finely grated rind of 1 small
lemon
1 egg, beaten
50 g (2 oz) cake crumbs
75 g (3 oz) ground almonds
1 tablespoon lemon juice
2 tablespoons strawberry jam
2 tablespoons lemon curd
15 g (½ oz) flaked almonds

Preparation time: 10 minutes,
plus making pastry
Cooking time: 35–40 minutes
Oven: 190°C, 375°F, Gas Mark 5

1. Roll out the pastry thinly and
use to line a 23 cm (9 inch) flan
tin. Trim, crimp edge neatly,
prick the base and chill.

2. Cream the butter and sugar
together with the lemon rind
until pale and fluffy. Beat in the
egg, cake crumbs, ground
almonds and lemon juice.

3. Spread the pastry case evenly
with the jam and lemon curd.
Spread the almond mixture on
top and scatter over the flaked
almonds.

4. Bake in the preheated oven
for 35–40 minutes, or until set
and golden brown.

Cheese Pastry

Use to make savoury flans.

225 g (8 oz) plain flour
a pinch of salt
a pinch of cayenne pepper
100 g (4 oz) butter
100 g (4 oz) finely grated
Cheddar cheese
1 egg yolk
1–2 tablespoons cold water

Preparation time: 30 minutes

1. Sift the flour with the
seasonings into a large bowl.
Cut the butter into small pieces
and add to the flour. Using two
round-bladed knives, cut the
butter into the flour, then rub
in with the fingertips until it
resembles fine breadcrumbs.

2. Add the grated cheese and
toss well to coat with flour and
separate the pieces.

3. Mix the egg yolk with one
tablespoon of water and stir in
to form a soft pliable dough.
Add the second tablespoon of
water, if necessary.

4. Turn out on to a lightly
floured surface and knead until
smooth. Wrap in cling film and
chill for 15–20 minutes.

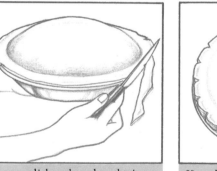

Lay on lid and seal and trim
the edges.

Knock up edges, decorate
top and glaze.

FLAKY PASTRY

This pastry has a light, flaky texture because of the way the fat is incorporated. It is similar to the classic Puff Pastry (see page 272) but it is much quicker and easier to make, though if the kitchen is warm it helps to chill the pastry between rollings. Use it for pies, meat or fish cooked 'en croûte', cream horns and pâtisserie.

225 g (8 oz) plain flour
pinch of salt
75 g (3 oz) butter
about 120 ml (4 fl oz) cold
*   water*
75 g (3 oz) lard

Preparation time: 30 minutes

1. Sift the flour and salt together in a mixing bowl. Cut half the butter into small cubes and rub into the flour until it resembles fine breadcrumbs.

2. Mix to a soft pliable dough with the water. Turn on to a lightly floured surface and knead until smooth.

3. Roll out the pastry to an oblong 10 × 30 cm (4 × 12 inches) and mark into 3 sections. Cut half the lard into small cubes and cover the top two-thirds of the pastry with these. Fold the bottom third over the centre and the top third over the

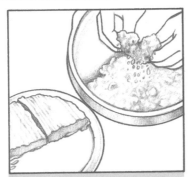

Rub in half the butter with fingertips.

Roll out the dough to a rectangle.

Cover two-thirds of the pastry with cubes of lard.

middle section and press the open ends together to seal.

4. Give the pastry a quarter turn and roll out again. Repeat twice more, using the second half of the butter and then the remaining lard in the same way. Roll again and fold as before, but without any fat. Chill for 10–15 minutes. Roll out and fold again if still streaky. Use as required.

Fold up to make a parcel.

Press the edges with rolling pin to seal.

Eccles Cakes

1 recipe quantity Flaky Pastry,
*   well chilled*
Filling:
25 g (1 oz) butter
25 g (1 oz) soft brown sugar
25 g (1 oz) chopped mixed peel
100 g (4 oz) currants, washed
a pinch of ground nutmeg
a pinch of ground mixed spice
Glaze:
beaten egg white
caster sugar

Preparation time: 10 minutes
Cooking time: 10–15 minutes
Oven: 220°C, 425°F, Gas Mark 7

1. Melt the butter in a pan, remove from the heat and add the sugar, mixed peel, currants and spices. Allow to cool.

2. Roll out the pastry thinly, and cut into rounds using a saucer as a guide for shape and size.

3. Put a tablespoon of filling in the centre of each round. Dampen the edges and gather together, like a bag, pressing the edges well together.

4. Turn over and, keeping their shape, gently flatten with a rolling pin, until the currants begin to show.

5. Make 3 small cuts across the top of each cake. Brush with beaten egg white, then dust with caster sugar.

6. Place on a baking sheet and bake in the preheated oven for 10–15 minutes until well puffed and golden brown.

SUET CRUST PASTRY

This is made by the same method as shortcrust, with twice as much flour as fat. Suet is the fat which surrounds ox kidney, and is easily available, ready shredded. Suet crust should be used immediately, once it is made. It can be baked or steamed and is used to make traditional Steak and Kidney Pudding and sweet puddings such as Jam Roly Poly.

350 g (12 oz) self-raising flour
pinch of salt
175 g (6 oz) shredded suet
175 ml (6 fl oz) cold water

1. Sift the flour and salt into a bowl. Stir in the suet until coated evenly.

2. Stir in the water with a knife to make a soft pliable dough. Knead on a floured surface until smooth, then roll out and use at once. (This pastry does not need to rest.)

Stir the suet into the flour until coated

Stir in the water with a knife

Knead until smooth. Roll out and use at once

Steak and Kidney Pudding

1 recipe quantity Suet Crust
Pastry
Filling:
675 g (1½ lb) stewing steak cut into 5 mm (¼ inch) cubes
225 g (8 oz) ox kidney cut into 5 mm (¼ inch) cubes
4 tablespoons seasoned flour
1 small onion, peeled and finely chopped
2 teaspoons chopped mixed herbs
1 teaspoon salt
freshly ground black pepper

Preparation time: 15 minutes, plus making pastry
Cooking time: 3–4 hours

1. Have ready a pan, large enough to hold a 1.7 litre (3 pint) pudding basin. Fill half-full with water and bring slowly to the boil.

2. Grease the basin well. Cut a third off the pastry and reserve for the lid. Roll the remaining piece into a 1 cm (½ inch) thick round, large enough to line the basin. Flour the round lightly, fold in four and lift into the basin, opening it up to press evenly over the base and sides.

3. Toss the steak and kidney in the seasoned flour, shake off excess flour, then put into the basin. Add the herbs, onion, salt and pepper and pour in enough cold water to fill the basin two-thirds full.

4. Roll out the remaining pastry to a round large enough to cover the pudding easily. Wet the edges and press the lid on firmly.

5. Cut a piece of greaseproof paper about 7.5 cm (3 inches) larger all round than the lid. Make a 5 cm (2 inch) pleat in the centre, to allow for rising, grease the paper lightly and lay over the pudding. Tie securely with string and trim off excess paper, about 2.5 cm (1 inch) from the string.

6. Stand the pudding in the pan of boiling water (the water should come three-quarters of the way up the sides) and cover with a lid. Boil steadily for 3–4 hours. Top up with boiling water when necessary. The pudding is cooked when the pastry is well puffed and dry-looking and the meat is tender. (Test by pressing a sharp skewer through the lid.)

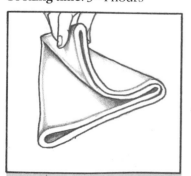
Fold the round of pastry into four.

Lift the folded pastry into the basin.

Lay the greaseproof over the lid.

Tie the paper securely with string.

ROUGH PUFF PASTRY

Rough Puff is a rich pastry with a high proportion of fat. The fat is rolled, not rubbed into the dough, to give a flaky texture. It is the quickest of the flaky pastries to make but is not so light as true flaky or puff pastry (see page 263 and page 272). It is best served hot and reheats successfully. It also freezes very well.

225 g (8 oz) plain flour
a pinch of salt
175 g (6 oz) butter
about 150 ml (¼ pint) cold
water

1. Sift the flour and salt together into a large bowl, cut the butter into 1 cm (½ inch) cubes and toss in the flour.

2. Stir in the water quickly, using a round-bladed knife, to a soft pliable dough. Turn on to a lightly floured surface and roll lightly and evenly into an oblong about 10 × 30 cm (4 × 12 inches).

3. Mark into three even sections, fold one end over the middle and the opposite end over that, to make an open-ended parcel. Seal the edges, turn so the fold is at the right, and roll and fold three times more. Chill before use.

Toss the butter cubes in the flour

Stir in the water with a round-bladed knife

Sausage Rolls

1 recipe quantity Rough Puff
Pastry
Filling:
450 g (1 lb) pork sausagemeat
1 small onion, peeled and
finely chopped
1 teaspoon chopped mixed
herbs
freshly ground black pepper
Glaze:
1 egg, beaten with salt

Preparation time: 20 minutes
Cooking time: 25 minutes
Oven: 220°C, 425°F, Gas Mark 7

1. Mix the sausagemeat thoroughly with the onion, herbs and seasoning.

2. Roll out the pastry to a large rectangle, about 5 mm (¼ inch) thick.

3. Place a roll of sausagemeat along one edge of the pastry, leaving about 5 cm (2 inches) of pastry for turnover. Brush the edge with beaten egg and fold the pastry over the sausagemeat. Press down well and cut off the long sausage-filled roll with a knife.

4. Continue until all the sausagemeat is used. Brush the rolls with beaten egg, cut into 5 cm (2 inch) lengths and place on a baking sheet. Cut a steam vent in the top of each roll and bake in the preheated oven for 20–25 minutes until puffed and golden brown. Remove and cool on a wire rack.

Roll out lightly to a rectangle

Make three sections and fold up to make a parcel

How to prepare vol-au-vent cases

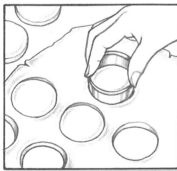
1. Roll out Flaky or Rough Puff Pastry 1 cm (½ inch) thick. Cut out rounds with a 6 cm (2½ inch) cutter and place on a damp baking sheet. Glaze with beaten egg.

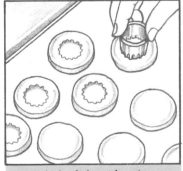
2. Mark the lids with a 4 cm (1½ inch) cutter, cutting only half-way through the rounds.

3. Bake in a hot oven (230°C, 350°F, Gas Mark 8). Carefully remove the lids and cool on a wire rack.

CONTINENTAL PASTRY

■

The French are the finest pastry-cooks in the world and this section shows why.
Step-by-step instructions and cook's tips ensure perfect results every time, whether
is is profiteroles, cream horns, éclairs or croissants. The section also includes hot-
water crust and strudel pastry, as well as cooking en croûte.

Basic rules

In French pastry-making, as in all pastry-making, the basic rules are much the same as those explained previously on pages 258–259.

■ Use plain flour (except in suet pastry and some specialist ones).

■ Keep everything cool, including work surfaces, ingredients, implements, hands etc.

■ Work quickly.

■ Use the fingertips only for working the soft ingredients, or use a pastry cutter. The mixture should never be allowed to come up into the palms of the hand.

■ Use iced water for mixing.

■ Add liquid gradually, because although more can be added, it cannot be taken away (and too much liquid gives a hard, tough pastry).

■ Always wrap pastry in cling-film, polythene or foil and chill for at least 20 minutes before rolling out – this gives time for the pastry to relax and firm up before rolling out.

Traditional French pastries

Basic pastries such as Shortcrust have been explained already but in this section many of the classic French pastries are covered. Pâte Brisée (the richer French version of shortcrust) and Pâte Sucrée (a sweet tart pastry for which there is no direct British equivalent) are pastries made by a method similar to a basic shortcrust. They are a granular combination of plain flour, fat (usually butter), and water or egg: sugar is an essential of Sucrée, optional in Brisée (which can be used for both savoury and sweet dishes). Both require that everything is cool – work surfaces, ingredients, implements and hands – and both need the lightest of touches, in the making and the rolling.

Pâte Feuilletée or puff pastry is the richest of the pastries that flake up in layers, as well as being the most complicated and lengthy to make. Made with equal proportions of butter and flour it too needs to be as cool as possible to achieve its buttery texture and lightness. The butter is kept whole and layered into the dough rather than broken down with the flour into the granular consistency of Pâtes Brisée and Sucrée. It is repeatedly folded, rolled and chilled until the butter is distributed in thin layers throughout the dough; it is this plus the sealing at the edges to trap the air in, that causes the expansion of steam and the pastry to rise into its spectacular layers (if the pastry is folded in three and rolled out six times, there will be over 700).

The 'rules' for Choux pastry are quite different. Heat rather than coolness is the first essential, for the fat is melted first into the water before the other ingredients are added. It is not rolled out but spooned or piped into the shapes characteristic of choux – the profiterole puff, gougère circle or éclair length. Choux has a high water content which is turned to steam during cooking and this forces the paste up and out until it is set by the heat of the oven.

Other pastries

The 'rules' for Strudel pastry are quite different again. The basic dough actually likes being handled heavily: it is thoroughly kneaded like a bread dough which allows the gluten in the (strong) flour to expand thus making the dough more elastic. Like filo pastry, its Middle Eastern counterpart, Strudel is then rolled out to an ethereal thinness and baked to a delicate crispness – either wrapped around a filling as in the classic strudels of Austria, or in the layers of the Greek Baklava.

Hot water crust pastry is rather the odd man out among this selection of Continental pastries, as it seems to be quintessentially British, its most famous manifestation being in the English pork pie. It is like choux pastry in that the fat is heated with the water before being mixed with the flour. It is a hard pastry because of its high proportion of water, which is why it's so often used to encase heavier mixtures like meat. Because it's made with lard, it is generally less tasty than the pastries made with a proportion of butter – and indeed some old recipes for meat pies recommended discarding the pastry uneaten once it had performed its duty as a baking container.

The ingredients

■ The flour used in pastry making should always be sifted to ensure that there are no lumps, and to incorporate air to make the pastry lighter. It should be plain flour, occasionally, strong plain flour. Wholemeal flour can be used for some pastries. It makes a deliciously nutty crust but, as it is more absorbent than plain, it requires more liquid which makes it harder. Equal proportions of wholemeal and plain flour work well.

■ It is the fat in pastry which dictates its eventual flavour. Butter is the tastiest, followed by hard margarine. Lard and other white fats give good texture but a pastry that lacks flavour: a combination of lard and butter produces a better result.

■ The less liquid used in pastry the better, in general. Some richer pastries need none at all, the butter and/or egg content allowing the flour to form a kneadable dough without any further liquid addition.

PÂTE BRISÉE

This is the French name for the traditional pastry, widely used for sweet and savoury dishes, which is similar in proportions to the English shortcrust or rich shortcrust pastry (see page 261). It is made the French way, which is on a board or marble slab, not in a bowl.

This pastry is made by using proportions of half fat to flour, or for a richer pastry three quarters fat to flour. For the best flavour use butter, but a good firm margarine can be used wholly or in conjunction with the butter. Many people prefer to use a mixture of half butter or margarine and half lard or other type of white fat. This combination gives the better texture.

---

225 g (8 oz) plain flour
50 g (2 oz) butter or
    margarine, diced
50 g (2 oz) lard or white fat,
    diced
1 egg and 1 tablespoon water
    or 1 egg yolk and 2
    tablespoons water
good pinch of salt
25 g (1 oz) sugar (optional for
    sweet dishes only)

Preparation time: about 10 minutes
Oven: 200°C, 400°F, Gas Mark 6

For perfect Pâte Brisée

■ Keep everything cool.
■ Use fat which is cool and firm but not too hard.
■ Use iced water or the coldest possible. A touch of lemon juice will give a good flavour.
■ Use as little water as possible. Although damper pastry is easier to handle, not being so crumbly, it will be tough when cooked.
■ Roll out on a cold surface – marble is best.
■ Wrap pastry and allow to relax in the refrigerator before rolling out.
■ Handle the pastry as little as possible.
■ Always roll the pastry in one direction only – straight ahead of you. Turn the pastry round as you roll, don't change the direction of rolling.
■ Never overstretch the pastry, it will only shrink back as it cooks.

1. Sift the flour on to a pastry board. Shape into a ring about 15 cm (6 inches) in diameter. Place the diced fats in the centre of the ring with the egg or yolk and water, the salt and the sugar if used.

3. With a palette knife bring the flour in over the wet ingredients and cut in very lightly.

2. With the fingertips of one hand only work the butter, egg, water, sugar (if used) and salt mixture until the butter is smooth and pliable.

4. As soon as the mixture is well coated use the heel of the hand to bring the pastry together, squeezing it firmly, letting go straight away and turning over as it falls.

5. Continue to work in this way until the pastry comes together adding a little more water if it seems very dry. Knead very lightly until smooth.

6. Wrap in foil or clingfilm and chill for at least 20 minutes. The pastry is then ready to use.

How much pastry to use

The following amounts of pastry are sufficient to line the different sizes of flan tins or dishes given below.
100 g (4 oz) flour etc. fits a
    15 cm (6 inch) flan tin.
150 g (5 oz) flour etc. fits an
    18 cm (7 inch) flan tin.
175 g (6 oz) flour etc. fits a
    23 cm (9 inch) flan tin.
225 g (8 oz) flour etc. fits a
    25 cm (10 inch) flan tin.

Rolling out the pastry

Turn the chilled pastry on to a very lightly floured surface and press lightly into a round or oval with the fingers. Use a lightly floured rolling pin to roll out the pastry in short sharp strokes away from you. Turn the pastry round carefully as you go, but do not alter the angle of rolling. Take care not to use too much extra flour when rolling or it will spoil the texture of the pastry.

Variations

Herb For savoury pies, add 1½–2 level teaspoons dried mixed herbs or any one herb to the flour.
Spicy For sweet pies and flans add 1 level teaspoon ground cinnamon or mixed spice to the flour.

Pear Tart

See page 260 for instructions on how to make decorative edges for pies and tarts.

Serves 6
1 recipe quantity Pâte Brisée, made with ½ level teaspoon ground cinnamon sifted with the flour
Filling:
300 ml (½ pint) water or water and white wine
175 g (6 oz) sugar
750 g (1½ lb) pears (firm dessert or cooking pears)
40 g (1½ oz) shelled walnuts, finely chopped
3–4 tablespoons thick double or clotted cream
egg white or milk to glaze
a little caster sugar for dusting

Preparation time: about 30 minutes, plus resting the pastry
Cooking time: about 40 minutes
Oven: 220°C, 425°F, Gas Mark 7

1. Make up the pastry, divide into one third and two thirds, wrap and leave to rest in the refrigerator for 30 minutes.

2. Put the water or wine and water and sugar into a saucepan and heat gently until dissolved. Peel, core and thickly slice the pears and poach in the syrup for 5 minutes or until tender. Drain and leave to cool.

3. Roll out the larger piece of the pastry and use to line a shallow pie tin or dish forming a good lip on the top edge. Spoon in the pears, add 2 tablespoons of the syrup and sprinkle with the nuts.

4. Roll out the remaining pastry for a lid that will just fit the tin. Cut out a 7.5 cm (3 inch) circle from the centre. Damp the edges of pastry with water and position over the pears. Press the edges together and crimp or flute to make a decorative edge.

5. Mark the surface of the pastry into a lattice design with the point of a sharp knife. Glaze with egg white and dust with caster sugar.

6. Cook the tart in a preheated oven for 35–40 minutes or until the top is well browned and the pastry is cooked through.

7. Leave to cool until just warm, then pour the cream into the flan through the central hole. If not serving straight away leave to go cold. When ready to serve, warm the tart through then pour cream into the flan through the central hole and serve immediately.

Tarte à l'Oignon

Alsace and Lorraine are the home of the quiche – an open-faced tart with a savoury filling set in an egg custard. This onion tart is one of the classics, with onions cooked in butter until they are meltingly soft and sweet. The tart can be served hot or cold.
See page 270 on how to line a flan tin.

Serves 6
1 recipe quantity Pâte Brisée
Filling:
50 g (2 oz) butter or margarine
750 g (1½ lb) onions, peeled and thinly sliced
3 eggs
85 ml (3 fl oz) milk
275 ml (9 fl oz) single cream
salt
freshly ground black pepper
pinch of freshly grated nutmeg
freshly chopped parsley, to garnish

Preparation time: about 30 minutes, plus chilling
Cooking time: about 50 minutes
Oven: 200°C, 400°F, Gas Mark 6

1. Melt the butter in a pan, add the onions and cook gently without colouring in a covered pan for about 20 minutes or until very soft, stirring from time to time. Leave to cool.

2. Roll out the pastry and use to line a 25 cm (10 inch) flan dish or a flan ring placed on a baking sheet. Prick the base and chill for 20–30 minutes.

3. Whisk the eggs, milk, cream, salt, pepper and nutmeg together.

4. Arrange the onions evenly in the bottom of the flan case and pour the custard on top.

5. Cook in a preheated oven for about 30 minutes or until the filling is golden brown and set. Remove the flan ring if serving straight away; if to be served cold, cool in the tin.

6. Sprinkle the top of the tart generously with parsley before serving.

Variations

There are many possible variations on this classic quiche.
Spinach Replace the onions with 275 g (10 oz) spinach, cooked with 2 tablespoons chopped shallots for 3 minutes and seasoned with salt, pepper and nutmeg. Stir into the custard and cook as above.
Mushroom Replace the onion with 450 g (1 lb) mushrooms sautéed in butter and 1 tablespoon lemon juice for 8 minutes until the liquid has evaporated. Stir into the custard, sprinkle with Gruyère cheese and bake as above.
Crab or Shrimp Replace the onions with 125 g (5 oz) cooked fresh or tinned crab, or diced cooked shrimps, cooked in the butter with 1 tablespoon dry white vermouth. Stir into the custard with 1 tablespoon tomato purée and bake as above.

PÂTE SUCRÉE

This is the famous French pastry which is crisp and thin when baked. It is used for the most delicate of sweet tarts and flans of Continental flavour. The pastry is made in the French way where only the fingertips should be used in mixing, and it is made on a board not in a bowl. It is very soft when made and must be wrapped and allowed to chill thoroughly for at least an hour after making or it will be difficult to roll out. This pastry should be rolled out very thinly.

Basic rules

■ It must be rolled thinly to achieve the crispness associated with this pastry. If this proves difficult, roll it between two sheets of non-stick baking paper or clingfilm.
■ Do not add a lot more flour to the surface or rolling pin as this will ruin the balance of ingredients.
■ Always use plain flour, butter and caster sugar. For this pastry the fat should be moderately soft, definitely not hard but neither too soft; it is important to use it at the correct temperature to achieve the necessary consistency.
■ Vanilla sugar, which is caster sugar with a vanilla pod stored in it, gives a good flavour to the pastry; a drop or two of vanilla essence may be added instead, but is not absolutely necessary.
■ Some recipes use icing sugar, but the pastry can turn out rather soft and is not suitable for lining into flans – too short in texture.

100 g (4 oz) plain flour
pinch of salt
50 g (2 oz) caster sugar
50 g (2 oz) butter (at cool room temperature)
2 egg yolks
2 drops vanilla essence (optional)

Preparation time: about 10 minutes

1. Sift the flour and salt into a pile on a working surface and make a well in the centre. Add the sugar, diced butter, egg yolks and vanilla essence, if using.

2. Using the fingertips of one hand only 'pinch and peck' the butter, sugar and yolks together until the mixture is smooth and pale. Try not to work too much flour in at this stage as it will toughen the finished pastry.

3. Clean the fingertips with a palette knife and then use the palette knife to draw the flour over the yolks. Use fingertips and then the heel of the hand to bring the pastry together in a ball. Knead lightly until smooth.

4. Shape into a flat round, wrap in clingfilm and chill for 1–2 hours before use. To use, roll out very thinly on a lightly floured surface.

Points to remember

■ Remember that because of the high fat content, no water is added to Pâte Sucrée.
■ The texture of Pâte Sucrée is quite different from Pâte Brisée. Because it is so crisp when baked, it is a better medium for runny fillings.
■ Never be tempted to use the fingers of both hands to make this pastry, otherwise the pastry will be sticky.
■ Pâte Sucrée can be made in a processor if liked, but it should be under- rather than overprocessed.
■ When this pastry is cooked it will be biscuit-coloured and rather soft. It will crisp up as it cools.

Strawberry Syllabub Tartlets

See page 259 for details of baking blind.

Serves 4
1 recipe quantity Pâte Sucrée
100 g (4 oz) strawberries, sliced
1 orange, peeled and
*   segmented*
50 g (2 oz) caster sugar plus 1
*   tablespoon*
1 egg white
finely grated rind of ¼ lemon
a little grated orange rind
2 teaspoons lemon juice
4 tablespoons dry white wine
150 ml (¼ pint) double cream
lemon slices, to decorate
*   (optional)*
Preparation time: about 25 minutes
Cooking time: about 20 minutes
Oven: 190°C, 375°F, Gas Mark 5

1. Make up the pastry, wrap and chill for an hour then roll out and use to line four individual flan tins or Yorkshire pudding tins 10–11 cm (4–4½ inches) in diameter.

2. Prick the bases and bake blind in a preheated oven for 15 minutes. Remove the paper and beans and return to the oven for 5–8 minutes or until set and a pale golden brown. Cool on a wire rack.

3. Put the sliced strawberries into a bowl. Cut each orange segment in half and add to the strawberries with 1 tablespoon sugar.

4. Whisk the egg white until very stiff then fold in the sugar followed by the fruit rinds, lemon juice and wine. Whip the cream until stiff and fold through the egg white mixture.

5. Divide the strawberries and orange between the pastry cases and spoon or pipe the syllabub on top. Decorate each with a twist of lemon, if liked, chill and serve within 30 minutes of assembling.

Normandy Apple Tart

Serves 4–5
1½ recipe quantity Pâte Sucrée
450 g (1 lb) cooking apples
2 tablespoons water
75 g (3 oz) apricot jam
65 g (2½ oz) caster sugar
2 large or 3 small dessert
*   apples*
1–2 tablespoons lemon juice
Glaze:
6 level tablespoons apricot jam
1 tablespoon water

Preparation time: about 1 hour
Cooking time: 40–45 minutes
Oven: 190°C, 375°F, Gas Mark 5

1. Make up the Pâte Sucrée, wrap in clingfilm and chill for at least an hour.

2. Peel, quarter, core and slice the cooking apples into a saucepan and cook with the water until very tender. Beat until smooth then add the apricot jam and 40 g (1½ oz) of the sugar and cook for 2–3 minutes. Leave to cool.

3. Peel, quarter, core and slice the dessert apples and put in a bowl with the lemon juice and remaining sugar; toss well until evenly coated.

4. Roll out the pastry and use to line an 18 cm (7 inch) flan tin, dish or deep plate. Prick the base and chill for 20 minutes, then spoon in the apple purée.

5. Arrange the dessert apples in overlapping slices in circles over the apple purée. Cook in a preheated oven for 40–45 minutes or until the apples are lightly browned and the pastry cooked through. Remove from the oven and unmould from the flan ring or tin on to a serving dish.

6. For the glaze: melt the jam in the water and bring slowly to the boil. Rub through a sieve and use to brush all over the apple slices while they are still warm. Serve warm or cold with cream.

How to line flan tins

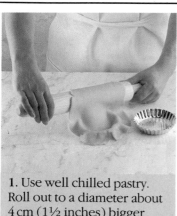

1. Use well chilled pastry. Roll out to a diameter about 4 cm (1½ inches) bigger than the flan tin or ring. Lift up the pastry on the rolling pin and lay centrally over the tin.

2. Ease the pastry down into the ring. Make a small ball of pastry (about the size of a marble) from the trimmings. Dip it in flour and use to press the dough into the bottom edge of the tin. Use the rolling pin to roll off the excess pastry round the top edges.

Top: Strawberry syllabub tartlets
Bottom: Normandy apple tart

PÂTE FEUILLETÉE

This is the richest and most flaky of all the 'flaky' (layered) pastries, and it gives the most even rise when baked. It is considered to be the most difficult pastry, because of the care that needs to be taken during rolling, and the time involved in the many stages of folding, rolling and chilling. However, the end result can be quite magnificent, with the cooked pastry puffing up into literally hundreds of crisp, buttery layers.

General method

Puff pastry is made by folding together layers of pastry dough with butter (for preference, although a combination of fats can be used); at the same time as much air as possible should be incorporated so that when baked the pastry puffs up into separate thin crisp layers or leaves. It is a rich pastry because it uses equal quantities of fat and flour (plain, as with most of the pastries). Puff pastry usually has 6 rollings, with a 30-minute chilling after each 2 rollings. The first rollings of the pastry should be used for vol-au-vents, cream slices, jalousie etc., whilst the trimmings (which have been neatly layered up, *not* squashed into a ball) can be rerolled carefully to use for small pastries such as Eccles cakes, palmiers, sausage rolls, sacristans etc.

225 g (8 oz) plain flour
1/2 teaspoon salt
225 g (8 oz) butter, firm but not too hard
about 150 ml (1/4 pint) iced water with a squeeze of lemon juice added

Preparation time: about 50 minutes, plus chilling time
Oven: 220–230°C, 425–450°F, Gas Mark 7–8

1. Sift the flour and salt into a bowl. Take about 40 g (1½ oz) of the butter and rub into the flour until the mixture is like fine breadcrumbs.

2. Use the iced water to bind to a fairly soft dough (it doesn't always take all the liquid). Knead lightly in the bowl until smooth. Wrap in clingfilm and chill for 15 minutes.

3. Soften the butter by beating between two sheets of clingfilm or greaseproof paper with a rolling pin, and form into an oblong block about 20 cm (8 inches) by 10 cm (4 inches).

6. 'Rib' the pastry by pressing the rolling pin across the pastry at regular intervals. This helps to distribute the air evenly through the pastry and makes the butter easier to roll out.

7. Roll the pastry into a long thin strip straight in front of you so that it is three times as long as it is wide, to measure approximately 10 cm (4 inches) by 30 cm (12 inches).

8. Fold the bottom third of the strip upwards and the top third downwards over the rest of the pastry, so it is quite even.

9. Seal the edges with the rolling pin and 'rib' it as before. Put into a polythene bag and chill for 15–20 minutes.

Basic rules

■ Puff pastry takes time and patience to make well. It should on no account be hurried or any of the chilling times cut out or cut down or the layers will not form correctly.

■ As the aim is to form those layers without the fat softening too much – or indeed melting – it is easier to make this pastry on a cool day rather than in hot weather when everything tends to soften too quickly.

■ It is best to make the pastry the day before it is required, which gives it time to relax and chill thoroughly before rolling out. If you are likely to be short of time on the day you want to cook the pastry, you can make the pastry as far as the 4th rolling on one day, and then complete the rolling and folding and shaping on the next day.

■ When correctly made this pastry when cooked should rise up to twice the thickness of the raw dough.

Storage and freezing

Once made the pastry will keep in the refrigerator for 2–3 days before use if well wrapped in foil or polythene; it also stores very well in the freezer for up to 6 months. Because of the time and effort involved it is a good idea to make the pastry in larger batches and freeze some for later use. Thaw it out completely, preferably in the refrigerator or a very cool place before use. It is also a good idea to allow the rolled out and shaped pastry to rest and chill slightly before cooking.

For perfect puff pastry

■ Everything must be as cool as possible before you start – ingredients, work surface, implements and hands, so that the butter stays in firm layers, giving the pastry its traditional layered effect when baked.

■ Always handle the pastry as lightly and as little as possible.

■ The flour and water paste should be firm enough to hold the butter but not so firm that it is difficult to roll out or so soft that the butter sinks into it rather than forming layers.

■ The butter should be cold and firm but not too hard; neither should it be too soft. The dough and the butter should be of the same consistency. If the butter is too hard it can be gently softened with a rolling pin and reshaped, but take care not to *over* soften it.

■ Only roll in one direction – straight in front of you – and use quick short movements which are quite light but firm enough to roll the pastry. If rolled too hard, the butter will be pushed out from between the layers.

■ Do not turn pastry over – it should only be rolled on one side.

■ Take care when folding the dough to keep it even; uneven layers will give an uneven rise during baking.

■ Make sure the fat does not come through the pastry dough during the first few rollings or it spoils the texture. If the fat does come through, dust the dough with flour, brush off surplus and chill for 10 minutes before continuing.

■ Use extra flour only very sparingly as this too spoils the texture and will not correct the problem.

■ When chilling the pastry make finger marks on the pastry to indicate the number of rollings given – it is easy to forget where you are when doing other things at the same time.

■ Use a sharp knife or cutter for cutting the dough so that the layers are not torn.

■ Sprinkle the baking sheet with water before putting the pastry on.

4. On a lightly floured surface roll out the pastry to a square of about 23 cm (9 inches) and about 1.5 cm (½ inch) thick. Peel off the clingfilm, and place the butter on the pastry.

5. Fold the pastry over corner by corner to form an 'envelope', enclosing the butter. Seal the edges of the pastry with the rolling pin.

10. Repeat the rollings and foldings (steps 7 and 8) 4 times more, giving the pastry a quarter turn each time so that the fold is always on the right. Wrap and chill for 30 minutes after every 2 rollings. If the pastry is still streaked with fat, give it a further rolling and folding.

11. Mark the dough each time with finger prints to show how often it has been rolled. Wrap in clingfilm and chill for 30 minutes before the final shaping.

Mille-Feuille

As its name implies this is a concoction of thousands of leaves or layers of pastry which are then sandwiched together with a variety of fillings, including Crème Pâtissière, whipped cream, jam or a fruit purée. The top may be simply dredged with icing sugar, or covered with a glacé icing. It should be assembled 2–3 hours before serving so that the pastry is easy to cut into slices.

Serves 8
¹/₂ recipe quantity Pâte Feuilletée (see page 272)
Glacé icing:
100 g (4 oz) icing sugar, sifted
1–2 tablespoons lemon juice or warm water
toasted chopped hazelnuts to decorate
Filling:
1 recipe quantity Crème Pâtissière (see page 242)
150 ml (¹/₄ pint) double cream, whipped
225 g (8 oz) good raspberry jam or other preserve; or 225 g (8 oz) strawberries, sliced or raspberries

Preparation time: about 30 minutes, not including pastry making
Cooking time: about 40 minutes
Oven: 230°C, 450°F, Gas Mark 8

1. Roll out the chilled pastry to a rectangle and trim to 30 × 38 cm (12 × 15 inches). Cut this into three rectangles of 30 × 12.5 cm (12 × 5 inches). Place on a dampened baking sheet and prick well.

2. Bake in a preheated oven for 15–20 minutes or until well puffed up and golden. Turn over and cook for 10–15 minutes on the other side. Cool on a wire rack. Place the 3 strips on top of each other and trim.

3. For the glacé icing, sift the icing sugar into a bowl and beat in sufficient lemon juice or water to give a spreading consistency.

4. Meanwhile make up the Crème Pâtissière and leave to cool in a covered bowl. Whip the cream until thick but not too stiff and fold evenly through the Crème Pâtissière.

5. Select the best of the pastry strips for the top layer and spread evenly with the icing. Sprinkle with the nuts and leave to set.

6. To assemble, place one of the pastry strips on a serving dish and spread first with the jam and then with a good layer of the cream mixture. If using fruit, put the cream on first and then layer with the fruit.

7. Cover with another piece of pastry and repeat with the filling. Finally add the iced lid and it is ready to serve.

Variations

Marron Mix a can of sweetened chestnut purée with the Crème Pâtissière and whipped cream, and flavour with rum. The icing can be flavoured with rum instead of lemon juice and the hazelnuts replaced by pieces of marron glacé.
Chocolate and Nut Flavour the Crème Pâtissière with cream, brandy or rum and add 175 g (6 oz) coarsely grated plain chocolate and 50 g (2 oz) toasted chopped almonds or hazelnuts. Cover the top of the pastry with a chocolate icing – using a quarter of the icing for the Sachertorte (see page 252).
Chocolate and Vanilla Cover the top of the pastry lid with vanilla-flavoured glacé icing, then decorate with chocolate glacé icing in a feathered design (see page 319).

Jalousie

A jalousie or galette jalousie is a dessert made of puff pastry which is like a semi open-topped pie. It is always a long rectangle and the pastry 'lid' is cut in a special way so that it opens out during baking to reveal the filling.

A thick jam or curd is often used for the filling but apples and jam or marmalade give more interest and make it a dessert rather than just a teatime treat.

Once cooked, the jalousie can be frozen for up to 3 months, packaged carefully in a rigid container.

Serves 6

1 recipe quantity Pâte
Feuilletée (see page 272)
175 g (6 oz) thick apricot jam
or chunky orange
marmalade
450 g (1 lb) cooking apples
egg white or milk to glaze
25 g (1 oz) caster sugar for
dredging

Preparation time: about 30 minutes, not including pastry making
Cooking time: about 30 minutes
Oven: 220°C, 425°F, Gas Mark 7

1. Divide the chilled pastry in two, one piece slightly larger than the other. Roll out the smaller piece thinly to a rectangle and place on a dampened or lightly greased baking sheet.

2. Spread the jam or marmalade over the pastry on the baking sheet, leaving a 2.5 cm (1 inch) margin all round. Peel, core and slice the apples and arrange the slices over the jam.

3. Roll out the second piece of pastry 2.5 cm (1 inch) larger all round. Flour well and fold in half lengthwise. Using a sharp knife cut into the fold at 5 mm (¼ inch) intervals, to within 2.5 cm (1 inch) of the edges and ends.

4. Brush the pastry margin with water and position the lid on top, carefully unfolding it to completely enclose the filling. Brush off the surplus flour.

5. Align the pastry margins and trim, then press well together and flake all round the sides with a sharp knife. Scallop with the back of a knife to complete the decoration.

6. Bake in a preheated oven for 20 minutes then remove from the oven. Glaze the pastry all over with lightly beaten egg white or milk and then dredge with the sugar.

7. Return to the oven and bake for another 10 minutes or until the pastry is well risen and golden brown. If it is browning too quickly, lay a sheet of greaseproof paper over the top.

8. Serve hot or cold in slices.

Cream Horns

These are a favourite teatime delicacy made from Pâte Feuilletée with a Crème Chantilly and jam filling. They can also be served with a savoury filling when they make an excellent starter.

Makes 8
½ recipe quantity Pâte Feuilletée (see page 272) or 225 g (8 oz) puff pastry trimmings
1 egg, beaten
Filling:
250 ml (8 fl oz) whipping or double cream
about 1 tablespoon vanilla sugar (flavoured with a vanilla pod, for preference)
raspberry or strawberry jam, or lemon curd, marmalade or any well flavoured fruity jam
chopped pistachio nuts (optional)
icing sugar (optional)

Preparation time: about 20 minutes, not including pastry making
Cooking time: about 5 minutes plus time for making the Crème Chantilly
Oven: 220°C, 425°F, Gas Mark 7

1. Lightly grease 8 metal cream horn tins. Roll out the pastry thinly to a strip measuring approximately 63 × 11 cm (25 × 4½ inches) and cut into long strips 1.5 cm (½ inch) wide.

2. Brush the strips with beaten egg and then wind one strip carefully around each horn tin, beginning at the tip and keeping the glazed side outwards; overlap slightly each time.

3. Place the horns on a greased baking sheet and keep the pastry join underneath. Glaze again.

4. Cook in a preheated oven for about 10 minutes or until well puffed up and golden brown. Cool on a wire rack for a few minutes to allow the pastry to shrink slightly from the tins.

5. Twist the tins slightly to slip the horns out. Return to the turned-off oven for 5 minutes to dry out the insides. Cool on a wire rack.

6. For the Crème Chantilly whip the cream until stiff and then fold in the vanilla sugar to taste.

7. Fill a piping bag with the cream. Put a teaspoon of the chosen jam into the tip of each pastry horn.

8. Pipe cream on top, using a large star nozzle. A little more jam can be put on top of the cream for decoration or a few chopped pistachio nuts may be sprinkled over the cream. Lightly dredge with sifted icing sugar before serving, if liked.

Savoury Horns

These are made in the same way but should only be glazed with beaten egg or egg white and not dredged with sugar. They may be lightly sprinkled with coarse sea salt or sesame seeds before baking which gives both texture and flavour to the finished horns. Use a well flavoured white sauce for the basis of the filling which can be meat, poultry, game, eggs, cheese, vegetables etc. Do not over fill and serve either hot, warm or cold.

Top: Mille-feuille Bottom: Cream horns

CHOUX PASTRY

Choux pastry is different from all other types of pastry; it is much softer in texture, and is often known as a paste rather than a pastry. Instead of the dough being rolled out, it is piped or spooned on to dampened baking sheets. Used for both sweet and savoury dishes, it can also be deep fried, eg, for beignets or aigrettes.

General method

There are two main ways of baking choux pastry. For éclairs, profiteroles and choux rings etc. it is simply piped or spooned on to baking sheets and baked in a hot oven. When extra rise is required, as for cream puffs, an inverted tin is sometimes placed over the piped or spooned buns.

This in turn creates extra steam inside and puffs the mixture up twice as much as usual. Care must be taken that the tins fit well: they must not be moved during cooking and there should be no looking to check progress until you can hear the buns sliding around on the baking sheet. If you lift the tins to have a look too soon, the buns will simply collapse.

Basic rules

■ Care is needed when making choux pastry although once prepared, it will wait for several hours before baking. (Cover with clingfilm and store in a cool place.)
■ Butter is used for flavour and it is important to add the well sifted flour all at once and beat it in as quickly as possible to form a ball that leaves the sides of the pan clean.
■ The flour should be tipped into the pan whilst it is still on the heat so the liquid is still boiling, then it is taken from the heat and beaten quickly. Do not over-beat the mixture or it will become oily and begin to separate; as a result it will not rise properly and the

---

65 g (2½ oz) plain flour
pinch of salt
50 g (2 oz) butter
150 ml (¼ pint) water
2 eggs, beaten

Preparation time: about 15 minutes, plus cooling

1. Sift the flour and salt on to a piece of greaseproof paper. Put the butter into the saucepan with the water.

2. Heat gently until the butter melts then bring quickly to the boil.

3. Add the flour to the pan all at once and mix in with a wooden spoon or spatula.

Freezing choux pastry

Choux buns or other shapes can be piped and then open frozen before baking but they must be thawed completely before baking. Alternatively, pipe, bake, cool and then open freeze. After thawing, they are then best placed in a hot oven (200°C, 400°F, Gas Mark 6) for 2–3 minutes to crispen before filling. Choux pastry will freeze for up to 3 months.

4. Beat until the mixture is smooth and forms a ball, leaving the sides of the pan clean. Do not over-beat. Remove quickly from the heat and spread the paste out evenly over the base of the pan. Leave to cool for about 10 minutes.

5. Beat the egg vigorously into the paste, a little at a time, to give a smooth glossy paste. A hand-held electric mixer is best for this as it helps to incorporate the maximum amount of air required for a good rise. The paste may not take the last spoonful of beaten egg.

6. It must be a dropping consistency, but remain stiff enough to pipe or spoon and hold its shape. The pastry is now ready for use.

cooked texture will be cake-like. Not adding the flour correctly or over-beating the flour mixture are the most common faults when making choux pastry.

■ Beat in as much air as possible with the eggs to give a smooth and glossy piping consistency. Let the paste cool first though, or the eggs will scramble. A hand-held electric mixer is ideal, although a wooden spoon and plenty of elbow grease will do. But, beating by hand you will not be able to incorporate quite as much air or beaten egg.

■ Choux pastry is baked in a hot oven (220–230°C, 425–450°F, Gas Mark 7–8) with the temperature lowered for the latter part of the cooking in some recipes. Take care not to open the door of the oven during cooking – any slight draught will cause the dough to sink rapidly.

For perfect choux pastry

■ Sift the flour once or twice and use plain flour.
■ Add the flour all at once and quickly.
■ The liquid must be boiling when the flour is added.
■ Beat the flour into the liquid only until smooth and formed into a ball; over-beating will spoil the texture.
■ Use a hand-held electric mixer for the best results when adding the egg.
■ The mixture will absorb more of the egg when using an electric mixer than when beating by hand; don't worry if it will not take all the egg.
■ Add the egg a little at a time in case the mixture cannot absorb it all – this will ensure that the consistency does not become too soft.
■ Do not open the oven door during cooking until you think the pastry is almost ready or it will surely sink.

Chocolate Éclairs

The size of the éclairs is adjusted simply by cutting the mixture at the desired length. For ease, a ruler can be placed on the baking sheet so each one is cut to the same length; and if the mixture tends to get messy when cutting, wipe the knife after each cut and dip it in cold water before cutting again. Makes about 12 traditional éclairs (more if smaller).

1 recipe quantity Choux Pastry
250 ml (8 fl oz) double or
*   whipping cream, or 1 recipe*
*   quantity Crème Pâtissière*
*   (see page 242)*
Chocolate satin icing:
50 g (2 oz) plain chocolate
25 g (1 oz) butter
120 g (4½ oz) icing sugar,
*   sifted*
3 tablespoons milk

Preparation time: about 40 minutes, plus cooling time for pastry
Cooking time: about 30 minutes, or 40 minutes if making Crème Pâtissière
Oven: 220°C, 425°F, Gas Mark 7

1. Put the choux pastry into a piping bag fitted with a plain 1 cm (½ inch) piping nozzle. Pipe the mixture on to greased baking sheets keeping a straight line and cutting the mixture off sharply with a knife to give éclairs of approx. 6 cm (2½ inches). It is very important that they are all the same length but they can be longer or shorter if preferred. Keep them well apart on the baking sheets.

2. Cook in a preheated oven for 25–30 minutes or until well risen, firm and golden.

3. Make a split in the side of each one for the steam to escape and return to the oven for a few minutes to dry out. Cool on a wire rack.

4. Just before serving, whip the cream until stiff and use to fill the éclairs either by spreading or piping in through the split. If using Crème Pâtissière beat it until smooth and use in the same way to fill the éclairs

5. For the icing, melt the chocolate and butter in a heavy-based saucepan or in a basin over a pan of gently simmering water. Stir until it is quite smooth then stir in the icing sugar, followed by the milk.

6. Either spread the icing quickly over the tops of each éclair or dip the top into the icing. Leave to set.

Beignets with Apricot Sauce

Another way of serving choux pastry as a dessert when it is deep fried and then tossed in flavoured sugar. Cook and serve as soon afterwards as possible.

Serves 5–6
1 recipe quantity Choux Pastry
oil or fat for deep frying
25 g (1 oz) caster sugar
½ teaspoon ground
*   cinnamon or mixed spice*
good pinch of ground allspice
Apricot sauce:
425 g (15 oz) can apricot
*   halves*
1½ teaspoons arrowroot
2 tablespoons brandy
2 tablespoons brown sugar
pinch of grated lemon rind
1 tablespoon lemon juice

Preparation time: about 30 minutes
Cooking time: about 30 minutes

1. First make the choux pastry and then the sauce. Take 2 tablespoons apricot juice and blend it with the arrowroot.

Drain the apricots and sieve or purée them with about 4 tablespoons juice. Put into a small pan with the brandy, sugar, lemon rind and juice and bring to the boil. Stir in the slaked arrowroot and bring back to the boil, stirring continuously. Cook until thickened, then leave to cool.

2. Put the choux pastry into a piping bag fitted with a large star vegetable nozzle.

3. Heat the oil to about 180°C, 350°F and when ready pipe lengths of choux mixture measuring about 2.5 cm (1 inch) into the fat cutting them off with a sharp knife. Cook about 6–7 at a time.

4. Cook for about 5 minutes or until well puffed up and browned.

5. Drain on absorbent kitchen paper and toss immediately in a mixture of caster sugar and the spices. Serve hot with the sauce.

Variations

Coffee Éclairs Make the éclairs in the same way but cover the tops with coffee glacé icing made by mixing 175 g (6 oz) sifted icing sugar with 2–3 teaspoons strong black coffee or coffee essence with sufficient warm water to give a consistency that will coat the back of a spoon.
Lemon or Orange Use lemon or orange glacé icing made as above but replacing the coffee essence with orange or lemon juice. The cream may have a little grated fruit rind and a touch of sugar added.

Paris-Brest

This Paris speciality, a choux pastry confection, is sprinkled with almonds. After baking it is split open and filled with praline flavoured Crème Pâtissière with added whipped cream.

It can be baked in one large ring, as below, or as small individual rings. For individual Paris-Brests pipe the mixture out into 8 circles of about 9–10 cm (3½–4 inches) in diameter, sprinkle with almonds and cook as below but for only about 30 minutes, or until crisp and dry. Split and fill as below.

Serves 8
*1½ recipe quantities Choux
    Pastry (see page 278)
25 g (1 oz) flaked or chopped
    blanched almonds
1 recipe quantity Crème
    Pâtissière (see page 242)
300 ml (½ pint) double or
    whipping cream
icing sugar, for dredging
strawberries, for decoration
    (optional)*
Praline:
*75 g (3 oz) unblanched
    almonds
75 g (3 oz) caster sugar*

Preparation time: about 45 minutes, plus cooling
Cooking time: about 45 minutes
Oven: 220°C, 425°F, Gas Mark 7

1. Make up the choux pastry. Draw a 23 cm (9 inch) circle on a sheet of non-stick baking paper and place on a baking sheet.

2. Spoon the choux pastry into a piping bag fitted with a plain 1.5 cm (½ inch) nozzle. Pipe a ring of pastry on top of the drawn circle, then pipe another one inside the first. Pipe a third ring to cover the join.

3. Alternatively, put spoonfuls of mixture in small balls all around to make a ring, just inside the drawn circle. Sprinkle with the almonds.

4. Bake in a preheated oven for about 40 minutes or until well risen and golden brown. Cover the top with greaseproof paper if the nuts begin to brown too much. Cool on a wire rack.

5. To make the praline, put the almonds and sugar into a small heavy-based pan and heat gently until the sugar has melted. Turn the almonds in the syrup and cook slowly until golden brown, allowing about 10 minutes.

6. Turn the mixture quickly on to an oiled baking sheet and leave until cold and set. Crush with a rolling pin or grind in a small grinder to a fine powder.

7. Split the ring in half horizontally and scoop out any damp pastry. Beat the Crème Pâtissière and praline together until smooth. Whip the cream until stiff and fold through the mixture.

8. Stand the base on a serving dish and pipe or spoon in the praline cream.

9. Replace the lid and dredge with sugar. If liked, fill with strawberries.

Top: Paris-Brest
Bottom: Chocolate éclairs

Profiteroles

This is one of the traditional ways of serving choux puffs. They can also be used to make Croquembouche (see page 257), or served with a variety of fillings. For savoury puffs, see page 283.

Serves 6
1 recipe quantity Choux Pastry (see page 278)
Chocolate sauce:
225 g (8 oz) plain chocolate, broken into pieces
8 tablespoons water
50 g (2 oz) butter
1–2 tablespoons rum (optional)
Filling:
450 ml (¾ pint) double or whipping cream
icing sugar, to dredge

Preparation time: about 30 minutes, plus cooling time
Cooking time: about 40 minutes
Oven: 220°C, 425°F, Gas Mark 7

1. Spoon the choux pastry into a piping bag fitted with a 2 cm (¾ inch) plain vegetable piping nozzle.

2. Pipe out walnut-sized balls of mixture on to dampened or lined baking sheets, leaving a space between each one. Bake in a preheated oven for about 25 minutes or until well puffed up, golden brown, and firm to the touch.

3. Remove from the oven and pierce each one close to the base with a skewer or sharp knife to allow the steam to escape. Return to the turned-off oven for 2–3 minutes to dry out. Cool on a wire rack.

4. Whip the cream until stiff and put into a piping bag fitted with a 5 mm (¼ inch) plain piping nozzle. Fill the choux buns with cream by inserting the nozzle into the hole pierced to allow the steam to escape. Alternatively the buns can be cut in half, filled with the cream and reassembled.

5. For the sauce, place the chocolate and water in a bowl over a pan of gently simmering water or in a microwave oven set to cool. Stir until smooth then add the butter a little at a time, continuing to stir until smooth. Add rum to taste. Pour into a serving jug and cover until required.

6. Arrange the buns on a serving plate, piling them up carefully into a pyramid shape. Dredge fairly heavily with sifted icing sugar and serve with the chocolate sauce. A little of the sauce may be poured over the profiteroles in the pyramid with the rest served separately.

Variations to fillings

Marron Turn the contents of a 225 g (8 oz) can sweetened chestnut purée (or two 100 g (4 oz) tubes of purée) into a bowl and mix with 300 ml (½ pint) whipped cream and 1 tablespoon rum or other liqueur. Spoon into a piping bag and fill as above.
Chocolate Chip and Nut Finely grate 50 g (2 oz) plain chocolate and add to the cream with 50 g (2 oz) finely chopped toasted hazelnuts or toasted blanched almonds.
Orange Finely grate the rind of 1 orange and add to the whipped cream with 1–2 tablespoons orange liqueur and 1 tablespoon clear honey. Alternatively add the grated rind of 1 orange to the chocolate sauce, above.
Ice cream Put 350 ml (12 fl oz) chocolate or vanilla ice cream into the refrigerator to soften. Just before serving, spoon the ice cream into a piping bag and pipe the ice cream into the choux buns.

Savoury Choux Puffs

Choux pastry can also be made to serve as a savoury pastry. It is ideal for cocktail 'bites' with a variety of savoury fillings. The puffs can be made the day before if necessary. They should then be crispened in a warm oven on the day, before filling.

Makes 18–25
1 recipe quantity Choux Pastry (see page 278)
salt
freshly ground black pepper
1 tablespoon grated Parmesan cheese (optional)
Filling:
225 g (8 oz) full fat soft cream cheese
75 g (3 oz) softened butter
1 garlic clove, crushed
1 teaspoon lemon juice
75 g (3 oz) blue cheese, crumbled or grated
1 tablespoon snipped chives or freshly chopped parsley
salt
freshly ground black pepper
1/2 small onion, peeled and very finely chopped
100 g (4 oz) chicken livers, washed and dried
1/2 teaspoon ground coriander

Preparation time: about 30 minutes, plus cooling
Cooking time: about 50 minutes
Oven: 220°C, 425°F, Gas Mark 7

1. Make up the choux pastry as usual but season with salt and pepper and beat in the Parmesan cheese, if liked. Put the mixture into a piping bag fitted with a 2–2.5 cm (3/4–1 inch) plain nozzle and pipe out walnut-sized balls on to greased baking sheets leaving space between each.

2. Bake in a preheated oven for about 25 minutes as for profiteroles and pierce and cool in the same way.

3. Make the fillings whilst the choux buns are cooking: first cream half the cheese with half the softened butter until smooth then beat in a touch of garlic, the lemon juice, blue cheese and chives with seasonings to taste.

4. For the second filling melt the remaining butter in a pan and fry the garlic and onion until soft. Add the chicken livers and cook for about 5 minutes, mashing them up as they cook. Season well, beat in the coriander and leave to cool. When cold mash thoroughly and beat into the remaining cream cheese.

5. To fill: either make a hole in the base of each bun and pipe in the filling; or cut each in half, spoon or pipe in the filling and reassemble.

Cheese Aigrettes

This method of deep frying small balls of choux pastry which have been flavoured is a very versatile way of using the pastry. It is ideal for hot cocktail snacks, quick snacks or light lunches or as an accompaniment to a meal instead of a vegetable. They should be served hot or warm and as soon after cooking as is convenient; if kept too long they will lose their crispness. Aigrettes can be served alone or with a flavoured dip to blend with or contrast with the filling.

Makes about 25–30
1 recipe quantity Choux Pastry (see page 278)
2 tablespoons grated Parmesan cheese
50 g (2 oz) mature Cheddar cheese or Stilton, grated
salt
freshly ground black pepper
pinch of cayenne pepper
oil or fat for deep frying

Preparation time: about 30 minutes, plus cooling
Cooking: about 30 minutes

1. Make up the choux pastry in the usual way and then beat in the cheeses, seasonings and cayenne.

2. Put the mixture into a piping bag fitted with a 1.5 cm (1/2 inch) plain nozzle or a large star vegetable nozzle. Heat the oil or fat until a cube of bread browns in about 30 seconds (about 180°C, 350°F).

3. Pipe small balls of the mixture about 1.5 cm (1/2 inch) in diameter into the hot fat – about 6 at a time – and cook until well puffed up and golden brown all over, turning over during cooking, if necessary. They should take 3–4 minutes.

4. Drain on paper towels and keep warm whilst frying the remainder. Serve with a flavoured mayonnaise or any suitable sauce for dipping. Tomato, herb, curry, horseradish, mustard etc. can all be used.

Variations

Cheese and Bacon Fry or grill 175 g (6 oz) streaky bacon rashers until very crispy, then crumble or chop finely. When cold beat into the choux mixture.
Smoked Mackerel or Salmon Add about 100 g (4 oz) finely flaked or chopped smoked mackerel or smoked salmon to the choux mixture. The cheese may be omitted if preferred.
Curried Prawn Add 1–2 teaspoons curry powder to the choux mixture along with 100 g (4 oz) finely chopped peeled prawns or potted shrimps.

Perfect profiteroles and éclairs

■ With profiteroles and éclairs make a small hole in the side of base when cooked to allow steam to escape, and if necessary return to the oven for 3–4 minutes to dry out.
■ Large éclairs should be split in half and returned to the oven, split side uppermost, to dry out the inside for a few minutes before cooling on a wire rack to prevent them becoming soggy. Any remaining damp or uncooked pastry should be scooped out, as with Paris-Brest.

STRUDEL PASTRY

The strudel is the national cake (or pastry) of Bavaria. Strudel dough is noted for its strength and elasticity, which allows it to be stretched out paper-thin to make the characteristic light, flaky pastry rolled around a filling.

The Greek version of this pastry is filo (made with strong flour but no eggs) which is widely available ready-made.

General method

It is made with a type of noodle pastry, which is rolled out as thinly as possible and then worked until it is even thinner by stretching the dough over the backs of the knuckles – until it is thin enough to read a newspaper through!

Strudel fillings are always sweet, and although the traditional one is spiced apple (sometimes with dried fruits and/or chopped nuts), many others can be invented or adapted to fill strudels; in fact a wide variety of flavours blend and bake well in strudel pastry.

The idea is to spread or scatter the thin pastry with a filling, fold in the edges to enclose it, and roll up. This ensures that the pastry and filling are evenly distributed, and that the layers of pastry will be crisp when baked. An extra layer of unfilled pastry for the last roll helps keep the strudel in shape, while moving to the baking sheet, and for holding the filling without splitting.

Large strudels can be baked in a straight line, divided in two or curved into a horseshoe shape. Strudels are usually served cold or just warm, often heavily dredged with sifted icing sugar and served with single cream.

225 g (8 oz) plain strong
   flour
a good pinch of salt
1 egg, beaten
2 tablespoons vegetable oil
4 tablespoons warm water
about 40 g (1½ oz) butter,
   melted
extra flour, for rolling

Preparation time: about 45 minutes, plus resting time

1. Sift the flour and salt into a bowl. Make a well in the centre and add the egg, oil and water.

2. Mix by hand to form a soft sticky dough, scraping it up with your fingers. Turn on to a floured surface and knead well by hand for about 15 minutes.

3. Work the dough by throwing it hard on to the work surface, gather up and repeat until the dough becomes very smooth and loses any stickiness.

6. Spread out a clean cotton tablecloth or sheet on the table or working surface and sprinkle all over with 2–3 tablespoons flour. Place the dough in the centre of the cloth and roll out carefully to a rectangle about 3 mm (⅛ inch) thick.

7. Now gently stretch the dough using the backs of the hands, putting them under the dough but over the cloth. Work from the centre outwards, carefully pulling it gently but evenly, until it is thin enough to see the texture or the pattern of the cloth through it.

8. Move round the table or work surface, stretching a section of dough at a time. It should be evenly thin all over but the edges will remain thicker. It should measure approx. 90 × 70 cm (36 × 28 inches) at least. Trim off the thick edges and brush with melted butter. The dough is now ready for shaping and filling.

Cream Cheese Strudel with Cherry Sauce

Baked strudels will freeze for up to 2 months if packed in rigid containers.

Basic rules

■ Use a good quality flour with a high gluten content to give a dough that is strong enough to be stretched thinly without tearing too easily.
■ The stretching process can be done by one person but it is easier and quicker if there are two of you. Be careful though, as over-enthusiasm will only cause it to tear.

4. Alternatively, put the dough into a large electric mixer fitted with a dough hook and knead for about 5 minutes, or until the dough is smooth and even.

5. Shape into a ball, place in an oiled polythene bag and leave to rest in a warm place for about 1 hour.

Serves 8–10
1 recipe quantity Strudel Pastry
butter
icing sugar, to dredge
Filling:
350 g (12 oz) cream cheese
75–100 g (3–4 oz) caster sugar
1 egg
1 egg yolk
grated rind of ½ lemon
75 g (3 oz) hazelnuts, toasted and chopped
1 × 425 g (15 oz) can pitted black cherries in syrup
Cherry sauce:
1½ teaspoons arrowroot
1–2 tablespoons brandy, Kirsch or water

Preparation time: about 50 minutes, plus resting
Cooking time: about 30 minutes
Oven: 190°C, 375°F, Gas Mark 5

1. Make the strudel pastry and while it is resting before stretching out, make the filling.

2. Cream the cheese with the sugar until smooth; then beat in the egg, egg yolk, lemon rind and nuts. Fold in half the drained cherries.

3. Roll and stretch the pastry as in the basic recipe. Cut in half and brush each half with melted butter. Dot the cream cheese mixture over one third of each piece of pastry, leaving the margins free.

4. Tuck in the sides and roll up as shown on page 287. Place both strudels on well greased baking sheets. Brush again with melted butter and bake in a preheated oven for about 30 minutes, or until golden brown and crisp.

5. While the strudel is cooking make the cherry sauce. Pour the cherry juice into a pan and bring to the boil. Blend the arrowroot with the brandy, Kirsch or water and add to the juice with the remaining

cherries. Bring back to the boil, stirring continuously until clear and slightly thickened.

6. When cooked, cool the strudels slightly and then transfer carefully to a wire tray to cool. Dredge with sifted icing sugar and serve in slices with the cherry sauce, either warm or cold.

Variation

75–100 g (3–4 oz) sultanas and 40–50 g (1½–2 oz) chopped mixed peel can be added to the cream cheese mixture, and the lemon rind can be replaced with orange rind for a change.

For perfect Strudel Pastry

■ Strudel pastry breaks many of the rules of pastry-making in general. It does not need light handling. Instead, knead it like a bread dough and allow to relax so it loses some of its springiness.
■ It should be worked in a warm atmosphere with warm cloths and warm rolling pin and even warm water and warm hands, which help to give the pastry elasticity.
■ Use a high gluten plain flour for the best results and most 'stretch'.
■ Once you begin to stretch the dough continue until it is

completed; do not even stop to answer the telephone or it will begin to dry and cease to yield as it should.
■ If you have long fingernails, do clench your fist when stretching the dough to prevent tears.
■ Allow lots of time for making strudel pastry and have plenty of patience. It is very worthwhile in the end.
■ It is easiest made on a table, so that you can walk around it to stretch it.
■ Make sure the cloth used is large enough and freshly laundered. Two tea towels

placed lengthwise in front of you are probably best, particularly if you are going to cut the dough in half and make two strudels. Otherwise use a small tablecloth.
■ Trim the edges off the strudel pastry before rolling it up. If it is a little thick, or forms a rim, it will spoil the texture and shape of the finished strudel.
■ Tilt the cloth to help roll up the strudel, especially if it is a large one. This is not necessary with small individual strudels which can be rolled by hand.

Baklava

Filo pastry is the Middle Eastern equivalent of strudel, but instead of being wrapped round the filling, the delicately thin sheets of pastry are buttered and layered, several at a time, with the filling sandwiched in between. As well as the delicious sweet Baklava, filo is also used to make savoury pies, such as the famous spanakopitta (cheese and spinach pie) which is popular all over Greece.

Serves 6
450 g (1 lb) ready-made filo pastry (defrosted if frozen)
250 g (9 oz) unsalted butter, melted
Syrup:
250 g (9 oz) sugar
150 ml (5 fl oz) water
2 teaspoons lemon juice
1 tablespoon clear honey
1 tablespoon rosewater
1 tablespoon orange-flower water
Filling:
450 g (1 lb) walnuts, almonds or pistachios, chopped
2 tablespoons sugar
1 tablespoon ground cinnamon

Preparation time: 45 minutes, plus cooling and chilling
Cooking time: 1 hour
Oven: 160°C, 325°F, Gas Mark 3

Top: Baklava
Bottom: Cream cheese strudel with cherry Sauce

1. Make the syrup: simmer the sugar and water with the lemon juice until it will coat a spoon. Remove the pan from the heat, then stir in the rest of the ingredients and chill.

2. Mix the filling ingredients thoroughly together.

3. Prepare the pastry: brush a 40 × 23 cm (16 × 9 inch) roasting tin with melted butter and place a filo sheet in the tin so that it covers the bottom. Fold the edges so that they cover the sides of the tin and brush all over with more butter.

4. Repeat the procedure until you have 5 or 6 sheets, each brushed thoroughly with melted butter. Keep the remaining sheets covered with a damp tea towel.

5. Sprinkle the top sheet with a quarter of the filling ingredients, then continue adding filling every fifth sheet, till the filling is used up, finishing with a layer of pastry.

6. Trim the edges of the pastry, overlapping the edges of the tin, with a sharp knife. Score the pastry into the traditional diamond shape.

7. Bake the Baklava for 45 minutes. If it has not begun to brown, raise the temperature a little and bake for a further 15 minutes.

8. Remove from the oven and pour the cold syrup over the Baklava, then let it cool.

Apfelstrudel

Apple pie the Austrian way with melt-in-the-mouth pastry and a spicy apple filling. The instructions below are for 2 smaller strudels; for one large curved strudel use all the pastry dough rolled up with the filling, and transfer very carefully to a greased baking sheet, cutting to fit if necessary. For individual strudels, cut the stretched out dough into pieces approx. 23 × 15 cm (9 × 6 inches). Position the filling to the narrow end of each piece, fold in the margins and roll up as before. Brush with butter and bake as in the recipe below.

Serves 8–10
*1 recipe quantity Strudel Pastry
   (see page 284)
50 g (2 oz) butter, melted
icing sugar, to dredge*
Filling:
*900 g (2 lb) cooking apples
40 g (1½ oz) raisins
40 g (1½ oz) currants
75 g (3 oz) sugar (caster or
   light soft brown)
½ teaspoon ground
   cinnamon or mixed spice
100 g (4 oz) ground almonds
   or breadcrumbs*

Preparation time: 1 hour, plus resting time
Cooking time: about 30 minutes
Oven: 190°C, 375°F, Gas Mark 5

1. Make the strudel pastry and whilst it is resting before stretching out prepare the filling.

2. Peel and core the apples and slice very thinly into a bowl. Add the raisins, currants, sugar and spice and mix lightly.

3. Roll out the dough and stretch on a sheet or tablecloth as described in the basic method. Trim off the thick edge all round the pastry so it is even. Brush with half the melted butter then sprinkle evenly with the ground almonds or breadcrumbs.

4. Spoon the filling along the width of the pastry, leaving a margin of about 2.5 cm (1 inch) at each side (see below).

5. Carefully use both hands to lift the cloth, and slowly roll up the strudel away from you, keeping it even and fairly tightly rolled. Continue until completely rolled. Cut the strudel in two.

6. Still with the help of the cloth remove the strudels to two greased baking sheets, keeping the join underneath. Use the remaining butter to brush all over the strudels.

7. Bake in a preheated oven for about 30 minutes or until golden brown and crisp. Cool slightly on the baking sheet then remove carefully with the help of fish slices to a wire rack to cool.

8. To serve, dredge with sifted icing sugar and serve cold or warm with pouring cream.

Variations

Mincemeat: Add 6–8 tablespoons mincemeat to the apple and dried fruit mixture.
Cranberry: Omit the dried fruit and spices. Increase the sugar to 175 g (6 oz) and add 100–175 g (4–6 oz) cranberries and the grated rind of ½–1 orange. The almonds may be omitted if preferred.
Apricot and Walnut: Omit the dried fruit, spices and ground almonds, and use only 750 g (1½ lb) apples. Add 100 g (4 oz) chopped walnuts, 100 g (4 oz) soaked and chopped dried apricots and 2 tablespoons honey to the apples.

How to roll a strudel

1. Brush the pastry with melted butter and sprinkle with breadcrumbs. Spoon the filling along the width of the pastry in a 7.5 cm (3 inch) wide band, about 7.5 cm (3 inches) in from the edge. Leave a margin of about 2.5 cm (1 inch) at each side and tuck in the ends if necessary to prevent the filling leaking out.

2. Using both hands, lift up the cloth and flip the edge of the dough over the filling. Pull the cloth towards you and continue to flip the pastry over so that it rolls round the filling. Finally, use the cloth to help tip the fully rolled strudel on to a baking tray.

For perfect Filo

■ Filo is available, fresh and frozen, from delicatessens and specialist food stores. If frozen, it should be allowed to thaw in its covering, otherwise it might dry out and crack. Once thawed, it should be kept covered.
■ It is important to follow instructions carefully for brushing each sheet of filo pastry with melted butter, otherwise the pastry may become brittle and crack.

HOT WATER CRUST

This is a unique pastry used for making raised pies. It breaks all the usual pastry rules by requiring everything to be warm instead of cold. It is made by adding melted lard and boiling water to the flour (rather like choux). This forms a strong dough which can then be moulded or 'raised' to make a pie crust that will hold its shape – because of the high proportion of water – during baking and become hard on cooling. After mixing, the pastry must be used quickly.

Basic method

Pies made from hot water crust pastry are almost always savoury. They can look most spectacular on a cold buffet table, especially when baked in one of the elaborate game pie moulds that are available. These moulds are tins which are either hinged or held together with clips and which come apart from the base, to make it easier to move the pie from the tin when it is cooked.

These tins are either oval or round in shape, but it is just as easy (if not so decorative) to use a round or square cake tin – usually about 18–20 cm (7–8 inch) – and preferably with a loose base. Even a 900 g (2 lb) loaf tin can be used.

Although traditionally all hot water crust pies were raised by hand, large pies are probably baked more often nowadays in tins: individual and smaller pies can more easily be moulded by hand.

The most famous pie using this pastry is the pork pie from Melton Mowbray, but other fillings can be used: chicken, veal and ham, mutton (for individual raised pies popular in Scotland), and game. Sometimes hard-boiled eggs are buried in the filling to give an attractive appearance when the pie is cut.

Lard is the usual fat for this pastry but sometimes a mixture of lard and butter is used. The fat is mixed with water or a combination of milk and water. It must be melted slowly in the liquid and only then brought to the boil, for if the liquid is allowed to boil too hard or too long whilst the fat melts, the liquid will evaporate and upset the proportions of the pastry. The whole process does have to be carried out fairly speedily.

Hot water crust pastry is one of the quickest pastries to make, and it is fairly easy to use, but it must be kept covered in a bowl while waiting to be used. The bowl should stand on something warm, or over a pan of hot water. As the pastry cools it sets and becomes more difficult and finally impossible to mould.

This pastry does not freeze as well as most other pastries but it can be kept in the freezer for a short time if necessary. It tends to crumble badly when cut after thawing.

To raise a pie by hand

1. Reserve a quarter to one-third of the dough for the lid and keep this warm in a covered bowl.

2. Roll out the remainder of the pastry and stand a cake tin of the required size in the centre of the pastry (dip it in flour first to prevent the pastry sticking).

3. Gradually work the pastry up the sides, using the balls of the thumbs. Trim the top with a sharp knife. The pastry will firm up as it cools.

4. Turn the tin on its side and roll a few times to smooth the outside and loosen the tin. Gently work the tin out – the pastry case will now remain standing. To fill, stand on a greased baking sheet.

---

450 g (1 lb) plain flour
1½ teaspoons salt
100 g (4 oz) lard
200 ml (7 fl oz) water or milk
    and water mixed

Preparation time: about 15 minutes

1. Make the filling for your pie before starting the pastry.

2. Sift the flour and salt into a bowl and make a well in the centre.

3. Put the lard and water into a saucepan and heat gently until the lard melts, then bring slowly to the boil.

4. Pour the boiling liquid all at once into the well in the flour.

5. Mix quickly to form a soft dough with a wooden spoon or spatula.

6. Knead the dough until smooth and even. Form into a ball and cover with a hot damp cloth to keep warm.

Melton Mowbray Pie

This pie, whose origins go back to the Middle Ages, was originally devised to satisfy keen appetites after a hard day's hunting. Traditionally the pie was always raised by hand (see below left for instructions) but it can equally well be made in a cake tin or hinged pie mould.

1.25 kg (2½ lb) lean pork, diced
salt
freshly ground black pepper
2 tablespoons freshly chopped parsley
600 ml (1 pint) jellied pork or Veal Stock (see page 27)
1 recipe quantity Hot Water Crust Pastry
beaten egg, to glaze

Preparation time: about 1 hour
Cooking time: about 1¾–2 hours
Oven: 200°C, 400°F, Gas Mark 6; then: 180°C, 350°F, Gas Mark 4

1. Mix together the diced pork, salt and pepper to taste, and parsley.

2. Grease a loose-bottomed cake tin or pie mould, measuring approximately 23 × 13 cm (9 × 5½ inches).

Make the pastry and use three-quarters of it to line the mould. Keep the remainder warm. Trim the top edge so that it stands about 1 cm (½ inch) above the rim. If raising the pie by hand, use a cake tin of the same dimensions to shape the pastry.

3. Spoon the filling into the pie case but do not press down too firmly except into the bottom corners. Roll out the remaining pastry for a lid, damp the edges and put into position. Press together, trim if necessary and crimp. Make a hole in the centre of the lid. Roll out the pastry trimmings and cut leaves to decorate around the central hole.

4. Glaze thoroughly with beaten egg and cook in a preheated oven for 30 minutes.

5. Reduce the oven temperature, glaze the pie again, and cook for a further 1 hour 15 minutes.

6. If using a cake tin or pie mould, carefully remove the sides 30 minutes before the end of the cooking time, brush the sides all over with beaten egg and return to the oven.

7. Remove the pie from the oven and cool slightly. Melt the jellied stock and pour into the pie through a funnel inserted into the central hole, until the pie is full. Cool and then chill thoroughly to allow the stock to set.

Variation:

Game Pie Mince 225 g (8 oz) each of pie veal and cooked ham and 350 g (12 oz) game (pheasant, grouse, wild duck etc) and mix with 1 small finely chopped onion, salt and pepper and a good pinch of ground mace or nutmeg. Cook as above but, if possible, make a good game stock using the carcass of the game used. It will need 2 teaspoons powdered gelatine dissolved in it to make it set.

For perfect Hot Water Crust

■ Keep everything warm for the pastry.
■ Prepare the filling before starting the pastry and have the tin greased and ready.
■ If the pastry is too hot to handle, a pair of scrupulously clean rubber gloves make the task much easier!
■ Keep the pastry warm in the bowl whilst it is waiting or it will harden and crack and be impossible to use. Once it has hardened too much there is nothing you can do to repair it.
■ When raising pies by hand it is a good idea to tie a double thickness of greaseproof paper around the outside of the pie before putting into the oven. This will help to keep the shape until the pastry has set; the paper can then be removed.
■ Don't try to raise a very large pie by hand, it is very difficult and may well collapse. Use a tin or pie mould.
■ Put an attractive decoration of pastry leaves on top of the pie. The pastry can still be rolled out for this purpose if it has become cold and hard. Glaze the pie with beaten egg several times during baking to achieve the traditional glossy surface.
■ Fill up the cooked pie through the central hole with a well-flavoured jellied stock or one which has been mixed with gelatine. Start adding the liquid while the pie is still hot and continue adding more as it cools, until it is full. If the pie springs a leak at this stage, plug it with some butter coloured with gravy powder or browning.
■ Chill the pie completely – preferably for at least 12 hours or longer – to make sure it will cut well.

How to line a hinged pie mould

1. Cut a strip of pastry to fit the sides. Roll up like a bandage, then unroll against the sides, pressing into the corners.

2. Cut a piece of pastry to make a lid. Lay in position, wetting the edges, and trim off the excess.

3. Unmould the sides 30 minutes before it has finished cooking and brush the sides with beaten egg.

COOKING EN CROÛTE

This is a method of cooking food – whether meat, poultry, game, fish or pâté – completely enclosed in a shell of puff pastry. (Sometimes other pastries or a Brioche dough, see page 304, are used.) This is less of an aid to the cooking of the food: more a way of presentation that looks spectacular when served. Almost anything can be baked en croûte, and a simple puff pastry casing can magically transform even the humblest chop.

Successful cooking en croûte

■ Make sure the meat, poultry, game or fish is completely boneless and free from sinews etc.
■ Keep the bones and trimmings to make stock for a sauce or gravy.
■ Part-cook meat, poultry and game by roasting, or seal in hot fat if individual portions or a quick cooking meat such as steak, but do not pre-cook fish. Cool quickly and refrigerate until ready to wrap and cook.
■ Remove all strings and skewers used to hold a joint or bird together during the initial cooking before wrapping in pastry.
■ Make a really tasty stuffing with which to stuff the food or to spread around the food, so that it is between the food and pastry.
■ If possible, chill the pastry-clad food for at least 30 minutes before baking.
■ Make several slashes in the pastry to allow the air to escape and prevent the pastry from bursting or splitting badly.
■ When the pastry is sufficiently browned, lay a sheet of wet greaseproof paper carefully over it to prevent overbrowning.

General method

The food used must be boneless for even cooking and for ease of later carving or division into portions. A leg of lamb, for instance, will be boned and rolled into a neat shape as will venison. Poultry and game birds will need to be completely boned (see page 68). Even chops need to be boned and well trimmed. Fish too, will need to be initially skinned, filleted and boned. In

Boeuf en Croûte

Beef Wellington

This is the classic fillet of beef cooked in a pastry case with a layer of mushrooms and pâté around the beef.

Serves 6
1 kg (2 lb) fillet of beef (thick end)
50 g (2 oz) butter
2 tablespoons brandy
freshly ground black pepper
Stuffing:
2 large onions, peeled and chopped
225 g (8 oz) mushrooms, chopped
2 tablespoons freshly chopped parsley
salt
1/2 teaspoon ground coriander
1 recipe quantity Pâte Feuilletée (see page 272)
75 g (3 oz) liver pâté, sliced
beaten egg, to glaze
To garnish:
watercress
lemon wedges

Preparation time: about 30 minutes, plus cooling
Cooking time: about 1 hour
Oven: 220°C, 425°F, Gas Mark 7

1. Tie the piece of fillet into a neat shape, keeping it of even thickness where possible. Melt the butter in a pan and fry the meat quickly, turning frequently to brown on all sides and seal in the juices.

2. Remove from the pan, put on a dish, pour the brandy over and ignite. Season with pepper and leave to cool.

3. For the stuffing, fry the onions in the same pan until soft, then add the mushrooms and continue frying for a few minutes. Turn into a bowl and add the parsley, salt, pepper and coriander and leave to cool.

6. Fold the pastry around the meat, turning up the ends first and then the sides, so they just overlap; press well. Place on a greased baking sheet with the joins underneath. Glaze with beaten egg.

7. Roll out the trimmings, cut into leaves and use to decorate the top of the pastry. Glaze again and make 2 slits in the pastry. Chill for 30 minutes.

general, it is the prime cuts of meat and the best fish that are cooked en croûte.

Many foods to be cooked en croûte are stuffed before wrapping in pastry. The bone cavity of a leg of lamb could be filled with a savoury stuffing before being rolled; a boned chicken or game bird will also be stuffed, both for flavour and to help retain the shape of the bird. Often a stuffing is merely wrapped around the meat to be

cooked en croûte as in the classic Beef Wellington. A prime fish, however, requires little more than a sprinkling of herbs and some butter. Most larger joints or birds must be par-cooked before being encased in pastry. The exception is fillet of beef, normally served rarer, which needs only an initial browning before being cooked en croûte. Fish requires no prior cooking at all.

4. Roll out the pastry on a lightly floured surface to a rectangle large enough to enclose the beef. Spread the mushroom mixture down the centre. Lay the pâté slices on the mushroom mixture and top with the beef.

5. Cut a 4 cm (1½ inch) square from each corner of the pastry and keep on one side. Brush round the edges of the pastry with beaten egg.

8. Bake in a preheated oven for just under an hour for steak which is pink in the centre. If you prefer it more cooked, continue for 15–20 minutes and carefully place a sheet of wet greaseproof paper over the pastry to prevent it overbrowning. Serve at once accompanied by Béarnaise Sauce (see page 46), and garnished with watercress and lemon wedges.

Individual Beef Wellingtons

These look spectacular at a dinner party, can be prepared in advance to put in the oven when required, and do away with any carving problems at the table.

Serves 6
6 tournedos or fillet steaks, about 100 g (4 oz) each
freshly ground pepper
50 g (2 oz) butter
stuffing (see Boeuf en Croûte)
75 g (3 oz) liver pâté (optional)
6 cap mushrooms
1½ recipe quantity Pâte Feuilletée (see page 272)
beaten egg, to glaze
To garnish:
watercress
chicory spears

Preparation time: about 30–40 minutes, plus cooling
Cooking time: 25–45 minutes
Oven: 200°C, 400°F, Gas Mark 6

1. Trim the steaks, wipe dry on kitchen paper and season lightly with pepper.

2. Melt the butter in a pan and quickly brown each steak on all sides to seal in the juices. Remove from the pan.

3. Make up the stuffing and leave to cool. Divide the pâté (if used) into 6 equal slices. Trim the stems of the mushrooms level with the caps.

4. Divide the pastry into three and roll each piece out to a rectangle about 36 × 28 cm (14 × 11 inches) and then cut in half. Divide the stuffing between these 6 pieces of pastry, add a slice of pâté (if used) and top with a steak and mushroom cap.

5. Brush round the edges with beaten egg. Fold the pastry over the meat to enclose the filling, trimming off any excess pastry, and sealing the edges well. Stand on a greased baking sheet with the join underneath. Glaze with beaten egg and decorate with leaves made from the pastry trimmings. Glaze again. Chill for at least 30 minutes and up to 3 hours.

6. Glaze again and bake in a preheated oven allowing 25 minutes for rare cooked steaks, 28–30 minutes for medium cooked steaks, and 40–45 minutes for well cooked steaks. Serve immediately with a garnish of watercress and chicory spears. Offer a selection of mustards as accompaniments or Béarnaise Sauce (see page 46).

Leg of Lamb en Croûte

Serves 6–8
*1 leg of lamb about 2.25 kg
    (5 lb), boned*
salt
freshly ground pepper
a little oil or dripping
Stuffing:
40 g (1½ oz) butter
*1 onion, peeled and finely
    chopped*
*4 rashers bacon, rinded and
    chopped*
*225 g (8 oz) mushrooms,
    chopped*
50 g (2 oz) fresh breadcrumbs
*1 tablespoon freshly chopped
    mint*
*1 dessert apple, peeled, cored
    and grated*
*1½ recipe quantity Pâte
    Feuilletée (see page 272)*
beaten egg, to glaze
To garnish:
*100 g (4 oz) button
    mushrooms, lightly sautéed
    in a little butter*
fresh mint or parsley
cooked carrot sticks

Preparation time: about 1¼
hours, excluding boning
Cooking time: about 2¾ hours
Oven: 220°C, 425°F, Gas Mark 7
then: 180°C, 350°F, Gas Mark 4

1. Roll the boned leg of lamb
and secure with string or
skewers. It should weigh 1.75–
2 kg (4–4½ lb). Stand in a
roasting tin, season with salt
and pepper and pour over a
little oil. Roast in a preheated
oven for 1¼ hours, basting
once or twice.

2. Remove the lamb to a plate
and leave until quite cold. The
joint may be chilled overnight.
When cold, remove any string
and/or skewers. The pan juices
may be used to make a gravy
which can be reheated when
required.

3. For the stuffing, melt the
butter in a pan and fry the
onion and bacon gently until
soft. Add the mushrooms and
continue frying for 3–4
minutes. Turn into a bowl and
leave until cold. Add
seasonings, the breadcrumbs,
mint and apple and mix well.

4. Roll out the pastry on a
lightly floured surface, until
large enough to enclose the
joint. Spread the stuffing down
the centre of the pastry and
place the joint in the centre.
Wrap up to enclose completely
in pastry brushing the edges
with beaten egg. Stand, seam
side downwards, in a greased
roasting tin and brush all over
with beaten egg. Re-roll the
pastry trimmings and cut out
pastry leaves to decorate the
pastry. Glaze with beaten egg
again. Chill for 30 minutes.

5. Cook in a preheated hot
oven for 30 minutes. Reduce
the oven temperature, glaze
the pastry again and cook for a
further hour, covering the
pastry carefully with a wet
sheet of greaseproof paper
when sufficiently browned.

6. When ready, transfer the
pastry parcel to a warmed
serving dish and garnish with
sautéed mushrooms, fresh
mint (or parsley) and carrot
sticks. Carve in slices and serve
with a thick gravy if liked, made
from the pan juices.

Salmon en Croûte

Cooking salmon or sea trout en
croûte really does the fish
justice, for not only have all the
bones been removed but the
natural juices are all held into
the fish by the pastry. It may be
served hot or cold.

Serves 6
*1.5 kg (3–3½ lb) salmon or
    sea trout, head removed and
    cleaned*
juice of 1 lemon
salt
freshly ground pepper
50 g (2 oz) butter, softened
*1 tablespoon chopped fresh dill
    (or 1 teaspoon dried)*
*1 recipe quantity Pâte
    Feuilletée (see page 272)*
beaten egg, to glaze
*Hollandaise Sauce (see page
    44), to serve*
To garnish:
lemon slices
cucumber slices
watercress

Preparation time: about 1 hour
Cooking time: about 50
minutes
Oven: 220°C, 425°F, Gas Mark 7
then 190°C, 375°F Gas Mark 5

1. Divide the fish into two
fillets by carefully taking the
fish off the bone (see page
71), then remove the skin.
Rub the fillets all over with
lemon juice and season
lightly with salt and pepper.

2. Lay one fillet on a board
and spread with the butter.
Sprinkle with the dill and
cover with the second fillet
to reshape the fish.

Variations

Venison en Croûte Use a
boned and rolled haunch of
venison weighing about 1.75–
2 kg (4–4½ lb) when boned.
Wrap the joint completely in
rinded streaky bacon rashers
and secure with string. The
stuffing can be virtually the
same as for the lamb but
replace the mint with 1
teaspoon dried basil and omit
the apple. Complete as for the
lamb. Use the bones to make a
stock for the gravy, which
should be flavoured with red
wine or port, redcurrant or
cranberry jelly, and orange
juice. Garnish with slices of
orange and watercress.
**Chicken or Pheasant en
Croûte** Use a completely
boned out chicken of about

1.75 kg (4 lb) and use the same
stuffing to fill the bird, then
truss and cover in rinded
streaky bacon as for the
venison. Roast for only 1 hour,
chill and then wrap in pastry
without any more stuffing.
Remember to have the joins
under the bird. Cook for 30
minutes in a hot oven and then
for about 40 minutes in a
moderate oven. When using
pheasants it would be best to
bone out 2 birds and sandwich
them together with the stuffing
before the first roasting.

6. Bake in a preheated hot oven for about 30 minutes. Reduce the temperature and bake for a further 20 minutes or until golden brown. If overbrowning, cover with a sheet of greaseproof paper and continue cooking until ready.

7. Serve garnished with lemon slices, cucumber and watercress. Serve the Hollandaise Sauce in a sauceboat so it is just warm.

3. Roll out about three-quarters of the pastry thinly and use to enclose the fish, keeping to the shape as much as possible and sealing the edges with water or beaten egg.

4. Place the fish on a greased baking sheet with the join underneath; glaze all over with beaten egg. Roll out the remaining pastry thinly together with the trimmings and use to cut into scales. Arrange these all over the fish, starting from the head and working to the tail.

5. Cut out a slightly enlarged pastry 'tail' and position. Also cut an eye for the head. Glaze all over with beaten egg.

BREAD

Bread-making is one of the most satisfying of activities, yet most people are frightened of ever trying it. Follow the guidelines for using yeast, be patient, and you will find it surprisingly easy.

Bread is basically a mixture of flour and water, leavened with yeast and baked in the oven. Yet the amount of variations that can be made in this simple formula are amazing. Bread can be made with wheat, rye or barley flour; you can also use buckwheat flour, cornmeal or even rice or potato flour. Bread can be spiced, sweetened or enriched with butter or eggs. It can even be cooked without yeast (unleavened) or risen with baking soda instead of yeast.

The most important lesson in bread-making is to learn about yeast and its properties (see page 295). It is essential to give yeast time to do its work properly if the end result is to be satisfactory. You must wait for the yeast to be activated; allow the dough time to rise properly; and wait for the dough to prove after shaping. In fact, you could say that patience is the secret of bread-making.

Yeast doughs can also be used for a variety of cakes and pastries (see pages 300–309).

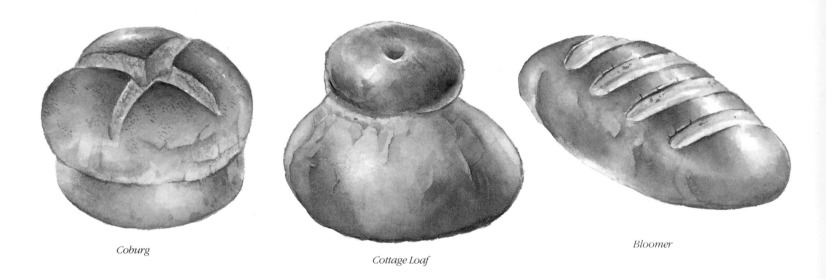

Coburg

Cottage Loaf

Bloomer

Cob

Plait

Vienna Loaves

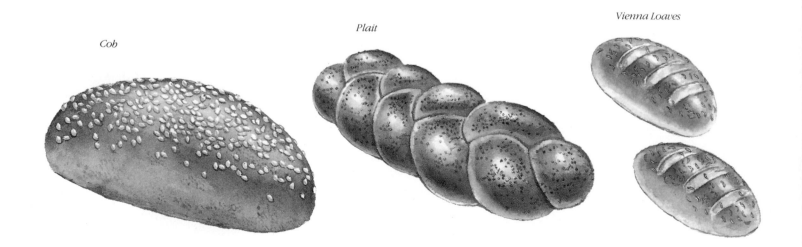

YEAST

In general, there are two types of yeast suitable for breadmaking or any yeast baking in general – fresh and dried. Brewer's yeast is not suitable for breadmaking.

Fresh yeast is the yeast most often used by bakers, and is sometimes also known as pressed or moist yeast. It is putty-coloured, smooth textured and moist, and will cut easily with a knife, or will crumble readily when broken. It should smell fresh and slightly fruity, rather like wine. If it is already crumbly, dark or spotty, it is stale and not suitable for use. It is available in health-food shops and some baker's shops.

It stays fresh for 2–3 weeks if stored in a loosely tied polythene bag in the refrigerator; or for 4–5 days in a cool place. It will freeze for up to 6 months if wrapped first

Cream fresh yeast with warm water

Leave dried yeast mixture until frothy

in clingfilm or polythene and then in foil. Always package it in usable amounts – 25 g (1 oz) packets, say – so it can be taken from the freezer, thawed and used at once. To reconstitute it, simply blend with the warm liquid and add to the dry ingredients.

Dried yeast comes as small granules of compacted yeast and is sold in tins or packets which will keep for up to 6 months after opening if put in an airtight container. There are always activating instructions on the packet or tin, and it is essential that it is properly activated before adding to the dry ingredients or the dough will not rise.

It can be reconstituted in warm liquid with a little sugar added. It is then left in a warm place until the granules have dissolved and the liquid froths up – this usually takes 10–20 minutes. It can also be mixed into a flour, sugar and milk and/or water batter which should be left for 20–30 minutes in a warm place to froth up; this method is more often used for the richer doughs. If the yeast does not froth up it is a sign the yeast is stale and should be discarded. Dried yeast is widely available from supermarkets, chemists, healthfood stores etc. Like herbs, yeast should not be kept on your shelves too long.

The batter method of activating yeast

Instant dried yeast is a new kind of granular dried yeast which is quick-acting and does not need to be reconstituted with liquid. It is simply mixed into the flour before the liquid is poured in. There are several varieties on the market, so simply follow the manufacturer's instructions.

Yeast quantities The quantity of yeast required varies with the type of dough being made, but if using dried yeast and the recipe only states a quantity for fresh yeast, then use half as much: 25 g (1 oz) fresh yeast = 15 g (½ oz) or 1 level tablespoon dried yeast, plus 1 teaspoon caster sugar.

For plain bread doughs –

those without extra fat added – allow 15 g (½ oz) fresh yeast or 1½ teaspoons dried and 1 teaspoon sugar to 450–675 g (1–1½ lb) white flour. For 1.5 kg (3 lb) flour, allow 25 g (1 oz) fresh or 1 tablespoon dried yeast plus 1 teaspoon sugar.

Wholemeal flour requires a higher proportion of yeast to flour; always half as much again and sometimes up to double the amount for white dough. Enriched doughs also need more than plain doughs because the extra fat, sugar, eggs, and/or fruit retard the growth of the yeast: if extra were not added, it would take forever to rise to even half the size it should.

INGREDIENTS

Flour A strong white gluten flour called a bread or strong flour should be used for breadmaking. The higher gluten content of strong flour allows more absorption of liquid thus giving a greater volume and lighter bread. A soft or household flour absorbs more fat but less liquid, giving a smaller volume and a closer, and shorter texture to most breads; however, this latter type of flour is sometimes preferred for rich fancy breads.

Quite apart from the plain strong white flours, numerous other types of flour are available: brown, wholewheat, wheatmeal, granary, etc.

Liquid The liquid for breadmaking is usually water, milk or a mixture of the two; sometimes beaten egg forms part of the liquid content. The liquid or part of it is used to dissolve the yeast, and it must be warm – between 37–43°C/ 98–110°F – to make the yeast work. If it is too cool, the yeast will not be activated, and if too

hot will simply kill the yeast.

Milk adds extra food value and strengthens a dough, and the fat content in the milk gives the bread a better keeping quality; it also gives a closer crumb and softer textured crust. You need approximately 300 ml (½ pint) liquid for each 450 g (1 lb) strong flour.

The liquid should always be added at the same time in breadmaking – even if done gradually to make sure the correct consistency is obtained – so that the dough is mixed evenly. Extra flour can be kneaded in quite easily, but adding extra water later, after kneading, usually results in a lumpy dough.

Fat A small amount of fat is often rubbed into the flour to help keep it moist and to help it keep longer, but it is not essential. Lard is usual, but butter or margarine can also be used. With the richer doughs more fat is required and it can be melted, softened or rubbed in, depending on the recipe.

BREAD-MAKING TECHNIQUES

Kneading All doughs must be kneaded after mixing to strengthen and develop the gluten in order to give a good rise and even texture to the baked loaf.

To knead dough, you form the dough into a ball and punch it down and away from you using the palm of your hand, then fold it over towards you and give it a quarter turn. Repeat until smooth and even and the dough feels elastic and is no longer sticky. This should take about 10 minutes (or as the recipe directs), and as you knead, it is possible to develop a rhythmic, rocking movement. Knead on a lightly floured surface, using as little extra flour as possible. You can also use an electric mixer's dough hook. Switch to the lowest speed for 3–4 minutes, following the instructions for the maximum amount the machine can safely handle.

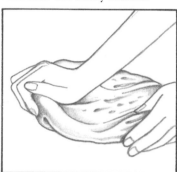

1. Kneading by hand

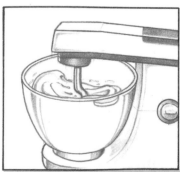

2. Kneading with the dough hook of an electric mixer

Rising All yeast doughs must rise at least once before baking. After kneading, the dough should be shaped into a ball and placed in a large lightly oiled polythene bag loosely tied at the neck. It could also be put into a lightly greased bowl or plastic storage container. This must be large enough for

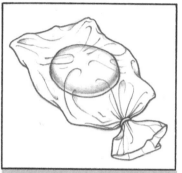

1. Place dough in oiled polythene bag to rise

the dough to double in size at least, and it must be kept covered to prevent a skin forming; either use a damp cloth, polythene which has been lightly oiled, or cling-film.

Rising times vary with room temperature, but the dough needs enough time to rise to double its size, and it should spring back when lightly pressed with a floured finger. Allow 45–60 minutes in a warm place; 2 hours at room temperature; up to 12 hours in a cold room or larder; or up to 24 hours in the refrigerator. Remember that chilled dough must be allowed to return to room temperature before shaping.

Surplus dough can be stored in a closed polythene bag or container in the refrigerator for up to 24 hours before use.

Freezing Doughs can very successfully be frozen at this stage. Allow the dough to begin rising to ensure that the yeast is working then wrap in cling film and place in the freezer. It can

be stored in the freezer for 3 months.

Knocking back This is simply a short second kneading of the dough to knock out the air bubbles and make it smooth and even, ready for shaping. It should only take 1–2 minutes: push down into the risen

2. Leave until doubled in size

dough with your closed fist, then push the sides into the

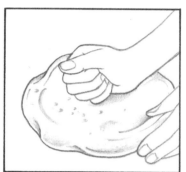

Knocking back after rising

centre. In the case of very rich doughs there is then a second rising – this develops a very fine even-grained texture.

Shaping and proving The dough is now ready for shaping. Follow the recipe instructions for whatever type of dough you are making. The shaped dough then requires a second rising (or proving). Proving usually takes 10–15 minutes in a warm kitchen. Put

the loaf tins, cake tins or baking sheets into large oiled polythene bags or lay a sheet of oiled polythene loosely over them to prevent a skin forming; put in a warm place until the dough has doubled in size again and springs back when lightly pressed with a floured finger. Remove the polythene before baking.

Glazing A glaze can be added to loaves, rolls or cakes before baking. Beaten egg, milk, salted water or a dredging of flour each give different finishes, and they can further be sprinkled with poppy seeds, sesame seeds, cracked wheat, oatmeal etc.

Baking Most bread doughs are baked in a hot to very hot oven with the plainer doughs requiring the hottest temperature. Richer doughs are sometimes baked in a moderately hot to fairly hot oven to prevent overbrowning.

A cooked loaf should shrink slightly from the sides of the tin. When it is turned out, the base should sound hollow when tapped with the knuckles. If the loaf is cooked, cool on a wire rack. If it is not cooked, replace in the tin and continue cooking for a few minutes. (Some loaves benefit from a few minutes baking *out* of the tin: this gives a good crust.)

Loaf should sound hollow when tapped on base

SHAPING LOAVES

There are many shapes of loaf which can be made simply from the basic white bread dough.

Coburg Shape half the recipe quantity of risen bread dough into a round ball. This is done by rolling the dough in a circular movement with the palm of your hand and gradually easing the pressure to give a smooth round ball – it takes practice to perfect. Place

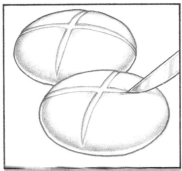

Mark the Coburg with a cross on top

on a greased baking sheet and, if liked, brush all over with milk or beaten egg. With a sharp knife, cut a cross on top of the loaf taking it from side to side. Put to prove as usual.

Cob This is a plain round loaf, again using half the basic recipe of risen bread dough. It is usually glazed and sprinkled with seeds, and used to be mainly made of brown dough. Sometimes the top of the loaf is slashed once across the top before proving.

Cottage The famous round loaf with a top-knot. Use a recipe quantity for a large loaf or divide it in 2 for smaller loaves. Remove one-third of the dough for the top-knot. Shape both pieces into round balls and place the larger piece on a greased baking sheet and flatten it slightly. Damp the base of the top-knot and

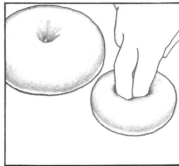

1. Shape loaf and topknot and make indentations

position it centrally on top of the large ball of dough; secure it by pushing your first finger and thumb right through the centre of the loaf to the base, taking care to keep the top-knot quite central. Brush with beaten egg or salted water and put to prove.

For a fancy notched cottage loaf, after shaping make slashes all round the lower part of the loaf at an angle; and then around the topknot.

Plait For whatever sized loaf you require, divide the dough into 3 equal portions and with the palms of the hands roll them into fairly thin, even sausage shapes of equal length. For thicker plaits simply roll the sausages thicker. Place the 3 pieces of dough next to each other on a greased baking sheet straight in front of you. Beginning in the centre, plait the pieces evenly towards you

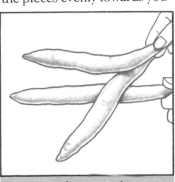

1. Begin plaiting in the centre of the 3 strands

2. Place topknot on loaf and push fingers through to base

and pinch the ends together firmly. Carefully turn the baking sheet round so that the unplaited strands face you. Complete the plaiting, secure the ends by pinching together, and tuck the ends underneath the loaf. Plaits can be baked plain or glazed with milk, beaten egg or salted water, and then sprinkled with poppy or sesame seeds for variety.

Crescent This loaf is a little more difficult to shape evenly and will take a little practice. Use half the recipe quantity of risen dough and roll it out on a lightly floured surface to an oval shape. Leave to rest for 5 minutes; then beginning at a wide edge, roll the dough up tightly to form a sausage, taking care to keep the middle very tight or the sausage will 'bulge' Bend into a crescent shape and put on to a greased baking sheet. Prove and then bake for

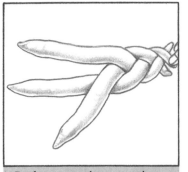

2. Plait towards you and pinch ends together

about 25 minutes.

Bloomer This is a long fat baton-shaped loaf with diagonal slashes along the top. It is usually crusty and can be sprinkled with poppy or sesame seeds. Use 1 recipe quantity of risen dough or half the dough for smaller loaves. Shape each piece into an even thickness baton by rolling the dough backwards and forwards with the palms of the hands. Tuck the ends underneath and place on a greased baking sheet. If liked, brush with milk, beaten egg or salted water, then cover with oiled polythene and put to prove until doubled in size. Remove the polythene, cut diagonal slashes all along the top of the loaf with a very sharp knife and bake for 30–40 minutes depending on size.

These loaves can be 'batch' baked by putting the pieces of dough quite close to each other so they join up during proving and baking. The baked loaves are then pulled apart to reveal soft crustless sides; they will still have crusty tops.

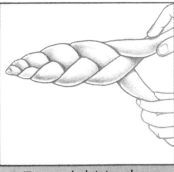

3. Turn and plait in other direction

White Bread

*750 g (1½ lb) strong white
  bread flour*
1–2 teaspoons salt
15 g (½ oz) lard
*15 g (½ oz) fresh yeast, or 1½
  teaspoons dried yeast plus 1
  teaspoon caster sugar*
*450 ml (¾ pint) warm water
  (about 43°C/110°F)*
*beaten egg or milk, to glaze
  (optional)*
*poppy or sesame seeds
  (optional)*

Preparation time: about 30
minutes, plus rising times
Cooking time: about 35–40
minutes
Oven: 230°C, 450°F, Gas Mark 8

1. Sift the flour and salt into a
bowl. Add the lard and rub in
finely.

2. If using fresh yeast, dissolve
in the warm water. For dried
yeast, dissolve the sugar in the
water and sprinkle the yeast on
top; leave in a warm place for
about 10 minutes or until
frothy.

3. Add the yeast liquid to the
dry ingredients all at once and
mix to form a firm elastic
dough, using a palette knife or
spatula.

4. Turn out on to a lightly
floured surface and knead the
dough for about 10 minutes or
until smooth and no longer
sticky (see page 296).
Alternatively the dough can be
mixed and kneaded in a large
electric mixer fitted with a
dough hook for 3–4 minutes.

5. Shape the dough into a ball,
place in a large oiled polythene
bag and tie loosely at the top,
or put into a floured bowl and
cover with a damp cloth or
piece of clingfilm. Put to rise in
a warm place for about an hour
until the dough has doubled in
size, and it springs back when
lightly pressed with a floured
finger. (Or put to rise at the
other suggested places and
times, see page 296.)

6. Remove the dough from the
bag, turn out on to a lightly
floured surface and 'knock
back' by kneading until smooth
and even again, and the air
bubbles have been knocked out.

7. The dough is now ready for
shaping. Grease 2 loaf tins – a
900 g (2 lb) and a 450 g (1 lb)
tin, or 3 of the smaller tins.
Divide the dough into 2
portions – two-thirds and one-
third, depending on the
number of tins – and shape
each piece to fit a tin by
kneading and rolling to give a
shape as wide as the tin and a
little longer. Tuck the ends
under and place evenly in the
tin.

8. Lay a sheet of oiled
polythene lightly over the
loaves and put to rise in a warm
place until the dough reaches
the tops of the tins.

9. They may be brushed with
beaten egg or milk and
sprinkled with poppy or
sesame seeds; if left plain, do
not glaze but dredge lightly
with flour.

10. Bake in a very hot oven for
35–40 minutes for the larger
loaf and about 30 minutes for
the smaller one (to test, see
page 296). Turn out on to a
wire tray and leave to cool.

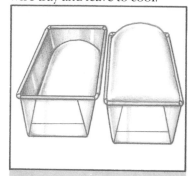

Put dough to rise in tins
until it doubles in size

Short-Time White Bread

This way of making bread is
really a cheat for the dough has
only one rising. The flavour is
good, though, but the keeping
quality is quite severely cut.
However, it will keep for a
couple of days and can be
frozen successfully, to take out
of the freezer and use at once.

*450 g (1 lb) strong plain white
  bread flour*
1½ teaspoons salt
2 teaspoons sugar
15 g (½ oz) lard
*15 g (½ oz) fresh yeast, or 2
  teaspoons dried yeast plus 1
  teaspoon sugar*
*300 ml (½ pint) warm water
  (about 43°/110°F)*
salted water, to glaze

Preparation time: about 20
minutes, plus rising time
Cooking time: about 25–30
minutes
Oven: 230°C, 450°F, Gas Mark 8
then: 200°C, 400°F, Gas Mark 6

1. Sift the flour and salt into a
bowl, add the sugar and then
rub in the lard finely.

2. If using fresh yeast, dissolve
it in the warm water; or for
dried yeast, dissolve the sugar
in the water, sprinkle the yeast
on top, and leave in a warm
place for about 10 minutes or
until frothy.

3. Add the yeast liquid to the
dry ingredients all at once, and
mix to form a fairly firm dough.
Turn on to a floured surface
and knead for about 10
minutes or until smooth and
no longer sticky.

4. Shape into 1 or 2 loaves.
Place on a greased baking sheet
and brush the tops with salted
water.

5. Put to rise in a warm place
until doubled in size. Remove
the polythene and bake in a
very hot oven for 15 minutes,
then reduce the temperature to
moderately hot, and continue
for about 10 minutes for the
smaller loaves, or about 20
minutes for the large loaf. The
base should sound hollow when
tapped. Cool on a wire tray.

FREEZING

Most yeasted breads, rolls and
cakes freeze satisfactorily after
cooking. When cooking for the
freezer do not over-bake to a
very crisp crust, as it may crack
and shell off in the freezer.
They should be cooled quickly,
wrapped tightly in foil or heavy
weight polythene and frozen at
once. Storage times vary from
1–2 months for very rich or
spicy recipes, to up to 6 months
for plain loaves. Thaw out
completely before use.
  Raw bread dough can be
frozen too. For unrisen dough,
form into a ball, place in a
greased polythene bag and
freeze immediately. Store plain
doughs for up to 2 months,
enriched doughs for up to 5
weeks. To thaw, tie the bag
loosely to allow room for rising
and leave for 5–6 hours at
room temperature, or
overnight in the refrigerator
Knock back and continue as
usual.
  Risen bread dough after
knocking back can be shaped
into a ball, placed in a greased
polythene bag and frozen
immediately. Store for up to 4
weeks for brown and white
doughs. Thaw as for unrisen
dough.

Vienna Loaves

It is almost impossible to achieve the flavour and texture of a true French baguette loaf in a domestic cooker, but this recipe, together with the bowl of water in the oven for part of the cooking time, helps to create the steamy atmosphere necessary to give the crisp but soft-textured crust and soft crumb of the French loaf. This loaf is best eaten on the day it is baked, but unlike the true French loaf, it is still edible the next day.

450 g (1 lb) strong white flour
1½ teaspoons salt
1 teaspoon caster sugar
25 g (1 oz) lard or margarine
*25 g (1 oz) fresh yeast, or 1
    tablespoon dried yeast plus 1
    teaspoon sugar*
*300 ml (½ pint) warm milk
    and water mixed (about
    43°C/110°F)*
poppy seeds (optional)

Preparation time: about 30 minutes, plus rising times
Cooking time: about 30 minutes
Oven: 230°C, 450°F, Gas Mark 8

1. Sift the flour, salt and sugar into a bowl and rub in the fat.

2. Blend the fresh yeast with the warm milk and water; or for dried yeast, dissolve the sugar in the liquid, sprinkle the yeast on top and leave in a warm place until frothy – about 10 minutes.

3. Add the yeast liquid to the dry ingredients and mix to form a fairly soft dough. Turn on to a lightly floured surface and knead until smooth and even – about 10 minutes by hand or 3–4 minutes in a large electric mixer fitted with a dough hook.

4. Shape into a ball, place in an oiled polythene bag and put to rise until doubled in size.

5. Remove from the bag, knead until smooth, and divide into 2 or 3 pieces. Roll each piece out thinly to an oval, keeping the rolling pin well floured to prevent tearing the dough; to about 30 cm (12 inches) for the larger loaf or 23 cm (9 inches) for the smaller ones.

6. Beginning at a long side roll up each piece evenly and fairly tightly to the shape of a baguette. Place on greased baking sheets either straight or curved, keeping the join underneath. Cover with oiled polythene and put to prove in a warm place for about 30 minutes or until doubled in size and puffy.

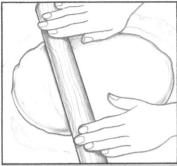
Roll out thinly to an oval

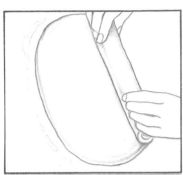
Roll up dough beginning at a long side

7. Remove polythene, make several slashes diagonally along the top of each loaf and sprinkle with poppy seeds if liked. Put a large tin of hot water in the bottom of a very hot oven to produce a steamy atmosphere. Leave for 10 minutes then put the loaves in the oven and bake for 15 minutes. Open the door, let out the steam and take out the tin of water. Close the oven and cook for a further 10–15 minutes or until the crust is crispy and a dark golden brown. Cool on a wire tray.

Wholemeal Bread

This bread can be made using any of the plain brown bread flours or a mixture of them. Some of the rougher flours will give a coarser textured loaf with a little less volume. For a lighter brown loaf use half brown and half white flour.

Brown bread may need a little more water than white flour as it has a slightly higher absorption rate. Do not allow the dough to be too dry or it will take a very long time to rise.

*750 g (1½ lb) wholemeal,
    wholewheat or any other
    plain brown flour*
1½ level teaspoons salt
1 tablespoon caster sugar
25 g (1 oz) lard
*25 g (1 oz) fresh yeast or 1
    tablespoon dried yeast plus 1
    teaspoon sugar*
*450 ml (¾ pint) warm water
    (about 43°C/110°F)*

Preparation time: about 30 minutes, plus rising times
Cooking time: about 30–40 minutes
Oven: 230°C, 450°F, Gas Mark 8

1. Put the flour into a bowl (do not sieve it or all the healthy bran etc. will be sifted out). Mix in the salt and sugar and rub in the lard.

2. Blend the fresh yeast with the warm liquid; or for dried yeast, dissolve the sugar in the liquid, sprinkle the yeast on top and leave in a warm place until frothy – about 10 minutes.

3. Add the yeast liquid to the dry ingredients and mix to form a pliable dough which leaves the sides of the bowl clean. If too dry add a little more warm water as you are mixing.

4. Turn on to a lightly floured surface and knead until smooth and even, and no longer sticky. Shape into a ball, place in an oiled polythene bag and put to rise until doubled in size.

5. Remove the dough from the bag, knock back and knead until smooth.

6. Shape to fit 1 greased 900 g (2 lb) loaf tin or 2 greased 450 g (1 lb) tins, or bake in any of the shapes already described.

7. Put to prove until the dough almost reaches the top of the tins and then bake in a very hot oven for 30–40 minutes in a tin (a little less for those without tins), or until the base sounds hollow when tapped.

This dough can also be shaped into rolls.

Yeast Doughs

There's much more to using yeast than just baking bread. Sticky buns, pastries and babas, light brioches and flaky croissants . . . success with yeast is guaranteed once you've mastered a few basic, all-important techniques. Full instructions are given here for perfect results.

Detailed instructions on using yeast and the method for the basic yeast dough have been explained previously on pages 295–296.

In this section, we continue on from the basic dough to enriched yeast doughs, which are used for Brioches, Croissants, Savarin and other delights.

Basic rules

There are two types of yeast to use for bread-making, namely fresh or dried (or the new instant dried). Both are readily available and give excellent results, but with dried or instant yeast always follow the manufacturer's instructions. Do not use brewer's yeast (for wine or beer) for bread-making.

A strong plain flour, called bread flour by bakers, should be used to achieve the best results. Strong flour has a higher gluten content than ordinary household flour, and this allows a higher absorption of liquid, resulting in a greater volume and lighter bread. The only exception to this rule is Danish pastry dough, which is made with household flour.

Where possible the liquid should be added all at once to the dry ingredients. Extra flour can be added if the dough is too sticky but adding extra water usually causes lumps and unevenness which are difficult to remove even during kneading.

Enriched Bread Dough

Rich bread doughs have a high proportion of butter and sugar, if appropriate, and usually are made with milk and eggs instead of water. Because of this, a large amount of yeast is required to raise the dough. All of these extra properties result in a bread which is moister, with a closer texture than usual, and a softer crust. It is almost cake-like in texture and can be used for richer bread and rolls.

The dough is made by the batter method. Because of this, dried yeast can be used, for this can be reconstituted during the batter fermentation, not as a separate process.

The dough can be baked in a tin, or shaped and baked on a baking sheet without a tin. It can be glazed with beaten egg, salted water or milk, and can be topped with poppy seeds, sesame seeds, caraway or fennel seeds as well as cracked wheat, oatmeal or crushed sea salt as liked. It is cooked in a moderate oven, for it would over-brown and dry in a hot oven, at the usual bread-baking heat.

Makes 1 large crown loaf or 2 small crown loaves
450 g (1 lb) strong white flour
1 teaspoon caster sugar
25 g (1 oz) fresh yeast or 1 tablespoon dried yeast
250 ml (8 fl oz) warm milk (43°C/110°F)
1 teaspoon salt
50 g (2 oz) butter or margarine
1 egg, beaten
Glaze:
1 egg, beaten
1 tablespoon water
poppy or sesame seeds (optional)

Preparation time: about 30 minutes, plus risings
Cooking time: about 50–60 minutes
Oven: 190°C, 375°F, Gas Mark 5

1. Put 150 g (5 oz) of the flour into a bowl with the sugar, yeast (fresh or dried) and the warmed milk. Mix lightly and leave in a warm place for about 20 minutes for fresh yeast – 30 minutes for dried – until frothy. Grease one 23 cm (9 inch) round deep sandwich tin, or two 15 cm (6 inch) round tins.

2. Sift the remaining flour and salt into a bowl and rub in the fat until the mixture resembles fine breadcrumbs. Add the yeast batter and beaten egg and mix well with a wooden spoon to form a fairly soft dough.

3. Turn on to a lightly floured surface and knead well until smooth and even and no longer sticky – about 10 minutes by hand or 3–4 minutes in a large electric mixer fitted with a dough hook. Shape the dough into a ball and place in a lightly oiled bowl or polythene bag. Put to rise in a warm place for about an hour or until doubled in size.

4. Remove dough from the bowl or polythene bag, put onto a very lightly floured surface, and knock back and knead until smooth – about 2 minutes.

Fat is added in small amounts to plain yeast mixtures to help keep it moist; but richer mixtures require a larger proportion which may be rubbed in, added in a melted state, or put on the rolled-out dough in flakes or softened form to fold and roll in like the flaked pastries.

All yeast mixtures need warmth, at least at some stage. For best results warm the bowl and flour slightly and make sure the liquids for activating the yeast are hand-hot – 43°C/110°F.

Kneading

All doughs require kneading after mixing to strengthen and develop the gluten in order to give a good rise and even texture to the baked loaf. Knead by folding the dough towards you, then push down and away, using the knuckles and heel of the hands. Give the dough a quarter turn and repeat the process, developing a rocking action. Knead by hand for about 10 minutes until the dough is smooth and even, on a very lightly floured surface, using as little extra flour as possible.

Kneading a yeast dough can be carried out in a large electric mixer using the special dough hook with the machine running at the slowest speed for 3–4 minutes.

Rising

All yeast doughs must rise at least once before baking. After kneading they should be shaped into a ball and put in a bowl covered with a damp cloth, until doubled in size. Some rich doughs are simply beaten and left to rise in the bowl. The dough then needs knocking back to remove air bubbles and make it smooth and even ready for shaping. Do not knead in any extra flour at this stage or it will spoil the colour and texture of the crust of the loaf.

Details for shaping, proving and baking are given with each individual recipe (see also pages 295–296).

For perfect Yeast Dough

■ Use a strong white flour for the best results. Some of the white flour may be replaced by a proportion of up to half of a brown or granary flour. This must be a strong flour too.

■ Make sure the liquid is no hotter than 43°C/110°F, or the yeast may be killed.

■ Do not cut down on the kneading process either by hand or in an electric mixer, or the gluten will not develop properly.

■ Choose the type of rising to suit your time schedule.

Quick rise 45–60 minutes in a warm place.

Slower rise About 2 hours at room temperature.

Overnight rise Up to 12 hours in a cold larder.

Refrigerator rise Up to 24 hours in the refrigerator. (Remember that refrigerated doughs need to 'come to' for about an hour at room temperature before proceeding.)

■ Make sure you don't knead too much extra flour into the dough, especially after the first rising, for it will spoil the texture, toughen the crumb and often give a speckled appearance to the crust.

■ Don't be tempted to bake loaves or rolls until doubled in size. The dough should be springy and leave a slight indentation when lightly pressed with a finger.

5. Divide the dough into 12 even-sized pieces and roll each into a ball. For a large crown place a circle of dough balls around the edge of the large tin with three or four in the centre; whilst for the smaller tins, arrange five balls around the outside with one in the centre.

6. Make the glaze by beating the egg and water together and use to brush all over the loaf. Sprinkle with poppy or sesame seeds, if used. Place in a large oiled polythene bag, or cover lightly with a sheet of oiled polythene and put to rise in a warm place until doubled in size.

7. Remove the polythene and bake in a preheated oven for 50–60 minutes for the large loaf or 30–40 minutes for the smaller loaves, or until a good golden brown. The base of the loaf should sound hollow when tapped. Cool on a wire tray.

Variations

Vienna Rolls. Divide the dough into 50 g (2 oz) pieces and shape into ovals with tapered ends. Place well apart on greased baking sheets. Cover lightly with oiled polythene and put to rise in a warm place until they have doubled in size. With a sharp floured knife make deep lengthwise slashes down the centre of each roll and brush with a glaze of 1 egg white beaten with 1 tablespoon water. Sprinkle with caraway or fennel seeds. Bake for 10–15 minutes until well risen.

Twists. Use 75–100 g (3–4 oz) pieces of dough and divide each piece in half. Roll each piece out to a sausage shape about 15 cm (6 inches) long. Pinch pairs of ropes together at one end and then carefully and evenly twist the two pieces together to seal. Place on greased baking sheets, either in straight lines, twisted into circles, or tied in knots. Cover with oiled polythene and put to rise in a warm place until doubled in size. Brush with beaten egg, sprinkle with sesame seeds and bake as above.

Knots. Roll out 50 g (2 oz) pieces of dough into sausage shapes of about 15 cm (6 inches) long. Tie the pieces into various knots, and place on greased baking sheets. Cover with oiled polythene and continue as for Twists.

Chelsea Buns

These originated at the old Chelsea Bun House where thousands of the buns – which came to be known by the same name – were baked every day at the height of its fame in the eighteenth century.

Makes 9
225 g (8 oz) strong white flour
15 g (½ oz) fresh yeast or 1½
*   teaspoons dried yeast plus 1*
*   teaspoon caster sugar*
100 ml (3½ fl oz) warm milk
½ teaspoon salt
15 g (½ oz) butter
1 egg, beaten
about 50 g (2 oz) butter, melted
100 g (4 oz) mixed dried fruit
25–50 g (1–2 oz) chopped
*   mixed peel*
50 g (2 oz) soft brown sugar
clear honey, to glaze

Preparation time: about 30 minutes, plus rising
Cooking time: about 30–35 minutes
Oven: 190°C, 375°F, Gas Mark 5

1. Grease an 18 cm (7 inch) square cake tin. Put 50 g (2 oz) of the flour into a bowl with the fresh yeast or dried yeast plus sugar and the warm milk, mix to a batter and leave in a warm place until frothy, about 10–20 minutes.

2. While the yeast froths, sift the remaining flour and the salt into a bowl and rub in the 15 g (½ oz) butter.

3. Pour the yeast batter into the flour mixture, add the egg, and mix thoroughly to form a soft dough. Turn on to a lightly floured surface and knead until smooth and elastic – this should take about 5 minutes by hand or 2–3 minutes in a large electric mixer fitted with a dough hook.

4. Shape into a ball and place in a lightly oiled polythene bag tied at the neck. Put to rise in a warm place until doubled in size, about 1–1½ hours. (This is a rich dough so it takes longer to rise.) Remove from the bag, knock back and knead until smooth.

5. Roll out to a rectangle about 30 × 23 cm (12 × 9 inches). Brush the whole surface with melted butter and sprinkle with the mixed fruit and peel, and finally with the sugar. Beginning with a long edge, roll up the dough like a Swiss roll, keeping it even, and seal the end with water. Brush with melted butter.

6. Cut into 9 even-sized slices and place, cut side downwards, in the prepared tin. They should not quite touch each other. Cover with oiled polythene and put to rise in a warm place until they feel springy to the touch (about 15–20 minutes). They will now have joined together.

7. Remove the polythene and bake in a preheated oven for 30–35 minutes or until golden brown and firm to the touch. Turn the buns out, still in one piece, on to a wire tray and whilst still warm, brush the tops with clear honey. Pull apart when cold.

Danish Pastries

These are made with a special soft-textured yeasted pastry which is an exception to the general yeast rule. Ordinary plain flour should be used instead of strong bread flour for the best results.

Makes 24–28 pastries
25 g (1 oz) fresh yeast or 1
*   tablespoon dried yeast plus 1*
*   teaspoon caster sugar*
150 ml (¼ pint) warm water
*   (43°C/110°F)*
450 g (1 lb) plain white flour
1 teaspoon salt
50 g (2 oz) lard
25 g (1 oz) caster sugar
2 eggs, beaten
275 g (10 oz) butter

Preparation time: about 1½ hours, plus rising
Cooking time: about 1¼ hours
Oven: 220°C, 425°F, Gas Mark 7

Fillings

Spiced Nut Toast 50 g (2 oz) hazelnuts or almonds, and chop roughly. Mix with 25 g (1 oz) each of butter and soft brown sugar and ½ teaspoon mixed spice.
Ginger Beat 25 g (1 oz) caster sugar into 25 g (1 oz) butter, with ½ teaspoon ground ginger and 40–50 g (1½–2 oz) finely chopped crystallized, preserved or stem ginger.
Apple Peel, core and slice 2 large cooking apples and cook in the minimum of water to a pulp, then beat until smooth. Stir in a knob of butter and sugar to taste. Flavour with a good pinch of cinnamon, mixed spice, allspice etc; or add a few currants, raisins, sultanas or chopped nuts.
Marzipan Mix together 50 g (2 oz) each of ground almonds and caster or icing sugar, and bind to a pliable paste with a few drops of almond essence and beaten egg or egg yolk.
Mixed Fruit Beat 25 g (1 oz)

1. Blend the fresh yeast with the water; or, for dried yeast, dissolve the sugar in the water, sprinkle the yeast on top. Leave in a warm place for about 10 minutes or until frothy.

4. Soften the butter by beating with a rolling pin between 2 sheets of greaseproof paper, until it can be shaped into an oblong measuring approximately 25 × 10 cm (10 × 4 inches). Remove the dough from the bag and roll it out to a 28 cm (11 inch) square. Spread the butter down the centre.

soft brown sugar into 25 g (1 oz) butter and work in a large pinch of ground allspice or cinnamon and 25 g (1 oz) each of currants, sultanas and chopped mixed peel until well mixed.
Confectioner's Custard Heat 300 ml (½ pint) milk gently. Beat together 50 g (2 oz) caster sugar, 20 g (¾ oz) flour and 15 g (½ oz) cornflour with 1 egg and 1 egg yolk until

Shaping Danish Pastries

2. Sift the flour and salt into a bowl, rub in the lard and mix in the sugar. Add the yeast liquid and the beaten eggs and mix to form a soft elastic dough, adding a little more water if necessary.

5. Enclose the butter by folding the wider flaps of dough to overlap in the middle; seal the top and bottom with the rolling pin, then roll out, folds at the sides, to a strip three times as long as it is wide. Fold the bottom one-third of the strip upwards and the top third downwards and seal the edges. Chill for 10 minutes.

smooth and creamy, then beat in a little of the milk. Whisk the mixture back into the rest of the milk and cook gently, stirring continuously until it thickens and comes to the boil. Boil for 1 minute then stir in a few drops of vanilla essence and a knob of butter. Cover with cling film and leave to cool.

3. Turn the dough on to a lightly floured surface and knead by hand until smooth – this will take 3–4 minutes. Shape the dough into a ball and put into a lightly oiled polythene bag. Chill the dough in the refrigerator for at least 10 minutes.

6. Repeat the rolling, folding and chilling process three more times, giving the pastry a quarter turn each time so that the last fold is always at the right-hand side. Chill for 30 minutes and the pastry is then ready for use. The dough may be frozen at this stage for up to 4 months.

7. Danish pastries are made in a variety of traditional shapes. See right for instructions on making 3 different ones. Fillings are equally varied. See page 302 for some of the most popular ones.

Toppings

Use plain or toasted blanched almonds, flaked, nibbed, split or chopped; chopped or sliced glacé cherries; chopped angelica; toasted hazelnuts, which have been roughly chopped; pieces of chopped crystallized or preserved ginger; clear honey, apricot jam and glacé icing; melted chocolate.

Pinwheels

Makes 8

1. Roll out a quarter of the dough thinly to a rectangle and trim to measure 30 × 20 cm (12 × 8 inches).

2. Spread all over with mixed fruit or ginger filling. Roll up like a Swiss roll, beginning at the narrow end; seal with beaten egg. Cut into 2.5 cm (1 inch) thick slices and place them cut side downwards on a

Windmills or Imperial Stars

Makes 12–16

1. Roll out half the dough thinly and cut into 10 cm (4 inch) squares. Make diagonal cuts from each corner to within 1 cm (½ inch) of the centre.

2. Put a small piece of marzipan in the centre then fold one corner of each cut to the centre and seal with beaten egg.

3. Place on greased baking sheets and cover with oiled polythene. Put to rise, and then bake for about 20 minutes.

4. Whilst still warm partly cover with glacé icing or brush with honey or apricot jam. For

Cock's Combs

Makes 6–8

1. Roll out a quarter of the dough thinly and cut into strips measuring 11 × 13 cm (4½ × 5 inches).

2. Spread half the width of each strip with any one of the fillings on the left and fold over the other half to enclose the filling. Seal with egg. Make four or five cuts with a sharp knife into the folded edge and place the pastries on a lightly greased baking sheet, curving each one a little to open out the comb.

lightly greased baking sheet. Flatten slightly with a palette knife.

3. Put to rise then brush with beaten egg and bake in a preheated oven for 15–20 minutes or until puffed up.

4. Remove to a wire rack and drizzle with glacé icing or spread with honey or jam and sprinkle with nuts and/or cherries. Leave until cold.

windmills, sprinkle with toasted nuts and/or cherries etc; for imperial stars, add glacé icing to the projections and a spoonful of confectioner's custard and a halved glacé cherry to the centre. Leave to set.

3. Put to rise, then glaze and bake as for the pinwheels for about 20 minutes.

4. Brush with honey or jam or spread with glacé icing while still warm.

BRIOCHE

Brioche is light, enriched yeast dough traditionally baked in deep fluted patty tins (or one larger tin). It is a traditional favourite for Continental breakfasts, eaten either warm or cold with chilled unsalted butter and a fruit conserve, along with plenty of hot coffee or chocolate.

Brioche can be used as the basis for savoury or sweet fillings. Some of the dough from the centre is removed and replaced with a filling of choice – seafood is particularly good. For desserts, fill with a Crème Chantilly and fresh fruit in season along with a liqueur to complement the fruit.

There are two methods of making brioche dough. In the first – the traditional French method – the yeast is mixed with the flour to make a paste, then is put into a bowl of warm water to rise; it is then added to the rest of the ingredients which have been formed into a dough. The other method is to sift flour and salt into a bowl and make a well in the centre. Warm the milk to blood heat, then add the eggs, sugar and yeast (crumbled) and pour into the well in the flour. Mix well. When very smooth add the creamed butter and work well. Put into an oiled bowl and continue from Step 9.

Makes 10–12
225 g (8 oz) strong white flour
15 g (½ oz) fresh yeast
about 2 tablespoons warm
*   water*
½ teaspoon salt
1 tablespoon caster sugar
2 eggs
2–4 tablespoons milk
75 g (3 oz) well softened butter
beaten egg, to glaze

Preparation time: about 1 hour, plus rising (it is easier if you start the day before)
Cooking time: 20–30 minutes
Oven: 220°C, 425°F, Gas Mark 7

1. Sift the flour into a heap on a working surface. Divide into four equal portions and pull one-quarter away from the rest. Shape the smaller portion into a pile and make a hole in the centre.

2. Crumble the yeast finely into this hole and add the water. Using your fingers gradually work the flour together with the yeast and water to form a smooth, soft dough. If too firm add a little extra water as you mix. Knead lightly until just smooth and shape into a ball with your hands.

3. Either snip a cross in the top of the dough or cut one with a sharp knife. Place in a bowl of warm water (baby bath hot).

4. The dough will sink to the bottom and gradually float back to the surface as the yeast makes the dough rise. It should take 5–8 minutes and the dough will look rather like a cauliflower.

7. Work in the softened butter piece by piece, pushing it into the dough with the heel of your hand. Smear the dough along the work surface – it will be very sticky and messy until it begins to absorb the butter. Work quickly until all the butter has been absorbed.

8. Lift the yeast cake from the water and drain it thoroughly on a slotted spoon or on a piece of muslin. Add to the dough, kneading it as before. The dough should be smooth and elastic.

9. Put the dough into a lightly greased or floured bowl and cover the bowl with clingfilm. Put into the refrigerator and leave to rise for at least 6–8 hours, or preferably overnight, until it has doubled in size.

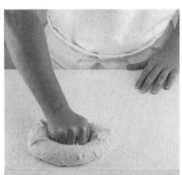

10. Turn on to a lightly floured surface and knock back. Knead lightly and divide into 10–12 pieces. Shape three-quarters of each piece into a ball and place in well greased individual fluted patty tins. Shape the remaining pieces of dough into balls with small tails.

Cheese Brioches

Makes 10–12
*1 recipe quantity Brioche
  dough*
*75 g (3 oz) Gruyère cheese,
  finely grated*
beaten egg, to glaze

Preparation time: about 1
hour, plus risings
Cooking time: about 15
minutes
Oven: 220°C, 425°F, Gas Mark 7

1. Make up the dough as usual
and beat in the cheese until
well blended.

2. Shape into individual
Brioches as Steps 10 and 11.

3. Glaze with beaten egg and
bake in a preheated oven for
about 15 minutes or until a
good golden brown.

5. While waiting for the yeast
dough to rise, gather the rest
of the flour on the work
surface into a heap and
make a well in the centre.
Add the salt, sugar and eggs
and mix to a fairly firm
dough with your fingers,
adding the milk as
necessary.

6. Gather up the dough and
throw it on to the surface,
take it up again with a twist
of the wrist and throw it
again. Do not bother to
scrape the dough off your
fingers. Continue until the
paste is shiny and elastic.

11. Make a hole in the
centre of the dough in the
tins with a finger and insert
the 'tail' of the smaller piece
of dough. Push down well.
Put to rise in a warm place
for 50–60 minutes, then
brush with beaten egg and
bake in a preheated oven for
about 20–30 minutes.

For a Large Brioche

Brush a 1.2 litre (2 pint)
capacity fluted mould with oil
or melted butter. Shape three-
quarters of the dough into a
ball and place in the tin. Shape
the remainder into a small ball
with a tail and put on top as for
the small Brioches. Put to rise
for 50–60 minutes, then glaze
and bake as for individual
Brioches but for 30–40
minutes.

Large Fruit Brioche

Serves 6–8
*1 recipe quantity Brioche
  dough*
beaten egg, to glaze
Filling:
*4 tablespoons orange Curaçao
  or other liqueur*
*200 ml (7 fl oz) double or
  whipping cream*
*40 g (1½ oz) toasted
  hazelnuts, chopped*
1 tablespoon icing sugar
*225 g (8 oz) raspberries or
  strawberries*

Preparation time: about 1 hour
plus rising, plus about 30
minutes
Cooking time: about 20–25
minutes
Oven: 220°C, 425°F, Gas Mark 7

1. Use the dough to make a
large Brioche (see below). Turn
out and cool on a wire rack.

2. For the filling, remove the
top-knot from the Brioche and
scoop out three-quarters of the
dough with a grapefruit knife.
Sprinkle the liqueur over the
inside of the Brioche.

3. Whip the cream until stiff
then fold in the hazelnuts and
icing sugar.

4. Layer up the hazelnut cream
and raspberries or sliced
strawberries in the Brioche so
it is over full. Replace the top-
knot.

For perfect Brioches

■ Use a strong white bread
flour with a high gluten
content for the best results.
■ Fresh yeast gives a better
result for this particular type
of Continental bread.
■ If the water for the yeast
dough is too hot it will kill the
yeast; if too cold the dough
will be too slow to rise. The
temperature should be about
that of a baby's bath. Do not
put it over direct heat whilst
the yeast dough is in it or
when the yeast cake sinks to
the bottom; it will become
over-heated and the yeast will
die.
■ Work as quickly as possible
when kneading in the butter,
especially if the kitchen is
warm. Be sure you are using
the heel of your hand (not the
palm) to smear the butter

pieces into the dough.
■ The dough will be very
messy and sticky at first. Use a
spatula to scrape it together
and then smear in more
butter. The kneading is
finished when the dough
draws back into shape.
■ The long rising of this
dough in the refrigerator
gives by far the best results
and so it is best to begin the
brioche dough the day before
required. The dough should
be cold when shaped so that
it is easy to handle and not
too sticky.
■ If to be eaten as they are,
brioches are much better
served fresh. If to be filled
with a savoury filling, they can
be frozen for up to 1 month.
Thaw completely before
adding the filling.

CROISSANTS

These classic French pastries are made from a crisp type of yeast dough. It is rolled out, cut into triangles and rolled up in the traditional manner with curved ends, ready to bake.

The yeast pastry dough is made in a similar way to flaky pastry with the butter spread over it, and several foldings, rollings, and chillings are necessary before shaping.

The baked croissants should be eaten as fresh as possible, but they freeze well, provided they are packed in a rigid container to prevent damage. If ready baked the croissants can be thawed out overnight, or even first thing in the morning, for they thaw quickly. Alternatively the dough may be made the night before with a slow rise in the refrigerator overnight ready to roll out, shape and bake as required.

Croissants are traditionally eaten for breakfast with butter (preferably unsalted) and jams, preserves or honey. They may be served warm or cold. They are also excellent lunchtime fare served with cheeses and pickles. Fillings may also be added: the most popular is chocolate, but others such as chopped nuts in spicy butter, or Stilton cheese can be used equally well. The fillings must be totally enclosed in the pastry to achieve the desired result. See below, page 307, for recipes for these various fillings.

Makes 10
350 g (12 oz) strong white flour
1 teaspoon salt
250 g (9 oz) butter, softened
25 g (1 oz) fresh yeast or 1 tablespoon dried yeast plus 1 teaspoon caster sugar
250 ml (8 fl oz) warm water (43°C/110°F)
1 egg, beaten
Glaze:
1 egg, beaten
2 teaspoons cold water
½ teaspoon caster sugar (optional)

Preparation time: about 2 hours, plus chilling and rising time
Cooking time: about 20 minutes
Oven: 220°C, 425°F, Gas Mark 7

1. Sift the flour and salt into a bowl and rub in 25 g (1 oz) of the butter until the mixture resembles fine breadcrumbs. Blend the fresh yeast with the warm water, then add to the dry ingredients with the egg and mix to a soft dough. With dried yeast, put the sugar and warm water into a basin, sprinkle the yeast on top and leave in a warm place until frothy. Continue as above.

2. Knead the dough on a lightly floured surface for about 10–15 minutes. Put in a polythene bag and chill.

3. Roll out the dough to a rectangle approximately 50 × 20 cm (20 × 8 inches). Soften the butter a little and divide into three. Use one portion to spread over two-thirds of the pastry leaving a small margin free round the edge.

4. Fold the plain third of pastry over the buttered pastry and then bring the other third over to make a neat parcel (as for flaky pastries). Turn the dough so that the fold is to the right-hand side. Seal the edges firmly with the rolling pin.

6. Wrap the folded dough in polythene or foil and chill for 30 minutes. Roll out and fold 3 times more (but without adding any fat), and then wrap in polythene and chill for at least an hour. (It can be left overnight at this stage.) If the dough becomes very soft between the rollings, chill between each for 10 minutes.

7. Roll out to a rectangle about 55 × 33 cm (22 × 13 inches) and cover loosely with a sheet of clingfilm. Leave to rest for 10 minutes.

8. Trim off the edges neatly and then cut in half lengthwise. Cut each strip into 5 triangles.

9. For the glaze, beat all the ingredients together and use to brush over the dough. Then roll up each triangle loosely starting at the wide base and finishing with the tip folded under the roll. Curve each Croissant into a crescent shape and glaze.

To make perfect Croissants

■ Use a strong plain flour for the best results. The high gluten content is necessary to cope with the rolling, folding and rising.
■ Fresh yeast is best for croissants but dried yeast can be used if reconstituted correctly (see method).
■ Make sure the water is at the correct temperature of 43°C/110°F, which is warm. If too hot it will kill the yeast and if too cool, the yeast will not work.
■ Always use butter for the best flavour (although a hard margarine will work).
■ Try to roll out on a surface only very lightly dusted with flour, as incorporating too much extra flour into the dough will spoil the texture.
■ Do not cut down on the suggested resting times in the refrigerator, or the butter will not firm up sufficiently to form good layers, and the dough will not rise well.
■ Longer chilling may be necessary if the kitchen is very hot or the atmosphere warm and sticky. The dough may be chilled between each rolling for about 10 minutes if it becomes very soft and sticky.
■ If there is time, make the dough and then allow it to chill overnight in the refrigerator so that it is cold when the butter is added.
■ Do not roll or press the pastry too firmly whilst shaping or the butter will burst through.

5. Reshape the dough to a long narrow strip which is at least three times as long as it is wide by pressing the dough fairly gently at regular intervals until the required size. Do not roll or press too hard or the fat will come through the pastry and make it very difficult to roll and shape. Repeat the rolling, spreading with butter and folding with the two remaining portions of butter, giving the dough a quarter turn each time so the folded edge is always to the right.

10. Place on greased baking sheets. Cover with oiled polythene and leave to rise for about 30 minutes.

11. Remove polythene, glaze and bake in a preheated oven for 15–20 minutes until well risen and golden brown.

Variations

Chocolate Croissants. Make as above, but put 1–2 teaspoons coarsely grated plain or milk chocolate at the base of each triangle of dough and roll it up so it is completely enclosed. Continue as above.
Spiced Nut Croissants. Cream 40 g (1½ oz) butter with 25 g (1 oz) light soft brown sugar and 1 teaspoon mixed spice or ground cinnamon. Add 50 g (2 oz) finely chopped nuts – almonds, hazelnuts, pecans, walnuts or unsalted peanuts – and add to the croissant dough triangles as for Chocolate Croissants.
Stilton Croissants. Grate about 75 g (3 oz) Stilton cheese and sprinkle it evenly over the dough triangles, keeping a narrow margin clear all round. Then roll up as usual, glaze, put to rise and bake as for normal croissants. (A strong Cheddar cheese can be used in the same way.)

SAVARIN

This is a yeasted cake which is baked in a round-based ring mould and soaked in a well flavoured sweet syrup containing rum, Kirsch or other liqueur, or brandy. The centre of the ring is usually filled with some type of fruit, often with plain whipped cream or Crème Chantilly used as part of the filling or for decoration.

The mixture is more like a thick batter than a dough and is beaten either with the hand or a wooden spoon rather than turned out and kneaded as for most yeast doughs.

Bake either in one large ring tin, in two smaller ones (a particularly good idea if you want to add more filling to the percentage of cake), or in 14–16 individual ring tins.

After soaking, the finished Savarin can be made to look even more spectacular by spiking it all over with blanched almonds cut into strips. If you are using just one large Savarin, extra fruit used in the filling may be served in a bowl to add to each portion.

Serve with whipped cream. For variations dried chopped fruits or nuts can be added to the dough before baking – Rum Babas have currants – along with any spices you may like to use.

Serves 8–10
225 g (8 oz) strong white flour
25 g (1 oz) fresh yeast or 1
  tablespoon dried yeast plus 1
  teaspoon caster sugar
6 tablespoons warm milk
a pinch of salt
2 tablespoons caster sugar
4 eggs, beaten
100 g (4 oz) butter, softened
Syrup:
6 tablespoons clear honey
6 tablespoons water
3–4 tablespoons brandy, rum,
  Kirsch or other liqueur
Filling:
225 g (8 oz) strawberries,
  halved, if large
2 kiwi fruit, peeled and sliced
2 oranges, peeled and
  segmented, free of
  membrane
2 tablespoons caster sugar
150–300 ml (¼–½ pint)
  double or whipping cream

Preparation time: about 30 minutes, plus risings
Cooking time: about 40 minutes
Oven: 190°C, 375°F, Gas Mark 5

1. Sift 50 g (2 oz) of the flour into a bowl. Blend the fresh yeast with the milk until smooth, add to the flour and beat well until smooth. If using dried yeast, mix the 50 g (2 oz) flour, yeast, 1 teaspoon sugar and the milk together. Leave in a warm place until frothy – about 20 minutes for fresh yeast, 30 minutes for dried yeast. Thoroughly butter a 20 cm (8 inch) round-based ring mould, or two 15 cm (6 inch) ring moulds.

2. Add the remaining sifted flour to the yeast mixture together with the salt, sugar, eggs and softened butter. Beat hard with your hand or a wooden spoon for 4–5 minutes until the dough is a thick smooth batter.

3. Pour the dough into the tin(s) to fill no more than just over half full. Cover the tin(s) lightly with oiled clingfilm and put in a warm place to rise.

7. Put a tray under the Savarin (still on the rack) and prick all over with a fine skewer. Immediately spoon the hot syrup over the warm Savarin. Spoon up any syrup on the tray and pour back over the Savarin; then leave until quite cold.

8. To serve, stand the Savarin on a serving dish. Mix the strawberries, slices of kiwi fruit and orange segments together and sprinkle with the sugar. Use to fill the central hole of the Savarin, piling it well up in the centre. Any extra fruit may be served separately in a bowl or arranged attractively around the base of the Savarin.

9. Whip the cream until stiff and put into a piping bag fitted with a large star vegetable nozzle. Pipe a heavy twisted row of cream around the top of the Savarin and another around the base. Alternatively, serve all the cream in a bowl. (See page 251 for an illustration of a Savarin filled with fruit and cream.)

For a perfect Savarin

■ Use strong white flour for the best results.
■ If using dried yeast make sure it is completely reconstituted (see method).
■ Grease the chosen tins really thoroughly to prevent sticking – butter will give the best colour and flavour.
■ With individual tins, only fill to half-full or they will overflow and spoil the shape. A larger tin may be filled up to almost two-thirds full.
■ When baked, turn the Savarin upside down in its tin on a wire rack. The steam rising in the tin will help to loosen the sponge.
■ The syrup soaks in better if poured over the Savarin whilst it is hot.

■ Add a brushing of sieved warm apricot jam or glaze to the soaked Savarin to give an attractive shiny appearance, if liked.
■ If the Savarin is to be frozen, cool rapidly, do not soak with syrup, and then, when cold, wrap and freeze immediately. When required, thaw completely, heat gently in a cool oven, prick all over with a thin skewer and then soak with the hot syrup.
■ If using fruits which might stain the Savarin (such as cherries), do not add the filling until the last possible minute and spread a layer of cream over the cake to keep the coloured fruit from actually touching it.

4. When the dough has fully risen, remove the clingfilm and bake in a preheated oven for about 40 minutes or until golden brown and the mixture is just beginning to shrink away from the sides of the tin.

5. Invert on to a wire rack and leave until the sponge drops out.

6. Put the honey and water into a saucepan, bring to the boil and simmer. Add the alcohol.

Variations

Winter Fruit Savarin. Soak 75 g (3 oz) dried apricots overnight in water, drain, chop finely and add to the Savarin dough before baking. Soak with a syrup made using apricot brandy (or apricot juice from a can of apricots and brandy). Fill the centre with a drained 425 g (15 oz) can apricot halves mixed with 100 g (4 oz) soaked and poached prunes, 2 dessert apples, peeled, cored and sliced and dipped in lemon juice, 1 sliced banana dipped in lemon juice and 1 stoned and sliced peach (or a 200 g (7 oz) can of peach slices).
Chestnut Cherry Savarin. Drain a 425 g (15 oz) can of black cherries and bring the juice up to the boil. Add 4 tablespoons brandy and use to soak the Savarin (it will change colour!) Mix a 200 g (7 oz) can (or two smaller tubes) sweetened chestnut spread with 300 ml (½ pint) whipped double cream and use some of it to half fill the hole in the Savarin. Reserve 10 cherries for decoration and put the rest on top of the cream mixture. Use the rest of the cream mixture to fill the central hole and pipe an attractive topping to the Savarin. Use the reserved cherries to decorate the cream.

Rum Babas

Makes 14–16
1 recipe quantity Savarin dough
100 g (4 oz) currants
Syrup:
8 tablespoons clear honey
8 tablespoons water
4 tablespoons rum
To serve:
300 ml (½ pint) double or whipping cream
14–16 whole glacé cherries
angelica leaves (optional)

Preparation time: about 30 minutes, plus rising
Cooking time: about 15–20 minutes
Oven: 200°C, 400°F, Gas Mark 6

1. Make up the dough as for Savarin and then beat in the currants.

2. Thoroughly butter 16 individual ring tins about 9–10 cm (3½–4 inches) wide. If you only have 8 tins then bake in 2 batches. Half fill the tins with the mixture and stand on baking sheets. Cover with oiled polythene and leave to rise in a warm place until the tins are two-thirds full.

3. Bake in a preheated oven for 15–20 minutes until well risen and golden brown. Cool for a few minutes in the tins, loosen the sides and turn out on to a wire tray.

4. For the syrup, heat the honey and water and bring to the boil for 1 minute or so. Add the rum and reheat. Prick the babas all over with a fine skewer and stand the wire tray over a tray or lipped baking sheet. Soak each baba thoroughly in syrup and spoon up any excess from the tray. Leave until cold.

5. To serve, whip the cream until stiff and pipe a large whirl into each one to fill the central hole. Decorate each with a glacé cherry and angelica leaves, if liked.

CAKES & ICINGS

There are four main methods of cake-making, all of them simple and easy to do at home: creamed mixtures, suitable for all kinds of cakes, whisked sponges, rubbed-in mixtures, for plain cakes and buns, and all-in-one mixtures, for quick-mix cakes.

The subject of cakes and biscuits and indeed baking generally is a very wide one, There are many different methods of preparing and making all types of cakes. There are those which are quick and easy and known as 'quick-mix' because everything is put into one bowl and mixed together rather than each stage being carried out separately, and at the other extreme there are rich celebration cakes for Christmas and other special occasions.

Biscuits too can be very simple or really quite complicated, but they are all made by similar methods to cakes – creamed, rubbed-in or all-in-one mixtures. Cake and biscuit making may sound daunting but if the beginner takes scrupulous care to follow all instructions exactly, good results should be assured. It is never worth cutting corners with cake-making.

Basic rules

Before you actually make the cake it is very important to prepare the tin properly and line it where necessary. This will ensure the cake will turn out easily when baked and will prevent it from getting thick and hard on the outside. There are many types of cake tin available, some of which have a special non-stick coating which does help prevent the cakes from sticking, and if you have this type, then follow the manufacturer's instructions for preparing them for use.

However, if making a rich fruit cake it is necessary to line even these tins for the extra protection required during the long cooking time necessary.

With all other types of cake tins it is necessary either to grease them thoroughly and then dredge with flour (knocking off the surplus) or grease, line with greaseproof paper and then grease again. If you prefer to use non-stick silicone paper there is no need to grease at all. Use oil, lard, margarine or butter (though this may stick) for greasing; avoid any fat with a strong flavour of its own.

Rich fruit cakes need a double thickness of paper for lining, all other types of cake need just a single thickness. Use melted lard, oil, margarine or butter for greasing with a preference for lard or margarine or oil.

Oven

The oven must be put on in good time at the temperature required. It is no good turning it on when the cake is ready to go in the oven for once made, apart from a few exceptions, a cake should be cooked immediately or it will spoil. This applies particularly to cakes which are whisked or have whisked egg whites folded into them.

The centre shelf or the one above this should always be used for cake baking. Position the shelf before turning the oven on. Do not open the oven door any more than is

Dundee cake

Chocolate sponge with swirled butter icing

Victoria sponge with feathered icing

Rock buns

Swiss roll

Fairy cakes

necessary whilst cooking a cake for the sudden draught is likely to make it sink and spoil all your efforts. Always shut the door very carefully when you have looked at the cake, and should the cake itself need moving, do that very carefully too. Any sharp or sudden movement can be very damaging to a cake.

Testing

When a baked cake is ready it should be well risen and firm to the touch, but it is also wise to check with a clean straight skewer which is pressed right down into the centre of the cake and should come out clean. If it comes out at all sticky, it means the cake is not quite ready, so cook for a further 5–10 minutes and test again. Light sponge cakes should not be tested with a skewer. They should be a golden brown, well risen, shrinking from the sides of the tin and leave no fingermark when lightly pressed in the centre. Sometimes a cake really looks done but when it is turned onto a wire rack it begins to sink, and this could be prevented by testing it properly before turning out. It is best to allow a cake to stand in the tin for a couple of minutes, before turning it out, this allows it to shrink slightly from the edge of the tin and come out cleanly; however there are exceptions here for rich cakes are best left in the tin until cold before turning out. The one which requires the most haste is a Swiss roll which must be turned out, paper stripped off, sides trimmed and rolled up almost immediately, or the cake will crack and not roll up as it should.

Storing

Once baked most cakes will store satisfactorily for several days. The exceptions are the whisked fatless cakes which are best eaten on the day baked or the next. Others should be kept in an airtight container or wrapped in foil. On average whisked cakes should be eaten within 24–48 hours; creamed mixtures keep well for 7–10 days; rubbed-in cakes for up to a week (although scones are best eaten within 2 days). The richest fruit cakes will keep for well over 3 months before eating providing they are well wrapped and preferably have been pricked with a skewer and had brandy poured into them at least once – if possible this should be repeated once a month to help with the maturing process. In fact rich cakes for weddings are best made at least 3 months and often longer before the date, and then the top tier may be kept for a year or so even after it has been iced and decorated.

Freezing cakes

Many cakes will freeze well too although it is often best to add the icing when the cake has been thawed. Butter cream does freeze very well and cakes either filled or topped with this icing can be frozen complete provided they are packed in a rigid container for protection. An un-iced cake can be wrapped in foil or thick polythene or put into a rigid container; and if layered these should be separated with waxed, non-stick or greaseproof paper before packing. Individual cakes can be frozen in polythene bags or rigid containers and can be open frozen first on a tray, if liked. Plain cakes will store in the freezer for 6–9 months, only the highly spiced ones are best used within 2 months, and the individuals are best not kept for too long.

To base line round or square cake tins

This method is used to prevent the cake bottom from falling out or sticking to the tin and is used for sponge and sandwich mixtures and some light fruit cakes which have been rubbed in; but not for rich mixtures or heavily fruited cakes.

1. Cut a single piece of greaseproof paper to fit the bottom of the tin by standing the tin on the paper and drawing around it. Cut it out inside the pencil line.

2. First grease the inside of the tin, put in the paper so that it fits neatly to the edges, but does not bend up the sides, and then grease the paper.

   Some recipes will then call for the tin to be floured and in some special cases a layer of sugar is put in before the flour. This gives a firmer crust.

To line a shallow rectangular tin

It is wise to line shallow tins used for Swiss rolls, batch bake cakes etc for easy removal.

1. Cut a piece of greaseproof paper about 7.5 cm (3 inches) larger than the tin (and larger still if the sides of the tin are deeper than about 2.5 cm (1 inch).

2. Stand the tin on the paper so it is quite central and then cut from the corners of the paper to the corners of the tin.

3. Grease inside the tin, put in the paper so it fits neatly, overlapping the paper at the corners to give sharp angles, and then grease again.

To line a loaf tin

Use the same method as for lining a shallow rectangular tin but cut the paper at least 15 cm (6 inches) larger than the top of the tin. Grease the tin, position the paper, again fitting the corners neatly, and grease again.

For perfect cake-making

■ Always read the recipe right through to make sure you have all the necessary ingredients; and check you have the correct sized tin.
■ Weigh out the ingredients absolutely accurately and use the ingredients stated; don't make substitutes unless you are a very experienced cake maker, or there may be trouble with the result.
■ Stick rigidly to either metric or Imperial weights. Any combination of the two will almost certainly prove disastrous.
■ Keep a supply of everyday cake decorations in your store cupboard if you are a keen cake maker.
■ When cold, put the cake into an airtight container until ready to ice it and again after icing, to keep it fresh.
■ Do not store cakes and biscuits in the same container for the moisture from the cake will make the biscuits turn soggy.

BASIC CREAMED MIXTURE

The Victoria sandwich cake is the most famous of the creamed cakes, which use equal quantities of fat and sugar, self-raising flour and eggs. It gives a very light and airy textured cake with good flavour and one that keeps well. It can be flavoured in numerous ways and have a variety of different icings and toppings added.

The basic method of creaming is used for other cakes too, but these are not so rich, having a higher proportion of flour and usually some sort of liquid apart from the other ingredients.

Most creamed cakes use self-raising flour, although the odd one may have a proportion of plain flour added. In the case of rich fruit cakes which are also creamed (see the recipe for Dundee Cake, opposite) only plain flour is used.

The following recipe for Victoria Sandwich can be baked in a variety of shapes and sizes and the mixture is easy to double or treble up without upsetting the balance. It also makes a very good birthday or other celebration cake for those who don't like fruit cake.

Victoria Sandwich

175 g (6 oz) butter or soft
margarine
175 g (6 oz) caster sugar
3 eggs (size 1, 2 or 3), beaten
175 g (6 oz) self-raising flour
few drops vanilla essence
1 tablespoon cold water

Preparation time: about 30 minutes
Cooking time: about 25 minutes
Oven: 190°C, 375°F, Gas Mark 5

1. Grease two 20 cm (8 inch) round sandwich tins and line the bases with greased greaseproof paper or non-stick silicone paper.

2. Beat the fat thoroughly until well softened then add the sugar gradually, incorporating it into the fat and cream together using a wooden spoon or hand-held electric mixture until the mixture is very light and fluffy and pale in colour. It is very important to cream sufficiently at this stage or the mixture will not accept the rest of the ingredients as it should.

3. Beat in the eggs, gradually, until completely incorporated.

4. Sift the flour and fold into the creamed mixture, using a metal spoon for preference, alternating with the essence and water. The mixture should be a soft dropping consistency, i.e. when it drops easily off the spoon neither too firm nor too soft.

5. Divide the mixture between the tins and level the tops, spreading out from the centre with a round-bladed knife, but only very lightly or some of the air will be forced out.

6. Bake in a moderately hot oven for 20–25 minutes until the cakes are well risen, just firm to the touch and golden brown. Cool in the tins briefly until the sides of the cakes just begin to shrink from the tin. Turn out carefully onto a wire rack and then invert quickly on to another rack so they are the right way up. Leave until cold.

7. For a plain cake simply sandwich together with jam and dredge the top of the cake with caster or sifted icing sugar. For butter cream and other toppings see pages 318–319.

Beat the butter until soft.

Cream the butter and sugar together.

Gradually add the beaten eggs.

Sift the flour and fold in.

Mixture should have a soft dropping consistency.

Level the mixture in the tins.

Variations

Chocolate – replace 25 g (1 oz) of the flour with sifted cocoa powder and add ½ teaspoon baking powder.
Coffee – omit the vanilla. Dissolve 2 tablespoons instant coffee in 1 tablespoon boiling water, cool and use.

Dundee Cake

225 g (8 oz) plain flour
1 teaspoon mixed spice
50 g (2 oz) blanched almonds,
  chopped
225 g (8 oz) currants
225 g (8 oz) sultanas
225 g (8 oz) raisins, seedless or
  stoned
100 g (4 oz) cut mixed peel
grated rind of 1 orange and 1
  lemon
225 g (8 oz) butter
225 g (8 oz) soft brown sugar,
  light or dark
4 eggs
1–2 tablespoons lemon juice
50 g (2 oz) whole blanched
  almonds

Preparation time: 40 minutes, plus cooling
Cooking time: 2½–3 hours
Oven: 160°C, 325°F, Gas Mark 3

1. Grease a deep 20 cm (8 inch) round cake tin and line with greased greaseproof paper. Sift the flour and spice together.

2. Mix together the almonds, currants, sultanas, raisins, mixed peel and orange and lemon rind.

3. Cream the butter and sugar together in a mixing bowl until very light, pale and fluffy. Beat in the eggs one at a time, folding in a tablespoon of flour after each addition.

4. Fold in the remaining flour followed by the dried fruit mixture and enough lemon juice to give a dropping consistency.

5. Turn the mixture into the prepared tin and make a slight hollow in the centre. Arrange the whole blanched almonds in circles over the top of the cake. Bake in a preheated moderate oven for 2½–3 hours or until a warmed fine skewer inserted into the centre of the cake comes out clean. Cover the cake with a sheet of foil if it appears to be overbrowning.

6. Cool in the tin for about 15 minutes then turn on to a wire rack.

Perfect fruit cakes

■ With dried fruits always buy a good brand which looks plump and juicy. If they do need washing, do so carefully, picking out any foreign bodies which might appear and then drain well and dry by spreading out over blotting paper or clean tea towels and leaving overnight, but do not put over direct heat or they will dry out hard and spoil. The drying is essential and cannot be hurried. If used wet, the fruit will sink in the cake.
■ With nuts of all types make sure they are in good condition and fresh. In the case of almonds, if they need blanching, do so before you begin the recipe, so it doesn't hold up the cake.

Lining a deep cake tin

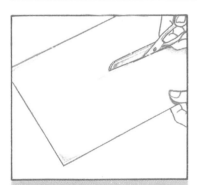

Cut 2 strips of greaseproof paper.

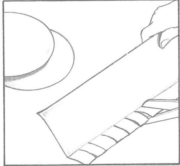

Fold and make slanting cuts.

1. For rich mixtures that require long cooking, you should use a double thickness of greaseproof paper and line both the sides and base of the tin. For a less rich cake, use only a single thickness. Both are lined in the same way.

2. Cut one or two strips of double greaseproof paper long enough to reach around the outside of the tin with sufficient to overlap and wide enough to come 2.5 cm (1 inch) above the rim of the tin.

3. Fold the bottom edge up about 2 cm (¾ inch) and crease it firmly. Open out and make slanting cuts into the folded strip with scissors at 2 cm (¾ inch) intervals.

4. Stand the tin on a double thickness of greaseproof paper and draw round the base. Cut out the circles.

5. Grease the inside of the tin thoroughly and place one circle in the base then grease the edge of the paper.

6. Place the long strips in the tin, pressing them against the sides with the cut edges spread out over the base. Grease all over the side paper.

7. Finally position the second circle in the base and grease again.

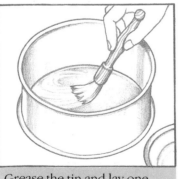

Grease the tin and lay one circle in base.

Place the long strips in the tin.

Place second circle in the base.

WHISKED SPONGE

These can either be made with or without butter, those having the added fat will keep better, but none of the whisked sponges have a very long shelf life and are far better if eaten on the day baked.

The success of this type of cake depends on the amount of air whisked into the mixture of eggs and sugar at the initial stage and then the folding in of the flour which must be light and even so as not to knock out all the added air. Heavy-handedness will simply produce a heavy cake with a strange heavy and rather soggy texture.

It is easier to use an electric mixer for making these cakes and, if using a hand-held one, the mixture must be put in a heatproof bowl over a pan of gently simmering water whilst it is being whisked to gain maximum volume. If you use a large free-standing electric mixer, no heat is required for it works that much faster, but warming the bowl before you start does hasten the process. Also make quite sure you use eggs which are at room temperature, not ones which have been taken straight from the refrigerator.

Chocolate Chestnut Cake

A whisked sponge without the added fat, but it is soaked in liqueur to help keep it moist.

3 eggs
110 g (4½ oz) caster sugar
75 g (3 oz) plain flour
15 g (½ oz) cocoa powder
Filling:
about 200 g (7 oz) can
   sweetened chestnut purée or
   two tubes chestnut purée
300 ml (½ pint) double cream
3–4 tablespoons liqueur or
   brandy
1 chocolate flake bar

Preparation time: about 30 minutes
Cooking time: about 30 minutes
Oven: 190°C, 375°F, Gas Mark 5

1. Grease and line a 20 cm (8 inch) round cake tin with single thickness greaseproof paper, which should then be greased and floured.

2. Whisk the eggs and sugar together in a heatproof bowl over a pan of hot water until very pale in colour and the whisk leaves a heavy trail when lifted. Remove from the heat and continue to whisk until the bowl is cold. If a large electric mixer is used, no heat is required.

3. Sift the flour and cocoa together twice and then fold quickly and evenly through the mixture, using a large metal spoon.

4. Turn into the prepared tin and level the top. Bake in a moderately hot oven for 25–30 minutes until well risen and firm to the touch.

5. Turn out onto a wire rack and leave to cool. Strip off the paper from the cake.

6. Put the chestnut purée into a bowl and beat until smooth. Whip the cream until stiff and fold about one third through the chestnut mixture.

7. Split the cake into three horizontally. Place the bottom layer on a serving dish and sprinkle with some of the liqueur. Spread with half the chestnut cream and then top with another layer of cake. Sprinkle this cake with liqueur and then spread this with the rest of the chestnut cream.

8. Top the cake with the last layer and cover with most of the remaining cream.

9. Put the remaining cream into a piping bag fitted with a large star nozzle and pipe a series of whirls round the top edge of the cake.

10. Complete the decoration by adding a piece of chocolate flake to the top of each whirl of cream.

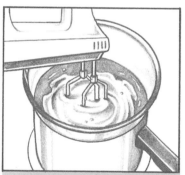
Place eggs and sugar in a bowl over hot water.

Whisk to the ribbon-like trail.

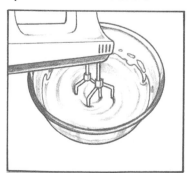
Remove from heat and whisk until cold.

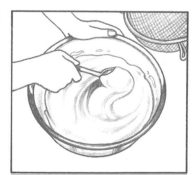
Fold in flour with a metal spoon.

For a richer cake add melted butter.

Swiss Roll

4 eggs
100 g (4 oz) caster sugar
100 g (4 oz) plain flour, sifted
    twice
25 g (1 oz) butter, melted and
    cooled
about 225 g (8 oz) jam for the
    filling
icing or caster sugar, for
    dredging

Preparation time: about 30 minutes
Cooking time: about 20 minutes
Oven: 190°C, 375°F, Gas Mark 5

1. Grease a Swiss roll tin or shallow rectangular tin about 30 × 25 cm (12 × 10 inches) with greased greaseproof paper or non-stick silicone paper or make a paper case.

2. Put the eggs and sugar into a large heatproof bowl and stand the bowl over a saucepan of gently simmering water. Whisk the mixture until it is very thick and pale in colour, at least doubled in bulk and the whisk leaves a heavy trail when lifted, about 7 minutes. Remove from the heat and continue whisking until the bowl is cool, about 7–10 minutes. If using a large electric mixer, no heat is required.

3. Sift the flour onto the mixture and fold in very quickly and evenly using a large metal spoon. Add the cooled but still runny butter and fold through the mixture.

4. Pour into the prepared tin and spread out evenly making sure there is plenty of mixture in the corners.

5. Bake in a moderately hot oven for 15–20 minutes or until the mixture is a pale golden brown and just firm to the touch.

1 Trim the edges of the roll.

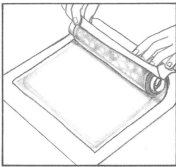
2 Roll up while hot with greaseproof paper inside.

3 Unroll, spread on filling, and roll up again.

6. Lay a sheet of non-stick silicone paper or greaseproof paper on a flat surface and dredge lightly with sugar. (This is not essential if using non-stick paper.) Turn the cake straightaway onto this paper and peel the paper off it very quickly. With a sharp knife cut off all the edges of the cake neatly.

7. Make a shallow cut across the cake about 2 cm (¾ inch) from one long end and spread thickly with jam. Roll the cake up quickly, trim the edges and dredge with icing sugar. If you want to fill the cake with cream or butter cream then put a second piece of paper on the surface of the cake and roll up

the cake very quickly and neatly with the paper still inside. Then fold back the top layer of the paper to prevent it sticking to the roll. Stand on a wire rack and leave to cool. This whole process of taking the cake from the oven to rolling it up must be done very swiftly or the cake will crack and not roll up as it should.

8. When the cake is cold, carefully unroll it, remove the paper and spread the inside with cream, cream and jam or butter cream. Reroll the cake, trim the ends and dredge with icing or caster sugar.

Variations

Coffee – sift 2–3 teaspoons instant coffee powder with the flour.
Chocolate – replace 1 tablespoon flour with cocoa powder.
Spicy – sift ½ teaspoon ground cinnamon or mixed spice with the flour.
Ginger – sift ½–1 teaspoon ground ginger with the flour.
Nutty – fold in 40 g (1½ oz) very finely chopped or ground walnuts, hazelnuts or toasted almonds with the melted butter.
Orange or Lemon – fold in the very finely grated rind of ½–1 small orange or 1 small lemon with the melted butter.

For perfect Whisked Sponges

■ It is important to whisk well to achieve maximum volume.
■ Warm the bowl before you start to whisk and make sure the eggs are at room temperature.
■ Whisk over hot water, but do not let the mixture become too hot or the sponge will be tough.
■ Use a bowl that will fit snugly over the pan of hot water, but make sure that the bottom of the bowl does

not touch the water or the eggs will cook.
■ The mixture should be thick enough to leave a trail when the whisk is lifted.
■ When butter is added to a whisked sponge it becomes a Genoese sponge, the kind which is layered with fruit and cream for gâteaux.
■ Sift the flour at least twice.
■ The flour should be plain and as fine as possible.
■ Fold in the flour gently a little at a time. If you add it

all at once, or fold it in too vigorously, the air will be lost and the cake will be heavy.
■ Use caster sugar which is quite free of lumps. Granulated sugar is too coarse and does not dissolve completely when beaten with the eggs. If the sugar is not dissolved, the cake will have a speckled appearance.
■ Sponges should be made with the finest ingredients to help their keeping qualities.

RUBBED-IN CAKES

This method of cake making is for plainer, coarser textured cakes which make very good 'cut and come again' cakes as well as the base for many types of teabread, scones and biscuits. The fat must be rubbed into the flour with the fingertips (or in a food processor or mixer) until the mixture resembles fine breadcrumbs.

The proportions of fat to flour vary with the type of cake being made, with scones only a quarter fat to flour and some cakes as much as two-thirds. The rubbed-in mixture will keep in a sealed container in the refrigerator for several days before baking; and the baked cake will keep well for over a week, but scones only last for a couple of days and small buns are best eaten within 4–5 days. The rubbed-in method is also used for biscuits, which should be stored in an airtight tin.

Scones

The secret of good scones is to handle the dough as little as possible after mixing, and to simply pat it out with the palms of the hands rather than use a rolling pin to reach the correct thickness for stamping out.

Makes about 10 scones
225 g (8 oz) self-raising flour
pinch of salt
50 g (2 oz) butter or margarine
1–2 tablespoons caster sugar
1 egg, beaten
about 5 tablespoons milk or
*   sour milk*
beaten egg or milk to glaze or
*   flour for dredging*

Preparation time: about 15 minutes
Cooking time: about 15 minutes
Oven: 230°C, 450°F, Gas Mark 8

1. Either grease a baking sheet or dredge it with flour.

2. Sift the flour and salt into a bowl and add the fat. Rub in until the mixture resembles fine breadcrumbs. This process can be done in a food processor when it should be switched on in short bursts until the required texture.

3. Stir in the sugar then add the egg and sufficient milk to mix quickly to a fairly soft but not sticky dough using a palette knife or spatula.

4. Turn out onto a lightly floured surface and pat out the dough until it is about 2 cm (¾ inch) thick. Stamp out scones of 4–5 cm (1½–2 inches) using a plain or fluted cutter. Re-form the dough and pat out to cut out further scones.

5. Place the scones on the prepared baking sheet and either glaze with beaten egg or milk, or dredge with sifted flour.

6. Bake in a very hot oven for 12–15 minutes until well risen, golden brown and just firm to the touch. Remove the scones to a wire rack and leave to cool.

7. All scones are best served on the day they are baked, either warm or cold and split and spread with butter and jam or with jam and whipped cream. They can be kept in an airtight container for 2–3 days but should be warmed through before serving. They will freeze for up to 3 months.

Variations

Fruit – add 50 g (2 oz) currants, sultanas or raisins to the dry ingredients, after rubbing in.
Orange or Lemon – add the finely grated rind of 1 orange or lemon to the dry ingredients with dried fruit as well, if liked.
Cheese – omit the sugar and add a pinch of dry mustard and 40–50 g (1½–2 oz) finely grated mature Cheddar cheese and 1 tablespoon grated Parmesan cheese to the dry ingredients.

Rock Buns

Makes 12–16 buns
225 g (8 oz) self-raising flour
pinch of salt
½ teaspoon mixed spice
½ teaspoon ground
*   cinnamon*
100 g (4 oz) butter or
*   margarine*
50 g (2 oz) currants
50 g (2 oz) raisins or sultanas
50 g (2 oz) cut mixed peel
100 g (4 oz) demerara or light
*   soft brown sugar*
grated rind of ½ lemon or
*   orange*
1 egg, beaten
2–3 tablespoons milk

Preparation time: about 20 minutes
Cooking time: about 20 minutes
Oven: 200°C, 400°F, Gas Mark 6

1. Grease two baking sheets or about 16 patty tins. Sift the flour, salt and spices into a bowl and add the butter cut into small pieces. Rub in until the mixture resembles fine breadcrumbs.

2. Stir in the currants, raisins, peel, sugar and fruit rind, then add the egg and sufficient milk to mix to a stiff dough.

3. Put the mixture into 12–16 rough heaps on the baking sheets or divide between the patty tins.

4. Bake in a fairly hot oven for about 20 minutes until lightly browned and just firm to the touch. Do not overcook. Leave to cool on a wire rack.

1. Pat out the dough to a round.

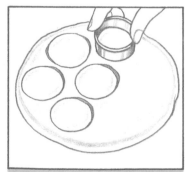

2. Stamp out rounds with a cutter.

QUICK-MIX CAKES

These are made by putting all the ingredients into the mixing bowl together and beating hard until thoroughly blended. The cake rises because it contains both self-raising flour and baking powder and for the cake to work you must use a soft tub margarine rather than any other type of fat. It has a rather close texture which will keep well for at least a week, but it does not have the extra lightness and airiness of the true Victoria sandwich.

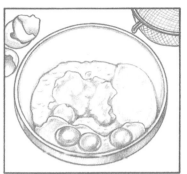

Place all the ingredients in the bowl together

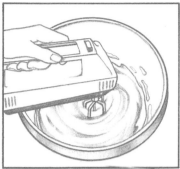

Beat well until smooth and glossy

175 g (6 oz) soft tub margarine
175 g (6 oz) caster sugar
3 eggs
175 g (6 oz) self-raising flour
1½ teaspoons baking powder
few drops vanilla essence

Preparation time: about 10 minutes
Cooking time: 30–35 minutes
Oven: 180°C, 350°F, Gas Mark 4

1. Grease two 20 cm (8 inch) round sandwich tins and line the bases with discs of greased greaseproof paper.

2. Put the margarine, sugar and eggs into a large mixing bowl. Sift in the flour and baking powder and add the essence. Mix together with a wooden spoon or hand-held electric mixer until all incorporated and then beat hard for about 2 minutes until smooth and glossy.

3. Turn into the prepared tins and level the tops. Bake in a moderate oven for about 30–35 minutes or until well risen, firm to the touch and golden brown; and they are just beginning to shrink from the sides of the tins.

4. Cool in the tin for a few seconds then turn out on to a wire rack, remove the paper from the base and invert the cakes onto another rack and leave to cool.

5. Sandwich together or cover with Butter Cream (see page 318).

Variations

Chocolate – add 1½ tablespoons cocoa powder sifted with the flour.
Coffee – omit the vanilla essence and add 1 tablespoon instant coffee powder sifted with the flour.
Orange or Lemon – omit the vanilla and add the finely grated rind of 1 orange or lemon to the mixture.

Butterscotch Quick-Mix Cake

100 g (4 oz) soft tub margarine
100 g (4 oz) light soft brown sugar, sieved
2 eggs
100 g (4 oz) self-raising flour
1 teaspoon baking powder
Icing:
50 g (2 oz) butter
100 g (4 oz) icing sugar, sifted
1 tablespoon golden syrup
2–3 butterscotch sweets for decoration

Preparation time: about 20 minutes
Cooking time: about 45 minutes
Oven: 180°C, 350°F, Gas Mark 4

1. Grease a 20 cm (8 inch) square cake tin and line the base with greased greaseproof paper.

2. Sift the flour and baking powder into a bowl and then add the margarine, sugar, and eggs. Mix well and then beat hard for 2 minutes until smooth and glossy.

3. Turn into the prepared tin and level the top. Bake in a moderate oven for about 45 minutes or until well risen and firm to the touch. Turn out onto a wire rack and leave to cool.

4. For the icing: cream the butter until soft and then beat in half the sugar, then the syrup and then the rest of the sugar.

5. Spread the icing over the top of the cake and then swirl it attractively with a round-bladed knife. Sprinkle with crushed butterscotch sweets and leave to set.

Choosing ingredients

■ Use ingredients which are fresh and have not been stored at the back of the larder since goodness knows when, for they are more than likely stale and the flavour will have deteriorated.
■ Select the correct sugar; but in most cases a light soft brown sugar can be substituted for caster sugar, or for at least part of it, provided it is not too sticky.

Coarse sugars make good toppings to bake into cakes.
■ Spices and essences do go 'off' after a while, especially if they are not kept in good airtight containers. Use up spices and renew when necessary. With flavourings it is very much better if you can obtain the true essences rather than the cheap flavourings which can taste very artificial.

SIMPLE ICINGS

Possible icings range from rich butter creams and frostings to traditional royal icing and moulded fondant icing. In this chapter we cover the simpler, easy-to-apply icings – Butter Cream and Glacé Icing. See pages 320–329 for details of how to make and apply Marzipan, Royal Icing and Fondant as well as making icing decorations.

Butter Cream

This is the standard soft icing used on so many cakes both for fillings and toppings and it will pipe very easily. Butter does of course give the best flavour, and once made it will keep for a week in the refrigerator.

Sufficient to cover the top and sides or top and fill a 20 cm (8 inch) round sandwich cake.

100 g (4 oz) butter
175–225 g (6–8 oz) icing sugar, sifted
few drops vanilla essence
1–2 tablespoons top of the milk, milk or lemon juice
colourings (optional)

Preparation time: 10–15 minutes

Cream the butter until very soft then gradually beat in the sugar, a little at a time adding the essence and sufficient milk or other liquid to give a fairly firm, but spreading consistency. It is now ready for use or for adding flavourings.

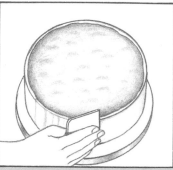

1. Spread sides with a knife or icing comb.

2. To decorate, roll sides in nuts or chocolate.

3. Spread icing over top of cake.

Variations

Chocolate – add 25–40 g (1–1½ oz) melted plain chocolate, or dissolve 1–2 tablespoons cocoa powder in a very little hot water to give a paste and, when cool, beat into the icing.
Coffee – omit the vanilla essence and replace 1 tablespoon of the milk with coffee essence or very strong black coffee, or beat in 2–3 teaspoons instant coffee powder.
Orange or Lemon – omit the essence, replace the milk with orange or lemon juice and add

4. Run knife backwards and forwards to decorate.

5. Making a pattern with a knife.

the finely grated rind of 1 orange or lemon with a few drops of orange or yellow

food colouring, if liked.

To ice a cake with Butter Cream

1. Stand the cake on a plate or cake board and remove any loose crumbs. If it is very crumbly a layer of Apricot Glaze (see overleaf, page 320) will make it easier.

2. Using a palette knife, spread a layer of butter cream all round the sides of the cake until evenly covered. If you have an icing turn-table and a serrated edged icing comb, it can be pulled around the sides to give a patterned finish. If not, a simple pattern can be made with a fork, or by using the round-bladed knife. Alternatively roll the side of the cake in chopped nuts, grated chocolate or toasted coconut.

3. For the top of the cake put the butter cream into the centre of the cake and spread it out gradually from the centre.
a) Starting at one side of the cake run a small round-bladed knife or palette knife backwards and forwards across the top of the cake to give a smooth row of lines.
b) Take a fork or palette

knife and rough up or swirl the icing all over the top.
c) Take the round-bladed knife and pull the blade in curves from the centre to the edge of the cake.

4. The top of the cake may then be finished by adding decorations such as glacé cherries, walnuts, lemon or orange jelly slices, etc.

Glacé Icing

Glacé icing is another simple topping for a cake. It is the simplest of icings to make but needs to be used up rapidly as it dries very quickly and tends to crack if the cake is moved before it has set and also if handled roughly once set. While working with the icing, to prevent it setting stand the bowl of icing in a larger bowl containing hot water.

225 g (8 oz) icing sugar, sifted
2–4 tablespoons hot water
food colourings and/or
*   flavourings (optional)*

Preparation time: about 5 minutes

1. Put the icing sugar into a bowl and gradually beat in sufficient water to give a smooth icing, thick enough to coat the back of a spoon. Extra water or sugar may be added to achieve the correct consistency.

2. Add a few drops of colouring and/or flavouring and stir until evenly distributed.

3. Use at once, or stand over a bowl of hot water for just a short time.

Variations

Coffee – use a little coffee essence or strong black coffee in place of the water.
Chocolate – dissolve 2–3 teaspoons sifted cocoa powder in the water and add to the icing sugar.
Lemon or Orange – use strained lemon or orange juice, heated gently, in place of the water and food colourings to match, if liked.

1. Tie collar round cake to ice top only.

2. Stand cake on rack and pour on icing.

How to apply Glacé Icing

When icing the top of a cake with glacé icing, tie a strip of non-stick silicone paper around the sides of the cake to come about 2.5 cm (1 inch) above the top, and tight enough to prevent the icing running down between the cake and paper. Pour the icing over the top of the cake, let it settle, pop any air bubbles with a darning needle and leave to set; only remove the paper when the icing has set.

For the whole cake, stand it on a wire tray over a plate. Pour almost all the icing over the middle of the cake, and spread it out evenly, allowing it to run down the sides. Use a palette knife dipped in hot water to help the icing cover the sides. Fill in any gaps with the reserved icing. Leave to set then trim off drips from under the tray and remove the cake carefully. Add decorations just as the cake is setting.

To decorate with feather icing

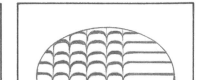

1. Pipe straight lines across the top.

2. Draw a skewer across the lines.

Make up the amount of glacé icing required for the cake plus an extra 50 g (2 oz) icing sugar. Remove about 2 tablespoons icing and colour it a fairly bright colour. Put the coloured icing into a greaseproof paper icing bag (see page 329) without cutting the tip off or adding a nozzle. Use the white icing to coat the top of the cake then immediately cut the tip off the coloured icing bag and pipe straight lines across the top of the cake at 1–2 cm (½–¾ inch) intervals. Immediately draw a skewer or the point of a knife across the lines at right angles about 2.5 cm (1 inch) apart. Quickly turn the cake

3. Draw skewer back in opposite direction.

round and draw the skewer across again in between the first lines but in the opposite direction to complete the feathered effect.

Decorating a cake without icing

Select a paper or plastic doily and put it centrally on top of the cake. Dredge the cake heavily with sifted icing sugar and then very carefully lift off the doily to reveal the pattern underneath. The doily should be slightly larger than the cake.

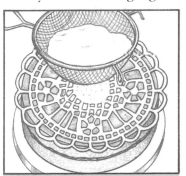

1. Sift icing sugar over doily.

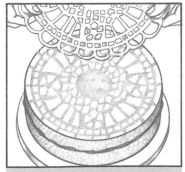

2. Remove doily to reveal pattern.

CAKE DECORATION

Decorating a cake beautifully is a real art. Once you have learned the basics of covering cakes with marzipan and making and applying royal and fondant icing, you can progress to more intricate work with a full range of piping techniques.

To those who enjoy making – and eating – cakes, decorating them is a major pleasure. Although a plain sponge filled with nothing more sophisticated than whipped cream can be attractive and delicious, a special occasion cake with royal icing and piped coil borders, central lattices and a decoration of piped roses and leaves looks spectacular, and gives as much satisfaction to the maker as it does to the eater. This is quite an art, however, something that takes time to learn, and requires plenty of practice as well as endless patience.

The simple icings and decorations such as Glacé Icing and Butter Cream, are described on pages 318–319. This section covers the more advanced techniques such as marzipan, fondant icing and royal icing. Finally, the icing techniques are covered in detail, ranging from how to fill and hold a basic piping bag, to how to pipe a Christmas rose.

Moulding Fondant Icing

This is available ready-made from cake specialist shops and is becoming a very popular way of covering formal cakes. Some supermarkets also sell it either plain white or coloured and flavoured. It comes ready to roll out to cover the cake (in a similar way to marzipan), but in one piece and without any joins. It is attached direct to the cake with apricot glaze, or with egg white if the cake is covered with marzipan. It is smoothed by rubbing in a circular movement with the fingers which have been dipped in a mixture of cornflour and icing sugar. It is easy to colour, but does take a little practice to achieve a perfect result. It can be used for moulding flowers and other shapes as well, and for cutting out shapes and plaques.

Fondant can also be made at home with icing sugar, egg whites and liquid glucose.

When added to cakes, it needs 2–3 days to dry and much longer if to be used with a tiered cake. In fact for large tiered cakes, it is better to add a layer of royal icing *under* the fondant icing so it will take the weight of the other tiers without either sinking or cracking.

Fondant Icing

Makes sufficient to cover a 20 cm (8 inch) round cake
450 g (1 lb) icing sugar
1 egg white
50 g (2 oz) liquid glucose
food colouring and/or flavouring (optional)

Preparation time: about 15 minutes

1. Sift the icing sugar into a mixing bowl and make a well in the centre.

2. Add the egg white and liquid glucose and beat with a wooden spoon, gradually pulling the icing sugar from the sides of the bowl to give a stiff mixture.

3. Knead the mixture thoroughly, mixing in any remaining icing sugar in the bowl to give a smooth and manageable paste.

4. Add colouring and flavouring if liked, and knead until evenly distributed.

5. The icing is now ready for use and can be stored in a tightly sealed polythene bag or a plastic container in a cool place for 2–3 days before use.

Apricot Glaze

The first basic is that all cakes are crumbly. To avoid crumbs being pulled into the icing, a layer of apricot glaze must be brushed over the surface. Apricot glaze is easily made and will store in a cool place or the refrigerator for 7–10 days; it should be boiled up and cooled before use after storage.

175–225 g (6–8 oz) apricot jam
2–3 tablespoons water or lemon juice

Preparation time: about 15 minutes

1. Put the jam and water into a saucepan and heat gently until the jam has melted, stirring occasionally.

2. Rub through a sieve and return to a clean saucepan.

3. Bring back to the boil and simmer until the required consistency is obtained.

Left: Wedding cake with royal icing
Right: Flower garden cake with moulded fondant icing

Applying Fondant Icing

1. If the cake is covered with marzipan first brush with egg white; otherwise brush with apricot glaze.

2. Roll out the icing on a surface dredged with a mixture of icing sugar and cornflour or between two sheets of polythene, to a round or square about 10–13 cm (4–5 inches) larger than the top of the cake.

3. Supporting the icing on a rolling pin, carefully place it centrally over the cake.

4. First dip your fingers in icing sugar and cornflour, then press the icing onto the sides of the cake. Work the icing evenly to the base of the cake using a circular movement.

5. Continue with the circular movements until the icing is smooth and even. Cut off the excess icing from the base of the cake. Leave to dry.

For square cakes you may need to cut a piece of icing from each corner, though it is possible, with care, to mould without cutting. The top edge of a cake covered in this type of icing is rounded not sharp and square as with royal icing.

MARZIPAN

Marzipan or almond paste is a mixture of ground almonds and sugar (usually icing sugar or equal quantities of icing and caster sugar) with a few drops of almond essence and lemon juice. It is bound to a pliable paste with beaten egg, egg yolks or egg white, depending on whether you want pale or bright yellow Marzipan.

It is used for covering all fruit cakes which are to be covered with royal icing or moulding fondant icing to give protection to the icing. It keeps the fruit mixture from seeping into the icing and discolouring it – as well as adding its own inimitable flavour. It can be used on all types of sponge cake, Madeira, quick mix and other cakes too, and any type of icing can be put on top of it.

When used in this way it should be allowed to dry for at least 3 days or up to a week before adding the icing, if it is for a formal cake. This is to prevent the oils from the almonds and egg seeping into the white icing. If to be used on a sponge or other cake with a soft icing, it really only needs about 24 hours to dry sufficiently, for if left too long the cake would stale and not be good to eat. Marzipan can also be used as a decorative top covering in its own right (see Simnel Cake, right) with an attractive design marked on it with a knife, and the edges fluted or crimped between fingers and thumb.

General method

To make a white marzipan mix with egg whites; for the traditional bright yellow commercial coloured marzipan it is necessary to use only egg yolks plus yellow colouring. Good commercial marzipan can be bought easily, either in traditional yellow or the white varieties, but home-made has a better flavour. Commercial marzipan is good for colouring and moulding purposes.

Homemade marzipan can be made and wrapped securely in polythene for about 24 hours before use. It is best if made and used straightaway, however, as it tends to dry out a little and crumble, and over-kneading will cause it to go oily.

There are several cakes which traditionally have marzipan as one of the main ingredients, eg. Battenburg Cake, or Simnel Cake (see right) which has both a middle layer of marzipan cooked with the cake and a topping of marzipan as well.

Marzipan

This quantity will cover a 15 cm (6 inch) square cake or an 18 cm (7 inch) round cake.

Makes 450 g (1 lb)
100 g (4 oz) icing sugar
100 g (4 oz) icing or caster sugar
225 g (8 oz) ground almonds
1 teaspoon lemon juice
a few drops of almond essence
1 egg, or 2 egg yolks, or 2 egg whites

Preparation time: about 10 minutes

1. Sift the icing sugar into a bowl, add the caster sugar if using, then stir in the almonds until evenly blended.

2. Combine the lemon juice, almond essence and beaten egg, yolks or whites. Add sufficient to the dry ingredients to give a fairly firm but manageable dough.

3. Knead very lightly until smooth and even. The marzipan is now ready for use. Wrap in polythene before using as required.

4. Marzipan is very versatile and can be easily coloured by kneading in liquid food colourings, powder or paste to give the required shade. This coloured marzipan can then be used for moulding all manner of things such as flowers, leaves, animals etc. It can also be rolled out thinly (between two sheets of polythene, to prevent it sticking and keep it even) to cut out numerous shapes for decorating.

Applying Marzipan to a cake

1. Place almost half of the marzipan on a working surface dredged with icing sugar, or if preferred between two sheets of polythene. Roll out the marzipan evenly to about 2.5 cm (1 inch) larger than the top of the cake.

1. Use a rolling pin to lay the marzipan on top of the cake.

2. Fit the marzipan on the side of the cake.

3. Smooth the joins with a palette knife.

2. Fill any dents or dips in the top of the cake with trimmings of marzipan or if preferred turn the cake upside down and cover the flat base. Brush all over the surface of the cake with apricot glaze (see page 320).

3. Using the rolling pin, lay the marzipan on top of the cake. Cut around it with a sharp knife allowing a narrow margin of marzipan all round. Using a small palette knife, smooth the marzipan around the edges of the cake so it is even.

4. Stand the cake on a cake board which is 5 cm (2 inches) larger than the cake. Brush the sides with apricot glaze.

5. Cut two pieces of string, one the exact height of the cake and the other the complete circumference. Roll out the remaining marzipan to a strip the circumference and height of the cake, or in two shorter strips, if easier.

6. Loosely roll the marzipan strip(s) into a coil. Place one end on the side of the cake and unroll carefully, moulding to the side of the cake (whatever the shape) and making sure the marzipan touches the cake board.

7. Using a palette knife, smooth the join(s) at the ends of the strip and where the strip meets the marzipan on top of the cake. If the marzipan is too moist, rub the surface with sifted icing sugar.

8. Store the cake, uncovered, in a warm dry place for at least 24 hours before applying icing.

Simnel Cake

In the late 19th century servant girls used to take home a Simnel cake to their mothers on the 4th Sunday in Lent (Mothering Sunday). The 11 marzipan balls on top symbolize Christ's 11 faithful disciples.

225 g (8 oz) plain flour
a pinch of salt
1 teaspoon baking powder
1 teaspoon ground cinnamon
a good pinch of ground
*   nutmeg and/or ground*
*   allspice*
175 g (6 oz) butter
175 g (6 oz) soft brown or
*   caster sugar*
3 eggs
2 tablespoons milk or lemon
*   juice*
100 g (4 oz) currants
175 g (6 oz) raisins
100 g (4 oz) sultanas
50 g (2 oz) chopped mixed peel
50 g (2 oz) glacé cherries,
*   quartered, washed and*
*   dried; or crystallized or*
*   preserved ginger, finely*
*   chopped*
grated rind of 1 orange
grated rind of 1 lemon
1 recipe quantity Marzipan
a little apricot jam or glaze
yellow ribbon, about 2.5 cm
*   (1 inch) wide*

Preparation time: about 40 minutes
Cooking time: about 2 hours
Oven: 160°C, 325°F, Gas Mark 3

1. Sift the flour, salt, baking powder and spices together. Cream the butter and sugar together until pale and fluffy.

2. Beat the eggs into the creamed mixture one at a time, following each with a spoonful of the flour mixture. Fold in the remainder of the flour, alternating with the milk or lemon juice.

3. Stir the dried fruits, peel, cherries or ginger, and fruit rinds into the mixture.

4. Grease and double line an 18 cm (7 inch) round cake tin with greased greaseproof paper or non-stick silicone paper, and spread half the mixture into the tin, levelling the top.

5. Roll out one-third of the marzipan and trim to an 18 cm (7 inch) circle to fit the cake tin. Lay this circle on the cake mixture in the tin, without pressing it down, and then cover with the remaining cake mixture. Level the top.

6. Bake in a preheated oven for about 2 hours or until cooked through. The cake will begin to shrink slightly from the sides of the tin, and a skewer inserted in the centre will come out clean (apart from traces of marzipan). Cool in the tin for 10 minutes, then turn on to a wire tray and leave until cold.

7. For the decoration, roll out just over half of the remaining marzipan to a round to fit the top of the cake. Brush the top of the cake with apricot jam or glaze, and position the marzipan circle. Make a criss-cross pattern on the round with a sharp knife and crimp the edge with a finger and thumb.

8. Roll the rest of the marzipan into 11 even-sized balls and arrange around the top edge of the marzipan circle, attaching each with a dab of jam or water.

9. Place the cake carefully under a moderately heated grill and, watching it constantly, cook until the top is lightly browned. (Brown the balls separately, if liked.) Leave until cold, then tie a ribbon around the sides of the cake, protecting it with a strip of greaseproof paper from becoming grease-stained.

ROYAL ICING

Royal icing and moulded fondant icing are both used to cover formal cakes after the layer of marzipan, ready for the final decorations. Royal icing is made with egg whites, lemon juice (for flavour and to help keep the colour) and icing sugar, with a touch of glycerine to prevent the icing from over-hardening and making it difficult to cut.

It can be made up in any quantity you like, provided you use 1 egg white to each 225 g (8 oz) icing sugar. However, it is often better to make up in fairly small quantities of, say, not more than 4 egg whites to use up fairly quickly, unless you need to base-ice a large batch of cakes.

General method

Royal icing can be made in a large electric mixer or by using a hand-held electric mixer, but it is by far the best if made by hand and given a thorough beating with a wooden spoon. Electric mixers incorporate large quantities of air which turn to air bubbles in the icing; these are difficult to disperse, and can easily spoil the smooth surface of a cake.

Powdered egg albumen (white) is available from specialist cake-decorating shops and distributors, and can be used in place of fresh egg whites for royal icing and meringues – the instructions are simple and come with the powder. It is also possible to buy packets of instant royal icing which come looking just like icing sugar and simply need to be reconstituted with water, but it needs very careful preparation to achieve the correct consistency.

3 egg whites
about 675 g (1½ lb) icing
  sugar, sifted
2–3 teaspoons strained lemon
  juice
1–1½ teaspoons liquid
  glycerine (optional)

Preparation time: about 20 minutes, plus standing

1. Beat the egg whites until frothy, then gradually beat in half the sugar using a wooden spoon.

2. Add the lemon juice and half the remaining sugar and beat well until smooth and very white. Gradually beat in more of the icing sugar until it will just stand in soft peaks.

3. Beat in the glycerine, if using and a little more icing sugar if necessary to achieve the same soft peak consistency.

4. Put the icing into an airtight container or cover the bowl with a damp cloth and/or clingfilm and leave for several hours. This is to allow most of the air bubbles to come to the surface and burst.

5. The icing is now ready for coating a cake, or, thickened with a little sifted icing sugar, to use for piping. At this stage the icing may be coloured with liquid food colourings.

APPROXIMATE QUANTITIES OF ICING SUGAR REQUIRED TO MAKE ROYAL ICING

Square		15 cm (6 inch)	18 cm (7 inch)	20 cm (8 inch)	23 cm (9 inch)	25 cm (10 inch)	28 cm (11 inch)	30 cm (12 inch)
Round	15 cm (6 inch)	18 cm (7 inch)	20 cm (8 inch)	23 cm (9 inch)	25 cm (10 inch)	28 cm (11 inch)	30 cm (12 inch)	
Icing Sugar	450 g (1 lb)	575 g (1¼ lb)	675 g (1½ lb)	900 g (2 lb)	1 kg (2¼ lb)	1.25 kg (2½ lb)	1.4 kg (3 lb)	1.6 kg (3½ lb)

The above quantities give two thin coats of icing on round, square and other shaped cakes. Sometimes a wedding cake will require a third coat on the top and this will require extra quantities of icing, as will the piped decorations.

Flat icing a cake ready for decoration

First cover the cake with apricot glaze and marzipan if using.

Some people prefer to ice the top and then the sides; others do it the other way round. It really doesn't matter so long as you add several thin layers of icing rather than one thick coat, as this gives the smoothest surface. It is advisable to add a layer to the top or sides and then let it dry before adding another, and make sure it is dry before adding a third coat.

An ordinary royal-iced cake requires two coats on the top and sides. Sometimes a third coat is needed on the top, if it is not as smooth as you would like.

With a wedding cake it is best to add three coats all over with an extra coat on the top of the lower tiers. Remember also to add no glycerine to the icing for the lower tiers, as the icing may crack or sink when the heavy tiers are placed on top of each other.

1. Place the cake on a cake board about 5 cm (2 inches) larger than the cake (if not already on one), attaching with a dab of icing. Stand the cake board on an icing turntable, if possible. Put a quantity of icing in the centre of the cake and smooth it out with a palette knife using a paddling

movement. Remove surplus icing from the edges.

2. Draw an icing ruler or long palette knife across the cake towards you, carefully, and evenly, keeping the ruler or knife at an angle of about 30°. Do not press heavily.

3. Remove surplus icing by running the palette knife around the top edge of the cake, holding it at right angles to the cake.

4. If the icing is not sufficiently smooth, cover with a little more icing and draw the ruler or knife across the cake again until smooth. This process can be repeated several times until you are satisfied with the result. Leave to dry.

5. Spread a thin but covering layer of icing all round the sides of the cake, again using a paddling action to push out as much air as possible, keeping the icing fairly smooth.

6. Hold an icing comb, or scraper or palette knife at an angle of about 45° to the cake. Starting at the back of the cake, with your free hand slowly rotate the cake, at the same time moving the comb slowly and evenly round the sides of the cake.

7. Remove the comb at an angle and fairly quickly so the join is hardly noticeable. Lift any excess icing from the top of the cake using a palette knife, again rotating the cake. If not sufficiently smooth, wipe the comb and repeat, adding extra icing as and when required. Leave to dry.

Second and third layers or coats

1. Repeat the same method for the top and sides when applying each subsequent coat, but make sure each previous layer is thoroughly dry first. This will take from 3–4 hours but can vary according to the room temperature.

2. If there is unevenness on the cake from the previous coats pare it off before adding the next coat, using either fine sandpaper, an emery board or a finely serrated-edged knife. This will help achieve a perfectly covered cake.

3. Leave the base iced cake to dry completely, uncovered, for 24 hours before adding the decoration. However, any decorations to be piped and stuck on to the cake may be made so they are ready when the cake is ready.

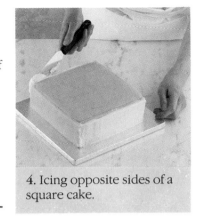

4. Icing opposite sides of a square cake.

For square cakes

For a square cake, ice the 2 opposite sides first, and then when dry ice the other 2. Spread some icing on one side, then draw the comb or palette knife up towards you, keeping the cake still.

Cut off the icing down the sides in a straight line and also off the top and base of the cake.

Repeat with the opposite side and then leave to dry. Repeat the process with the two remaining sides, keeping the corners neat and tidy. Leave to dry.

For petal, oval and rectangular cakes

Simply ice in the same way, using a combination of the round or square methods, and making sure you keep corners square and straight, and curves or indents evenly covered.

Icing the cake board

When the cake has been completely iced, coat the cake board with 2 thin layers of icing. Hold the scraper at an angle on the icing and turn the turntable one revolution to smooth the surface. Remove surplus icing on the edge of the cake board with a palette knife.

1. Use an icing comb to smooth the sides

2. Smooth out icing on top with a paddling movement.

3. Draw the icing ruler towards you at an angle.

ICING TECHNIQUES

The decoration of a wedding or other special occasion cake is an art, but there are degrees of difficulty when it comes to choosing the design and adding it to the cake. A beginner with a little knowledge can produce a really pretty, simply designed cake, but with practice will soon be able to attempt more complicated designs.

Equipment

A good turntable is necessary for more advanced work. It should be firm standing and heavy enough so it turns easily with a simple flick of the fingers. For simpler work an upturned plate can be used.

Greaseproof, waxed and non-stick silicone papers and kitchen foil are all widely used in cake decoration. Run-outs and flowers are made on non-stick papers, and waxed paper is ideal for separating them, when dry, for storage. Always buy the best quality, so it won't tear or let you down at a vital moment.

Piping nozzles

A selection of piping nozzles is essential too (see opposite). Again, buy the best quality, and either plain or screw-on types depending whether you are going to use greaseproof icing bags for decorating (which are by far the easiest to handle), or a plastic or nylon bag with a special nozzle fitting or a more cumbersome icing pump. See page 329 for instructions on making a greaseproof paper icing bag.

The range of nozzles is huge, and they are sold by number. Unfortunately, the manufacturers have not got together so nozzles are not all numbered similarly, which can cause confusion. So pick one make and begin with a selection of the writing nozzles from No. 1 as the finest up to No. 4, a thick plain rope suitable for large dots and base borders. Get too some star nozzles in two or three shapes and sizes, along with a petal nozzle for making flowers. The nozzles must not be damaged or have badly fitting seams or the piped shape will be misshapen and spoil the appearance of your cake.

Larger nozzles – called 'large', 'vegetable' or 'meringue' – are available in metal or plastic, and are used for heavy decoration such as on gâteaux with whipped cream or butter cream apart from their other uses. They need to be used with a nylon bag.

Plain Nozzles Select a fine, medium or thick writing nozzle and place it in the piping bag. Half fill the bag with icing, fold down and make sure the tip is clean and free from any trace of icing or it will not be easy to start the piping.

Straight Lines Put the tip of the nozzle where the line is to begin. Press the icing out slowly and lift the nozzle about 2.5 cm (1 inch) above the surface. Move your hand in the direction of the line to be piped, using the other hand to guide the bag, and keeping the icing flowing evenly. About 1 cm (½ inch) from where it should finish, stop squeezing and bring the tip of the nozzle gently back to the surface. Break off the icing by touching the nozzle onto the hard surface. By holding the icing above the surface it helps even the shakiest hands to keep straight lines – with a little practice. It is easiest to pipe in a line towards you but some find it easier to pipe from left to right or vice versa. If you finish a line with a blob, remove it carefully with a fine skewer or small sharp knife. If the whole line is wrong, lift it off carefully with a skewer.

Dots Hold the nozzle upright and just touching the surface. Squeeze the bag gently, at the same time lifting the nozzle to allow the icing to flow out. Stop squeezing when you have the size of dot you require, and remove the nozzle quickly with a slightly down and up movement to prevent leaving a tail. Use a hat pin to remove the tail, if one appears.

Dots can be piped in any size and by themselves or in varying groups. Two-tier dots can be made by dipping the nozzle downwards fairly firmly into the icing halfway through icing the dot. Dots are widely used for overpiping in a colour for emphasis and extra decoration. Any size of nozzle can be used for making dots, depending on what you want to achieve.

Lattice This is the most attractive way of using straight lines, and can be worked in many ways. It is done by first piping a series of straight lines, parallel to each other, over the given shape or area, keeping in one direction and keeping them evenly spaced. Leave to dry then turn the cake and pipe a second layer of parallel lines over the first but at right angles or an angle of 45° to the first ones. This creates squares or diamonds.

The design can be left at this but it is better with a third layer piped over the first two to give a raised and almost 3-D effect. With very fine work the lattice is often worked up to 5 layers. Let each layer dry before starting the next for if a mistake is made the wet layer will easily lift off without disturbing the rest of the icing. Many other designs can be worked using curved and other shapes.

Curved Lines These can be worked quite easily once you have mastered the early stages of icing. For curves you really need a template which is a piece of stiff paper or card cut with the shape to be iced. This is then placed on top of the cake and gives a shape to ice next to. All manner of shapes can be piped on to the tops and sides of cakes with the help of a template.

For practice before icing the actual cake, draw curves on paper and ice over them. For curves, place the tip of the nozzle at the beginning of the curve, lift it up above the surface as for straight lines and allow the icing to follow the curve round, allowing the nozzle to lower and touch the surface between each scallop. Various sizes of nozzle can be used for curves and with them you can also make scrolls and coils.

Writing The design to be piped should first be written on greaseproof paper to exactly the size and style you want. This design is then put on top of the cake, and the main parts of the letters pricked out using a pin. The pattern is removed to reveal guide lines for the writing. It is wise to pipe the words first in icing the same colour as the cake itself and then, when dry, over-pipe in the chosen colour of the decoration. If there are any mistakes, the icing can be removed without leaving marks of another colour. Practise writing on a table. All manner of styles can be used for writing on cakes, from neat print to your own handwriting.

Lacework This is an attractive

and fairly simple freehand design added to lots of cakes using a fine or very fine writing nozzle. It is like scribbling and is as easy to add to the top as to the sides of cakes, and it is often used to decorate right over the edge. Hold the nozzle almost upright and just above the surface so that the icing flows out, and move the nozzle around quickly and easily to form the pattern. If the icing is too stiff, it will be difficult to get the freehand effect and smooth lines.

Star nozzles

These vary widely in size and shape of the star or shell they produce. A medium to fine nozzle is the most versatile.

Stars Place the nozzle in the bag and fill as usual. Hold the bag upright and just above the surface. Pipe out sufficient icing to form the star and sharply lift the nozzle away with a down and up movement. Stars should sit fairly flat on the surface, not pulled up into a point in the centre.

Rosettes or Whirls These are piped with the same star nozzles but in a circular movement like making a big dot. Begin just above the surface and move the nozzle in a complete circle to enclose the middle and finish off quickly to leave a slightly raised point in the centre, but not a 'tail'. They can be made in varying sizes and slightly differing shapes depending on the nozzle you choose.

Shells Use either a star nozzle or a special shell nozzle, both of which make good shells once you know how. Hold the icing bag at an angle to the surface and a little above it. Start in the centre of the shell and first move the nozzle away from you, keeping an even pressure of icing, then back towards you with a little more

pressure for the 'fat' part of the shell. Release pressure and pull off sharply to form a point. To make a shell edging, simply repeat the shells, linking them in a line by beginning the next shell over the tail of the previous one. It is very important to finish off each shell and lift the nozzle between each one, or a bulky and uneven border will result. Shells can form a variety of borders and designs for cakes.

Scrolls These are useful for the tops and sides of cakes, but do need a lot of practice, for they are quite difficult to keep even, especially when they are complicated and twisted. A simple scroll edging can be worked using either a star or shell nozzle, but the large or individual scrolls need a template, so they are piped and kept exactly even. Hold the bag as for a straight line and, with the nozzle almost on the surface, work a question mark shape beginning with a fairly thick head and gradually releasing the pressure while finishing off in a long pointed tail. A series of scrolls can be worked in the same way.

1st row: Fine writing nozzle, Medium writing nozzle, Forget-me-not nozzle, Fancy star nozzle
2nd row: Fine 6-point star nozzle, Fine 8-point star nozzle, Medium 8-point star nozzle, Shell nozzle
3rd row: Fine 5-point star nozzle, Fancy shell nozzle, Ribbon nozzle, Leaf nozzle

Coils This is a border or edging and is made using a star nozzle. Begin just touching the surface and continue making small circular movements in an anti-clockwise direction. Coils can be worked from left to right, or vice versa as you prefer. If liked, a decoration on top using a writing nozzle can be added.

Petal, rose or leaf nozzles

These are used for making flowers and leaves. To make flowers, you need an icing nail or a cork impaled on a short skewer and a quantity of non-stick silicone paper or waxed paper cut into 2.5–5 cm (1–2 inch) squares. Secure each piece of paper to the icing nail with a dab of icing. The flower is piped and then left undisturbed until dry.

Leave all flowers to dry for 24 hours before peeling off the paper. They may be stored in an airtight container for several months provided they are quite dry when stored.

Leaves There is a special piping nozzle available for making leaves and they can be worked separately to add to the cake or straight onto the cake when you are sufficiently proficient at making them. Usually they are made in white or green icing. Begin with the nozzle touching the paper or cake and the end turning up a fraction. Press gently and as the icing begins to come out of the bag, raise it slightly. When the leaf is large enough, break the icing off quickly leaving a point. The bag can be gently twisted or moved up and down to give different shapes and twists to the leaves and the size can be increased by using extra pressure. Leave to dry. A leaf border can be worked around the top and base edges of cakes by working each leaf separately onto the cake so the left tips are left showing. To obtain a vein effect on the leaves if it is not clear enough, simply run a wooden cocktail stick or darning needle along the main vein.

Rose The most popular flower to make in royal icing is a rose (see top right).

Daisy A fairly simple flower to make and one that looks good on many cakes. Use either white or coloured royal icing for the basic flower and when dry add a centre of a contrasting colour or white if a coloured flower.
Pipe 6 slightly rounded but pointed petals, each separate from its neighbour, but all touching in the centre, by holding the nozzle with the thick end to the centre and completely upright. Squeeze each petal out and pull off the icing quickly and evenly. Leave to dry then, using a medium writing nozzle, pipe a large dot in the centre of the flower (or several dots), using a contrasting colour.

Primrose Use pale yellow icing to make this 5 petalled flower. Begin with the thick edge of the petal nozzle to the centre. Keep the nozzle flat and work each petal separately. Gently squeeze the icing, take the nozzle outwards to a point, still keeping it flat, then dip it towards the centre slightly and take it out again and then bring it back towards the centre, twisting it slightly and gradually releasing the pressure; break off. This gives a slightly heart-shaped petal; work 4 more evenly to complete the flower. Leave to dry.
Work a few tiny dots in the centre using a fine writing nozzle and deep yellow or orange icing.

Christmas Rose These look good on a Christmas cake, along with holly leaves and berries. Another flat flower made in a similar way to the primrose but without the indentation in the petals. They are slightly tilted upwards at the edges and rounded to the 'tea-rose' shape. The centre is filled with a lot of pale to deeper yellow dots for the stamen. If liked the centre of the petals can be tinted pale mauve using a fine paint brush and mauve and pink liquid food colourings to make Lenten lilies.

Making piped roses

1. Fill a piping bag fitted with a petal nozzle no more than half full

2. Hold the piping bag so the thin edge of the petal nozzle is inwards. Squeezing evenly and twisting the nail at the same time, pipe a tight coil for the centre of the rose.

3. Continue to add 3–6 petals, one at a time, piping the icing and twisting at the same time, but taking each petal only about three quarters of the way round the flower. Begin in a different part of the flower each time, and keep the base of the nozzle in towards the centre of the flower or the rose will lose its shape. The petals can also be kept tight to form a rose bud.

How to make basketwork

Ribbon or Basket Nozzles are thick, with either one or both sides serrated, and are flat to produce a ridged ribbon of icing. They are used for flat or pleated ribbon edging which is worked continuously by simply overlapping each pleat, as well as for basket work or 'weaving'.

1. Fill 1 icing bag with a medium writing nozzle and the other with the basket nozzle.

Building up a basketwork pattern.

Hold the basket nozzle sideways to the cake and at an angle, and pipe 3 short lines the same length as each other, one above the other, and with the width of the tip of the nozzle between each one.

2. Pipe a straight vertical line with the writing nozzle along the edge of the 3 ribbon lines.

3. Pipe 3 more straight lines with the basket nozzle of the same length as the first ones to fill in the gaps but beginning halfway along those and covering the straight line.

4. Pipe another vertical line at the end of these lines and continue building up first with the basket nozzle and then the vertical line until you join up with the start. The weave can be worked to any depth you like and can be used round all shapes and sizes of cakes.

4. One or two really open petals can be worked at the base of the flower especially when making large flowers with a large petal nozzle.

Consistency of the icing

It is most important to use icing of the correct consistency for the job to be done. For dots, shells, rosettes, etc, royal icing should be stiff enough to stand in well formed but not hard peaks, but for writing or trellis it must be slacker or the icing will constantly break. It must not be too soft or it will not hold its shape.

Colouring icings

Liquid food colourings in highly concentrated form are available in a huge variety of colours and shades. Take care when using blue colouring for it is most difficult to obtain a good true blue: so often it gives a grey-blue and rather dirty effect. Blue colourings do vary in shades from turquoise through a purple tone.

Powder and paste colours are also available and these also give true colours.

The easiest way to add any colouring to icing, a little at time, is to dip the tip of a skewer into the bottle of colouring and then touch the surface with the colour. Stir each addition in fully until the correct colour is achieved. Remember it is easy to add more colouring but impossible to take it away!

Chocolate decorations

All types of chocolate can be used for decorations but plain varieties set firmer than milk chocolate.

Curls For chocolate curls, (caraque) spread a thin layer of melted chocolate on a firm surface such as marble or formica. Holding a straight-bladed sharp knife at the point and at the handle, place it across the chocolate at an angle of about 45°. Gently draw the knife towards you, carefully shaving off a curl of chocolate.

Leaves Select perfect rose leaves (or other leaves), wash and dry carefully, and then paint the underside of the leaf with melted chocolate, using a fine paint brush. Chill and then add a second coat. Chill again and when quite set carefully peel off the leaves to reveal a chocolate leaf.

Cut-outs Spread melted chocolate thinly and evenly on a sheet of kitchen foil or non-stick silicone paper, keeping it absolutely flat. Leave until it is barely set and cut out whatever shapes you fancy using metal cutters.

Lacework Using a plain writing nozzle, fill a piping bag with melted chocolate. Draw an outline of the shape required on greaseproof paper and pipe over it. Allow to dry then fill the inside of the shape with a freehand 'scribbled' design. Allow to dry then lift off the paper with a palette knife.

Making a paper icing bag

1. Cut a piece of good quality greaseproof paper to a square of about 25–30 cm (10–12 inches). Cut in half to make 2 triangles.

2. Hold the triangle with the right-angled (centre) point towards you, gripping it by the thumb. Take the left hand acute-angled point and bring it loosely up and round to meet the centre point so that it forms a cone shape. If you make sure the smaller point fits exactly into the right-hand half of the centre point, you will have a perfect cone.

3. Take the right-hand point and bring it over the outside of the cone and round to the back

until it fits the other half of the larger angle.

4. Tuck over the flap where the points meet and crease it firmly or fasten it with sticky tape.

5. Cut a little off the tip of the cone and fit in a piping nozzle, cutting off more if the hole is too small.

Preparing the icing bag

1. Insert the nozzle and half to two-thirds fill with royal icing.

2. Push the icing well down into the tip of the bag then close the bag by folding over the top carefully and pushing the icing downwards.

3. Do the same if using a nylon icing bag after fitting the special screw collar connector and nozzle. Do not overfill.

4. The easiest way to fill a nylon bag is to place the nozzle between the finger and thumb of your left hand and fold the rest of the bag over your hand so it is inside out; in this way as you spoon the icing in with the right hand it can be pressed down to the tip by the left hand and the outside of the bag stays clean and free of icing.

Holding the icing bag

1. For paper bags, open your hand and place the bag across the palm with the tip towards the ends of your fingers. Place the thumb on the folded end of the bag (to keep in the icing), then fold over the other four fingers to hold the bag tightly. Use the other hand to steady it, then apply a steady pressure to the bag until the icing begins to come out of the nozzle.

2. With a nylon bag, place the

thumb and forefinger round the icing in the bag and twist the bag tightly two or three times to prevent the icing moving up and coming out of the bag.

3. Then hold the bag tightly over the twist, again with the thumb and forefinger, with the rest of the fingers folded over the bag. Apply pressure with the other hand.

SUGAR SYRUPS & CANDIES

Sugar syrups are the base for an astonishing range of dishes and confections: luxurious fruit salads, a variety of icings, ice creams and sorbets, caramel, toffee and spun sugar. This section explains all you need to know about ingredients, equipment and technique.

Basic sugar syrups are used in many different ways – for poaching fruit, making fruit salads, ice creams, water ices and jellies; and when sugar is boiled to a higher temperature, sweets or candies, fondant icing and caramels are obtained.

Basic rules

When making sugar syrups or caramels, it is better to use coarse grain or lump sugar which hold less dust and impurities, and therefore give a clearer result. The amount of sugar used can vary from 75–100 g (3–4 oz) per 300 ml (½ pint) water for a light syrup (for poaching fruit) to 450 g (1 lb) sugar to 150 ml (¼ pint) water for a heavy syrup (for fondant). The results required depend entirely on the proportions of sugar to water, and on how long the mixture is boiled and to what temperature.

Great care must always be taken when dissolving the sugar in water to ensure that the sugar does not crystallize later on in the boiling syrup.

Once the sugar is dissolved, the liquid is boiled for a couple of minutes to form a syrup which is then used as required. Sugar syrups can be boiled to higher temperatures when they will begin to change colour and then into caramel. Caramel is usually allowed to set hard and is used for decoration or for adding texture (as in ice creams) when crushed, or it can be shaped into baskets. If a small amount of hot water is added to the hot caramel this will prevent it from setting, and a caramel syrup will form, such as that used in Oranges in Caramel (see page 333).

Fondant icing

There are two types of fondant. Fondant icing (see opposite) is made by boiling sugar syrup and then cooling and working it on marble. It is used diluted to ice large and small cakes and sometimes fruits. Cold fondant (see page 320) is made with icing sugar, liquid glucose and egg whites and is a much firmer icing that is rolled out, placed on top of the cake and moulded into shape.

SUGAR BOILING CHART

TEMPERATURE	USES
THREAD: 107°C/225°F Using a small spoon or fork remove a little of the syrup and allow it to fall from the spoon or fork. It should form a fine thin thread.	Spun sugar; ice cream base; mousse-line mixtures
SOFT BALL: 113–118°C/235–245°F Drop a small amount of the syrup into iced water. Mould the sticky syrup into a soft ball with the fingers. Remove the ball from the water. It should immediately lose its shape.	Fudge; fondant
HARD BALL: 120–130°C/248–266°F Drop a little syrup into iced water, then mould into a ball and remove from the water. It should feel firm and quite sticky.	Butterscotch
SOFT CRACK: 132–142°C/270–286°F Drop a little syrup into iced water. Remove from the water and gently stretch it between the fingers. It should form hard but elastic strands, and only feel slightly sticky.	Soft toffee; frostings
HARD CRACK: 149–154°C/300–310°F Drop a little syrup into iced water. Remove from the water. It should form brittle threads which snap easily between the fingers.	Hard toffee
CARAMEL: 160–177°C/320–350°F Using a small spoon pour a little syrup on to a white saucer. It should be a light golden brown.	Sauces; moulds; crème caramel

Thread stage

Soft ball

Hard ball

Soft crack

Fondant

Makes 450 g (1 lb)
450 g (1 lb) sugar lumps
150 ml (¼ pint) water
a good pinch of cream of tartar
dissolved in 1 teaspoon of
water

Preparation time: 5 minutes,
plus 10–15 minutes scraping
the syrup.
Cooking time: about 30
minutes

A sugar thermometer is
essential for this, and it should
be warmed in hot water before
adding to the hot syrup. For
general sugar boiling rules see
page 333

1. Place sugar lumps and water
into a deep pan and place over
a low heat to dissolve the sugar
without boiling.

2. Gently shake the pan to
encourage the sugar to dissolve
and use a wet pastry brush to
brush down the sides of the
pan. This will rinse down any
sugar crystals. When all the
sugar has dissolved add the
cream of tartar, put the lid on
the pan, bring to the boil and
boil rapidly for 2 minutes.
Remove the lid.

3. Place the warmed sugar
thermometer in the sugar
syrup and continue to boil
rapidly to 116°C/240°F. This
will take about 7 minutes.
When the temperature is
reached, immediately check

the cooking by sitting the pan
in a bath of cold water.

4. When the bubbling has
subsided pour from a height in
a thin steady stream on to a
dampened marble slab or
suitable heatproof working
surface. Pour slowly to ensure
the syrup does not spread too
rapidly. Leave to cool for
several minutes.

5. Using a sugar scraper, palette
knife or wooden spoon, start to
push the sugar syrup into the
centre of the slab, lifting and
working all of the syrup.
Gradually it will start to turn
opaque.

6. When the mixture becomes
white and is cool enough to
handle roll into small balls and
store in an airtight container.

7. To use fondant for icing,
place in a bowl over hot water.
Add colouring, if liked, and
soften with about 2
tablespoons of sugar syrup
until the fondant will coat the
back of a spoon and is the
consistency of thick cream.
Heat until just tepid and pour
over a cake set on a rack, or use
for dipping fruits.

Hard crack

Caramel

Chocolate Fudge

450 g (1 lb) granulated sugar
300 ml (½ pint) water
1 tablespoon golden syrup
50 g (2 oz) butter
50 g (2 oz) cocoa powder

Preparation time: 5 minutes,
plus cooling
Cooking time: 30 minutes

1. Place the sugar and water in
a deep-sided saucepan. Add the
syrup, butter and cocoa
powder and place over a gentle
heat.

2. When the sugar has
dissolved boil rapidly to 115°C/
238°F – about 7 minutes. Be
careful as the mixture will boil
up the sides of the pan. If no
sugar thermometer is available,
test as outlined for the soft ball
stage.

3. Draw the pan off the heat
and leave to cool for about 5–
10 minutes, stirring
occasionally. As the mixture
begins to thicken, beat
constantly until it starts to hold
its shape and become slightly
granular.

4. Pour into a lightly buttered
Swiss roll tin. Leave until just
set, mark into squares, and
leave until cold.

5. Cut the fudge into squares
and remove from the tin.

Peppermint Cushions

350 g (12 oz) granulated sugar
120 ml (4 fl oz) water
1½ tablespoons liquid glucose
(available from chemists)
25 g (1 oz) butter, melted and
cooled
2–3 teaspoons peppermint
essence

Preparation time: 15 minutes
Cooking time: about 15–20
minutes

1. Place the sugar and water in
a deep pan and dissolve the
sugar over gentle heat,
brushing down the sides of the
pan with a wet pastry brush.
Add the liquid glucose and boil
to 115°C/238°F.

2. Add the butter and continue
to boil to 143°C/290°F.

3. Pour on to an oiled surface
and leave to cool for several
minutes.

4. Using a sugar scraper or
palette knives, lift and work the
mixture as for fondant, adding
the peppermint essence.

5. As soon as you can handle
the mixture, begin to stretch
and work it with oiled hands.
Fold and stretch the mixture
into a long roll and as soon as it
is smooth and about 2 cm (¾
inch) in diameter, cut off the
first 'cushion' using scissors.
Give the roll a 90° turn and cut
off the second cushion. Turn
again and cut and repeat until
all the roll has been cut. It is
essential to work quickly

6. Allow to cool and serve
immediately.

CARAMEL

There are two types of caramel: a 'wet' caramel and a 'dry' caramel. Wet caramel is, as the name implies, made using sugar plus water, whereas dry caramel is made using sugar only. Caster sugar is usually used for a dry caramel, as it melts more easily. Below we show how to make a wet caramel and use as a glaze.

150 g (5 oz) caster sugar
85 ml (3 fl oz) water

Dry caramel should be made on a low heat and it is possible to turn the sugar to a rich brown colour without it boiling: this is an advantage when the caramel is to be poured over the top of a cake or used as a dip.

General Method

When making caramel, the darker it is the more bitter it will be; if not dark enough, however, the caramel will be too sweet and not have an effective colour. The colour and flavour of the caramel are determined by what it is being used for – sweet recipes can take a slightly darker caramel than dishes which are less sweet. Caramel can be used either as a syrup, or set hard and used as a decoration, flavouring or mould.

Moulded caramel shapes are made by pouring the liquid caramel syrup into a lightly oiled metal tray. When it is on the point of setting, the caramel can be lifted into an oiled mould and shaped.

1. Dissolve the sugar in the water in a heavy-based pan without boiling. When all the sugar is dissolved bring to the boil and boil rapidly.

2. As the bubbles slow down the sugar syrup will begin to turn a green/gold round the edge of the pan. Shake the pan to encourage even colouring of the caramel. Use a wet pastry brush to brush down the sugar from the sides of the pan.

3. Continue to cook until the sugar is a good dark golden caramel colour. For set caramel, check cooking by dipping pan into cold water and then pour on to a lightly oiled metal tray and leave until set.

For perfect Caramel

■ When making caramel, boil the sugar syrup until it starts to turn to a pale golden brown then shake the pan and cook gently, shaking occasionally, until it becomes a dark golden brown.
■ To stop caramel cooking any further, put the base of the pan into a bowl of cold water.
■ Pour a caramel on to an oiled tin tray and leave to set. If a liquid caramel is required add about 85 ml (3 fl oz) hot water quickly to the caramel. Again be careful, as it will splutter. Shake the pan to mix the water through the caramel.
■ Use a heavy-based pan, preferably cast aluminium. When making caramels the sugar can reach as high a temperature as 190°C (374°F) and less strong pans may burn or linings may crack.

4. To keep the caramel liquid do not check the cooking in cold water but add 85 ml (3 fl oz) water or boiling water to the hot caramel. Add it all at once and shake the pan well to mix. If the caramel thickens as it cools, add a little more hot water.

5. The caramel can be used to glaze fruit. To dip stemmed fruit, such as grapes, catch the stems with the prongs of a fork. Hold over the pan until excess syrup drains off, then cool on a wire rack.

Pineapple Fruit Salad with Spun Sugar

Spun sugar must not be prepared more than an hour before it is required, and must be kept dry, not in a steamy kitchen.

1 large ripe pineapple
a good selection of ripe fruit
(strawberries, lychees, kiwi
fruit, black grapes etc.)
25–50 g (1–2 oz) caster sugar
liqueur to flavour (Kirsch,
Grand Marnier etc.)
Spun sugar:
150 g (5 oz) lump sugar
75 ml (2½ fl oz) water
a pinch of cream of tartar,
dissolved in 1 teaspoon
water

Preparation time: 40 minutes
Cooking time: 10 minutes

1. Carefully halve the pineapple lengthways and, using a grapefruit knife, loosen and lift out the two halves of the fruit leaving the skins intact. Cut each half fruit into two parts lengthways. Cut out the core and slice the fruit. Combine with the other chosen prepared fruits, and sprinkle with sugar and liqueur. Chill fruits and the skins of the pineapple.

2. An hour before serving, start to prepare the spun sugar. Dissolve the sugar in the water in a shallow pan without boiling. Add the cream of tartar, and boil the sugar syrup to 110°C/230°F, to the thread stage, or until a very pale golden colour. Check the cooking in a bath of cold water.

3. While the syrup is boiling lay plenty of paper over the floor and rest 2 lightly oiled wooden spoon handles 30 cm (12 inches) apart over the edge of the table, holding them in position with a chopping board.

4. As soon as the syrup is ready, take 2 forks and, holding them together, dip into the syrup. Using a good wrist action, flick the falling syrup very quickly backwards and forwards over the spoon handles. Continue in this way until the syrup is used up and there are plenty of sugar strands over the spoon handles.

5. Carefully lift the spun sugar off the spoons and roll up into a large oval.

6. Spoon the fruit salad into the pineapple skins and place on a large oval serving dish. Place the spun sugar on top.

Oranges in Caramel

6 large seedless oranges
100 g (4 oz) granulated sugar
85 ml (3 fl oz) cold water
85 ml (3 fl oz) hot water

Preparation time: 30 minutes
Cooking time: 15 minutes

1. Remove a little of the rind from the skin of one orange and cut into very fine julienne shreds, about 4 cm (1½ inches) in length. Cook in boiling water for 1–2 minutes. Drain and set on one side.

2. Dissolve the sugar in the cold water over gentle heat. Bring to the boil and boil to a rich brown colour.

3. Draw off the heat and quickly add the hot water all at once, doing so carefully as it will splutter. Shake the pan to mix evenly and leave to cool.

4. Meanwhile remove all the peel and pith from the oranges. Slice and re-assemble, securing each orange with a cocktail stick. Arrange in a serving bowl.

5. If the caramel syrup has thickened too much, add a little more hot water to correct the consistency. Pour over the oranges and chill for several hours.

6. Just before serving stir the juices in the bowl together and sprinkle over the prepared orange rind. Use to decorate the oranges.

Crunchy Blackberry and Apple Fruit Salad

100 g (4 oz) granulated sugar
300 ml (½ pint) water
4 dessert apples (Cox or
Granny Smith), peeled, cored
and quartered
225 g (8 oz) blackberries (fresh
or frozen)
Caramel:
100 g (4 oz) granulated sugar
60 ml (2 fl oz) water

Preparation time: 15 minutes
Cooking time: 30 minutes

1. Make a sugar syrup first by dissolving the first quantity of sugar slowly in the 300 ml (½ pint) water in a wide pan. Bring to the boil and boil rapidly for 2 minutes.

2. Place the apples, rounded side down, into the syrup and cook very slowly until soft – about 20–25 minutes.

3. Lift the apples into a serving dish and add the blackberries to the pan. Cook for 5 minutes. Leave to cool.

4. Meanwhile dissolve the sugar for the caramel in the water and boil rapidly to a rich brown colour, pour on to a lightly oiled tray and leave until cold. Break up with the end of a rolling pin and crush lightly.

5. Pour the blackberries and syrup over the apple, scatter with the caramel pieces, and chill for an hour or so before serving.

For perfect Sugar Syrups

■ When the sugar proportion is very high, it is a good idea to use a wet pastry brush to wash down the sides of the pan when dissolving the sugar to ensure all the sugar is properly dissolved.

■ When making sugar syrup, allow the syrup to boil a little before use so that it thickens slightly.

■ For some sugar syrups and toffee recipes, a sugar thermometer is required to measure the temperature of the sugar – fondant icing and fudge.

■ Always use a coarse grain or lump sugar to obtain a clear syrup or caramel.

■ Dissolve the sugar slowly in the water, stirring as little as possible. It is usually sufficient to swish the water gently round the pan to help dissolve the sugar. It is important that the water does not boil until the sugar is completely dissolved, as this could cause the sugar to crystallize and form white flakes in the syrup.

Jams & Preserves

For centuries the surplus fruits of summer have been preserved by turning them into jams, jellies, curds and cheeses. These traditional skills are easily learned, enabling you to enjoy the flavour of homemade jams and marmalades all year.

Preserving is a method of keeping food, in this case fruit, for a longer time than it would last if fresh, and it can cover a multitude of processes. The most familiar are jams, jellies and marmalades, but fruit can also be made into conserves or fruit curds. A jam is made from crushed or whole fruit and is runnier than jelly, which is made from strained fruit juices. Marmalade is jam made exclusively of citrus fruit. Conserves are normally jams containing a mixture of whole fruit and which set less stiffly than jam, while curd is made from fruit with the addition of butter and eggs, and thus will not keep as long as the other preserves.

EQUIPMENT NEEDED

Preserving pan A preserving pan should be made of aluminium or tin-lined copper. It should be thick based, and narrower at the bottom than at the top, which in turn should be wide enough to allow good evaporation. If a preserving pan is not available, use a large saucepan, but this will not give such a good result, as the fruit needs to be boiled longer to give a set.

Jars should be very clean and free of cracks and chips. They can be special preserving jars, but you can use the jars from commercial jams. The 450 g (1 lb) size is the best. Always have *more* ready for use than you think you will need to avoid a last-minute rush: jam will generally yield a greater quantity than jelly. After washing and drying the jars, put them into a preheated cool oven, and fill them while they are hot to prevent them cracking.

Jam covers are necessary to seal the preserve. Waxed paper discs are the best. They are placed wax side down on to the hot jam. These in turn are covered with dampened cellophane covers which are secured with elastic bands. Labels are needed, but apply only when the jam is cool. Store jars in a dark cupboard or larder.

A **slotted spoon** is useful to skim the surface of the jam, especially for fruits with stones, when the stones come to the surface. A long-handled spoon will prevent scalds when stirring.

Jelly bag A very clean sterile cloth or jelly bag and some sort of stand (see page 336) will be needed for jellies to allow them to drip through.

Jam funnel A jug and special jam funnel are useful for filling the jars.

Sugar thermometer Essential if an accurate test is to be done for setting, though most jam makers manage without one. See opposite for other ways of testing for a set.

BASIC REQUIREMENTS FOR SETTING

Jams, like jellies and marmalades, are made by boiling fruit or fruit juices with sugar, until the sugar, fruit, pectin and acid combine together to set the mixture when it is cold. All four are vital in combination for successful setting: pectin is a substance contained in the cell walls of most fruit and it reacts with the natural acids of the fruit to form a jelly-like set; the sugar, a natural preservative, also helps the pectin form a set.

Fruits vary in their concentration of pectin and acid. Fruits high in both and which give a good set are gooseberries, currants, damsons, apples, Seville oranges, lemons, limes and some plums. Those that give a medium set are greengages, some plums, raspberries, apricots and loganberries. Fruits that lack pectin and acid are strawberries, melon, rhubarb, cherries, blackberries and pears.

The latter fruits will require the addition of a fruit which is high in pectin and acid; the juice of 1–2 lemons, for instance, can be used per 1.75 kg (4 lb) of fruit. Commercial pectin is readily available and, if used, you should follow the manufacturer's instructions. There is also a special preserving sugar available with pectin already added to it.
The pectin content can be tested to see if it is sufficiently high to set the fruit. When the fruit has been cooked until it is soft, before adding the sugar, remove about 1 teaspoon juice from the pan. Pour 3 tablespoons of methylated spirits into a glass, and drop in the cold juice. If the juice clots into a jelly ball, the pectin content is good. If the juice does not clot, or forms more than a couple of jelly balls, extra pectin or acid will be required.
Sugar Basically, any sugar can be used in preserves. Preserving sugar gives the clearest result, but it is more expensive than granulated. Brown sugar will give a darker colour to the jam.

Sugar has a hardening effect on fruit, so it should only be added to fruit which has been thoroughly softened. The exception is soft fruit like strawberries, which can be 'hardened' by the sugar to help them retain their shape and remain whole.

Homemade pectin extract

Wash 1 kg (2 lb) sour crab apples or cooking apples well, and cut them up roughly. Do not peel or core. Add 600–900 ml (1–1½ pints) water to cover the fruit in a saucepan. Stew the fruit gently until very soft, for about 45 minutes, then strain through a jelly bag.

As a guide, use 150–300 ml (¼–½ pint) pectin extract per 1.75 kg (4 lb) of fruit low in pectin (see above for a list of fruits that lack pectin).

Jam-Making

The fruit must be firm, and slightly under-ripe to just ripe, with absolutely no blemishes. Never use over-ripe fruit, which will contain less pectin and acid.

1. Pick over the fruit and prepare it according to type. Wipe it if dusty and dry thoroughly. Do not wash unless absolutely necessary, as water will dilute the pectin and acid. The boiling process will purify the fruit.

2. Put the fruit into the preserving pan, pour over the water (if specified in the recipe), and bring to the boil. Simmer until the fruit is tender.

3. Heat the sugar in a cool oven (140°C, 275°F, Gas Mark 1) for 10 minutes, to help it dissolve more quickly.

4. Stir the warmed sugar into the pan, and heat gently until the sugar has dissolved. Stir occasionally.

5. When the sugar has dissolved (there should be no crystals on the spoon), boil rapidly, uncovered, stirring occasionally, until the jam sets when it is tested. This varies from about 3–20 minutes, depending on the type of fruit and quantity. Start timing when the jam reaches a fast boil. Put the jam back to boil if the tests prove the setting point has not been reached.

6. Once a set has been reached take the jam off the heat, and skim off any scum.

7. Arrange the hot jars on a baking sheet. Ladle the jam into a jug (or use a jam funnel), and pour the hot jam into the jars right up to the neck. Be very careful as the jam will be extremely hot. Whole fruit jams and marmalades should be cooled for 15 minutes before potting so that the fruit does not rise in the jars.

8. Cover the hot jam with the waxed discs, waxed side down, then wipe the rim of the jars with a slightly damp hot cloth.

9. Dampen the top of cellophane covers, making sure that the underside is dry, then stretch over the top of the jars. Secure with elastic bands. When the covers are cold they should shrink tightly around the jars.

10. Wipe the outside of each jar with a damp cloth, and leave to cool.

11. When cool, label with the name and date. Store in a cool, dry, dark place.

Strawberry Jam

This jam requires extra acid and pectin to make a good set. You can either use your own homemade pectin extract (see page 334) or commercial bottled pectin. If using the latter, follow the manufacturer's instructions. The soft-skinned strawberries are cooked first with the sugar to harden them so that they retain their shape, remain whole, and look good.

Makes 2.25 kg (5 lb)
1 kg (2 lb) small whole strawberries, hulled
1.5 kg (3 lb) preserving or granulated sugar
juice of 1 large lemon
175 ml (6 fl oz) pectin extract

Preparation time: 20 minutes
Cooking time: 25 minutes

1. Put the strawberries into the preserving pan, and add the warmed sugar and lemon juice.

2. Very slowly heat until the sugar has dissolved, stirring occasionally.

3. Bring to the boil and boil for 5 minutes.

4. Remove from the heat and stir in the pectin extract.

5. Cool for 15 minutes, then stir.

6. Pot and cover in the usual way.

Testing for a set

There are three ways of testing for a set.

Wrinkle test Place a small quantity of jam (about 1 teaspoon) on to a cold saucer. Cool it quickly – in the freezer perhaps – then push the tip of a finger through the surface of the jam. If the slight skin wrinkles whilst still tepid, the jam will set.

Temperature test This is the most accurate method. Place a sugar thermometer in the preserving pan. When the temperature reaches 104°C/220°F, a set will be obtained. Some fruit, however, requires a degree above or below this so it is best to combine this test with one of the others.

Flake test Stir the jam with a long-handled wooden spoon. Hold a spoonful of jam horizontally above the pan to cool it a little, then tip the spoon to allow the jam to run off it. If the jam sets partly on the spoon and falls away in large flakes rather than drops, it is ready. If the jam runs in an unbroken single stream, it needs further boiling before being tested again.

Wrinkle Test

Temperature Test

Flake Test

MARMALADE-MAKING

The name marmalade comes from the Portuguese *marmelada* – a preserve made from quinces – but now the name is almost exclusively applied to preserves made from citrus fruits.

General method

Marmalade-making is very similar to jam-making, but as the rind of citrus fruit is much tougher and thicker it requires longer cooking to soften it. This should be thinly pared away from the white pith (keep the pith) and then shredded finely, either by hand or by machine. (Soaking it in cold water overnight can help to soften it, but this is not essential.)

The cooking time is also longer than for jams because the water content is so much higher. The liquid should be reduced by half by the end of the first cooking stage, by which time the fruit rind should be really soft. A pressure cooker is ideal for speeding up this process – allow about 15 minutes.

The pectin in marmalades is contained in the white pith and the pips, which are carefully saved after removing the rind and squeezing the juice. They are tied in a muslin or gauze bag, which is attached to the handle of the preserving pan and suspended in the marmalade. It is vital that the bag is totally submerged in the liquid at all times during the cooking.

Seville Orange Marmalade

Makes 4.5 kg (10 lb)
1.5 kg (3 lb) Seville oranges
juice of 2 lemons
3.5 litres (6 pints) cold water
2.75 kg (6 lb) preserving or
* granulated sugar*
knob of butter (optional)

Preparation time: 30 minutes
Cooking time: about 3½ hours

1. Wash, scrub and dry the fruit well.

2. Halve the fruit, squeeze out the juice, and reserve the juice and the pips.

3. Remove the white pith from the rind and cut it up roughly. Put the pith and pips into a square of muslin and tie up.

4. Shred the rind, finely, medium or fairly thickly, as liked.

5. Put the juice, shredded rind and water into the preserving pan. Tie the pith and pips bag

to the handle of the pan and suspend in the liquid. Bring to the boil and simmer for about 2 hours (depending on the thickness of the peel) until the peel is really soft.

6. Remove the muslin bag, leave to cool a little, then squeeze it well into the pan to extract all the juices. Do this by hand or between 2 saucers or plates.

7. Stir the sugar into the pan and heat gently, until it has dissolved.

8. Boil rapidly until setting point has been reached (see page 113).

9. Skim if necessary (or stir in a tiny knob of butter).

10. Leave to stand for 15–20 minutes until a skin has formed on top. Pot and cover in the usual way. Store in a cool, dry, dark place.

JELLY-MAKING

The rules for making jelly are similar to those for jam-making, but the amount of sugar should be calculated from the yield of strained juice from the fruit, and on the richness of the pectin content (the more pectin, the more sugar and thus the greater amount of successful jelly). An *exact* quantity of jelly to be made cannot be quoted, therefore, as it all depends on the fruit used, and the amount of juice.

Fruits that are high in pectin and acid are obviously the best for making jellies, but fruits with a low pectin content may

be combined with those high in pectin to give a fairly satisfactory set.

Ready-made jelly bags with stands are available, but you can improvise with a doubled fine cloth or teatowel. Turn a stool or chair upside down, and secure the corners of the cloth firmly to each of the legs of the chair or stool. Place a bowl underneath to catch the jelly as it drips through. The bag or cloths must be completely sterile first. To do this, pour boiling water through it twice, allowing it to drip through.

General method

1. Check over the fruit, discarding any that are damaged or bruised.

2. Large fruit such as apples and plums need to be roughly chopped. There is no need to peel, core or stone the fruit, as they will be separated from the juice when it is strained.

3. The fruit should be covered with water, but the juicier the fruit the less the liquid required. Soft fruits may be cooked without a lid, but hard fruit should be covered.

4. Cook the fruit very slowly to extract as much juice as possible – this will take about 45–60 minutes.

5. Have ready the sterilized jelly bag, jelly cloth or doubled thickness of teatowel with a bowl underneath. Pour the cooked fruit and water into it and allow to drip through. *Do not* squeeze the bag or touch it in any way as this will cloud the jelly.

6. When the bag has stopped dripping – it can take several hours – the juice is measured then mixed with the appropriate amount of sugar – allowing 450 g (1 lb) sugar for every 600 ml (1 pint) of juice – and the process is finished as for jam (see page 113).

7. When setting point is reached (see page 113), the scum should be removed, and if necessary the jelly should be strained.

8. Pot and cover in the usual way, but do not move the jar until the jelly is completely cold. Store in a cool, dry, dark place.

CONSERVES

Conserves are whole fruits cooked with sugar, and are similar to jams, but they do not set as stiffly. The same basic jam-making rules apply for conserves (see page 335), but their shelf-life is shorter, and they should be eaten within 6 months. As well as being spread on scones or bread, conserves are often used as a sauce, with ice cream, sponges or milk puddings. They are also delicious as a filling for gâteaux and sponges.

Store conserves in a cool, dry, dark place – or in the refrigerator. Conserves do not keep as well as jams, so the jars should be checked regularly.

Fresh Fig Conserve

Makes about 1.75 kg (4 lb)
1 kg (2 lb) fresh figs, quartered
finely grated rind and juice of
*   2 lemons*
2 tablespoons water
1 kg (2 lb) sugar

Preparation time: 20 minutes
Cooking time: 40 minutes
Oven: 140°C, 275°F, Gas Mark 1

1. Put the figs into a preserving pan with the lemon rind and juice, and pour over the water.

2. Very slowly bring the figs to the boil, lower the heat immediately, and simmer for 20 minutes until they are soft.

3. Meanwhile, put the sugar into an ovenproof bowl, in a preheated oven, for 20 minutes.

4. Stir the warm sugar into the figs, and stir over heat until dissolved.

5. Bring to the boil and boil rapidly until setting point has been reached (see page 335).

6. Cool for 10 minutes, then pot and cover in the usual way.

Black Cherry Conserve

Makes about 1–1.25 kg (2–2½ lb)
500 g (1¼ lb) ripe black
*   cherries, stoned*
450 g (1 lb) preserving sugar
150 ml (¼ pint) plus 2
*   tablespoons water*
450 g (1 lb) redcurrants, stalks
*   removed*
2 tablespoons brandy

Preparation time: 20 minutes, plus standing overnight
Cooking time: about 30 minutes

As cherries contain little or no pectin or acid, redcurrant juice needs to be added to give a set.

1. Drain the cherries and put them into a bowl.

2. Put the sugar and the 150 ml (¼ pint) cold water into a saucepan, and stir over a gentle heat until the sugar has dissolved. Slowly bring to the boil and simmer for 2 minutes.

3. Pour over the cherries, cover and leave to stand for 24 hours.

4. Meanwhile, place the redcurrants in a saucepan with 2 tablespoons of water, and cook them for 15 minutes until very soft, stirring occasionally to prevent them sticking.

5. Pour the redcurrants into a sterilized jelly bag (see page 336) and allow to drip through. There should be about 150 ml (¼ pint) juice.

6. Place the cherries and their syrup in a preserving pan, add the redcurrant juice, and bring to the boil. Simmer for 8–10 minutes until the cherries are soft.

7. Using a slotted spoon, lift the cherries from the pan, letting the syrup drop back into the pan. Put the cherries into hot jars.

8. Boil the syrup until setting point has been reached (see page 113).

9. Skim off the scum using a perforated spoon, then stir in the brandy. Pour the syrup over the cherries, and pot and cover in the usual way.

FRUIT CURDS

Curds are a liaison of eggs, sugar, butter and fruit juice, and the most famous as well as the most satisfactory are lemon or orange based. Unlike jams, jellies and marmalades, fruit curds need to be cooked at a very low temperature, so that the egg mixture does not scramble. For best results, they should be cooked in a double saucepan or a bain-marie (see page 74), and great care should be taken that the water in the bain-marie is only at a low simmer.

As curds do not have a long shelf-life, it is best to make a little at a time. They will store for up to 1 month in a dark cupboard or larder, or for 2 months in the refrigerator. They are delicious on bread or scones, or can be used as cake fillings or in lemon or orange meringue pies and pastry tarts or spread in a Queen of Puddings. Lemon Cheese is similar and the two names are often confused but properly a cheese is much firmer in texture and is made with a higher proportion of sugar and no eggs.

Always wash lemons before use, as they are commonly sprayed with chemicals. Lemon Curd freezes very successfully for up to 3 months.

Lemon Curd

Makes about 450–750 g (1–1½ lb)
100 g (4 oz) unsalted butter
350 g (12 oz) granulated sugar
finely grated rind and juice of
*   3 lemons*
8 egg yolks

Preparation time: 10 minutes
Cooking time: 30 minutes

For orange curd, replace the lemons by 3 small oranges.

1. Put the butter, sugar, lemon rind and juice into the top of a double saucepan or into a bain-marie.

2. Heat gently and stir occasionally until the butter has melted and the sugar has dissolved.

3. Lightly whisk the egg yolks together, and stir into the lemon mixture.

4. Continue stirring over very gently simmering water until the mixture thickens, about 20 minutes.

5. Pot and cover in the usual way.

FOOD GARNISHES

A well-made garnish can greatly enhance food, ensuring that it both appeals to the eye and whets the appetite. Garnishes are intended for savoury food – meat, poultry, game, fish, vegetables and eggs – and this selection is suitable for them all.

Croûtons

1. Use a 1.5 cm (½ inch) thick slice of day-old bread, remove the crusts and cut into even dice.

2. Heat equal quantities of butter and oil and when very hot fry the dice until golden brown. Alternatively deep fry in oil. Drain immediately on paper towels. Use for soups and salads.

Cucumber, lemon and orange peel spirals

1. Holding a canelle knife firmly use the notch to remove a strip of skin or peel. Continue to remove the skin or peel in a spiral fashion from the vegetable or fruit. Arrange attractively over the side of a glass or over a dessert.

2. Use cucumber, lemon and orange spirals for drinks and lemon and orange spirals for poached pears.

Pommes de terre noisette

1. Peel large potatoes and press a parisienne cutter/melon baller right into the potato until a half circle is made. Scoop out small balls.

2. Blanch for 2 minutes then drain and dry thoroughly on paper towels.

3. Fry in hot butter in a shallow pan for 5–7 minutes shaking from time to time until golden brown and tender. Drain well, Serve them with steaks or lamb cutlets. Keep uncooked noisettes in water.

Game chips

1. Peel the potatoes and slice evenly and very thinly using a sharp knife or a mandolin (taking care to keep fingers well away from the blade).

2. Soak in cold water for 10 minutes to remove the starch. Drain and dry thoroughly on paper towels.

3. Fry in hot fat in a chip pan or deep fryer for 3 minutes or until golden brown. Drain well and sprinkle with salt. Serve with roast chicken, game and dips.

Anchovy lattice

1. Soak the anchovies in milk for about 15 minutes to remove excess salt. Dry well on paper towels.

2. Cut lengthwise into thin strips.

3. Arrange in a lattice design and use on egg mayonnaise or tomato salad. This goes well with any bland creamy food.

Cutlet frills

1. For a cutlet or poultry frill, use a piece of plain white paper about 25 cm (10 inches) long and cut a strip 9 cm (3½ inches) wide.

2. Fold lengthwise to within 1.5 cm (¾ inch) of the top of the paper.

3. Make a series of thin cuts 3.2 cm (1¼ inches) in from the folded edge along the length of the paper.

4. Open out the strip and refold inside out, lining up the edges.

5. Fold back 1.5 cm (¾ inch) to form a cuff.

6. Cut to the required length. Roll into a frill with the cuff outside. Cut two nicks and tuck the tab inside to secure. A ham frill is made in the same way but using a much larger piece of paper. Use to decorate any exposed bone such as the end of lamb cutlets on guard of honour or rack of lamb or the end of the drumstick on poultry. Put them on only after cooking.

Tomato water-lily

1. Hold the tomato between the thumb and forefingers and with a small sharp knife make zig zag cuts around the middle.

2. Carefully separate the two halves and place a small sprig of parsley in the centre of each.

Use for salads and cold meats.

Tomato rose

1. Use a firm tomato. With a sharp knife, remove the skin in a continuous strip about 1 cm (½ inch) wide, starting at the smooth end.

2. With the flesh side inside, start to curl from the base end, forming a bud shape between the fingers.

3. Continue winding the strip of skin into a rose. Use for salads and cold meats.

Tomato cups

Cut tomatoes in half, scoop out the inside and leave upside down to drain for ½ hour. Fill with peas or sweetcorn and serve, warmed, round a joint.

Radish rose and radish water-lily

1. For a radish rose, remove the stalk and with the pointed end of a small sharp knife cut a row of petal shapes round the radish keeping them joined at the base.

2. Cut a second row of petal shapes in-between and above the first row and continue cutting rows of petals until the top of the radish is reached.

1. For a radish water-lily, remove the stalk and, using a small sharp knife, cut through 4–6 times, keeping the radish joined at the base.

Place both radish rose and water-lily in iced water for several hours to open out. Use for salads and oriental dishes.

Lemon, orange and cucumber slices

1. Holding a canelle knife, firmly use the notch to remove strips of skin at regular intervals down the cucumber.

2. Cut into even slices. Prepare orange or lemon in the same way, removing any pips when slicing. Use for garnishing fish or for drinks.

Polonaise

1. Finely chop some fresh parsley. Chop the white of a hard-boiled egg.

2. Sieve the yolk of a hard-boiled egg.

3. Fry some breadcrumbs in butter.

4. Sprinkle in layers over a vegetable, such as cauliflower, cabbage or Brussels sprouts. Keep ingredients separate, ready to be assembled.

Butter curls and butter balls

1. For butter curls, using a block of cold butter and a butter curler, draw the curler across the surface.

1. For butter balls, using a block of cold butter press a parisienne cutter, melon or butter baller right into the block and scoop out butter balls.

2. Drop each curl or ball into iced water to keep its shape.

Pommes de terre duchesse border

1. Fill a nylon piping bag containing a large rosette nozzle with a duchesse potato mixture (see page 181).

2. For a border, butter the edge of the serving dish and pipe a design round it.

3. Brush lightly with beaten egg and brown in the top of a preheated hot oven (220°C, 425°F, Gas Mark 7) for about 10 minutes. Use the border for lamb or poached fish.

Gherkin fan

1. Using a sharp knife, slice through the gherkin at regular intervals, keeping it joined at the base.

2. Gently pull the slices to form a fan. Use for cheeseboard or hors d'oeuvre.

Flavoured butters

1. Mix softened butter with one or more of the following: chopped fresh tarragon, parsley or another herb; anchovy essence; finely chopped walnuts or hazelnuts; finely grated lemon or orange rind; crushed garlic; paprika.

2. Shape the flavoured butter into a sausage shape on a piece of greaseproof paper and roll up securely, twisting the ends of the paper like a cracker, so as to condense the butter and seal it tightly – ideally the sausage of butter should be about 1.5 cm (¾ inch) in diameter.

3. Chill in the refrigerator until firm. Serve sliced on top of grilled fish, steaks or chops.

Pastry fleurons

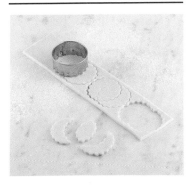

1. Cut a strip of flaky or puff pastry 5 cm (2 inches) wide. Using a 4 cm (1½ inch) diameter fluted cutter, start at the base of the strip of pastry and remove crescent shapes.

2. Brush with beaten egg and bake in a preheated hot oven (220°C, 425°F, Gas Mark 7) for about 10 minutes. Arrange around vegetable and fish dishes or casseroles.

Spring onion tassels

1. Remove the root from the spring onions and trim to about 7.5 cm (3 inches). Cut lengthwise through the stalk several times to within 4 cm (1½ inches) of the end.

2. Place the tassels in iced water for about 1 hour to open out. Use to garnish dips and oriental dishes.

Flower design

1. Blanch strips of red or green pepper, carrot, orange or lemon rind for 1 minute. With an aspic cutter or a small sharp knife, cut into petal shapes. Work out a flower design using a strip of tarragon, cucumber skin or chive to make leaves and a stem.

2. Dip in liquid aspic and transfer the design to the food. Use to decorate food in aspic, the base of moulds or terrines which will become the top when turned out and chaudfroid joints of chicken.

MICROWAVE COOKING

A microwave cooker can be the busy cook's best friend. Use it not just for cooking, but also for defrosting and reheating frozen food. As with freezers, it is important to learn how to manage it efficiently.

How Microwaves Cook

In the microwave cooker a 'magnetron' converts electricity into electromagnetic waves, or 'microwaves'. Microwaves pass through most objects without affecting them at all, but are reflected by metal and absorbed by food. The microwaves penetrate food to a depth of about 5 cm/2 inches and cause the moisture molecules to vibrate, generating heat within the food.

Power Output

The microwave oven's power output varies from 450 to 700 watts.

Some microwave cookers, suitable for defrosting, reheating and simple cooking, have only full power (100%) or low power (30%). Others have completely variable power, permitting much more versatile cooking.

Additional Features

Extra features include: **removable shelf**, allowing several dishes to be cooked. **temperature probe**, to control the internal temperature you wish food to reach – specially useful when cooking meat. **programmable memory**, which allows you to control the oven's starting time and temperature, and to change temperatures during cooking, all in advance. For example you can set it to start cooking on high power to heat food quickly and then reduce power to cook gently or simmer.

food browners – small grills or integral convection ovens because most food cooks too quickly to have time to brown.

Cooking Containers

These must be microwave transparent.
Do use: heat-resistant glass, china, firm plastics and polythene, roasting and boiling bags, paper, wood, wicker (the last three for warming foods).
Do not use: crystal or cut glass, unglazed earthenware and pottery, soft polythene, metal, foil, dishes with silver or gold trims.

To check if a dish is suitable for microwaving, place a glass jug half full of water in the dish and microwave on full power for 1 minute. The dish should be cool; if it is hot it should not be used. Some plastics melt when the food gets very hot. This is especially a problem when cooking foods with a high fat or sugar content, and these should only be cooked in heat-resistant glass or pottery.

Special Microwave Ware

Specially designed microwave cookware includes some particularly useful items:
Browning Dishes: these are used to brown and crisp foods.
Cooking Racks: good for cooking meat, bacon and poultry.

Cooking by Microwave

Because microwaves penetrate the food from the outer edge first, foods arranged in a circle cook most evenly.

Foods also cook more evenly if stirred or rearranged during microwaving. Foods which can't be stirred, should be rotated unless you have a turntable to do it for you and, if possible, turned over at least once during cooking. Unevenly shaped foods can be placed so the thinner parts are in the centre where they receive less energy.

Because metal reflects microwaves, in many makes of microwave oven (but first check your manufacturer's instructions) it is possible to use very small pieces of *smooth* aluminium foil to protect thin parts of larger items such as the tails of whole fish. Foil should be removed halfway through cooking.

Almost all foods are covered before microwaving. A solid lid or microwave-suitable cling-film cover which holds steam in to keep the food moist, speed cooking and stop splattering, is used for vegetables, fruits, fish, casseroles, pasta and rice. Absorbent paper is used to cover foods such as bacon, sausages and chops to stop them spattering and to wrap breads and cakes to absorb excess moisture.

Vegetables and fruits such as potatoes, tomatoes and apples can be cooked uncovered, though the skins must be pricked before microwaving to prevent them bursting. Soups and sauces are sometimes microwaved without a lid, either to reduce the quantity or because they need stirring.

Calculating Cooking Times

The more food you put in the microwave at one time, the longer it takes to cook. If you double the quantities in a recipe you will need to add about one third to a half to the times given. Conversely, if you reduce the quantity you will also need to reduce the time.

The shapes of food and dishes also affects the cooking time, with shallow dishes and thin foods cooking more quickly than thicker foods.

The starting temperature of food makes a noticeable difference when microwaving because cooking times are so much shorter. Most microwave recipes give times for food at room temperature, so food taken straight from the refrigerator will need a longer cooking time.

All food continues to cook for a short time after the microwave has been switched off. In this time the heat on the outside is conducted to the centre of the food so food should be removed before it is completely cooked and cooking allowed to finish during 'standing' time.

What Not To Do

■ Do not deep-fry – you can't control the fat temperature.
■ Do not cook eggs in their shells (they will explode).
■ Do not switch on the microwave when empty – this will damage the magnetron.
■ Do not use ordinary thermometers – use a special microwave thermometer.

COOKING CHARTS

Fish and vegetables are among the foods that cook particularly well in the microwave. Fish turns out succulent and full-flavoured without the need for additional cooking fat – a real plus point for anyone who is aiming to keep the fat content of their diet under control.

Vegetables can be cooked to perfection – not soggy but crisp and just tender, retaining the maximum nutrient content and looking colourful. They can be cooked in suitable serving dishes, without too much added liquid. If small amounts are to be cooked, then several different vegetables can be cooked at the same time.

Tender poultry and game also cook well in the microwave but they do not brown (unless you have a combination model which offers the facility for using conventional heat simultaneously with the microwaves). Whole chickens or ducks can be prepared, cooked, then browned under the grill if liked. In some cases this browning is not necessary – for example, chicken breasts or joints cooked in flavoursome sauces can be served without the need for additional browning. If the bird is to be served with the skin on then it is best to brown it first.

The charts below and on the following pages offer guidance on the cooking times for fish, poultry and vegetables. Obviously you can extend your repertoire of microwave cooking beyond these basics but because these are foods that cook successfully, they are good items to select for your first experiments with this new cooking method.

Remember the few points that always apply to microwave cooking: the more food you put in, the longer the cooking time; unless otherwise stated cover food to keep it moist during cooking; and – very important – do not overcook food, it is better to reduce the cooking time if you are unsure of the process, then put the food back for a few seconds or minutes to complete the cooking. Timings given are for a 650 watt oven.

COOKING FISH IN THE MICROWAVE

		Quantity	Cooking time on Full Power	Preparation
Bass	whole	450 g/1 lb	5–7 minutes	Shield the head and tail with foil. Cut the skin in two or three places to prevent it from bursting.
Cod	fillets	450 g/1 lb	5–7 minutes	Place the fillet tails to the centre of the dish or shield with foil. Cut the skin in two or three places to prevent it from bursting.
	steaks	450 g/1 lb	4–5 minutes	Cover with greaseproof paper before cooking.
Haddock	fillets	450 g/1 lb	5–7 minutes	Place the fillet tails to the centre of the dish or shield with foil. Cut the skin in two or three places to prevent it from bursting.
	steaks	450 g/1 lb	4–5 minutes	Cover with greaseproof paper before cooking.
Halibut	steaks	450 g/1 lb	4–5 minutes	Cover with greaseproof paper before cooking.
Kippers	whole	1	1–2 minutes	Cover with cling film and snip two holes in the top to allow the steam to escape.
Red Mullet and Red Snapper	whole	450 g/1 lb	5–7 minutes	Shield the head and tail with foil. Cut the skin in two or three places to prevent it from bursting.
Salmon	steaks	450 g/1 lb	4–5 minutes	Cover with greaseproof paper before cooking.
Salmon Trout	whole	450 g/1 lb	7–8 minutes	Shield the head and tail with foil. Cut the skin in two or three places to prevent it from bursting.
Scallops		450 g/1 lb	5–7 minutes	Cover with dampened absorbent kitchen paper.
Smoked Haddock	whole	450 g/1 lb	4–5 minutes	Cover with cling film, snipping two holes in the top to allow the steam to escape.
Trout	whole	450 g/1 lb	8–9 minutes	Shield the head and tail with foil, cut the skin in two or three places to prevent it from bursting.

COOKING VEGETABLES IN THE MICROWAVE

	Quantity or weight	Cooking time on Full Power	Preparation
Artichokes, globe	1 medium	8–10 minutes	Add 4 tablespoons water. Cook in large covered dish or cook-bag.
Artichokes, Jerusalem	450 g/1 lb peeled	10–12 minutes	Add 2 tablespoons lemon juice and 25 g/1 oz butter.
Asparagus	450 g/1 lb medium spears, trimmed	5–7 minutes	Add 2 tablespooons water. Cook in flan dish or cook-bag.
Beans, broad	450 g/1 lb (shelled weight)	5–7 minutes	Add 2 tablespoons water.
Beans, French	450 g/1 lb	7–8 minutes	Add 3 tablespoons water.
Beans, runner	450 g/1 lb sliced	5–7 minutes	Add 3 tablespoons water.
Beetroot	4 medium	10 minutes	Add 4 tablespoons water.
Broccoli	450 g/1 lb	7–8 minutes	Add 3 tablespoons water.
Cabbage	450 g/1 lb shredded	10 minutes	Add 2 tablespoons water.
Carrots	225 g/8 oz in 1-cm/½-inch slices	5 minutes	Add 2 tablespoons water.
Cauliflower	225 g/8 oz broken in florets	5 minutes	Add 4 tablespoons water.
Corn on the cob	2 cobs, with husks removed	8–10 minutes	Add 3 tablespoons water.
Courgettes	450 g/1 lb sliced	3 minutes plus 10 minutes standing time	Add 25 g/1 oz butter.
Leeks	450 g/1 lb sliced	5–7 minutes	Add 25 g/1 oz butter.
Mushrooms, button	225 g/8 oz whole	1½ minutes	Add 25 g/1 oz butter.
Onions, whole	175 g/6 oz each (2 at a time)	10 minutes	Add 2 tablespoons water.
Parsnips	450 g/1 lb sliced	10 minutes	Add 2 tablespoons water.
Peas	450 g/1 lb (shelled weight)	8 minutes	Add 2 tablespoons water.
Potatoes, baked	1 kg/2 lb (4 large, even-sized)	18–20 minutes	Place the potatoes on double-thick kitchen paper.
Potatoes, boiled	450 g/1 lb (in 50-g/2-oz pieces)	5–7 minutes	Add 3 tablespoons water.
Potatoes, new	450 g/1 lb (even-sized)	5 minutes	Add 4 tablespoons water.
Spinach	450 g/1 lb	5–6 minutes	Place in large dish or cook-bag.
Spring greens	450 g/1 lb	8 minutes	Place in large dish or cook-bag.
Swede	450 g/1 lb (in 25-g/1-oz pieces)	10 minutes	Add 2 tablespoons water.

COOKING POULTRY AND GAME IN THE MICROWAVE

	Cooking time on Full Power per 450 g/1 lb	Cooking time on Medium Power per 450 g/1 lb	Preparation
Chicken whole	6–8 minutes	9–10 minutes	Shield the tips of the wings and legs with foil. Place in a roasting bag in a dish with 2–3 tablespoons stock. Give the dish a half turn halfway through the cooking time.
pieces 1 2 3 4 5 6	2–4 minutes 4–6 minutes 5–7 minutes $6\frac{1}{2}$–10 minutes $7\frac{1}{2}$–12 minutes 8–14 minutes		Place the meatiest part of the chicken piece to the outside of the dish. Cover with greaseproof paper. Give the dish a half turn halfway through the cooking time.
Duck whole	7–8 minutes	9–11 minutes	Shield the tips of the wings, tail end and legs with foil. Prick the skin thoroughly to help release the fat. Place in a dish in a roasting bag on a trivet or upturned saucer and turn over halfway through the cooking time.
Grouse, guinea fowl, partridge, pheasant, pigeon, poussin, quail and woodcock	6–8 minutes	9–11 minutes	Shield the tips of the wings and legs with foil. Smear the breast with a little butter and place in a roasting bag in a dish. Turn the dish halfway through the cooking time.
Turkey	9–11 minutes	11 13 minutes	Shield the tips of the wings and legs with foil. Place in a roasting bag in a dish with 2–3 tablespoons stock. Turn over at least once during the cooking time and give the dish a quarter turn every 15 minutes.

FREEZING

To get the best out of your freezer it is important to buy the correct model for your needs and the size of your kitchen, whether you are a busy mother, dedicated home-grower or working woman. Manage it efficiently and it will prove invaluable.

Choosing a freezer

When deciding which freezer to buy, consider the available space, cost (both purchase price and running costs), the size of your family and the purpose for which you require the freezer. As a general guide, allow a minimum of 56 litres (2 cu ft) of freezer space for each member of the family, remembering that 28 litres (1 cu ft) should hold about 9 kg (20 lb) of food.

Chest freezers with top-opening hinged lids are less expensive to buy than uprights per litre/cu ft; they are are also less expensive to run because they use less electricity.

Upright freezers tend to be more expensive to buy and run than chest freezers, but they are more convenient to use in kitchens – some are even small enough to stand on top of units or other appliances.

Look for a model with shelves on runners to make it easier and therefore quicker to find things.

Combination refrigerator/freezer If your kitchen is small, this is an ideal model to buy because the two units together take up only the floor space of one.

Defrosting

Regular defrosting is essential if the freezer is to run efficiently. It is impossible to say exactly how often this is necessary but, on average, it should be two or three times a year for an upright, once or twice for a chest. As a general guide, when the ice has built up to a thickness of more than 5 mm (¼ inch) inside the cabinet, it is time to defrost.

Defrost when stocks are low and the weather is cold.

Labelling

It is essential to have a log book in which to keep records of food as it is put into the freezer, so that you know what is in the cabinet, when it was frozen and the date it needs to be consumed by. Label the food packets themselves, too. Write clearly and include the type of food, number of servings or amounts, as well as the date of freezing.

Thawing

Once food has been fully thawed, it should be used as soon as possible – do not leave it lying around at room temperature. Never refreeze thawed food.

Meat

Raw meat is best thawed slowly in its wrapping in the refrigerator so it absorbs as much of its juices as possible. But it is a slow process: you should allow 5 hours per 450 g (1 lb) to thaw completely. Thawing at room temperature is much faster – 2 hours per 450 g (1 lb) – but it is not advisable for pork.

However, with the exception of boned and rolled meat (when there is a possibility that micro-organisms may have been transferred to the inside of the meat during boning and rolling) joints can be cooked straight from frozen, providing an adequate cooking time is allowed. Cooking from frozen may, however, result in tougher meat.

Approximate roasting times and temperatures when cooking from frozen.
Beef joints: 160°C, 325°F, Gas Mark 3. 30 minutes to the 450 g (1 lb) plus 30 minutes over.
Lamb joints: 160°C, 325°F, Gas Mark 3. 35 minutes to the 450 g (1 lb) plus 35 minutes over.
Pork joints: 190°C, 375°F, Gas Mark 5. 40 minutes to the 450 g (1 lb) plus 40 minutes over.

Freezing terms and techniques

Batch cooking This means to cook a 'batch' or large quantity of the same dish, then to divide it into smaller usable quantities to freeze for future use.

Blanching This procedure is essential for many vegetables to preserve their quality in the freezer, and when specified in freezing instructions it should not be disregarded.

Cooling This is one of the most vital stages in the preparation of cooked food for the freezer. Food that is placed in the freezer must be as cold as possible to prevent moisture being trapped inside packages.

Open freezing Food is frozen without wrappings for a short time until solid, then wrapped and sealed for the freezer. Use for: cream rosettes, gâteaux, cheesecakes, casseroles, bakes, mousses, etc.

Overwrapping This is used to prevent cross-flavouring of strong-smelling foods. To overwrap, pack items in the normal way, then wrap again in foil or in a polythene bag.

Preforming A way of packaging food for the freezer that makes economic use of freezer space and containers. Pour liquid food such as soup, stocks, stews and casseroles into a rigid container lined with a polythene bag, open freeze until solid, then remove the bag, seal and store in the freezer.

Refreezing Refreezing food that has thawed is not recommended because it can be harmful and is certainly likely to spoil the quality of food.

Sterilizing As a precaution against harmful bacteria, it is a good idea to sterilize all containers before reusing them for the freezer.

Storage times Storage times recommended in freezing instructions and recipes and by manufacturers of commercial goods err on the safe side. Food will not normally be harmful if eaten shortly after the recommended date, but the quality in terms of colour, flavour and texture will not be as good.

Food that will not freeze successfully: eggs, cream of less than 40% butterfat, fruit high in water content, bananas, avocado pears, celery, boiled potatoes (but mashed ones are all right), salad vegetables, tomatoes, custards, jelly, yogurt, soured cream, soft meringue, icings, mayonnaise, carbonated drinks.

INDEX